THE COMPLETE GUIDE TO
FIGHTERS
&BOMBERS
OF THE WORLD

THE COMPLETE GUIDE TO
FIGHTERS
&BOMBERS
OF THE WORLD

FEATURES 1200 WARTIME AND MODERN IDENTIFICATION PHOTOGRAPHS

An illustrated history of the world's greatest military aircraft, from the pioneering days of air fighting in World War I through to the jet fighters and stealth bombers of the present day

FRANCIS CROSBY

HERMES
HOUSE

This book is dedicated to my daughter Gemma

This edition is published by Hermes House

Hermes House is an imprint of
Anness Publishing Ltd
Hermes House
88–89 Blackfriars Road
London SE1 8HA
tel. 020 7401 2077
fax 020 7633 9499
info@anness.com

A CIP catalogue record for this book
is available from the British Library.

Publisher: Joanna Lorenz
Editorial Director: Judith Simons
Project Editor: Felicity Forster
Designers: Steve West and Ian Sandom
Copy Editors: Judy Cox, Peter Moloney,
Jeremy Nicols and Alan Thatcher
Editorial Readers: Joy Wotton and Rosanna Fairhead
Production Controller: Don Campaniello

Previously published as two separate volumes, *Fighter Aircraft* and *The World Encyclopedia of Bombers*

1 3 5 7 9 10 8 6 4 2

PAGE 1: **Junkers Ju 52.**
PAGE 2: **Saab Gripens.**
PAGE 3: **North American P-51 Mustang.**
PAGE 4: **Panavia Tornado.**

Contents

BOMBERS

A–Z of Modern Bombers: 1945 to the Present Day

Introduction

The mobilization of combat aircraft is often one of the first highly visible indications when tensions rise between nations or opposing factions. Centuries ago, fleets of warships would have been despatched as a show of strength to an enemy. Today the deployment of a flight of high-performance combat aircraft can be enough to deter would-be aggressors. Often the fact that the aircraft are simply there and serviceable, or that an aircraft carrier is within range to launch its warplanes is sufficient to prompt a rethink on the part of a potential opponent. Such is the influence of modern combat aircraft.

Although technological advances have revolutionized combat aircraft design, the basic principles of the functions of bomber and fighter aircraft established in World War I remain unchanged. What has changed, however, is the ability for certain nations to unleash truly horrific damage upon an enemy through the use of nuclear weapons that could be dropped by a single bomber aircraft. Even the development of so-called "smart" weapons has increased the ability of small numbers of combat aircraft to cripple an enemy's infrastructure.

The differentiation between fighter and bomber aircraft has become increasingly blurred since World War II, when pioneering multi-role aircraft such as the de Havilland Mosquito made air force planners strive to acquire aircraft that

TOP: **The Avro Lancaster, one of the most famous bomber aircraft of all time, was derived from an earlier lacklustre design and then itself spawned derivative types.** ABOVE: **The Bristol Fighter was, as its name suggests, developed as a fighter aircraft but even this early type was capable of carrying two 51kg/112lb bombs beneath its wings.**

were masters of all trades. There have been many subsequent examples of aircraft that can be excellent fighters and effective ground attack aircraft. In the 1950s the USAF were acquiring aircraft designed as fighters that were capable of delivering tactical nuclear weapons, but it has proved impossible to produce a truly multi-role aircraft that could serve as a long-range bomber aircraft and be used to defend its home airspace. Extraordinarily capable and high-performance aircraft such as the F-15 can, however, fight its way to a target that it will then bomb before fighting its way home. Few nations today can afford to sustain the large fleets of bomber aircraft that once equipped many world air forces. It is interesting to note that due to the vast research and financial resources needed to develop new strategic bombers from scratch, the B-52 Stratofortress is expected to remain with front-line USAF units until 2045, 90 years after entering front-line service. To place this remarkable fact in context, it is the equivalent of the Vickers Vimy remaining in RAF service until 2008.

Some analysts believe that the B-1 and B-2 are the world's last long-range strategic bombers, and that their place will be taken ultimately by space-based weapon systems or ultra-"smart" precision ordnance launched hundreds of miles away from airliner airframes refined for military use. Until then, however, air strikes will be carried out by the few remaining strategic bomber types or relatively short-range types, which require "tanking" by inflight refuelling tankers.

Technology – specifically the development of the jet engine – and a greater understanding of aerodynamics have pushed fighters and bombers higher, faster and over greater distances. It is difficult to believe now that while Frank Whittle was trying to develop his revolutionary jet powerplant in the 1930s, he was met with indifference from officialdom. Meanwhile, German engineers were well resourced, and produced the Messerschmitt Me262, the world's first operational jet-powered combat aircraft. When it took to the skies in anger in July 1944 with a top speed around 25 per cent greater than Allied fighters, the Messerschmitt effectively rendered piston-powered fighter aircraft obsolete.

Fighter aircraft now need high speed only to get swiftly within missile-firing range of multiple targets that can be attacked simultaneously. Meanwhile, the materials from which fighter and bomber aircraft can now be built enable some to evade or confound the most complex defensive systems. However, the crews of these computer-screen equipped aircraft remain as human as the goggles-wearing, oil-soaked aerial warriors that first did battle almost a century ago.

ABOVE: **The Saab Gripen is a splendid marriage of advanced aerodynamics, materials and engine technology.** BELOW: **The remarkable Northrop Grumman B-2 Spirit revisited a flying wing design developed by Northrop over four decades earlier.** BELOW LEFT: **A Sea Harrier demonstrates the revolutionary VTOL capability of the type.**

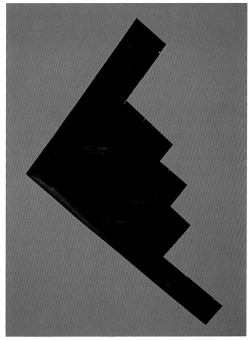

The performance figures quoted in this book should be seen as a broad indicator of an aircraft's capabilities. Aircraft performance and capabilities can vary considerably, even within the same marks of an aircraft type. If bombs are carried, for example, maximum speed can be reduced. Also the maximum speeds quoted are top speeds achieved at the optimum altitude for that particular aircraft type and should not be seen as the definitive top speed for the aircraft at all altitudes.

ABOVE: **The Hawker Hurricane, the RAF's first 482kph/300mph aircraft.**

FIGHTER AIRCRAFT

Introducing fighters

" It is not to be expected that aircraft will be able to carry out their duties undisturbed. In war, advantages must be fought for and the importance of aerial reconnaissance is so great that each side will strive to prevent the other side making use of it." Royal Flying Corps manual, 1914.

This observation predates the first true fighter aircraft but neatly sums up how fighter aircraft came to be. World War I reconnaissance aircraft, "scouts", began to gather increasingly valuable information for their forces and effective armament became a necessity so they could carry out their work unmolested. Initially scout crews armed themselves to take the occasional shot at other scouts. The aeroplane, once no more than a sporting contraption, had become a weapon, and a special type of military aircraft soon evolved – the fighter.

From simple beginnings over the bloody trenches of World War I, fighter aircraft have developed into the extraordinarily complex machines in service today. Although air fighting is only a phenomenon of the last century, it is now central to securing military victory on the ground. In 1940, Hitler's Luftwaffe needed to gain control of the sky over southern England before Germany could mount an effective invasion of Britain. Without air superiority Germany risked their ground

TOP: **The Hurricane (top) and Spitfire, two of World War II's classic fighting aircraft.** ABOVE: **A classic fighter pilot pose – an RAF pilot with his Curtiss P-40 Kittyhawk.**

troops coming under constant attack from British bombers. The fighters of Britain's Royal Air Force defended their country's sky in what has become an almost legendary campaign in the summer of 1940 – The Battle of Britain – and Germany's planned invasion was thwarted.

The weapons with which the Spitfires and Messerschmitts fought each other during the Battle of Britain would have been recognized by the pilots from World War I – machine-guns and cannon, the latter basically a heavy machine-gun that fired explosive shells. Although many modern fighters still carry guns, primary weaponry is now the guided air-to-air missile, some with such long ranges that in recent air combats, pilots have seen an enemy only as a blip on their radar screen before loosing off a missile.

In terms of pilot workload, modern fighters are very demanding and in reality today's fighter pilot spends more time managing computerized weapons systems than flying the aircraft, much of which is done by on-board computers. Where fighters once had mechanical linkages from control columns to control surfaces, fighters now employ electronic signalling to move control surfaces. Computer and electronic systems control the fighters of today and pilots manage these systems.

This section of the book attempts to tell the story of fighter aircraft and how they evolved, and highlights particular episodes of history in which fighters have played a key role, such as the Battle of Britain in 1940. The A–Z listing of fighters does not include every fighter aircraft that was ever built or that saw action. Instead, it presents the individual stories of what the author believes to be the most significant fighters.

TOP: **The McDonnell Douglas F-4 Phantom typified the 1950s trend for higher and faster flying fighters.** ABOVE: **The unique V/STOL Harrier gave military leaders the capability to operate fighters from virtually anywhere.** LEFT: **Bristling with air-to-air missiles, the Saab Gripen is one of the world's most modern fighters.**

It makes interesting reading when one compares the size, weight and capability of aircraft as diverse as the Fokker Dr.I triplane, the P-51 Mustang and the Eurofighter Typhoon. As will be seen, fighter aircraft have come in many different shapes, sizes and configurations.

Despite the predictions of some in the 1950s that the fighter aircraft was obsolete, the lack of flexibility afforded by a surface-to-air anti-aircraft missile requires that fighter aircraft remain in use. The Soviet bombers that frequently probed UK airspace during the Cold War simply needed to be escorted away by RAF fighters – a far less provocative act than loosing off a missile that could not be recalled.

The History of Fighter Aircraft

The fighter aircraft, born in World War I, has played a crucial role in modern history. Fighter aircraft have won wars, possibly prevented wars and defended nations from aggressors. Multi-role fighters of today can range over vast areas of airspace and, if required, unleash a range of "smart" weaponry against the enemy. This is a far cry from the first pistol shots exchanged between "scout" aircraft over the trenches of World War I.

Although the speed of fighter aircraft increased remarkably from World War I through to the 1960s, improved agility and manoeuvrability became the goals of the last quarter of the 20th century. This was made possible by the development of special materials allowing large thin wings to be built, optimizing manoeuvrability and aerodynamics without compromizing the strength of the aircraft.

Fighters can be used to protect national airspace, escort bomber aircraft on hazardous missions and, with the dawn of true multi-role aircraft, carry out reconnaissance or ground attack missions themselves. As long as air superiority is a military necessity, there will always be fighter aircraft.

LEFT: **Two classic European fighter aircraft, the Tornado ADV (top) and the legendary Spitfire (bottom).**

Birth of the fighter

TOP: **The Wright Brothers, Wilbur (second from left) and Orville (far right) and their Wright Military Aeroplane, 1909.**
ABOVE: **Lt Harvey-Kelly's B.E.2a was the first British aircraft to land in France after World War I began.**

Although the Wright Brothers pioneered sustained and controllable powered flight in 1903, they were not the first builders of military aircraft. The first contract for a military aeroplane was awarded to Frenchman Clément Ader in February 1892 for the construction of a two-seater capable of lifting a 75kg/165lb bombload. The aircraft failed to fly but the precedent was set – the military were interested in the aeroplane as a weapon.

In 1907 the US Army released the first ever specification for a military aeroplane issued for commercial tender. Within the specification were the requirements that the aircraft should have a speed of at least 64kph/40mph and that it should be designed to carry two persons having a combined weight of 159kg/350lb for 201km/125 miles.

A key year in the development of military air power was 1910. Missiles were first dropped from an aeroplane in January 1910 when Lt Paul Beck of the US Army released sandbags representing bombs over the city of Los Angeles, but, more importantly for this book, the first military firearm to be fired from an aeroplane was a rifle used by Lt Jacob Earl Fickel of the United States Army from a two-seat Curtiss biplane on August 20, 1910. Equally significant was a German patent, taken out in 1910, for a device that allowed a fixed machine-gun to be fired from an aeroplane.

The first British aeroplane built as an armed fighting machine was the Vickers Destroyer E.F.B.1 ordered by the British Admiralty in November 1912. A year later, in November 1913, the first aerial combat between aircraft took place during the Mexican civil war – pistol shots were exchanged and, although none seemed to hit the mark, the aircraft was now seen as a weapon of war. But at the outbreak of World War I, military aircraft had a long way to go before they could be described as effective fighting machines.

When World War I broke out in 1914, Britain's Royal Flying Corps had five squadrons. Most of these B.E.2s, Blériot monoplanes, Farman biplanes, Avro 504s and B.E.8s were sent to France in mid-August 1914 – all were unarmed. Blériot had conquered the English Channel just five years earlier and crossing that expanse of water to France by air was still a risky undertaking. When the first Royal Naval Air Service aircraft arrived in France in late August they were promptly fired on by their own troops. British Union Jack flags were quickly painted beneath the wings of British aircraft, being soon replaced by the roundels developed for the Allies.

Arming these early military aircraft was not easy, and a stray friendly bullet could have easily damaged a vital bracing wire or wooden support, not to mention the wooden propeller. At first, aircrew were armed with hand-held weapons – pistols and rifles. Early use of machine-guns like the Lewis gun were not immediately successful as the weapon's weight severely hampered the aircraft's performance. On August 22, 1914 RFC aircraft were scrambled to challenge a German Albatros – a Farman armed with a Lewis Gun took half an hour to reach 305m/1000ft and on landing the pilot was ordered to remove the Lewis and only carry a rifle. Machine-guns were however soon acknowledged to be the best armament and were gradually fitted to the sturdier aircraft entering service on both sides of World War I.

Mounted cavalry did see action early in World War I but the mechanized battlefield was no place for these warriors of another age and the mounted cavalry were driven from the field of combat forever. By early 1915, aircraft began to take over the reconnaissance role of the cavalry. Whereas cavalry could not ride through enemy positions defended by barbed wire and machine-guns, aircraft could simply fly over these positions and gather intelligence about the enemy – the military aircraft was beginning to define its role.

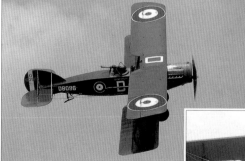

TOP: **This dramatic painting of World War I combat shows aircraft attacking out of the sun.** ABOVE: **The Sopwith Camel was another classic British fighter – note the guns, synchronized to fire between the spinning propeller blades.** LEFT: **The Bristol Fighter's arrival over the Western Front was bad news for enemy aircrews.** BELOW: **The Albatros D.Va was the ultimate Albatros D. fighter but was soon outclassed as better Allied aircraft appeared to counter it.**

By mid-1915, "fighting scout" aircraft were being used to accompany reconnaissance and artillery-spotting aircraft. When these escorting fighting scouts clashed and tried to destroy their respective charges, the first true dogfights began. Whereas early aircraft with poor performance had avoided aerial confrontation, pilots equipped with more able fighting machines began to go on the offensive – the fighter was born.

The first aces

World War I was a conflict fought on a truly massive scale – the devastation and loss of life on all sides was fantastically high. Almost as an antidote to the grim reports of mass slaughter, the stories of daring pilots in their magnificent machines, locked in aerial combat with a deadly foe, gripped the people back home on all sides of the conflict. The new knights were the men who did battle flying the new, dangerous yet glamorous aeroplane.

Albert Ball – Britain

Ball was the first British ace idolized by the public and was the darling of the British press. An engineering student when the war began, he transferred from the regular army to the Royal Flying Corps in 1915. From his arrival in France in February 1916, Ball established a reputation as a fearless pilot and excellent shot, achieving his first confirmed victory in late June. In just three months over the Somme, he scored 30 victories. With the introduction of the S.E.5, he reluctantly gave up his Nieuport XVII and on May 6, 1917 claimed his 44th and last victim, a German Albatros D.III.

The S.E.5s of Ball's flight encountered Manfred von Richthofen's unit, the all-red Jasta 11 on the evening of May 7, 1917 and Ball was last seen entering a thundercloud. Moments before Ball crashed, a German officer on the ground witnessed Ball's undamaged inverted aircraft emerge alone from the clouds, 61m/200ft above the ground with a dead propeller. He was only 20 years old and was posthumously awarded the Victoria Cross. Ball's death profoundly affected the morale of the Royal Flying Corps.

Manfred von Richthofen – Germany

The most famous ace of World War I, Manfred von Richthofen, joined a cavalry regiment in 1911. He transferred to the German Air Service in May 1915, initially as an observer, and earned his pilot's wings in December that year. After brief service on the Russian Front he transferred to France in August 1916 and on September 17, 1916 claimed the first of his 80 confirmed victories.

On January 16, 1917 he was given command of his own squadron, Jagdstaffel 11 and on June 26 that year, the command of Jagdgeschwader 1, a wing of four staffeln (squadrons) that came to be known as Richthofen's Flying Circus. The wing was made up of Germany's flying élite and Richthofen was keen to let the enemy know they were dealing with the "top guns" of the time – his personal Albatros D.III was painted all red and his men's aircraft were equally conspicuous, earning him the Red Baron nickname. Richthofen was almost killed in a dog-fight in July 1917 – he received a serious head wound but managed to crash-land his Albatros D.V. On September 2, 1917, flying the new Fokker Dr.I triplane, he scored his 60th kill. The Red Baron's score continued to climb and on April 20, 1918 he claimed his 80th and last victim, an RAF Sopwith Camel.

TOP: **Captain Albert Ball VC, DSO, MC – Britain's first aviation hero of the Great War.** ABOVE: **The Albatros D.V was the type being flown by the "Red Baron" in mid-1917.** RIGHT: **Pilots of Jagdstaffel 11 with von Richthofen in the cockpit of the Albatros D.III.**

Richthofen was killed the next day as he flew over the trenches in pursuit of Canadian Wilfrid May in his R.E.8. Evidence suggests Richthofen was hit by a single bullet, possibly fired from a machine-gun in the trenches. Richthofen's loss devastated German morale and far outweighed the military value of any further victories he might have achieved.

Edward Rickenbacker – USA

A celebrated racing driver before World War I, Eddie Rickenbacker first went to France in 1917 as the personal chauffeur of General Pershing. Eager to see action, he transferred to the US Army Aviation Section, initially as an engineering officer. After learning to fly, he joined the 94th Aero Squadron in March 1918.

He first flew Nieuport 28s and then SPADs and by the end of the war he had built up the impressive total of 26 victories, even more remarkable as he was hospitalized for two of his eight months of combat flying. Rickenbacker took over as commanding officer of the 94th in September 1918, and having been born in 1890, Rickenbacker was an old man compared to many of the pilots he commanded. Unlike many other famous World War I fighter pilots, he survived the war and returned to a hero's welcome in the USA as America's leading fighter ace.

Charles Nungesser – France

Like Rickenbacker, Charles Nungesser had been a racing driver, and by the end of World War I Nungesser was officially France's third-ranking fighter ace. While racing in South America, the Frenchman learned to fly and on returning to France in 1914 he joined the army. Nungesser got a transfer to the Flying Service and by 1915 he was a reconnaissance pilot, albeit a very aggressive example. In November that year he was posted to a fighter squadron and began to build his impressive total of 45 victories, most of which he won flying Nieuports bearing his favoured skull and crossbones motif.

On January 29, 1916 Nungesser was in a serious crash and broke both legs, but he was flying again within two months. He

was wounded many times and in-between his numerous crashes and visits to the hospital, Nungesser was taking his toll of German aircraft – by December 1916, a total of 21 victories.

At one point a German aircraft dropped a message on his aerodrome challenging him to a "duel". When Nungesser arrived at the appointed place he was ambushed by six German fighters. He shot two of them down and the others fled. On the same day, the Frenchman was attacked in the air by an RFC pilot who clearly had poor recognition skills – the British pilot persisted and Nungesser reluctantly shot him down too. The sky over the Western Front was full of danger. By mid-August 1917 he was so physically exhausted that he had to be carried to his aircraft, such was his desire to fight. Nungesser continued the familiar pattern of crashes, injuries and more victories until the war's end.

Although he survived the war, he disappeared over the Atlantic in 1927 while trying to fly from France to the USA.

TOP: **The Fokker Dr.I Triplane was von Richthofen's last mount.** ABOVE: **With his matinee idol looks and outstanding combat record Eddie Rickenbacker was the all-American hero.** LEFT: **Pictured with his Nieuport, Nungesser started the war as a cavalry officer and began his military flying in 1915.**

LEFT: **The cockpit of this Bristol Scout replica is equipped with all the original instruments a 1914 pilot had.** BELOW: **Woodworking tools outnumbered metalworking tools in the early aircraft factories.** BOTTOM: **With two wings generating more lift than one, the biplane was a popular configuration.**

Fighter aircraft technology up to 1945

When Orville and Wilbur Wright built their pioneering Wright Flyer in 1903, they used wood as the main material for wings and fuselage, braced by wires for added strength. By the end of World War II, most fighters were all-metal and flew at speeds the Wrights could have only dreamed of. The Wright Flyer was a biplane and a pusher aircraft, that is the propeller was used to push from behind rather than pull from the front as in later tractor aircraft.

The pusher arrangement was retained for some early fighters, in the days before the invention of interrupter gear, so that a forward-firing gun could be used with no propeller, which had tended to get in the way of the bullets. With no propeller in the way, the front seat was given to the gunner/observer while the pilot occupied the rear seat. The pusher arrangement was ultimately unsuitable for higher-per-formance fighters and dangerous – in the event of a nose-down crash, the engine and associated fuel tended to land on top of the two-man crew. The tractor configuration therefore became the norm for fighters and other aircraft.

The Wrights' aircraft's roll was controlled by wing warping, that is, bracing wires were pulled to twist the wing's outer sections. When World War I broke out, most aircraft designers were favouring the conventional tailplane and fin arrangement using trailing edge ailerons to effect roll in place of the limited wing warping.

As engine technology improved and speeds increased, drag on early aircraft became an issue and aircraft frames were increasingly covered and enclosed with taut fabric for streamlining. This technique was used into the mid-1930s, but by the time of World War II most new

fighter aircraft were of all-metal "monocoque" construction. Whereas early fabric-covered fighters got their structural strength from taut metal bracing wires, the metal skin of the monocoque fuselage and ultimately wings and tail, welded or riveted to a light metal interior framework provided an incredibly strong construction.

The Wrights chose a biplane configuration for their Flyer and this form was used in most early World War I fighters as two pairs of wings generated much more lift than a monoplane. A series of pre-World War I accidents had led Britain's government to ban the Royal Flying Corps from using the apparently unstable and unsafe monoplane, and it was not until 1937 that the Royal Air Force deployed a monoplane fighter – the Hurricane. The Hawker Hurricane was an interesting aircraft and was a "crossover" design as it incorporated old and new aircraft construction techniques – it was a monoplane but its fuselage had a metal framework covered with wooden formers with a fabric covering.

As biplanes had succeeded in the first air combats, it was therefore inevitable that triplanes appeared, and in the cases of the Fokker Dr.I and the Sopwith Triplane were very successful.

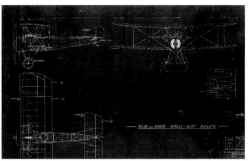

LEFT: **Compare the complexity of this 1945 Grumman Tigercat cockpit with that of the 1914 Bristol Scout.** BELOW: **By the end of World War II, the wood and fabric fighter construction technique was obsolete.**

Sets of two or three wings had to be braced by fairly substantial wires and joined together with interplane struts which in themselves generated drag. A single wing of the same area would generate much less drag and being more aerodynamic would allow the aircraft to go that much faster.

Engine technology developed at an incredible pace in the first four decades of the 20th century. The 1914 Vickers F.B.5 with a top speed of 113kph/70mph was powered by a 100hp rotary engine, and less than three decades later the engine that powered the 697kph/433mph P-47 Thunderbolt was rated at 2535hp. Rotary engines, the principal combat aircraft engine when war broke out, reached their developmental peak by the end of World War I. Although relatively small and light, power output of the rotary dropped off with increased altitude.

By the end of World War I, air-cooled radials and in-line piston engines were clearly the way ahead. Both types of engine had much to commend them and both were developed to the maximum until the jet engine ultimately replaced them both. The importance of engine development in the evolution of fighters cannot be overemphasized. More powerful and efficient engines coupled with improved aerodynamics enabled fighters to fly higher and faster. Without a Merlin engine, would the Spitfire have been the fighter it became?

Although World War I had clearly demonstrated the military value of aircraft, in the years immediately after, fighter development was neglected – it was peacetime uses of aircraft that taxed the designers' ingenuity. However, speed competitions like the Schneider Trophy challenged designers to develop small, fast aircraft. With national pride at stake, these competitions generated huge amounts of worldwide interest. The Schneider Trophy races held annually from 1919 to 1931 did much to encourage innovation in engine and airframe design and showed that fuel science and super-charging were vital elements in the engine equation. Britain won the Schneider Trophy in 1931 with a Supermarine racing floatplane, a design that led directly to the legendary Spitfire.

ABOVE: **A Royal Air Force Spitfire. By 1945, piston engine technology had effectively reached its evolutionary limit.**

But what use is an engine without a good propeller? This vital but often overlooked element of the fighter aircraft "package" was itself dramatically improved between World War I and 1945. World War I fighters had two blades but late mark Spitfires had five-blade examples. As a propeller spins it generates thrust in the same way as a wing develops lift. Early propellers were fixed pitch but in the late 1930s variable-pitch propellers were introduced so the pilot could mechanically adjust the propeller blades' angle for maximum efficiency at different speeds.

Towards the end of World War II, German and British jet-powered aircraft appeared and showed aircraft designers around the world the way ahead. The Messerschmitt Me262 could reach speeds of 870kph/540mph compared to the P-51 Mustang's top speed of 703kph/437mph. Designers knew that these early jet engines could take aircraft to speeds almost 25 per cent faster than the best piston-engined fighters in the world. The jet engine was the powerplant of the future.

Fighter armament: 1914–45

At the outbreak of World War I, aircraft armament was non-existent or ad hoc. The first fighters were armed with revolvers, rifles or shotguns carried by the pilots or observers but the importance of reliable hard-hitting armament was soon appreciated. Once weapons like the 7.7mm/0.303in Lewis machine-gun were proven, their use was then perfected. At first the guns were mounted on pivot pins or flexible mounts, aimed by the observers or pilots but they became truly effective once the guns were fixed to the aircraft and were synchronized to fire between the spinning propeller blades. To aim at a target, the pilot simply had to fly straight at it.

During World War I, two rifle-calibre machine-guns were usually enough to inflict serious damage on canvas-covered mainly wooden aircraft. By the mid-1930s this was clearly inadequate to destroy the larger, metal bombers coming off the drawing boards at the time. Consequently, more and bigger guns were used to arm fighter aircraft but where was the best location for them? Guns synchronized to fire through the propeller arc usually experienced a 10 per cent reduction in the rate of fire, and the numbers of guns that could be clustered around an engine was physically limited. The other option was to mount the guns in the wings – a far cry from the early days of air fighting when the gun's breech had to be within reach of the pilot so he could free jammed bullets. The down side of the wing-mounted gun, especially as wings became thinner, was the limited amounts of ammunition that could be physically fitted in the wing.

Most British World War I fighters were armed with 7.7mm/0.303in Vickers machine-guns and these remained the standard British armament until the mid-1930s when the Browning 7.7mm/0.303in was adopted. The Browning could fire 1100–1200 rounds per minute compared to the 750rpm of the Lewis. The muzzle velocity of the Browning was also greater than that of the Vickers – 811m/2660ft per second compared to 683m/2240ft per second. These performance figures are important because in most combats, pilots only have time for perhaps a second's burst as an enemy aircraft flashes by.

BELOW: **The synchronizing of fighter aircraft guns eased aiming for the pilots and thus improved the effectiveness of the early fighters.**

TOP LEFT: **Rearming an RAF Hurricane – two of the aircraft's four hard-hitting wing-mounted 20mm/0.78in cannon.** ABOVE: **Preparing to load the guns in USAAF P-51 Mustangs.**

During World War I, experiments had been carried out to see if large calibre weapons (cannon) firing explosive ammunition could destroy enemy aircraft. Early British tests found that the recoil of these comparatively large weapons was enough to stop a slow-moving firing aircraft in flight, let alone inflict damage on an enemy. French development work was more successful and a 37mm/1.45in cannon was used in combat by French aces Guynemer and Fonck, both of whom destroyed German aircraft with the weapon. Germany's World War I Becker cannon was later used as the basis for the early 1930s French Hispano-Suiza cannon that became the hugely successful Type 404 Moteur Canon.

In the mid-1930s Britain was behind the other major air forces in the procurement of cannon armament for fighter aircraft so it eventually licence-built the French Hispano-Suiza cannon.

When the legendary Spitfire first went to war its original armament was eight 7.7mm/0.303in Browning machine-guns but as the German Luftwaffe provided their aircraft with more armour and self-sealing fuel tanks it was apparent that the Spitfire's eight machine-guns were not adequate to inflict enough damage on enemy aircraft. Some Spitfire pilots were amazed to learn that enemy bombers claimed as "probably destroyed" had managed to limp home having suffered perhaps over 100 hits from 7.7mm/0.303in ammunition rounds. The Germans' ingenious self-sealing tanks, made of lightweight metal coated with layers of vulcanized and non-vulcanized rubber, must have saved many such aircraft from becoming airborne infernos. When the fuel tank was punctured by a bullet or shrapnel, the leaking fuel reacted with the non-vulcanized layer making it swell thereby plugging the hole. In spite of this, a hit from an exploding cannon round would have caused irreparable damage.

Aircraft like the early Hurricane with its eight machine-guns could unleash 160 bullets per second on a target whereas a 20mm/0.78in cannon carried by a Messerschmitt Bf109 could fire five shells per second – quantity versus destructive capability. The best solution was a compromise and so later Spitfires and Hurricanes carried a combined machine-gun/cannon armament.

During World War I, pilots had aimed their guns using a ring bead sight but that kept them too focused on the target, unable to see what else was going on in the sky ahead. In the mid-1930s the electric reflector sight was introduced and was a simplistic forerunner of today's Head-Up Display. A bright circle of light with an aiming dot in the centre was projected on to a small glass screen in front of the pilot. As the image was focused on infinity, it also allowed the pilot to be aware of what else was in the sky ahead.

Although the machine-gun and cannon were the most significant air-to-air weapons in the period, unguided rockets were highly developed by the end of World War II. Soviet fighters had in fact been experimentally armed with bomber-destroying 82mm/3.23in unguided rockets in the late 1930s. This Russian rocket was typical of most unguided rockets, having impact-fused explosive warheads that could inflict major damage on a bomber. During World War II, Germany was equally advanced in the development of unguided missiles and was eager to produce any means of knocking enemy bombers from the sky. The Luftwaffe initially used adapted surface-to-surface 21cm/8.27in rockets with 10.22kg/22.5lb high-explosive warheads detonated by a timed fuse. By the end of the war, Luftwaffe fighters were routinely armed with up to 24 unguided air-to-air rockets which, fired as a salvo, represented a deadly threat to Allied bombers. More impressive was the crude but effective radar-linked fire control computer that tracked an enemy aircraft and then launched an unguided missile at optimum range. Luckily for the Allies, Germany's comprehensive guided missile programme did not result in production weapons before the war's end.

LEFT: **In World War I, formal uniforms were the normal flying dress, however impractical they were.**
BELOW: **In winter conditions and as aircraft ceilings increased, thick flying suits were introduced on both sides during World War I.**

Pilot equipment up to 1945

What kind of equipment was at the early fighter pilot's disposal?

Early cockpits had very few instruments – an airspeed indicator, altimeter, fuel and oil pressure gauges and little else. As fighters were able to climb higher and higher, so the aircrew had to wear more and more clothes to counter the effect of the bitter cold. A pilot's efficiency also suffers above heights of 3050m/10,000ft and pressurized oxygen is required above 5,500m/18,000ft or they will ultimately pass out. Face masks were developed to provide oxygen under these conditions and continue to be used today. Cockpit heating was not much use if the pilot's "office" was open to the elements but it did make a difference when enclosed cockpits were introduced.

Before World War I, aircraft had carried radio receivers and transmitters only for experimental purposes – the first use of radio between an aircraft and the ground was in the USA in 1910. Before the days of transistors, those early radios were large heavy pieces of equipment weighing up to 114kg/250lb and as weight was a crucial factor in early aircraft, they were just not practical. When radios were installed they were normally only capable of receiving or sending Morse code signals. The other complication was that due to the wavelengths in use at the time, a trailing aerial of 91m/300ft length had to be used. Improved technology was required to make radio more practical and by the mid-1930s, relatively clear speech exchanges over the air were becoming the norm. Leather flying helmets were produced with earpieces stitched in, while the oxygen mask also had a built-in microphone.

On March 1, 1912 Captain Albert Berry of the United States made the first parachute jump from an aircraft, and from the start of World War I observation balloon crews were equipped with parachutes. The life-saving devices were not, however,

LEFT: **By the end of World War II more practical flying clothing was the norm, as were the parachutes denied to pioneer fighter pilots.** BELOW: **This Spitfire pilot sports the standard RAF oxygen mask with inbuilt microphone fixed to his helmet featuring in-built headphones.** BOTTOM: **The ultimate emergency exit. This unknown pilot leaves his stricken aircraft and prepares to open his 'chute.**

issued to aircrew and this led to many unnecessary deaths on both sides. Early 'chutes were heavy and bulky and would have added greatly to the overall weight of an aircraft. There was also a ludicrous belief among British military leaders that parachutes would undermine a pilot's fighting spirit and that they would "take to the silk" when faced with danger.

By the last year of World War I, however, aircraft performance and better parachute design made the parachute a more practical piece of equipment. Germany had led the way and issued parachutes to its crews in the summer of 1918. The first time a pilot used a parachute as a means of escape and survived was on August 22, 1918 – Lt Frigyes Hefty of the Austro-Hungarian Air Corps left his burning fighter after a dogfight with Italian aircraft, landed safely and lived to tell the tale.

As the higher speed jet fighters entered service towards the end of World War II, parachutes were found to be unsuitable for emergency escape. The high speed airflow made it very difficult and dangerous to bail out in the traditional manner. In the same way that they had led the way with parachutes, the Germans pioneered the use of what came to be known as "ejection seats" that propelled the pilot clear of their aircraft's tail, usually approaching very rapidly from the rear. A Heinkel He219A-0 was experimentally fitted with compressed air ejection seats for both crew, believed to be the first of their kind in service. The Heinkel 280 jet prototype's seat was also fired with compressed air, as opposed to the explosive charges in use today. In January 1942, during a test flight of the Heinkel jet, the pilot lost control of the aircraft and successfully ejected. The pilot, Flugkapitan Otto Schenk, was the first of thousands of aircrew to have their lives saved by ejection seats.

Blitzkrieg fighters

When Germany invaded Poland on September 1, 1939, precipitating World War II, a Blitzkrieg (lightning war) was unleashed on the ill-prepared Poles. The Blitzkrieg strategy was devised to create psychological shock and chaos in enemy forces through the use of surprise, speed and superiority. Proven by the Germans during the Spanish Civil War in 1938, the Blitzkrieg against Poland saw totally co-ordinated air (fighters and bombers) and land forces paralyse Poland's capacity to defend.

The best fighter aircraft in the Polish inventory was the P.Z.L. P.11 – with a top speed of 390kph/242mph the P.11 was still no match for the German Messerschmitt Bf109E that could fly over 177kph/110mph faster than the Polish fighter.

ABOVE: **The Messerschmitt Bf109, one of the all-time great fighter aircraft, was at the forefront of the Blitzkrieg, blasting ill-prepared opposition from the air.**
BELOW: **By the time the Luftwaffe reached France, it met more effective fighters – the Dewoitine D.520s.**

That said, the Polish P.11 pilots made the most of their out-moded machines. Some sources claim that 114 of the P.11s were destroyed in the air battles that raged at the time of the invasion – although the defence of Poland failed, the P.11s did claim 126 Luftwaffe aircraft in the process.

The Luftwaffe deployed 200 Bf109E fighters and fighter-bombers for the invasion of Poland and the more manoeuvrable Bf109 was also better armed than the P.11 and Poland's even more antiquated P.7 fighters. The P.11s were however very nimble and not to be taken lightly, a mistake made by a number of Luftwaffe twin-engine fighter crews.

The Polish air defence ultimately failed partly because of the inflexible military structure of the Polish armed forces. Many fighter and bomber units were assigned to different armies tasked with defending different parts of the country and so there was no co-ordinated fighter response to the armadas of German bombers. A very significant element of the Polish fighter force was the Pursuit Brigade solely tasked with the defence of Warsaw.

The Nazi Propaganda Ministry had claimed that the Polish Air Force had been destroyed on the ground in the first day of battle but this was far from the truth. A formation of Heinkel He111 bombers trying to attack an airfield near Warsaw, was mauled and six were destroyed, the first falling to P.11 pilot Lt Aleksander Gabszwicz. On the afternoon of September 1, 1939, He111 bombers again headed for Warsaw, escorted by Bf109s and Bf110s. The air combats that followed after defending P.11 fighters were scrambled saw six German bombers shot down for the loss of five Polish fighters. So committed were the Polish defenders that one pilot rammed a Bf109 and baled out. The Polish defenders had prevented the Luftwaffe from dropping a single bomb on Warsaw.

The fighters attached to the armies saw much action and accounted for many German aircraft. In the first six days of war, army units claimed 63 Luftwaffe aircraft while the Pursuit Brigade claimed 42. From September 8, as the Germans pushed through and the Polish forces fell back towards Warsaw, the Poles' ability to defend themselves in a concerted manner was severely undermined. As the Polish infrastructure was dismantled by the Blitzkrieg, and starved of fuel, their fighter forces dissolved into chaos. On September 17, Soviet forces, acting in concert with Germany, also crossed into Poland, sealing the fate of the beleaguered nation.

The P.11s and P.7s continued to fight as they could until being ordered by General Rayski, Polish Commander-in-Chief, to evacuate to Romania. Many desperate and courageous Polish pilots had continued to attack large Luftwaffe formations on what were ultimately suicide missions. A number of Polish pilots escaped so they could continue to fight Germany from friendly countries. Some enlisted in the French Air Force and after the Fall of France made their way to Britain to join RAF Fighter Command.

Poland had fallen to the might of the Nazi war machine with Luftwaffe fighters playing a vital role in neutralizing resistance in the air. Blitzkrieg tactics were subsequently employed in the German invasions of Belgium, the Netherlands and France in 1940.

TOP: **German nightfighters, primarily developed to counter the RAF night-time bombing offensive, gave the Luftwaffe the ability to fight around the clock.** ABOVE: **The P.Z.L. P.11 fighters of Poland were not able to repulse the might of the Nazi Blitzkrieg.** LEFT: **Armadas of Heinkel He111 bombers, having honed their skills in Spain, carried the Blitzkrieg across Europe.**

The Battle of Britain

By June 1940 Belgium, Holland and France had fallen to German forces. The British Army withdrew from the Continent and the British Prime Minister, Winston Churchill, declared "the Battle of France is over; the Battle of Britain is about to begin". The so-called "phoney" war was over and the Third Reich's next objective was the subjugation of Britain. Churchill refused to consider peace on German terms and Hitler realized that he might have to invade Britain, which was protected from the German Army by the waters of the English Channel. On July 16, 1940 Hitler issued a directive ordering the preparation and execution of a plan to invade Britain. With Britain's large and powerful navy to contend with, an amphibious invasion of Britain would only be possible if the Luftwaffe could establish control of the air over the Channel and southern England. The Luftwaffe planned to destroy British air power in a wave of massive raids and clear the way for the invasion. As the Luftwaffe bombing attacks started in July 1940, Goering, leader of the German Air Force, thought that the Luftwaffe would easily beat the Royal Air Force, and so the German Army and Navy prepared to invade. Invasion barges were assembled in Channel ports.

ABOVE: **The Spitfire's well-documented role in the summer of 1940 earned it a place in world history.**

The forces deployed in the Battle of Britain were surprisingly small. The RAF had around 600 front-line fighters, mainly Spitfires and Hurricanes, to defend their country. The Germans had around 1300 bombers and dive bombers, and about 900 single-engined and 300 twin-engined fighters. Despite the importance of the campaign as a prelude to invasion, the Luftwaffe had no systematic or consistent plan of action. In contrast, RAF Fighter Command had prepared themselves for exactly the type of battle that took place. Britain's radar early warning, the most advanced operational system in the world, gave the RAF notice of where and when to direct their fighter forces to repel German raids, thus avoiding costly and misplaced standing patrols. This was a vital lesson which is as valid today as in 1940.

German bombers lacked the bomb-carrying capacity to mount truly strategic bombing raids against key military targets, and British radar largely prevented them from exploiting the element of surprise. Long-range Luftwaffe fighter cover was only partially available from German fighter aircraft, since the latter were operating at the limit of their flying range from bases across the English Channel.

Between July 10 and August 11, German air attacks were directed on ports and most importantly on fighter airfields to draw Fighter Command into combat. From August 12 to 23 the battle became more intense as the Luftwaffe launched Adlerangriff (Eagle Attack) hitting radar stations and trying to destroy Fighter Command in combat – inland airfields and communications centres were still heavily attacked. Up to September 6, RAF Fighter Command came close to defeat as the Germans intensified their efforts to destroy Fighter Command and obliterate British defences. Although British aircraft production increased and the Luftwaffe had lost more than 600 aircraft, RAF pilots were being killed more quickly than replacements could be trained. The RAF's effectiveness was further hampered by bombing damage done to the vital radar stations.

At the beginning of September the British retaliated by unexpectedly bombing Berlin, which so angered Hitler that he ordered the Luftwaffe to shift its attacks from Fighter

Command installations to London and other cities. Although this led to many civilian casualties, it gave Fighter Command a short respite and time to regroup. In reality, the Luftwaffe's raids were somewhat formulaic which allowed Fighter Command to concentrate its fighter strength for the first time. By September 6, a huge German invasion fleet appeared to be ready to sail and British forces were put on "Alert No.2" meaning that an attack was probable in the next three days.

On September 15, the RAF's Spitfires and Hurricanes destroyed 185 German aircraft, showing the Luftwaffe that it could not gain air ascendancy over Britain. British fighters were simply shooting down German bombers faster than German industry could produce them. After the decisive RAF victories on September 15, the threat of invasion faded. The Battle of Britain was won, principally by the fighters of the Royal Air Force, and Hitler's invasion of Britain was postponed indefinitely.

ABOVE: **Messerschmitt Bf109s on patrol over the English Channel.** ABOVE RIGHT: **The fate of many Luftwaffe aircraft during the Battle.** RIGHT: **The Hawker Hurricane in fact destroyed more enemy aircraft than Spitfires, balloons and anti-aircraft defences combined. This photograph shows No.310 (Czechoslovakian) Squadron, Duxford 1940.**

Nightfighters

As early as World War I, German night bombing of Britain had been countered by defending fighters such as the Bristol Fighter and Sopwith Camel. Relying only on their eyesight and the hope of a bright moon, early nightfighter pilots did not constitute a practical deterrent and achieved only marginal success.

By World War II, defenders were assisted by ground radars, which could guide nightfighters to the general area where the enemy might be found, again by visual means. Truly effective night interception had to await the development of a radar small enough to be carried by the fighter itself. An airborne radar of this kind could aid in finding, stalking and bringing the nightfighter into firing range.

The USA, Germany, and Britain were all developing airborne radar early in World War II. Britain modified existing aircraft to fill the nightfighter gap. The Bristol Blenheim could not match the performance of day fighters like the German Bf109 so many became nightfighters, ultimately carrying the new and highly secret airborne radar. But even before the Blenheim IFs were equipped with radar, the RAF achieved some night-time victories – in June 1940 No.23 Squadron destroyed a Heinkel 111 bomber over Norfolk. However, the first radar interception came in late July 1940 when a Blenheim IF of the RAF's Fighter Interception Unit destroyed a German Dornier Do 17.

ABOVE: **The only specialized equipment carried by early nightfighters like the Bristol Fighter was the pilot's keen eyesight.** BELOW: **The Spitfire, with its narrow undercarriage track, was far from ideal for night operations.**

The Bristol Beaufighter was the world's first high-performance purpose-designed nightfighter and was a very advanced aircraft for its time. At the time of its combat début in 1940 the Beaufighter's devastating armament of four 20mm/0.78in cannon and six 7.7mm/0.303in machine-guns was the heaviest carried by any front-line aircraft. The closing months of 1940 saw the machine-guns fitted to the

LEFT: **The Northrop P-61 Black Widow – the first purpose-designed US nightfighter.** BELOW: **Only a handful of the Focke Wulf Ta154 dedicated nightfighters were ever built but indicated the realization that nightfighting was a specialized business.**

ABOVE: **A Junkers Ju 88 D-1 nightfighter.** RIGHT: **As aircraft were developed for nightfighting, so the cockpit began to accumulate new forms of equipment. The right seat position of this RAF Mosquito XIII nightfighter is dominated by the viewing apparatus of the AI Mk VIIIB radar.**

Beaufighters and, after a period of trial and error mastering the new radar with its range of 6.4km/4 miles, the aircraft's night victories began to increase.

Meanwhile, the United States directed its attentions to the interim Douglas P-70 and to the new Northrop P-61 Black Widow, the first US aircraft designed from the outset as a nightfighter. Lacking sufficient suitable US aircraft, USAAF units in Europe operated the British Beaufighter and later the Mosquito with good effect. In the Pacific, USAAF nightfighter squadrons operated the P-70 nightfighter version of the Douglas A-20 until P-61s could be delivered in 1944. By the end of World War II, the P-61 was the standard USAAF nightfighter and was in service with 15 of the 16 nightfighter squadrons operating in combat theatres worldwide.

German nightfighting began in the same way as the British – day fighters used in conjunction with a pilot's eyesight and searchlights on the ground below as the only means of seeing enemy aircraft in the dark. But by the summer of 1942

dedicated nightfighter groups were equipped with airborne radar. The RAF then began to use "Window", bundles of aluminium strips which, when dropped from the bombers, filled the sky with erroneous radar targets rendering German radar useless at a stroke. The Luftwaffe response in mid-1943 was the Wilde Sau nightfighters (Bf109 and Fw190) that relied on the illumination of enemy bombers by flares, searchlights or fires from below. Fighters guided from the ground by radar and helped by the ground lighting were then able to engage the enemy. German flak units were ordered to limit their fire to altitudes of 7000m/22,967ft so that the friendly nightfighters could operate in safety. Messerschmitt Bf110 and Junkers Ju 88 nightfighters equipped with radar and upward firing cannon did take a heavy toll of Allied bombers – literally hundreds were shot down.

The first uncertain steps in nightfighting led to the radar-equipped fighters of today, equally at home in day, bad weather and night conditions.

Fleet fighters: the rise of naval air power

The year 1910 was a key year in the development of military air power. On November 14 that year a Curtiss biplane became the first ever to take-off from a ship. The aircraft flown by Eugene B. Ely flew from a 25.3m/83ft platform built over the bows of the US Navy cruiser USS *Birmingham*. Within two months Ely had succeeded in landing a Curtiss on a ship, this time the USS *Pennsylvania*. These feats were considered by many as nothing more than stunts but Ely had shown that aircraft actually did not need dry land from which to operate. By combining one of man's oldest means of transport, the boat, with his newest, the aeroplane, a new means of waging war was born.

Britain's first deck take-off came on January 10, 1912, when the Royal Navy's Lt C.R. Samson flew a Short biplane from staging erected over the gun turret of the cruiser HMS *Africa*. By 1915 Britain had two ships with 36.6m/120ft-long flying-off decks but they were far from operational. Flying-off platforms were, however, fitted to a handful of Royal Navy ships and a Sopwith Pup using the HMS *Yarmouth* flying platform was launched against and subsequently destroyed a German Zeppelin – this action is believed to have been the earliest use of a "carrier-borne" fighter for air defence.

The first significant use of carrier-borne air power came in the 1931–2 war between China and Japan. In January 1932, carrier-borne aircraft operated in support of Japanese land forces in action near Shanghai. It was not, however, until World War II that aircraft carriers and fighters came into their own.

TOP: **Three thoroughbred Grumman fighters – the Hellcat (foreground), Bearcat and Wildcat (rear).** ABOVE: **Early fleet fighter – a Sopwith 1½ Strutter takes off from the deck of HMS *Argus*.**

The carrier was vital in the World War II Japanese campaigns in the Pacific and enabled them to project power over vast distances. Carriers were able to make or break campaigns by providing strike aircraft and air cover for other ships, convoys and assault ships, making their protection vital. Each carrier had fighter aircraft to defend the ships and carriers from air attack. The US Navy developed defensive fighter "nets" over carrier groups to protect them from enemy aircraft by a combination of radar early-warning and standing patrols of fighters, some up to 64km/40 miles away from the carrier. A carrier that could be protected from air attack was a massive strategic asset in any theatre of war.

LEFT: **A typical scene from the flight deck of a Pacific theatre carrier.**

ABOVE: **Martlet/Wildcats prepare for take-off from the deck of a Royal Navy carrier.** RIGHT: **The deck of a wartime carrier was fraught with dangers. Here a US Navy Hellcat burns while another, wings folded, awaits orders.**

While Britain at first had second-rate or obsolete aircraft deployed as carrier-borne fighters, other nations developed high-performance hard-hitting fighters designed from the outset as carrier aircraft. One of the first true fighters deployed by the Royal Navy was the Sea Hurricane, the navalized version of the famous Battle of Britain fighter. RAF Hurricanes had flown on and off HMS *Glorious* during the Norwegian campaign in 1940 and shown that high-performance fighters could be operated from carriers. It was followed into Royal Navy service by the American-built Grumman Martlet (known as the Wildcat in the US Navy and later in the Royal Navy). The Wildcat proved itself almost immediately in its first carrier deployment on convoy protection in September 1941 by driving away or destroying enemy aircraft. Meanwhile the Sea Hurricanes soldiered on, tackling German torpedo aircraft while newer high-performance fighters were awaited from America.

World War II Japanese carrier-borne air power was formidable. Six aircraft carriers took part in the devastating December 1941 attack on Pearl Harbor which devastated the US Pacific Fleet. In this and other attacks, Japanese strike aircraft were only able to carry out their deadly missions because they were escorted by fighters such as the Mitsubishi Zero that fought with the defending fighters. The Zero was a formidable enemy to take on but its excellent manoeuvrability was achieved at the price of pilot safety. Every weight-saving measure was taken – there was no armour protecting the pilot and often there was not even a radio in the aircraft.

ABOVE: **Dramatic rocket-sled take-off by an early Sea Hurricane. Launched from a ship without a flight deck, the pilot had to find land or ditch.**

One carrier fighter in particular could be described as a war winner – the Grumman F6F Hellcat. Following its arrival in combat in August 1943, this tough fighter was able to turn the tables on the Zero and gave US Navy and Marine Corps pilots the upper hand until the end of World War II. Aircraft carriers had been shown to be as good as their defences, and in particular the fighters that protected them.

Higher and faster

By the end of World War II, the piston-engined fighter had effectively been developed to the limits of its possibilities. The future lay with a greater knowledge of aerodynamics and fighters with jet power. Less than a decade after the end of the war, there were fighter aircraft on the drawing board that were planned to travel at up to three times the speed of sound. But jet propulsion also opened up new horizons for bomber aircraft design. While bombers were designed to go higher and faster, fighters were also developed to go higher and faster to intercept and destroy them. Speeds that man had only dreamed of were now within reach.

Whereas propellers would not have looked out of place on some early straight-wing jet fighters, aerodynamicists began to understand more about the special design requirements of high-speed jet aircraft. Wartime German research had found that by sweeping back the wings and tailplanes, the buffeting, vibration and drag experienced by early jets near the speed of sound could be reduced. Designers hoped that this feature could help the aircraft ease through the Mach 1 sound barrier.

TOP: **The Panavia Air Defence Tornado is capable of patrolling and defending huge expanses of airspace.** ABOVE: **The BAC Lightning reached RAF units in 1960. It was the fastest British fighter ever.**

At the same time the experts were trying to get their aircraft higher and higher. The fast climb was essential because it gave defending fighters the chance to reach the "high ground" from which to mount the most effective attack on enemy fighters and bombers – the aim of fighter pilots since World War I.

During the Korean War of 1950–3, the North American F-86 Sabre and the MiG-15 represented the state of the art and both had been designed with the benefit of wartime German research data. Both of these highly successful fighters tried to use their performance to achieve a height advantage

LEFT: **The F-16 has a maximum speed of 2125kph/1320mph and a ceiling in excess of 15,250m/50,000ft which it can reach in one minute.**
BELOW: **The ubiquitous MiG-21, still widely deployed today, was one of the first high-performance all-weather fighters.**

ABOVE: **Much of the performance data of the Saab Gripen remains secret.**

over the enemy, with the result that most fighter actions were fought 8–13km/5–8 miles above the ground. The Korean War had shown that the straight-wing jets had had their day and that high-performance and therefore the most effective fighters would have swept wings and other aerodynamic innovations.

Third-generation jet fighters such as the F-100 Super Sabre and MiG-19 were the first production jet fighters capable of supersonic speeds in level flight but were still essentially fair-weather fighters. It was not until the next wave of jet fighters that the interceptor was born. High-performance fast-climbing aircraft such as the MiG-21 and F-104 could reach speeds of Mach 2 and operate in all weathers.

The 1950s was the golden age of the strategic bomber – the USA, USSR and Britain all had fleets of long-range strategic bombers. High-performance, fast-climbing radar-equipped interceptors such as the English Electric Lightning and Convair F-102 appeared, and in the case of the Lightning could climb at 15,240m/50,000ft per minute.

In 1957 Britain's Defence Minister, Duncan Sandys, said the manned fighter would soon be a thing of the past, replaced by missiles. While this debate raged in the UK, elsewhere larger, often two-seat, fighters armed with missiles were in favour.

While Mach 2 performance and rapid climb are taken for granted in modern fighters, manoeuvrability is just as important. Modern interceptors like the Tornado ADV, F-16 and Gripen have an advantage over even slightly older fighters in that although they have to be able to climb quickly to high altitudes, the pilots don't actually have to see the enemy target aircraft. The powerful radars carried by today's fighters can pick up "bogies" over great distances and air-to-air missiles can be launched at targets beyond visual range.

Korea: the first jet v. jet war

Although jet fighter aircraft did enter service with Germany, Britain and the United States towards the end of World War II, it was not until the Korean War of 1950–3 that jet fought jet in the first major air war since World War II. When the war broke out following the North Korean invasion of South Korea on June 25, 1950, both sides were equipped with piston-powered aircraft, the North Korean Air Force having among other combat aircraft a total of 70 aged Soviet Yakovlev Yak-9 fighters. The Communist aggression against South Korea, whose air arm consisted of 16 unarmed trainers, drew the United States and the United Nations to the aid of the South.

The early days of the air war saw World War II types like F- (formerly P-) 51 Mustangs taking on Lavochkin La-7s although the USAF quickly deployed the F-80, the USAF's main fighter in the theatre. This straight-winged jet arrived just too late to see action in World War II but by 1950 was virtually obsolete. Nevertheless it began to rack up significant numbers of kills against the older North Korean types.

On July 3, US Navy jets flew in anger for the first time ever as F9F-3 Panthers escorted a bombing mission. Although the Panther too was a straight-wing jet, it remained the standard US Navy fighter throughout the conflict.

And so for the first six months of the war, the UN were to retain the upper hand in the air and on the ground. But then on November 1, 1950 some USAF Mustang pilots reported coming under fire by six swept-wing jet fighters that had flown across the Yalu river from Manchuria – the Russian-built Mikoyan-Gurevich MiG-15 was in the Korean War. The first jet

against jet air combat soon followed on November 8, when four MiGs were seen to fly into Korean air space and were challenged by F-80Cs of the 51 Fighter-Interceptor Wing. Lt Russell J. Brown attacked and destroyed one of the MiGs in mid-air. This historic combat was followed next day by the first jet kill by a US Navy jet when a Panther flown by Lt Commander

TOP: **Two classic jet fighters – the F-86 Sabre (left) and MiG-15.** ABOVE: **Royal Navy Lt Peter Carmichael on the day he downed a MiG jet with his piston-powered Sea Fury.**

W.T. Amen shot down another MiG-15. The Russian jets were starting to enjoy victories of their own against USAF B-29 bombers which had previously operated in relative safety. Flying from Chinese bases immune from UN attack, the MiGs were used to defend North Korean installations and represented a major threat to UN air superiority in the north where they created the very dangerous "MiG Alley". UN aircraft could range across the battlefields but faced deadly opposition when they neared areas in range of the MiG bases.

The USAF were quick to respond to the MiG threat and on November 8 ordered the F-86 Sabre-equipped 4th Fighter Group from the USA to Korea. The 27th Fighter-Escort Wing and their F-84 Thunderjets followed soon after. The F-86A was the most modern USAF fighter available but was later shown

TOP: **The F-51 Mustang was widely deployed by the USAF in the early days of the air war.** ABOVE: **A Sea Fury FB Mk II of No.804 Sqdn. Royal Navy leaves the deck of HMS *Glory*.** LEFT: **The remarkable F-82 Twin Mustang was among the first USAF aircraft to operate over Korea.**

to have a slightly inferior performance to that of the MiG. The Sabre's armament of six 12.7mm/0.5in machine-guns was no match for the two 23mm/0.9in and one 37mm/1.46in cannon of the MiG although the Sabre was a steadier gun platform. Tactically, the Communist pilots did themselves no favours, preferring to fly in gaggles of 20 or more aircraft compared to the section of four favoured by Western tacticians.

The first Sabre versus MiG air battle occurred on December 17, 1950 when four F-86s came upon four MiGs at an altitude of 7620m/25,000ft. Lt Colonel Bruce H. Hinton, leader of the F-86 section, fired 1500 rounds of ammunition and sent one MiG down to its destruction. On December 22, eight Sabres took on 15 MiGs and in the dogfights that followed from 9145m/30,000ft down to 305m/1000ft, the USAF pilots destroyed no fewer than six of the MiGs.

The Royal Australian Air Force, initially equipped with F-51 Mustangs, converted to Gloster Meteor F.8s but they were no match for the fast and manoeuvrable MiGs, which inflicted unacceptable losses on the F.8s.

The Republic F-84 Thunderjet was widely used in the war as a fighter-bomber and is credited with a number of air-kills, the first of which came on January 21, 1951. During a dive-bombing attack, F-84s were bounced by MiGs and in the dogfights that followed, Lt Colonel William E. Bertram scored the F-84's first MiG kill.

The MiGs did well to avoid all UN aircraft, not just the jets. The Hawker Sea Fury, operated by the Royal Navy, is known to have destroyed more Communist aircraft than any other non-US type and even shot down a number of North Korean MiGs. During August 1952, while flying the piston-engined Sea Fury off HMS *Ocean*, Royal Navy Lt Peter Carmichael destroyed a MiG-15 jet and earned himself a place in history.

By the end of the Korean War, USAF Sabres had achieved 757 victories for 103 losses. The first jet versus jet war was over and had demonstrated that tactics were as vital as effective weaponry. Straight-winged jets such as the F-80, F-84 and Meteor were shown to have had their day and the swept-winged fighters were on the ascendancy.

Fighter aircraft technology: 1945 to the present day

For most of the latter half of the 20th century, the designers of fighter aircraft continued to do what their predecessors had done – improve performance through more powerful engines and a better understanding of aerodynamics. Piston-engined fighters had virtually reached the end of their evolutionary line by 1945 although many remained in service for some years after the end of World War II. Jet powered fighters began to make their mark toward the end of the war, and within a decade supersonic speeds were regularly achieved, albeit in dives.

A greater understanding of "area rule" – the design technique that produces a fuselage contour with the lowest possible transonic wave drag – came in the 1950s and helped aircraft designers break through the "sound barrier" and produce aircraft capable of supersonic speeds in level flight. The quest for performance as opposed to manoeuvrability was typified by the Lockheed F-104 Starfighter that first flew in 1954.

Jet engine technology progressed rapidly in the 1950s resulting in engines like the F-104's General Electric 7076kg/15,600lb afterburning thrust J79 turbojet. This engine generated more than twice the output of the F-86 Sabre's 3402kg/7500lb thrust J47 turbojet. Compare them both to the 11,340kg/25,000lb thrust engines that power the F-15s in service today. Afterburner or reheat capability was developed in the late 1940s to give fighters an emergency boost of energy if required. When a pilot engages afterburner, additional fuel is simply burned in the jetpipe to generate extra thrust. This does consume considerable amounts of fuel and is used sparingly.

At first, jet fighters continued to use the construction techniques and materials employed on piston-engined aircraft. With the dawn of high speed flight and the extreme stresses placed on an airframe, designers began to look beyond aluminium and magnesium alloys and used titanium alloys and specially developed steel. Carbon or graphite fibre composites are also now commonly used and weigh half as much as

aluminium alloys but have three times the strength. This major weight saving reduces the overall weight of fighters and allows them to carry more fuel or weaponry if required.

Jet fighter designers have always grappled with the problem of trying to reduce the take-off and landing runs of high speed swept-wing aircraft and thus enable fighters to operate from shorter runways or even sections of road.

A truly innovative solution was the development of swing-wing or variable geometry in which the wings can move automatically from the swept to the spread position to maximize the aircraft's aerodynamic performance as required.

On take-off the spread position generates more lift and gets the aircraft off the ground sooner. Once in the air, the wings can be swept back for high-speed performance. Only a handful of swing-wing fighters have entered service – the F-14 Tomcat, the MiG-23 and the Tornado.

The ultimate solution to the short take-off requirement is the Harrier – the only single-engined vertical or short take-off and landing (V/STOL) aircraft in service. The key to the Harrier's truly remarkable vertical take-off capability lies with the vectored thrust from the Harrier's Rolls-Royce Pegasus engine, directed by four jet nozzles. The nozzles swivel as one, directing thrust from directly to the rear to just forward of vertical. In air combat the nozzles can be used to rapidly decelerate the aircraft so that an enemy aircraft, previously on the Harrier's tail, shoots by, unable to stop, thus becoming the Harrier's prey instead.

Where fighters once had mechanical linkages from control columns to control surfaces, modern fighters have fly-by-wire. This form of electronic signalling eliminates the need for mechanical linkages and a control column – the F-16 for example has a small side stick instead. Computers are now as fundamental to fighters as engines and weapons.

FAR LEFT: **The revolutionary vertical take-off Harrier is equally at home operating from an airfield or a supermarket car park.** INSET LEFT: **The Lockheed F-104 epitomized the quest for better performance.** BELOW: **A Rolls-Royce Spey jet engine. The development of powerplants such as these gave designers the thrust to achieve the required performance.**

Fighter armament: 1945 to the present day

In the years immediately after World War II it became apparent that jet fighters needed better armament than the machine-guns then available, some of which were based on World War I designs. By the end of World War II, Germany was leading the way in fighter armament development and some of their weapons were adopted and improved by the Allies after the war. The highly advanced Mauser MG-213 cannon for example was copied by the USA, Switzerland, France, the Soviet Union and Britain amongst others, and equipped most of the world's air forces in the post-war period. The British version of the Mauser gun, the Aden, is still used today. Even highly evolved cannon have their limitations and cannot for instance be effective over great distances.

The single most important development in aircraft armament since World War II has in fact been the guided Air-to-Air Missile (AAM) with its high explosive warhead. Unguided missiles, many of them developed in World War II, continued to be used into the 1950s. Perhaps the most remarkable of all unguided missiles was the Douglas Genie AAM which to this day is undoubtedly the most devastating of all AAMs. First tested in 1957, the Genie had a 1.5 kiloton nuclear warhead (equivalent to 1500 tons of TNT) with a lethal radius in excess of 305m/1000ft. The launch aircraft's

TOP: **A Royal Air Force Harrier looses off a Sidewinder AAM.** ABOVE: **A Matra Magic II AAM carried by a French Navy Super Etendard.**

on-board computer used radar to track the target and detonated the warhead at the optimum time. Pinpoint accuracy was not necessary with warheads of such destructive power.

Guided air-to-air missiles are now used by fighters to attack enemy aircraft from a minimum of 1.6km/1 mile away and up to distances in excess of 161km/100 miles. Air-to-air missiles

LEFT: **A Tornado F.3 armed with four Sky Flash and two Sidewinder AAMs.** BELOW: **A Royal Air Force F-4 Phantom pictured in 1974 with its armament of SRAAM Sidewinders under the wing, MRAAM Sparrows on the trolley and to the extreme right the pod-mounted 20mm/0.78in Vulcan gun.**

were first used in anger in 1958 when Taiwanese F-86 Sabres clashed with MiG-15s of the People's Republic of China. Armed with early examples of the AIM-9 Sidewinder, the F-86s downed a number of Chinese MiGs with the new weapon.

Modern AAMs are usually infra-red (IR) guided (the missile sensors make it follow a high temperature source such as an engine exhaust) or radar guided (the missile homes in on a target illuminated by a radar from the aircraft, and then follows on its own radar). The latter type normally uses a technique called Semi-Active Radar Homing which allows the radar to operate in pulses, to avoid making itself a target to radar-homing missiles. Some missiles use both the IR and radar guidance methods being radar-guided to within a few miles range and then IR guided to terminate in destruction.

Whatever the guidance, the AAM must reach its target quickly as most only have enough fuel for a few minutes' run. In those missiles with speeds of three or four times the speed of sound, the run can be counted in seconds.

AAMs are usually proximity armed, and, having detected that they are within lethal range, explode rather than having to hit the target. This is to counter last second evasive manoeuvres by the target aircraft and even if a missile just misses the target, the detonation will still cause substantial damage.

Air-to-air missiles are categorized according to their range, into short-range missiles (SRAAMs), medium-range missiles (MRAAMs), and long-range missiles (LRAAMs).

The SRAAM is designed for use in close air combat and distances up to 18km/11 miles and a typical SRAAM would be the well-known and widely used American Sidewinder (AIM-9) series.

The Medium-Range Air-to-Air Missile is mainly used to intercept targets beyond SRAAM range and uses a radar homing system with a greater detection range and better all-weather properties than the infra-red guidance system.

Long-Range Air-to-Air missiles are truly remarkable weapons and perhaps the most impressive of all is the Phoenix carried exclusively by the US Navy F-14 Tomcat. Probably the world's most sophisticated and expensive AAM the Phoenix has a speed of five times the speed of sound, and can be launched from over 200km/124 miles distance from a target, before the F-14 has even appeared on an enemy aircraft radar screen.

With no real alternatives on the horizon, air-to-air missiles will remain the prime armament of fighters for some years to come.

LEFT: **An artist's impression of a Saab Gripen test firing a BVRAAM (Beyond Visual Range Air-to-Air Missile).**

Fighters at war: 1950s–70s

M any fighters developed since the end of World War II have never fired a shot in anger. However, wars have raged around the globe since then, and those that did not directly involve the superpowers often became testing grounds for their equipment. Fighter aircraft have played a key part in most of these conflicts from the Arab-Israeli War to the Falklands, and from the Indian-Pakistan wars to the Gulf War. The performance of these fighters influenced fighter design.

After Korea, the next significant use of fighters came in the 1958 exchanges between Taiwan and the People's Republic of China over disputed territory. In a replay of some of the classic air battles of the Korean War, Taiwanese F-86s took on Chinese MiG-15s. This time the Sabres were armed with air-to-air missiles as well as guns.

India and Pakistan's first air battles took place in 1965. While the Indians deployed the Hawker Hunter, Folland Gnat, Mystère IV and MiG-21, Pakistan had Lockheed F-104s and Sabres which, like the Taiwanese examples, were armed with Sidewinders. Although the Mach 2 F-104 was able to shoot down two Indian Mystères it was shown to be no dogfighter. Indian Hunters were able to outperform enemy Sabres but the F-86 air-to-air missile capability more than evened up the fight.

Fighters entered the fray in Vietnam from 1965 and battled almost constantly until 1973. North Vietnam relied on Soviet equipment including the MiG-17 much favoured by North Vietnam's aces. The MiGs were agile and very dangerous in close combat whereas the USA deployed large, complex missile-armed fighters like the F-4 Phantom designed to hit enemy aircraft from some distance away. The US Navy Crusader, known as the last of the gunfighters, actually achieved 19 out of 20 air victories using AAMs. Despite claims that the dogfight was a thing of the past, Vietnam proved that close air combat expertise was still a vital skill for modern fighter pilots. The US Navy was so concerned with the poor air-combat results from early in the Vietnam War that it set up the now famous Top Gun programme. US Navy pilots were taught how to fight and not just how to fly, and the programme continues to this day.

When the Arab-Israeli War erupted in 1967 the Israelis had Mirage IIIs and, later, the F-4 Phantom, while their Arab opponents flew MiG-19s and MiG-21s. The Mirage III was able to outfly and outgun any aircraft it met in the war and when the F-4 entered Israeli service, the nation had one of the most potent and combat experienced fighter forces in the world. In September 1973 a patrol of Arab MiG-21s attacked a flight of Israeli Mirages and Phantoms off the Syrian coast – 13 MiGs were lost for one Mirage. Fighter aircraft had come a long way since the Korean War but were still only as good as the air fighting system that backed them.

LEFT: **Royal Air Force F-4s. The Phantom saw considerable combat in Vietnam and the Middle East.** TOP AND UPPER MIDDLE: **The MiG-15 (top) and F-86 Sabre (upper middle) had a post-Korea rematch in air battles between Taiwan and the People's Republic of China.** LOWER MIDDLE: **The Hawker Hunter, widely exported from Britain, was used in action by the Indian Air Force during the Indo-Pak war of 1965.** BOTTOM: **The ubiquitous MiG-21.**

Fighters at war: 1980s–90s

Israel's fighter actions against Syria over the Lebanon in 1982 demonstrated how fighters, as part of an integrated strike plan, can win wars. Eighty-two Syrian fighters, mainly MiG-21s and -23s were destroyed without loss by the Israeli fighter force of F-15s and F-16s. Israeli use of all-aspect Sidewinder air-to-air missiles for the first time in combat, allowed their fighters to attack enemy aircraft from any angle and not just the traditional "six o'clock" position to the rear. Ground radar, AWACS and ELINT aircraft all passed information to the Israeli fighters bestowing their pilots with exceptional situational awareness – in short, they knew exactly where the Syrian fighters were and what they were doing.

In 1982 the Falklands War between Britain and Argentina also broke out. Compared to other conflicts, fighter operations over the Falklands were limited but nevertheless absolutely determined the outcome of the war. Fighting a numerically superior enemy, the British pilots had to achieve air superiority over the islands so the ground campaign could begin. British Sea Harriers were tasked with defending the British fleet and

ABOVE: **The swing-wing F-14 Tomcat.** BELOW: **The Mirage 2000, deployed during the Gulf War by France, is an extraordinarily manoeuvrable fighter. Although it has been flying since 1978, the 2000's agility stops the show when it appears at air displays.**

faced the Argentine Mirage IIIs and Daggers. The Argentine fighters, forced to withdraw to the mainland after RAF Vulcan bombing raids on the Port Stanley runway, were operating hundreds of miles from their home bases. In the air combats that took place, British Sea Harriers accounted for 23 enemy aircraft including the very capable Mirages and Israeli-built Daggers – no Sea Harriers were lost in air combat. If the Sea Harriers had not protected the British Task Force so effectively,

ABOVE: Clearly illustrating the appalling operating conditions in the South Atlantic during the Falklands air war, these Sea Harriers are seen battered by the elements. Nevertheless the Sea Harriers of the Task Force kept the Argentine fighters at bay. LEFT: The MiG-21 was widely deployed by a range of air arms in the 1980s and '90s. BELOW: The highly capable and potent MiG-29 (this is a German Luftwaffe example) was in the Iraqi Air Force inventory during the Gulf War of 1991.

Britain's attempt to retake the Falklands could have ended in defeat with the Task Force at the bottom of the South Atlantic.

The rather more one-sided Gulf War of 1991 saw Iraq take on most of the Western world as a result of their invasion of Kuwait. The best fighter in the Iraqi inventory was the Mach 2 plus MiG-29. This very capable, incredibly agile high-performance fighter was developed in the Cold War to take on the best of the West's fighters. With a radar that can track ten targets simultaneously up to 245km/152 miles away, the MiG-29 pilot's helmet-mounted sight allows them to direct air-to-air missiles wherever the pilot looks. Complemented by MiG-21s, -23s, -25s and Mirage F1s, the Iraqi fighter force of MiG-29s was not to be taken lightly. The coalition forces boasted a fighter force of Tornado F.3s, Mirage 2000Cs, F-15Cs, F-16Cs, F-14s and F/A-18s provided by the United States (Air Force, Navy and Marine Corps), Britain (Royal Air Force), Saudi Arabia, France, Qatar and Canada. Although the Iraqi aircraft were very capable in absolute terms, compared to the highly trained coalition pilots backed by the biggest military machine since World War II, Iraqi pilots had little chance of success. The coalition had systematically destroyed the Iraqi military infrastructure piece by piece using bombs and cruise missiles. Despite the massive deployment of coalition fighters only 45 victories were achieved because most Iraqi fighters had fled to safe havens as soon as the shooting began. Without their complex support system, the Iraqi fighters would have been sitting ducks. Thirty-six of the victories were achieved by USAF F-15 Eagles, demonstrating the war-winning ability of the McDonnell Douglas fighter. A further two "kills" were credited to a single Royal Saudi Air Force F-15 that simultaneously shot down two Iraqi Mirage F1s with air-to-air missiles.

The overwhelming weight of coalition fighter power drove the Iraqi Air Force from the sky and allowed the Allied air attacks to continue unopposed. The cease-fire was signed on March 3, 1991 and the fighter had once again helped bring a war to a swift conclusion.

Inflight refuelling

Inflight refuelling (IFR) is vital to the world's major air forces and most recently played a key role in NATO's 1999 air offensive over the Balkans. In the early days of military aviation however, the refuelling of aircraft in flight was seen as nothing more than a stunt and it took some time for the military to be convinced of its value.

In June 1923 the US Army Air Service (USAAS) used two DH4 biplanes to prove a workable, if risky, system consisting of 500 litres/110 gallons of fuel, large funnels, and a 15.25m/50ft hose with an "on/off" nozzle on the end. Despite the dangers, by 1935 the record for sustained flight courtesy of inflight refuelling was pushed to 653 hours and 33 minutes – a record that stands to this day.

Although the USA had an early lead it was Britain's Sir Alan Cobham who turned IFR from a stunt to a workable technique. In 1934 Cobham's company Flight Refuelling Ltd developed a system consisting of a weighted cable let out from the tanker and a grapnel fired from the receiving aircraft to grab the cable. The hose was then drawn into the receiver aircraft – it was known as the looped hose system. However, just as World War II was coming to an end, Flight Refuelling perfected a new technique, still in use today – the probe and drogue

TOP: **A Royal Navy Sea Harrier tops up its tanks from a Royal Air Force VC-10 tanker using the probe and drogue technique.** ABOVE: **A USAF "flying boom" prepares to connect to an F-16.**

method. The tanker aircraft trails a hose with a stabilizing conical drogue at its end. Receiving aircraft are fitted with fixed probes which accept fuel flow when connected to the drogue. Valves are automatically opened on the probe and drogue when locked together and shut once contact is broken.

LEFT: **Converted Handley Page Victor bombers served as RAF tankers.**
BELOW: **Tanker operations have been central to fighter operations in a number of conflicts. Here a KC-135 refuels a USAF F4E during the Vietnam War. Two F4Ds (foreground) and two more F4Es (background) await their turn.**

The probe and drogue method was developed and perfected in the late 1940s and was widely adopted, representing a major improvement on the old line and grapnel method. On August 7, 1949 an RAF Meteor Mk 3 was kept airborne for 12 hours and 3 minutes and pilot comfort appeared to be the only limiting factor. In 1951 a specially modified USAF B-29 bomber with three refuelling points became the world's first triple point tanker. In spite of trials in which this B-29 simultaneously kept six RAF Meteor 8s aloft for four hours at a time, the RAF appeared to lose interest in IFR. The triple point tanker was however taken up by the USAF and in the mid-1950s, unlike their British counterparts, all new American fighters were built with IFR probes.

The US Navy also adopted the probe and drogue system in 1954. The Douglas company created the "buddy pack" so that aircraft could carry an air refuelling pod as an external store as easily as a drop tank. This makes for wonderful flexibility as any "buddy-equipped" aircraft can be a tanker or receiver. From the mid-1950s most US Navy and Marine aircraft were also fitted with folding probes.

Meanwhile in the USA, the Boeing company set about developing their own system to improve on the British technique. They wanted to pass fuel at a faster rate down a shorter hose which ultimately evolved into a rigid pipe. So was born the flying boom method used by the USAF today.

The rigid pipe is actually telescopic and joined to the tanker by a universally pivoted coupling. The boom is pressurized by the fuel itself and has aerodynamic control surfaces near the "business" end, controlled by a boom operator or "boomer" who "fires" the telescopic boom to make a fuel-tight seal.

The Boeing KC-135 tanker, developed from the 707 airliner, first flew in August 1956 and swiftly took its place as the tanker aircraft of all time. The KC-135 had a performance that allowed it to fuel thirsty aircraft at jet speed and heights using a high-speed boom transferring 3773 litres/1000 US gallons of fuel per minute. The French Air Force were so impressed by the KC-135 they ordered 12, modified for probe and drogue use, to exclusively refuel the Armée de l'Air Mirage IVA nuclear attack force. In Vietnam, KC-135s transferred almost 3.6 billion kg/8 billion lb of fuel in over 160,000 missions. USAF KC-135s are still in widespread use today and were in the air around the clock during the 1999 NATO action against Serb forces.

During the Gulf War in 1990–1 and the extensive 1999 air campaign against Serb forces, IFR was used throughout both to keep the Allies' aircraft aloft. As long as combat aircraft cannot carry enough fuel to complete lengthy missions, the flying fuel stations of the world's air forces will remain crucial to the plans of aerial warfare strategists.

Pilot equipment in the 21st century

No matter how advanced fighters may become in years to come, as long as there are human pilots they will always need a means of safely abandoning the aircraft in an emergency. One of the most fundamental pieces of pilot equipment is the ejection seat, pioneered during World War II. They are more than just a means of getting pilots and other aircrew out of the aircraft in an emergency – they also have to be comfortable and will be sat on, possibly for thousands of hours without ever being fired. When an ejection seat is fired usually by a handle between the legs or on top of the seat headrest, it draws the occupant's legs in close to the seat with garters (through which the legs are threaded) to keep them from harm's way as the seat rockets from the aircraft. The garters release at the same time as the main harness holding the pilot in the seat is opened.

For a seat to be a true life-saver it must be capable of being fired from ground level and propel itself high enough for the parachute to deploy while not subjecting the pilot to unacceptably dangerous acceleration forces. If a high altitude ejection takes place, modern ejection seats carry their own supply of oxygen so the occupant can breathe easily as soon as ejection has occurred. In reality many aircrew lose their face masks on ejection – some even lose their boots, such can be the violence of an ejection.

When the seat falls below 3050m/10,000ft a barostatic gauge senses the altitude and releases a drogue chute to draw

ABOVE: **Split-second decisions are essential in combat. The Head-Up Display of modern fighters projects vital data on to an angled screen so that the pilot does not waste time constantly looking down at an instrument panel.** LEFT: **A true life-saver – although ejection is a physically traumatic experience, it gives aircrew a means of escape from a striken aircraft at virtually any altitude.**

out the main parachute. Another drogue chute is deployed as soon as the seat leaves the aircraft and slows the seat's descent. All of these functions are automatic in case the occupant is unconscious.

Once clear of the aircraft, the seat automatically releases the occupant from the seat and deploys the main parachute. Although aircrew can suffer injuries due to the rapid acceleration during ejection and the battering they receive as they hit the airflow, possibly at hundreds of miles per hour, they do at least have a means of escape, unlike their 1914 counterparts.

The future?

Cockpit instrumentation has been revolutionized in recent years to relieve the pilot's workload as much as possible so that they can manage the aircraft's systems and fight more effectively.

Helmet-mounted sights have been in use since the mid-1990s but helmet-mounted displays are likely to become the only means of providing the pilot with information. Computers will "clean" the information so that the pilot does not become overloaded with data. A 3-D moving map, painted on the pilot's retina using eye-friendly lasers, will maximize a pilot's situational awareness letting them know exactly where they are in relation to potential enemies.

Pilots are already bombarded with huge volumes of data from on board and other sensors, all of which has to be assimilated by the pilot whilst flying and perhaps fighting.

ABOVE: **Radar equipment carried by today's fighters is far more powerful than that carried during World War II.**

There is however a limit to the amount of information and activities a human can handle simultaneously. Incredibly intelligent software will ultimately be able to provide pilots with instantaneous decision support by assimilating information and recommending an action.

Pilots have relied mainly on sight for flying and fighting whereas systems already under development for the Space Shuttle and the US Navy's Joint Strike Fighter use other senses. Pilots wear a vest bristling with what the manufacturers call "tactors" that vibrate against the pilot's body as a non-visual means of providing information on aircraft orientation. If the aircraft rolls left a tactor vibrates against the pilot's left side and so on.

Complementing visual displays, 3-D audio can also make fuller use of the pilot's senses – a left engine failure for

TOP: **The Eurofighter cockpit is dominated by a wide-angle Head-Up Display and three colour monitors displaying all instrument information and flight data. The pilot has a helmet-mounted sight for weapon aiming and direct voice input allows the pilot to control certain aspects of the flight just by talking to the aircraft.** ABOVE: **Helmet-mounted sights were introduced in the mid-1990s.**

example could be signalled to the pilot via an audible tone in the left ear.

Some experts are claiming, not for the first time in the history of fighter aircraft, that the days of the manned fighter may be coming to an end. Time will tell, but for the foreseeable future, air combat will be fought with humans in the cockpit.

A–Z of World War Fighter Aircraft

1914–45

At the outbreak of World War I there were no fighter aircraft as such. Early aerial battles between aircraft with top speeds of around 135kph/84mph consisted of the pilots or observers shooting at their opposite number with pistols or hand-held rifles. Armed reconnaissance aircraft gave way to fighting scouts, the first true fighter aircraft. By the end of the war, one of the fastest fighters was the SPAD S.XIII with a top speed of 215kph/134mph. Compare this to the 660kph/410mph Gloster Meteor that flew into action late in World War II or the remarkable rocket-powered Messerschmitt Me163 Komet, which could reach 960kph/596mph.

These remarkable advances were made in only three decades. Piston engines were developed to their limits and jet engines, like those that equipped the Meteor, were produced as viable powerplants. Biplanes eventually gave way to monoplanes, and pilots came to be enclosed in heated cockpits as air fighting was forced higher and higher by attackers trying to evade defenders. But by the end of World War II, new aircraft designs and other technological advances were under development that would make the finest World War II fighters seem primitive by comparison.

LEFT: **A pair of North American P-51 Mustangs.**

LEFT: **The widely produced Albatros D.Va was an early example of fuselage streamlining.**
BELOW: **In early 1917 the D.I won air superiority for the Germans over the Western Front.**

Albatros D. Fighters — I, II, III, V, Va

The D series of Albatros fighters illustrates very well just how short-lived air superiority could be over the Western Front in World War I. As one side introduced a more effective type and achieved the upper hand, the enemy would develop a superior aircraft and very quickly redress the balance. The D.V was the last of a line of Albatros fighters that began with the D.I, developed into the D.II and then the D.III. As each version joined the fray it enjoyed only relatively short-lived success.

The Albatros D.I was introduced by the Germans to counter the Allied de Havilland and Nieuport fighting scouts, which had ended the "Fokker Scourge" of early 1916 and regained air superiority from the Germans. The D.I played a major role in swinging the pendulum back in favour of the Germans in early 1917. Apart from the fuselage, the D.I was built using components or building methods employed in the Albatros C series. The fighter's fuselage was elliptical in section and represented an advance in aerodynamic design over the earlier models.

The aircraft was powered by either a Benz Bz.III or a Mercedes D.III engine, which were then the most powerful engines fitted in a scout. This, coupled with the fact that the D.I was armed with

two synchronized machine-guns, made it a hard-hitting fighter capable of climbing to 1000m/3280ft in six minutes – an impressive climb rate for the time. These factors made it attractive to the German "top guns" of the time, such as von Richthofen and Boelcke, who used the aircraft to regain air superiority for the Germans over the Western Front.

The D.II introduced a few fundamental improvements, including the lowering of the top wing so that the pilot could see over it and the aerodynamically improved installation of the radiator in the upper wing centre section. Climbing to 1000m/3280ft now took a mere five minutes.

The D.III was an improved version of the D.II, designed for better manoeuvrability. Changes to the wing set-up required the introduction of v-shaped struts between the upper and lower wings to improve rigidity. By late 1917 the D.III was in turn outclassed by the newer Allied fighters like the S.E.5 and was replaced by the D.V, the ultimate Albatros. The D.V had a wonderfully streamlined plywood-skinned fuselage and was produced in vast numbers. Over 1500 alone served on the Western Front, making up for any combat shortcomings by sheer weight of numbers. Heavy losses were

experienced, not only as a result of enemy action but also to the Albatros's tendency to break up in flight, due to inherent structural weaknesses in the lower wing.

ABOVE: **The D.II had its upper wing lowered so that the pilot could see over the top.**

Albatros D.V

First flight: Spring 1917
Power: Mercedes 180hp DIIa six-cylinder in-line engine.
Armament: Two belt-fed fixed 7.92mm/0.31in Spandau machine-guns
Size: Wingspan – 9.05m/29ft 8in
 Length – 7.33m/24ft 0.5in
 Height – 2.7m/8ft 10.25in
 Wing area – 21.28m²/229sq ft
Weights: Empty – 687kg/1511lb
 Maximum loaded – 937kg/2061lb
Performance: Maximum speed – 187kph/116mph
 Ceiling – 5700m/18,700ft
 Range – 2 hours endurance
 Climb – 1000m/3280ft in 4 minutes

LEFT: **An all-metal Siskin IIIA of No.49 Squadron Royal Air Force, pictured in 1929.**

Armstrong Whitworth Siskin IIIA

First flight: October 20, 1925
Power: Armstrong Siddeley Jaguar IV radial piston engine
Armament: Two synchronized 7.7mm/0.303in Vickers machine-guns in forward fuselage
Size: Wingspan – 10.11m/33ft 2in
Length – 7.72m/25ft 4in
Height – 3.1m/10ft 2in
Wing area – 27.22m²/293sq ft
Weights: Empty – 935kg/2061lb
Maximum loaded – 1366kg/3012lb
Performance: Maximum speed – 251kph/156mph
Ceiling – 8230m/27,000ft
Range – 1 hour, 12 minutes at full throttle
Climb – 3050m/10,000ft in 6 minutes, 20 seconds

Armstrong Whitworth Siskin

This fighter had its origins in the Siddeley Deasy S.R.2 Siskin, produced by Armstrong Whitworth's parent company in 1919 and constructed mainly of wood. Britain's Air Ministry only wanted all-metal fighters and so the Siskin was redesigned. When the Siskin III joined No.41 Squadron at Northolt in May 1924 it became the first all-metal fighter in RAF service.

In total, 465 Siskin IIIs were produced, including some examples for export to Estonia and Canada. The improved Siskin IIIA, powered by a supercharged Armstrong Siddeley Jaguar IV engine, first flew in October 1925 and went on to equip eleven RAF squadrons from September 1926 – the newer model can be identified by the lack of the ventral fin beneath the tail.

Royal Air Force Siskin squadrons pioneered aerobatics in the service, some Siskins even being flown literally tied together at the famous Hendon Air Displays.

The last Siskin in RAF service was phased out in October 1932, although IIIAs supplied to the Royal Canadian Air Force soldiered on until replaced by Hawker Hurricanes in 1939.

LEFT: **The Avia 534, arguably the best fighter of its time.**

Avia 534

First flight: August 1933
Power: Hispano-Suiza 850hp HS 12Ydrs in-line piston engine
Armament: Four fixed 7.7mm/0.303in synchronized machine-guns in front fuselage plus underwing racks for six 20kg/44lb bombs
Size: Wingspan – 9.4m/30ft 10in
Length – 8.2m/26ft 10.75in Height – 3.1m/10ft 2in
Wing area – 23.56m²/253.61sq ft
Weights: Empty – 1460kg/3219lb
Maximum loaded – 2120kg/4674lb
Performance: Maximum speed – 394kph/245mph
Ceiling – 10,600m/34,775ft
Range – 580km/360 miles
Climb – 900m/2953ft per minute

Avia B. 534-IV

This little-known fighter has been described as the finest fighter aircraft of its time, because of its combination of impressive armament, excellent handling and high speed. It was certainly the most important Czech aircraft of the inter-war years and was almost at the pinnacle of biplane fighter design, lacking only a retractable under-carriage. Construction of the 534 was an

interesting combination of steel wings covered with fabric, and a fuselage of riveted and bolted steel tubes covered with metal panels or fabric. In April 1934 the second prototype set a Czech national speed record of 365.74kph/227.27mph.

Front-line Czech fighter units were equipped with over 300 of these fine aircraft during the Munich Crisis of

September 1938, and after the German occupation of Czechoslovakia, Slovak Air Force units flew 534s against the Red Army in July 1941.

The Avia 534 interested the Luftwaffe sufficiently for it to form in late 1939, albeit briefly, a unit equipped solely with the captured Czech fighter. These robust and manoeuvrable fighters were later relegated to target towing duties.

LEFT: **The P-39, widely used by the Soviet Union.**

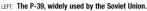

Bell P-39M Airacobra

First flight: April 6, 1938
Power: Allison 1200hp V-1710-83
in-line piston engine
Armament: One 37mm/1.46in T9 cannon,
two 12.7mm/0.5in machine-guns and four
7.62mm/0.3in machine-guns
Size: Wingspan – 10.36m/34ft
Length – 9.19m/30ft 2in Height – 3.61m/11ft 10in
Wing area – 19.79m^2/213sq ft
Weights: Empty – 2545kg/5610lb
Maximum take-off – 3810kg/8400lb
Performance: Maximum speed – 621kph/386mph
Ceiling – 10,970m/36,000ft
Range – 1046km/650 miles
Climb – 4575m/15,000ft in 4 minutes, 30 seconds

Bell P-39 Airacobra

The P-39 was the first fighter with a tricycle undercarriage. The type was also unorthodox because its engine was installed behind the pilot, as it was armed with a large-calibre cannon that fired through the propeller hub. The aircraft had in fact been designed around the 37mm/1.46in weapon from the outset. Initially ordered for the French Air Force, the aircraft were instead supplied to Britain.

The P-39 entered USAAF service in February 1941, and in September the same year, No.601 Squadron became the first and only RAF unit to operate the type. During the aircraft's test programme, a decision was made to exclude the engine's turbocharger and the consequent relatively poor performance did not endear the P-39 to the RAF, who only used the type for

ground attack missions between October and December 1941. The USAAF, however, did use the P-39 with some success in North Africa in a ground attack role and around 5000 were supplied to the USSR, where they were used for similar missions. From 1942–4 the P-39, together with the P-40, were the main front-line USAAF fighters in the Pacific theatre.

LEFT: **At first the F4B had no engine cowling, but later a ring cowling was added to improve streamlining. The F4B equipped both the US Navy and Marine Corps, while the P-12 variants were operated by the USAAC.**

Boeing F4B

First flight: June 25, 1928
Power: Pratt and Whitney 550hp R-1340-16
Wasp nine-cylinder radial engine
Armament: Two fixed forward-firing 7.62mm/0.3in
machine-guns
Size: Wingspan – 9.14m/30ft
Length – 6.12m/20ft 1in
Height – 2.84m/9ft 4in
Wing area – 21.13m^2/227.5sq ft
Weights: Empty – 1068kg/2354lb
Maximum loaded – 1638kg/3611lb
Performance: Maximum speed – 303kph/188mph
Ceiling – 8200m/26,900ft
Range – 595km/370 miles
Climb – 1525m/5000ft in 2 minutes, 42 seconds

Boeing F4B/P-12

Boeing developed the F4B as a private venture to possibly replace the US Navy's Boeing F2B and F3B. The new aircraft was smaller and lighter than its forerunners but retained the Wasp engine of the F3B and included some design changes that together resulted in improved performance. Accordingly the

F4B was ordered in great quantities for the US Navy and, later, the US Army who gave it the designation P-12. Both the US Navy and Army utilized a host of different variants many of which served on into World War II. Brazil was the only major customer outside the USA. Total production reached 586.

Boeing P-26

The "Peashooter" as it was known, was an aircraft that spanned two eras. America's first all-metal fighter produced in quantity is also notable as it was the last to have a fixed undercarriage and open cockpit. Boeing first proposed the P-26 to the US Army in 1931 having designed it around the trusted Pratt and Whitney R-1340 radial engine. The first prototype was built and flown in only nine weeks, taking to the air for the first time in March 1932 at Wright Field. The P-26's top speed of 365kph/227mph may seem sedate by today's transonic standards but it represented an increase of over 20 per cent compared to the performance of the P-12 it replaced. The order placed by the US Army Air Corps (USAAC) in January 1933 was at the time the biggest ever for a US military aircraft.

By the time the P-26 joined the USAAC squadrons in early 1934, a number of refinements and improvements had been incorporated including strengthening of the pilot's headrest fairing. An early version of the

aircraft had overturned after landing on soft ground, killing the pilot as the headrest collapsed. The Peashooter was popular with pilots as it was light and responsive, and it was the fastest USAAC fighter until 1938. It remained in service until as late as 1942.

Boeing widely exported the P-26, but the aircraft had a high landing speed for the time, around 117kph/73mph, which was found to be rather high for the rough airfields of foreign air forces. Split landing flaps were fitted to reduce the speed at the critical landing time. In September 1934 the first of ten examples sold to China arrived at Canton. Over the next year or so the Peashooters were in action against the invading Japanese on an almost daily basis and succeeded in destroying some of the enemy's aircraft in air combat. Ex-USAAC P-26s were also supplied to Guatemala where they comprised the Guatemalan Military Air Corps' first fighter unit and remained in service until 1955.

TOP: **The Peashooter was the fastest USAAC fighter aircraft until 1938, and the type remained in Guatemalan service until 1955.** ABOVE: **The agile P-26 was America's first mass-produced all-metal fighter.**

Boeing P-26A

First flight: March 20, 1932
Power: One Pratt and Whitney 500hp nine-cylinder air-cooled radial piston engine
Armament: Two synchronized forward-firing 7.62mm/0.3in machine-guns on sides of nose
Size: Wingspan – 8.52m/27ft 11.5in
Length – 7.26m/23ft 10in
Height – 3.17m/10.5ft
Wing area – 13.89m²/149.5sq ft
Weights: Empty – 1031kg/2271lb
Maximum take-off – 1366kg/3012lb
Performance: Maximum speed – 365kph/227mph
Ceiling – 8350m/27,400ft
Range – 579km/360 miles
Climb – 719m/2360ft per minute

LEFT: **Defiants of No.264 Squadron, RAF.**

Boulton Paul Defiant Mark II

First flight: August 11, 1937
Power: Rolls-Royce 1280hp Merlin XX piston engine
Armament: Four 7.7mm/0.303in machine-guns in power-operated dorsal turret
Size: Wingspan – 11.99m/39ft 4in
Length – 10.77m/35ft 4in
Height – 3.45m/11ft 4in
Wing area – 23.23m²/250 sq ft
Weights: Empty – 2849kg/6282lb
Maximum loaded – 3821kg/8424lb
Performance: Maximum speed – 504kph/313mph
Ceiling – 9250m/30350ft
Range – 748km/465 miles
Climb – 580m/1900ft per minute

Boulton Paul Defiant

The Defiant was the RAF's first four-gun fighter in squadron service, making its first flight in August 1937. Tactically, the Defiants were a departure for two-seat fighters as all of their firepower was concentrated in the rear turret and no forward armament was carried. They went into action for the first time on May 12, 1940 and by the end of the month had destroyed 65 enemy aircraft over France. The success was partly due to the devastating fire-power that could be unleashed on any fighter that got on a Defiant's tail. The "honeymoon" was soon over. In dogfights the Defiant was no match for the Luftwaffe's best fighters and losses began to increase. With no front-firing guns, the Defiant was vulnerable to head-on attacks and in August 1940 they were withdrawn.

Defiants were then "recycled" as nightfighters and fitted with the new and highly secret Airborne Interception radar. Over the winter of 1940–1 the Defiant had more kills per interception than any other RAF type. At the height of their use, Defiant nightfighters equipped 13 RAF squadrons, and played a vital role in the night defence of Britain.

LEFT: **Buffaloes entered RAF service in 1940.**

Brewster F2A-3 Buffalo

First flight: December 1937
Power: Wright 1200hp R-1820-40 Cyclone radial piston engine
Armament: Four fixed forward-firing 12.7mm/0.5in machine-guns
Size: Wingspan – 10.67m/35ft
Length – 8.03m/26ft 4in Height – 3.68m/12ft 1in
Wing area – 19.41m²/208.9sq ft
Weights: Empty – 2146kg/4723lb
Maximum take-off – 3247kg/7159lb
Performance: Maximum speed – 517kph/321mph
Ceiling – 10,120m/33,200ft
Range – 1553km/965 miles
Climb – 935m/3070ft per minute

Brewster F2A Buffalo

The F2A was designed to meet a US Navy specification for a carrier-based monoplane and was awarded the contract, making it the Navy's first monoplane fighter. Of the 54 ordered only 11 made it into service, the rest being sold to Finland. Further contracts from the US Navy brought the F2A-2 and the more heavily armed and armoured F2A-3 into service. US Marine Corps aviators used the Buffalo to the best of their ability in the first Battle of Midway, when 13 out of 19 were destroyed.

Orders placed by Britain (where the F2A was named Buffalo by the RAF and was found to be inadequate for the war in Europe) and the Netherlands East Indies brought more Buffaloes to the war in the Far East, where they were out-classed by Japanese fighters. The aircraft's failure was due to its poor manoeuvrability, heavy weight and basic instability. In spite of this, by the time of the fall of Singapore in February 1942, RAF Buffaloes had destroyed 30 Japanese aircraft in the air.

Only in Finland did the Buffalo hold its own, when from mid-1941 until September 1944 it successfully opposed Soviet forces in the Russo-Finnish War.

Bristol Beaufighter

The Beaufighter was not designed to an official specification – the Bristol company simply proposed a versatile heavily armed aircraft that they thought the RAF needed. Britain's Air Ministry was impressed by the proposal and the devastating fire power this aircraft could unleash, realizing they had found the heavily armed long-range fighter missing from the RAF inventory. Using the major airframe elements of the Beaufort torpedo-bomber already in production, the two-seat Beaufighter was produced quickly and joined front-line squadrons at the height of the Battle of Britain in 1940, only 13 months after the prototype first flew.

The "Beau" was the world's first high-performance purpose-designed nightfighter and was a very advanced aircraft for its time. At the time of its combat début with the Fighter Interception Unit in 1940, the Beaufighter's armament of four 20mm/0.78in cannon and six 7.7mm/0.303in machine-guns was the heaviest carried by any front-line aircraft. Crews found the "Beau" to be quite fast

and manoeuvrable and experienced Blenheim pilots were able to manage the aircraft's demanding take-off swing. When Beaufighters joined front-line Royal Air Force squadrons in early September 1940, most only carried their cannon armament – the much needed machine-guns were retained for the all-important Spitfires and Hurricanes, should a shortage have arisen. The closing months of 1940 saw machine-guns fitted to the Beaufighters and, after a period of trial and error mastering the new AI radar, the aircraft's night victories against the Luftwaffe began to increase.

Day fighter versions saw action in the Western Desert and Malta while RAF Coastal Command also used the "Beau" to great effect, particularly over the Bay of Biscay against Luftwaffe Junkers Ju 88s. Bomber and torpedo-carrying versions also saw wartime service with the RAF and after the war's end, Beaufighters served with Coastal Command and in the Far East until 1950 and as target towing aircraft until 1960.

TOP: **A Beaufighter of No.235 Squadron RAF.**

ABOVE: **Nicknamed "Whispering Death" by the Japanese, the Beaufighter was a robust aircraft well suited to hot and tropical conditions.**

LEFT: **A well-worn Beaufighter IIF.**

Bristol Beaufighter VIF

First flight: July 17, 1939

Power: Two Bristol 1,635hp Hercules VI 14-cylinder air-cooled sleeve valve radials

Armament: Four 20mm/0.78in cannon in nose, plus six 7.7mm/0.303in machine-guns in wings

Size: Wingspan – 17.65m/57ft 10in
Length 12.6m/41ft 8in
Height – 4.84m/15ft 10in
Wing area – 46.74m^2/503sq ft

Weights: Empty – 6631kg/14,600lb
Maximum take off – 9810kg/21,600lb

Performance: Maximum speed – 536kph/333mph
Ceiling – 8083m/26,500ft
Range – 2381km/1480 miles
Climb – 4575m/15,000ft in 7.8 minutes

Bristol Blenheim

The three-seat Bristol Blenheim first flew in 1935 and was a technological quantum leap among RAF aircraft at the time. With a top speed of around 428kph/266mph, the Blenheim bomber was considerably faster than the 290kph/180mph Hind biplane it replaced and it could outrun many contemporary fighters. The first Blenheim fighter, the IF, was proposed as a long-range fighter that could escort bombers over hostile territory and also carry out ground attack missions of its own. Around 200 Blenheims were modified for these

TOP: **This Blenheim, preserved and flown in the UK is a rare survivor.** ABOVE: **A Blenheim Mk IF of No.248 Squadron RAF – note the ventral gun pack beneath the rear of the cockpit area.**

fighter duties, additionally armed with a gun pack beneath the fuselage consisting of four machine-guns.

The type had first entered service in December 1938 and by September 1939 there were 111 Blenheim fighters in use with the RAF. Unfortunately the Blenheim could not match the performance of aircraft such as the Messerschmitt Bf109 and so many became nightfighters, ultimately carrying the new and highly secret airborne radar.

Even before the IFs were equipped with radar they achieved some night-time victories – in June 1940 No.23 Squadron destroyed a Heinkel 111 bomber over Norfolk. The first ever radar interception came in late July when a Blenheim IF of Tangmere's Fighter Interception Unit destroyed a Dornier Do 17 near Brighton.

The pioneers of the Blenheim nightfighters were a flight of No.25 Squadron who were in fact the first unit in the world to operate radar-equipped nightfighters. But Blenheim fighters continued to operate in daylight too and as late as August 15, 1940, during the Battle of Britain, No.219 Squadron were in action

against a German raid on north-east England. Between November 1939 and March 1940, RAF Coastal Command also operated IFs, providing top cover for shipping. The Mark IVF was again a long-range fighter version of the Mark IV bomber, carrying the same gun pack. Around 125 served with Coastal Command, providing shipping with air cover, as had the IF. In April 1940 a pilot of No.254 Squadron shot down a Heinkel 111 that posed a threat to British ships off the coast of Norway.

Bristol Blenheim IF

First flight: April 12, 1935

Power: Two Bristol 840hp Mercury VIII nine-cylinder air-cooled radial engines

Armament: Four 7.7mm/0.303in Browning machine-guns in ventral gun pack, plus one Browning gun in port wing and one in gun turret

Size: Wingspan – 17.17m/56ft 4in
Length – 12.12m/39ft 9in Height – 3m/9ft 10in
Wing area – 43.57m²/469sq ft

Weights: Empty – 3674kg/8100lb
Maximum take-off – 5670kg/12,500lb

Performance: Maximum speed – 458kph/285mph
Ceiling – 8315m/27,280ft
Range – 1810km/1125 miles
Climb – 4570m/15,000ft in 11 minutes, 30 seconds

LEFT: **The prototype Bulldog II, J9480. The Bulldog was an unequal span biplane with a metal frame and a fabric covering.** BELOW: **A Bulldog IIA, preserved at a UK aviation museum. The type was the standard RAF fighter for seven years.**

Bristol Bulldog II

First flight: May 17, 1927
Power: Bristol 440hp Jupiter VII radial piston engine
Armament: Two fixed forward-firing synchronized Vickers machine-guns
Size: Wingspan – 10.34m/33ft 11in
  Length – 7.62m/25ft
  Height – 3m/9ft 10in
  Wing area – 28.47m²/306.6sq ft
Weights: Empty – 998kg/2200lb
  Maximum loaded – 1583kg/3490lb
Performance: Maximum speed – 280kph/174mph
  Ceiling – 8230m/27,000ft
  Range – 443km/275 miles
  Climb – 6096m/20,000ft in 14 minutes, 30 seconds

Bristol Bulldog

The Bulldog was designed in response to a 1926 Air Ministry specification for a single-seat day- or nightfighter armed with two Vickers machine-guns able to take on the bombers of the era. The Mark I was used for development and it was the Mark II that replaced the RAF's Siskins and Gamecocks and first entered RAF service with No.3 Squadron at Upavon in June 1929. The Bulldog's fuselage was all-metal with a fabric covering, and it had a shock-absorbing tail skid, as operations were still exclusively from grass strips. Innovations for the Bulldog included an oxygen supply for the pilot and a short-wave two-way radio.

By 1932 the Bulldog equipped ten RAF squadrons and it remained the service's standard fighter until 1936. The 312 Bulldogs that entered service comprised about 70 per cent of the UK's air defence capability.

The last RAF Bulldogs were phased out in 1937, being replaced by Gloster Gauntlets. Many were exported to other countries, including Australia, Denmark, Siam (now Thailand), Sweden, Estonia and Finland. A two-seat trainer version was also produced.

Bristol Fighter

The arrival of the Bristol F.2B Fighter, powered by the new Rolls-Royce Falcon engine, over the Western Front ultimately proved to be very bad news for the German opposition. The aircraft had two crew – a pilot and an observer gunner in the rear cockpit. Each could engage an enemy aircraft independently – the pilot with a fixed forward-firing machine-gun and the observer with a Lewis gun (or two if he was strong).

Designed by Capt. Frank Barnwell around the Falcon engine, the armament of the Bristol Fighter was integral to its design from the outset, crew visibility was excellent and they had an unobstructed field of fire. The April 5, 1917 combat début of the "Brisfit" at the Battle of Arras was, however, far from successful as the Royal Flying Corps pilots used the standard two-seater tactic of leaving the aircraft's defence with the observer. This tactical error, coupled with oil freezing, which rendered a number of observers' guns useless, led to the loss of four out of six Brisfits on their first mission. Within days, the British pilots began to use the aircraft's forward-firing Vickers gun to full effect and flew the F.2B as if it were a single-seat fighter – the aircraft became something to be feared. The Bristol Fighter was to become the best two-seat fighter of World War I. When the Royal Air Force was established on April 1, 1918 it was a Bristol Fighter that flew the first combat mission of Britain's newly formed independent air arm. It proved popular with pilots because it was fast, manoeuvrable, could dive faster than any other aircraft in the theatre and it could take a lot of punishment.

The Vickers machine-gun mounted on the Bristol Fighter's centreline was beneath the engine cowling. Its location required a "tunnel" to be provided for the gun through the upper fuel tank.

Post-war the type was used as an Army co-operation aircraft and a trainer. Production of the Bristol Fighter continued until 1927 and the RAF took

TOP: **The combat début of the Bristol Fighter in April 1917 was far from auspicious, with four out of six aircraft being lost on their first mission.** ABOVE: **When both crew members used their guns, the Brisfit was a formidable fighter to contend with.**

delivery of its last Bristol Fighter in December 1926. Fourteen foreign air forces, including Canada, Greece and Mexico, also operated the type. Fifteen years after entering RFC service, the

Brisfit was still serving with the RAF in Iraq and India, at which time they were replaced by Fairey Gordons. The Royal New Zealand Air Force continued to operate Bristol Fighters until 1938.

TOP: **The Bristol Fighter equipped RAF units in Turkey, India, Iraq, Palestine, Egypt and Syria.** ABOVE: **The Brisfit went on to become one of the best two-seat fighters of World War I.** BELOW: **Pilots and observers of No.22 Squadron of the newly formed Royal Air Force, pictured at Vert Galland on April 1, 1918.**

Bristol F.2B Fighter

First flight: September 9, 1916

Power: Rolls-Royce 275hp Falcon III in-line piston engine

Armament: One fixed forward-firing synchronized Vickers machine-gun and one or two "flexible" 7.7mm/0.303in Lewis guns in rear cockpit

Size: Wingspan – 11.96m/39ft 3in
Length – 7.87m/25ft 10in
Height – 2.97m/9ft 9in
Wing area – 37.63m²/405 sq ft

Weights: Empty – 975kg/2150lb
Maximum loaded – 1474kg/3250lb

Performance: Maximum speed – 198kph/123mph
Ceiling – 5485m/18,000ft
Range – 3 hours endurance
Climb – 3048m/10,000ft in 11 minutes, 30 seconds

Bristol Scout

The Scout was derived from a pre-World War I racing aircraft and, had it been designed with armament from the outset, could have been a great fighter. Widely described as a very "clean" design, the Scout was certainly fast for its day and was used initially as a fast "scout", or reconnaissance aircraft. Soon after its appearance at the Front in February 1915, with its high performance, single-seat Scouts were allocated to two-seater squadrons as escorts. Armament on these first fighters varied widely at first, sometimes simply consisting of rifles bolted to

ABOVE: **5574 was a Scout D, the version that introduced a synchronized Vickers machine-gun.** BELOW: **A replica Scout D. Once the type was withdrawn from front-line duties the Scout was used for training purposes, and later a number were sold for civil use.**

the sides of the fuselage. In spite of this, on July 25, 1915 Captain L.G. Hawker used his Bristol Scout C to shoot down three enemy aircraft, themselves armed with machine-guns. For this action he was awarded the Victoria Cross, the first for aerial combat. At this point, Scouts equipped both the Royal Flying Corps and the Royal Naval Air Service, the latter using the Scout for anti-Zeppelin patrols armed with explosive "darts" thrown over the side.

When No.11 Squadron RFC was formed in February 1915 equipped with, among other types, Bristol Scouts, its sole purpose was the interception and destruction of enemy aircraft – it was one of the first true fighter squadrons. The British ace Albert Ball served with No.11 and liked to fly the Scout D which entered service in November 1915, equipped with a synchronized Vickers machine-gun. During one week in May

1916 Albert Ball used his Scout D, serial number 5326, to drive down four enemy aircraft and remove them from the war.

In all, around 370 Scouts were delivered. From mid-1916 they were gradually withdrawn from front-line duties to become training aircraft.

Bristol Scout

First flight: February 23, 1914 (Scout A)
Power: Le Rhône 80hp rotary piston engine
Armament: One 7.7mm/0.303in Lewis machine-gun or local combinations of small arms
Size: Wingspan – 8.33m/27ft4in
　　　Length 6.02m/19ft 9in
　　　Height – 2.59m/8ft 6in
　　　Wing area – 18.39m^2/198sq ft
Weights: Empty – 345kg/760lb
　　　Maximum loaded – 567kg/1250lb
Performance: Maximum speed – 161kph/100mph
　　　Ceiling – 4267m/14,000ft
　　　Range – 2.5 hours endurance
　　　Climb – 3050m/10,000ft in 18.5 minutes

LEFT: **The large and remarkable R. 11.**

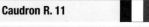

Caudron R. 11

First flight: March 1917
Power: Two Hispano-Suiza 215hp 8Bba in-line
piston engines
Armament: Five 7.7mm/0.303in Lewis machine-guns
– two each in front and rear gunner positions, plus
an additional "stinger" under the aircraft nose
Size: Wingspan – 17.92m/58ft 9.5in
Length – 11.22m/36ft 9.5in
Height – 2.8m/9ft 2.25in
Wing area – 54.25m²/583.96sq ft
Weights: Empty – 1422kg/3135lb
Maximum take-off – 2167kg/4777lb
Performance: Maximum speed – 183kph/114mph
Ceiling – 5950m/19,520ft
Range – 3 hours endurance
Climb – 2000m/6560ft in 8 minutes, 10 seconds

Caudron R.11

The R.11 was designed in 1916 by
René Caudron as a heavily armed
reconnaissance-bomber, but the twin-
engined biplane found its niche as
a formidable escort fighter over the
Western Front. Armed with five Lewis
machine-guns, and fully aerobatic, the
R.11 could escort French bombers to
targets deep in enemy territory and dish
out considerable punishment to German
fighters that came near. The three-seat
R.11, twice the size of other escort
fighters in use at the time, built up an
impressive tally of enemy aircraft kills.

A number of features make the R.11
stand out from many aircraft of the time.
The engines were housed in streamlined
nacelles to minimize drag, and both
could be fed from one of two main fuel
tanks as required. In late model R.11s
the rear sections of the engine nacelles
could be jettisoned, together with the
auxiliary fuel tanks they contained.
Another innovation was the provision of
dual controls in the rear gunner's cockpit
so that the gunner could take control if
the pilot was incapacitated. The R.11
protected France until July 1922.

LEFT: **Developed from an aircraft which was itself
derived from another, the Boomerang proved to be
a very worthwhile fighter. The example pictured,
sole survivor of the type, is preserved in Australia.**

Commonwealth
Boomerang II

First flight: May 29, 1942
Power: Pratt & Whitney 1200hp R-1830-S3C4
Twin Wasp radial piston engine
Armament: Four 7.7mm/0.303in machine-guns
and two 20mm/0.78in cannon in wings
Size: Wingspan – 10.97m/36ft
Length – 7.77m/25ft 6in
Height – 2.92m/9ft 7in
Wing area – 20.9m²/225sq ft
Weights: Empty – 2437kg/5373lb
Maximum take-off – 3742kg/8249lb
Performance: Maximum speed – 491kph/305mph
Ceiling – 10,365m/34,000ft
Range – 2575km/1600 miles
Climb – 896m/2940ft per minute

Commonwealth Boomerang

The Boomerang was born of
desperation and the sudden need
in December 1941 to defend Australia
from the Japanese. The aircraft was
based on the Commonwealth Aircraft
Corporation's earlier Wirraway which
was in turn developed from the North
American NA-16 trainer. The Wirraway's
wing, undercarriage and tail were mated
to a new fuselage and the resulting
Boomerang prototype was produced
in only three months. The Twin Wasp
engine was considered too low powered
for fighters elsewhere but the
Boomerang design team used it to
power their aircraft, which entered
service in October 1942. This well-
armed, tough and manoeuvrable aircraft
first flew into action in April 1943
and proved to be an adversary to be
reckoned with. As other fighter types
became available the Boomerang was
quickly replaced, having served in
New Guinea and defended western
and northern Australia in the country's
time of need.

Curtiss P-36 Hawk

Design work on the second family of Curtiss Hawks began in 1934 and led to the P-36 Hawk, which first flew in May 1935. It incorporated advanced features for the time, including an enclosed cockpit and retractable landing gear. The aircraft impressed the US Army Air Corps so much that Curtiss received an order for 210 machines, the largest peacetime order ever placed by the USAAC for a fighter. Deliveries began in April 1938 but by the time America entered World War II in December 1941, the aircraft was already thought to be obsolete, although some did see early action against the Japanese. P-36As were the main fighters defending Hawaii at the time of Pearl Harbor in December 1941.

Export versions of the P-36, the H75, were supplied to France where they saw limited action before the fall of France in 1940. One Armée de l'Air Hawk claimed the first German aircraft to fall to a French fighter in World War II. Most of the French Hawks were, however, transferred to the UK , where the Royal Air Force designated them "Mohawks". Some of the Hawks seized by the Germans were supplied by them to Finland after being used by the Luftwaffe as fighter trainers.

A further 100 Mohawks came to the UK direct from the USA between July and December 1940. Some were shipped to the Middle East and others were dispatched to India, where they entered service in December 1941. At one point, the fighter defence of the whole of north-east India was provided by just eight Mohawks. The last RAF unit to fly them was No.155 Squadron, which relinquished them in January 1944.

Hawks were also supplied to Norway (and the Free Norwegian Forces based in Canada), the Netherlands (diverted to the Netherlands East Indies) and Persia (now Iran). Vichy France, Finland, India and Peru also operated the type.

In 1937 a less sophisticated version of the P-36, the Hawk 75, was developed for export and supplied to China, Siam (now Thailand) and Argentina, where a further 20 were built. Chinese and Siamese 75s were used against the Japanese.

TOP: **A French H75, the export version of the P-36.** ABOVE: **One of the French H75s transferred to the RAF after the fall of France.**

Curtiss P-36G Hawk

First flight: May 1935
Power: Wright 1200hp R-1820-G205A Cyclone piston radial engine
Armament: Four wing-mounted 7.62mm/0.3in machine-guns, plus two fuselage-mounted 12.7mm/0.5in machine-guns
Size: Wingspan – 11.28m/37ft
Length – 8.69m/28ft 6in
Height – 2.82m/9ft 3in
Wing area – 21.92m²/236sq ft
Weights: Empty – 2121kg/4675lb
Maximum loaded – 2667kg/5880lb
Performance: Maximum speed – 518kph/322mph
Ceiling – 9860m/32,350ft
Range – 1046km/650 miles
Climb – 4570m/15,000ft in 6 minutes

Curtiss P-40 Warhawk/Kittyhawk

The next version in the Hawk family tree was the P-40 Warhawk, which mainly differed from the Hawk by having an Allison liquid-cooled engine instead of the air-cooled Wright Cyclone radial. This model, more aerodynamically efficient than the Hawk due to the use of flush rivets, became the principal fighter of US Army Air Corps pursuit (fighter) squadrons. France had placed an order, which was instead sent to the UK after Germany invaded France. Britain had also ordered the new P-40s and designated them "Tomahawks". For the RAF, the Allison engine failed to provide the performance required for air combat in Europe in 1941 and RAF Tomahawks were used purely as low-level tactical reconnaissance aircraft. However, 100 British Tomahawk IIs were diverted to the American Volunteer Group operating in China, where they achieved many victories against Japanese aircraft.

The P-40D first flew in May 1941 and was a major improvement on previous models, with a new, more powerful Allison engine. The nose cross-section was reduced and the guns formerly carried in the nose were dropped. Main armament was now four 12.7mm/0.5in machine-guns in the wings and a rack could be added beneath the fuselage to carry a 227kg/500lb bomb. It was the British who ordered the P-40D and coined the name "Kittyhawk" for their version of the Curtiss fighter. (The name Kittyhawk is often mistakenly applied to the whole Warhawk range.) By now, however, the P-40 was way behind in contemporary fighter performance and it was not capable of holding its own against crack pilots. Nevertheless, the later P-40E model was also supplied to the American Volunteer Group in China, where it continued to achieve kills. Even in the Western Desert, where the RAF's Kittyhawks' fighter-bomber achievements are well known, the type had many victories in the air. Legendary British test pilot Neville Duke scored 12 air victories while flying Kittyhawks there, as well as the five kills he achieved whilst flying Tomahawks, also in the Western Desert.

Total production of the P-40 exceeded 16,800.

ABOVE: **This P-40, preserved in the USA, is painted as an aircraft of the American Volunteer Group.**

BELOW: **A fine wartime photograph of an RAF Kittyhawk in the Western Desert.**

P-40N/Kittyhawk IV

First flight: October 1938 (XP-40)

Power: Allison 1360hpV-1710-81 in-line piston engine

Armament: Six 12.7mm/0.5in machine-guns in wings and provision for one 227kg/500lb bomb under fuselage

Size: Wingspan – 11.42m/37ft 4in
Length – 10.2m/33ft 4in Height – 3.77m/12ft 4in
Wing area – 21.95m^2/236sq ft

Weights: Empty – 2724kg/6000lb
Maximum loaded – 4018kg/8850lb

Performance: Maximum speed – 609kph/378mph
Ceiling – 11,630m/38,000ft
Range – 386km/240 miles
Climb – 4590m/15,000ft in 6 minutes, 42 seconds

LEFT: **A French Air Force D.500.**

Dewoitine D.501

First flight: Early 1934
Power: Hispano-Suiza 690hp 12Xcrs in-line
   piston engine
Armament: One 20mm/0.78in Oerlikon cannon firing
   through propeller hub, plus two wing-mounted
   7.55mm/0.295in machine-guns
Size: Wingspan – 12.09m/39ft 8.25in
   Length – 7.56m/24ft 9.75in
   Height – 2.7m/8ft 10.25in
   Wing area – 16.5m²/177.61sq ft
Weights: Empty – 1287kg/2837lb
   Maximum loaded – 1787kg/3940lb
Performance: Maximum speed – 335kph/208mph
   Ceiling – 10,200m/33,465ft
   Range – 870km/541 miles
   Climb – 1000m/3280ft in 1 minute, 20 seconds

Dewoitine D.500 series

The French D.500 may have been the most modern-looking fighter of its day but it was a transition design, bridging the gap between open-cockpit fabric-covered biplanes and the new all-metal monoplanes. The D.500, the prototype for the series, was made entirely of light alloy and first flew in 1932, attracting much overseas interest. It was a low wing monoplane with a fixed tailwheel. The D.501 was the first

production version of a series that differed in engine and armament installation, resulting in a host of variants.

The ultimate version was the D.510 which, together with a few D.501s, was in widespread use in the French Air Force at the outbreak of World War II. Compared with the earlier models in the series, the D.510 had a more powerful engine and greater fuel capacity but with a top speed of 400kph/249mph, it would

have been no match for Hitler's more modern and capable fighters.

It was transferred to French squadrons overseas before the German attack of May 1940. Some exported Dewoitines did battle in China until late 1941.

LEFT: **The long nose of the D.520 presented the pilot with a very poor view from the cockpit, so techniques used by RAF Spitfire pilots were employed – weave while taxiing and sideslip in to land.**

Dewoitine D.520

First flight: October 2, 1938
Power: Hispano-Suiza 850hp 12Y-45 12-cylinder
   liquid-cooled piston engine
Armament: One 20mm/0.78in cannon firing through
   propeller hub, plus four 7.5mm/0.295in machine-
   guns in wings
Size: Wingspan – 10.2m/33ft 5.5in
   Length – 8.76m/28ft 8.75in Height – 2.57m/8ft 5in
   Wing area – 15.95m²/171.7sq ft
Weights: Empty – 2125kg/4685lb
   Maximum take-off – 2790kg/6151lb
Performance: Maximum speed – 535kph/332mph
   Ceiling – 10,250m/33,639ft
   Range – 1540km/957 miles
   Climb – 4000m/13,125ft in 5 minutes, 48 seconds

Dewoitine D.520

The D.520, with the look of a racing aircraft, was certainly the most capable fighter available to the French Armée de l'Air at the start of World War II. Production, in the face of initial official indifference was problematic, but they were rolling off the line at a healthy rate by the time France fell to the Germans. Some did reach French fighter units before the fall, and accounted for 147 German aircraft. Henschel 126s, Messerschmitt Bf109s

and Bf110s, and Heinkel 111s all fell to the guns of the outnumbered D.520s.

Vichy forces used the D.520 extensively and with some success against Allied aircraft in the 1941 Syrian campaign and the North African landings of November 1942. D.520 production continued in Occupied France and these aircraft together with captured examples were supplied to Germany's allies, including Italy, Romania and Bulgaria.

The Luftwaffe itself was also quick to realize the D.520's potential as a fighter-trainer. These aircraft were later seized back by French forces after D-Day in 1944, had their German markings painted over, and were used against Germans in southern France. Post-war, the French Air Force operated D.520s until 1953.

de Havilland/Airco DH.2

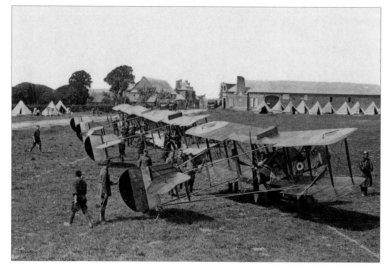

LEFT: **Four DH.2s of No.32 Squadron, Royal Flying Corps at Vert Galland, France, 1916.** BELOW: **A replica DH.2, showing the gun fixed in the front of the aircraft.** BOTTOM: **The DH.2 was vital to winning back control of the air in early 1916.**

In June 1914 Airco hired talented young designer Geoffrey de Havilland, later founder of the company that bore his name, to head their design department and the DH.2 was his second project for the company. The first had been the DH.1 two-seat reconnaissance fighter and the DH.2 was simply a smaller version of it for a one-man crew. The DH.2 used an air-cooled rotary engine instead of the DH.1's water-cooled in-line engine but kept the "pusher" configuration, with the propeller facing behind the aircraft. This was due to the fact that in early 1915 a means had not yet been perfected that would allow a gun to shoot forwards between spinning blades of propeller blades.

The armament arrangement seems bizarre by today's standards, consisting of a Lewis gun which could be mounted on either side of the cockpit as the pilot wished. He did of course have to manhandle the gun (that weighed 8kg/17.5lb) to the other side if an enemy presented himself there, all while still trying to control the aircraft. The gun was later mounted at the front of the aircraft on the centre line and was normally used as a fixed weapon, aimed by aiming the aircraft itself.

Nevertheless the DH.2 was praised by its pilots for its responsiveness and excellent rate of climb, and the aircraft was certainly central to winning back control of the air over the Western Front in early 1916.

Around 450 were built, but the tide began to turn again, and the DH.2 was outclassed by the latest German fighters by late 1916. The type was eventually withdrawn from March 1917 but not before No.29 Squadron lost five out of six DH.2s in one engagement, with five of the new Albatros D.IIIs on December 20, 1916.

Airco DH.2

First flight: Spring 1915
Power: Gnome Monosoupape 100hp nine-cylinder rotary piston engine
Armament: One 7.7mm/0.303in Lewis machine-gun
Size: Wingspan – 8.61m/28ft 3in
Length – 7.68m/25ft 2.5in
Height – 2.91m/9ft 6.5in
Wing area – 23.13m²/249sq ft
Weights: Empty – 428kg/943lb
Maximum take-off – 654kg/1441lb
Performance: Maximum speed – 150kph/93mph
Ceiling – 4265m/14,000ft
Range – 2 hours, 45 minutes endurance
Climb – 1830m/6000ft in 11 minutes

de Havilland Mosquito

The Mosquito was a true multi-role combat aircraft, which started life in late 1938 as an outline design for a bomber-reconnaissance aircraft that could fly so fast and high that no defensive armament was needed. The far-sighted design avoided the use of strategic materials, instead using wood for virtually the whole aircraft – this later led to the nickname the "Wooden Wonder". Even so, it was only after World War II began that Britain's Air Ministry seriously considered the proposal, and then with some caution, but in November 1940 the Mosquito first flew and convinced the sceptics that it was a remarkable aircraft. Priority production was ordered for the bomber version and meanwhile the photo-reconnaissance and fighter prototypes were prepared.

The Mosquito fighter prototype flew in May 1941 and was immediately developed as a nightfighter equipped with the latest secret Airborne Interception (AI) radar. It also differed from the bomber version by having strengthened wing spars for air combat and a flat bullet-proof windscreen.

Armed with four cannon in the floor beneath the nose and four machine-guns in the nose itself, the two-man Mosquito NF.II entered Fighter Command service in January 1942, gradually replacing the Beaufighter as the RAF's standard UK-based nightfighter. From December that year, No.23 Squadron's NF.IIs operated from Malta, and in the first few months of 1943 shot down 17 enemy aircraft. They were

TOP: **The bomber version of the Mosquito appeared first.** ABOVE: **The Mosquito sting – four 20mm/0.78in cannon below the cockpit. Later nightfighters had radomes like this NF.XIX, eliminating the external "antler" aerials.**

equally active in daylight and also flew train-busting missions over Italy, Sicily and North Africa, clearly demonstrating the versatility of the Mosquito as a fighter-bomber. The purely dayfighter version was shelved after one prototype, such was the effectiveness of the nightfighter and the later fighter-bomber versions.

The radar carried by nightfighter Mosquitoes was constantly improved (Marks NF.XII, XIII and XVII) and the nose-mounted machine-guns were eventually deleted, leaving four cannon as the only armament. The crews became very adept at finding and destroying enemy aircraft under cover of darkness. On March 19, 1944 a Mk XVII of No.25 Squadron shot down three

Junkers Ju 188s on a single sortie over the Humber. Some of the XVIIs were equipped with a tail-mounted warning radar so that they could themselves avoid becoming the prey.

Fighter-bomber versions were also developed and the FB.Mk VI became the most widely used of all Mosquito fighters. This version was a day or night intruder, able ultimately to carry two 227kg/500lb bombs as well as the usual fighter armament. RAF Coastal Command were quick to see the potential of the type and soon began using the VI, armed with underwing rockets, as a maritime strike aircraft.

Mk VIs were equally at home defending the UK as nightfighters or flying deep into German airspace, wreaking havoc on their nightfighters. Mosquito VIs were also capable of catching and destroying the German V-1 flying bombs that rained down on parts of Britain from June 1944. In all, Mosquito fighters destroyed 428 V-1s, the first being claimed by Flight Lt J.G. Musgrove on the night of June 14–15.

ABOVE: **All Royal Australian Air Force Mosquitoes carried the A52 serial prefix denoting the aircraft type. DH Australia produced a total of 212 Mosquitoes during World War II.** BELOW: **Covered with matt black paint and with aerial arrays on the nose, the NF.II entered service in January 1942.**

In March 1944, a modified IV became the first British twin-engine aircraft to land on an aircraft carrier. This trial, on board HMS *Indefatigable*, proved the feasibility of the Sea Mosquito which, equipped with folding wings and a modified undercarriage, joined the Royal Navy in 1946.

The ultimate wartime Mosquito nightfighter was the NF.30 high-altitude version, which regularly escorted Royal Air Force bombers on missions over Germany. As one pilot later said, "The fact that we might have been there on their tail made some Luftwaffe pilots think twice before attacking our bomber boys".

Post-war, the Mosquito NF.36, fitted with American Mk 10 AI radar, appeared and an export version equipped with British AI radar was supplied to Yugoslavia. The NF.36 was the only all-weather fighter available to the RAF until 1951–2, when the nightfighter Meteors and Vampires entered service. It is hard to think of the Mosquito as a Cold War aircraft but it came to be so due to a technology deficit in the UK.

The last de Havilland Mosquito, out of a total production run of 7781 planes, was an NF.38, completed at Chester in November 1950.

de Havilland Mosquito NF.30

First flight: May 15, 1941 (fighter prototype)
Power: Two Rolls-Royce 1690hp Merlin 113/114 in-line piston engines
Armament: Four 20mm/0.78in cannon
Size: Wingspan – 16.5m/54ft 2in
Length – 13.57m/44ft 6in
Height – 3.81m/12ft 6in
Wing area – 42.19m²/454sq ft
Weights: Empty – 6086kg/13,400lb
Maximum take-off – 9810kg/21,600lb
Performance: Maximum speed – 655kph/407mph
Ceiling – 11,590m/38,000ft
Range – 2091km/1300 miles
Climb – 869m/2850ft per minute

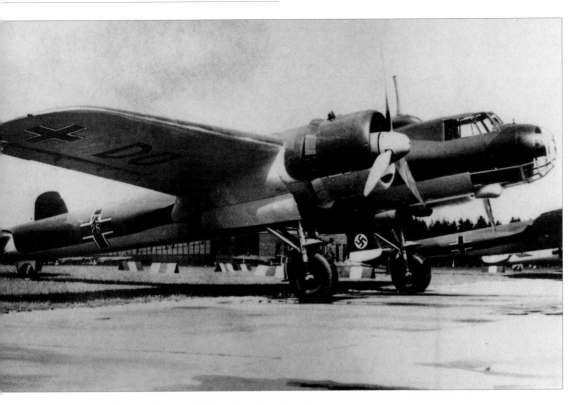

Dornier Do 17 nightfighters

Nicknamed the "Flying Pencil", Germany's Do 17 was a medium bomber developed from a Dornier high-speed mailplane, whose performance caused much concern outside Germany when it appeared in 1934. The concern was well placed as the Do 17 was extensively used by the Luftwaffe as a bomber, reconnaissance aircraft and glider tug through much of World War II.

The first Do 17 nightfighter variant was the experimental Do 17Z-6 Kauz (Screech Owl), which married a Do 17Z-3 airframe to the nose and forward-firing armament (three MG15 machine-guns and a 20mm cannon) of the Ju 88C-2.

The production Do 17Z-10 Kauz II had a completely new purpose-designed nose, housing four machine-guns, four cannon and an infra-red (IR) detector. Rear-firing machine-guns were retained from the bomber version.

The first unit to operate the three-seat Do 17 Kauz II was 4/NJG 1 based at Deelen, and on October 18, 1940 the Do 17 nightfighter claimed its first kill when a Royal Air Force Wellington bomber was destroyed.

The 4/NJG 1 also achieved some success in the east of England by attacking the streams of bomber aircraft returning to home airfields after night missions over Europe. The vulnerable RAF bombers were classic sitting targets as they dropped their undercarriages for the safe landing that never came.

A small but significant number of Kauz IIs remained active until early 1942. Versions of the Do 17 that had more powerful engines and were designed for export to Yugoslavia were designated Do 215. In all only ten Do 17 nightfighters were built and remained active until early 1942.

ABOVE: **The versatile Dornier Do 17 "Flying Pencil" spawned the very useful nightfighter variants. Although produced in small numbers, they were very effective against RAF bombers. Although only in use for around two years, the Do 17 nightfighters proved the value of dedicated nightfighters.**

Dornier Do 17Z-10 Kauz II

First flight: Early 1938 (Do 17 prototype)
Power: Two Bramo 1000hp 323P radial piston engines
Armament: Four 7.92mm/0.31in machine-guns and four 20mm/0.78in cannon
Size: Wingspan – 18m/59ft 1in
Length – 15.8m/51ft 10in
Height – 4.55m/14ft 11in
Wing area – 55m²/592sq ft
Weights: Empty – approx 5700kg/12,545lb
Maximum take-off – 9000kg/19,841lb
Performance: Maximum speed – 450kph/280mph
Ceiling – 9500m/31,170ft
Range – 1609km/1000 miles
Climb – 1000m/3280ft in 4 minutes, 30 seconds

Dornier Do 217 nightfighters

The Do 217 was derived from the highly successful Do 17/215 series of bombers, but was very different from the earlier aircraft. The 217 was initially developed as a bomber that could carry a greater load than any other German bomber of the time. Variants soon followed, including the three-seat 217J fighter-bomber and nightfighter versions. Both differed from the 217 bomber by having a solid nose in place of the "greenhouse" nose for a bomb aimer.

The J-1 was a fighter-bomber, operational from February 1942, armed with four nose-mounted 7.92mm/0.31in machine-guns and four 20mm/0.78in cannon, in addition to dorsal and ventral gun positions, each mounting a pair of 13mm/0.51in guns.

The J-2 was an interim nightfighter, armed like the J-1 but without a bomb bay and equipped with the Lichtenstein radar. Both J models entered service in summer 1942 but only over Germany. The Italian Air Force, the Regia Aeronautica, also operated J models over Italy and the Mediterranean.

July 1942 saw the test flight of the improved Do 217N four-seat nightfighter. Powered by higher-performance engines and carrying more "black box" radar equipment than the J-2, the N model also had its rear bomb bay reinstated for missions over the Eastern Front. The upper and lower gun positions were deleted and faired over and this weight reduction improved performance. Replacement fire-power was in the form of four oblique, upward-firing 20mm/0.78in cannon. The 217N was used operationally in the Mediterranean as well as over Germany and in the occupied countries.

In 1943 Hauptmann Hans Krause was awarded the Iron Cross after destroying 12 Allied aircraft over Hungary and the Adriatic while flying Do 217Ns.

Dornier Do 217N-2

First flight: July 31, 1942
Power: Two Daimler Benz 1750hp DB 603A 12-cylinder liquid-cooled engines
Armament: Four 7.9mm/0.31in machine-guns in nose, four 20mm/0.78in cannon in lower nose, four 20mm/0.78in cannon firing obliquely upwards (70 degrees) from centre fuselage
Size: Wingspan – 19m/62ft 4in
Length – 18.9m/62ft, including radar aerials
Height – 5m/16ft 5in Wing area – 57m²/614sq ft
Weights: Empty – 19,780kg/43,607lb
Maximum take-off – 13,700kg/30,202lb
Performance: Maximum speed – 425kph/264mph
Ceiling – 8418m/27,600ft
Range – 1755km/1090 miles
Climb – 6000m/19,685ft in 17 minutes

A total of 364 J and N models were produced and they were replaced by mid-1944.

BELOW: **The distinctive aerials of the Lichtenstein C-1 radar on the Do 217J-2 were the nightfighters' eyes in the black of night.**

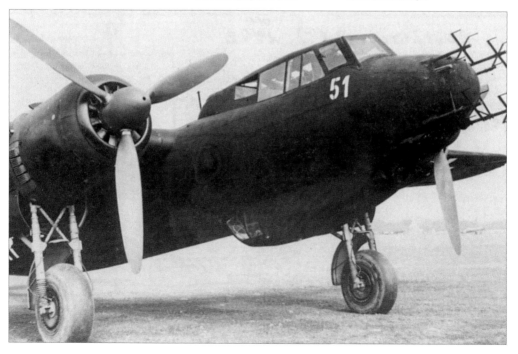

Fairey Firefly

From 1926 Britain's Fleet Air Arm deployed a series of fast two-seat fighter reconnaissance aircraft, and the Fairey Firefly continued the tradition, first flying in December 1941. It replaced the Fairey Fulmar as the Royal Navy's principal carrier-borne fighter from July 1943 and first saw action during attacks on the *Tirpitz* in July 1944. The Firefly's elliptical wings could be folded back manually for beneath-deck stowage and were hydraulically locked into the extended flying position.

Although the Griffon-engined Firefly Mk 1 was around 64kph/40mph faster than the Merlin-engined Fulmar, it was still slower than most contemporary fighters. The Firefly did however have better armament, in the form of four hard-hitting 20mm/0.78in cannons in place of the Fulmar's eight machine-guns. It also had great low-speed handling characteristics – vital for carrier-borne fighters.

Firefly nightfighter variants were developed early in production of the type and carried airborne interception radar in small wing-mounted radomes. The associated extra equipment affected the aircraft's centre of gravity and necessitated a lengthening of the fuselage by 45.7cm/18in. This version of the F.1, the N.F.2, was only produced in limited quantities because an alternative means of accomodating the radar equipment was developed that did not require major structural work. Radar was then being fitted as standard to Fireflies and the non-lengthened Firefly N.F.1 was the nightfighter version of the F.R.1, which was itself basically an F.1 fitted with radar. All Firefly nightfighters were equipped with exhaust dampers so that the glowing exhausts of the Griffon engine would not show up in darkness.

Although the Firefly was never a classic fighter, it excelled in the strike and armed reconnaissance role. The first Firefly air combat victory occurred on January 2, 1945 during a Fleet Air Arm attack on oil refineries in Sumatra, when a No.1770 Squadron aircraft shot down a Japanese "Oscar", a very capable dogfighter.

In the weeks immediately after VJ Day (September 2, 1945), Fleet Air Arm Fireflies carried out supply drops to POW camps on the Japanese mainland. Royal Navy Fireflies went on to see action in the Korean War and then, in 1954, in the ground-attack role in Malaya. Royal Netherlands Air Force Firefly AS4s were in action in Indonesia in early 1962.

ABOVE: **The early Fireflies had the radiator beneath the engine.** BELOW: **Later versions had wing leading edge radiators, changing the look of the aircraft.**

Fairey Firefly F.1

First flight: December 22, 1941
Power: Rolls-Royce 1990hp Griffon XII engine
Armament: Four 20mm/0.78in cannon in wings
Size: Wingspan – 13.56m/44ft 6in, spread
4.04m/13ft 3in, folded
Length – 11.46m/37ft 7in
Height – 4.14m/13ft 7in
Wing area – 30.48m²/328sq ft
Weights: Empty – 4423kg/9750lb
Maximum take-off – 6360kg/14,020lb
Performance: Maximum speed – 509kph/316mph
Ceiling – 8534m/28,000ft
Range – 2092km/1300 miles
Climb – 4575m/15,000ft in 9.6 minutes

Fiat CR.32

This biplane fighter, which first flew in 1933, has been described as one of the greatest ever aircraft in its class. The highly manoeuvrable all-metal aircraft proved itself during the Spanish Civil War, when around 380 flew in support of the Nationalist forces. It was more than a match for the Republicans' Polikarpov I-15 and I-16 monoplanes, and Spain built its own under licence as the Hispano Chirri. Other Fiat-built machines were supplied to China, Hungary and various South American countries. Even as late as 1940 the

CR.32 was widely deployed by Italy's Regia Aeronautica. They were by then outclassed by contemporary fighters but some were modified as nightfighters and others soldiered on, some being used against British troops in Libya. Some of the Spanish Chirri models remained in service up to 1953 as aerobatic trainers.

Fiat CR.32

First flight: April 28, 1933
Power: Fiat 600hp A.30 V-12 water-cooled in-line piston engine
Armament: Two synchronized 7.7mm/0.303in machine-guns
Size: Wingspan – 9.5m/31ft 2in
length, 7.45m/24ft 5.25in
Height – 2.63m/8ft 7.5in
Wing area – 22.1m²/237.89sq ft
Weights: Empty – 1325kg/2921lb
Maximum take-off – 1850kg/4079lb
Performance: Maximum speed – 375kph/233mph
Ceiling – 8800m/28,870ft
Range – 680km/422 miles
Climb – 907m/2000ft per minute

Fiat CR.42 Falco

Italy's air ministry, impressed by the performance of the CR.32 in the Spanish Civil War, believed the biplane fighter still had a place in modern air war. The Falco was really of another age by the time it entered service. With many air forces planning to equip with closed-cockpit metal monoplanes, the fixed-undercarriage Falco was virtually obsolete before it had flown. Nevertheless, the CR.42 was not only ordered for Italy's Regia Aeronautica but also for the air forces of Sweden, Belgium and Hungary. When Italy went to war in June 1940, Falcos flew as

escorts on bombing missions over France. In late 1940 the biplane fighters were based in Belgium for Italian bomber attacks on Britain. This often forgotten aspect of the post-Battle of Britain period climaxed on November 11 when the only major Italian raid saw the Italian attackers severely mauled – Falcos were no match for Hurricanes.

Fiat CR.42 Falco

First flight: May 23, 1938
Power: Fiat A.74 R1C 14-cylinder radial piston engine
Armament: Two fixed synchronized 12.7mm/0.5in machine-guns
Size: Wingspan – 9.7m/31ft 10in
Length – 8.27m/27ft 1.5in
Height – 3.59m/11ft 9.25in
Wing area – 22.4m²/241.12sq ft
Weights: Empty – 1782kg/3929lb
Maximum take-off – 2298kg/5060lb
Performance: Maximum speed – 430kph/267mph
Ceiling – 10,200m/33,465ft
Range – 775km/482 miles
Climb – 6000m/19,685ft in 8 minutes, 40 seconds

Fiat G.50 Freccia

The G.50 was the Regia Aeronautica's first all-metal retractable undercarriage monoplane fighter. Early models were combat-tested in the Spanish Civil War: pilots talked of its manoeuvrability and speed. The pilots did not, however, like the "greenhouse" cockpit canopy and, remarkably, the next 200 G.50s built had an open cockpit. About 120 were in service when Italy entered World War II and some were used on raids against France. G.50s also took part in the Italian Air Force raids on Britain in late

1940 and later participated in the Greek and Western Desert campaigns, sometimes in the fighter-bomber role. Only a handful were left in service at the time of the Italian armistice.

In 1939 Finland bought 35 Freccias (Arrow) and used them in action against the Soviet Union in the Russo-Finnish War between 1941 and 1944.

Fiat G.50 Freccia

First flight: February 26, 1937
Power: Fiat A.74 RC38 14-cylinder radial piston engine
Armament: Two synchronized 12.7mm/0.5in machine-guns
Size: Wingspan – 10.96m/35ft 11.5in
Length – 7.79m/25ft 6.75in
Height – 2.96m/9ft 8.5in
Wing area – 18.15m²/195.37sq ft
Weights: Empty – 1975kg/4354lb
Maximum take-off – 2415kg/5324lb
Performance: Maximum speed – 472kph/293mph
Ceiling – 9835m/32,265ft
Range – 670km/416 miles
Climb – 6000m/19,685 in 7 minutes, 30 seconds

Focke-Wulf Fw190

The Fw190, considered by many to be the finest Luftwaffe fighter of the war, was first flown in June 1939 and swiftly proved that single-seat fighters powered by air-cooled radials could still take on the best of the in-line engined fighters. When the Fw190 appeared in combat over France in September 1941 claiming three Spitfires, it proved to be bad news for the RAF whose Spitfire V had ruled the sky since its appearance in February 1941. The 190 was more manoeuvrable than the Spitfire V, except in its turning circle, and had a higher top speed. The Focke-Wulf fighter had a considerable period of dominance in the west and was only seriously challenged when the improved Spitfire IX appeared in quantity in the autumn of 1942.

In February 1942 the Fw190A had its combat début, providing air cover for the German battle-cruisers *Scharnhorst* and *Gneisenau* and the heavy cruiser *Prinz Eugen* as they tried to reach north German ports. In one engagement, 190s destroyed all six attacking Royal Navy Swordfish.

From 1942, the 190A began to appear in quantity on all major fronts and in the West served in both the air defence and fighter/bomber roles. Fw190s were in the thick of one of the fiercest air battles of World War II, over the British and Canadian landings at Dieppe on August 19, 1942. Fw190s were in action throughout the day, by the end of which their pilots had claimed a total of 97 RAF aircraft destroyed. One pilot alone, Josef Wurmheller, claimed seven Spitfires.

The A-model was constantly improved, carrying heavier armament and sometimes equipped with water-methanol or nitrous-oxide injection. Over 30 different variants appeared from the simple fighter to torpedo-carriers.

ABOVE: **The Fw190F was a fighter-bomber version. This example, captured by US forces, is seen awaiting evaluation at Freeman Field in the USA, September 1945.**

In the later war years, the Fw190 became the standard home defence fighter for Germany and was in constant action against the Allied bomber streams. On August 17, 1943 a USAAF bomber force was intercepted by over 300 Fw190 fighters who accounted for 60 American bombers destroyed and 100 damaged. Some of the 190s were specially equipped with 210mm/8.19in rockets used to blow the defensive formations apart, making the bombers easier targets for the conventionally armed Fw190s.

In June 1943 a dedicated Fw190 nightfighter unit was formed but the aircraft were not fitted with radar, instead relying on intercepting the bombers over targets where they might be illuminated by flares, searchlights or the light of the fires below. Over 200 RAF heavy bombers are believed to have been destroyed by these aircraft.

In 1943, the Luftwaffe was faced with an urgent need for fighters with better high-altitude performance to face not just the threat of Allied bombers but also the American B-29 that was known to be coming into service. The existing Fw190 was thought to be incapable of intercepting this new American bomber and so Focke-Wulf, under the leadership of Kurt Tank, undertook the development of a high altitude version of his Fw190 fighter to meet the threat.

The result was the long-nosed D model, or "Dora", and the first production version was the Fw190D-9, which attained production status in the early summer of 1944. The Fw190D

LEFT: **The versatile Fw190 was an excellent fighter-bomber. This example is shown carrying a bomb below its centre line.** BELOW: **The D model, or "Dora" was introduced to counter the anticipated threat of USAAF B-29s.**

BELOW RIGHT: **A captured Ta152H-1 in RAF markings. The Ta152 was an even longer-nosed derivative of the Fw190D.** BELOW: **This Fw190A-3 landed in the UK by mistake during June 1943, giving the Allies all the information they needed about the type.**

was the first production Fw190 fitted with a liquid-cooled engine and was a very good high-altitude interceptor, equal to the P-51D or Spitfire Mk XIV and without the altitude limitations of the Fw190A.

Delivery of the Fw190D-9 began in August 1944 and the first Gruppe (group) to convert to the Dora-9 was 3/JG 54. Their first mission was to provide top cover for Me 262 jet fighters during take-off when they were at their most vulnerable. The general opinion of the Fw190D-9 pilots was that it was the finest Luftwaffe propeller fighter of the entire war and many considered it more than a match for the P-51 Mustang.

The D model was the stepping-stone to the high-flying Focke-Wulf Ta152 that saw service in limited numbers towards the end of the war.

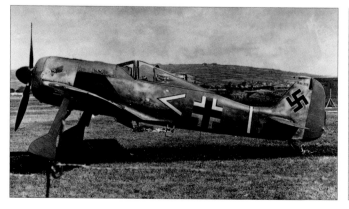

Focke-Wulf 190D-9

First flight: June 1, 1939 (Fw190)
Power: Junkers 1776hp Jumo 213A-1 inverted V piston engine
Armament: Two 13mm/0.51in machine-guns, two 20mm/0.79in cannon plus one 500kg/1102lb bomb
Size: Wingspan – 10.5m/34ft 5.5in
Length – 10.2m/33ft 5.5in
Height – 3.35m/11ft
Wing area – 18.3m²/197sq ft
Weights: Empty – 3490kg//7694lb
Maximum take-off – 4848kg/10,670lb
Performance: Maximum speed – 685kph/426mph
Ceiling – 12,000m/39,370ft
Range – 835km/519 miles
Climb – 6000m/19,685ft in 7 minutes, 6 seconds

Fokker Eindecker

The Fokker E (Eindecker or monoplane) was significant because it was the first combat aircraft to be equipped with interrupter gear that allowed bullets from a fixed machine-gun to be fired safely between the spinning blades of a propeller. This gave the Eindecker pilots a significant advantage over their Allied adversaries, who still had to manoeuvre their aircraft into a firing position and then aim their moving guns manually. The interrupter gear synchronized the Eindecker's single gun with the propeller blades so that once the aircraft was pointed at a target, so was the gun.

The Eindecker, not a remarkable aircraft, was developed from the pre-war M.5 design and relied on "wing-warping" for lateral control, but the technical advantage of a single synchronized gun allowed its pilots to rack up a significant number of aerial victories, beginning on August 1, 1915, when the legendary German ace Max Immelmann achieved his and the Eindecker's first "kill". Over the following weeks Royal Flying Corps pilots were alarmed to come across these single-seat "fighters" that could fire along their own line of flight. This was the beginning of a period of German air supremacy over the Western Front that came to be known as the "Fokker Scourge". The Eindecker, with its innovative armament, gave pilots like Immelmann and Oswald Boelcke a string

of victories that made them national heroes in their homeland and possibly the first well-known fighter aces.

In spite of this, for a number of reasons the Eindecker never reached its full potential as a weapon. German paranoia about the "secret" of the interrupter gear falling into British hands made them forbid the use of the Eindeckers over enemy territory. Also, the Eindeckers were only allocated as individual aircraft to fly escort for two-seater aircraft. Production problems meant that even though they were clearly very significant aircraft, there were less than a hundred in service by the end of 1915. Nevertheless, Eindecker pilots honed their tactics and eventually began to operate in fours, while a more organized ground control system had them vectored to airspace where enemy aircraft were known to be. The result was that by the end of 1915 a small number of Eindeckers had effectively removed the enemy's ability to carry out reconnaissance missions. Meanwhile two lone Eindeckers on the Eastern Front kept the Imperial Russian Air Service in their area at bay.

The tactical advantage enjoyed by the Fokker E series (later Es, the EII, III and

TOP: **The very effective Fokker Eindecker destroyed over 1000 Allied aircraft.** ABOVE: **The period of Eindecker supremacy over the Western Front was known as the "Fokker Scourge".**

IV had more powerful engines and/or an additional gun) came to an end, as Allied designers produced purpose-built fighters to counter the "Fokker Scourge" and Eindeckers were gradually replaced during 1916, but they are thought to have destroyed over 1000 Allied aircraft in their short time of supremacy.

Fokker Eindecker

First flight: 1913 (M.5)
Power: Oberursel 100hp U.I nine-cylinder rotary piston engine
Armament: One fixed forward-firing 7.92mm/0.31in machine-gun
Size: Wingspan – 9.5m/31ft 2.75in
Length – 7.2m/23ft 7.5in
Height – 2.4m/7ft 10.5in
Wing area – 16m²/172.23sq ft
Weight: Empty – 399kg/880lb
Maximum take-off – 610kg/1345lb
Performance: Maximum speed – 140kph/87mph
Ceiling – 3500m/11,480ft
Range – 1.5 hours endurance
Climb – 3000m/9845ft in 30 minutes

Fokker Dr.I Triplane

The Dr.I, chosen by the Germans to counter the threat posed by the British Sopwith Triplane, was rushed into production in 1917 and reached front-line units in October that year. Although extremely manoeuvrable the Dr.I (Dr. was short for Dreidecker or triplane) had an enormous amount of induced drag from its three wings and was consequently not as fast as most of the fighter aircraft then in front-line service. It was, however, extremely manoeuvrable and became the mount of some of Germany's finest World War I aces. The Dr.I will be forever linked with the "Red Baron", Manfred von Richthofen.

Lt Werner Voss scored ten victories flying a prototype Dr.I between September 3 and September 23, 1917 when he died in a dogfight with a Royal Flying Corps S.E.5a. Production models first joined Manfred von Richthofen's Jagdgeschwader (fighter squadron) 1 in mid-October but were grounded after a series of fatal crashes. Investigations found defective wing construction and

the Dr.Is were back in action from the end of November only after all wings had been checked and if necessary rebuilt. Its career was, however, short-lived and production ceased in May 1918, at which time all remaining Dr.Is were withdrawn for the air defence of Germany. Although it was manoeuvrable, the Fokker was outclassed in many

other ways and was really the last of the line of rotary-engined fighters. Richthofen, however, liked its agility and excellent climb rate and was flying his personal scarlet machine when he was shot down and killed in April 1918.

Lt Carl Jacobs was the highest scoring Imperial German Air Force Triplane pilot, credited with 41 victories.

ABOVE: **Perhaps best known as the type made famous by the Red Baron, the Dr.I was one of the rotary-engined fighters.** LEFT: **The Fokker Triplane was introduced to counter the British Sopwith Triplane, which was very manoeuvrable.**

Fokker Dr.I Triplane

First flight: June 1917

Power: Oberursel Ur.II nine-cylinder rotary piston engine

Armament: Two fixed forward-firing 7.92mm/0.31in machine-guns

Size: Wingspan – 7.2m/23ft 7.5in
Length – 5.77m/18ft 11.25in
Height – 2.95m/9ft 8.25in
Wing area – 18.7m^2/201.29sq ft

Weights: Empty – 406kg/895lb
Maximum take-off – 585kg/1290lb

Performance: Maximum speed – 165kph/103mph
Ceiling – 6095m/20,000ft
Range – 1.5 hours endurance
Climb – 1000m/3280ft in 2 minutes, 54 seconds

Fokker D. VII

The D. VII followed the Dr.I into production at the Fokker factory and went on to become the most famous German fighting scout aircraft of World War I. Like the Dreidecker before it, the D. VII was largely designed by Fokker designer Reinhold Platz and shared a number of common components and features with it. The 160hp engine fitted to early D. VIIs was, however, a major step forward in terms of power and the first test flight was carried out by Manfred Richthofen. It first entered service in April 1918 with Jagdgeschwader 1, Richthofen's old unit, commanded by Hermann Goering after the "Red Baron's" death.

The D. VII was popular with its pilots, who described it as responsive and easy to fly. Pilots of this last World War I Fokker fighter achieved many aerial victories in a short period. Germany's first true naval fighter unit Marine-Feld-Geschwader was formed in May 1917 and it was this unit which on August 12, equipped with D. VIIs, shot down 19 British aircraft without loss to itself. The only Allied aircraft that could match the D. VII were the Sopwith Snipe and the SPAD S.XIII.

It is believed that over 1000 were built by the time of the Armistice in November 1918. It is interesting to note that one of the conditions of the Armistice Agreement was that "... especially all first-line D. VII aircraft" were to be handed over to the Allies, such was the regard for the Fokker fighter.

The Fokker company had been founded by Dutchman Anthony Fokker, who having had some of his designs rejected by Britain, among others, offered his services to the Central Powers. At the end of World War I, Fokker managed to smuggle some disassembled D. VIIs and components into Holland, where he went on manufacturing D. VIIs after the war. The Dutch Air Force continued to fly D. VIIs in the Netherlands East Indies until the late 1920s. Ex-German D. VIIs also served with many European air forces after the war.

TOP: **The Fokker D. VII was such a potent fighter that it was specifically mentioned in the Armistice Agreement.** ABOVE: **Oberleutnant Ernst Udet with his personal D. VII. His personal "LO" markings are just visible on the side of the fuselage.**

Fokker D. VII

First flight: January 1918
Power: BMW 185hp six-cylinder in-line piston engine
Armament: Two fixed forward-firing 7.92mm/0.3in machine-guns
Size: Wingspan – 8.9m/29ft 2.5in
 Length – 6.95m/22ft 9.5in
 Height – 2.75m/9ft 0.25in,
 Wing area – 20.5m²/220.67sq ft
Weights: Empty – 735kg/1620lb
 Maximum take-off – 880kg/1940lb
Performance: Maximum speed – 200kph/124mph
 Ceiling – 7000m/22,965ft
 Range – 1.5 hours endurance
 Climb – 5000m/16,405ft in 16 minutes

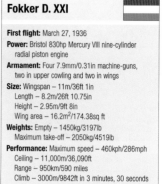

Fokker D. XXI

First flight: March 27, 1936
Power: Bristol 830hp Mercury VIII nine-cylinder
radial piston engine
Armament: Four 7.9mm/0.31in machine-guns,
two in upper cowling and two in wings
Size: Wingspan – 11m/36ft 1in
Length – 8.2m/26ft 10.75in
Height – 2.95m/9ft 8in
Wing area – 16.2m^2/174.38sq ft
Weights: Empty – 1450kg/3197lb
Maximum take-off – 2050kg/4519lb
Performance: Maximum speed – 460kph/286mph
Ceiling – 11,000m/36,090ft
Range – 950km/590 miles
Climb – 3000m/9842ft in 3 minutes, 30 seconds

Fokker D. XXI

Although the D. XXI was designed to meet a Netherlands East Indies Army Air Service requirement, it became the standard fighter for three European countries – Holland, Finland and Denmark. The first Dutch Air Force aircraft flew in mid-1938 and all were in service by early September 1938. The Dutch Air Force had 28 D. XXIs deployed when Germany invaded the Netherlands in May 1940. During the five days before Holland surrendered, the Fokker fighters were pitched against overwhelming odds, but on May 10 they destroyed 37 German Junkers 52 transports in one morning. The brave Dutch D. XXI pilots flew on until their ammunition ran out.

Finnish licence production ran from 1939 until 1944, and a number of these machines were modified to take the 825hp Pratt and Whitney Twin Wasp Junior or the Bristol Pegasus engines. Finnish aircraft also differed from the others by having all four guns mounted in the wings, and "snow shoes" for winter operations.

Denmark operated both Dutch-built and Danish licence-built D. XXIs, which saw action in World War II, opposing the German invaders in March 1940.

LEFT: **Royal Air Force Gauntlet Is. The type was
replaced by Gladiators, Spitfires and Hurricanes
from 1938, but soldiered on in RAF service overseas
until late 1940.**

Gloster Gauntlet II

First flight: October 1934 (Gauntlet I)
Power: Bristol 640hp Mercury VIS nine-cylinder
radial piston engine
Armament: Two fixed forward-firing 7.7mm/0.303in
machine-guns
Size: Wingspan – 9.99m/32ft 9.5in
Length – 8.05m/26ft 5in
Height – 3.12m/10ft 3in
Wing area – 29.26m^2/315sq ft
Weights: Empty – 1256kg/2770lb
Maximum take-off – 1801kg/3970lb
Performance: Maximum speed – 370kph/230mph
Ceiling – 10,210m/33,500ft
Range – 740km/460 miles
Climb – 701m/2300ft per minute

Gloster Gauntlet

The Gauntlet was the last open-cockpit biplane fighter with the RAF, entering service in 1935. It was the fastest single-seat fighter in service until 1937, when the Hurricane appeared, and served as a day- and nightfighter.

Gauntlets went on to equip 14 squadrons of RAF Fighter Command and remained a front-line aircraft in the UK until June 1939. However, the type soldiered on with No.6 Squadron in Palestine until April 1940 and a flight of four fought the Italians in East Africa during September-November 1940. On September 7 a Gauntlet downed an Italian Caproni Ca133 bomber.

In November 1937 it was a Gauntlet of No.32 Squadron that became the first fighter ever to carry out an interception under the direction of ground radar.

Seventeen Gauntlets were produced under licence in Denmark, and ex-RAF Gauntlets were supplied to the Royal Australian Air Force, Finland, Rhodesia and South Africa. The Finnish Gauntlets were fitted with ski landing gear.

Gloster Meteor

The Gloster Meteor was the first jet aircraft in RAF squadron service and also the only Allied jet to see action in World War II. The Meteor beat Germany's Messerschmitt Me262 into squadron service and entered the history books by a matter of days to become the world's first operational jet fighter.

The Meteor was designed by George Carter, who began design work in 1940 and chose the twin-engine layout because of the poor thrust produced by the turbojets of the time. The first Meteor to be built was powered by two Frank Whittle-designed W2B turbojets, but the aircraft was only taxied as the engines failed to produce more than 454kg/1000lb of thrust. So when, on March 5, 1943 the first Meteor flew, it was powered by two Halford H1 engines, forerunners of the Goblin engine later used in the de Havilland Vampire, each providing 681kg/1500lb of thrust. Other prototypes soon took to the air, powered by different engines as the most reliable and efficient powerplant was sought. Development and manufacture of the Whittle-designed engine had passed to Rolls-Royce, who produced it as the 772kg/1700lb thrust W2B/23 Welland engine and it was two of these powerplants that took the fourth Meteor prototype into the air for the first time in June 1943. The Welland was subsequently chosen to power the production Meteor I.

The first RAF Meteor squadron was No.616, who received their first delivery of the futuristic fighters on July 12, 1944 and wasted no time in putting the Meteor to the test. The first

TOP: **A Meteor F.8, the only British jet type to see action in the Korean War.**

ABOVE: **Over 1000 Meteor F.8s were in service with the RAF between 1950 and 1955.**

sortie flown by a Meteor was not against manned aircraft but actually against the deadly V-1 flying bombs that began to rain down on Britain in 1944. Problems with the guns frustrated Britain's first jet pilots but on August 4 Flying Officer Dean succeeded in tipping a V-1 over in flight after his guns had jammed. By the end of the month, with gun problems resolved, No.616 had destroyed a total of 13 flying bombs. As the Allies pushed into Europe after D-Day, the next Meteors were readied for fighter v. fighter combat, possibly against the new twin-engined Me262 recently deployed by the Germans. In fact only one inconclusive encounter with Focke-Wulf Fw190s is recorded. As World War II came to an end, the Meteor F. Mk III was the standard version in service, with more powerful Derwent engines and a sliding canopy. These aircraft remained in RAF service for some years after the war and formed the backbone of Fighter Command in the post-war years, retaining the standard wartime armament of four 20mm/0.78in Hispano cannon, carried on the sides of the fuselage forward of the cockpit.

Between 1947 and 1948 the Mk III was superseded in front-line units by the F. Mk 4, which was powered by uprated Derwent 5 engines and which went on to equip 22 RAF squadrons. The F. Mk 8, developed from the F.4 had a longer fuselage, extra internal fuel tankage and an ejection seat as standard. The latter safety feature is taken for granted these days but it was not so in the early days of jet fighter aircraft. The Mk 8 had a top speed of 965kph/600mph and from 1950 until 1955 was the RAF's main day interceptor with a staggering 1090 in service to counter the Soviet bomber threat.

Although not used there by the RAF, F.8s of the Royal Australian Air Force became the only British jet aircraft to see action in Korea, though their performance gave the enemy MiG-15s little to worry about. After the type's poor showing against the MiGs in Korea, many air forces applied the Meteor to the ground-attack role, armed with small bombs and air-to-ground rockets. The Meteor's performance was improved during its operational life but by the early 1950s it was outclassed by swept-wing fighters.

RAF F. Mk 8s were replaced by Hunters from 1955 but some were converted for use as target tugs and continued to fly in the RAF until 1977.

TOP: **The F.4 entered RAF service in 1947 and equipped 22 Fighter Command units.** ABOVE: **The Meteor F. Mk III was in RAF service by the end of World War II.** BELOW: **The Meteor was widely exported and equipped the air arms of at least 13 other nations.**

Over 350 Gloster Meteors were exported to at least 13 other nations (NATO air forces included Belgium, the Netherlands and Denmark) and more than 240 were built under licence by Belgium's Avions Fairey. Total UK production of Meteors reached 2920, and a few aircraft dayfighters of the era remained in service for three decades.

Gloster Meteor F. Mk I

First flight: March 5, 1943
Power: Two Rolls-Royce 772kg/1700-lb-thrust W2B/23 Welland turbojets
Armament: Four 20mm/0.78in cannon
Size: Wingspan – 13.11m/43ft
Length – 12.57m/41ft 4in
Height – 3.96m/13ft
Wing area – 34.74m^2/374sq ft
Weights: Empty – 3692kg/8140lb
Maximum take-off – 6268kg/13,800lb
Performance: Maximum speed – 660kph/410mph
Ceiling – 12,190m/40,000ft
Range – 1610km/1000 miles
Climb – 657m/2155ft per minute

Gloster Gladiator

The Gloster Gladiator was the RAF's last biplane fighter and entered service in February 1937, by which time it was already obsolete. Although largely replaced by the start of World War II, the Gladiators of Nos.607 and 615 auxiliary squadrons were deployed to France with the Air Component of the Allied Expeditionary Force in November 1939. The RAF fighter squadrons were converting to Spitfires and Hurricanes when the German attack in the west was launched in May 1940, and the Gladiators proved to be no match for the modern Luftwaffe fighters.

Meanwhile in Norway, No.263 Squadron Gladiators were in action defending British forces and one pilot, Flying Officer Jacobsen, destroyed at least five German aircraft on one remarkable mission. Tragically all of No.263's aircraft and all but two of its pilots were lost when the ship carrying them home following the British withdrawal from Norway was sunk by German battleships.

Even during the Battle of Britain, No.247 Squadron's Gladiators based at Roborough protected Plymouth and its dockyard from German attackers.

In June 1940 a handful of Gladiators were responsible for the defence of Malta and the type was also in action against Italian forces in Egypt. Elsewhere, Gladiators served in the Western Desert until early 1942.

Some Gladiators were fitted with arrester hooks and served with the Fleet Air Arm from December 1938, while fully navalized Sea Gladiators equipped for catapult launches were developed. After withdrawal from front-line duties, Gladiators continued to fly as communications and meteorological aircraft until 1944.

LEFT: **Three RAF Gladiators, literally tied together for the ultimate test of formation flying, practice for the Hendon Air Display.** BELOW: **This Gladiator, preserved in the UK by the Shuttleworth Collection, is shown painted as an aircraft of No.247 Squadron at the time of the Battle of Britain.**

Gloster Gladiator Mk I

First flight: September 12, 1934
Power: Bristol 840hp Mercury IX air-cooled radial piston engine
Armament: Two 7.7mm/0.303in machine-guns in nose, plus two more mounted in wing
Size: Wingspan – 9.83m/32ft 3in
Length – 8.36m/27ft 5in
Height – 3.15m/10ft 4in
Wing area – 30.01m^2/323sq ft
Weights: Empty – 1565kg/3450lb
Maximum take-off – 2155kg/4750lb
Performance: Maximum speed – 407kph/253mph
Ceiling – 10,060m/33,000ft
Range – 547km/340 miles
Climb – 6095m/20,000ft in 9 minutes, 30 seconds

Grumman Biplane fighters

The Grumman company's long association with the US Navy began in March 1931, when the Navy ordered a prototype two-seat biplane fighter, the XFF-1. The all-metal XFF-1 had a top speed of 314kph/195mph and was faster than the Navy's standard fighter of the time, the Boeing F4B-4. The Navy ordered the Grumman biplane and it entered service as the FF-1 from April 1933. Canadian licence-built versions, known as Goblins were supplied to the Royal Canadian Air Force, Nicaragua and Japan. Spanish Republican Forces also acquired 40 of them and the two-seaters were in action against Spanish Nationalist forces between 1936 and 1939, during the Spanish Civil War.

The FF-1 was certainly a winning design and Grumman unsurprisingly began to develop a lighter, single-seat version, which became the F2F-1.

The single-seater was lighter than the FF1, had a top speed of 383kph/238mph and entered US Navy service during 1935, replacing the F4B. The F2F-1 remained in front-line service aboard USS *Lexington* until late September 1940, at which point it became an advanced trainer.

The F2F-1 had exhibited some inherent directional instability, which Grumman sought to eradicate in an improved design, the F3F. With a longer fuselage and wings, together with other aerodynamic refinements, the F3F-1 prototype first flew in March 1935 but crashed two days later, killing the pilot, when the engine and wings detached themselves in a test dive. Wing and engine fittings were strengthened on the second prototype which also crashed, on May 17, after the pilot was unable to recover from a flat spin. Remarkably, this crashed aircraft

ABOVE AND LEFT: **The Grumman F3F was in US Navy service from 1936 until 1941. The family resemblance to the later Wildcat monoplane is clear.**

was rebuilt and was back in the air after just three weeks, fitted with a small ventral fin beneath the tail to aid spin recovery.

The F3F-1 entered US Navy service aboard USS *Ranger* and USS *Saratoga* in 1936 and US Marine Corps unit VMF-211 was the last to retire the F3F, in October 1941.

Grumman F2F-1

First flight: October 18, 1933
Power: Pratt & Whitney 650hp R-1535-72 Twin Wasp Junior radial piston engine
Armament: Two 7.62mm/0.3in machine-guns
Size: Wingspan – 8.69m/28ft 6in
    Length – 6.53m/21ft 5in
    Height – 2.77m/9ft 1in
    Wing area – 21.37m²/230sq ft
Weights: Empty – 1221kg/2691lb
    Maximum take-off – 1745kg/3847lb
Performance: Maximum speed – 383kph/238mph
    Ceiling – 8380m/27,500ft
    Range – 1585km/985 miles
    Climb – 939m/3080ft per minute

Grumman F4F Wildcat

If the Wildcat looks like a biplane missing a set of wings there is a good reason – it was originally conceived as a biplane but was redesigned as a monoplane, the F4F, in 1936. Its industrial appearance, due to the entirely riveted fuselage, masked an aircraft with excellent speed and manoeuvrability.

In early 1939 the French Aéronavale placed the first order for the type with Grumman and this was followed in August that year by an order from the US Navy. After France fell, aircraft destined for the Aéronavale were diverted to Britain, where the first machines for Britain's Fleet Air Arm arrived in

July 1940. The British named the F4F the "Martlet" and put the type into service almost immediately with No.804 Squadron in the Orkneys. In December 1940 two of these Martlets became the first US-built fighters in British World War II service to destroy a German aircraft. In September 1941 No.802 Squadron became the first FAA unit to go to sea with Martlets, aboard HMS *Audacity*, and on the 20th, two of the aircraft shot down a Focke-Wulf 200 that was shadowing their convoy. Martlets of the Royal Naval Fighter Unit saw action over the Western Desert and shot down an Italian Fiat G.50 on September 28, 1941.

In May 1942 over Madagascar, FAA Martlets saw action against Vichy French aircraft and in August that year, while escorting a convoy to Malta, they tackled Italian bombers over the Mediterranean. By now the Martlet/Wildcat was known as a formidable fighter aircraft. Pilots praised its hard-hitting firepower but knew it was a tricky aircraft to fly and to handle on the ground too.

When the USA entered World War II in December 1941 the F4F, by now known as the Wildcat, was the most widely used fighter on US aircraft carriers and also equipped many

LEFT: **Despite its origins in a biplane design, the F4F went on to be one of the most effective carrier fighters of World War II.** BELOW: **Impressed by the performance of the Wildcat prototype, the US Navy ordered 78 of the type in 1939.**

LEFT: **To survive the harsh environment of carrier operations, naval fighters have to be supremely rugged and the Wildcat was just that.** BELOW: **Royal Navy Wildcats, initially named Martlets, saw widespread action in World War II and destroyed many enemy aircraft.** BOTTOM: **British Fleet Air Arm Wildcats destroyed four Luftwaffe fighters over Norway in March 1945.**

land-based US Marine Corps units. This tough, hard-hitting and highly manoeuvrable aircraft was the US Navy's only carrier-borne fighter until the 1943 arrival of the Hellcat. Wildcats were central to some of the war's most remarkable heroic actions involving US Navy and USMC pilots.

USMC Wildcats operated extensively from land bases, one of which was Henderson Field on Guadalcanal and it was from here that the Americans mounted their first offensive action of the war in the Pacific. One USMC Wildcat pilot, Captain Joe Foss, a flight commander with Marine Fighting Squadron VMF-121, led his flight of eight Wildcats from Guadalcanal to 72 confirmed aerial victories in a matter of sixteen weeks. Foss himself shot down a total of 26 Japanese aircraft, including five in a single day, and was awarded the Congressional Medal of Honor.

Although in a straight fight Wildcats could not cope well with Japanese Zeros, the Grumman fighter's armour plating and self-sealing fuel tanks, together with its pilot's tenacity made it a potent adversary in a dogfight. US Navy Wildcats were phased out in favour of the Grumman Hellcat in late 1943 but Britain's Fleet Air Arm continued to operate the Wildcat to the end of the war. In March 1945 Wildcats (the British abandoned the name Martlet in January 1944) of No.882 Squadron destroyed four Messerschmitt Bf109s over Norway in what was the FAA's last wartime victory over German fighters.

Those Wildcats built by General Motors were designated FM-1 and -2.

Grumman FM-2 Wildcat

First flight: March 1943 (FM-2)
Power: Wright Cyclone 1350hp R-1820-56 nine-cylinder air-cooled radial engine
Armament: Six 12.7mm/0.5in machine-guns in outer wings, plus two underwing 113kg/250lb bombs or six 12.7cm/5in rockets
Size: Wingspan – 11.58m/38ft
  Length – 8.8m/28ft 11in
  Height – 3.5m/11ft 5in
  Wing area – 24.16m²/260sq ft
Weights: Empty – 2226kg/4900lb
  Maximum take-off – 3367kg/7412lb
Performance: Maximum speed – 534kph/332mph
  Service ceiling – 10,576m/34,700ft
  Range – 1,448km/900 miles
  Climb – 610m/2000ft per minute

Grumman F6F Hellcat

The F6F Hellcat has been rightly described as a war-winning fighter. Developed from the F4F Wildcat, designed and produced in record time, the Hellcat's combat début in August 1943 swung the Pacific air power balance firmly in favour of the United States. From then on all the major Pacific air battles were dominated by the F6F. In its first big air battle, in the Kwajalein area on December 4, 1943, 91 Hellcats fought 50 Japanese A6M Zeros and destroyed 28 for the loss of only two. Powered by the Pratt and Whitney R-2800 Double Wasp engine, the robust Hellcat was credited with 75 per cent of all enemy aircraft destroyed by US Navy carrier pilots, with an overall F6F kills-to-losses ratio in excess of 19:1. The Hellcat was America's all-time top "ace-making" aircraft, with no less than 307 pilots credited with the destruction of five or more enemy aircraft while flying the Grumman fighter. US Navy pilot Lt Bill Hardy became an ace on the day of April 6, 1945, when in a single 70-minute sortie he engaged and destroyed five Japanese aircraft.

Effective at any altitude, the Hellcat's unusual features included backwards-retracting landing gear and a distinctive $31.13m^2/334sq$ ft wing, larger than that of any other major single-engined fighter of World War II. The outer sections of the folding wings each contained three 12.7mm/0.5in machine-guns, with 400 rounds each.

Nightfighter versions equipped with radar appeared in early 1944 and ensured that the Hellcats were an ever-present threat to their enemies. The Hellcat omnipresence in Pacific combat zones night or day came to be known as "The Big

TOP: **The Hellcat turned the tide in favour of the USA in the Pacific air war during World War II.** ABOVE: **The XF6F-4, the Hellcat prototype.** LEFT: **During World War II the F6F was the single-engine fighter with the largest wing area.**

Blue Blanket". US Navy ace Lt Alex Vraciu destroyed 19 Japanese aircraft while flying Hellcats, including six in one spectacular eight-minute engagement, and later described the F6F Hellcat as "tough, hard-hitting, dependable – one hell of an airplane".

From April 1943 Britain's Fleet Air Arm received 252 F6F-3s under the Lend Lease programme. Initially renamed the "Gannet" in Royal Navy service, British F6Fs saw a lot of combat in actions off Norway, in the Mediterranean and the Far East, including the final assault on Japan. By late 1945 the Hellcat was virtually completely replaced in Royal Navy service, although a senior Fleet Air Arm officer is known to have had a personal F6F until 1953.

When the last aircraft rolled off the production line in November 1945 it made a total Hellcat production figure of 12,272, of which 11,000 were built in just two years. Swift production of the Hellcat has been attributed to the soundness of the original design, which required few engineering changes while production was underway.

Other nations that operated the Hellcat included France, whose Aéronavale used them in Indo-China, while the Argentine and Uruguayan navies used them until 1961.

Some US Navy Hellcats were converted into drones packed with explosives, and in August 1952 six of these remotely controlled F6F-5Ks were directed on to North Korean targets.

ABOVE: **During the last two years of World War II the Hellcat was credited with 75 per cent of enemy aircraft shot down by US Navy pilots.** BELOW: **In all, the F6F destroyed over 5000 enemy aircraft.** BOTTOM: **US Navy ace Lt Alex Vraciu pictured with his personal Hellcat. This historic aircraft, also pictured below, is preserved in flying condition in the UK.**

Grumman F6F-5 Hellcat

First flight: June 26, 1942
Power: Pratt and Whitney 2000hp R-2800-10W 18-cylinder two-row air-cooled radial piston engine
Armament: Six 12.7mm/0.5in Browning machine-guns, plus provision for bombs up to 907kg/2000lb
Size: Wingspan – 13m/42ft 10in
    Length – 10.2m/33ft 7in
    Height – 3.96m/13ft
    Wing area – 31m²/334sq ft
Weights: Empty – 4152kg/9153lb
    Maximum take-off – 6991kg/15,413lb
Performance: Maximum speed – 621kph/386mph
    Ceiling – 11,369m/37,300ft
    Range – 1674km/1040 miles on internal fuel
    Climb – 1039m/3410ft per minute

Grumman F8F Bearcat

The Grumman Bearcat was the last in the Grumman series of carrier-based fighters that had started back in 1931 with the Grumman FF. It was one of the fastest piston-engined aircraft ever and was built to a specification calling for a small, light fighter aircraft to be powered by the mighty R-2800 Double Wasp engine that had been used in the Hellcat and Tigercat.

The Bearcat was 20 per cent lighter than the Hellcat and had a 30 per cent greater rate of climb than its Grumman stablemate. These factors, together with its excellent manoeuvrability and good low-level performance made it an excellent fighter aircraft in all respects. It is worth noting that in comparative

trials the Bearcat's impressive performance allowed it to outmanoeuvre most of the early jet fighters. The first production aircraft (the F8F-1) were delivered in February 1945, a mere six months after the prototype test flight.

In May 1945 US Navy fighter squadron VF-19 became the first unit to equip with the Bearcat but the type arrived too late to see action in World War II. Production nevertheless continued until May 1949, by which time 24 US Navy squadrons were operating Bearcats. The F8F-1B version (of which 100 were built) was armed with four 20mm/0.78in cannon instead of the four 12.7mm/0.5in machine-guns of the F8F-1. Almost 300 examples of the F8F-2 were built with 20mm/0.5in cannon armament as standard. Small numbers of radar-equipped nightfighter and photo-reconnaissance versions were also made.

The Bearcat was phased out of front-line US Navy use by 1952 but around 250 were refurbished and sold as F8F-1Ds to the French Armée de l'Air, who used them in Indo-China. Many of these aircraft were later acquired by the air forces of both North and South Vietnam. The Royal Thai Air Force was also supplied with about 130 Bearcats.

TOP: **The Bearcat was the fastest piston-engined production aircraft ever built and was loved by its pilots.** ABOVE: **Too late for wartime service, the Bearcat remained in front-line US Navy service until the early 1950s.** LEFT: **Due to its high performance, the Bearcat has become a favourite of air racers and warbird collectors.**

Grumman F8F-1B Bearcat

First flight: August 21, 1944
Power: Pratt & Whitney 2100hp R-2800-34W Double Wasp 18-cylinder radial piston engine
Armament: Four 20mm/0.78in cannon, plus provision for two 454kg/1,000lb bombs or four 12.7cm/5in rockets under wings
Size: Wingspan – 10.92m/35ft 10in
Length – 8.61m/28ft 3in Height – 4.2m/13ft 10in
Wing area – 22.67m²/244sq ft
Weights: Empty – 3206kg/7070lb
Maximum take-off – 5873kg/12,947lb
Performance: Maximum speed – 677kph/421mph
Ceiling – 11,795m/38,700ft
Range – 1778km/1105 miles
Climb – 1395m/4570ft per minute

Hawker Fury

The Fury was loved by its pilots, who praised its light and sensitive controls and excellent rate of climb. This small biplane first flew in March 1931 and on entering Royal Air Force service in May that year, became the first RAF fighter to exceed 322kph/200mph. Displays of aerobatics by RAF Furies were for some years the highlight of the famous Hendon Air Pageants – on some occasions three Furies were literally tied together for a full aerobatic routine, demonstrating how stable and responsive the aircraft could be.

An improved performance version powered by the Kestrel VI engine entered RAF service in early 1937 as the Fury II – this was to serve as a stop gap while the Hurricane was developed. Although the Fury II could fly 10 per cent faster than the Mk I it had 10 per cent less range than the earlier model.

Furies were the main RAF fighters in the mid-1930s and some remained in the RAF front line until 1937, when they were replaced by Gladiators. When World War II broke out in September 1939, around 50 Fury IIs were still in service with training units.

Export versions were supplied to South Africa, Spain, Norway, Persia

ABOVE: **This preserved Fury I is a regular at British air shows.** RIGHT: **The Fury was the first Royal Air Force fighter to exceed 322kph/200mph.** BELOW: **Furies were exported to a number of nations including Yugoslavia, who operated the machine pictured.**

(Iran), Portugal and Yugoslavia. Three squadrons of South African Furies saw action in East Africa early in World War II, while Yugoslav Furies were pitched against the Luftwaffe during the German invasion of April 1941. The Mk I examples supplied to Persia in 1933 were powered with Pratt and Whitney Hornet or Bristol Mercury radial engines and the RAF came up against some of these Furies during a revolt in 1941.

Hawker Fury II

First flight: March 25, 1931 (Fury I)
Power: Rolls-Royce 640hp Kestrel VI 12-cylinder
    V piston engine
Armament: Two synchronized forward-firing
    7.7mm/0.303in machine-guns
Size: Wingspan – 9.14m/30ft
    Length – 8.15m/26ft 9in
    Height – 3.1m/10ft 2in
    Wing area – 23.41m²/252sq ft
Weights: Empty – 1245kg/2743lb
    Maximum take-off – 1637kg/3609lb
Performance: Maximum speed – 359kph/223mph
    Ceiling – 8990m/29,500ft
    Range – 435km/270 miles
    Climb – 3050m/10,000ft in 3.8 minutes

Hawker Hurricane

Comparison of the Hurricane and the earlier Hawker Fury's fuselages explains why the embryonic Hurricane was initially known as the Fury Monoplane. The aircraft that only became known as the Hurricane in June 1936 first flew in November 1935, retaining the metal tube construction with fabric covering used by Hawkers since the late 1920s, and not the more modern and complicated stressed-metal fuselage. War clouds were forming in Europe and it was important to get the RAF's first eight-gun monoplane fighter into production and into service as quickly as possible. Stressed-metal covered wings became standard after early Hurricane models appeared with fabric-covered wings.

When the Hurricane entered RAF service, replacing No.111 Squadron's Gloster Gauntlets at Northolt in December 1937, it became the first RAF aircraft able to exceed 482kph/ 300mph. In February 1938 a 111 Squadron Hurricane flew into the record books by making a nightflight from Edinburgh to RAF Northolt at a very impressive average speed of 656kph/408mph.

Hurricanes outnumbered Spitfires in RAF Fighter Command by about two to one when war broke out and so bore the brunt of early wartime fighter operations. Four squadrons operated in France and on October 30, 1939 a Hurricane of No.1 Squadron destroyed the first German aircraft of World War II, a Dornier Do 17.

It was, however, during the Battle of Britain in 1940 that the Hurricane earned its place in history, accounting for more enemy aircraft than all other defences, ground and air combined. In August of that historic year, Hurricane pilot

TOP: **Preserved in the UK, this Hurricane is painted as a nightfighter of No.87 Squadron, one of the longest serving RAF Hurricane nightfighter units.**
ABOVE: **The number of airworthy Hurricanes is growing.**

Flight Lt J.B. Nicholson of No.249 Squadron was awarded Fighter Command's only Victoria Cross for attacking a Luftwaffe Messerschmitt Me110 after his own aircraft had caught fire.

While the Battle of Britain raged, on August 2, 1940 Hurricanes of No.261 Squadron began their defence of Malta against Italian bombers. Hurricanes took on the Italians again, but this time over Britain, in November 1940, during a little-known episode of World War II. Italian bombers made their one and only en masse appearance over the UK and were badly mauled by the Hurricanes of Nos.46, 249 and 257 Squadrons. Seven out of ten Fiat BR.20 bombers were shot down, together with four Fiat CR.42 escort fighters.

The Mk II Hurricane reached RAF squadrons from September 1940 and differed from the Mk I by having a two-stage supercharged Merlin XX engine instead of the

ABOVE: **The world's only surviving Sea Hurricane is preserved in the UK.**

Merlin III. Armament on the Mk II varied between the eight machine-guns of the IIA to the 12 7.7mm/0.303in machine-guns of the IIB. The Mk IIC joined the squadrons in April 1941 and carried four 20mm/0.78in guns.

Nightfighter and navalized versions appeared later and ground-attack variants, some carrying two devastating 40mm/0.79in anti-tank guns (the Mk IID), were widely used in North Africa. Hurricanes operating in Burma became the leading RAF fighter against the Japanese. The last version to enter service was the Mk IV, which equipped the RAF's last Hurricane squadron, No.6, until January 1947. A total of 14,231 Hurricanes were built in Britain and Canada and a handful remain flying today.

In 1941 the Royal Navy began to use Hurricanes fitted with catapult and arrester gear. Known as Sea Hurricanes, they served with the Merchant Ship Fighter Unit and also the Fleet Air Arm from carriers. The former versions were carried on ships on rocket sleds and were launched when a threat appeared. When unable to recover to land or to a carrier the aircraft simply ditched in the sea.

As a fighter, the aircraft was extremely popular with pilots since it was fast, agile and, as celebrated Hurricane pilot Robert Stanford Tuck recalled, "The Hurricane was solid and could obviously stand up to a lot of punishment. It was steady as a rock and an excellent gun platform. Pilot visibility was better than the contemporary Spitfires as the nose sloped more steeply from the cockpit to the spinner and this of course made shooting rather easier".

Hawker Hurricane Mk I

First flight: November 6, 1935
Power: Rolls-Royce 1030hp Merlin III 12-cylinder
  liquid-cooled engine
Armament: Eight 7.7mm/0.303in Browning
  machine-guns with 334 rounds per gun
Size: Wingspan – 12.19m/40ft
  Length – 9.57m/31ft 5in
  Height – 4.m/13ft 1.5in
  Wing area – 24m²/258sq ft
Weights: Empty – 2260kg/4982lb
  Loaded – 2924kg/6447lb
Performance: Maximum speed – 511kph/318mph
  Ceiling – 10,970m/36,000ft
  Range – 740km/460 miles
  Climb – 770m/2520ft per minute

TOP: **Turkey was one of the export customers for the Hurricane.** MIDDLE: **Though eclipsed by the Spitfire, the Hurricane was central to the British victory in the Battle of Britain.** BOTTOM: **A pre-war examination of a No.1 Squadron RAF aircraft.**

Hawker Tempest

The Tempest was developed from the Typhoon and differed from its predecessor mainly by its lengthened fuselage and a new thin-section laminar flow wing intended to improve on the Typhoon's disappointing climb and altitude performance. Five versions were planned to test various engine installations but only three ever saw service – the Mks II, V and VI. On the Mk II Tempest the radiator was moved from beneath the engine to the wing leading edges and fuel tankage moved from the wing to the longer fuselage. The first Tempest to fly, the Mk V, was a modified Typhoon which took to the air in September 1942.

The V was powered by a Napier Sabre II engine, while the Mk VI had the 2340hp Sabre V. Only the Tempest Mk V, retaining the Typhoon's distinctive chin radiator, saw wartime service, the first RAF Tempest wing being formed in April 1944. After initial train-busting and ground-attack duties, the Tempest V was used to tackle the V-1 flying bombs and excelled in the role. The Tempest V was the fastest fighter to be responsible for British air defence and destroyed 638 V-1s between June 13 and September 5, 1944.

Later, as part of the 2nd Tactical Air Force, Tempest Vs destroyed 20 Messerschmitt Me262s in air combat. Post-war, a number of Tempest Vs continued to serve as target tugs, and the Tempest VI was the RAF's standard Middle East fighter until the Vampire replaced them in 1949.

The Tempest II looked very different from the earlier Typhoon and was powered by a 2520hp Centaurus engine. It was designed for operations against the Japanese but the war ended before they could be deployed as part of the planned Tiger Force.

The Mk II first entered RAF service in November 1945 and the majority served overseas. Three Tempest II squadrons were based in Germany in 1946–8 and during the Berlin Airlift in 1948–9 Tempests of No.33 Squadron were based at Berlin's RAF Gatow to demonstrate the RAF's fighter potential in the area. No.33 later operated their Tempest IIs in the Far East and some saw action against Malayan terrorists in 1950–1.

ABOVE: **The Tempest's Typhoon origins are clear in this photograph of a Mk V – note the bubble canopy introduced in later Typhoons for improved pilot view.** BELOW: **Post-war, this Tempest V was used for target towing duties.**

Hawker Tempest V

First flight: September 1942
Power: Napier 2180-hp Sabre II 24-cylinder piston engine
Armament: Four 20mm/0.78in cannon in wings and provision for rocket-projectiles or 908kg/2000lb of bombs beneath wings
Size: Wingspan – 12.5m/41ft
Length – 10.26m/33ft 8in
Height – 4.9m/16ft 1in
Wing area – 28.06m²/302sq ft
Weights: Empty – 4082kg/9000lb
Maximum take-off – 6142kg/13,500lb
Performance: Maximum speed – 686kph/427mph
Ceiling – 11,125m/36,500ft
Range – 1191km/740 miles
Climb – 4575m/15,000ft in 5 minutes

Hawker Typhoon

The Typhoon was plagued with engine problems and structural weaknesses in its early days and failed to perform adequately for its intended role as a wartime interceptor. Nevertheless it went on to become an extremely effective fighter-bomber, accompanying the Allied advance through France and Holland in the later stages of World War II in 1944.

The Typhoon was born of a British Air Ministry specification for an interceptor designed to make the most of the new Rolls-Royce and Napier 24-cylinder 2000hp engines then under development. The Typhoon was paired with the Napier Sabre engine and flew for the first time in February 1940. Continued development and production problems delayed the Typhoon's delivery to the RAF until August 1941, when it became the RAF's first 643kph/400mph fighter. The price to pay for the high speed was

ABOVE: **A Typhoon IB of No.175 Squadron RAF is checked and armed for another D-Day period mission.**
BELOW LEFT: **This unusual trials Typhoon IB, built by Gloster Aircraft, is shown with a four-blade propeller.**
BELOW RIGHT: **A No.183 Squadron Typhoon IB – the "Tiffie" was the only RAF fighter with the speed to stop Fw190 hit-and-run raids on Britain.**

a low rate of climb and lacklustre performance at altitude, all due to the unreliable Sabre engine, which simply entered service before it was ready. A hazard unrelated to engine problems for early Typhoon pilots was a structural weakness in the tail, which cost the lives of a number of pilots – this problem was later rectified.

The whole Typhoon fleet was almost withdrawn from service, such was the effect of the combined problems, but these were fixed and a use was found for the Typhoon's high low-level speed. German Focke-Wulf 190s had been carrying out hit-and-run raids along Britain's south coast – the Typhoon with

its top speed of 664kph/412mph was the only RAF fighter that could catch them and destroyed four within days of being deployed.

From 1943, "Tiffies" went on the offensive, attacking targets in France and the Low Countries. When late in 1943 the Typhoons began carrying rocket projectiles, they proved to be truly devastating aircraft. The relentless day and night attacks by RAF Typhoon squadrons on German communications targets greatly aided the D-Day operations. The aircraft that was once almost scrapped from RAF service ultimately equipped no fewer than 26 squadrons of the 2nd Tactical Air Force.

Hawker Typhoon IB

First flight: May 27, 1941 (Production IA)
Power: Napier 2180hp Sabre IIA 24-cylinder sleeve-valve liquid-cooled piston engine
Armament: Four 20mm/0.78in cannon in outer wings and racks for eight rockets or two 227kg/500lb bombs
Size: Wingspan – 12.67m/41ft 7in
Length – 9.73m/31ft 11in
Height – 4.67m/15ft 4in
Wing area – 25.92m²/279sq ft
Weights: Empty – 3992kg/8800lb
Maximum take-off – 6010kg/13,250lb
Performance: Maximum speed – 664kph/412mph
Ceiling – 10,730m/35,200ft
Range – 821km/510 miles (with bombs)
Climb – 914m/3000ft per minute

Heinkel He162 Salamander

The He162 story shows what desperate means the German military conceived to stem the tide of the Allied advance in 1944. One solution was this small, cheap and easy-to-build jet fighter designed to attack the fleets of Allied bombers that pounded the Third Reich on a daily basis. The official requirement was issued on September 8, 1944 and the whole programme, not the aircraft, was given the name Salamander. Popularly known as the Volksjäger (people's fighter), it flew for the first time on December 6, 1944, incredibly only 38 days after detailed plans were passed to the factory. Total time from the start of design work to test flight was just over three months.

The light metal alloy streamlined fuselage had a moulded plywood nose and the one-piece wooden wing was tipped with metal. The He162 cockpit was modern-looking with an upward hinged canopy and an ejection seat. Maintenance was not judged to be an issue because damaged or unserviceable aircraft would be replaced by one of the many new ones in mass production.

The engine was top mounted to save design and construction time creating an aircraft around an engine, plus its intake and jet pipes. Fixed to the aircraft by three large bolts, the engine's location did not cause aerodynamic problems but did affect stability making the aircraft difficult to fly and fight in. An onboard two-stroke piston engine was used as a starter motor. During the first flight in December 1944 one of the main

TOP: **The He162 took to the air only 38 days after the design was handed to the factory.** ABOVE: **Planned mass production was expected to create 4000 examples of the Volksjäger (people's fighter) each month.**

undercarriage doors failed and broke away. The door was made of adhesive-bonded wood, as were the wings and fins. Investigation showed that the wood adhesive contained acid that was slowly eating into the wood of the aircraft. While a new adhesive was sourced for the production aircraft, the test flights had to continue and on December 10, 1944 the prototype crashed after the wing came apart in flight.

Production, fed by a network of sub-contractors including woodworkers and furniture makers, was expected to reach a peak of 4000 per month. Hundreds of factories were to take

part in the mass production of the Volksjäger. By February, about 100 He162s had been built but pilot training was not in step with aircraft production. Huge numbers of workers had been organized to build the He162 before the design was finished. Meanwhile Hitler Youth were being quickly trained in gliders as pilots for the new interceptor – their training was to be completed by flying the He162 in combat. Experienced fighter

TOP: **This captured He162, shown here with RAF markings, was shipped to Farnborough in Britain for evaluation – it crashed in November 1945.** ABOVE: **Only 200 were completed, but a further 800 incomplete examples were found when underground factories were captured by the Allies.** LEFT: **The type was equipped with an ejection seat – this example was a more aerodynamically refined He162A-2.**

pilots may have been able to manage the handful that the He162 certainly was, poorly trained Hitler Youth would have fared much worse.

In keeping with the breakneck speed of the programme, the first aircraft were delivered for operational evaluation and trials in January 1945. In February 1945 1/JG1 became the first unit to relinquish (some pilots reluctantly) their Fw190s, to begin conversion on the He162. One Gruppe (group) of three squadrons was formed on May 4, 1945 at Leck in Schleswig-Holstein but the airfield was captured by the British only four days later. Fuel shortages and general chaos had prevented the fighter from ever firing its twin 20mm/0.79in cannon in anger.

Although around 200 were completed, a further 800 were under production at underground factories when they were captured. Post-war, 11 Salamanders were taken to Britain for evaluation by the RAF.

Heinkel He162 Salamander

First flight: December 6, 1944
Power: BMW 800kg/1764lb thrust 0030A-1 turbojet
Armament: Two 20mm/0.78in cannon
Size: Wingspan – 7.2m/23ft 7.5in
Length – 9.05m/29ft 8.25in
Height – 2.55m/8ft 4.5in
Wing area – 11.2m²/120.56sq ft
Weights: Empty – 2050kg/4520lb
Maximum take-off – 2695kg/5941lb
Performance:
Maximum speed – 840kph/522mph (6000m)
Ceiling – 12,040m/39,500ft
Range – 695km/434 miles
Climb – 1280m/4200ft per minute

Heinkel He219

Heinkel's excellent nightfighter began as project P.1060 in 1940 as a high-speed multi-role aircraft. There was little interest in the design until late 1941, when RAF Bomber Command's raids began to have a strategic impact on the German war machine. Ernst Heinkel was then asked to produce his design as a nightfighter and so it first flew in November 1942. Among the design innovations were a tricycle undercarriage (the first operational Luftwaffe aircraft to have one) and ejection seats (the first anywhere in an operational aircraft) that accommodated the pilot and navigator in tandem but back to back.

The second prototype was evaluated in mock combat against other Luftwaffe types and was so successful that a production order was placed immediately.

The He219 Uhu (eagle-owl), equipped with radar that could find enemy bombers in the dark and a formidable armament with which to destroy them, was clearly a fearsome night-fighter and the Luftwaffe were keen to get it into service. So keen in fact that even the early prototypes were sent to form a trials unit at Venlo in Holland in April 1943. On the night of June 11, Major Werner Streib shot down five RAF Lancaster bombers in one sortie, thus proving the military value of dedicated nightfighter aircraft. During the first six night missions an incredible 20 RAF bombers were claimed as destroyed, among them six Mosquitoes. Despite this success, the He219 was never produced in adequate numbers, mainly because a bewildering profusion of sub-types appeared, with different armament and "black box" installations, to prove the aircraft's worth to sceptical officials. From November 1944 virtually the only aircraft being produced were jets and so the He219 only ever totally equipped one unit, 1/NJG 1, based at Venlo. Individual aircraft were attached to other units but the type was never used strategically. The Uhu was another fine German design that did not reach its potential due to the short-sightedness or sheer incompetence of the decision-makers within the Luftwaffe and government.

TOP: **The He219 was an extremely effective nightfighter that wreaked havoc among RAF bombing raids.** ABOVE: **This He219A-7, an aircraft operated by 3/NJG (Nachtjagdgeschwader – nightfighter wing) 3, was evaluated after the war by the RAF.** LEFT: **One of many sub-types, the prototype A-5/R1.**

Heinkel He219A-7/R2 Uhu

First flight: November 15, 1942
Power: Two Daimler-Benz 1800hp DB603E 12-cylinder engines
Armament: Four 20mm/0.78in cannon – two in underbelly "tray" and two in wing roots. Two 30mm/1.18in cannon, mounted to fire obliquely forward from rear of cockpit
Size: Wingspan – 18.5m/60ft 8.3in
Length – 16.34m/53ft 7.25in
Height – 4.1m/13ft 5.4in
Wing area – 44.5m²/478.99sq ft
Weights: Empty – 8345kg/18,398lb
Maximum take-off – 15,100kg/33,289lb
Performance: Maximum speed – 460kph/286mph
Ceiling – 9800m/32,150ft
Range – 1850km/1150 miles
Climb – 552m/1810ft per minute

LEFT: **The I.A.R. 80 was a lesser-known fighter type that served for some years after World War II.**

I.A.R. 80

First flight: April 1939
Power: I.A.R. 1025hp K14-1000A radial piston engine
Armament: Four 7.92mm/0.31in machine-guns in wings
Size: Wingspan – 10.5m/34ft 5.25in
Length – 8.9m/29ft 2.5in Height – 3.6m/11ft 9.75in
Wing area – 15.97m²/171.9sq ft
Weights: Empty – 1780kg/3924lb
Maximum take-off – 2550kg/5622lb
Performance: Maximum speed – 550kph/342mph
Ceiling – 10,500m/34,450ft
Range – 940km/584 miles
Climb – 4500m/14,760ft in 5 minutes, 40 seconds

I.A.R. 80

The I.A.R. 80 was derived from the Polish-designed P.Z.L. P-24 fighter and was designed to replace the P-24. Development work was exclusively Romanian and began in 1938. The resulting fighter that first flew in April 1939 was tough and offered a drastically improved performance over the P-24. The front and rear of the two aircraft were almost identical. The significant difference was in the wholly new centre section. The bubble-type canopy was very advanced for the time and offered the pilot excellent visibility. Production was carried out on German authority and later models carried the German Mauser cannon. Strangely the type had a skid instead of a tailwheel.

About 250 were built in a number of versions and most served on the Eastern Front from May 1942. From 1943 all were based in Romania defending the country from US bomber attacks.

About half of all produced survived the war and served in the Romanian Air Force, this time under Soviet control, until they were replaced by Soviet fighters from 1949. A number were converted into two-seat dual control trainers and were in service until 1952.

LEFT: **A Ju 88 nightfighter bristling with radar aerials. The Ju 88 was the most versatile combat aircraft in the wartime Luftwaffe inventory.**

Junkers Ju 88G

First flight: December 21, 1936 (Ju 88 prototype)
Power: Two BMW 1700hp 801D-2 14-cylinder radials
Armament: Two 30mm/1.18in and up to six 20mm/0.78in cannon
Size: Wingspan – 20m/65ft 7in
Length – 14.54m/47ft 8in
Height – 4.85m/15ft 11in
Wing area – 54.5m/586.6sq ft
Weights: Empty – 9081kg/20,020lb
Maximum take-off – 14,690kg/32,385lb
Performance: Maximum speed – 573kph/356mph
Ceiling – 8840m/29,000ft
Range – 4 hours endurance
Climb – 504.78m/1655ft per minute

Junkers Ju 88

The Ju 88 is widely described as the "German Mosquito" because, like the de Havilland Mosquito, the Ju 88 was an extremely versatile design. It was first designed as a high-speed bomber but was then developed for dive-bomber, torpedo-bomber, close support, reconnaissance, heavy fighter and nightfighter roles. The Ju 88's speed, almost as good as fighters of the time, led to the C-series of heavy fighters and the first, the Ju 88C-0, made its maiden flight in July 1939. Large numbers of C-series fighters were eventually built, powered by Jumo 211 or BMW 801 engines, with solid noses housing a battery of cannon and machine-guns.

The Ju 88G was the definitive radar-equipped three-seat nightfighter, with typical armament of two 30mm/1.18in plus four to six 20mm/0.78in cannon all firing diagonally forward and upwards to destroy bombers with a short but deadly burst of fire from below.

Ju 88 nightfighters were one of the most effective German defences against enemy bombers.

Kawanishi N1K1-/K2-J

Land-based aircraft have often been turned into floatplanes, but in the case of the Kawanishi N1K1-J Shiden (violet lightning), it was uniquely a landplane derived from a floatplane fighter. Codenamed "George" by the Allies, it entered service during the last year of World War II, appearing throughout the Pacific from May 1944. In spite of production problems and shortages of parts caused by B-29 raids on the Japanese homeland, over 1400 were built and were formidable foes. Manoeuvrability was dramatically enhanced by unique automatic combat flaps that increased lift during extreme combat manoeuvres. The George proved to be one of the best all-round fighters in the Pacific theatre but lacked the high-altitude performance needed to counter the devastating B-29 raids.

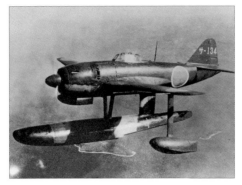

Early versions had poor visibility due to the mid-mounted wing and inadequate landing gear and so the N1K2-J version known as the Shiden-Kai was produced. The main difference was the moving of the wing from mid to low position, which reduced the need for troublesome long landing gear. The prototype of this variant first flew in December 1943, and was soon adopted as the standard Japanese land-based fighter and fighter-bomber. The N1K2-J could be built in half the

LEFT: **The N1K1 Kyofu (mighty wind) floatplane fighter from which the "George" derived.**
BELOW: **The Shiden-Kai was an excellent fighter, but a number were used as kamikaze aircraft.**

Kawanishi N1K2-J

First flight: December 31, 1943
Power: Nakajima 1990hp NK9H Homare 21 radial piston engine
Armament: Four 20mm/0.78in cannon in wings plus two 250kg/551lb bombs under wings
Size: Wing span – 12m/39ft 4.5in
Length – 9.35m/30ft 8in
Height – 3.96m/13ft
Wing area – 23.5m²/252.96sq ft
Weights: Empty – 2657kg/5858lb
Maximum take-off – 4860kg/10,714lb
Performance: Maximum speed – 595kph/370mph
Ceiling – 10,760m/35,300ft
Range – 2335km/1451 miles with drop tanks
Climb – 1000m/3300ft per minute

time of the earlier version and became a truly outstanding fighter aircraft, which could hold its own against the best of Allied fighters.

Kawasaki Ki-45 Toryu

In 1937, the Imperial Japanese Army issued a requirement for its first long-range twin-engine fighter and Kawasaki's proposal was the Ki-45, which first flew in January 1939. Continued problems with engines

year and first saw combat in October 1942. The fast and manoeuvrable Ki-45, codenamed "Nick" by the Allies, achieved a number of victories over USAAF B-24s – the aircraft was then modified for nightfighter duties when the American bombers began to operate at night. It proved so successful as a night-fighter that a specially developed nightfighter version (Kai-C) was produced, fitted with cannon that fired obliquely upward for attacks from below. On the night of June 15, 1944 alone, seven B-29s were claimed by Ki-45s.

delayed production until September 1941, when the aircraft was designated Ki-45 Kai Toryu – kai was short for kaizo (modified) and Toryu means "dragon slayer". The two-seat Toryu finally entered service in August the following

In May 1944 four Ki-45s carried out the first kamikaze (divine wind) suicide attacks against Allied ships. More conventional anti-shipping and ground attack variants were also produced. Around 1700 Ki-45s were built.

TOP: **The Imperial Japanese Army's first long-range twin-engine fighter.** ABOVE: **The type was one of the most successful Japanese nightfighters.** LEFT: **Note the two obliquely firing cannon between the cockpits.**

Kawasaki Ki-45 Kai-C Toryu

First flight: January 1939

Power: Two Mitsubishi 1080hp Ha-102 14-cylinder two-row radial piston engines

Armament: Two 12.7mm/0.5in machine-guns, installed at 30 degrees between cockpits, two 12.7mm/0.5in machine-guns and one 20mm/0.78in or 37mm/1.46in cannon in nose, plus one rear-firing 7.92mm/0.31in machine-gun

Size: Wingspan – 15.05m/49ft 4.5in
Length – 11m/36ft 1in Height – 3.7m/12ft 1.5in
Wing area – 32m²/344.46sq ft

Weights: Empty – 4000kg/8820lb
Maximum take-off – 5500kg/12,125lb

Performance: Maximum speed – 545kph/339mph
Ceiling – 10,000m/32,810ft
Range – 2000km/1243 miles
Climb – 700m/2300ft per minute

Kawasaki Ki-61 Hien

The Kawasaki Ki-61 Hien (swallow) fighter was a major departure in Japanese fighter aircraft design in World War II. While other Japanese fighters were designed with air-cooled radials, the Ki-61 used a licence-built Daimler-Benz 601A liquid-cooled in-line engine and was designed for speed. The Ki-61 was so radically different from other Japanese fighters that when the type was first encountered in combat in June 1943, the Allies thought it was a licence-built German or Italian fighter, the latter theory earning Hien the Allied codename of "Tony".

The very different nature of the design makes sense, given that from 1923 to 1933 Kawasaki Aircraft Engineering Company's head designer was Dr Richard Vogt, a German who returned to his homeland in 1933 for a similar role at Blohm und Voss during World War II. Kawasaki continued to be influenced by Vogt's design work long after he left.

The Hien was in constant use from its entry into service in August 1942 until the end of the war, but found itself increasingly outclassed. The Ki-100 was a "Tony" with a radial engine and proved to be an extremely good fighter.

ABOVE: **At one time the Ki-61 was thought to be a version of the Messerschmitt Bf109.** BELOW: **This captured "Tony" was taken for evaluation to the US Naval Air Station Patuxent River.** BOTTOM: **The Ki-61 was Japan's only in-line engined fighter in service during World War II.**

Kawasaki Ki-61-Ic Hien

First flight: December 1941

Power: Kawasaki 1175hp Ha-40 V12 liquid-cooled piston engine

Armament: Two 12.7mm/0.5in machine-guns on top of engine, plus two wing-mounted 20mm/0.78in cannon

Size: Wingspan – 12m/39ft 4.5in
Length – 8.95m/29ft 4.25in
Height – 3.7m/12ft 1.75in
Wing area – 20m^2/215.29sq ft

Weights: Empty – 2630kg/5798lb
Maximum take-off – 3470kg/7650lb

Performance: Maximum speed – 560kph/348mph
Ceiling – 10,000m/32,810ft
Range – 1900km/1181 miles
Climb – 675m/2200ft per minute

Lavochkin LaGG-3 and La-5

The stopgap Lavochkin LaGG-3, built almost entirely of wood, was probably the greatest under-achiever of the early World War II fighters and was easily outclassed by the Messerschmitt Bf109 and Focke-Wulf 190. Even the few Italian Macchi 202s that served on the Russian Front outclassed the Lavochkins.

In 1941 development began on upgrading the powerplant of the LaGG-3's sound airframe by a shift from in-line V-12 engines to an M-82 14-cylinder, twin-row radial engine. Various changes were made to improve both performance and range, and the ever-present need for the use of strategically non-important materials was observed. The resulting aircraft, the La-5, was the first in a series of excellent radial-engined thoroughbred

fighters. The Lavochkin La-5FN, again constructed almost wholly of wood, became one of the best Soviet fighters of World War II. The Shvestov M-82 engine had a two-stage supercharger and gave the La-5FN a maximum speed of 648km/403mph. The fighter was responsive, could outperform any other Soviet fighter and, more importantly, almost all of its opponents. Armed with two 20mm/0.9in cannon, the La-5FN could deliver a small but deadly punch. After service with the Russians in World War II, the La-5FN went on to serve for a decade or so with various Soviet bloc countries, until being replaced by jets.

Further improved performance for the La-5 was, however, achieved by weight-saving and aerodynamic fine-tuning undertaken in late 1943, resulting in the high-altitude interceptor designated La-7. Over 5500 of these improved Lavochkins were built by 1946 and saw extensive wartime use.

TOP: **The LaGG-3's all-wooden construction was, among fighters, unique for its time.** ABOVE: **An La-5 of the 1st Czech Fighter Regiment, pictured in the Ukraine.** LEFT: **The higher flying La-7 was built in great quantities.**

Lavochkin La-5FN

First flight: January 1942

Power: Shvetsov 1330hp M-82A 14-cylinder two-row radial engine

Armament: Two 23mm/0.9in cannon, plus underwing bombs

Size: Wingspan – 9.8m/32ft 2in
Length – 8.46m/27ft 10.75in
Height – 2.84m/9ft 3in
Wing area – 17.5m^2/188.37sq ft

Weights: Empty – 2800kg/6173lb
Maximum take-off – 3360kg/7407lb

Performance: Maximum speed – 648kph/403mph
Ceiling – 9500m/31,170ft
Range – 765km/475 miles
Climb – 5000m/16,405ft in 4 minutes, 42 seconds

Lockheed P-38 Lightning

The P-38 Lightning's radical twin-boom, twin-engine configuration was Lockheed's answer to an exacting US Army Air Corps specification, in February 1937, for a high-performance long-range interceptor capable of flying at high altitude and high speed for at least an hour.

The P-38 was Lockheed's first purely military type and the prototype, the XP-38, first flew in January 1939. It made headlines almost immediately when it set a new record of 7 hours, 2 minutes for a transcontinental flight across America, even though at 6713kg/14,800lb it weighed more than most American light bombers of the time. From the outset the P-38 was designed as a hard-hitting fighter, being armed with a cannon and four machine-guns in the nose.

In spite of some official misgivings about its high cost and the sheer number of innovations incorporated into the P-38, it entered USAAC service in August 1941. The British had expressed interest in the P-38 but the American ban on the export of superchargers to Europe left the aircraft underpowered in the view of British test pilots. Aircraft were already on the production line earmarked for the RAF but these were diverted for US use when British interest waned. The British apparently named the P-38 "Lightning" and the name was already in widespread use.

Most early models were used for evaluation in the USA but during 1942–3 12 squadrons were equipped with P-38Es in the South West Pacific and the Aleutians. Even before that, an Iceland-based P-38E had claimed the first USAAF destruction of an enemy aircraft in World War II on December 7, 1941. A Focke-Wulf Condor was destroyed only hours after America's declaration of war.

TOP: **The radical twin-boom P-38 was a hard-hitting fighter capable of going deep into enemy territory.** ABOVE: **Regular P-38 combat missions were first flown from Africa.**

By this time the P-38's outstanding performance had unsurprisingly led to a reconnaissance version, known as the F-4, and later the F-5, armed only with cameras.

The P-38 came to be deployed extensively in the Pacific, Mediterranean and Europe where the P-38's speed, performance and firepower soon prompted the nickname "fork-tailed devil" from the Germans.

The J model of the P-38 had improved airscrews for better speed and climb at altitude and carried more fuel than earlier versions. With drop tanks, the P-38J had a range of around 3700km/2300 miles, enabling it to fly deep into the heart of enemy territory, engage in ten minutes of air combat and then make it back to the UK. Top speed of the P-38J was 666kph/414mph but in combat dives, pilots frequently exceeded 885kph/550mph. At that speed the aircraft's handling proved difficult and hydraulically assisted control systems were introduced, becoming one of the first examples of power-assisted controls in a combat aircraft.

Some P-38Js were modified to two-seaters equipped with a Norden bombsight, carried a bombardier and led formations of Lightning fighter-bombers on high-altitude precision bombing missions. As the P-47 and P-51 fighters appeared in huge numbers, the Lightnings in Europe were used more and more in the ground-attack and tactical bombing role.

However in the Pacific theatre, the Lightning equipped 27 USAAF squadrons and was credited with the destruction of more enemy aircraft than any other type. As a long-range fighter it was peerless. The top US ace of World War II, Major Richard Bong, earned all his 40 kills flying Lightnings in the Pacific. The most celebrated P-38 mission was probably the interception and destruction of the aircraft carrying Japan's Admiral Yamamoto. The P-38s responsible for this daring mission were from 339th Fighter Squadron on Guadalcanal, operating some 805km/500 miles from their base, using drop tanks to get the extra range. The 347th Fighter Group pilot credited with this remarkable feat was Lt Thomas G. Lanphier, who went on to become a Lockheed test pilot.

ABOVE: **In the Pacific Theatre the P-38 equipped 27 USAAF squadrons. The P-38 destroyed more enemy aircraft than any other Allied fighter.**

RIGHT: **The five-gun nose armament is clear on this aircraft painted as the aircraft of P-38 ace Jack Ilfrey.** BELOW: **The P-38's long range made it ideal for the war in the Pacific, where combats were fought over great distances.**

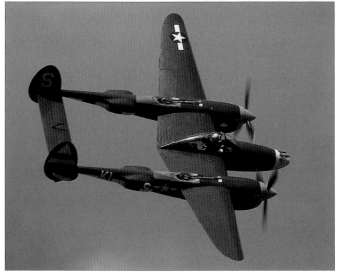

Lockheed P-38J Lightning

First flight: January 27, 1939
Power: Two Allison 1425hp V-1710-89 in-line piston engines
Armament: One 20mm/0.78in cannon, plus four 12.7mm/0.5in machine-guns in nose, up to 908kg/2000lb of bombs and ten 12.7cm/5in rocket projectiles
Size: Wingspan – 15.85m/52ft
Length – 11.52m/37ft 10in
Height – 2.99m/9ft 10in
Wing area – 30.42m²/327.5sq ft
Weights: Empty – 5707kg/12,580lb
Maximum take-off – 9798kg/21,600lb
Performance: Maximum speed – 666kph/414mph
Ceiling – 13,411m/44,000ft
Range – 3636km/2260 miles
Climb – 1524m/5000ft in 2 minutes

Macchi M.C.200 Saetta

The Saetta (lightning) was one of the principal fighters with which Italy joined World War II. It was developed in the mid-1930s in response to an Italian Air Force (Regia Aeronautica) requirement for a new single-seat fighter. The new fighter was part of a programme intended to re-equip the Regia Aeronautica following the end of Italy's military activity in East Africa. The prototype made its first flight in December 1937, and by the time of Italy's entry into World War II in June 1940 some 156 were in service. The M.C.200 was first employed against the British at Malta and eventually saw service in Greece, North Africa, Yugoslavia and the Soviet Union. Saettas were deployed against US forces in North Africa and in defence of Italy itself. A total of 1151 were built in all.

Macchi M.C.200

First flight: December 24, 1937
Power: FIAT 870hp A.74 RC38 double row, 14-cylinder, air cooled radial engine
Armament: Two 12.7mm/0.5in synchronized machine-guns
Size: Wingspan – 10.58m/34ft 8.5in
Length – 8.19m/26ft 10.25in
Height – 3.5m/11ft 5.75in
Wing area – 16.8m^2/180.84sq ft
Weights: Empty – 1895kg/4178lb
Maximum take-off – 2590kg/5710lb
Performance: Maximum speed – 502kph/312mph
Ceiling – 8900m/29,200ft
Range – 870km/540 miles with extra tanks
Climb – 3000m/9840ft in 3 minutes, 24 seconds

LEFT: **Early versions of the Saetta had a modern enclosed cockpit which was, by Italian pilot demand, deleted on later versions.** BELOW: **After the Italian Armistice of September 1943, a number of M.C.200s were flown to Allied airfields and were later flown with the Allies by the Italian Co-Belligerent Air Force.**

LEFT: The C.202 was an excellent fighter.

Macchi C.202 Folgore

First flight: August 10, 1940
Power: Alfa Romeo 1175hp RA.1000 RC 41-I
(licence-built DB-601A) inverted V-12 piston engine
Armament: Two 12.7mm/0.5in machine-guns in
engine cowling
Size: Wingspan – 10.58m/34ft 8.5in
Length – 8.85m/29ft 0.5in
Height – 3.04m/9ft 11.5in
Wing area – 16.8m^2/180.84sq ft
Weights: Empty – 2350kg/5181lb
Maximum take-off – 3010kg/6636lb
Performance: Maximum speed – 595kph/370mph
Ceiling – 11,500m/37,730ft
Range – 765km/475 miles
Climb – 3000m/9840ft in 2 minutes, 28 seconds

Macchi C.202 Folgore

This fighter, often neglected by historians, is said by many to have been the best Italian Air Force fighter of World War II. The Folgore (thunderbolt) was derived from the Macchi M.C.200 and married its airframe to the proven Daimler-Benz DB 601 liquid-cooled engine. No indigenous in-line engine of sufficient power was available when the war started and in early 1940 Macchi

imported the German engine. Flight testing began in August 1940 and results were impressive – the Folgore was almost 97kph/60mph faster than the M.C.200.

By November 1941 the C.202 was deployed in Libya against RAF aircraft and was clearly superior to both the Curtiss P-40 and the Hawker Hurricane. In fact the Italian fighter outperformed

all comers except the Spitfire and P-51 Mustang. When supplies of DB 601 engines ran out, Alfa Romeo built a copy under licence and by late 1942 Folgores outnumbered all other fighters in the Italian Air Force – the Regia Aeronautica. Folgore production reached about 1200 but only two survive.

The Germans also operated the C.202 in limited numbers.

LEFT: After World War I, the many surplus
Buzzards were sold around the world.
Civilianized and floatplane versions were
among the variants produced.

Martinsyde F.4 Buzzard

First flight: May 1918
Power: Hispano-Suiza 300hp V-8 piston engine
Armament: Two forward-firing synchronized
7.7mm/0.303in machine-guns
Size: Wingspan – 9.99m/32ft 9.5in
Length – 7.77m/25ft 5.75in
Height – 3.15m/10ft 4in
Wing area – 29.73m^2/320sq ft
Weights: Empty – 776kg/1710lb
Maximum take-off – 1038kg/2289lb
Performance: Maximum speed – 233kph/145mph
Ceiling – 7620m/25,000ft
Range – 2 hours, 30 minutes endurance
Climb – 3050m/10,000ft in 7 minutes, 54 seconds

Martinsyde F.4 Buzzard

The Martinsyde F.4 single-seat biplane fighter was the ultimate model of the Martinsyde F series fighters and first flew in May 1918. The F.4 was really a production version of the fine F.3 that was thoroughly tested and even deployed on home defence duties by the Royal Flying Corps.

In tests carried out by the Royal Air Force the aircraft's performance and

handling were so good that large-scale production was ordered immediately. A total of 1450 aircraft were ordered but due to delays in engine deliveries only a handful of aircraft were handed over to the Royal Air Force before the end of World War I at which point the order was cancelled. Martinsyde had however completed around 370 F.4s but as the F.4 was among the best fighters of the

World War I period there was no shortage of customers for the excellent fighting aircraft. F.4s were widely exported to countries including Spain, Ireland, Japan, Latvia, the Soviet Union (100 aircraft), Portugal and Finland where they were used as trainers as late as 1939.

Messerschmitt Bf109

TOP AND ABOVE: **Two photographs of the very rare Messerschmitt Bf109G owned by the Royal Air Force Museum and returned to flying condition in the 1990s. Unfortunately the aircraft was damaged in a crash landing and will not fly again.**

The Messerschmitt Bf109, the most famous German fighter of the World War II era, remained in production over a decade after the regime that spawned it was crushed. It first flew in September 1935, powered by a Rolls-Royce Kestrel engine and incorporating features of the Messerschmitt Bf108 four-seat touring aircraft. Messerschmitt 109Bs were first delivered to the Luftwaffe in 1937, to its "top guns" in Jagdgeschwader 132 "Richthofen". Later that year the 109 earned its spurs when it made its combat début with Germany's Condor Legion in the Spanish Civil War. This was invaluable, not only as combat experience for Germany's fighter pilots but also to help with developing and improving what was clearly already an exceptional fighter aircraft.

In November 1937 the 109 flew into the record books by setting a new world landplane speed record of 610.55kph/ 379.38mph. B, C and D versions all saw service but the type really came into its own with the definitive E model that appeared in late 1938 and was widely deployed at the outbreak of World War II, when the Luftwaffe had around 1000 of these fast and manoeuvrable fighters in service.

The 109E was in action throughout the Blitzkrieg and in this first year of the war outclassed all the fighters it encountered, except the Spitfire. Like the famous Supermarine aircraft, the Messerschmitt 109 will be forever associated with the air fighting that took place in the Battle of Britain in 1940. In fact the 109's first action against the RAF had been on December 18, 1939, when 109Es attacked unescorted Vickers Wellington bombers on a daylight bombing mission over Wilhelmshaven.

Numerous versions of the 109E were in use during the Battle of Britain, including the E-4/B fighter-bomber. The 109 had two main advantages over the British Spitfires and Hurricanes. One was that the cannon armament carried by the Messerschmitt had a longer range and was more damaging

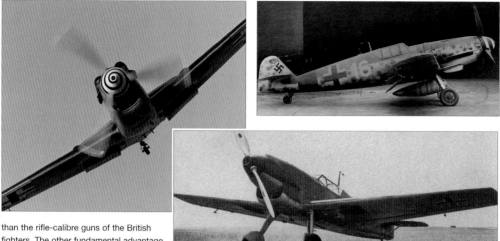

than the rifle-calibre guns of the British fighters. The other fundamental advantage enjoyed by the 109 was the fuel-injection system of its Daimler-Benz engine, which continued to supply fuel no matter how violent the aircraft's manoeuvres. The Merlin engines of the RAF fighters, at the time equipped with carburettors, could, in contrast, be momentarily starved of fuel and cut out if the aircraft was pushed into a steep dive, thus generating negative gravity. RAF pilots soon developed the technique of rolling their aircraft over at the critical time and diving upside down so as not to lose the upper hand in what was often a kill or be killed air combat situation.

TOP LEFT: **Incredibly, Spanish-built 109s (Buchons), powered by Rolls-Royce Merlins, were still being built in the mid-1950s.** TOP RIGHT: **The Bf109 was the principal fighter of the wartime Luftwaffe and destroyed more aircraft in combat than any other German fighter.** ABOVE: **Ten prototype Bf109s were built to prove the design in 1935–6 and the type entered Luftwaffe service in 1937.** BELOW: **One of the most widely produced fighter aircraft in history, the Bf109.**

By early 1941 the "Emil", as the E model was widely known, had appeared in the Mediterranean theatre and tropicalized versions were serving in North Africa. After the success of the E model the 109F was developed and is considered by many to be the best version of all because of its high speed and excellent all-round performance. While in the West the 109F was able to outclass the Spitfire V, on the Eastern Front it spearheaded the attack on the USSR. At this stage in the 109 story it is worth making the point that throughout its life the 109 was fitted with a bewildering array of armament options, the F-model more than most.

After 1942 the G ("Gustav") became the standard model in Luftwaffe use and was numerically the most important version. Although well-armed, the Gustav needed great attention from the pilot and was particularly difficult to land satisfactorily. It served on all fronts in roles that included fighter-bomber, ground-attack and interceptor.

Post-war, the 109 remained in production, thanks to the Czech firm Avia who had an intact Bf109 factory. In 1948, Israel bought some 109s and used them in combat, while the Spanish Air Force also operated Spanish-built versions. In 1953, Spanish manufacturers began fitting Merlin engines to produce the Buchón (pigeon) and the last new-build 109 was test-flown in 1956. Total production exceeded 35,000.

Messerschmitt Bf109E-7

First flight: September 1935
Power: One Daimler-Benz 1200hp DB 601N liquid-cooled inverted-V 12-cylinder piston engine
Armament: One hub-firing 20mm/0.7in cannon and four 7.9mm/0.31in machine-guns, two in engine cowling and two in wings
Size: Wingspan 9.86m/32ft 4.5in
Length – 8.74m/28ft 8in Height – 3.4m/11ft 2in
Wing area – 16.16m²/174sq ft
Weights: Empty – 2014kg/4440lb
Maximum take-off – 2767kg/6100lb
Performance: Maximum speed – 578kph/358mph
Ceiling – 11,125m/36,500ft
Range – 1094km/680 miles
Climb – 1006m/3300ft per minute

Messerschmitt Bf110

The Bf110 was designed to a Luftwaffe specification for a heavy fighter that could also be used as a high-speed bomber and the prototype flew in 1936. It was intended to escort bombers deep into enemy territory and what it may have lacked in manoeuvrability,

it made up for with firepower. The 110 first saw action during the invasion of Poland and made its mark as a bomber-destroyer in December 1939, when it was used against a force of 22 RAF Wellington bombers and shot down nine. With its capability proven, production was stepped up and over 100 were produced each month during 1940. It was, however, during 1940 that the

Bf110 began to suffer heavy losses to more modern fighters such as the Spitfire and Hurricane. Although largely withdrawn as a day fighter, some persisted in this role against better aircraft until 1944, sustaining increasingly heavy losses. After a period of use on bombing and reconnaissance, the type found its niche during the winter of 1940–1 as a nightfighter defending Hitler's Reich.

At first the three-man crews had no special equipment for night operations and relied on their eyes alone to find enemy aircraft in the dark. Ground-controlled interception began from mid-1941, and the 110 began to take its toll of RAF bombers and was soon an aircraft to be feared. Airborne radar was used experimentally during 1941, effective up to a maximum distance of 3.5km/2.2 miles and capable of bringing the 110 to within 200m/655ft of a target. Front-line units received the radar from July 1942. By this time the standard version of the nightfighter was the Bf110F-4, with the usual armament of four 7.92mm/0.31in machine-guns and two 20mm/0.78in cannon. The usual means of attack was from below, the target bomber being raked across the belly and wing fuel

tanks with high explosive and incendiary ammunition as the Bf110 pilot pulled the aircraft up. In 1943 the armament was supplemented by upward-firing cannon, which meant the Bf110 only had to formate below the target aircraft to achieve a first-rate firing position.

These nightfighters continued to defend Germany right through to the end of the war and one pilot, Major Heinz-Wolfgang Schnaufer, claimed no less than 121 night kills while flying the Bf110.

LEFT: **This Bf110 nightfighter is preserved by the RAF Museum in Britain.** BELOW: **The Bf110 was a key aircraft in the Blitzkrieg.**

Messerschmitt Me410

On the basis of the Bf110's early successes, its manufacturers were asked to design a successor – this became the Me210. The aircraft was certainly a handful on its test flight and was essentially unstable, being prone to stalling and spinning. In spite of this it was ordered into production and 200 were built before it was abandoned in favour of a new production run of Bf110s.

The Me210 design was salvaged with a redesigned, longer, rear fuselage and automatic leading edge slats to counter the stall tendency. Fitted with more powerful engines than the original Me210, the new two-seat heavy fighter aircraft was designated Me410 and called Hornisse (Hornet).

The first Me410As reached front-line Luftwaffe units in January 1943, replacing Dornier Do 217s and Junkers Ju 88s. They were at first used as nightfighter-bombers over Britain and then as bomber-destroyers in the Mediterranean theatre. From Spring 1944 the Hornisse began to replace the Bf110 in bomber-destroyer (Zerstörer) units in defence of the Reich and also served as a nightfighter on the Eastern Front.

The Me410A-1/U4 bomber-destroyer carried a 50mm/2in gun beneath the fuselage that weighed 900kg/1984lb and had a recoil effect of seven tons. Carrying 21 rounds, the effect of the weapon on enemy bombers would have been devastating while the effect on Me410 crews was at best startling and at worst terrifying.

The Me410 was no more effective than the Bf110 it was designed to replace but over 1100 were built before production ceased in September 1944.

TOP: **This excellent preserved example of an Me410 is part of the Royal Air Force Museum collection in Britain.** ABOVE: **The Hornisse was almost identical to the earlier Me210.** LEFT: **This Me410A-3 was captured in Italy and evaluated by the RAF while bearing the serial TF209.**

Messerschmitt Me410A-1/U2 Hornisse

First flight: Late 1942

Power: Two Daimler-Benz 1850hp 603A inverted V-12 in-line piston engines

Armament: Four 20mm/0.78in cannon and two 7.93mm/0.31in machine-guns, plus two 13mm/0.51in remotely controlled rear-firing barbettes

Size: Wingspan – 16.35m/53ft7.75in
Length – 12.48m/40ft 11.5in
Height – 4.28m/14ft 0.5in
Wing area – 36.2m^2/389.67sq ft

Weights: Empty – 7518kg/16,5/4lb
Maximum take-off – 9650kg/21,276lb

Performance: Maximum speed – 625kph/388mph
Ceiling – 10,000m/32,180ft
Range – 1690km/1050 miles
Climb – 6700m/22,000ft in 10 minutes, 42 seconds

Messerschmitt Me163

When the German Komet first attacked USAAF bomber formations in July 1944 it struck fear into the Allies. This extremely high-performance rocket-powered fighter flew almost twice as fast as any Allied fighters and was a truly radical design. The very small and agile Komet was developed from designs originated by the brilliant Dr Alexander Lippisch, who joined the Messerschmitt company in 1939, having pioneered tailless gliders in the 1920s. The first step toward the revolutionary Me163 was an adaptation of the tailless all-wood DFS 194 research glider, powered by a Walter rocket motor. Fuel for the motor consisted of two hypergolic (spontaneously igniting) liquids, T-Stoff and Z-Stoff, which when mixed reacted violently, the resulting controlled explosion producing around 400kg/882lb of thrust. The rocket-powered glider was test flown at the secret Peenemünde research establishment in June 1940 and the pilot Heini Dittmar reported that the aircraft handled superbly. In later test flights the trailblazing prototype reached 547kph/340mph in level flight and amazed all with its steep climb capability.

The success of the test flights led to six Me163A prototypes, the first of which flew with rocket power in mid-1941. By now the Walter rocket motor had been developed to deliver 750kg/1653lb of thrust, pushing the Komet through the air at 885kph/550mph. One 163A, towed to 4000m/13,125ft before

ABOVE: **The revolutionary Komet was certainly the most futuristic form in the sky during World War II.**

the engine was fired, reached speeds of around 1003kph/623mph (greater than the world speed record of the time) before stability was affected. Minor design changes to the wing eradicated that problem, but others were experienced that plagued the Komet throughout its short service life. Its glider origins resulted in the Komet taking off from a wheeled "dolly", which was jettisoned once the aircraft was off the ground, while for landing the Komet landed on a sprung skid. The take-off and landing phases both held their own hazards for the Komet pilot due to the extremely dangerous nature of the fuels, but the percentage of landing accidents for the Komet, though high, was less than that of the Bf109.

The main production version was the Me163B, equipped with a more powerful rocket motor and armed with two 30mm/1.18in cannon in the roots of the swept wooden wings. The Komet first flew in anger on July 28, 1944, when six aircraft of 1/Jagdgeschwader 400 attacked a formation of USAAF Flying Fortresses heading for the Leuna-Merseburg oil refineries. The attack was ineffective as the pilots were not able to bring their guns to bear, mainly due to the very high closing speeds on the targets. At best the Komet pilot could

LEFT: **The Me163 was one of the first combat aircraft with swept wings.** BELOW: **The aircraft took off from a wheeled "dolly" and landed on the skid beneath the aircraft.**

fire his cannon for three seconds before his pass was over and, in addition, the guns only had 60 rounds each.

The preferred method of attack was to take-off when the enemy was known to be nearby, fly above it at very high speed then make a high speed gliding dive on the targets. The maximum period of powered flight was only 7.5 minutes and after the combat the Komet would then make an unpowered glide back to base for a risky landing. The bat-like glider was an absurdly easy target on approach to landing as it could do nothing but land, even if under attack.

The Me163 was used to test an ingenious air-to-air weapon, the SG 500 Jagdfaust (Fighter fist) which consisted of five vertically firing tubes in each wing root. Each tube carried a single 50mm/ 1.97in shell and all ten would be fired as a salvo when triggered by the shadow of a bomber passing over the Komet, activating a photo-electric cell. All the Komet had to do was fly, top speed, under an enemy aircraft, and the system was proven on April 10, 1945, when a B-17 was destroyed in mid-air by a Jagdfaust-equipped Komet.

In late 1943, Japan negotiated manufacturing rights for the Me163 (as the Mitsubishi J8M1 for the Navy and the Mitsubishi Ki-200 for the Army) but one of the two submarines bringing the technical information to Japan was sunk. With incomplete drawings the Japanese still managed to produce prototypes, one of which flew before the end of the war.

Although around 300 entered service, the Komet never reached its potential and destroyed only nine Allied bombers. It was however by far the most futuristic aircraft in service during World War II.

Messerschmitt Me163B-1a Komet

First flight: June 23, 1943 (powered)
Power: Walter 1700kg/3748lb-thrust HWK 509A-1 rocket motor
Armament: Two 30mm/1.18in cannon
Size: Wingspan – 9.4m/30ft 7.3in
Length – 5.85m/19ft 2.3in
Height – 2.76m/9ft 0.6in
Wing area – 18.5m²/199.1sq ft
Weights: Empty – 1900kg/4190lb
Maximum take-off – 4310kg/9502lb
Performance: Maximum speed – 960kph/596mph
Ceiling – 16,500m/54,000ft
Range – 100km/62 miles or 2 minutes,
30 seconds from top of powered climb
Climb – 5000m/16,400ft per minute

Messerschmitt Me262

The Me262 was the world's first operational jet aircraft and many Germans believed it was a war-winning aircraft. Design work began on the revolutionary aircraft in late 1938 and power was to be provided by ground-breaking gas turbines under development by BMW. The aircraft was ready before its engines and was test-flown with a single Jumo piston engine in the nose on April 18, 1941. The first test flight with the jet engines installed took place in March 1942. As a safety measure, the piston engine was retained in the nose

and the prototype took off under power of all three engines. The two jets seized shortly after take-off and the pilot was lucky to land the aircraft safely. The engines had to be redesigned and the test programme continued with the Me262 powered by two heavier Junkers turbojets. The development of this

remarkable aircraft was not considered a top priority by the German High Command and the Messerschmitt company were more concerned with improvements of existing proven combat aircraft such as the Bf109 and Bf110. One of the greatest boosts to the Me262 programme came in May 1943 when legendary Luftwaffe ace General der Jagdflieger (fighter general) Adolf Galland flew the aircraft for the first time.

ABOVE: **The trailblazing Me262 was the first operational jet aircraft and the Third Reich had high hopes for the futuristic fighter.** LEFT: **On July 25, 1944 the Me262 became the first jet to see combat.**

He advocated the mass production of the aircraft as soon as possible but then the whole programme was delayed again by devastating August 1943 Allied bombing raids on the Regensburg factories housing the Me262 production lines. Messerschmitt then moved its jet development operation to Bavaria where a shortage of skilled labour delayed production again by several months. Hitler's oft-quoted ruling that the high-performance aircraft should also be used as a bomber was not the only reason that the 262 entered service late in the war – apart from enemy action, the unreliability and poor performance of the early jet engines were major factors.

And so it was not until July 1944 that the Me262, by now named Schwalbe (swallow), entered front-line service and on July 25 an Me262 became the first jet aircraft used in combat when it attacked a British photo-reconnaissance Mosquito flying over Munich. By late 1944 the Me262 was deployed in three forms – fighter-bomber, pure interceptor and an unarmed reconnaissance version. The first dedicated Me262 interceptor unit went into action for the first time on October 3, 1944. Although it arrived too late to make a real difference to the air war, the 262 was a deadly bomber-killer, equipped with 24 rockets and four 30mm/1.18in cannon. In combat with high-performance P-51 Mustangs, the Me262 sometimes came

LEFT: **Two-seat radar-equipped nightfighter versions were also developed.** BELOW: **Reliability problems plagued the pioneering jet fighter.**

off worse because of the inferior manoeuvrability compared to the piston-engined aircraft. It was however faster and better armed than the British Meteor jet fighter but the two trailblazing jets never met in air combat.

As a fighter, the German jet scored heavily against Allied bomber formations, but although more than 1400 Me262s were produced by VE Day, less than 300 saw combat as hundreds were destroyed on the ground by Allied bombing. Most stayed firmly on the ground awaiting conversion to bombers or were unable to fly because of lack of fuel, spare parts or trained pilots. The German jet engines were unreliable and engine failures took their toll of the pioneer jet pilots. The under-carriage was prone to collapse and the guns regularly jammed making the pilots vulnerable in a dogfight.

The one period of concerted Me262 fighter activity came between March 18–21, 1945 when some 40 fighter sorties were flown daily against American bombers. It was however too little too late.

Although Germany never realized the potential of the 262, this revolutionary aircraft inspired British, American and Soviet designers and directly affected worldwide jet fighter design for years to come.

FAR LEFT: **The radical design of the Me262 is evident in this study.** LEFT: **A captured Me262A-1 shipped to Wright Field in the USA for evaluation.**

Messerschmitt Me262A-1a

First flight: July 18, 1942, solely on jet power
Power: Two Junkers 900kg/1984lb thrust Jumo 004B-1 turbojets
Armament: Four 30mm/1.18in cannon in nose plus up to 12 air to-air rockets under each wing
Size: Wingspan – 12.48m/40ft 11.5in
Length – 10.6m/34ft 9.5in
Height – 3.84m/12ft 7in
Wing area – 21.7m²/233.58sq ft
Weights: Empty – 3800kg/8378lb
Maximum take-off – 6400kg/14,110lb
Performance: Maximum speed – 870kph/540mph
Ceiling – 11450m/37,565ft
Range – 1050km/653 miles
Climb – 1200m/3937ft per minute

Mikoyan-Gurevich MiG-3

The MiG-3 interceptor was the third aircraft designed by Artem Mikoyan and Mikhail Gurevich and was developed from their MiG-1, which first flew in April 1940. The MiG-3 incorporated many improvements over the MiG-1, including a new propeller, a modified wing, greater

range, better armour and increased armament. The new MiG was first delivered to front-line units in April 1941 at the same time as the MiG-1, which remained in production despite its shortcomings. The Russians knew the MiG-1

was inadequate in many ways but any aircraft were better than none when facing the military might of the Third Reich.

Even the improved MiG-3 was no low-level fighter and was better suited to altitudes over 5000m/16,405ft. Although tricky to fly, the MiG-3's speed enabled it to give the Luftwaffe a real fight for air superiority over the Eastern Front.

Total production of the MiG-1 and -3 amounted to 3422 when MiG-3 production ceased in 1942. By 1942 the latest Luftwaffe fighters were generally getting the better of the long-nosed MiGs, so the type was progressively removed from front-line fighter units during the winter of 1942–3 and went on to be used mainly for armed reconnaissance and close support missions.

Mikoyan-Gurevich MiG-3

First flight: Late 1941
Power: Mikulin 1350hp AM-35A V-12 piston engine
Armament: One 12.7mm/0.5in and two 7.62mm/0.3in machine-guns in nose, plus up to 200kg/441lb of bombs and rockets under wings
Size: Wingspan – 10.2m/33ft 5in
Length – 8.3m/27ft 1in
Height – 3.5m/11ft 6in
Wing area – 17.44m²/187.73sq ft
Weights: Empty – 2595kg/5721lb
Maximum take-off – 3350kg/7385lb
Performance: Maximum speed – 640kph/398mph
Ceiling – 12,000m/39,370ft
Range – 1195km/743 miles
Climb – 1200m/3937ft per minute

LEFT: **The Soviet MiG-3 was a handful for its pilots, but did much to protect the USSR.**
BELOW: **A replica MiG-3 proudly displayed at a museum in Moscow, the city that the type was designed to protect above all else.**

Mitsubishi A5M

The 350kph/217mph top speed specified in a 1934 Imperial Japanese Navy fighter specification seemed to be a tall order at the time. To ease the designers' burden, the need to operate the new fighter from aircraft carriers was not even written into the specification. However, Mitsubishi's offering was the Ka-14, which, having flown in February 1935, showed a top speed of 450kph/280mph. It was designed with minimum drag in mind – the fuselage had a small cross-section, the aluminium skin was flush-riveted and the fixed undercarriage had streamlining spats. It was perhaps too complex a design and the inverted gull-wing that caused some handling headaches was replaced with a more conventional low wing. With this change and powered by a 585hp Kotobuki 2-KAI-1 engine, the type was ordered into production as the Navy Type 96 Carrier Fighter Model 1 (Mitsubishi A5M1) and began to enter service in early 1937. The subsequent A5M2a (basically the same aircraft powered by a 610hp KAI-3 engine) and A5M2b (with the 640hp Kotobuki 3 engine) became the most important Navy fighters during Japan's war with

China. Until the A5M2a arrival in theatre, the Japanese were suffering heavy losses but after only a short time the A5M2a achieved total air superiority. Experience of air operations in China speeded up development of the A5M2b, which boasted the luxury of an enclosed cockpit and a three-bladed propeller driven by the more powerful engine. The greenhouse-style canopy was actually unpopular with pilots and was omitted on late-build A5M2bs. The A5M2s were so effective in China that all Chinese air units were withdrawn out of range of the Japanese fighters.

The final, best-known and most numerous production version was the A5M4, which was developed in response to the Chinese withdrawal – greater range was the most important consideration. The A5M4 looked identical to the late-production open-cockpit A5M2bs but was powered by the 710hp Nakajima Kotobuki 41 engine and carried a 160 litre/35.2 gallon drop tank. It entered service in China in 1938 and with its longer range greatly extended the area of Japanese air superiority while driving the less able Chinese air units even further away from the battle area.

ABOVE: **A5M4 of the 14th Kokutai, pictured in 1940.**

Codenamed "Claude" by the Allies, the A5M4 was in front-line use at the start of the Pacific War but it was soon withdrawn for second-line duties (including advanced fighter training) as it was no match for the newer Allied fighters. As the war in the Pacific approached its desperate end, remaining A5M4s were used in kamikaze (divine wind) attacks against Allied ships off the Japanese coast.

Mitsubishi A5M4

First flight: February 4, 1935 (Ka-14)

Power: Nakajima 710hp Kotobuki 41 (Bristol Jupiter) nine-cylinder radial piston engine

Armament: Two 7.7mm/0.303in machine-guns firing on each side of upper cylinder of engine, plus two racks for two 30kg/66lb bombs under outer wings

Size: Wingspan – 11m/36ft 1in
Length – 7.55m/24ft 9.25in
Height – 3.2m/10ft 6in
Wing area – 17.8m²/191.6sq ft

Weights: Empty – 1216kg/2681lb
Maximum take-off – 1707kg/3763lb

Performance: Maximum speed – 440kph/273mph
Ceiling – 10,000m/32,800ft
Range – 1200km/746 miles
Climb – 850m/2790ft per minute

Mitsubishi A6M Zero-Sen

Japan's most famous wartime aircraft and the first shipboard fighter capable of beating its land-based opponents had its origins in a 1937 Japanese Navy requirement for a new fighter with a maximum speed exceeding 499kph/310mph to replace the Mitsubishi A5M carrier fighter. The new aircraft had to climb to 3000m/9840ft in 3.5 minutes, and have manoeuvrability and range exceeding any existing fighter together with the impressive armament of two cannon and two machine-guns. Only Mitsubishi accepted the challenge and design work began under the direction of Jiro Horikoshi. The prototype was completed on March 16, 1939, first flew on April 1 and was accepted by the Navy on September 14, 1939 as the A6M1 Carrier Fighter. The chosen powerplant was the lightweight Mitsubishi Zuisei, later replaced by the more powerful Nakajima Sakae (Prosperity) 925hp radial which was only slightly larger and heavier than the original Zuisei. With its new-found power, the fighter amply exceeded the original performance requirements regarded as impossible only a few months earlier. At this time, production models of Navy aircraft were assigned type numbers based on the last number of the current Japanese year in which production began, and as 1940 was the year 2600 in the Japanese calendar, the A6M series was known as the Zero-Sen (Type 00 fighter).

ABOVE: **The A6M Zero-Sen – Japan's finest wartime fighter aircraft.** BELOW: **More Zero-Sens were produced than any other Japanese wartime aircraft.**

Even before the final acceptance of the A6M2 as a production fighter, the Japanese Navy requested that a number of machines be delivered for operational use in China to meet growing aerial resistance. So 15 A6M2s were delivered for service in China and first appeared over Chungking in August 1940 when the new Zeros shot down all the defending Chinese fighters. Washington were informed about the new high-performance Japanese fighter but no heed was taken and so its appearance over Pearl Harbor came as a complete surprise to the American forces. Its subsequent appearance in every major battle area in the opening days of the war seemed to indicate that Japan possessed almost unlimited supplies of the high-performance fighter. In fact in December 1941 the Japanese Navy had well over 400 Zero fighters. In 1941–2 the Zero certainly got the better of all opposing fighters whether it flew from carriers or had to operate over long distances from land bases. During a Japanese carrier-raid on Ceylon (now Sri Lanka), Zeros easily out-turned opposing RAF Hawker Hurricanes, aircraft which until then had been regarded as outstandingly manoeuvrable.

In mid-1942 the Allies eventually acquired an intact specimen and found that the Zero possessed many shortcomings. It was shipped to the USA where exhaustive tests revealed the fighter's faults and shattered the myth that surrounded it. The tables were turned when the Mitsubishi fighter finally came up against a new generation of US Navy and Army fighters, with powerful engines and heavy protection for their pilot and fuel tanks. Against them the Zero, still basically the design which had flown first in April 1939 offered minimal protection for pilot and fuel tanks and from 1943 the Zeros fell like flies. The installation of the 1560hp Kinsei engine brought the A6M8, the ultimate Zero, closer to the performance of Allied fighters but it was too late. The value of the fighter declined steadily and its lowest point was reached when it was selected as the first aircraft used intentionally as suicide attack (kamikaze or divine-wind) planes. The outstanding success of this form of attack led to the formation of dedicated Kamikaze units, and the bomb-carrying Zeros became the prime suicide attack bombers of the Navy.

More Zero-Sens were produced than any other wartime Japanese aircraft. Mitsubishi alone produced 3879 aircraft of this type, Nakajima built 6,215 which, together with the 844 trainer and floatplane variants produced by Sasebo, Hitachi and Nakajima, brought the grand total of A6M series aircraft to 10,938.

TOP LEFT: **The Zero was of great interest to Japan's enemies. A rare picture of an A6M2 in Chinese Nationalist markings – note the US serviceman by the tail.** TOP RIGHT: **This A6M3 in USAAF markings was assembled from five Zeros captured by the USA in December 1942.** ABOVE LEFT: **These captured Zeros pictured in 1946 were evaluated by the RAF in the Far East while flown by Japanese pilots.** ABOVE RIGHT: **An evaluation A6M3 in USAAF markings pictured over the USA on July 1, 1944.**

Mitsubishi A6M5 Zero-Sen ●

First flight: August 1943
Power: Nakajima 1130hp NK1C Sakae 21 14-cylinder two-row radial piston engine
Armament: Two 20mm/0.78in cannon in wing, two 7.7mm/0.303in machine-guns in fuselage, plus two 60kg/132lb bombs on underwing racks
Size: Wingspan – 11m/36ft 1in
Length – 9.06m/29ft 9in Height – 2.98m/9ft 8in
Wing area – 21.3m^2/229.28sq ft
Weights: Empty – 1876kg/4136lb
Maximum take-off – 2733kg/6025lb
Performance: Maximum speed – 570kph/354mph
Ceiling – 11,500m/37,500ft
Range – 1920km/1200 miles with drop tanks
Climb – 6000m/19,685ft in 7.05 minutes

LEFT: **This J2M had clearly seen better days.**

Mitsubishi J2M3 Raiden

First flight: March 20, 1942 (J2M1)
Power: Mitsubishi 1820hp MK4R-A Kasei 23a
14-cylinder two-row radial piston engine
Armament: Four 20mm/0.78in cannon,
plus two 60kg/132lb bombs
Size: Wingspan – 10.82m/35ft 5.25in
Length – 9.95m/32ft 7.75in Height – 3.95m/
12ft 11.5in Wing area – 20.05m^2/215.82sq ft
Weights: Empty – 2460kg/5423lb
Maximum take-off – 3945kg/8695lb
Performance: Maximum speed – 595kph/370mph
Ceiling – 11,700m/38,385ft
Range – 1055km/655 miles
Climb – 1170m/3838ft per minute

Mitsubishi J2M Raiden

The J2M, designed by the same team as the Zero, was the Japanese Navy's first interceptor, being designed to operate from shore bases to destroy enemy bombers. Breaking with the Japanese tradition of manoeuvrability above all else, the Raiden (thunderbolt) was built for speed and climb. Among the design points of interest were a streamlined nose, retractable tailwheel and a laminar flow wing with "combat" flaps for improved agility. The small aerodynamic nose was achieved by connecting the propeller to the engine (which was set further back in the fuselage) by an extension shaft. Early J2M1 versions flew in March 1942 but proved troublesome and did not meet the Navy's requirements, consequently an improved Kasei 23a-engined J2M2 was ordered for production in October 1942. Continued technical difficulties meant the aircraft did not enter service until December 1943 and then as the improved J2M3 version with four wing-mounted cannon.

Codenamed "Jack" by the Allies, the Raiden played a key role in the defence of the Japanese homeland in the closing months of World War II.

LEFT: **A captured Ki-46 with US markings.**

Mitsubishi Ki-46-III Kai

First flight: October 1944
Power: Mitsubishi 1500hp Ha-112II piston engines
Armament: Two 20mm/0.78in cannon in nose and
one 37mm/1.46in oblique forward-firing cannon
in upper fuselage
Size: Wingspan – 14.7m/48ft 2.75in
Length – 11.48m/37ft 8.25in
Height – 3.88m/12ft 8.75in
Wing area – 32m^2/344.46sq ft
Weights: Empty – 3831kg/8446lb
Maximum take-off – 6228kg/13730lb
Performance: Maximum speed – 630kph/391mph
Ceiling – 10,500m/34,450ft
Range – 2000km/1243 miles
Climb – 600m/1970ft per minute

Mitsubishi Ki-46-III Kai

As Japan was forced on the defensive by the Allies, the Imperial Staff recognized the need for heavy fighter-interceptors to defend against Allied bombers. Since the very high-performance Ki-46 reconnaissance aircraft was some 83kph/53mph faster than the Army's standard twin-engine fighter (the Ki-45), the Ki-46 was selected for development as a stop-gap high-altitude interceptor. The development work, carried out by the Army Aerotechnical Research Institute, began in June 1943.

Photographic equipment was removed from the nose and replaced by two forward-firing 20mm/0.78in cannon, complemented by an obliquely forward-firing 37mm/1.46in cannon in the upper fuselage. Around 200 interceptor versions were built.

The aircraft appeared from October 1944 and saw service in November, but proved disappointing against B-29 daylight raids mainly due to its climb rate. When B-29 gunners found their mark, the Ki-46 was very vulnerable because of its lack of armour and self-sealing fuel tanks.

When the American bombers switched to night operations the Ki-46 proved to be even less effective as it was never fitted with radar for operational use.

Mitsubishi Ki-109

In 1943 the B-29 Superfortress was causing great concern among the Japanese military. The new super-bomber would have to be stopped and one of the means considered was a bomber hunter-killer developed from the fast and agile Mitsubishi Ki-67 heavy bomber. Initial plans called for a hunter version equipped with radar and a powerful searchlight that would have operated in concert with a killer version that would have destroyed the enemy aircraft. The scheme was then simplified to a large-calibre cannon-armed day interceptor.

The main offensive armament was a manually loaded 75mm/2.95in anti-aircraft cannon that could be fired out of range of the B-29's defending guns. The first prototype was completed in August 1944, two months after the dreaded B-29s carried out their first bombing raid on Japan.

Production versions had improved engines over the original bomber version and the sole defensive armament was a 12.7mm/0.5in machine-gun in the tail

TOP: **The Ki-109 was developed from the Ki-67 heavy bomber. Two versions were originally planned to work as a team – one radar-equipped hunter and a heavily armed killer. Only the armed version appeared.** ABOVE: **The Ki-109 differed from the Ki-67 pictured by mounting a 75mm/3in cannon in the nose.**

turret. Although it still lacked high-altitude performance, 22 examples of the highly manoeuvrable Ki-109s entered service, but by then the B-29s had switched to low-level night operations anyway.

Mitsubishi Ki-109

First flight: August 1944
Power: Two Mitsubishi 1900hp Ha-104 piston engines
Armament: One 75mm/2.95in cannon in nose and one 12.7mm/0.5in machine-gun in tail
Size: Wingspan – 22.5m/73ft 9.75in
Length – 17.95m/58ft 10.75in
Height – 5.8m/19ft 1in
Wing area – 65.85m^2/708.8sq ft
Weights: Empty – 7424kg/16367lb
Maximum take-off – 10,800kg/23,810lb
Performance: Maximum speed – 550kph/342mph
Ceiling – 9470m/31,070ft
Range – 2200km/1367 miles
Climb – 450m/1476ft per minute

Morane-Saulnier M.S.406

Morane-Saulnier built the 406 in response to a 1934 French Air Ministry requirement for a single-seat fighter. It first flew in August 1935 and was unusual for its Plymax construction – plywood with a light alloy sheet glued to the outside made up most of the aircraft except for the fabric-covered rear fuselage. Although the aircraft had a retractable undercarriage, it also had a tail-skid instead of a tailwheel.

The design was thoroughly tested by the M.S.405 series of pre-production aircraft, and in March 1938 Morane-Saulnier got an order for 1000 examples of the production M.S.406C-1, the first of which flew in January 1939. Export orders were secured from China, Finland, Lithuania, Turkey, Poland and Yugoslavia. Swiss acquisition of two early examples led to the licence-built EFW D-3800 versions in that country.

Production problems with the 12Y engine meant that only 572 completed aircraft had been delivered to the French Air Force by the time war broke out. The brave French pilots soon found that their fighters, though only six years old as a design, were from an earlier age compared to the Messerschmitts that they had to fight. More than 400

ABOVE: **The M.S.406's fuselage is reminiscent of the Hawker Hurricane.** BELOW: **A row of M.S.406s of the Polish Air Force.**

M.S.406s were lost against 175 enemy aircraft in the Battle of France.

Although deliveries continued to the French Air Force and over 1000 had been delivered by the fall of France, only one group of the Vichy French Air Force operated the M.S.406 after the armistice.

Morane-Saulnier M.S.406

First flight: August 8, 1935
Power: Hispano-Suiza 860hp 12Y-31 V-12 liquid-cooled engine
Armament: One 20mm/0.78in cannon firing through propeller hub and two 7.5mm/0.295in machine-guns in wings
Size: Wingspan – 10.6m/34ft 9.75in
Length – 8.16m/26ft 9.25in
Height – 2.83m/9ft 3.75in
Wing area – 16m²/172.23sq ft
Weights: Empty – 1900kg/4189lb
Maximum take-off – 2470kg/5445lb
Performance: Maximum speed – 485kph/302mph
Ceiling – 9400m/30,840ft
Range – 800km/497 miles
Climb – 850m/2789ft per minute

Morane-Saulnier Type N

The Type N, nicknamed "Bullet" by the Royal Flying Corps, was a neat little mid-wing monoplane that became the first French fighter aircraft – the British used the type due to the shortage of good British fighting scouts at the time. It first flew in July 1914, with the famous French pilot Roland Garros at the controls.

A huge metal propeller spinner, designed to streamline the front of the aircraft, earned the Type N its nickname but also caused engines to overheat because it so effectively deflected air around the aircraft instead of over the engine. As a result the spinner was often deleted from 1915 and in fact caused little loss of performance.

The N was armed with a fixed machine-gun, but without a synchronization gear, as the Allies had yet to develop it. Instead the N used metal bullet-deflectors on the propeller blades, an installation pioneered by Garros on a Type L. This technique was far from ideal as the impact of the bullets on the deflectors could still shatter the propeller or weaken the engine mount with disastrous results. There were also occasional ricochets of the bullets back at the pilot. With a high, for the time, landing speed, the Type N was a handful and required a skilful pilot at the controls.

The Type N was less popular than the earlier Morane-Saulnier Type L Parasol and as the Type N did not do well against the Fokker Eindecker, only 49 were built in 1917. In spite of that, the RFC Type Ns saw plenty of action as did those that flew with the French and the Russians.

At that point in aviation history, aircraft development proceeded so fast that most fighter planes were virtually obsolete by the time they reached the front-line squadrons.

Morane-Saulnier Type N

First flight: July 1914
Power: Le Rhône 110hp 9C rotary piston engine
Armament: One fixed forward-firing 7.7 or 8mm/0.303 or 0.315in machine-gun
Size: Wingspan – 8.3m/27ft 2.75in
Length – 6.7m/21ft 11.75in
Height – 2.5m/8ft 2.5in
Wing area – 11m^2/118.41sq ft
Weights: Empty – 288kg/635lb
Maximum take-off – 444kg/979lb
Performance: Maximum speed – 165kph/102.5mph
Ceiling – 4000m/13,123ft
Range – 225km/140 miles
Climb – 250m/820ft per minute

LEFT: **Complete with huge spinner, the Type N experienced engine overheating problems.**
BELOW: **The earlier M.S Type L Parasol.**
BOTTOM: **With the spinner removed, the Type N experienced no further overheating problems.**

Nakajima Ki-27

The Nakajima Ki-27 was derived from a private venture all-metal stressed-skin aircraft called the PE designed by Nakajima in 1935. When the company was invited by the Imperial Japanese Army to tender a design for an advanced fighter, a revised PE was submitted as the Ki-27.

The prototype made its first flight in October 1936 and was accepted by the Army, after comparative trials with other prototypes, in December 1937. It was called the Army Type 97 Fighter Model A – the 97 refers to the year it went into

service which was the Japanese year 2597. The Ki-27 was the Imperial Japanese Army's first monoplane fighter but it had fixed landing gear. The fighter was basic in many ways – it had a skid instead of a heavier tailwheel, no pilot armour or self-sealing fuel tanks, nor did it have a starter motor. This left the aircraft very light and incredibly manoeuvrable.

The Ki-27, codenamed "Nate" by the Allies, made its combat début over northern China in early 1938 and retained air superiority until the Chinese deployed the Polikarpov I-16. Nates later took part in the invasion of Burma, Malaya and the Philippines.

At the outbreak of the Pacific War most front-line Japanese fighter units were equipped with the Ki-27 and the type did prove to be initially very

Nakajima Ki-27a

First flight: October 15, 1936
Power: Nakajima 710hp Ha-1b air-cooled radial piston engine
Armament: Two 7.7mm/0.303in machine-guns in nose
Size: Wingspan – 11.31m/37ft 1.5in
Length – 7.53m/24ft 8.5in
Height – 3.25m/10ft 8in
Wing area – 18.55m^2/199.68sq ft
Weights: Empty – 1110kg/2447lb
Maximum take-off – 1790kg/3946lb
Performance: Maximum speed – 470kph/292mph
Ceiling – 12,250m/40190ft
Range – 635km/389 miles
Climb – 900m/2953ft per minute

LEFT: **The first monoplane fighter of the Imperial Japanese Army, the Ki-27.** BELOW: **The Ki-27 was a very basic light fighter equipped with a tail skid in place of a tailwheel.**

effective against the Allies, but once they were pitched against the more modern Western fighters, they were withdrawn to the Japanese mainland where they served until 1943. Nates did however continue in Japanese service in Manchuria until the end of World War II. Home-based examples were also used as advanced trainers and even as Kamikaze aircraft.

Nakajima Ki-43 Hayabusa

In 1937, when the Japanese Imperial Army decided to acquire a fighter with a retractable undercarriage to succeed the Ki-27, it turned to the Nakajima company for a replacement, which emerged as the Ki-43 Hayabusa (peregrine falcon). Like the Ki-27 before it, lightness and manoeuvrability were central to the design of the Ki-43 so it had no pilot armour, self-sealing fuel tanks or starter motor. It was, however, disappointing in flight tests during early 1939

and development was abandoned until spring 1941, when combat flaps were added, thus increasing the wing area as required and creating a fighter that could turn inside the highly manoeuvrable Zero. This modified version, which could dogfight with the best of the Allies' fighters, went into service in June 1941 and proved very successful despite its light armament. Most of Japan's Army fighter aces built up their scores while flying the Ki-43.

After encounters with the newer Allied fighters, armour and self-sealing fuel tanks were added, together with a more powerful engine to produce the II version, a clipped-wing variant of which was widely produced. The Ki-43 was in action throughout the Pacific theatre

in World War II and in the final days was used in the defence of Tokyo and for kamikaze (divine wind) missions. Almost 6000 were built in all – this aeroplane, codenamed "Oscar" by the Allies, was deployed in greater numbers than any other Imperial Army fighter and was second only to the Navy's Zero in terms of sheer numbers in the Japanese inventory.

As an interesting post-war footnote, in late 1945 the French Armeé de l'Air flew captured Oscars painted in

ABOVE: **The Ki-43 was in service throughout the war in the Pacific. LEFT: A Ki-43-II captured by the Allies before the end of World War II, rebuilt for evaluation.**

French markings in the ground support role against Viet Minh forces in Indochina. Captured Hayabusas were also operated by the Indonesian People's Security Forces against the Dutch in the same period.

Nakajima Ki-43-II Hayabusa

First flight: January 1939

Power: Nakajima 1150hp Ha-115 air-cooled radial piston engine

Armament: Two 12.7mm/0.5in synchronized machine-guns, plus two 30kg/66lb or 250kg/551lb bombs

Size: Wingspan – 10.84m/35ft 6.75in
Length – 8.92m/29ft 3.3in
Height – 3.27m/10ft 8.75in
Wing area – 21.4m²/230.4sq ft

Weights: Empty – 1910kg/4211lb
Maximum take-off – 2925kg/6450lb

Performance: Maximum speed – 530kph/329mph
Ceiling – 11,200m/36,750ft
Range – 1760km/1095 miles
Climb – 5000m/16,405ft in 5 minutes, 49 seconds

123

Nakajima Ki-44 Shoki

The Ki-44 was designed purely as an interceptor, so high speed and good climb were sought at the expense of manoeuvrability. The type first flew in August 1940 and when tested against an imported Messerschmitt Bf109E was shown to be superior in performance.

The Shoki (demon) did not enter production until mid-1942 and finally reached a production total of 1225. Virtually all were used in the defence of the Japanese home islands and in one defensive mission on February 19, 1945

a small number of Shokis attacked a force of 120 B-29s, destroying ten of the US bombers. The Allied codename for the Ki-44 was "Tojo".

TOP: **The Shoki was a good fighter, but high landing speeds demanded respect for the type from its pilots.** ABOVE: **The Allied codename for the Ki-44 was "Tojo".**
LEFT: **Total production of the Ki-44 exceeded 1200.** BELOW: **The Ki-44 was an effective interceptor that could have wreaked havoc among enemy bomber formations, had it been deployed effectively in sufficient numbers.**

Nakajima Ki-44-IIb Shoki

First flight: August 1940
Power: Nakajima 1520hp Ha-109 radial piston engine
Armament: Four forward-firing 12.7mm/0.5in machine-guns
Size: Wingspan – 9.45m/31ft
Length – 8.8m/28ft 10.5in
Height – 3.25m/10ft 8in
Wing area – 15m²/161.46sq ft
Weights: Empty – 2105kg/4641lb
Maximum take-off – 2995kg/6603lb
Performance: Maximum speed – 605kph/376mph
Ceiling – 11,200m/36,745ft
Range – 1700km/1056 miles
Climb – 1200m/3940ft per minute

ABOVE LEFT: **A Ki-84 of the 11th Sentai.** ABOVE: **The Ki-84 was a formidable fighter aircraft with an excellent performance.**

Nakajima Ki-84 Hayate

Introduced in mid-1944, the Nakajima Ki-84 Hayate (gale) was numerically the most important fighter that served with the Japanese Army Air Force during the last year of the war in the Pacific. If it had been available in larger numbers earlier in the war, the Hayate could have been a major obstacle for Allied aircraft to overcome. It was the equal of the most advanced Allied fighters including the P-51 and P-47 and in many cases had better climb and manoeuvrability. Japan was so desperate for Ki-84s in the last months of the war that underground factories were being built with a planned output of 200 aircraft per month.

The Ki-84 began in 1942 when the Nakajima Aeroplane Co. began to design a replacement for its Ki-43 Hayabusa. The JAAF wanted a high-performance long-range fighter that could outperform those of the Allies.

The Ki-84 prototype flew for the first time in March 1943 and was quickly shown to be the best-performing Japanese fighter aircraft then available for production.

Service tests of the Ki-84 began in Japan under operational conditions in October 1943 and the type was accepted for production as the Army Type 4 Fighter Model 1A Hayate (gale) or Ki-84-Ia.

Production aircraft began to roll off the assembly lines in April 1944. In March 1944 the experimental squadron that was conducting the service test trials of the Ki-84 was disbanded, and its personnel transferred to the 22nd Sentai which was re-equipped with production Hayates and transferred to China in August 1944 for combat against the USAAF's 14th Air Force. The Ki-84-Ia swiftly established itself as a formidable foe that compared very well with the best Allied fighters of the time.

The Hayate exhibited an excellent performance and climb rate, and unlike most earlier Japanese fighters, it was well armoured for pilot protection.

The Ki-84 proved faster than the P-51D Mustang and the P-47D Thunderbolt at all but the highest altitudes while at medium height the Hayate was so fast that it was virtually uncatchable.

Fighter-bomber versions of the Ki-84 also proved to be formidable combat aircraft. On April 15, 1945 a flight of 11 Hayates made a surprise air attack on American airfields on Okinawa damaging or destroying many aircraft on the ground.

The Hayate did have some handling idiosyncrasies. Taxiing and ground handling were generally hazardous and on take-off, the considerable engine torque caused a swing to port once the tail came up.

Most Ki-84 defects were simply due to poor quality control in a country under siege. Later examples had progressively poorer performance and mechanical reliability – the metal of the landing gear struts inadequately hardened during manufacture, which made them likely to snap on landing. Production of the aircraft never reached the desired levels because the Nakajima factory was regularly bombed by US B-29 Superfortresses.

Nakajima Ki-84-Ia Hayate	

First flight: March 1943
Power: Nakajima 1900hp Ha-45 radial piston engine
Armament: Two 12.7mm/0.5in machine-guns plus two 20mm/0.78in cannon and two underwing 250kg/551lb bombs
Size: Wingspan – 11.24m/36ft 10.5in
Length – 9.92m/32ft 6.5in
Height – 3.39m/11ft 1.5in
Wing area – 21m²/226sq ft
Weights: Empty – 2660kg/5864lb
Maximum take-off – 3890kg/8576lb
Performance: Maximum speed – 631kph/392mph
Ceiling – 10,500m/34,350ft
Range – 2168km/1347 miles
Climb – 1100m/3600ft per minute

ABOVE: **This Hayate was shipped to Wright Field in the USA for post-war evaluation by the USAAF.**

Nieuport fighting scouts

The Nieuport fighting scouts earned a fine reputation for both their designer Gustave Delage and the company that built them. The Nieuport XI was developed from the 1914 Bébé racer aircraft and retained the earlier aircraft's name as a nickname. By the summer of 1915 the first Bébés were in service in France and the Dardanelles with Britain's Royal Flying Corps and Royal Naval Air Service and were one of the first true fighters used by the British. In the hands of an experienced pilot, the tiny Nieuport XI had no problem outmanoeuvring an Eindecker and bringing it down. Powered by an 80hp Gnome or Le Rhône engine, the aircraft were much better than what was in use at the time. They were highly agile fighters with good rates of climb and speed but the chief problem lay in the fragility of the wing structure which could fail in flight.

They were armed with a single Hotchkiss or Lewis machine-gun mounted on the top wing but the Nieuport XI could also carry eight Le Prieur rockets for attacking balloons. In addition to French production, the Nieuport XI was also built in Russia, Spain and the Netherlands, as well as being copied by German designers.

> ### Nieuport XI
>
> **First flight:** Early 1915
> **Power:** Le Rhône 80hp 9C rotary piston engine
> **Armament:** One 7.7mm/0.303in Lewis gun
> **Size:** Wingspan – 7.55m/24ft 9in
> Length – 5.8m/19ft 0.75in
> Height – 2.45m/8ft 0.5in
> Wing area – 13m^2/139.94sq ft
> **Weights:** Empty – 350kg/772lb
> Maximum take-off – 480kg/1058lb
> **Performance:** Maximum speed – 155kph/97mph
> Ceiling – 4500m/14,765ft
> Range – 2 hours, 30 minutes endurance
> Climb – about 200m/660ft per minute

ABOVE: **The Nieuports were one of the most successful "families" of World War I aircraft.** BELOW AND BOTTOM: **The Nieuport XI was one of the earliest fighter aircraft used by Britain's RFC and RNAS. Though manoeuvrable, the type's wings were fragile.**

The Nieuport XVII was one of the most famous fighter aircraft of World War I and was a significant improvement on the Bébé. The type first appeared with the French on the Western Front in May 1916, and was a direct development of the XI. It had a more powerful engine, larger wings and a stiffening of the entire structure. It first had the 110hp Le Rhône 9J rotary engine, and then was upgraded to the more powerful 130hp Clerget 9B. The XVII combined outstanding manoeuvrability with good speed and excellent climb, and influenced the design of many other aircraft – the German Siemens-Schuckert DI was, except for the tailplane, a direct copy of it.

Reloading of the top wing gun on this model was made easier by the Foster gun mount, a curved metal rail along which the gun could be pulled back and down – the pilot could then reach the magazine on top of the machine-gun but this was a difficult feat in anything but straight and level flight. Nevertheless many World War I Allied aces flew these aircraft, including René Fonck, Georges Guynemer, Charles Nungesser, Albert Ball and Billy Bishop.

The Nieuport 28 first flew in June 1917 and was the first fighter aircraft flown in combat by pilots of the American Expeditionary Forces (AEF) in World War I. Its second armed patrol with an AEF unit on April 14, 1918 resulted in two victories when Lts Alan Winslow and Douglas Campbell (the first American-trained ace) of the 94th Aero Squadron each downed an enemy aircraft. The 28 was very different to the earlier Nieuports and lost the familiar slim lower wing in favour of a lower wing almost as large as the top one.

By the time the Nieuport 28 was in service it had been overtaken in terms of performance by the SPAD, but American pilots maintained a good ratio of kills to losses while flying the Nieuport. The Nieuport was more manoeuvrable than the sturdier SPAD XIII that replaced it, but had a reputation for fragility and a tendency, in a dive, to shed the fabric covering its upper wing. Even so, many American aces of World War I, including Eddie Rickenbacker with 26 victories, flew the French-built Nieuport 28. Post-war, many Nieuport 28s continued to fly in air forces around the world.

Nieuport XVII

First flight: January 1916
Power: Le Rhône 120hp rotary piston engine
Armament: One 7.7mm/0.303in Lewis gun on flexible top wing mount plus one 7.7m/0.303in synchronized machine-gun
Size: Wingspan – 8.2m/26ft 10.75in
Length – 5.96m/19ft 7in
Height – 2.44m/8ft
Wing area – 14.75m^2/158.77sq ft
Weights: Empty – 374kg/825lb
Maximum take-off – 560kg/1235lb
Performance: Maximum speed – 170kph/106mph
Ceiling – 5350m/17,550ft
Range – 250km/155 miles
Climb – 4000m/13,125ft in 19 minutes, 30 seconds

ABOVE: **Around 90 examples of the 120hp or 130hp engined Nieuport 27 were in service briefly with the RFC from mid-1917 April 1918.** BELOW: **The ultimate Nieuport – the 28. As well as extensive wartime service, the type was also widely used post-World War I.**

Nieuport 28

First flight: June 14, 1917
Power: Gnome 160hp 9N rotary piston engine
Armament: Two fixed 7.7mm/0.303in machine-guns
Size: Wingspan – 8m/26ft 3in
Length – 6.2m/20ft 4in
Height – 2.48m/8ft 1.75in
Wing area – 20m^2/215.29sq ft
Weights: Empty – 532kg/1172lb
Maximum take-off – 740kg/1631lb
Performance: Maximum speed – 195kph/121mph
Ceiling – 5200m/17,060ft
Range – 400km/248 miles
Climb – 5000m/16,405ft in 21 minutes, 15 seconds

North American P/F–51 Mustang

Considered to be one of the greatest US fighters ever, the first Mustangs were actually designed and built in the United States with Allison engines to a British specification for the Royal Air Force. Designed and built in the remarkably short time of 117 days, the new fighter was test flown in October 1940. The Mustang could outperform contemporary American fighters but the Allison's lack of power in the climb and at altitude led to the early Mustang's use in the European theatre being limited to armed tactical reconnaissance. In October 1942 RAF Mustangs attacked targets on the Dortmund-Ems canal and became the first British single-engined aircraft over Germany in World War II. The A-36 Invader was the dedicated dive-bomber version of the early Mustang and equipped the USAAF in Sicily, where it was used to devastating effect.

When in 1942 the Mustang airframe was matched with the proven Rolls-Royce Merlin, the "Cadillac of the skies" was born and the P-51 Mustang became one of the most successful fighter aircraft of all time. In October 1943, as a result of unacceptable losses, unescorted US daylight bomber

ABOVE: With its long range, the P-51 Mustang enabled the resumption of US bombing missions deep in enemy territory. BELOW: This preserved P-51 is painted as the personal aircraft of US wartime ace Clarence "Bud" Anderson.

missions deep into enemy Europe were suspended. No Allied fighter had the range to defend and escort the American bombers all the way to the target. The arrival of the Mustang, with its US-built Merlin engines and droppable wing tanks enabled the bombers to resume their daylight missions, safe in the knowledge that their "little buddies" could fly with them all the way to Berlin and back. Even at that range, the P-51's performance was superior to that of its Luftwaffe adversaries. The Mustang allowed the Allies to gain command of the daylight sky over Germany and as a result made a major contribution to the defeat of Nazi Germany.

The Mustang was a very comfortable long-range aircraft and pilot visibility was excellent. Cockpit ergonomics were well thought out, with everything readily to hand. It was so aero-dynamically clean that it was capable of higher speeds than

Spitfires fitted with the same engine. Although manoeuvrable it demanded, however, great physical effort from the pilot to get the best from the aircraft at high speed.

The P-51D was produced in greater numbers than any other model but improvements continued to be made to the design, culminating in the P-51H, which was 454kg/1000lb lighter than the D model and was the fastest Allied piston-engined aircraft of the war.

Total production amounted to 15,586 and after World War II the Mustang was operated by at least 55 air forces, making it the world's most widely used fighter at the time. Licence-built versions were also produced in Australia in the late 1940s.

Always thought of as a World War II fighter, the P-51 was in action for many years after 1945. Mothballed USAF P/F-51s returned to service for the Korean War as fighter-bombers and also scored a number of air-to-air victories. South African and Australian Mustangs also served in the conflict until being replaced by jets.

Dutch P-51Ds and Ks were in combat in the Dutch East Indies in 1946 and following the withdrawal of Dutch forces the P-51s were given over to the embryonic Indonesian Air Force, who operated the type into the 1970s. The Israeli Air Force fielded Mustangs during the 1956 Arab-Israeli conflict and on January 15, 1962 Indonesian F-51Ds provided top cover for a failed attempt to invade Dutch New Guinea. Dutch Hawker Hunter F. Mk 4s were ready to engage the Mustangs when negotiations halted what could have been a remarkable air combat episode.

Such was the quality and longevity of the original design that the P-51 was put back into production in 1967 as a turboprop-powered counter-insurgency aircraft.

TOP: **The Cadillac of the skies – looking every inch a thoroughbred.**
ABOVE: **Where it all began – a Mustang I of No.2 Squadron RAF. Due to the low altitude power ratings of the Allison engines installed, the type was initially limited to armed tactical reconnaissance.** BELOW: **Drop tanks gave the Mustang even longer legs, and helped the type regain control of the sky over Europe from the Luftwaffe.**

North American P-51D Mustang

First flight: October 26, 1940
Power: Packard 1590hp V-1650-7 Merlin piston engine
Armament: Six 12.7mm/0.5in machine-guns and up to 454kg/1000lb of bombs or rockets in place of drop tanks
Size: Wingspan – 11.29m/37ft
Length – 9.85m/32ft 3in
Height – 4.16m/13ft 8in
Wing area – 21.83m²/235sq ft
Weights: Empty – 3230kg/7125lb
Maximum take-off – 5262kg/11,600lb
Performance: Maximum speed – 703kph/437mph
Ceiling – 12,771m/41,900ft
Range – 3347km/2080 miles with drop tanks
Climb – 1060m/3475ft per minute

129

Northrop P/F-61 Black Widow

Northrop P-61B
Black Widow

First flight: May 21, 1942 (XP-61)
Power: Two Pratt & Whitney 2000hp R-2800-65
  Double Wasp 18-cylinder radial piston engines
Armament: Four 12.7mm/0.5in machine-guns in
  upper turret, four 20mm/0.78in cannons in belly,
  plus up to 2905kg/6400lb of bombs
Size: Wingspan – 20.11m/66ft 0.75in
  Length – 15.11m/49ft 7in
  Height – 4.47m/14ft 8in
  Wing area – 61.53m²/662.36sq ft
Weights: Empty – 10,637kg/23,450lb
  Maximum take-off – 16,420kg/36,200lb
Performance: Maximum speed – 589kph/366mph
  Ceiling – 10,060m/33,000ft
  Range – 2172km/1350 miles
  Climb – 637m/2090ft per minute

The large and heavily armed twin-engine twin-boom Black Widow was the first ever aircraft specifically designed as a nightfighter and was built to meet a specification issued in October 1940, following the early successes of RAF nightfighters against the Luftwaffe. In the nose it carried the then new radar equipment, which enabled its crew to locate enemy aircraft in total darkness and manoeuvre into an attacking position. The XP-61 was flight-tested in 1942 and delivery of production aircraft began in late 1943, following hold-ups due to technical challenges of both aircraft and radar that had to be overcome.

The P-61A flew its first operational intercept missions as a nightfighter in Europe in July 1944 and destroyed four German bombers in the type's first engagement. Black Widows were also credited with the destruction of nine V-1 flying bombs in Europe. Meanwhile in the Pacific, a Black Widow claimed its first kill on the night of July 6–7, 1944. As the P-61s became available, they replaced the stop-gap Douglas P-70s in all USAAF nightfighter squadrons.

Armament was carried below the nose and in a remotely controlled barbette at top centre of the fuselage – the latter was deleted early in production of the A model due to buffeting problems when pointed at right angles to the aircraft's centre line. The dorsal barbette was later reinstated during production of the B-model, which differed from the A model by being 20.3cm/8in longer and having the ability to carry four 726kg/1600lb bombs or 1136 litre/300 US gallon drop tanks. 200 P-61As were built, while B model production reached 450. After feedback about the P-61's combat performance, the P-61C was developed, powered by turbo-supercharged R-2800-73 engines with an emergency output of 2800hp apiece. As the take-off weight of the type increased to 18,144kg/40,000lb,

a recommended take-off run of 4.8km/3 miles was required.

A number of Black Widows continued to serve until 1950 in USAF service (by then designated F-51s) and in 1949 were the first aircraft of the embryonic US Air Defense Command, founded to defend the USA from Soviet air attack.

BELOW: **The P-61 Black Widow was the first ever purpose-designed nightfighter, and proved the value of the dedicated nightfighter aircraft.**

Petlyakov Pe-3

Originally designed as a high altitude interceptor (designated VI-100), the Pe-2 became one of the most significant aircraft in the wartime Allied inventory. The prototype flew in mid-1939 and its high speed and high altitude capability would indeed have made it a very effective interceptor. However, early in 1940 the decision was taken to develop the type as a bomber as a priority over a high flying interceptor. It performed outstandingly as a tactical/dive-bomber and was very fast for the time. Two RAF Hurricane squadrons were sent to Russia in the autumn of 1941 to strengthen the Soviet defences, and when escorting the Pe-2 on bombing missions found it very hard to keep up.

When an early Pe-2 dive-bomber was modified as a multi-role fighter prototype it was given the designation Pe-3. It first flew in early 1941 and was structurally similar to the bomber version. The fighter had a two-man crew (as opposed to three for the bomber) and they sat back to back with the observer gunner facing backwards. Additional fuel was carried in the main bomb bay and the small bomb bays in the rear of the two engine nacelles. Only 23 examples were built prior to the German invasion of Russia at which point production ceased.

The Pe-2 did however make it into production as a fighter in the summer of 1941. Every second aircraft on the Pe-2 production line was hastily modified to fighter configuration and were designated Pe-3bis. Armament consisted of two 20mm/0.78in cannon carried in the bomb bay. The bomber's nose armament of two 7.62mm/0.31in machine-guns were sometimes replaced by two harder-hitting 12.7mm/0.5in cannon, while the bomber's 12.7mm/0.5in cannon in the dorsal turret was retained. Front-line units had deliveries from August 1941 and those aircraft used in the nightfighter role were equipped with special equipment. Around 300 aircraft were built in all.

TOP: **The Pe-3 bristled with offensive armament.** ABOVE: **From mid-1941, every alternate Pe-2 on the production line was made as a fighter.**

Petlyakov Pe-3bis

First flight: December 22, 1939 (VI-100 prototype)
Power: Two Klimov 1260hp VK-105PF V12 piston engines
Armament: Two 20mm/0.78in cannon in bomb bay, two 7.62mm/0.31in machine-guns or two 12.7mm/0.5in cannon in nose, plus one 12.7mm/0.5in cannon in dorsal turret
Size: Wingspan – 17.16m/56ft 3.6in
Length – 12.6m/41ft 4.5in
Height – 3.42m/11ft 2.6in
Wing area – 40.5m²/435.95sq ft
Weights: Empty – 5870kg/12,941lb
Maximum take-off – 8040kg/17,725lb
Performance: Maximum speed – 530kph/329mph
Ceiling – 8800m/28,700ft
Range – 1700km/1056 miles
Climb – 5000m/16,405ft in 10 minutes, 12 seconds

Pfalz D.III

The D.III appeared in mid-1917 and was built with the experience gained by Pfalz while producing LFG-Roland fighters. The D.III biplane fighter, the design of which owed much to the LFG-Roland D.I and D.II, was a competent, agile fighter aircraft that was also strong, easy to fly and popular with pilots. About 600 were built and supplied at least at first, only to Bavarian

fighter units in the German Air Force – this was no doubt due to the fact that the Pfalz factory was run by the Bavarian government. The excellent Pfalz D.XII was a development of the D.III and was, in 1918, accepted by the German High Command for mass production.

Among the refinements was the removal of the radiator from the top wing

ABOVE: **D.XIIs were in action on the Western Front from October 1918, but could do little to affect the final outcome of World War I.**

to the engine to prevent unfortunate pilots from being scalded by a punctured cooling system. Although the D.XII was powered by the same Mercedes engine as the D.III, it had a slightly higher top speed than the earlier mark.

ABOVE: **A Pfalz D.IIIa. By the end of 1917 some 275 were in action at the Front, but by April 1918 this number had risen to 433.**

Pfalz D.IIIa

First flight: Summer 1917
Power: Mercedes 180hp D.IIIa in-line piston engine
Armament: Two fixed 7.92mm/0.31in machine-guns
Size: Wingspan – 9.4m/30ft 10in
Length – 6.95m/22ft 9.5in
Height – 2.67m/8ft 9in
Wing area – 22.1m²/237.89sq ft
Weights: Empty – 695kg/1532lb
Maximum take-off – 935kg/2061lb
Performance: Maximum speed – 165kph/103mph
Ceiling – 5180m/17,000ft
Range – 2 hours, 30 minutes endurance
Climb – 250m/820ft per minute

Polikarpov I-15

LEFT: **The I-15 fought from Manchuria to Spain.**

Developed from the earlier I-5 fighter, the agile little Polikarpov I-15 biplane actually replaced the monoplane I-16 in service in parts of the USSR. Having first flown during October 1933 in prototype TsKB-3 form, production of the I-15 Chaika (gull) began in 1934 and continued for three years.

The I-15 was used extensively by the Republicans during the Spanish Civil War (1936–9) and earned the nickname "Chato", meaning flat-nosed. The first I-15s arrived in Spain during October 1936 and during the subsequent combats earned a reputation as a tough opponent. In addition to the imported examples, Spanish government factories also licence-built some 287 examples and many fell into the hands of the Nationalists when the war ended in March 1939.

The improved I-15bis was tested in early 1937 and was distinguished by a longer cowling (covering a more powerful engine), and streamlining spats on the undercarriage legs. Over 2400 examples had been built by the time production ceased in early 1939. By then it had also seen action against the Japanese in Manchuria. In the Winter War of 1939–40, the I-15bis was extensively used against the Finns. The few examples of the improved version that made it to fight in Spain were nicknamed "Super Chatos" by the Spanish.

In 1937–8, the I-15bis was sent in quantity, with pilots, to help Chinese Nationalists fight the Japanese who were invading. It was during these air battles that the tough biplane began to meet its match in some of the Japanese mono-planes. Nevertheless over 1000 I-15bis fighters were still in Soviet Air Force use in mid-1941 although most were used for ground attack. By late 1942 all were relegated to second-line duties.

Polikarpov I-15bis

First flight: October 1933 (prototype)
Power: M-25V 775hp radial piston engine
Armament: Four 7.62mm/0.3in machine-guns plus bombload of up to 150kg/331lb
Size: Wingspan – 10.2m/33ft 5.5in
Length – 6.27m/20ft 6.75in
Height – 2.19m/7ft 2.25in
Wing area – 22.53m^2/242.52sq ft
Weights: Empty – 1320kg/2910lb
Maximum take-off – 1900kg/4189lb
Performance: Maximum speed – 370kph/230mph
Ceiling – 9500m/31,170ft
Range – 530km/329 miles
Climb – 765m/2500ft per minute

Polikarpov I-16

LEFT: **The classic I-16 fighter was in the front line on at least four battle fronts.**

The tiny I-16, reminiscent of the American Gee Bee racing aircraft, was one of the most important and innovative fighters of its time. With a wooden fuselage, it was also the first widely used low-wing cantilever mono-plane with retractable landing gear. It first flew in December 1933, and in the mid-1930s this aircraft was one of the world's best fighters – it had a good top speed some 123kph/70mph faster than its contemporaries, and was well-armed and highly manoeuvrable. It remained in production until 1939 by which time a host of variants had been developed.

It was not until the Spanish Civil War that the I-16 came to the attention of the Western world. The Republicans were supplied with 278 I-16s from October 1935. Hispano-Suiza also licence-built the I-16 for the Republicans in Spain but after their surrender, others were produced for the Franco régime. Many of the I-16s that saw action in Spain were flown by volunteer Soviet pilots.

In 1937, Soviet I-16s also saw service in China against the Japanese. From 1938 the Chinese flew the type and by 1939, Soviet I-16s were locked in fierce air battles with the Japanese on the Manchurian border.

The 1939–40 Winter War with Finland saw the Soviet I-16s in action again but by the time of the German invasion of Russia, the I-16 was seriously out-classed. Though suffering large losses, the I-16 fought on in the battles of 1941 with the often desperate heroism displayed by the Soviet pilots – some I-16s are known to have resorted to ramming enemy aircraft in attempts to stem the invasion. It was not until late 1943 that the I-16 was withdrawn from Soviet front-line service.

The I-16 was an excellent fighter for its time period, and fought on long after it should have been retired.

Polikarpov I-16 Type 24

First flight: December 31, 1933
Power: M-62 1000hp radial piston engine
Armament: Four 7.62mm/0.3in machine-guns – two in wings and two synchronized housed in forward fuselage
Size: Wingspan – 8.88m/29ft 1.5in
Length – 6.04m/19ft 9.75in
Height – 2.41m/7ft 10.75in
Wing area – 14.87m^2/160sq ft
Weights: Empty – 14/5kg/3252lb
Maximum take-off – 2060kg/4542lb
Performance: Maximum speed – 490kph/304mph
Ceiling – 9470m/31,070ft
Range – 600km/373 miles
Climb – 850m/2790ft per minute

LEFT: The Potez 63.11 variant was a
tactical reconnaissance/ground version
of the series.

Potez 631

First flight: April 25, 1936 (Potez 630)
Power: Two Hispano-Suiza 725hp 14AB 14-cylinder
two row radials
Armament: Two forward-firing 20mm/0.78in cannon
and a flexibly mounted 7.5mm/0.3in machine-gun
in the rear cockpit plus four 7.5mm/0.3in machine-
guns mounted under the wings
Size: Wingspan – 16m/52ft 6in
Length – 11.07m/36ft 10.5in
Height – 3.04m/9ft 11.6in
Wing area – 32.7m²/351.99sq ft
Weights: Empty – 2838kg/6256lb
Maximum take-off – 3760kg/8289lb
Performance: Maximum speed – 442kph/275mph
Ceiling – 10,000m/32,800ft
Range – 1200km/758 miles
Climb – 4000m/13,125ft in 5 minutes, 56 seconds

Potez 630/631

The three-seat Potez 630 was built to a demanding French air ministry specification for a twin-engine strategic fighter and first flew in April 1936. It was for its time a thoroughly modern design, powered by slim engines and boasting the far from standard retractable under-carriage. The first production version was the 630, all 80 of which were grounded for a time due to a series

of catastrophic engine failures. Their generally poor performance soon took them into second-line training duties. The 631 however, powered by Gnome-Rhône engines was a great success and over 200 were built for both the Armée de l'Air and the French Navy. During the Battle of France, 631s flying in both day- and nightfighter units accounted for 29 Luftwaffe aircraft. After the fall of

France, surviving 631s were for a time operated by Vichy forces but were later seized and passed on to Romania as trainers and target tugs.

LEFT: The P.Z.L. P.11 was no match for the Luftwaffe
fighters it faced in the Blitzkrieg.

P.Z.L. P.11c

First flight: August 1931
Power: P.Z.L./Bristol Mercury 645hp VI.S2 radial
piston engine
Armament: Two 7.7mm/0.303in machine-guns
plus light bombs carried beneath wings
Size: Wingspan – 10.72m/35ft 2in
Length – 7.55m/24ft 9.25in Height – 2.85m/
9ft 4.25in Wing area – 17.9m²/192.68sq ft
Weights: Empty – 1147kg/2529lb
Maximum take-off – 1630kg/3594lb
Performance: Maximum speed – 390kph/242mph
Ceiling – 8000m/26,245ft
Range – 700km/435 miles
Climb – 800m/2625ft per minute

P.Z.L. P.11

As the Germans prepared to invade Poland in September 1939, the bulk of the poorly organized fighter force that faced them was made up of around 160 P.11s. These aircraft were derived from the Polish-designed P.6 and P.7 fighters that first flew in 1930. Pilot forward view from the cockpit of the P.7 was compromised by the large radial engine that powered it. Smaller diameter

engines were tested to improve the view and this together with other refinements led to the P.11 that was produced in three differently engined versions. The major variant was the P.11c powered by Skoda or P.Z.L-built Bristol Mercury radials and deliveries to the Polish Air Force were complete by late 1936.

When the Germans launched their invasion of Poland, the P.11 pilots fought

well and made the most of their outmoded machines. Some sources claim that 114 of the P.11s were destroyed in the air battles that raged at the time of the invasion – although the defence failed, the P.11s did destroy 126 Luftwaffe aircraft. A more heavily armed version of the P.11 was tested but finished aircraft did not reach the Polish fighter squadrons before the German invasion.

Reggiane Re.2000 fighters

Development of the Re.2000 began in 1937 and was clearly influenced by the chunky radial-engined fighters being developed in the USA at the time. When the Re.2000 Falco I prototype flew in 1938, the Italian Air Force appeared to show little interest, but the Italian Navy

did order Serie II and Serie III versions for catapult launching and long-range missions respectively. The Hungarian Air Force also bought some Re.2000s and a few were manufactured in Hungary under licence – in Hungary the type was known as Hejja (hawk). Sweden also ordered 60 for the Swedish Air Force who operated the type until 1945.

The German DB-601 in-line engine was trialled in a new version designated Re.2001 Ariete (ram) but Daimler-Benz had to focus on orders for the Luftwaffe. Accordingly a licence-built version made by Alfa Romeo was used to power the Ariete, 252 of which were built in three differently armed versions as well as fighter-bomber and nightfighter variants.

Following the Re.2002 fighter-bomber version, the end of the Re.2000 line came with the Re.2005 Sagittario which many consider to be the best Italian fighter of World War II. Powered by an in-line engine, the test flight took place in September 1942, and when it entered production it was powered by a licence-built DB 605. Although only 48 Sagittarios were built before the Allies overran the factories, these fighters were widely used to defend Naples, Rome and Sicily. As the Allies closed in on Berlin, a few fanatical pilots and their Re.2005s even fought on over the city.

TOP: **The US design influence is clear on this study of an early Re.2000.** ABOVE: **A few Re.2000s were exported to Sweden and Hungary; the latter nation also undertook its own production of the type.** LEFT: **Derivatives of the Re.2000 proved to be very potent fighter aircraft.**

Reggiane Re.2005 Sagittario

First flight: September 1942
Power: Fiat 1475hp RA.1050 RC.58 Tifone in-line piston engine
Armament: Three 20mm/0.78in cannon and two 12.7mm/0.5in machine-guns
Size: Wingspan – 11m/36ft 1in
Length – 8.73m/28ft 7.75in
Height – 3.15m/10ft 4in
Wing area – 20.4m^2/219.59sq ft
Weights: Empty – 2600kg/5732lb
Maximum take-off – 3560kg/7848lb
Performance: Maximum speed – 630kph/391mph
Ceiling – 12,000m/39,370ft
Range – 1250km/777 miles
Climb – 1100m/3600ft per minute

Republic P-47 Thunderbolt

When the P-47 first flew in May 1941 it was the largest and heaviest single-seat piston fighter ever produced – it still is. Later versions, when fully loaded, weighed more than a loaded Luftwaffe Dornier Do 17 bomber. It was also produced in greater numbers than any other American fighter and was one of the outstanding US fighters of World War II.

Considerable technical difficulties were overcome in the development of the P-47 – making sure that the massive 3.7m/12ft-diameter propeller cleared the ground was a major concern, calling for very long landing gear which had to retract inwards to leave room for the heavy wing armament of eight 12.7mm/0.5in machine-guns. The deep fuselage was made to accommodate the large pipes and ducts that fed exhaust gas to the turbocharger in the rear fuselage or fed high-pressure air back to the engine again. Among the cockpit innovations were cabin air-conditioning, variable gun-bay heating and electric fuel indicators.

The P-47B finally entered production in 1942 and Thunderbolts of the US Army Air Force began to arrive in Britain from early 1943 with the task of escorting Eighth Air Force B-17s and B-24s on hazardous daylight bombing raids over Europe. The first P-47 mission was in April 1943 and the "Jug" (short for juggernaut) excelled as a high-altitude escort fighter – in spite of its size it was agile and a favourite of pilots. P-47Cs introduced more powerful engines and

TOP: **The mighty P-47 was a truly big aircraft – compare it to the slender Spitfire.** ABOVE: **This example, based at the Imperial War Museum Duxford in the UK, is a very popular participant in European air shows.**

provision for a belly tank – these auxiliary droppable fuel tanks were carried from March 1944, giving the Jugs the range to get them all the way to Berlin.

Thunderbolts were also formidable ground-attack aircraft and pilots were encouraged to indulge in train-busting for which the robustly constructed aircraft was ideally suited. It was a "get-you-home" aircraft that could absorb considerable damage. P-47s were also widely used by the UK-based US Ninth (tactical) Air Force, escorting their Havocs and Marauders.

The P-47D, produced from early 1943, was the definitive Thunderbolt and featured a host of improvements – a more powerful engine equipped for water injection emergency boost, a more efficient turbocharger, better pilot armour and multi-ply tyres to survive landings on the roughest of airstrips. The D model was also the first able to carry a 454kg/1000lb bomb under each wing as well as a belly tank – with three tanks the Jugs could go deep into enemy territory. Part way into D model production, the bubble canopy was introduced, replacing the old greenhouse type, and the removal of the "razorback" eradicated a blind spot to the rear. Unpainted aircraft were now also supplied from the factories, improving top speed slightly.

ABOVE: **An early razorback version of the P-47 with the "greenhouse"-style canopy.**
LEFT: **A P-47 of the 78th Fighter Group, US Eighth Air Force, in World War II.**

A special "hot-rod" version of the P-47D, the P-47M, was built in limited numbers and made its appearance in December 1944, to catch and destroy the V-1 flying bombs that Germany was launching against Allied targets. With a

top speed of 756kph/470mph, the P-47M had airbrakes fitted to the wings so that it could decelerate once it had caught enemy aircraft. The P-47M certainly scored victories over German Me262 and Arado 234 jets.

The long-range P-47N, the ultimate Thunderbolt, was virtually a complete redesign, with long-span wings containing fuel tanks. Produced from December 1944, it was intended for long-range operations in the Pacific and had square-tipped wings for better roll.

The Royal Air Force also used Thunderbolts from September 1944, but exclusively in the Far East against the Japanese. Sixteen RAF squadrons operated the type in both ground-attack and bomber escort missions but rarely had the opportunity to engage in a dogfight. Two RAF Thunderbolt squadrons continued in service in India until 1946 when the Tempest replaced it in Royal Air Force service.

By the end of World War II the P-47 had flown 546,000 missions and in Western Europe alone destroyed 3752 aircraft in air combat. The Jug was truly one of the greatest fighters ever and continued to equip air forces until the mid-1950s. A total of 15,660 P-47s were produced, of which 12,602 were D models.

LEFT: **The Thunderbolt was equally at home in the low-level ground attack role.** ABOVE: **Preparing for another mission, these "razorbacks" are pictured just after D-Day.**

Republic P-47D Thunderbolt

First flight: May 6, 1941 (XP-47B)
Power: Pratt & Whitney 2535hp R-2800-59 Double-Wasp eighteen-cylinder radial engine
Armament: Eight 12.7mm/0.5in machine-guns, plus provision for external load of bombs or rockets to maximum of 1134kg/2500lb
Size: Wingspan – 12.4m/40ft 9in
  Length – 11.02m/36ft 1in Height – 4.47m/14ft8in
  Wing area – 27.87m²/300sq ft
Weights: Empty – 4513kg/9950lb
  Maximum take-off – 7938kg/17,500lb
Performance: Maximum speed – 697kph/433mph
  Ceiling – 12,495m/41,000ft
  Range – 3060km/1900 miles with three drop tanks
  Climb – 976m/3200ft per minute

Royal Aircraft Factory S.E.5a

The robust and long-lived S.E.5a was one of the few World War I aircraft to enjoy a lengthy production run, with over 5000 produced in all, compared to, for example, the mere 150 Sopwith Triplanes that entered service. The S.E.5a was developed from the S.E.5, designed to make maximum use of a new Hispano-Suiza engine that appeared in 1915. The unarmed prototype, made almost entirely of wood with a fabric covering, first flew in November 1916. Two versions of the engine (150hp and 200hp) were proposed for the aircraft and although early examples had the 150hp powerplant, the 200hp version soon became the standard engine.

The S.E.5 first entered service with the Royal Flying Corps' No.56 Squadron, but its operational use in France was delayed until April 1917 as a factory-fitted wrap-around windscreen was found to obscure the pilot's forward vision and had to be removed from all machines. About 60 of the 150hp S.E.5s were built but they were gradually replaced on the production line and in the squadrons by the 200hp-engined S.E.5a. Other improvements incorporated in the S.E.5a were shorter wings resulting from the rear spar being shortened for greater strength and a headrest and fairing behind the cockpit to improve pilot comfort and streamlining.

ABOVE: **The widely produced S.E.5a was a true classic fighter.** BELOW: **The air element of the American Expeditionary Force used the S.E.5a with great success.**

The S.E.5a reached front-line squadrons in France in 1917 and was soon found to be capable of outfighting most enemy aircraft. But by December that year, only five RFC squadrons were equipped with the S.E.5a, production delays being caused by the continued slow delivery of engines – literally hundreds of aircraft sat engineless. But when the S.E.5a finally reached the front line in quantity, the very capable fighter served extensively over the Western Front with British, Australian and American pilots of the US American Expeditionary Force. They were also deployed in Macedonia and on home defence duties in the UK. The S.E.5a, together with the Sopwith Camel which appeared a few months later, basically regained and maintained Allied air superiority until the end of the war.

The S.E.5a became the favoured mount of some of World War I's most successful Allied fighter pilots, including British flying ace Albert Ball, who initially described the S.E.5 as a "bloody awful machine". Other S.E.5 aces included Longton, Clayson, Shields, Maxwell, Mannock and McCudden.

LEFT: **Some of the Allies' highest scoring pilots owed their success to the performance of the S.E.5a.**
BELOW: **Victoria Cross recipient Captain Albert Ball pictured in the cockpit of a No.56 Squadron S.E.5a.**

By the time the war ended, 22 RFC and US Air Service units were flying the S.E.5a. Over 5000 had been built in just under 18 months by five companies – Austin, Bleriot & SPAD, Martinsyde, Vickers and Wolseley.

After World War I, hundreds of these fighters were passed on to air forces throughout the British Empire. The American Expeditionary Force had bought 38 S.E.5as in Britain during the war and the design was selected for US production. Wartime plans to licence-build 1000 examples of the S.E.5a in the USA for the US Air Service were scrapped after the Armistice. Only one Curtiss S.E.5a was completed in the USA but 56 more were completed in the 1922–3 period from components shipped from Britain. These were later converted for use as advanced trainers in the USA.

After the end of World War I the fighter was dropped from military inventories and hundreds were sold on to civilian operators. In 1921, one example went to Japan with the British aviation mission and is considered to have greatly influenced later single-seat fighter design in Japan. S.E.5as were also widely used to pioneer the advertising phenomenon of skywriting, spelling out company names in the air using trails of smoke.

LEFT: **Members of No.1 Squadron RAF and their S.E.5as pictured on July 3, 1918.**

ABOVE: **As well as their use on the Western Front, S.E.5as were also used defending Britain on home defence duties.**

Royal Aircraft Factory S.E.5a

First flight: November 22, 1916 (S.E.5)
Power: Wolseley 200hp Viper V-8 water-cooled engine
Armament: One synchronized 7.7mm/0.303in machine-gun, mounted off-centre on top of engine, plus another on a flexible mount in front of cockpit. Four 11.3kg/25lb bombs could be carried under the fuselage
Size: Wingspan – 8.12m/26ft 7.5in
Length – 6.38m/20ft 11in   Height – 2.9m/9ft 6in
Wing area – 22.67m²/44sq ft
Weights: Empty – 649kg/1430lb
Maximum take-off – 880kg/1940lb
Performance: Maximum speed – 222kph/138mph
Ceiling – 5180m/17,000ft
Range – 2.5 hours endurance
Climb – 3050m/10,000ft in 13.25 minutes

Royal Aircraft Factory F.E. series

The Royal Aircraft Factory first started building the F.E.2 (F.E. stood for Fighter Experimental) in 1913. The F.E.2 was what was known as a pusher aircraft, that is the propeller was used to push from behind rather than pull from the front as in tractor aircraft.

The pusher arrangement was born, in the days before the invention of interrupter gear, of the need for a forward-firing gun

and the removal of the propeller, which tended to get in the way of the bullets. With no propeller in the way, the front seat was given to the gunner/observer while the pilot occupied the rear seat. Disadvantages of the pusher arrangement included the danger of anything flying out of the aircraft hitting the propeller, sometimes damaging or destroying it. Although the engine could protect the pilot if attacked from behind, in the event of a nose-down crash the engine and associated fuel tended to land on top of the two-man crew.

Early Fees, as they were known, had a 100hp engine which was soon replaced in the F.E.2b by a 120hp Beardmore engine. This was itself later supplanted by 160hp Beardmores which improved the aircraft's top speed and performance. The ultimate development of the Fee was the F.E.2d powered by a 250hp Rolls-Royce engine.

In combat the F.E.2b, along with the Airco D.H.2, kept the Fokkers at bay and it was an F.E.2b that shot down the German ace Max Immelmann in June 1916. This version was however soon outclassed by the latest German Albatros and Halberstadt fighting scouts

Royal Aircraft Factory F.E.2b

First flight: August 1913 (F.E.)
Power: Beardmore 120hp in-line piston engine
Armament: Up to two 7.7mm/0.303in machine-guns
Size: Wingspan – 14.55m/47ft 9in
　　　Length – 9.83m/32ft 3in
　　　Height – 3.85m/12ft 7.5in
　　　Wing area – 45.89m²/494sq ft
Weights: Empty – 904kg/1993lb
　　　Maximum take-off – 1347kg/2970lb
Performance: Maximum speed – 129kph/80mph
　　　Ceiling – 2745m/9000ft
　　　Range – 3 hours endurance
　　　Climb – 3050m/10,000ft in 51 minutes, 45 seconds

so the F.E.2d was brought to the Front in 1916. F.E.2bs did however serve until the end of the war on UK home defence against Zeppelins and Gotha bombers.

ABOVE: **This F.E.2b, serial A5666, is shown minus the usual nosewheel installation.** LEFT: **A rare air-to-air shot of a "Fee" in its element.**

BELOW: **An F.E.2d of No.20 Squadron, Royal Flying Corps, pictured in 1916.**

The single-seat F.E.8 pusher biplane was developed again because of the lack of an effective British interrupter gear and entered service on the Western Front in August 1916. Although lighter and more manoeuvrable than the F.E.2, the F.E.8 was no better a fighter as the pilot had to deal with the machine-gun (which was prone to stoppages) while still flying the aircraft and looking for the enemy. Nine F.E.8s were effectively destroyed in a single engagement with a formation led by Baron von Richthofen and by mid-1917 all F.E.8s were withdrawn from front-line use.

Royal Aircraft Factory F.E.8

First flight: October 15, 1915
Power: Gnome Monosoupape 100hp rotary
　　　piston engine
Armament: One 7.7mm/0.303in machine-guns
Size: Wingspan – 9.6m/31ft 6in
　　　Length – 7.21m/23ft 8in
　　　Height – 2.79m/9ft 2in
　　　Wing area – 20.25m²/218sq ft
Weights: Empty – 406kg/895lb
　　　Maximum take-off – 610kg/1345lb
Performance: Maximum speed – 151kph/94mph
　　　Ceiling – 4420m/14,500ft
　　　Range – 2 hours, 30 minutes endurance
　　　Climb – 1830m/6000ft in 9 minutes, 28 seconds

Siemens-Schuckert D-series fighters

Throughout the history of aviation, good designs have both inspired competitors and been copied by enemies. The Siemens-Schuckert D-series of fighters began in 1916 with the D I that was an improved copy of the Nieuport XI. The arrival of the French fighter was a severe problem for Germany and, as no better aircraft was in the German design pipeline, they decided to copy it instead. Three German companies were ordered to produce improved copies of the Nieuport, and Siemens-Schuckert did the best job. Powered by a 110hp rotary engine and armed with one synchronized 7.9mm/0.31in machine-gun, the D I was otherwise identical to the French aircraft. During early tests in October 1916, the aircraft made an impressive climb to 5000m/16,405ft in 45 minutes. Although 150 aircraft were ordered, engine production problems delayed their delivery and by mid-1917 only 95 had been completed. By then other aircraft with better performance were available and so, when the D I finally made it to the Western Front, it was used mainly for training.

The Siemens-Schuckert D III with its circular section fuselage was built around the new 160hp Siemens-Halske Sh III rotary engine. The D III was derived from D II prototypes that first flew in June 1917. Just like the D I, engine development had delayed the D II programme and unreliability was initially a problem on the D III. However, when the engine's teething problems were resolved, the D III proved to have great potential as an interceptor due its good rate of climb. Unfortunately its level speed was not high enough for it to be a viable modern fighter, so the type was used to trial aerodynamic refinements which led to the D IV fighter version. The D IV had the same impressive climb as

ABOVE: **With its origins in a Nieuport XI copy, the D-series evolved into some worthwhile fighter types.**
LEFT: **A number of D-Series replicas fly in the USA.**

the D III and all-round performance was improved. The first of around 60 D IVs to see service reached front-line units in August 1918 but it was a case of too little too late to make a difference. Strangely, production of the D IV was allowed to continue after the Armistice until mid-1919.

Siemens-Schuckert D III

First flight: October 1917

Power: Siemens-Halske 160hp Sh III rotary piston engine

Armament: Two fixed forward-firing 7.92mm/0.31in machine-guns

Size: Wingspan – 8.43m/27ft 7.75in
Length – 5.7m/18ft 8.5in
Height – 2.8m/9ft 2.25in
Wing area – 18.9m²/203.44sq ft

Weights: Empty – 534kg/1177lb
Maximum take-off – 725kg/1598lb

Performance: Maximum speed – 180kph/112mph
Ceiling – 8000m/26,245ft
Range – 2 hours endurance
Climb – 5000m/16,400ft in 13 minutes

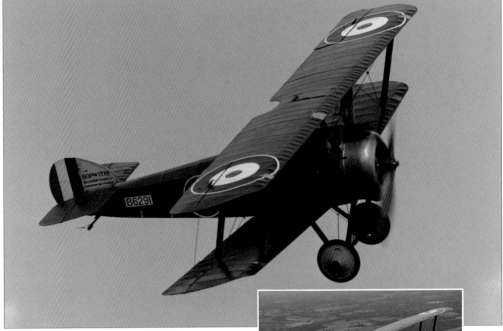

Sopwith Camel

The Camel, arguably the best-known aircraft of the World War I period, is now credited with the destruction of around 3000 enemy aircraft, making it by far the most effective fighter of the War. It evolved from the Sopwith Pup (which it replaced in service) and Triplane but was much more of a handful than its Sopwith stablemates. It was extremely sensitive on the controls and its forward-placed centre of gravity (due to the concentration of the engine, armament, pilot and fuel in the front 2.17m/7ft of the fuselage) made it very easy to turn. It earned a reputation for weeding out the less able student pilots in the most final of ways but in skilled hands the Camel was an excellent fighter and virtually unbeatable. Like the Pup, the Sopwith Biplane F.1 became better known by its nickname, in this case the Camel, and the official designation is largely forgotten.

The prototype, powered by a 110hp Clerget 9Z engine, first flew at Brooklands in February 1917 and was followed by the F.1/3 pre-production model. First deliveries were to the RNAS No.4 (Naval) Squadron at Dunkirk, who received their new fighter in June 1917. The first Camel air victory occurred on June 4, when Flight Commander A.M. Shook sent a German aircraft down into the sea – on the next day Shook attacked 15 enemy aircraft and probably destroyed two of them. The RFC's first Camel victory was achieved by Captain C. Collett on June 27.

TOP AND ABOVE: **Though replicas, these two aircraft salute World War I's most effective fighter aircraft, the Sopwith Camel.**

One manoeuvre unique to the Camel was an incredibly quick starboard turn, assisted by the torque of the big rotary engine. So fast was the right turn that pilots were able to use it to great advantage in combat, sometimes choosing to make three-quarter right turns in place of the slower quarter turn to the left. It was risky, however, as during the sharp right turns, the nose tried to go violently downwards and a left turn brought a tendency to climb, all due to the torque of the engine. Camels were built equipped with a variety of engines, including the Clerget 9B, Bentley BR1, Gnome Monosoupape and Le Rhône 9J.

In the Battle of Cambrai in March 1918, Captain J.L. Trollope of No.43 Squadron used his Camel to shoot down six enemy aircraft in one day, March 24. Later that year Camels were in the thick of what many historians believe to be the greatest dogfight of World War I. On the morning of November 4, 1918 Camels of Nos.65 and 204 Squadrons attacked 40 Fokker D. VIIs. The pilots of No.65 claimed eight

LEFT: **One of the very early Sopwith-built Camel F.1s, serial N6332.** ABOVE: **Major William Barker V.C., D.S.O., M.C., at one time commander of No.28 Squadron, with his personal Camel.**

RIGHT: **Credited with the destruction of around 3000 aircraft – the Camel. Note the Sopwith branding and address on the tail of this Camel.** BELOW: **A portrait of Major William Barker's Camel. Barker scored the first "kill" on the Italian Front, flying in the famous Sopwith fighter.**

destroyed, six out of control and one driven down while the pilots of 204 claimed two destroyed and five out of control. Perhaps the most famous single Camel victory is, however, that of Canadian Camel pilot Roy Brown, who was credited with the death of Manfred von Richthofen, the "Red Baron", on April 21, 1918.

Camels were also operated against the Austro-Hungarians on the Italian Front, and Major William Barker scored the first British victory in that theatre while flying a Camel on November 29, 1917.

By the end of 1917 over 1000 Camels were delivered and work began on sub-variants. Camels that went to sea on the early aircraft carriers had a removable tail for easy stowage. Those specially designed for shipboard use were designated 2F.1 Camel and were the last type of Camel built. Many stayed in use after the war. A ground-attack version with downward-firing Lewis guns was developed – called the TF.1 (trench fighter), it did not go into production.

Nightfighter Camels on home defence duties in the UK were powered by the Le Rhône engine and were armed with two

Lewis guns above the upper wing, in place of the usual twin-Vickers that fired through the propeller arc. They were widely used against the German Gotha bombers. As part of experiments to provide British airships with their own fighter defence, Camels were experimentally launched from a cradle beneath airship R.23.

In addition to the RFC, RNAS and RAF, Camels were also operated by Belgium, Canada, Greece and the air element of the American Expeditionary Force. The Slavo-British Aviation Group also operated Camels in Russia in 1918. Total Camel production was around 5500.

Sopwith F.1 Camel

First flight: February 26, 1917
Power: Clerget 130hp 9-cylinder air-cooled rotary piston engine
Armament: Two 7.7mm/0.303in synchronized Vickers machine-guns on nose, plus four 11.35kg/25lb bombs carried below fuselage
Size: Wingspan – 8.53m/28ft
Length – 5.72m/18ft 9in
Height – 2.6m/8ft 6in
Wing area – 21.46m²/231sq ft
Weights: Empty – 421kg/929lb
Maximum take-off – 659kg/1453lb
Performance: Maximum speed – 188kph/117mph
Ceiling – 5790m/19,000ft
Range – 2 hours, 30 minutes endurance
Climb – 3050m/10,000ft in 10 minutes, 35 seconds

Sopwith 5F.1 Dolphin

First flight: May 22, 1917
Power: Hispano-Suiza 200hp piston engine
Armament: Two forward-firing synchronized
    7.7mm/0.303in machine-guns plus one or two
    machine-guns mounted in front of the cockpit,
    fixed to fire obliquely forward
Size: Wingspan – 9.91m/32ft 6in
    Length – 6.78m/22ft 3in Height – 2.59m/8ft 6in
    Wing area – 24.46m²/263sq ft
Weights: Empty – 671kg/1480lb
    Maximum take-off – 911kg/2008lb
Performance: Maximum speed – 180kph/112mph
    Ceiling – 6095m/20,000ft
    Range – 315km/195 miles
    Climb – 260m/855ft per minute

Sopwith Dolphin

By the time the Dolphin first flew in May 1917, Sopwith had produced an impressive line of fighting aircraft, each benefiting from the experiences gained producing earlier models. With the Dolphin, prime design considerations were armament and pilot view from the cockpit. The pilot's all-round view was indeed excellent as his head poked through a gap in the centre section of the top wing which was mounted very close to the deep section fuselage.

The Dolphin Mk I entered service in 1917 and of the 1532 Dolphins produced a small number were also Mk II and Mk IIIs powered by different engines.

Dolphins were apparently not very popular with some pilots – their protruding head was vulnerable in nose-over landing incidents and the unusual back-staggered wing created odd stalling characteristics. Pilots' concerns for their safety led to the addition of a crash pylon above the top wing centre section, to prevent the aircraft slamming on to the top wing. Some pilots ran up impressive tallies of victories in Dolphins, including a Captain Gillett of No.79 Squadron who destroyed 14 enemy aircraft and three balloons.

Sopwith Pup

First flight: February 1916
Power: Le Rhône 80hp rotary engine
Armament: One forward-firing synchronized Vickers
    7.7mm/0.303 machine-gun, plus up to four
    11.3kg/25lb bombs on external racks
Size: Wingspan – 8.08m/26ft 6in
    Length – 6.04m/19ft 3.75in Height – 2.87m/9ft 5in
    Wing area – 23.6m²/254sq ft
Weights: Empty – 357kg/787 lb
    Maximum take-off – 556kg/1225 lb
Performance: Maximum speed – 180kph/112mph
    Ceiling – 5335m/17,500ft
    Range – 3 hours endurance
    Climb – 4911m/16,100ft in 35 minutes

Sopwith Pup

The Pup was the Allies' best answer to the Fokker Scourge and from late 1916 helped them turn the tide on the Western Front. Originally known as the Admiralty Type 9901, it retained the interplane struts (between the upper and lower wing) used on the Sopwith 1½-Strutter, but as its wings were 20 per cent smaller, the nickname of "Pup" was given and eventually kept as the official name. The Pup was manoeuvrable and a fine dogfighter. It entered Royal Naval Air Service (RNAS) and Royal Flying Corps service in 1916, soon earning a reputation as a formidable foe. It was responsive even at high altitude, and fully aerobatic up to 4575m/15,000ft. No.8 (Naval) Squadron accounted for 20 enemy aircraft with the Pup within little over two months in late 1916.

Production of this potent fighter exceeded 1770. Examples powered by the 100hp Gnome Monosoupape rotary engine were used for home defence in Britain, the larger engine markedly improving the Pup's performance.

RNAS Pup's were used to pioneer the use of aircraft from Royal Navy ships – one flown on August 2, 1917 became the first aircraft to land on a ship underway.

Sopwith Snipe

The Sopwith Snipe was the last significant aircraft produced by Thomas Sopwith during World War I. Designed and developed by Herbert Smith in late 1917, the Snipe was an improved version of the Sopwith Camel with a new engine, the 230hp Bentley rotary, which enabled it to fly faster and higher than its predecessor.

The Snipe was, by 1918, considered to be the best Allied fighter plane on the Western Front and was praised by pilots for its speed, strength and agility. The view from the cockpit was much better than that of the Camel which was particularly important on nightflying. Almost 500 Snipes were built in 1918 and eventually 1567 were delivered to the Royal Air Force.

The Snipe introduced a number of innovations including electric cockpit heating and pilot oxygen. Although the Snipe reached the front line only eight weeks before the end of the war, its few encounters with the enemy showed its clear superiority. On October 27, 1918 Major William Barker, in a Snipe of No.201 Squadron RAF, came upon no fewer than 60 Fokker D. VIIs, 15 of which attacked him repeatedly. He took them all on single-handed, destroyed four and probably two others before he crash-landed his bullet-ridden Snipe weak from loss of blood from wounds sustained in his epic aerial battle against seemingly overwhelming odds. Barker was awarded the Victoria Cross for his action.

Sopwith Snipe	

First flight: September 1917
Power: Bentley 230hp B.R.2 rotary piston engine
Armament: Two forward-firing synchronized 7.7mm/0.303in machine-guns
Size: Wingspan – 9.17m/30ft 1in
Length – 6.02m/19ft 9in
Height – 2.67m/8ft 9in
Wing area – 25.08m²/270sq ft
Weights: Empty – 595kg/1312lb
Maximum take-off – 916kg/2020lb
Performance: Maximum speed – 195kph/121mph
Ceiling – 5945m/19,500ft
Range – 3 hours endurance
Climb – 460m/1500ft per minute

After the war the Snipe remained the most important fighter in the RAF, and up until 1923 it constituted Britain's only fighter defence, remaining in service until 1927.

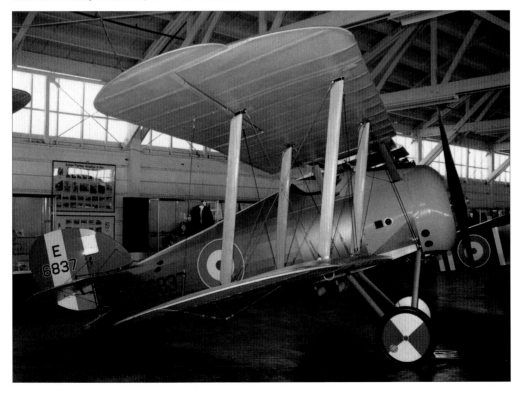

Sopwith Triplane

Following the success of the Sopwith Pup, the Sopwith Triplane was designed and built in 1916 and combined what were thought at the time to be the prime performance requirements for a fighter – high rate of climb and excellent manoeuvrability. In what was

really a daring experiment the new aircraft was built using a fuselage and tail unit similar to that of the Sopwith Pup, a more powerful engine and the all-important extra wing. Although it could not outmanoeuvre the earlier Pup, the Triplane could outclimb any other aircraft, friendly and hostile.

After its first flight in May 1916, the prototype was sent to France immediately for combat trials and became the first triplane fighter on the Western Front. Within only 15 minutes of its arrival in France, it was sent up to attack a German aircraft. Observers were amazed at the Triplane's ability to get to 3660m/12,000ft in only 13 minutes.

The enthusiastic response of its first pilots got the Sopwith rushed into production for service with the Royal Naval Air Service, who flew it with devastating effect between February and July 1917. The all-Canadian "B" Flight (nicknamed "Black Flight") of No.10 Squadron RNAS alone notched up 87 kills in Triplanes in less than 12 weeks. German pilots actively avoided flights of Triplanes. Such was the impact of the Tripehound, as the Sopwith came to be affectionately known, that the German High Command offered a substantial prize for an aircraft of equal capability. Anthony Fokker had set about designing his own triplane before a captured example

TOP: **In a climb, no contemporary fighter could match the performance of the "Tripehound".** ABOVE: **The Royal Naval Air Service was a very effective user of the Triplane.** LEFT: **The Triplane was so impressive in action that the Germans were desperate to develop their own equivalent, which resulted in the Fokker Dr.I Triplane.**

could be examined. It is hard to believe that this small fighter, of which only 140 examples were built, had the upper hand over enemy fighters for so long.

Sopwith Triplane

First flight: May 28, 1916
Power: Clerget 130hp rotary piston engine
Armament: One or two forward-firing synchronized 7.7mm/0.303in Vickers machine-guns
Size: Wingspan – 8.08m/26ft 6in
 Length – 5.74m/18ft 10in Height – 3.2m/10ft 6in
 Wing area – 21.46m^2/231sq ft
Weights: Empty – 499kg/1101lb
 Maximum take-off – 699kg/1541lb
Performance: Maximum speed – 188kph/117mph
 Ceiling – 6250m/20,500ft
 Range – 2 hours, 45 minutes
 Climb – 366m/1200ft per minute

SPAD S.XIII

First flight: April 4, 1917
Power: Hispano-Suiza 220hp 8Be piston engine
Armament: Two forward-firing synchronized
7.7mm/0.303 machine-guns
Size: Wingspan – 8.1m/26ft 6.75in
Length – 6.3m/20ft 8in
Height – 2.35m/7ft 8.5in
Wing area – 20.2m²/217.44sq ft
Weights: Empty – 601kg/1326lb
Maximum take-off – 845kg/1863lb
Performance: Maximum speed – 215kph/134mph
Ceiling – 6650m/21,815ft
Range – 2 hours endurance
Climb – 2000m/6560ft in 4 minutes, 40 seconds

SPAD S. series fighters

The SPAD (Société Pour l'Aviation et ses Dérivés) S.VII, the French company's first really successful military aircraft, took to the air for the first time in April 1916. It showed such promise that it was put into production immediately. The S.VII was an immediate success, mainly because of its sturdy construction, which permitted it to dive at high speeds without disintegrating. Two engine types were used to power the S.VII – the 150hp Hispano-Suiza 8Aa and the 180hp 8Ac.

By September 1916 it began to appear at the Front in both French and British (Royal Flying Corps and Royal Naval Air Service) fighter squadrons. The sought-after fighter was also operated by the Belgians, the Italians and the Russians. The famed Escadrille Lafayette, made up of American pilots, was operating the SPAD VII in February 1918 at the time it transferred from the French forces to the Air Service of the American Expeditionary Force (AEF) and became the 103rd Aero Squadron. More than 6,000 SPAD S.VIIs were built, of which 189 were purchased by the AEF.

The success of the S.VII inevitably led to developments of the aircraft, such as the S.XIII, designed in 1916 to counter the twin-gun German fighters. It had an increased wingspan and a more powerful engine, plus other aerodynamic refinements. The highly successful S.XIII doubled the firepower of the earlier S.VII by mounting

two 7.7mm/0.303in machine-guns. French test pilots enthused about the aircraft and the French government ordered more than 2000 – in the end almost 8500 were built. It began to enter service with French units on the Western Front late in May 1917, replacing S.VIIs and Nieuports, and became the mount of the French aces Nungesser, Fonck and Guynemer.

The Royal Flying Corps operated the S.XIII as did the air forces of Italy and Belgium. The US Air Service also began operating the S.XIII in March 1918, and by the end of the war in November 1918 it had acquired 893. Throughout 1917 and into 1918 the S.XIII held its own against German aircraft, but during the summer of 1918 it was outclassed by the new Fokker D. VII. Nevertheless, at the war's end,

TOP LEFT: **The French "Cicognes" Group de Chasse 12 were famed for the flying stork insignia carried on their aircraft.** ABOVE: **The SPAD S.XIII, a replica in this example, was a great fighter aircraft.**

BELOW: **Another distinctive scheme, the famous "hat in the hoop" insignia on this replica SPAD S. XIII was sported by aircraft of the 94th Squadron, US Air Service. This aircraft is painted as the personal aircraft of American ace Eddie Rickenbacker.**

outstanding orders for more than 10,000 examples were cancelled, such had been the demand for this excellent fighter aircraft.

Supermarine Spitfire

The Spitfire is perhaps the most famous combat aircraft of all time, and some would say the most beautiful. Spitfires first entered Royal Air Force service at RAF Duxford in August 1938 and it was on October 16, 1939 that a Spitfire of No.603 Squadron claimed the first German aircraft, a Heinkel He111, to be destroyed over Britain in World War II.

The Spitfire Mk I is the model inevitably associated with Britain's Finest Hour, but by the time the Mark Is were battling to keep the Germans from invading Britain, the Spitfire had undergone a series of modifications that made it quite different to the aircraft that first entered RAF service in 1938. At the start of the Battle of Britain, Fighter Command could field a total of 19 Spitfire squadrons. Although some Mk IIs reached squadron service during the battle, it is the Mk I Spitfire that will forever be considered the Spitfire that won the Battle of Britain. During 1941 the Spitfire Mk I was relegated from the front line but its work was done – the Spitfire had earned a special place in the nation's heart and it had already become a legend.

The Spitfire Mk V began to reach RAF squadrons in February 1941 and swiftly became Fighter Command's primary weapon. Six thousand Mk Vs entered service between 1941 and 1943 and the type equipped more than 140 RAF squadrons, as well as nine overseas air forces, including the USAAF in Europe. Throughout 1941 the Mk V took part in fighter sweeps over occupied Europe, its range boosted by drop tanks. In 1942

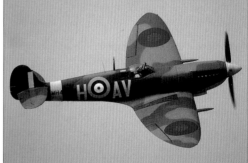

TOP: **R.J. Mitchell's classic design, the Supermarine Spitfire, is surely the most famous of all fighters and has earned itself a special place in history, not just for what it achieved but also for what it represented.** ABOVE: **This Mk IX, MH434, is operated in the UK by the Old Flying Machine Company and has delighted crowds at air shows for decades.**

Mk Vs were used in support of the Dieppe landings, fought in the North African campaign, defended Malta, took part in Operation Torch and were supplied to the USSR. In 1943 they even moved as far afield as Australia to defend against attack by Japanese aircraft.

When the Spitfire Mk IX was introduced in June 1942, it offered the RAF a much-needed counter to the deadly Focke-Wulf 190. With its armament of two 20mm/0.788in cannon, four .303 machine-guns and up to 2540kg/1000lb of bombs or rockets, the Spitfire Mk IX was indeed a potent fighting machine.

ABOVE: **The first of many – these early No.19** Squadron machines are shown with two blade propellers and unusual pre-war squadron numbers painted on the tails. BELOW: **MB882,** a late production Mk XII, in classic pose. Note the clipped wings, changing the distinctive "Spit" wing shape for better handling at low altitude.

ABOVE: **This Mk V, preserved in the UK by the Shuttleworth Collection, was operated by No.310 (Czechoslovakian) Squadron during World War II and is seen in its wartime scheme.**
LEFT: **An excellent wartime photograph of a Spitfire preparing to depart for another sortie.**

The Mk IX went on to equip around 100 RAF and Commonwealth fighter squadrons and later had the distinction of destroying several Me262 jets.

Designed to operate at high altitude, the Spitfire Mk XIV entered RAF service in January 1944 with 610 (City of Chester) Squadron. With a top speed of almost 724kph/450mph, it was capable of catching and destroying the V-1 flying bombs that were then menacing Britain. By the end of the war, the Mk XIV had accounted for more than 300 "doodlebugs". Compared to the early Merlin-engined Spitfire, the Mk XIV with its new fin

and larger rudder was almost 1m/3ft longer and weighed up to 1224kg/2700lb more. In October 1944 a Mk XIV claimed a Messerschmitt Me262 jet fighter, the first to be shot down by an Allied aircraft, and in December of that year RAF Spitfire Mk XIVs carried out the heaviest fighter-bomber attack of World War II on V-2 rocket sites. A total of 957 Spitfire Mk XIVs were built, and the later Mk XVIII was directly developed from this powerful fighting machine.

Post-war, the Spitfire was widely used by many air forces but the last operational sortie of an RAF Spitfire was by a PR.19 of No.81 Squadron in Malaya on April 1, 1954. In all, over 20,000 Spitfires and Seafires (the naval version) were built by the time production ceased in 1949.

Supermarine Spitfire Mk Va

First flight: March 5, 1936
Power: Rolls-Royce 1478hp Merlin 45 liquid cooled V-12 engine
Armament: Eight 7.7mm/0.303in machine-guns
Size: Wingspan – 11.23m/36ft 10in
Length – 9.12m/29ft 11in
Height – 3.02m/9ft 11in
Wing area – 22.48m²/242sq ft
Weights: Empty – 2267kg/4998lb
Maximum take-off – 2911kg/6417lb
Performance: Maximum speed – 594kph/369mph
Ceiling – 11,125m/36,500ft
Range – 1827km/1135 miles
Climb – 6100m/20,000ft in 7 minutes, 30 seconds

149

Vickers F.B.5

The Vickers F.B.5, nicknamed "Gun Bus", was directly developed from one of the world's first combat aircraft, the Vickers Destroyer, and was designed to meet a late 1912 British Admiralty specification for a machine-gun armed fighting aeroplane. It was the first British aircraft to mount a machine-gun. The two-seat F.B.5 was, like the F.E.2, a pusher aircraft, that is the propeller was used to push from behind rather than pull from the front. With no propeller in the way, the front seat was given to the gunner/observer while the pilot occupied the rear seat.

Although the first of these planes arrived on the Western Front in February 1915 it was not until July 25, 1915 that No.11 Squadron, Royal Flying Corps, arrived in France. No.11 was the world's first squadron formed for fighting duties and it was equipped throughout with one aircraft type – the Vickers F.B.5.

This slow but strong machine fought well but F.B.5 crews were wise to keep

ABOVE: **The relatively slow F.B.5 could be vulnerable. This No.18 Squadron RFC "Gun Bus" was shot down on December 29, 1915 by anti-aircraft fire.**

BELOW: **An F.B.5 replica pictured at the Royal Air Force Museum in Britain.**

away from the faster and better-armed Fokker E. Combat reports of the time regularly state that enemy aircraft simply got away due to their better speed.

After a few months of combat the F.B.5 was withdrawn from front-line duties and was used for training purposes back in Britain.

Vickers F.B.5

First flight: October 1914 (production F.B.5)
Power: Gnome Monosoupape 100hp rotary engine
Armament: One 7.7mm/0.303in machine-gun aimed from front cockpit
Size: Wingspan – 11.13m/36ft 6in
Length – 8.2m/27ft 2in Height – 3.51m/11ft 6in
Wing area – 35.5m^2/382sq ft
Weights: Empty – 553kg/1220lb
Maximum take-off – 930kg/2050lb
Performance: Maximum speed – 113kph/70mph
Ceiling – 2745m/9000ft
Range – 386km/240 miles
Climb – 122m/400ft per minute

Westland Whirlwind

The Whirlwind was the Royal Air Force's first single-seat twin-engine fighter and was designed to provide the RAF with a high-performance long-range escort-nightfighter. It was ahead of its time in many ways – the engine radiators were housed in the leading edges of the slim wings, pilot visibility was excellent thanks to the clear bubble hood and the armament housed in the nose was devastating. The Whirlwinds' shape was dominated by the two large engine nacelles, and entry into service was delayed by development troubles with the Peregrine engines they contained.

Whirlwinds first entered front-line Royal Air Force service with No.263 Squadron in December 1940 and it was used on offensive sweeps from June 1941. The aircraft proved to be unpopular with Fighter Command chiefs because it was underpowered and its Peregrine engines, the only ones used in the RAF, had constant servicing problems. Operational flexibility was further limited by the Whirlwind's high landing speed of 129kph/80mph, which required it to operate from long runways.

TOP: **Ahead of its time, the Whirlwind was only operated by two Royal Air Force units.** ABOVE: **Note the hard-hitting armament of four cannon in the nose of this aircraft being prepared for a cross-channel fighter-bomber mission.** RIGHT: **Only 112 Whirlwinds were produced for the RAF.**

Nevertheless, the Whirlwinds of No.263 escorted RAF bombers on daylight raids, the most famous being the Blenheim raid on Cologne in August 1941.

The second Whirlwind unit, No.137 Squadron, used Whirlwinds modified as fighter-bombers (Mark IAs) on low-level cross-Channel missions. By December 1943, both squadrons were re-equipped with other types, and in June 1944 the Whirlwind was declared obsolete.

Westland Whirlwind I

First flight: October 11, 1938

Power: Two Rolls-Royce 885hp Peregrine liquid-cooled piston engines

Armament: Four 20mm/0.78in cannon in nose

Size: Wingspan – 13.72m/45ft Length – 9.98m/32ft 9in
Height – 3.52m/11ft 7in
Wing area – 23.23m²/250sq ft

Weights: Empty – 3556kg/7840lb
Maximum take-off – 4658kg/10,270lb

Performance: Maximum speed – 580kph/360mph
Ceiling – 9144m/30,000ft
Range – Approx. 1290km/800 miles
Climb – 915m/3000ft per minute

Vought F4U Corsair

The Corsair was undoubtedly one of the greatest ever fighters. Designers Igor Sikorsky and Rex Beisel employed the largest propeller and most powerful engine ever fitted to a fighter aircraft, the latter a 2000hp Pratt and Whitney R-2800 Double Wasp. It was no surprise when, in 1940, the prototype Corsair exceeded 640kph/400mph, the first American combat aircraft to do so. It was equipped with a variety of armament over its long career but the Corsair was originally designed to carry two wing and two fuselage guns. Six 12.7mm/0.5in Browning machine-guns became standard, carried in the outer section of the foldable wings. Cannon and rockets were later added to the weapon options.

Ironically, as one of the fastest and most powerful fighters of World War II, the Corsair was originally rejected by the US Navy, who considered it unsuitable for carrier operations. Poor cockpit visibility and a tendency to bounce on landing meant that when, in February 1943 over Guadalcanal, the US Marines got the first chance to use the formidable fighter in action, it was as a land-based rather than carrier-based aircraft. It swiftly established itself as an excellent combat aircraft and the first Allied fighter able to take on the Japanese Zero on equal terms. The Corps was so impressed by the Corsair that all Marine squadrons re-equipped with the type within six months of its début. Marine Corsair pilot Major Gregory "Pappy" Boyington became the Corps' highest scoring pilot, ending the war with a total of 28 victories.

TOP: **The distinctive gull-wing of the Corsair is evident in this photograph of a preserved example.** ABOVE: **Initial US Navy reservations led to the type being considered unsuitable for operation from US carriers.**

By the end of the year the mighty bent-wing fighter, operating purely from land, had accounted for over 500 Japanese aircraft. It was nicknamed "Whistling Death" by Japanese troops, who came to fear the noise made by air rushing through the diving Corsair's cooler vents heralding a deadly attack. By the end of World War II, the Corsair's total tally had increased to 2140 enemy aircraft destroyed in air combat, with over 64,000 air combat and ground attack missions recorded.

The Corsair's first use as a carrier fighter was with Britain's Fleet Air Arm, who had each of the aircraft's distinctive gull-wings clipped by around 20cm/8in to allow its stowage in the below-deck hangars on Royal Navy carriers. This début, in April 1944, was an attack on the German battleship *Tirpitz*. The Corsair became the principal aircraft of the FAA in the Pacific and almost 2000 were supplied to the Royal Navy and the Royal New Zealand Air Force.

"In dogfights the Corsair could out-turn most contemporary aircraft and in a dive, she could out-run anything," said Keith Quilter, FAA Corsair pilot.

The Corsair's outstanding performance led to extensive post-war use, notably in Korea, where they flew 80 per cent of all US Navy and Marine close-support missions in the conflict's first year, 1950. Nightfighter versions were particularly successful during the conflict, and during daytime combats the Corsairs even engaged and destroyed MiG-15s.

When production ceased in 1952, over 12,500 had been built, giving the Corsair one of the longest US fighter production runs in history. The late F2G version was powered by the 3000hp Pratt and Whitney R-4350 Wasp Major engine, which was 50 per cent more powerful than the Corsair's original powerplant.

The Corsair continued to serve in the front line for a number of years, and French naval pilots operated Corsairs from land bases during the anti-guerrilla war against the Viet Minh in Indochina from 1952 to 1954.

The Corsair was built in a number of versions, from the F4U-1 to the F4U-7. The designation differed when aircraft were produced by other manufacturers – Brewster (F3A) and Goodyear (FG, F2G).

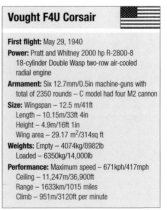

TOP: **The Corsair's designers utilized the most powerful engine available.** LEFT: **Fleet Air Arm Corsairs first went into action in April 1944.**

BELOW: **The space-saving effect of wing folding and the location of the six wing-mounted guns can be seen in this photograph.**

ABOVE: **Royal Navy versions of the Vought fighter had to be slightly clipped for Fleet Air Arm carrier use.**

Vought F4U Corsair

First flight: May 29, 1940
Power: Pratt and Whitney 2000 hp R-2800-8 18-cylinder Double Wasp two-row air-cooled radial engine
Armament: Six 12.7mm/0.5in machine-guns with total of 2350 rounds – C model had four M2 cannon
Size: Wingspan – 12.5 m/41ft
  Length – 10.15m/33ft 4in
  Height – 4.9m/16ft 1in
  Wing area – 29.17 m^2/314sq ft
Weights: Empty – 4074kg/8982lb
  Loaded – 6350kg/14,000lb
Performance: Maximum speed – 671kph/417mph
  Ceiling – 11,247m/36,900ft
  Range – 1633km/1015 miles
  Climb – 951m/3120ft per minute

Yakovlev wartime fighters

The Ya-26 fighter, made mostly of wood, was first flown in March 1939, having been designed to meet a Soviet requirement for a standard Soviet fighter. When it entered production it was as the I-26 but it was then redesignated the Yak-1. Production had barely begun when Germany invaded in June 1941. Designed to be as simple to manufacture as possible, the Yak was surprisingly agile and fast for its time. The Yak-1 had considerably closed the fighter gap that existed at the beginning of Russo-German hostilities and was able to hold its own to some degree with the Bf109. Total production was 8721.

Development was ongoing and the Yak-3 was a further development of a Yak-1 variant now referred to as the Yak-1M. First flown in late 1943, the Yak-3 proved to be an extremely capable dogfighter with outstanding manoeuvrability and a very high rate of climb. When it reached operational units in July 1944, the Luftwaffe knew it had met its match. On July 14, 1944 a force of 18 Yak-3s met 30 German fighters and destroyed 15 Luftwaffe aircraft for the loss of only one of their own. As the more powerful 1700hp VK-107 engine became available, Yakovlev installed a small number into existing airframes and the Yak-3 achieved ultimate capability with a top speed of 720kph/447mph.

TOP, ABOVE RIGHT AND ABOVE: **The Yak-3 was an excellent fighter aircraft that could give a very good account of itself against any enemy aircraft of the time. Since the end of the Cold War, more Yak-3s have been rebuilt to fly for customers in the West.**

Yakovlev Yak-3

First flight: Late 1943
Power: Klimov 1300hp VK-105PF-2 piston engine
Armament: One 20mm/0.78in cannon firing through the propeller hub, plus two synchronized 12.7mm/0.5in machine-guns
Size: Wingspan – 9.2m/30ft 2.25in
Length – 8.49m/27ft 10.25in
Height – 2.42m/7ft 11.25in
Wing area – 14.83m^2/159.63sq ft
Weights: Empty – 2105kg/4641lb
Maximum take-off – 2660kg/5864lb
Performance: Maximum speed – 655kph/407mph
Ceiling – 10,700m/35,105ft
Range – 900km/559 miles
Climb – 1300m/4265ft per minute

ABOVE: **Yak-7Bs of the Red Air Force. The B model was built in great numbers, with a total of around 5000 reaching front-line units.** RIGHT: **A Yak-3 of an unknown Soviet fighter regiment.** BELOW RIGHT: **Before it took delivery of Yak-9s, the Free French Normandie-Niemen Group were equipped with Yak-3s.**

The Yak-7 was designed as a dual control fighter trainer and displayed such excellent flying qualities (better than the Yak-1 fighter) that a single-seat fighter version was ordered into production and over 5000 were built in all.

The Yak-9 was designed in parallel with the Yak-3 and was a development of an experimental Yak-7. Production of the Yak-9 began in October 1942 and differed from the earlier Yak by having light metal alloy spars in the wings.

The type became a significant factor in the air battles over Stalingrad where it met and outclassed the Messerschmitt Bf109G. The Free French Normandie-Niemen Group that flew with the Soviet Air Force and Free Polish squadrons were both equipped with the Yak-9. By mid-1943, the aircraft was incorporating more and more aluminium to save weight and increase strength. Fitted with increasingly more powerful versions of the VK-105 engine, the various variants include the standard Yak-9M, the long-range Yak-9D. The very long-range Yak-9DD was used to escort USAAF bombers and some even flew from the Ukraine to southern Italy to aid partisans.

The final major variant of the Yak-9 was the all-metal Yak-9U, first flown in December 1943, that entered service in the latter half of 1944. At first the Yak-9U was fitted with the VK-105PF-2 engine but the VK-107A engine was introduced later giving a maximum speed of 698kph/434mph. Even the early -9Us were able to outfly any fighters the Germans cared to field. The Yak-9 remained in production well into 1946 and was the most numerous of all the wartime Yak fighters with 16,769 built. When the Korean War began in 1950, the post-war cannon-armed Yak-9P was the most advanced fighter in the North Korean Air Force inventory.

Total production of the wartime Yak fighter series was in excess of 37,000.

Yakovlev Yak-9U

First flight: Late 1943
Power: Klimov 1650hp VK-107A in-line piston engine
Armament: One 20mm/0.78in cannon firing through hub plus two 12.7mm/0.5in machine-guns and two 100kg/220lb bombs under wings
Size: Wingspan – 9.77m/32ft 0.75in
Length – 8.55m/28ft 0.5in
Height – 2.96m/9ft 8.5in
Wing area – 17.25m²/185.68sq ft
Weights: Empty – 2716kg/5988lb
Maximum take-off – 3098kg/6830lb
Performance: Maximum speed – 698kph/434mph
Ceiling – 11,900m/39,040ft
Range – 870km/541 miles
Climb – 1500m/4920ft per minute

155

A–Z of Modern Fighter Aircraft

1945 to the Present Day

By the end of World War II, piston-engined fighters had been developed as far as they could go. Although many remained in service for some years, jet fighters were clearly the way ahead and effectively rendered the piston fighter obsolete. After limited use towards the end of World War II, jets were within a decade regularly flying at supersonic speeds, if only in dives. Wartime German aerodynamic research and experiments revolutionized post-war fighter design, and as swept-wing fighters began to appear, supersonic flight became routine. Many of the fighters featured in the following pages were conceived in the Cold War to tackle fleets of enemy bombers carrying deadly nuclear cargoes. These sophisticated fighters were sometimes bigger than World War II bombers and weighed more than 20 times as much as World War I fighters. Some were never used in anger, possibly serving to deter their enemy from attack, while others have been used many times in conventional wars around the globe.

New ideas for fighter configurations, new materials and construction techniques, and even more complex on-board systems will shape the fighter aircraft of the future.

LEFT: **Lockheed P-80A Shooting Star, the first US jet fighter in military service.**

LEFT: **The US design influence on the Ching-kuo is clear in this photograph.**

AIDC Ching-kuo

First flight: May 28, 1989
Power: Two International Turbofan Engine Company 4269kg/9400lb afterbunning-thrust TFE1042-70 turbofans
Armament: One 20mm/0.78in cannon, plus six hardpoints for a variety of AAMs, anti-ship missiles and bombs
Size: Wingspan – 8.53m/28ft
Length – 13.26m/43ft 6in
Height – 4.65m/15ft 3in
Wing area – 24.3m²/261.1sq ft
Weights: Empty – 6485kg/14,300lb
Maximum take-off – 12,245kg/27,000lb
Performance: Maximum speed – 1295kph/804mph
Ceiling – 16,470m/54,000ft
Range – Approx. 965km/600 miles
Climb – 15,250m/50,000ft per minute

AIDC Ching-kuo

Also known as the Indigenous Defensive Fighter (IDF), the Ching-kuo (named after the late President Chiang Ching-kuo) was built in Taiwan with major technical help from US companies, notably General Dynamics. The aircraft bears more than a passing resemblance to the F-16 and is essentially a smaller version of the famous General Dynamics fighter. Development began after a 1982 arms embargo by the USA was imposed (to improve relations with China), prohibiting the import by Taiwan of US fighter aircraft. It did not however prohibit technical help, which is why the Ching-kuo is an F-20A Tigershark nose married to the body, wings and fin of an F-16.

Taiwan wanted the IDF to replace ageing F-5 and F-104 Starfighter fighters – the IDF accelerates faster than the F-104 and can turn inside an F-5.

The prototype first flew in May 1989, deliveries to the Republic of China Air Force began in January 1994 and the last of 130 examples was delivered in January 2000.

Armstrong Whitworth Meteor nightfighters

LEFT: **The NF.11 was the first Meteor nightfighter, and was built until 1954.**

Armstrong Whitworth Meteor NF.11

First flight: May 31, 1950
Power: Two Rolls-Royce 1588kg/3500lb static-thrust Derwent 8 turbojet engines
Armament: Four 20mm/0.78in cannon mounted in wings
Size: Wingspan – 13.11m/43ft
Length – 14.78m/48ft 6in Height – 4.24m/13ft 11in
Wing area – 34.75m²/374sq ft
Weights: Empty – 5451kg/12,091lb
Maximum take-off – 9088kg/20,035lb
Performance: Maximum speed – 933kph/580mph
Ceiling – 12,192m/40,000ft
Range – 1480km/920 miles
Climb – 9144m/30,000ft in 11 minutes, 12 seconds

Wartime Mosquitos were Britain's nightfighter defence from the end of the war until Meteor (and Vampire) nightfighters entered service in 1951.

The Meteor NF.11 was built as a stop-gap while delays of the all-weather Javelin dragged on. The NF.11 was basically a Meteor Mk 7 trainer with the new AI Mk 10 radar in an enlarged nose. The rear cockpit's dual-controls were replaced by navigator/radar operator equipment and displays. Cannon were moved from the nose out to the long span wing. The Meteor 8's tail completed the composite nightfighter which first flew in May 1950. Derwent 8s were the chosen powerplant and 335 NF.11s were produced up to 1954. The tropicalized version of the Mk 11 was the Mk 13, 40 of which were built – they only served with two RAF units in the Middle East and six were later sold on to Egypt.

The Mk 12 had improved American APS-21 radar and first flew in April 1953 powered by Derwent 9s – altogether 97 of these were built.

The Meteor NF.14 was the last of the line and can be identified by its clear vision two-piece canopy – the aircraft was also some 43.2cm/17in longer than previous NF marks. It was an NF.14 of No.60 Squadron in Singapore that flew the RAF's last Meteor sortie in 1961.

Armstrong Whitworth built a total of 547 Meteor nightfighters.

Armstrong Whitworth (Hawker) Sea Hawk

The Sea Hawk is remarkable for two reasons – it was the first standard jet fighter of Britain's Fleet Air Arm and it remained in front-line service long after swept-wing fighters equipped navies elsewhere. Also, the aircraft's layout was unusual in that the single jet engine jet pipe was bifurcated (split) to feed two exhaust ducts, one at each trailing-edge wing root. The leading-edge wing roots incorporated the two corresponding air intakes.

The first incarnation of the Sea Hawk was the Hawker P.1040, which flew in September 1947 and was proposed as a new fighter for both the Royal Navy and the RAF. Only the Navy placed orders for the Sea Hawk and after building just 35 production Sea Hawk fighters, Hawkers transferred production to Armstrong Whitworth, hence the

occasional confusion over the Sea Hawk manufacturer's identity. As a design the Sea Hawk certainly looked right, coming from the same team that designed the Hurricane and, later, the Hunter.

The first Royal Navy Sea Hawk squadron, No.806, formed in March 1953, carrying its distinctive ace of diamonds logo on its Sea Hawk Mk 1s. In February the following year, 806 embarked on HMS Eagle. The most widely-used Sea Hawk version was the Mk 3 fighter-bomber, capable of carrying considerable amounts of ordnance under its wings. This change in usage was due to the realization that the Sea Hawk's performance could not match that of potential enemies in air-to-air combat. That said, the Fleet Air Arm's Sea Hawks did see action in the ground-attack role during the 1956 Suez Crisis, with Sea Venoms as fighter escort. The type continued in front-line FAA service until 1960, but some continued in second-line roles until 1969.

Some ex-Royal Navy aircraft were supplied to the Royal Australian and Canadian navies but the biggest export customers were the West German naval air arm, Holland and the Indian Navy.

ABOVE: **The Sea Hawk was the Royal Navy's first standard jet fighter.** LEFT: **Fleet Air Arm Sea Hawks saw action during the Suez Crisis of 1956.**

Dutch aircraft were equipped to carry an early version of the Sidewinder air-to-air missile until their phasing-out in 1964. German Sea Hawks operated exclusively from land bases in the air defence role until the mid-1960s. The Indian Navy's Sea Hawks saw action in the war with Pakistan in 1971 and continued to be flown, remarkably, into the mid-1980s, when they were replaced by Sea Harriers.

Armstrong Whitworth (Hawker) Sea Hawk F. Mk 1

First flight: September 2, 1947 (P.1040)
Power: Rolls-Royce 2268kg/5000lb thrust Nene 101 turbojet
Armament: Four 20mm/0.78in Hispano cannon beneath cockpit floor
Size: Wingspan – 11.89m/39ft
Length – 12.08m/39ft 8in
Height – 2.79m/8ft 8in
Wing area – 25.83m²/278sq ft
Weights: Empty – 4173kg/9200lb
Maximum take-off – 7355kg/16,200lb
Performance: Maximum speed – 901kph/560mph
Ceiling – 13,176m/43,200ft
Range – 1191km/740 miles
Climb – 10,675m/35,000ft in 12 minutes, 5 seconds

Atlas/Denel Cheetah

The multi-role Cheetah was developed in response to a 1977 United Nations arms embargo against South Africa. At the time, the South Africans were hoping to import combat aircraft to replace their ageing 1960s Mirage IIIs but instead looked to develop and improve the existing airframes. State-owned Atlas already had experience of assembling imported Mirage F1 kits. Arguably the most comprehensive upgrade of the Mirage III achieved anywhere, the result was one of the world's most capable combat aircraft. Though never officially disclosed, the updates were undertaken with the assistance of IAI of Israel who had upgraded their own Mirages to Kfir standard.

Nearly 50 per cent of the airframe was replaced, canard foreplanes, new avionics and weapons systems were added, and more powerful engines were installed in two-seaters.

The first Cheetah unveiled in 1986 was the Cheetah D attack aircraft,

a two-seat upgraded version of the Mirage IIIDZ two-seater. Single-seat Cheetah fighters, declared operational in 1987, were designated EZ and kept the old Mirage SNECMA Atar 9C engine but this version led to the Cheetah C fighter, considered by many to be the ultimate Mirage upgrade. Developed in great secrecy, news of the C model only reached the outside world in the early 1995. With a powerful radar, state-of-the-art cockpit avionics and advanced self-defence systems, the Cheetah C's main armament is indigenous South African air-to-air missiles.

TOP: **The Cheetah is one of the world's most capable combat aircraft.** ABOVE: **The two-seat attack D version was developed from the Mirage IIIDZ.** BELOW: **The Cheetah is the ultimate Mirage III development.**

Atlas/Denel Cheetah EZ

First flight: Believed to be 1986
Power: SNECMA 6209kg/13,670lb thrust Atar 9C turbojet
Armament: One 30mm/1.18in cannon plus V3B Kukri, V3C Darter, Python and Shafrir air-to-air missiles as well as bombs/rockets
Size: Wingspan – 8.22m/26ft 11in
Length – 15.5m/51ft
Height – 4.5m/14ft 9in
Wing area – 34.8m²/374.6sq ft
Weights: Empty – 6608kg/14,550lb
Maximum take-off – 13,700kg/30,200lb
Performance: Maximum speed – 2338kph/1452mph
Ceiling – 17,000m/55,777ft
Range and climb data are not published but likely to be similar to Mirage IIIE, i.e. 1200km/745 miles and 7930m/26,000ft in 3 minutes

Avro Canada CF-100 Canuck

The CF-100 was the first combat aircraft of indigenous Canadian design and had its maiden flight in January 1950. This large and impressive interceptor was designed very quickly for the Royal Canadian Air Force (RCAF) to operate at night, in all weathers and with great range to protect the vast expanses of Canadian airspace.

The first true fighter version, the Mk 3, entered RCAF service in 1952, armed with eight machine-guns housed in a "belly" pack beneath the rear cockpit. The Mk 4 had a more powerful engine and was armed with wingtip pods, each containing 29 Mighty Mouse air-to-air rockets that could be fired by an on-board computer. Having steered the aircraft on a collision course with

the target using the radar housed in the nose, the computer could then fire the rockets at the optimum range. Additional rockets or guns could be carried in the belly.

In 1957 the joint Canadian/US North American Air Defense Command (NORAD) was established and the RCAF Canucks joined the USAF F-86s, F-89s and F-94s, ranged to protect North America against Soviet incursion from the north. The Canuck's short take-off run allowed it to fly from small airstrips and its good climb rate meant it could reach incoming Soviet aircraft very quickly if needed.

The ultimate CF-100, the Mk 5, had even more powerful engines and a 1.83m/6ft increase in wingspan for better high-altitude performance. Fifty-three of this final version were also supplied to Belgium, where they comprised the 1st All-Weather Interception Wing. These excellent and underrated fighters protected Canadian skies through to 1981.

ABOVE: **A Mk 4B of No.445 Squadron, Royal Canadian Air Force.** LEFT: **The underrated CF-100 was a key Cold War fighter.** BELOW: **This Mk 4 is preserved in the UK by the Imperial War Museum at Duxford.**

Avro Canada CF-100 Canuck Mk 5

First flight: January 19, 1950
Power: Two Orenda 14 3300kg/7275lb thrust turbojets
Armament: 58 Mighty Mouse 70mm/2.75in unguided air-to-air rockets, carried in two wingtip pods, 29 in each
Size: Wingspan – 17.7m/58ft
Length – 16.5m/54ft 1in
Height – 4.72m/15ft 7in
Wing area – 54.8m^2/591sq ft
Weights: Empty – 10,478kg/23,100lb
Maximum take-off – 16,783kg/37,000lb
Performance: Maximum speed – 1046kph/650mph
Ceiling – 16,460m/54,000ft
Range – 1046km/650 miles
Climb – 9144m/30,000ft in 5 minutes

BAE Systems Harrier/Sea Harrier

The Harrier is among the best examples of British innovation in the field of aircraft design. This truly remarkable aircraft, constantly improved and updated since its first hovering flight in October 1960, is still the only single-engined vertical or short take-off and landing (V/STOL) in service. It enables military planners to wield air power without the need for airfields.

During the Cold War it was obvious that the West's military airfields would have been attacked very early in any offensive. Dispersal of aircraft and equipment was one option of

response – the other was the Harrier, with its ability to operate from any small piece of flat ground. The Harrier is equally at home operating from a supermarket car park or woodland clearing as it is from conventional airfields. The fact that an aircraft can take off vertically with no need for forward movement still leaves spectators stunned over four decades after the prototype carried out its first uncertain and tethered hover.

The Harrier can take off and land vertically by the pilot selecting an 80-degree nozzle angle and applying full power. At 15–30m/50–100ft altitude, the nozzles are gradually directed

ABOVE: **Two Royal Navy Sea Harrier FRS. Mk 1s. Developed from the land-based Harrier, the naval versions of the type have been a great success.** LEFT: **Although it has an air-to-air combat facility, the Harrier GR.7 is a versatile all-weather ground-attack aircraft.**

rearwards until conventional wingborne flight is achieved. The key to the Harrier's vertical take-off lies with the vectored thrust from the aircraft's Pegasus engine, directed by four jet nozzles controlled by a selector lever next to the throttle in the cockpit. The nozzles swivel as one, directing thrust from directly to the rear to just forward of vertical. While hovering or flying at very low speeds, the aircraft is controlled in all planes of movement by reaction control jets located in the nose, wing and tail. These jets are operated by the Harrier's conventional rudder pedals and control column.

The Harrier's agility is legendary and it is able to make very tight turns by using the nozzles. In air combat the nozzles can be used to decelerate the aircraft rapidly so that an enemy aircraft, previously on the Harrier's tail, shoots by, unable to stop – it becomes the Harrier's prey instead.

The Harrier GR.1 first entered squadron service with the RAF in October 1969 and many were subsequently upgraded to GR.3 standard, with more powerful engines and a tail warning radar to alert pilots to hostile missiles locking on to their aircraft. Early in the Harrier's operational life, the US Marine Corps expressed an interest in the aircraft, leading to more than a hundred being built as the AV-8A by McDonnell Douglas in the USA. The USMC continue to operate Harriers today with the AV-8B variant, which is roughly equivalent to the GR.7 in current RAF service. The other customer for the early Harrier was the Spanish Navy, who ordered the US-built AV-8A and who subsequently sold some of the aircraft on to the Thai Navy in 1996. Manufacture of new AV-8Bs and GR.7s stopped in late 1997, when AV-8Bs were supplied to the Italian Navy. Many existing aircraft are, however, being upgraded to Harrier II Plus standard, allowing the Harrier to carry more weaponry over a greater distance. Improved radar and compatibility with the AMRAAM air-to-air missile can be part of the upgrade.

The Harrier's V/STOL capability was not lost on naval strategists and in February 1963 an early version of the Harrier landed on HMS *Ark Royal* at sea. The Royal Navy ordered a maritime version in 1975 and the Sea Harrier FRS. Mk 1 flew for the first time in August 1978. This aircraft was similar to the GR.3 but had a completely redesigned front fuselage, different avionics and was powered by a special version of the Pegasus engine (104), with improved corrosion resistance. Examples of this version were exported to the Indian Navy as FRS.51s. The Sea Harriers are true fighter aircraft, while the Harriers are close air support aircraft.

ABOVE: **Sea Harrier FA.2s pictured on the deck of Britain's HMS *Illustrious* in 1995.** LEFT: **The Harrier can provide versatile and flexible air power from small unexpected locations.**

The Sea Harrier FA.2 was a mid-life upgrade of the FRS.1, with changes to the airframe, armament, avionics, radar and cockpit. The FA.2 was the first European fighter to be equipped with the AIM-120 AMRAAM air-to-air missile. The Royal Navy's FA.2s made their combat début in August 1994 over Bosnia, operated by No.899 Squadron from the deck of HMS *Invincible*. Early versions of the Sea Harrier, however, had already been in action with the FAA 12 years earlier. In 1982 Britain's Task Force sailed south on its 12,872km/8000 mile journey to retake the Falkland Islands but it faced serious opposition from Argentine forces. Against considerable odds, the combined Harrier force of RAF and Fleet Air Arm pilots and machines flew a total of 1850 missions and destroyed 32 Argentine aircraft, 23 of them in air combat, including high-performance Daggers.

Two-seat trainer versions of all marks have been produced.

ABOVE: **Harriers are still flying more than 40 years after the prototype first took to the sky.** BELOW LEFT: **The distinctive nose of the FA.2 houses the advanced Blue Vixen radar.**

BAE Systems
Sea Harrier FA.2

First flight: September 19, 1988

Power: Rolls-Royce 9765kg/21,500lb-thrust Pegasus 106 turbofan

Armament: Four AIM-120 air-to-air missiles or two AIM-120s and four AIM-9 Sidewinders. Two 30mm/1.18in Aden cannon can also be carried on underfuselage stations, as well as up to 2270kg/5000lb of bombs, rockets and anti-ship missiles

Size: Wingspan – 7.7m/25ft 3in
Length – 14.17m/46ft 6in
Height – 3.71m/12ft 2in
Wing area – 18.7m²/201sq ft

Weights: Empty – 6374kg/14,052lb
Maximum take-off – 11,880kg/26,200lb

Performance Maximum speed – 1185kph/736mph
Ceiling – 15,555m/51,000ft
Range – 1300km/800 miles
Climb – 15,240m/50,000ft per minute at VTOL weight

McDonnell Douglas/Boeing F-15

The F-15 Eagle, designed to succeed the legendary F-4 Phantom, is an all-weather, highly manoeuvrable fighter originally designed to gain and maintain US Air Force air superiority in aerial combat. It is probably the most capable multi-role fighter in service today. Between entering service in 1974 and 2000, the F-15 has achieved an unprecedented air combat record with 100.5 victories for zero losses.

The first F-15A flight was made in July 1972, and the first flight of the two-seat F-15B trainer followed in July 1973. The first USAF Eagle (an F-15B) was delivered to the Air Force in November 1974. The first Eagle destined for a front-line combat squadron was delivered in January 1976, and some squadrons were combat-ready by the end of the year.

The Eagle's air superiority is achieved through a mixture of incredible manoeuvrability and acceleration, range, weapons and avionics. It can penetrate enemy defence and outperform and outfight any current enemy aircraft. The F-15 has electronic systems and weaponry to detect, acquire, track and attack enemy aircraft while operating in friendly or enemy-controlled airspace. The weapons and flight control systems are designed so one person can safely and effectively perform air-to-air combat.

The F-15's superior manoeuvrability and acceleration are achieved through high engine thrust-to-weight ratio and low wing loading. Low wing loading (the ratio of aircraft weight to its wing area) is a vital factor in manoeuvrability and, combined with the high thrust-to-weight ratio, enables the aircraft to turn tightly without losing airspeed.

The F-15's avionics system sets it apart from other fighter aircraft. It includes a Head-Up Display, advanced radar, ultra-high frequency communications, and an instrument landing system for automatic landings. The Eagle also has an internally mounted, tactical electronic-warfare system, "identification friend or foe" system, electronic countermeasures set and a central digital computer system.

The Head-Up Display projects on the windscreen all essential flight information gathered by the integrated avionics system. This display, visible in any light condition, provides the pilot with information necessary to track and destroy an enemy aircraft without having to look down at cockpit instruments.

ABOVE: **An F-15E – this two-seat Strike Eagle was based in the UK at RAF Lakenheath.** BELOW: **The F-15 is a world-class fighter with a remarkable combat record. The USAF will operate F-15s for some years to come.**

LEFT: **Widely deployed in Europe during the Cold War, the F-15 actually first saw combat in Israeli service in 1977.** BELOW: **F-15As of the 21st Tactical Fighter Wing based at Elmendorf AFB, Alaska, helped protect North America from an attack over the North Pole.**

The F-15's versatile pulse-Doppler radar can look up at high-flying targets and down at low-flying targets, detect and track aircraft and small high-speed targets at distances beyond visual range down to close range and at altitudes down to treetop level. The radar feeds target information into the central computer for effective weapons delivery. For close-in dogfights, the radar automatically acquires enemy aircraft, and this information is projected on the Head-Up Display. The F-15's electronic warfare system provides both threat warning and automatic countermeasures against selected threats.

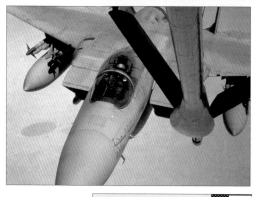

The single-seat F-15C and two-seat F-15D models entered the USAF inventory from 1979. Among the improvements were 900kg/2000lb of additional internal fuel and provision for "conformal" fuel tanks that fit flush with the fuselage.

The F-15E Strike Eagle, first flight July 1980, is a two-seat, dual-role fighter for all-weather, air-to-air and deep interdiction missions – the rear cockpit is reserved for the weapons systems officer. It can fight its way to a target

LEFT: **F-15s proved their worth during the Gulf War. Here a Royal Saudi Air Force F-15C is seen refuelling from a USAF tanker.**

over long ranges, destroy ground targets and fight its way out. Its engines incorporate advanced digital technology for improved-performance acceleration – from a standstill to maximum afterburner takes less than four seconds.

The F-15's combat début came not with the USAF but with export customer Israel who shot down four Syrian MiG-21s in June 1977. Unconfirmed numbers of Syrian fighters were also shot down by Israeli F-15s in 1982. USAF F-15C, D and E models were in action during the Gulf War where they proved their superior combat capability with a confirmed 36 air-to-air victories. Saudi F-15s also downed Iraqi aircraft in combat. In the 1999 Balkans conflict, USAF F-15s destroyed four Serb MiG-29s.

More than 1500 F-15s have been produced for the USA and international customers Israel, Japan and Saudi Arabia. The F-15I Thunder, a model designed for Israel, has been built in the USA, the first of 25 Thunders arriving in Israel in January 1998.

McDonnell Douglas F-15A

First flight: July 27, 1972

Power: Two Pratt & Whitney 11340kg/25000lb afterburning thrust F100-PW-100 turbofans

Armament: One 20mm/0.78in cannon, four AIM-7 Sparrow and four AIM-9 Sidewinder AAMs plus up to 7267kg/16,000lb of other weaponry on five hardpoints

Size: Wingspan – 13.04m/42ft 9.5in
Length – 19.44m/63ft 9.5in
Height – 5.64m/18ft 6in
Wing area – 56.48m²/608sq ft

Weights: Empty – 12,247kg/27,000lb
Maximum take-off – 25,402kg/56,000lb

Performance: Maximum speed – 2655kph/1650mph
Ceiling – 19,200m/63,000ft
Range – 966km/600 miles
Climb – 15,250m/50,000ft per minute

Boeing/McDonnell Douglas/Northrop F/A-18 Hornet

The twin-engine Hornet was developed for the US Navy from the YF-17 project that Northrop had proposed for the US Air Force. As the company had no experience building carrier-borne aircraft, it teamed up with McDonnell Douglas (now Boeing) to develop the F-17. Two versions, ground attack and fighter, were originally proposed but the two roles were combined in the very capable F/A-18, the first of which flew in 1978. With its excellent fighter and self-defence capabilities, the F/A-18 was intended to increase strike mission survivability and supplement the F-14 Tomcat in US Navy fleet air defence.

The F/A-18's advanced radar and avionics systems allow its pilots to shift from fighter to strike mode on the same mission by the flip of a switch, a facility used routinely by Hornets in Operation Desert Storm in 1991 – they fought their way to a target by defeating opposing aircraft and then attacking ground targets. This "force multiplier" capability gives more flexibility in employing tactical aircraft in a rapidly changing battle scenario.

ABOVE: **The remarkable F/A-18 is, at the flip of a switch, a fighter or a strike aircraft. The type was proven in combat during the Gulf War.** LEFT: **The Hornet was originally intended to support the F-14 in defending the US Fleet in the air.**

In addition to air superiority, fighter escort and forward air control missions, the F/A-18 is equally capable in the air-defence suppression, reconnaissance, close air support and strike mission roles. Designed to be reliable and easily maintainable, survivability was another key consideration and was proven by taking direct hits from surface-to-air missiles, recovering successfully, being repaired quickly and flying again the next day.

The F/A-18 Hornet was built in single- and two-seat versions. Although the two-seater is a conversion trainer, it is also combat capable and has a surprisingly similar performance to the single-seat version although with reduced range. The F/A-18A and C are single-seat aircraft while the F/A-18B and D are two-seaters. The B model is used primarily for training, while the D model is the current US Navy aircraft for attack, tactical air control, forward air control and reconnaissance squadrons.

In November 1989, the first F/A-18s equipped with night strike capability were delivered, and since 1991 F/A-18s have been delivered with F404-GE-402 enhanced-performance engines that produce up to 20 per cent more thrust than the previous F404 engines. From May 1994, the Hornet has been equipped with upgraded radar – the APG-73, which substantially increases the speed and memory capacity of the radar's processors. These upgrades and improvements help the Hornet maintain its advantage over potential enemies and keep it among the most advanced and capable combat aircraft in the world.

Apart from the US Navy and Marine Corps, the F/A-18 is also in service with the air forces of Canada, Australia, Spain, Kuwait, Finland, Switzerland and Malaysia.

Canada was the first international customer for the F/A-18, and its fleet of 138 CF-18 Hornets is the largest outside the United States. The CF-18s have an unusual element to their paint scheme in that a "fake" cockpit is painted on the underside of the fuselage directly beneath the real cockpit. This is intended to confuse an enemy fighter, if only for a split second, about the orientation of the CF-18 in close air combat. That moment's hesitation can mean the difference between kill or be killed in a dogfight situation.

The manufacturers have devised a life extension programme that will keep the Hornet in the front line until 2019.

The F/A-18E/F Super Hornet was devised to build on the great success of the Hornet and, having been test flown in November 1995, entered service for evaluation with US Navy squadron VFA-122 in November 1999. It was approved for US Navy service and the first Super Hornet fleet deployment was scheduled for 2002. Export versions were expected to be available in 2005. The Super Hornet is 25 per cent larger than its predecessor but has 42 per cent fewer parts. Both the single-seat E and two-seat F models offer increased range, greater endurance, more payload-carrying ability and more powerful engines in the form of the F414-GE-400, an advanced derivative of the Hornet's current F404 engine family that produces 35 per cent more thrust.

Structural changes to the airframe increase internal fuel capacity by 1633kg/3600lb which extends the Hornet's mission radius by up to 40 per cent. The fuselage is 86.3cm/34in longer and the wing is 25 per cent larger with an extra 9.3m²/100sq ft of surface area. There are two additional weapons stations, bringing the total to 11.

In the words of its manufacturers "The Super Hornet is an adverse-weather, day and night, multi-mission strike fighter whose survivability improvements over its predecessors make it harder to find, and if found, harder to hit, and if hit, harder to disable".

ABOVE: **The twin fins canted at 30 degrees are a prime recognition feature of the F/A-18.** LEFT: **A US Marine Corps F/A-18D. This versatile version is equipped for improved weapons delivery and has better radar and more effective armament.**

ABOVE: **US Marine Corps F/A-18 Hornets of VFA-25, pictured on the deck of USS** *Independence* **in 1991.**

Boeing/McDonnell Douglas/Northrop F/A-18C Hornet

First flight: November 18, 1978

Power: Two General Electric 7267kg/16,000lb thrust F404-GE-400 turbofans

Armament: One 20mm/0.78in cannon, nine hard points carrying up to 7031kg/15,500lb of weapons including AIM-7, AIM-120 AMRAAM, AIM-9 air-to-air missiles or other guided weapons, bombs and rockets

Size: Wingspan – 11.43m/37ft 6in
Length – 17.07m/56ft
Height – 4.66m/15ft 3in
Wing area – 37.2m²/400sq ft

Weights: Empty – 10,455kg/23,050lb
Maximum take-off – 25,400kg/56,000lb

Performance: Maximum speed – 1915kph/1189mph
Ceiling – 15,250m/50,000ft
Range – 3336km/2027 miles
Climb – 13,725m/45,000ft per minute

167

British Aircraft Corporation/English Electric Lightning

When the very high-performance Lightning joined front-line squadrons in 1960, it gave the RAF an interceptor capable of a performance way beyond any of its predecessors. During a lengthy development and testing programme, the Lightning became the first aircraft to exceed the speed of sound in level flight over the UK. With a top speed of around 2.5 times the speed of sound and a climb rate that few fighters have ever equalled, the Lightning was the fastest British fighter ever.

Design work for the aircraft began in 1947, when English Electric were awarded a study contract for a supersonic research aircraft. Extensive research into swept-wing fighters had been carried out in German wind tunnels during World War II, and the English Electric designers looked carefully at the data. The fruit of the study was the P.1A, which first flew in August 1954 and soon exceeded Mach 1, the speed of sound. The aerodynamics of the aircraft were considered to be so complex that Britain's first transonic wind tunnel was constructed to help with development. A scaled-down flying test bed was also built by Short Brothers to test the various swept-wing and tailplane configurations.

ABOVE: **XS897, a Lightning F.6 of No.56 Squadron, pictured in 1975. Note the phoenix and flames unit badge on the tail and the 1930s era chequerboard design by the roundel.** BELOW: **Range was always an issue with the Lightning – this F.3 has overwing ferry tanks as well as a large ventral fuel tank.**

The design was eventually refined and became the P.1B, powered by Avon turbojets, the two engines mounted one above the other with the nose acting as one large air intake. In November 1958, fitted with afterburning Avons, the P.1B topped Mach 2 for the first time. The Lightning, as it was then

LEFT: **Demonstrating the Lightning's unusual outboard retraction of the undercarriage, this aircraft has its burners lit and is preparing to go vertical.** BELOW: **This F.6, XS928, was based at RAF Binbrook for the last years of its RAF service.** BOTTOM: **The Lightning was the last all-British-built fighter in RAF service.**

called, was cleared for service shortly afterwards. The first RAF unit to receive the new Lightning was No.74 Squadron, based at Coltishall.

The Lightning was a relatively complicated aircraft compared to its predecessors, but it did give the RAF an all-weather fighter that could have held its own with any other fighters of the time. The radar, housed in the cone at the entrance to the air intake, could search above and below the horizon, take the aircraft to within firing range of a target and then automatically loose off two Firestreak or Red Top air-to-air missiles. Thus the Lightning was the RAF's first single-seat fighter integrated weapons system, as opposed to a simple gun platform.

Modifications to the Lightning throughout its service life improved its performance and it remained a viable air defence weapon until its retirement. When the F. Mk 1A was introduced it included an inflight refuelling capability, giving the Lightning the ability to transit over long distances such as the North Sea. The Lightning Mk 6 had a new wing that improved the aircraft's performance to the point where the fuel load could be doubled without significantly affecting performance.

A two-seat version, the T. Mk 5, was developed as a trainer and first flew in March 1962, accommodating the instructor and pupil side by side with duplicated instruments and controls. The change to the forward fuselage profile did nothing to slow the version down, as it was still capable of achieving Mach 2.3. Tornado F.3s finally replaced the last RAF Lightnings in 1988.

Saudi Arabia and Kuwait both operated export versions of the F. Mk 6, which served in the multi-role fighter and ground-attack roles. In 1969, Saudi Lightning F.53s flew ground-attack missions against targets in Yemen.

The Lightning was the last solely UK-designed fighter to enter RAF service and is considered by many to be the peak of UK fighter development.

BAC Lightning F. Mk 6

First flight: April 4, 1957 (P.1B)
Power: Two Rolls-Royce 7420kg/16,360lb-thrust Avon 301 afterburning turbojets
Armament: Two Red Top or Firestreak infra-red homing air-to-air missiles or two batteries of 22 50mm/2in unguided rockets. Twin 30mm/1.18in Aden cannon can also be carried in a ventral pack
Size: Wingspan – 10.62m/34ft 10in
Length – 16.84m/55ft 3in, including probe
Height – 5.97m/19ft 7in
Wing area – 42.97m^2/458.5sq ft
Weights: Empty – 12,717kg/28,041lb
Maximum take-off – 19,047kg/42,000lb
Performance: Maximum speed – 2112kph/1320mph
Ceiling – 16,770m/55,000ft
Range – 1290km/800 miles
Climb – 15,240m/50,000ft per minute

Convair F-102 Delta Dagger

In 1950 the US Air Force invited designs for a fighter that could exceed the performance of known Soviet bombers, but this aircraft would be ground-breaking because it was going to be just one part of a weapon package built around the Hughes Electronic Control System. The successful proposal came from Convair and led to the first fighter to be developed as part of an integrated weapons system, the F-102, and ultimately the F-106. Convair's design had an unorthodox delta (triangular) wing, which was, it turned out, a little ahead of its time. The company had some experience of deltas already, having produced the experimental XF-92 research aircraft inspired by the German wartime deltas of Dr Alexander Lippisch.

Development delays with the proposed Wright J67 engine and the various electronic "black boxes" forced the USAF to ask Convair to develop an interim version of the proposed new fighter, which was then designated F-102. The original design progressed to become the F-106. Far from being a spin-off or a poor relation, the F-102 became a very able combat aircraft and was the first fighter armed only with missiles, the AIM-4 and AIM-26 Falcon.

The F-102's development was far from painless – during its maiden flight in October 1953 it became apparent that the aircraft was incapable of exceeding the speed of sound in level flight, which had been a basic requirement from the

USAF. The design team had literally to go back to the drawing board to overcome the high levels of transonic drag. The fuselage was lengthened by 1.21m/4ft, the air intakes and the fin were made bigger and the wing was modified too. By then the Pratt and Whitney J57 engine had been chosen, to help

TOP: **The F-102 came about as an interim version of the F-106 but was a potent fighter in its own right.**
ABOVE: **A total of 875 F-102s were delivered to the US Air Force.**

the aircraft punch through the sound barrier. Test flights beginning in December 1954 showed the modifications had worked and the design could indeed fly faster than Mach 1. The first production version flew in June 1955, and the F-102 finally entered USAF service in April 1956, three years later than planned. In doing so it became the first supersonic delta-winged aircraft to reach operational status.

By 1958, 26 squadrons of F-102s equipped the USAF's Air Defense Command but this was the peak. The 102 was always seen as an interim aircraft by the USAF, plugging the gap while the F-106 was developed. The F-102 did, however, continue in the front line with the USAF in Europe, Alaska and the Pacific for some years and was the main fighter equipment of the Air National Guard through to the early 1970s. The last Air Defense Command unit to operate the F-102 was the 57th Fighter Interception Squadron, based at Keflavik in Iceland, who finally relinquished their machines in April 1973.

In the F-102 cockpit the pilot had two control columns to handle – one managed the aircraft's movements, while the other was used to control the impressive on-board radar, which could pick up an enemy aircraft and direct the aircraft to the target. Pilots then had to choose their weapons from between small unguided rockets, carried within the doors of the weapons bay, or Falcon air-to-air missiles, one of which could have been nuclear-tipped. The Falcons were stored in the aircraft's internal weapons bay until the pilot or the fire control system extended them for firing.

Exported models of ex-USAF Delta Daggers were supplied to the air forces of Greece and Turkey in the early 1970s. Around 200 ex-USAF F-102s also became pilotless target aircraft, helping the USAF's "top guns" perfect their weapon skills in the air and not in the classroom.

Convair F-102A Delta Dagger

First flight: October 24, 1953
Power: Pratt and Whitney 5307kg/11,700lb (7802kg/17,200lb afterburning) thrust J57P-23 turbojet
Armament: Three AIM-4C Falcon infra-red homing air-to-air missiles and one AIM-26A Nuclear Falcon or three AIM-4A semi-active radar homing and three AIM-4C infra-red air-to-air missiles
Size: Wingspan – 11.62m/38ft 1.5in
Length – 20.84m/68ft 5in
Height – 6.46m/21ft 2.5in
Wing area – 61.45m²/661.5sq ft
Weights: Empty – 8630kg/19,050lb
Maximum take-off – 14,288kg/31,500lb
Performance: Maximum speed – 1328kph/825mph
Ceiling – 16,460m/54,000ft
Range – 2173km/1350 miles
Climb – 5304m/17,400ft per minute

TOP: **This F-102A served with the 82nd Fighter Interception Squadron on Okinawa, Japan, and bears a typical camouflage scheme of the era.** ABOVE: **With its internal missile bays open, this F-102 shows some of the armament that made the Delta Dagger such a potent interceptor.**

Convair F-106 Delta Dart

Initially designated F-102B, the F-106 was conceived as the ultimate interceptor. Delayed engine and electronic development for what became the F-106 forced the development of the interim F-102. While the F-102 was developed, the USAF refined its requirements for the new super-fighter – it had to intercept enemy aircraft in all weathers up to 21,335m/70,000ft and be capable of Mach 2 interceptions up to 10,670m/35,000ft. Prototype flights between December 1956 and February 1957 were disappointing and the USAF almost scrapped the whole programme. Instead they reduced the order from 1000 aircraft to 350 to save spiralling costs. Engine and avionics improvements brought the F-106 up to an acceptable standard and the type entered operational service as the F-106A in October 1959. Production ceased in December 1960 but the F-106 remained in front-line service for more than 20 years thanks to constant updating programmes – it was finally phased out of Air National Guard service in 1988.

The F-106's Hughes MA-1 fire control system essentially managed all interceptions from radar-lock to missile firing while the pilot simply acted as a systems supervisor. Among the weaponry were two devastating Genie nuclear-tipped air-to-air missiles carried in an internal bomb-bay, which the computer would instruct the pilot to arm just prior to firing.

From 1973 F-106s were equipped with a multi-barrel "Gatling-gun" rotary cannon, reflecting the realization that fighters might once again need to tackle an enemy in close combat and not just from a stand-off position using long-range missiles. Pilots say the F-106 was a delight to fly and at its peak the F-106 equipped 13 US Air Defense Command squadrons.

TOP: **A fine air-to-air photograph of a New Jersey Air National Guard F-106A. The bump on the fuselage forward of the windscreen is a retractable infra-red detector.** ABOVE: **This F-106 is believed to have been used by NASA for some unmanned drone missions after its retirement from USAF Air Defense Command.**

Convair F-106A
Delta Dart

First flight: December 26, 1956
Power: Pratt & Whitney 11,113kg/24,500lb afterburning-thrust P-17 turbojet engine
Armament: One 20mm/0.78in cannon, four Falcon AAMs, plus two Genie unguided nuclear rockets
Size: Wingspan – 11.67m/38ft 2.5in
Length – 21.55m/70ft 8.75in
Height – 6.18m/20ft 3.3in
Wing area – 64.8m²/697.8sq ft
Weights: Empty – 10,800kg/23,814lb
Maximum take-off – 17,350kg/38,250lb
Performance: Maximum speed – 2393kph/1487mph
Ceiling – 17,680m/58,000ft
Range – 3138km/1950 miles with external tanks
Climb – 9144m/30,000ft per minute

Dassault Mystère/Super Mystère

LEFT: **Unusually, the Mystère IVs that joined the Armée de l'Air in 1955 were funded by the USA under a NATO Assistance Programme.**
BELOW: **A Super Mystère B2 of an Armée de l'Air "Tiger squadron" – not a usual paint scheme.**

Developed from the Dassault Ouragan, France's first jet fighter, the Mystère was essentially an Ouragan with swept wing and tail surfaces, and first flew in 1951.

The production version, the Mystère II, was one of the first swept-wing aircraft in production in Western Europe and entered Armée de l'Air service between 1954 and 1956, powered by the SNEC-MA Atar, the first French turbojet engine to be used in military aircraft. A Mystère IIA was the first French aircraft to break Mach 1 in controlled flight (in a dive), on October 28, 1952. The Armée de l'Air ordered 150 Mystère IICs and the last was delivered in 1957, by which time the type was already being relegated to advanced training duties. Even as the Mystère was becoming operational, the better Mystère IV was already flying. Mystère IIs remained in use as advanced trainers until 1963.

The Mystère IV was a new aircraft, having few common parts with the Mark II and had a new oval-section fuselage, thinner wings with greater sweep, and new tail surfaces. The first prototype was flown in September 1952, powered by an Hispano-built Rolls-Royce Tay 250 turbojet engine, as were the first 50 production examples – later examples were powered by the Hispano-Suiza Verdon. The production contract for 225 Mystère IVAs for the Armée de l'Air was paid for by the United States as part of the NATO Military Assistance Program. The first production Mystère IVA flew in late May 1954 and the type entered

service with the Armée de l'Air the following year. The Mystère IVA remained a first-line fighter with the Armée de l'Air until the early 1960s but continued to serve as an operational trainer until 1980.

Sixty Verdon-powered Mystère IVAs ordered by the French were sold on to Israel and the first batch of 24 arrived in April 1956, just in time for the war in October. In the hands of skilled Israeli pilots, they proved more than a match for Egyptian MiG-15s. The Indian Air Force also bought 110 all-new production Verdon-powered Mystère IVAs. First delivered in 1957, they were used in the close-support role during the 1965 Indo-Pakistan War.

The ultimate Mystère was the Super Mystère, which like the Mystère IV was largely a new aircraft. It was bigger and heavier than previous Mystères and was the first European production aircraft capable of transonic flight. The first prototype flew in March 1955 and had wings with a 45-degree sweepback and an F-100-like oval air intake. The prototype exceeded Mach 1 in level flight the day after it first took to the air. A total of 180 Super Mystère B2s were built for the Armée de l'Air, and the last was delivered in 1959. They were relegated to the attack role once the Mirage III was available and remained in French service

until late 1977. In 1958, 36 Super Mystères bought by the French were sold on to the Israelis who used them to counter the MiG-19s favoured by Arab nations. In the early 1970s, the Israelis upgraded surviving Super Mystères by retrofitting a non-afterburning Pratt & Whitney J52-P8A turbojet engine and 12 of these uprated Super Mystères were sold to Honduras, who operated them until 1989, when the operational career of the Mystère series came to an end.

Dassault Mystère IVA

First flight: February 23, 1951 (Mystère prototype)
Power: Hispano-Suiza 3500kg/7716lb-thrust Verdon 350 turbojet engine
Armament: Two 30mm/1.18in cannon, plus two 454kg/1000lb bombs or 12 rockets
Size: Wingspan 11.12m/36ft 6in
 Length – 12.85m/42ft 2in
 Height – 4.6m/15ft 1in
 Wing area – 32m²/344.46sq ft
Weights: Empty – 5886kg/12,950lb
 Maximum take-off – 9500kg/20,944kg
Performance: Maximum speed – 1120kph/696mph
 Ceiling – 15,000m/49,200ft
 Range – 912km/570 miles
 Climb – 2700m/8860ft per minute

Dassault–Breguet Mirage 2000

In December 1975 Dassault got the green light to proceed with what became the Mirage 2000 programme to develop a replacement for the Mirage F.1. With this design, Dassault revisited the delta wing shape of the Mirage III series and brought greatly improved manoeuvrability and handling thanks to fly-by-wire systems and a much greater knowledge of aerodynamics. Although the Mirage 2000 looks very similar to the Mirage III series, it is an entirely new aircraft. The prototype first flew in March 1978 and service deliveries began in 1983. For its secondary ground-attack role, the Mirage 2000 carries laser guided missiles, rockets and bombs.

The last of 136 single-seat Mirage 2000Cs were delivered to the Armée de l'Air in 1998 but foreign orders for this very capable fighter were secured some years before. Abu Dhabi, Greece, Egypt, Peru and India all operate export 2000 models.

There is a two-seat version of this aircraft, the 2000N, which has nuclear stand-off capability. The Mirage 2000D, derived from the Mirage 2000N operated by the French Air Force, is a two-seater air-to-ground attack aircraft that carries air-to-ground high precision weapons which can be fired at a safe distance, by day or by night. Its navigation and attack systems enable it to fly in any weather conditions, hugging the terrain at a very low altitude.

A modernized multi-role version, the Mirage 2000-5, was also offered from 1997, featuring improved more powerful

ABOVE: **The Mirage 2000 is a fine example of a very good aircraft being developed into a series of specialist variants.** BELOW: **The aircraft's M53-P2 turbofan generates 9917kg/21,835lb of afterburning thrust.**

radar, more powerful engine and compatibility with the Matra Mica air-to-air missile. The Mirage 2000-5 is a single-seater or two-seater fighter and differs from its predecessors mainly in its avionics and its new multiple target air-to-ground and air-to-air firing procedures. The aircraft has Hands On Throttle and Stick control, a Head-Up Display and five cathode ray tube multi-function Advanced Pilot Systems Interface (APSI) displays. The combined head-up/head-level display presents data relating to flight control, navigation, target engagement and weapon firing. The Taiwan Republic of China Air Force operates 60 Mirage 2000-5s while Qatar took delivery of 12 in 1997 having sold its Mirage 1s to Spain to finance the purchase.

Mirage 2000 has nine hardpoints for carrying weapon system payloads, five on the fuselage and two on each wing. The single-seat version is also armed with two internally mounted high-firing rate 30mm/1.18in guns. Air-to-air weapons include the MICA multi-target air-to-air intercept and combat missiles and the Matra Magic 2 missiles. The aircraft can carry four MICA missiles, two Magic missiles and three drop tanks simultaneously. The Mirage 2000-5 can fire the Super 530D missile or the Sky Flash air-to-air missile as an alternative to the MICA.

The Mirage 2000 is equipped with a multi-mode doppler radar which provides multi-targeting capability in the air defence role, and the radar also has a look down/shoot down mode of operation. The radar can simultaneously detect up to 24 targets and carry out track-while-scan on the eight highest priority threats, an invaluable tool for a pilot.

Armée de l'Air Mirage 2000Cs served as part of the UN peacekeeping force over Bosnia and Kosovo.

TOP: **A single-seat Mirage 2000C fighter is seen here armed with Matra Magic and Matra Super 530S air-to-air missiles.** ABOVE: **The Mirage 2000 is an incredibly agile aircraft which always thrills crowds.** BELOW: **The stork emblem on the tail of this two-seat Mirage 2000B identifies it as an aircraft of Escadron de Chasse 1/2 Cigognes.**

Dassault-Breguet Mirage 2000C

First flight: March 10, 1978
Power: SNECMA 9917kg/21,835lb afterburning thrust M53-P2 turbofan
Armament: Two 30mm/1.18in cannon, nine hardpoints capable of carrying 6300kg/13,890lb of weaponry including Super 530D, 530F, 550 Magic, Magic 2 AAMs, bombs and rockets
Size: Wingspan – 9.13m/29ft 11in
Length – 14.36m/47ft 1in   Height – 5.2m/17ft
Wing area – 41m²/441.4 sq ft
Weights: Empty – 7500kg/16,534lb
Maximum take-off – 17,000kg/37,480lb
Performance: Maximum speed – 2338kph/1452mph
Ceiling – 16,470m/54,000ft
Range – 1850km/1149 miles
Climb – 17,080m/56,000ft per minute

Dassault Etendard and Super Etendard

Dassault's private venture Etendard (standard) was designed to meet the needs of both French national and NATO programmes for new light fighters, reflecting air combat experiences during the Korean War. Dassault clearly adhered to the proven Super Mystère layout, although slightly scaled down, but various versions did not get beyond the prototype stage. Then the Etendard IV drew the attention of the French Navy as a multi-role carrier-based fighter, leading to the development of the Etendard IVM specifically for the Navy – it was the first naval aircraft developed by Dassault.

The Etendard IVM made its maiden flight in May 1958 and between 1961 and 1965, the French Navy took delivery of 69 Etendard IVMs that served on the French carriers *Foch* and

Clemenceau, as well as 21 reconnaissance Etendard IVPs. The Etendard IVMs continued to serve in the French Navy until July 1991, by which time they had logged 180,000 flying hours and made 25,300 carrier landings.

The search for an Etendard replacement led to Dassault proposing the Super Etendard, an updated and much improved aircraft based on the Etendard IVM but a 90 per cent new design. Designed for strike and interception duties, it featured the more powerful Atar 8K-50 engine and a strengthened structure to withstand higher-speed operations. The weapons system was improved through the installation of a modern navigation and combat management system centred on a Thomson multi-mode radar. The wing had a new leading edge and revised flaps which, with the newer engine, eased take-off with greater weight than the Etendard.

The aircraft prototype made its maiden flight on October 28, 1974 and the first of 71 production aircraft were delivered from mid-1978, again for service on the aircraft carriers *Foch* and *Clemenceau*. 100 Super Etendards were planned for the Navy but spiralling costs called for a reduction of the order. Armed with two 30mm/1.18in cannon, the Super Etendard could carry a variety of weaponry on its five hard points, including two Matra Magic air-to-air missiles, four pods of 18 68mm/2.68in

ABOVE: **The Etendard was designed to reflect the experiences of air combat during the Korean War.** BELOW: **The Etendard IVP reconnaissance version was in Aeronavale service for almost three decades.**

rockets, a variety of bombs or two Exocet anti-ship missiles. A number were also modified to carry the Aérospatiale ASMP nuclear stand-off bomb.

The Argentine Navy's use of the Super Etendard/Exocet combination during the Falklands War of 1982 proved devastating against British ships – Argentina had ordered 14 Super Etendards from Dassault in 1979 but only five had been delivered from 1981. These five strike fighters, with pilots unwilling to engage the agile British Harriers in air combat, were nevertheless a very potent element of the Argentine inventory.

A handful of Super Etendards were supplied to Iraq in October 1983 as the Iraqis were desperate to cripple Iran by attacking tankers in the Persian Gulf with Exocets. Around 50 ships were attacked in the Gulf in 1984, the majority of the actions apparently carried out by Iraqi Super Etendards.

Production of the Super Etendard ended in 1983 but from 1992 a programme of structural and avionics upgrading was undertaken to extend the service life of the "fleet" until 2008.

ABOVE: The Etendard IVP had a fixed refuelling probe and cameras in the nose. It could also carry a "buddy pack" and act as an inflight refuelling tanker.

Dassault Super Etendard

First flight: October 28, 1974
Power: SNECMA 5000kg/11,025lb afterburning thrust Atar 8K-50 turbojet engine
Armament: Two 30mm/1.18in cannon, plus 2100kg/4630lb of weapons, including Matra Magic air-to-air missiles, AM39 Exocet ASMs, bombs and rockets
Size: Wingspan – 9.6m/31ft 6in
Length – 14.31m/46ft 11.5in
Height – 3.86m/12ft 8in
Wing area – 28.4m²/305.71sq ft
Weights: Empty – 6500kg/14,330lb
Maximum take-off – 12,000kg/26,455lb
Performance: Maximum speed – 1205kph/749mph
Ceiling – 13,700m/44,950ft
Range – 650km/404 miles
Climb – 6000m/19,685ft per minute

Dassault Mirage F1

The swept-wing F1 multi-role fighter was developed as a successor to the excellent Mirage III and first flew just before Christmas in 1966. The first customer for the single-seat F1 was the French Armée de l'Air, who received the first of 100 F1Cs in May 1973. Later deliveries to the same service were of the F1C-200 version, which had a fixed probe for inflight refuelling. The F1 could carry a large offensive/defensive payload, handled well at low altitude and had a very impressive climb rate – all essential for truly great fighters. The aircraft's very good short take-off and landing performance (it could take-off and land within 500–800m/1640–2625ft) was produced by the wing's high lift system of leading-edge droops and large flaps.

The Mirage F1's turn-around time between missions was impressive, due to its onboard self-starter and a high-pressure refuelling system which filled all onboard tanks within six minutes. The F1 could be airborne within two minutes, courtesy of a special self-propelled ground vehicle that kept the aircraft's systems "alive", cooled or heated as required, and

ready to go. The ingenious vehicle also carried a cockpit sunshade on a telescopic arm so the pilot could sit at readiness in the cockpit for hours in the highest of temperatures. As soon as the aircraft started to taxi, the umbilicals were automatically ejected and the aircraft was on its own.

TOP: **A quarter of a century after it first flew, the Mirage F1 is still a very effective fighter in a number of air force inventories.** ABOVE: **This French Air Force F1 sports a very striking squadron anniversary paint scheme.**

The F1's Thomson-CSF Cyrano IV radar, housed in the glass-reinforced plastic nose, enabled the F1 pilot to intercept targets at all altitudes, even those flying at low level. A fire-control computer could then fire the appropriate weapons automatically, if required.

Although production of the F1 ceased in 1989, the F1 continues to be a key aircraft in French air defence strategy and upgrades of the popular jet will undoubtedly keep it in service with other air forces well beyond 2010.

France has exported the F1 to Ecuador, Greece, Jordan, Morocco, Spain, South Africa, Libya and Iraq. The last country, however, fielded the type without success during the Gulf War. The F1A was also built under licence by Atlas Aircraft in South Africa.

TOP LEFT: **The Spanish Air Force (Ejercito del aire) were a major export customer of the F1. The Spanish fleet was expanded in the 1990s by the acquisition of Qatar's F1 fleet.** TOP RIGHT: **The F1's stalky undercarriage is a distinctive identifying feature of the type.** ABOVE: **Jordan's F1s were gradually replaced by F-16s in the early 2000s.** BELOW: **The F1C-200 is equipped with a fixed but detachable inflight refuelling probe.**

Dassault Mirage F1

First flight: December 23, 1966
Power: One SNECMA 49kN/11,025lb
(70.2kg/15,785lb afterburning)
Atar 9K-50 turbojet engine
Armament: Two 30mm/1.17in DEFA 553 cannons in
fuselage and up to 4000kg/8818lb of other
weapons, including AIM-9 Sidewinder or Magic
air-to-air missiles on wingtips or R.530
or Super 530F radar-guided air-to-air missiles on
underwing or centreline hardpoints
Size: Wingspan – 8.4m/27ft 7in, excluding
wingtip missiles
Length – 15.3m/50ft 3in Height – 4.5m/14ft 9in
Wing area – 25m^2/269.1sq ft
Weights: Empty – 7400kg/16,315lb
Maximum loaded – 16,200kg/35,715lb
Performance: Maximum speed – 2338kph/1452mph
Ceiling – 20,008m/65,600ft
Range – 900km/560 miles with full weapon
load, unrefuelled
Climb – 12,789m/41,931ft per minute

Dassault Mirage III family

The delta-wing Mirage III is certainly one of the greatest ever combat aircraft and was produced in greater numbers than any other European fighter. The success of this aircraft brought France to the forefront of the military aircraft industry. It started as a Dassault private venture project and first flew in November 1956, having benefited from the testing of the small Mirage I experimental delta aircraft. After some refinements to the wing design, in October 1958 it became the first western European aircraft to reach Mach 2 in level flight. The aircraft's capability soon caught the attention of the French Armée de l'Air, who quickly ordered the high-performance aircraft as a new fighter for their inventory.

Foreign air forces were also very interested in the Mirage III and orders from Israel and South Africa followed in late 1960. By now the first production aircraft, the Mirage IIIC single-seat air defence fighter, was coming off the production line for the Armée de l'Air and the first were delivered in July 1961. Equipped with the Cyrano AI radar, the Mirage IIIC was armed with two 30mm/1.18in cannon and air-to-air missiles. Some of Israel's IIICs, well used in combat, were sold to Argentina in 1982, a country which already operated that type.

The Mirage IIIE was a long-range fighter-bomber version powered by the SNECMA Atar 9C turbojet. While the IIIC was a dedicated interceptor, the IIIE was designed and equipped for both air defence and all-weather ground attack and French

versions were equipped to carry a nuclear bomb. It was widely exported and was also built under licence in Australia and Switzerland. Although France has retired its Mirage IIIs, many air forces still operate the type, having upgraded it in many ways – Swiss and Brazilian IIIs, for example, have acquired canard wings to enhance their handling.

It was the IIIE that spawned the Mirage 5 ground-attack fighter, basically a simplified version of the IIIE, designed as

ABOVE: **The Belgian Air Force operated over 70 Mirages – a Mirage 5 is here seen nearing the end of its landing roll with braking parachute deployed.**
BELOW: **This 1966 photograph features an Armée de l'Air Mirage IIIC of Escadre de Chasse 3/2 "Alsace". The fin of this early paint scheme IIIC carries the Alsace coat of arms.**

a daytime clear weather ground-attack fighter in response to an Israeli Air Force request. The need for sophisticated radar was considered to be not so great in the Middle East and when the Israeli Mirage 5 first flew in May 1967 it was minus the Cyrano radar. The delivery to Israel was stopped for political reasons by President de Gaulle and the aircraft instead served as the Mirage 5F in the Armée de l'Air. Israel then decided to go it alone and developed their Mirage III into the Kfir.

Some 450 Mirage 5s were, however, exported to other nations and more advanced avionics were offered later. Belgium built their own Mirage 5s and upgraded them in the 1990s to keep them flying until 2005.

The Mirage 50 multi-mission fighter was created by installing the more powerful Atar 9K-50 engine in a Mirage 5 airframe. It first flew in April 1979 and boasted Head-Up Displays and a more advanced radar than the Mirage III. Chile and Venezuela both ordered Mirage 50s. Dassault offers the Mirage 50M upgrade for existing Mirage IIIs and 5s but several operator nations have undertaken local upgrade programmes with improved avionics and the addition of canard foreplanes.

In the 1967 and 1973 Arab-Israeli wars, the Israeli Mirage IIIs outclassed Arab-flown MiGs and generated lots of export sales, but Mirage pilots admit that the type did not have a great sustained turn capability due to the aerodynamic idiosyncrasies of the delta wing. Indeed three Mirages were shot down by Iraqi Hunters during the Six Day War of 1967. Nevertheless, the Mirage III series gave many air forces their first fighters capable of flying at twice the speed of sound and many upgraded examples around the world will be flying until at least 2005.

TOP: **The Swiss Air Force operated fighter and reconnaissance versions of the Mirage III.** ABOVE: **The Mirage III was undoubtedly one of the finest fighting aircraft ever built.**

ABOVE: **Two-seat trainer versions were supplied to most Mirage III/5 export customers.**

Dassault Mirage IIIC

First flight: November 18, 1956
Power: SNECMA 6000kg/13,228lb afterburning thrust Atar 9C turbojet engine
Armament: Two 30mm/1.18in cannon, plus two Sidewinder air-to-air missiles and one Matra R.530 air-to-air missile
Size: Wingspan – 8.22m/27ft
Length – 14.75m/48ft 5in
Height – 4.5m/14ft 9in
Wing area – 35m^2/375sq ft
Weights: Empty – 6575kg/14,495lb
Maximum take-off – 12,700kg/27,998lb
Performance: Maximum speed – 2112kph/1320mph
Ceiling – 20,000m/65,615ft
Range – 1610km/1000 miles
Climb – 5000m/16,400ft per minute

Dassault Rafale

Even as Mirage 2000 was entering service in the early 1980s, a successor was already being sought to be the prime French Air Force fighter. After France withdrew from what became the Eurofighter programme, attention was then focused on Dassault's Avion de Combat Experimentale (ACX) which first flew on July 4, 1986 and was later designated Rafale A. This demonstrator aircraft was used to test the basic design including the airframe, powerplant and the fly-by-wire system.

Directly derived from the slightly (3 per cent) larger Rafale A demonstrator, production Rafales appeared in three versions – the single-seat air defence Rafale C, the two-seater trainer/multi-role Rafale B and the single-seat Rafale M fighter for the Navy. The three versions were fitted with the same engines (the SNECMA M88-2), navigation/attack system, aircraft management system and flight control systems. The cockpit had Hands On Throttle

ABOVE: The Rafale is a twin-engined highly advanced fighter. The two-seat Rafale B can be a trainer or multi-role combat aircraft. LEFT: The Rafale's delta wing is complemented by small canards forward of the leading edge, resulting in outstanding agility.

and Stick (HOTAS) controls, a wide-angle Head-up Display (HUD), two multi-function display (MFD) monitors showing all flight and instrument information, and a helmet-mounted weapons sight. Voice recognition is planned to feature in future versions so the pilot will be able to issue orders to the aircraft simply by using his or her voice.

All three versions had the same 213kph/132mph approach speed and take-off/landing run of less than 400m/1312ft made possible by complementing the delta wing with canard foreplanes, which together optimize aerodynamic efficiency and stability control without impeding the pilot's visibility. The materials employed and the shapes that make up the aircraft were both carefully selected to minimize the aircraft's electro-magnetic and infra-red signature to make it as "stealthy" as possible. Carbon and Kevlar composites, superplastic-formed diffusion-bonded titanium and aluminium-lithium alloys have all been used in this aircraft.

The first production aircraft, Rafale B1, flew in December 1998 with a total of up to 234 aircraft to be delivered to the

French Air Force from 1998 to 2005. The total programme for the French Air Force and Navy is set at 294 aircraft.

The single-seat Rafale C (first flight May 19, 1991) is an air defence fighter with fully integrated weapons and navigation systems. Making full use of the latest technology, it is capable of outstanding performance on multiple air-to-air targets.

The two-seat multi-role Rafale B first took to the air on April 30, 1993 and retained most of the elements of the single-seater version, including its weapons and navigation system. The Rafale B could undertake an operational mission with just a pilot as crew or with a pilot and a weapons system operator. In Armée de l'Air service the B model is intended to replace the popular ground-attack Jaguar and can carry up to 8000kg/17,637lb of weaponry – in the air-to-air role this will include up to eight Matra Mica AAM missiles.

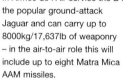

The Rafale M was ordered to replace the French Navy's ageing fleet of F-8 Crusaders, and is a single-seat fighter strengthened for seaborne use with a toughened undercarriage, arrester hook and catapult points for deck launches. This navalized Rafale first flew in December 1991. The first flight of a production Rafale M took place in July 1999, and on the same day a Rafale M prototype landed on France's nuclear-powered aircraft carrier *Charles de Gaulle*. The Navy's first Rafale unit of 12 aircraft was scheduled to embark on the carrier in 2002, the first of a total of 60 aircraft planned for the French Navy.

The first Rafale produced for the French Air Force, a two-seater, was handed over in December 1999.

ABOVE: **The Rafale's two engines generate an impressive combined thrust of 17764kg/39,110lb.** LEFT: **Proudly displaying the test flight running total, this navalized Rafale M is displayed with its range of available weaponry.**

RIGHT: **An early Rafale pictured the year after the type's test flight.** BELOW: **The Rafale was designed to be central to the French fighter force. Until the type is ready to equip the French Air Force and Navy, existing types such as the Mirage F1 and Mirage 2000 will continue to serve.**

Dassault Rafale C

First flight: May 19, 1991

Power: Two SNECMA 8882kg/19,555lb afterburning thrust M88-2 augmented turbofans

Armament: One 30mm/1.18in cannon, maximum of 14 hardpoints carrying a weapons load of up to 6000kg/13,228lb including eight Matra Mica AAMs, ASMP stand-off nuclear missile and other munitions

Size: Wingspan – 10.9m/35ft 9in
 Length – 15.3m/50ft 2in
 Height – 5.34m/17ft 6in
 Wing area – 46m²/495.1sq ft

Weights: Empty – 9060kg/19,973lb
 Maximum take-off – 21,500kg/47,399lb

Performance: Maximum speed – 2125kph/1320mph
 Ceiling – 20,000m/65,620ft
 Range – 1850km/1150 miles with maximum weapon load
 Climb – not published

LEFT: **Royal Navy Sea Hornet F.20s of No.728 Squadron, Fleet Air Arm.** BELOW: **Designed for combat in the Pacific Theatre, the Hornet arrived before the end of World War II. The photograph shows PX210, the first production Hornet F.1.**

de Havilland Hornet

Following the success of the Mosquito, the de Havilland design team turned their thoughts to a scaled-down single-seat Mosquito capable of taking on Japanese fighters in the Pacific. Very long range was a major feature of the design that came to be known as the Hornet and streamlining was seen as one way of achieving that. Rolls-Royce were involved from the outset and were responsible for developing Merlin engines with a

reduced frontal area to lessen the drag on the aircraft. Although inspired by the Mosquito, the Hornet was a completely new aircraft – the main similarity between the two types was the plywood-balsa-plywood technique for building the wooden fuselage. The Hornet wing also differed from that of the Mosquito in that it was made

of wood and metal – the Hornet was the first aircraft in which wood was cemented to metal using the pioneering Redux adhesive.

Geoffrey de Havilland Jr took the Hornet into the air for the first time in July 1944. Although the first production aircraft were delivered to the RAF in April 1945, the type did not see action in World War II. In fact the first RAF Hornet squadron, No.64, was not formed until May 1946. Hornets defended UK air space until replaced by Meteor 8s in 1951, but from 1949 they were switched from interceptor to intruder duties.

Most RAF Hornets joined the Far East Air Force in early 1951 for action in Malaya. Equipped with rocket projectiles or bombs, the Hornets proved very effective against terrorist targets in the jungle. The Hornets of No.45 Squadron became the last piston-engined fighters in RAF service and were finally replaced by Vampires in 1955.

A naval version was considered from the start and the production Sea Hornet had folding wings, arrester hook, plus naval radio and radar, as well as landing gear modified for deck landings. Sea Hornets appeared in day and two-seat

nightfighter versions, the latter version proving to be considerably slower. The Fleet Air Arm's No.801 Squadron operated Sea Hornet F.20s from the carrier HMS *Implacable* between 1949 and 1951.

ABOVE: **The engines dominated the Hornet from any perspective – a Hornet F.3 of the RAF Linton-on-Ouse Station Flight.** LEFT: **The Hornet/Sea Hornet pioneered the use of Redux adhesive in construction – Royal Navy Sea Hornet F.20s.**

de Havilland Hornet F. Mk 3

First flight: July 28, 1944 (prototype)
Power: Two Rolls-Royce 2030hp Merlin 130/131 in-line piston engines
Armament: Four 20mm/0.78in cannon in nose, plus provision for up to 908kg/2000lb of underwing bombs or rockets
Size: Wingspan – 13.73m/45ft
Length – 11.18m/36ft 8in
Height – 4.32m/14ft2in
Wing area – 33.54m²/361sq ft
Weights: Empty – 5850kg/12,880lb
Maximum take-off – 9493kg/20,900lb
Performance: Maximum speed – 759kph/472mph
Ceiling – 10,675m/35,000ft
Range – 4827km/3000 miles
Climb – 1220m/4000ft per minute

de Havilland Sea Vixen

The Sea Venom's successor in Royal Navy service was the impressive de Havilland Sea Vixen, which, when it first appeared in the early 1950s, was a match for any land-based fighter of the time. It gave the Royal Navy its first swept-wing two-seat all-weather fighter and was developed from the D.H.110 that was designed to meet Royal Navy and Royal Air Force requirements. Although it followed the Vampire/Venom-type twin-boom configuration, this was a

totally modern aircraft. Development delays following the high-profile and tragic 1952 crash of the prototype at Farnborough kept the Sea Vixen from entering Royal Navy Fleet Air Arm service until 1958. The aircraft became operational the following year and was

the mainstay of carrier-borne fighter squadrons for a decade. It was the first British interceptor to dispense with guns and was armed only with air-to-air missiles and rockets.

The Sea Vixen FAW. Mk 1 had a hinged radome, power-folding wings and a steerable nosewheel. The novel nose arrangement had the pilot's cockpit off-set to the port side to provide sufficient working space for a radar operator below and behind on the starboard side. The FAW. Mk 2 was an improved version, either upgraded from Mk 1 standard or built from new. More fuel was carried in the forward sections of the tail-booms, which were extended forward of the wings, and armament for this model was four Red Top air-to-air missiles in place of the Firestreaks carried by the FAW. Mk 1.

Despite the Sea Vixen's late entry into service, the aircraft gave the Royal Navy a formidable all-weather interception and surface-attack capability until the type was finally retired in 1972.

TOP LEFT: **This weary FAW. Mk 2 shows the extent of wing folding on the type.** ABOVE LEFT: **The Sea Vixen pilot's cockpit sat offset to the port side to make room for the fellow crew member.**

TOP: **The very capable Sea Vixen was the first British fighter to be armed exclusively with rockets and air-to-air missiles.** ABOVE: **An excellent photograph of a Royal Navy Sea Vixen buzzing the island of British aircraft carrier HMS *Hermes*, June 1961.**

de Havilland Sea Vixen FAW. Mk 2

First flight: September 26, 1951 (D.H.110)

Power: Two Rolls-Royce 5094kg/11,230lb-thrust Avon 208 turbojet engines

Armament: Four Red Top infra-red homing air-to-air missiles, plus two retractable nose pods with 28 51mm/2in rocket projectiles

Size: Wingspan – 15.54m/51ft
Length – 16.94m/55ft 7in
Height – 3.28m/10ft 9in
Wing area – 60.2m²/648sq ft

Weights: Empty – 9979kg/22,000lb
Maximum take-off – 16,793kg/37,000lb

Performance: Maximum speed 1110kph/690mph
Ceiling – 14,640m/48,000ft
Range – 1287km/800 miles
Climb – 12,200m/40,000ft in 8.5 minutes

de Havilland Vampire

The Vampire was Britain's first single-jet fighter and was probably the first aircraft whose designers thought the advent of the jet engine called for a rethink of aircraft layout. While many early jets were just modified ex-propeller-driven airframes, the de Havilland company produced instead a radical twin-boom design to accommodate the new form of propulsion – the jet engine.

The Vampire first flew in September 1943 with Geoffrey de Havilland at the controls, only 16 months after detailed design work began. It arrived too late to see action in World War II but joined RAF squadrons in 1946, becoming the second jet aircraft in Royal Air Force service. When the prototype jet fighter first took to the air it was powered by an engine with 1226kg/2700lb thrust, a far cry from, for example, the 6097kg/13,490lb-thrust Eurojet turbofans that power today's Eurofighter.

In the early post-war years, the Vampires of RAF Fighter Command played a key part in the first-line air defence of the UK, until they were replaced in this role by the Meteor 8 in 1951. By then the Vampire was in widespread use with the RAF's Middle East and Far East Air Forces until it was replaced by the de Havilland Venom, the second of de Havilland's distinctive twin-boom designs.

In December 1945 the world's first deck landing by jet was made by the prototype Sea Vampire, which was the first jet aircraft to go into service with any navy. This version was a modified Vampire F.B.5, strengthened to cope with the extra strain put on airframes during arrester-hook landings. It served in the Royal Navy as a much-needed trainer for the Fleet Air Arm's first generation of jet pilots.

Vampires continued to fly in air forces around the world until the mid-1970s and even into the early 1980s, in the cases of the Dominican Republic and, most famously, Switzerland.

In the early 1950s more than 430 Vampires were licence-built by SNCASE at Marseilles (and named the Mistral) giving France's aviation industry a much-needed post-war shot in the arm. Meanwhile Macchi built 80 in Italy and Switzerland produced 178.

Vampire NF. Mk 10 nightfighters also provided valuable service for the RAF. A total of 95 machines were built and some were later refurbished for sale to the Indian Air Force in the mid-1950s. Privately owned versions continue to fly.

ABOVE: **LZ551 was an English Electric-built prototype equipped with an arrester hook for deck trials.**

ABOVE: **Britain's first single-engine jet fighter, the Vampire, joined RAF squadrons in 1946. The twin-boom layout was a response to the revolutionary new form of propulsion, the jet engine.** RIGHT: **Vampire F.B.9s of No.8 Squadron RAF pictured over Kenya. The F.B.9 was a special version produced for use in tropical climates and had, among other innovations, much needed cockpit air-conditioning.**

de Havilland Vampire F.I

First flight: September 20, 1943
Power: de Havilland 1408kg/3100lb-thrust Goblin 1 turbojet
Armament: Four 20mm/0.78in cannon in nose
Size: Wingspan – 12.2m/40ft
Length – 9.37m/30ft 9in Height – 2.69m/8ft 10in
Wing area – 24.35m²/262sq ft
Weights: Empty – 2894kg/6372lb
Maximum take-off – 4760kg/10,480lb
Performance: Maximum speed – 868kph/540mph
Ceiling – 12,500m/41,000ft
Range – 1175km/730 miles
Climb – 1312m/4300ft per minute

Douglas F4D Skyray

German wartime aerodynamics experiments led the post-war US Navy to consider the use of a delta wing for a carrier-borne fighter. In 1947, the Douglas Corporation proposed the delta-winged XF4D-1 and, following US Navy approval, the prototype first flew in January 1951. The F4D's capabilities were evident when, on October 3, 1953, the second prototype set a new world air speed record of 1211.7kph/752.9mph.

Deliveries to the US Navy began in April 1956 and 17 front-line US Navy/USMC units, plus three reserve units, were eventually equipped with the Skyray.

The F4D-1 had an incredible climb rate for the time and on May 22 and 23, 1958 the Skyray piloted by Major Edward LeFaivre of the US Marine Corps broke five world records for time-to-altitude. This feat led to one US Navy unit, VFAW-3, based at Naval Air Station North Island in California, being part of North American Air Defense Command tasked with defending the USA against expected fleets of Soviet bombers.

This unusual aircraft was finally retired in the late 1960s, having been redesignated F-6A in 1962.

TOP: **This F4D is preserved at the Museum of Naval Aviation at Pensacola, Florida, in the United States.**
ABOVE: **The Skyray was a record-breaker and set a number of records for speed and time-to-altitude.**
BELOW: **Directly influenced by German wartime delta wing research, the Skyray entered US Navy service over a decade after the end of World War II.**

Douglas F4D Skyray

First flight: January 23, 1951
Power: Pratt & Whitney 6577kg/14,500lb afterburning thrust J57-P-8B turbojet engine
Armament: Four 20mm/0.78in cannon, plus up to 1814kg/4000lb of fuel or ordnance on six underwing hardpoints
Size: Wingspan – 10.21m/33ft 6in
Length – 13.93m/45ft 8.25in
Height – 3.96m/13ft
Wing area – 51.75m^2/557sq ft
Weights: Empty – 7268kg/16,024lb
Maximum take-off – 11,340kg/25,000lb
Performance: Maximum speed – 1162kph/722mph
Ceiling – 16,765m/55,000ft
Range – 1931km/1200 miles
Climb – 5580m/18,300ft per minute

Eurofighter Typhoon

In the modern world, few nations can "go it alone" and develop a new high-performance fighter aircraft. So in 1983 Britain, France, Germany, Italy and Spain issued a joint requirement for a highly agile single-seat fighter with a secondary ground attack capability. The French withdrew in 1985 to pursue their own indigenous design but the other nations continued with what became Eurofighter.

Development work was split between UK and Germany (33 per cent each), Italy (21 per cent) and Spain (13 per cent). Germany threatened to withdraw from the programme in 1992 unless spiralling costs were pegged. A lower specification Eurofighter was proposed, accepted by all partners, and the programme continued.

Eurofighter first flew in Germany in March 1994 and is optimized for air-dominance performance with high instantaneous and sustained turn rates. Special emphasis has been placed on

low wing loading, high thrust-to-weight ratio, excellent all round vision and ease of handling. The use of stealth technology is incorporated throughout the aircraft's basic design and it only needs a 700m/2300ft runway.

Eurofighter's high performance is matched by excellent all round vision and by sophisticated attack, identification and defence systems which include long-range radar, Infra-Red Search and Track, advanced medium and short-range air-to-air missiles and a comprehensive electronic warfare suite to enhance weapons system effectiveness and survivability. As well as the expected chaff and flare dispensers, towed decoys are carried in wingtip pods.

Eurofighter is aerodynamically unstable to provide extremely high levels of agility, reduced drag and enhanced lift. The unstable design cannot be flown by conventional means and the pilot controls the aircraft via a computerized "fly-by-wire" system. The pilot has an advanced cockpit dominated by a wide-angle Head-Up Display and three colour monitors displaying all instrument information and flight data, as well as a helmet-mounted sight for weapon aiming. Direct voice input allows the pilot to control aspects of the flight just by talking to the aircraft.

The Eurojet EJ200 turbofan combines high thrust with low fuel consumption and strength.

ABOVE: **The Eurofighter Typhoon is an excellent example of multi-national industry co-operation. The result is a very high-performance fighter that will equip a number of key European air arms for decades to come.** LEFT: **The Eurofighter Typhoon's two turbofans generate a combined thrust of 18396kg/40,500lb, comparable to that of the F-14 Tomcat. An unladen Eurofighter is, however, half the weight of an empty F-14.**

British Eurofighters will be assembled by BAE Systems from components manufactured by companies in the partner nations. In the other nations the respective partner companies will have their own assembly lines in Munich, Turin and Madrid.

Eurofighter Typhoon

First flight: March 27, 1994
Power: Two EJ200 9198kg/20,250lb afterburning thrust turbofans
Armament: One 27mm/1.05in cannon plus 13 hardpoints carrying up to 6500kg/14,330lb of ordnance including short- and medium-range AAMs plus a range of stand-off weapons, bombs, rockets
Size: Wingspan – 10.95m/35ft 11in
Length – 15.96m/52ft 4in
Height – 5.28m/17ft 7in
Wing area – 50m²/538.2sq ft
Weights: Empty – 9990kg/22,043lb
Maximum take-off – 21,000kg /46,297lb
Performance: Maximum speed – 2020kph/1255mph
Ceiling – 16,775m/55,000ft
Range – 1390km/863 miles
Climb – 10,670m/35,000ft in 2 minutes, 30 seconds

Fiat/Aeritalia G91

In response to a 1953 NATO specification for a light strike fighter with rough field capability that was still capable of 0.92 Mach, Fiat proposed the F-86 Sabre-inspired G91. Despite the loss of the prototype on its first flight (August 9, 1956), an accident which would cause

The Italian Air Force and the Luftwaffe took delivery of the G91R single-seat tactical reconnaissance/ground attack fighter version in the early 1960s. Dornier undertook some production in Germany historically making the G91 the first jet combat aircraft built in Germany since World War II. Some G91s were later transferred to the Portuguese Air Force in 1965.

The G91Y twin-engined fighter, first seen as a development of the G91R, was really a totally new design capable of carrying much greater

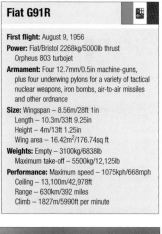

ABOVE: **A G91R of the Portuguese Air Force's Escuadra 121 "Tigres". Portugal operated around 40 of the type.** LEFT: **Resembling a late mark F-86 Sabre, the G91 was a straightforward design said by pilots to be easy to handle in the air.**

the French to refuse to purchase the aircraft, the G91 entered production for the Italian Air Force. While the design was intended for use by all the NATO countries, only Italy and Germany initially acquired the design.

military loads over much longer distances. Powered by two General Electric jet engines, the G91Y first flew in December 1966 and deliveries to the Regia Aeronautica took place between 1971–5.

Fiat G91R

First flight: August 9, 1956
Power: Fiat/Bristol 2268kg/5000lb thrust Orpheus 803 turbojet
Armament: Four 12.7mm/0.5in machine-guns, plus four underwing pylons for a variety of tactical nuclear weapons, iron bombs, air-to-air missiles and other ordnance
Size: Wingspan – 8.56m/28ft 1in
Length – 10.3m/33ft 9.25in
Height – 4m/13ft 1.25in
Wing area – 16.42m^2/176.74sq ft
Weights: Empty – 3100kg/6838lb
Maximum take-off – 5500kg/12,125lb
Performance: Maximum speed – 1075kph/668mph
Ceiling – 13,100m/42,978ft
Range – 630km/392 miles
Climb – 1827m/5990ft per minute

ABOVE: **The G91T two-seat trainer was developed to give pilots experience of flight at transonic speeds. The pre-unification Federal German Air Force took delivery of 66 trainer versions, 22 built under licence in Germany and the rest by Fiat in Italy.**

Folland/Hawker Siddeley Gnat

Best known as a jet trainer, the Gnat actually began life as a private-venture single-seat fighter, the Midge, which first took to the air in August 1954. While fighters around the world were getting more complex and heavier, the Gnat was designed by W.E.W. Petter as a lightweight jet fighter, making use of the smaller jet engines then available.

Although the British government ordered six Gnats for development flying, the Gnat failed to be adopted as an RAF fighter. By mid-1957 the Gnat's potential

as a two-seat trainer was recognized by the RAF, leading to orders for a total of 105 two-seat Gnat trainers for the RAF.

India had, however, been impressed by the Gnat as a fighter and had licence-built 213 of them by 1973. In the Indo-Pakistan war of 1971 the Indian Gnats proved most effective in close combat; then in 1974 Hindustan Aircraft Ltd signed an agreement to produce the Gnat II or Ajit (unconquerable). Finland also operated Gnat fighters between 1958 and 1972.

TOP: **The Gnat is best known as a mount of the world-famous RAF Red Arrows aerobatic team.** ABOVE: **Indian licence-built Gnats saw action against Pakistan in the early 1970s.** BELOW: **Where it all began – the private-venture Midge that first flew in 1954.**

Folland Gnat 1

First flight: July 18, 1955
Power: Bristol 2050kg/4520lb-thrust Orpheus 701 turbojet engine
Armament: Two 30mm/1.18in Aden cannon, plus underwing hardpoints for 454kg/1000lb bomb load
Size: Wingspan – 6.75m/22ft 2in
Length – 9.06m/29ft 9in
Height – 2.69m/8ft 10in
Wing area – 16.26m^2/175sq ft
Weights: Empty – 2200kg/4850lb
Maximum take-off – 4030kg/8885lb
Performance: Maximum speed – 1150kph/714mph
Ceiling – 15,250m/50,000ft plus
Range – 1900km/1180 miles
Climb – 6096m/20,000ft per minute

Gloster Javelin

Gloster Javelin F(AW). Mk 1

First flight: November 26, 1951
Power: Two Armstrong Siddeley 3629kg/8000lb-thrust Sapphire ASSa.6 turbojet engines
Armament: Two 30mm/1.18in cannon in each wing
Size: Wingspan – 15.85m/52ft
  Length – 17.15m/56ft 3in
  Height – 4.88m/16ft
  Wing area – 86.12m^2/927sq ft
Weights: Empty – 10,886kg/24,000lb
  Maximum take-off – 14,324kg/31,580lb
Performance: Maximum speed – 1141kph/709mph
  Ceiling – 16,000m/52,500ft
  Range – 1530km/950 miles with drop tanks
  Climb – 15,250m/50,000ft (Mk 9) in 9.25 minutes

The Javelin was the first British combat aircraft designed for the all-weather day and night role and was the first twin-engined delta-wing jet in service anywhere.

The design team began work on the Javelin in 1948 and the type first flew on November 26, 1951. After competitive trials with the de Havilland 110 (which led to the Sea Vixen) in July 1952 Britain's Air Ministry chose the Javelin to equip the RAF's all-weather fighter units. Following the loss of three prototypes in accidents and after much redesign, production finally got under way in 1954.

The Javelin was designed to have the very high performance and long endurance that would enable it to intercept high-speed, high-altitude Soviet bombers. With state-of-the-art electronics and radar, the two-seat Javelin was able to operate day or night in all weather conditions. The Javelin's large delta wing provided good high-altitude performance, while the massive swept vertical tail fin carried a delta tailplane on top which helped keep the aircraft's landing angle-of-attack within safe limits for night and all-weather landings.

When the Mk 1 Javelins entered RAF service in 1956, they were the first of 427 of a type that ultimately appeared in nine versions.

The Mk 2 entered service in August 1957 and had uprated engines (3770kg/8300lb, compared to the 3702kg/8150lb-thrust of the Mk 1) and an improved Westinghouse radar. Next came the T.3 dual control trainer, which had no radar but was armed with 30mm/1.18in guns.

Fifty examples of the pilot-friendly Mk 4 were built and with its all-moving tailplane it was much easier to fly. An extra 1137 litres/250 US gallons of internal tankage in a modified wing was the principal performance improvement on the Mk 5 while the Mk 6 was simply a Mk 5 equipped with American radar.

The Javelin FAW.7 was a major redesign and was produced in greater numbers (142) than the other versions. It boasted the much more powerful 4996kg/11,000lb-thrust Sapphire 203 engines and much-needed missile armament of four Firestreak infra-red homing air-to-air missiles in place of two of the 30mm/1.18in guns. This model entered front-line service in July 1958.

The Mk 8 had afterburners that increased thrust to 6082kg/13,390lb and the final variant was the Mk 9. This ultimate Javelin was a conversion of existing Mk 7s to Mk 8 standard and an inflight refuelling (IFR) probe. Four No.23 Squadron Javelins demonstrated the usefulness of IFR by flying non-stop to Singapore in 1960. FAW.9s were first delivered to No.25 Squadron at Waterbeach in December 1959.

Javelins were the last aircraft built by the famous Gloster company, and their last product was withdrawn from service in June 1967. At its peak, the Javelin equipped 14 Royal Air Force squadrons.

BELOW: **The Javelin was the world's first twin-engined delta jet fighter in service.**

Grumman F7F Tigercat

In 1941 Grumman began design work on a hard-hitting high-performance twin-engine fighter to operate from the Midway class of US aircraft carriers – the Tigercat. As the Tigercat developed it was apparent that it was going to be heavier and faster than all previous US carrier aircraft. It was also unusual in that it had a tricycle undercarriage,

although it retained the usual arrester hook and folding wings for carrier operations. Even before the prototype flew in December 1943, the US Marine Corps had placed an order for 500 of the F7F-1 version. They wanted to use the Tigercat primarily as a land-based fighter in close support of Marines on the ground. Although deliveries began in April 1944, the big fighter arrived too late to be cleared for use in World War II.

Wartime production had diversified to deliver the F7F-2N nightfighter, which differed from the F7F-1 by the removal of a fuel tank to make way for a radar operator cockpit and the removal of nose armament for the fitting of the radar.

An improved fighter-bomber version was also developed, the F7F-3, and had different engines for more power at altitude, a slightly larger fin and bigger fuel tanks.

Tigercat production continued after the war's end with F7F-3N and F7F-4N nightfighters, both having lengthened noses to house the latest radar and a few of these aircraft were strengthened and equipped for carrier operations. Some F7F-3s were modified for electronic and photographic reconnaissance missions.

Although it missed action in World War II, the Tigercat did see combat with the Marine Corps over Korea. USMC fighter unit VMF(N)-513 was based in Japan when the Korean War broke out. Equipped with Tigercat nightfighters, they went into action immediately as night-intruders and performed valuable service.

The US Marines were the only operators of the Tigercat.

TOP: **The fast and heavy F7F was only used by the US Marines.** ABOVE: **Despite its vintage, the high-performance Tigercat is a popular "warbird", and a number are preserved by collectors in the USA and Europe.** LEFT: **Too late for World War II, the F7F was widely used in the Korean War.**

Grumman F7F-3N

First flight: December 1943 (F7F-1)
Power: Two Pratt & Whitney 2100hp R-2800-34W Double Wasp radial piston engines
Armament: Four 20mm/0.78in cannon in wing roots
Size: Wingspan – 15.7m/51ft 6in
  Length – 13.8m/45ft 4in
  Height – 5.06m/16ft 7in
  Wing area – 42.27m²/455sq ft
Weights: Empty – 7379kg/16,270lb
  Maximum take-off – 11,666kg/25,720lb
Performance: Maximum speed – 700kph/435mph
  Ceiling – 12,414m/40,700ft
  Range – 1609km/1000 miles
  Climb – 1380m/4530ft per minute

Grumman F9F Cougar

Grumman, aware of wartime German swept-wing research, had considered a swept-wing version of the F9F in December 1945. In March 1950 the company sought official approval for a swept-wing version of the Panther – Grumman was given the green light for this logical and speedy development of an already successful programme.

Having been granted a contract in March 1951, Grumman tested the first swept-wing aircraft of the F9F family on September 20, 1951. It was different enough from the Panther to warrant the new name F9F-6 Cougar – in fact only the forward fuselage was retained from the original straight-winged aircraft. The wings had 35 degrees sweep and the wingtip fuel tanks were deleted – power was provided by the J48-8 engine with water/alcohol injection giving a thrust of 3289kg/7250lb. The Cougar entered US Navy service in late 1952.

The F9F-7 version, powered by the 2880kg/6350lb J33 engine, reached a production total of 168. The final Cougar version, the F9F-8 with its bigger wing, first flew in December 1953 and in

January 1954 exceeded the speed of sound in a shallow dive – 662 were built. This version was equipped to carry early Sidewinder missiles.

Many Cougars and Panthers were converted for use as target drones, and two-seat trainer versions of the Cougar were still flying in US Navy service in the mid-1970s.

ABOVE: **Two-seat conversion of Cougars flew on with the US Navy in the mid-1970s.**

BELOW: **Benefiting from wartime German swept-wing research, the Cougar was a swept-wing version of the Panther.**

Grumman F9F-8 Cougar

First flight: September 20, 1951 (F9F-6)

Power: Pratt & Whitney 3266kg/7200lb thrust J48-P-8A turbojet

Armament: Two 20mm/0.78in cannon plus 908kg/2000lb of underwing weapons

Size: Wingspan – 10.52m/34ft 6in
Length – 13.54m/44ft 5in, including probe
Height – 3.73m/12ft 3in
Wing area – 31.31m^2/337sq ft

Weights: Empty – 5382kg/11,866lb
Maximum take-off – 11,232kg/24,763lb

Performance: Maximum speed – 1041kph/647mph
Ceiling – 15,240m/50,000ft
Range – 1610km/1000 miles
Climb – 1860m/6100ft

Grumman F9F Panther

LEFT: **The folded wings of this F9F-2 betray its origins as a naval fighter.** BELOW: **In the Korean War the Panther flew 78,000 missions.** BOTTOM: **The Panther could carry up to 908kg/2000lb of bombs and rockets beneath its wings.**

The Panther was the US Navy's most widely used jet fighter of the Korean War.

Although it was mainly used in the ground-attack role, it did notch up some air combat successes against North Korean MiGs. On July 3, 1950 a Panther of US Navy unit VF-51 aboard USS *Valley Forge* scored the Navy's first aerial kill of the Korean War when it downed a Yak-9. By the end of the war the F9F had flown 78,000 combat missions.

Grumman's first jet fighter for the US Navy had its origins in the last days of World War II, when the US Navy Fighter Branch drew up a requirement for an all-weather/night radar-equipped carrier-borne fighter. As originally planned, Grumman's proposed XF9F-1 was powered by no less than four jet engines positioned in the wings. The high number of engines was dictated by the low power output of early turbojets. As many engines as this called for a wingspan of almost 17m/55.7ft, which worried Grumman – they knew that their twin-engine Tigercat had already proved somewhat large for carrier operations.

As better powerplants were available, the design was refined and when the prototype flew on November 24, 1947 it was powered by a lone Rolls-Royce Nene engine. The Panther's distinctive 454 litre/120 US gallon wingtip fuel tanks were first tested in February 1948 and were adopted as standard to extend the aircraft's range.

This straight-wing model, now called F9F-2, went into production and was equipping US naval units by May 1949, having completed carrier trials two months earlier.

The most produced Panther was the F9F-5, which featured water injection and the J48 engine of 3175kg/7000lb thrust. A total of 616 of this version were built and delivered between November 1950 and January 1953. Panthers continued in US Navy service until 1958, and in 1966 one batch was reconditioned as fighters for the Argentine Navy. Total Panther production was 1382.

Grumman F9F-2B Panther

First flight: November 24, 1947
Power: Pratt & Whitney 2586kg/5700lb-thrust J42-P-8 turbojet engine (licence-built Rolls-Royce Nene)
Armament: Four 20mm/0.78in cannon, plus underwing weapon load of up to 908kg/2000lb
Size: Wingspan – 11.58m/37ft 11.75in
Length – 11.35m/37ft 3in
Height – 3.45m/11ft 4in
Wing area – 23.22m²/250sq ft
Weights: Empty – 4533kg/9993lb
Maximum take-off – 8842kg/19,494lb
Performance: Maximum speed – 877kph/545mph
Ceiling – 13,600m/44,600ft
Range – 2177km/1353 miles
Climb – 1567m/5140ft per minute

Grumman F11F Tiger

While the Grumman Cougar was making its first flight, Grumman designers were already hard at work on a successor derived from the Cougar/Panther family. In the end, a totally new design was undertaken, with high performance in combat a major requirement. The resulting aircraft was the smallest and lightest airplane that could be designed for the dayfighter mission. The reduced size had another advantage – only the wingtips needed to be folded for carrier handling and storage, thus eliminating the need for complex heavy wing-folding gear.

The prototype flew in July 1954 but the overall performance was not enough

of an improvement over that of the Cougar – supersonic speed was the goal. The engine manufacturers Wright proposed that an afterburner version of the J-65 (which was a licence-built British Sapphire engine) could be developed and a complete redesign of the aft fuselage and tail surfaces followed. During the long and troubled development period that followed, the aircraft got a new designation – the F11F.

The afterburner problems continued and a de-rated engine was fitted to bring the aircraft into service. As a result, the expected performance was never achieved and production was limited to only 201 aircraft.

The Tiger entered US Navy service in March 1957. Easy to

TOP: **Pleasant to fly and well armed, the F11F was popular with pilots.**
ABOVE: **Like the Folland Gnat, the F11F was a diminutive fighter and the type was easy to operate from carriers.** BELOW: **Continued engine problems plagued the Tiger's short US Navy career.**

maintain and having pleasant flying qualities, it continued to be plagued by many engine problems. The last US Navy Tigers were phased out by April 1961, after only four years of service and were replaced by F-8 Crusaders.

Grumman F11F-1

First flight: July 30, 1954
Power: Wright 3379kg/7450lb-thrust J65-W-18 turbojet engine
Armament: Four 20mm/0.78in cannon and four Sidewinder air-to-air missiles under wings
Size: Wingspan – 9.64m/31ft 7.5in
Length – 14.31m/46ft 11.25in
Height – 4.03m/13ft 2.75in
Wing area – 23.23m²/250sq ft
Weights: Empty – 6091kg/13,428lb
Maximum take-off – 10,052kg/22,160lb
Performance: Maximum speed – 1207kph/750mph
Ceiling – 12,770m/41,900ft
Range – 2044km/1270 miles
Climb – 1565m/5130ft per minute

Grumman F-14 Tomcat

Despite its age, the swing-wing, twin-engine Grumman F-14 Tomcat is still one of the world's most potent interceptors. Its primary missions, in all weathers, are air superiority, fleet air defence and, more recently, precision strikes against ground targets. Continued developments and improvements have maintained its capabilities to the extent that it is still a potent threat and an effective deterrent to any hostile aircraft foolish enough to threaten US Navy aircraft carrier groups. Its mix of air-to-air weapons is unmatched by any other interceptor type, and its radar is the most capable long-range airborne interception radar carried by any fighter today. With its mix of weapons, it can attack any target at any altitude from ranges between only a few hundred feet to over 160km/100 miles away. It is already a classic fighter.

The F-14 had its beginnings in the early 1960s when Grumman collaborated with General Dynamics on the abortive F-111B, the carrier-based escort fighter version of the F-111. Even before the F-111B cancellation took place, Grumman began work on a company-funded project known as Design 303, a carrier-borne aircraft for the air superiority, escort fighter and deck-launched interception role.

Having flown for the first time on December 21, 1970, the first two US Navy F-14 squadrons were formed in 1972 and

ABOVE: **Wings sweeping back for high-speed flight – the F-14 is over three decades old but is still one of the finest interceptors in service today.**

went to sea in 1974, making the Tomcat the first variable geometry carrier-borne aircraft in service. Its variable-geometry wings are designed for both speed and greater stability. In full forward-sweep position, the wings provide the lift needed for slow-speed flight, especially needed during carrier landings. In swept-back position, the wings blend into the aircraft, giving the F-14 a dart-like configuration for high-speed, supersonic flight. Only a handful of swing-wing types are in service.

The F-14 Tomcat was designed to carry a million dollar missile, the AIM-54 Phoenix, and is the only aircraft that is armed with the AIM-54. With a range of over 200km/120 miles the AIM-54 gives the Tomcat a very long-range punch. Enemy aircraft can be engaged before the Tomcat even appears on their radar screens. Less expensive Sidewinders are also carried for close air fighting.

The F-14B, introduced in November 1987, incorporated new General Electric F-110 engines. A 1995 upgrade program was initiated to incorporate new digital avionics and weapons system improvements to strengthen the F-14s multi-mission capability. The vastly improved F-14D, delivered from 1990, was a major upgrade with F-110 engines, new APG-71 radar system, Airborne Self Protection Jammer (ASPJ), Joint Tactical Information Distribution System (JTIDS) and Infra-Red Search and Track (IRST). Additionally, all F-14 variants were given precision strike capability using the LANTIRN (Low Altitude Navigation and Targeting Infra-Red for Night) targeting system, night vision compatibility, new defensive countermeasures systems and a new digital flight control system. LANTIRN

pods, placed on an external point beneath the right wing, allow the F-14 to drop laser-guided bombs under the cover of darkness. The improved F-14B and F-14D have been built and deployed by the US Navy in modest numbers.

The Tomcat first got to prove itself in combat on August 19, 1981 when two F-14s from the USS *Nimitz* were "intercepted" by two Libyan Sukhoi Su-22 fighter-bombers. The Libyan jets apparently attacked the F-14s and were destroyed with ease. Again on January 4, 1989, two Libyan MiG-23 "Floggers" were engaged by two F-14s and shot down.

Tomcats also saw combat during Operation Desert Storm in 1991, providing top cover protection for bombers and other aircraft, and performing TARPS (Tactical Air Reconnaissance Pod System) missions – the F-14, equipped with TARPS, is the US Navy's only manned tactical reconnaissance platform.

In late 1995, the F-14 Tomcat was used in the bomber role against targets in Bosnia. Nicknamed "Bombcats", the F-14s dropped "smart" bombs while other aircraft illuminated the targets with lasers.

A total of 79 of the type were even exported to Iran before the downfall of the Shah in 1979 and a number were still in service in 2000, having been without the benefit of US technical back-up since 1980.

TOP: **The F-14 earned a much broader audience when it starred in the Hollywood film *Top Gun*.** MIDDLE: **A Tomcat of USS *George Washington*. Note the port of the single 20mm/0.788in cannon low down on the nose just ahead of the cockpit.** ABOVE: **This F-14 of US Navy fighter squadron VF-142 was based on the US Navy carrier USS *Dwight D. Eisenhower*.**

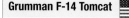

ABOVE: **On the deck of the USS *Nimitz*, this F-14 is about to be moved and prepared for take-off. The F-14 will continue to protect US Navy carrier groups and project American Air Power for the foreseeable future.**

Grumman F-14 Tomcat

First flight: December 21, 1970

Power: Two Pratt & Whitney 9480kg/20,900lb afterburning thrust TF30-P-412A turbofans

Armament: One 20mm/0.78in cannon plus six AIM-7F Sparrow and four AIM-9 Sidewinder AAMs, or six AIM-54A Phoenix long-range AAMs and two AIM-9s, or a variety of air-to-surface weapons up to 6575kg/14,500lb

Size: Wingspan – 19.55m/64ft 1.5in, unswept
Length – 19.1m/62ft 8in
Height – 4.88m/16ft
Wing area – 52.49m²/565sq ft

Weights: Empty – 18,036kg/39,762lb
Maximum take-off – 31,945kg/70,426lb

Performance: Maximum speed – 2486kph/1545mph
Ceiling – 18,290m/60,000ft
Range – 725km/450 miles
Climb – 18,290m/60,000ft in 2 minutes, 6 seconds

197

Hawker Hunter

The Hunter, the longest-serving British jet fighter aircraft, was designed to replace the Gloster Meteor in RAF service. Ultimately over 1000 Hunters were built for the RAF in five versions. The prototype flew in July 1951 powered by a 2948kg/6500lb thrust Avon 100 series turbojet and was supersonic in a shallow dive. The Hunter prototype WB188 appeared at the 1951 Farnborough SBAC show, and in April 1952 test pilot Neville Duke took the Hunter through the

TOP: **A Royal Jordanian Air Force FR. Mk 10. A number of Middle East nations were enthusiastic operators of Sidney Camm's classic fighter.** ABOVE: **A Royal Air Force F.6 wearing a "raspberry ripple" trainer paint scheme.**
LEFT: **The Hawker Hunter was claimed by its makers to be "the finest fighter in the world". In addition to its use by the RAF and Royal Navy, Hunters were exported to at least 19 other nations.**

much-publicized "sound barrier" for the first time. The first production F. Mk 1 flew on May 16, 1953, but this and a further 22 early production aircraft were used for development purposes.

The Hunter F.1 entered RAF service with 43 Squadron in July 1954, replacing their Meteor F.8s, providing the RAF with its long-awaited first transonic fighter. The interceptor capabilities of the Mk 1 were however drastically limited as cannon firing in this mark was restricted to altitudes below 9150m/30,000ft because exhaust gas from the guns caused the engine to flame out. Also, spent cartridge links being ejected by the guns and tumbling along the lower fuselage caused damage or could have even been ingested into the air intakes, so bulbous link collectors were fitted from the F.4 onwards, and were retro-fitted to earlier marks too.

While the F. Mk 1 and the F. Mk 4 that succeeded it were Avon powered, a parallel series of Hunters with the Armstrong Siddeley Sapphire turbojet was developed – the F. Mk 2 and F. Mk 5. The F.2 equipped the RAF's No.257 Squadron from September 1954 and was only produced in limited numbers, despite it not having the flame-out problem of the Mk 1. Both variants were however short-range interceptors and Hawkers

looked at ways to give the Hunter longer legs. The F.4 entered service with 111 Squadron in June 1955, replacing their F.1s. The new model, powered by Avon 115s instead of the problematic Avon 113s of the Mk 1, carried more fuel in strengthened wings which allowed carriage of bombs, rockets and drop tanks.

The Sapphire-powered F.5, otherwise similar to the Mk 4, entered service with 263 Squadron in April 1955 and was the first variant to see active service, being deployed against ground targets in Egypt during the Suez campaign.

Next came the Hunter F. Mk 6 with the 4536kg/10,000lb thrust Avon 203 engine that bestowed a much improved performance and an impressive climb. Although it was only transonic in a dive, the F.6 was built in greater numbers than any other version. Early examples of this high-powered Hunter had a tendency to pitch-up at high speeds, and this was cured by extending the leading edges of the outer portion of the wing, giving the saw-toothed look. F.6s could also scramble more quickly as they used an AVPIN starter system, enabling quicker engine start-up than the cartridge-started early variants. The Hunter F. Mk 6 entered front-line service in October 1956. With better performance at altitude, the Hunter was now able to hold its own with most contemporary fighters but this was shortlived. Britain's V-bombers could climb

beyond its reach and the new American fighters could outperform it. The arrival of the very high-performance Lightning in RAF service spelt the end for the Hunter as an interceptor and the last Fighter Command F.6s were replaced in April 1963. From then on the Hunter's role in the RAF was primarily ground attack, and so the next variant was the FGA.9 which served until 1970 when it was replaced by a mixture of Buccaneers, Phantoms and Harriers. Hunters continued to be used as weapons trainers in the RAF into the 1980s.

ABOVE: **At its peak use, over 1000 Hunters were in service with the RAF.** LEFT: **The Royal Navy used the two-seat Hunters for training pilots of transonic fighter types such as the Scimitar and Sea Vixen.**

The Hunter was of course a major export success and was used by at least 19 foreign air forces. In addition, licence production was carried out in Holland and Belgium. Sweden, Singapore, Denmark and Switzerland all operated Hunters; the latter nation proved to be a long-lived Hunter operator, flying theirs from 1958 until 1995. India made extensive use of the Hunter from 1957 to the early 1980s, and was the first export customer of the type. Participating in the 1965 and 1971 conflicts with Pakistan, the Indian Hunters proved to be a formidable ground attack aircraft and took part in air-to-air combat with Pakistani Sabres and even an F-104. In the 1971 IndoPak war, eight Sabres were claimed by Indian Hunters in air-to-air combat.

In the Middle East, Hunters were operated by Abu Dhabi, Qatar, Saudi Arabia and Kuwait. Jordan operated Hunters from 1958 until 1974, and their aircraft were the first Arab aircraft to attack Israeli territory in the Six Day War. The Lebanon and Zimbabwe were still operating front-line Hunters in early 2000.

ABOVE: **Early problems with gun firing were eliminated by simple modifications.** LEFT: **The first of the many – WB188 was the prototype P.1067 that first flew in July 1951. The basic design changed little for production versions.** BELOW: **An F.6, XF515, in the markings of No.43 Squadron RAF, "The Fighting Cocks". Note the unit insignia on the forward fuselage.**

Hawker Hunter F. Mk 6

First flight: July 20, 1951 (prototype)
Power: Rolls-Royce 4542kg/10,000lb thrust Avon 203
Armament: Four fixed 30mm/1.18in cannon in removable pack. Provision under wings for two 454kg/1000lb bombs, 5cm/2in or 7.62cm/3in multiple rocket batteries
Size: Wingspan – 10.2m/33ft 8in
Length – 14m/45ft 11in Height – 4.01m/13ft 2in
Wing area – 31.6m²/340sq ft
Weights: Empty – 5795kg/12,760lb
Maximum take-off – 8062kg/17,750lb
Performance: Maximum speed – 1150kph/715mph
Ceiling – 15,707m/51,500ft
Range – 2960km/1840 miles
Climb – 13,725m/45,000ft in 7.5 minutes

Hawker Sea Fury/Fury

The Fury was designed as a lighter, smaller version of the Hawker Tempest to a joint British Air Ministry and Admiralty wartime specification. The land-based Fury first flew in September 1944 but at the war's end RAF interest in the ultimate Hawker piston-engined fighter ceased. Development of the Sea Fury did, however, continue, following the version's test flight in February 1945. This aircraft was essentially a navalized land plane, complete with non-folding wings. The second prototype Sea Fury was a fully navalized aircraft, with folding wings and arrester hook and was powered by a Bristol Centaurus XV.

The production version, the Sea Fury Mk X, began to replace Fleet Air Arm Supermarine Seafires from August 1947. Meanwhile trials with external stores and rocket-assisted take-off equipment led to the Sea Fury FB. Mk 11. It was this aircraft that represented the ultimate development of British piston-engined fighters and the FB.11 proved to be an extremely capable combat aircraft. FAA Sea Furies were among the few British aircraft types that saw combat during the Korean War (1950–3), where they were mainly used in the ground-attack role, operating from HMS *Theseus*, HMS *Ocean*, HMS *Glory* and HMAS *Sydney*. Korea was the first true jet versus jet war but the Sea Fury is known to have destroyed more Communist aircraft than any other non-US type and even shot down a number of North Korean MiGs.

ABOVE: **SR661 was a prototype of the Mk X production version intended to replace Seafires in Fleet Air Arm service.** BELOW: **Certainly the ultimate British piston fighter and considered by some to be the best single-engine piston-powered fighter ever, the Hawker Sea Fury was a very capable fighting aircraft. The example pictured is an FB.11.**

While flying the piston-engined Sea Fury off HMS *Ocean*, Royal Navy Lt Peter Carmichael destroyed a MiG-15 jet and earned himself a place in the history books. "At dawn on August 9, 1952 I was leading a section of four aircraft on a patrol near Chinnampo. We were flying at 1068m/3500ft, looking for rail targets when my Number Two called out, 'MiGs five o'clock – coming in!' Eight came at us from the sun. One came at me head on and I saw his tracer coming over. I managed to fire a burst and then he flashed past. I looked over my shoulder and saw an aircraft going down. When all

LEFT: **The Iraqi Air Force operated a number of land-based Furies in the late 1940s and early 1950s while Pakistan had a number of the type in use into the 1970s.**

my section called in, I knew I'd bagged a MiG! I believe the Sea Fury is the finest single-seat piston fighter ever built".

The Sea Fury, the last piston-engined fighter in RN front-line service, continued flying with Royal Navy Volunteer Reserve units until 1957 and was replaced in FAA service by the Sea Hawk.

Although the RAF rejected the Fury design, a little-known contract with Iraq saw 55 land-based Furies and five two-seat trainers delivered to the Iraqi Air Force between 1948 and 1955. The IAF are known to have used the aircraft in a counter-insurgency role. Pakistan also received Furies and used them in action against India until 1973.

Sea Furies were also exported to Egypt, Burma, Canada, Australia and the Netherlands, where a number were also licence-built by Fokker. At the time of the Cuban Missile Crisis in 1962, Cuba's fighter defence centred on 15 FB.11s, which had been imported in the Batista period.

After their military service a number of these high-performance piston aircraft were snapped up for air racing in the United States, where they set world record speeds.

ABOVE: **The Royal Netherlands Navy was the only other European operator of the Sea Fury. Twenty-two aircraft were exported from the UK while a further 210 were built in Holland by Fokker.** BELOW: **The Royal Australian Navy's HMAS *Sydney* took its Sea Furies into combat during the Korean War.**

Hawker Sea Fury FB.11

First flight: September 1, 1944

Power: Bristol 2480hp Centaurus 18 two-row sleeve-valve radial engine

Armament: Four 20mm/0.78in cannon in outer wings, plus underwing provision for up to 907kg/2000lb of bombs or rockets

Size: Wingspan – 11.69m/38ft 4.75in, spread 4.9m/16ft 1in, folded
Length – 10.56m/34ft 8in
Height – 4.81m/15ft 10in
Wing area – 26.01m^2/280sq ft

Weights: Empty – 4090kg/8977lb
Maximum take-off – 5669kg/12,500lb

Performance: Maximum speed – 740kph/460mph
Ceiling – 11,000m/36,000ft
Range – 1223km /760 miles
Climb – 1320m/4320ft per minute

Hindustan HF-24 Marut	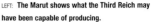

First flight: June 17, 1961
Power: Two HAL/Rolls-Royce 2200kg/4850lb-thrust Orpheus Mk 703 turbojet engines
Armament: Four 30mm/1.18in cannon, plus retractable pack of 50 68mm/2.68in rockets in belly, plus hardpoints to carry a variety of weapons
Size: Wingspan – 9m/29ft 6.25in
Length – 15.87m/52ft 0.75in
Height – 3.6m/11ft 9.75in
Wing area – 28m²/301.6sq ft
Weights: Empty – 6195kg/13,658lb
Maximum take-off – 10,908kg/24,048lb
Performance: Maximum speed – 1112kph/691mph
Ceiling – 12,200m/40,000ft
Range – 1000km/620 miles
Climb – 12,200m/40,000ft in 9 minutes 20 seconds

Hindustan HF-24 Marut

The Marut (spirit of the tempest) was the first fruit of the Indian Air Staff's desire for their country to be self-reliant in combat aircraft production. In mid-1950s India, however, there was little expertise in jet aircraft design so the famous Focke-Wulf designer Kurt Tank was invited to create a team (that ultimately included 18 German engineers) to work on the project in India. Design work began in 1957 with

the aim of building a Mach-2 capable all-weather multi-role aircraft.

The prototype first flew in June 1961, powered by two Rolls-Royce Bristol Orpheus 703 turbojets and the production aircraft had Indian licence-built Orpheus engines. The Marut finally entered service in April 1967 and was the first supersonic fighter built by a non-superpower.

By late 1975 about 100 aircraft had been delivered and had seen action

in the 1971 war against Pakistan, on some occasions dogfighting with enemy F-86 Sabres.

The Marut did not meet expectations as a fighter, but it served the Indian Air Force well until mid-1990.

IAI Kfir-C7	✡

First flight: October 19, 1970 (Kfir prototype)
Power: IAI/General Electric 8112kg/17,860lb after-burning thrust licence-built J79-JIE turbojet engine
Armament: Two 30mm/1.18in cannon, five underfuselage and two underwing hardpoints for AIM-9 Sidewinder, Python or Shafir air-to-air missiles or anti-radar missiles and bombs
Size: Wingspan – 8.22m/27ft
Length – 15.65m/51ft 4in
Height – 4.55m/14ft 11in
Wing area – 34.8m²/374.6sq ft
Weights: Empty –7285kg/16,060lb
Maximum take-off – 16,500kg/36,375lb
Performance: Maximum speed – Mach 2.3/2440kph/1515mph
Ceiling – 17,690m/58,000ft
Range – 882km/548 miles
Climb – 13,989m/45,866ft per minute

Israel Aircraft Industries Kfir

The original Kfir (lion cub) prototype that first flew on October 19, 1970 combined a French-built Mirage III airframe with the licence-built GE-J79 afterburning turbojet of the F-4 Phantom II. By the time the Kfir reached production in 1974–5, the airframe was a version of the Israeli-built Mirage 5 (Nesher), equipped with Israeli-built electronics. Only 27 Kfir-C1s were built and 25 were later sold on to the US

Navy and Marine Corps for use as "aggressor" aircraft, designated F-21A.

The first of 185 Kfir-C2s entered service in 1976, having first flown in 1974. It sported a canard mounted on the air-intakes. Virtually all C1s were upgraded to C2 standard.

The Kfir-C7 was introduced in 1983 and is an improved upgraded version of the C2, with a more powerful engine and improved performance. It can also

carry "smart" weapons, has a sophisticated cockpit and is equipped for inflight refuelling.

The Kfir, widely considered to be the most potent development of the Mirage, is expected to be phased out of IAF service in the early 2000s.

Lavochkin La-11

This aircraft was among the last Soviet piston-engined fighters produced and emerged into a world of jet aircraft. Developed from the earlier Lavochkin La-9, the La-11 was designed to escort Soviet bombers on their long missions. Although it had the same engine and the wing was similar to that of the La-9, other changes were incorporated. Auxiliary fuel tanks were added to the wingtips and the earlier aircraft's distinctive underbelly oil cooler was built into the engine cowling. Armament was reduced from four to three 23mm/0.9in cannon.

The new aircraft first flew in late 1944 and remained in production until 1951 by which time 1182 examples had been built. Both the North Korean and Chinese air forces were supplied with La-11s and the type was used in combat during the Korean War (1950–3). By the end of that conflict, the La-11 was being phased out as a fighter by all operating air arms but a number carried on in second-line training duties into the 1960s.

TOP: **The La-11 was the end of the line for Soviet piston-engined fighters, and saw action in the Korean War.** ABOVE: **This example crash-landed in Sweden during World War II.**

Lavochkin La-11

First flight: late 1944
Power: Shvetsov 1870hp ASh-82FNV radial piston engine
Armament: Three 23mm/0.9in cannon
Size: Wingspan – 9.95m/32ft 7.75in
Length – 8.6m/28ft 2.5in
Height – 2.95m/9ft 8in
Wing area – 17.7m²/190.53sq ft
Weights: Empty – 2770kg/6107lb
Maximum take-off – 3995kg/8807lb
Performance: Maximum speed – 690kph/429mph
Ceiling – 10,250m/33,630ft
Range – 750km/466 miles
Climb – 5000m/16,405ft in 6 minutes, 35 seconds

Lockheed F-80 Shooting Star

Lockheed began design work on a jet fighter as early as 1941 but abandoned it due to lack of the right powerplant. Work restarted in earnest in June 1943, when the British de Havilland Goblin jet engine (1361kg/3000lb thrust) became available. The first prototype was built and ready to fly in only 143 days but its maiden flight was delayed due to an engine

failure and the XP-80 finally took to the sky in January 1944. Later prototypes and the first P-80As were powered by a General Electric engine developed from Frank Whittle's W.1 turbojet. Early tests flights saw the aircraft attain speeds of 805kph/500mph, considerably faster than the piston-engined fighters in service at the time and the 660kph/410mph of the Gloster Meteor Mk 1.

ABOVE: **Too late for action in World War II, the Lockheed P-80 (later F-80) was the USA's first jet fighter.** BELOW LEFT: **The two-seater trainer version, the T-33, still flies with air forces around the world, and many are also in private hands.**

The sleek low-winged P-80 entered USAAF service in February 1945 and the first Shooting Stars, pre-production models, arrived in Italy before the end of World War II. By the end of the war a total of 45 had been delivered to the USAAF but they did not see service. The first unit solely to operate the P-80 was the 412th Fighter Group established at March Field in November 1945.

Post-war the P-80 was selected to re-equip pursuit (fighter) units of the USAAF and was the first jet fighter to be entrusted with the task of defending the USA, until being superseded by the F-86 Sabre.

In 1948, a wing of P-80As were deployed to Fürstenfeldbrück during the Berlin Airlift, in reaction to Yak-3s and La-5FNs buzzing Allied transport aircraft. As the USAF's first jet fighter, its deployment demonstrated the gravity with which the West viewed the situation. Also in 1948, the USAF (an independent service from September 1947, formerly USAAF) changed the designation of its pursuit aircraft to fighters and the P-80 became the F-80.

The last P-80A was built in December 1946 and was replaced on the production line by the much improved P-80B, which was some 454kg/1000lb heavier and powered by a better engine.

When the Korean War broke out in 1950 the F-80 was the principal USAF fighter in the theatre and ultimately the 8th,

35th, 49th and 51st Fighter Groups all flew Shooting Stars in Korea. On June 27, 1950 the first jet fighter combat involving US fighters saw four F-80s shoot down four North Korean Air Force Ilyushin Il-10 Shturmoviks.

By now the F-80C, the definitive fighter version of the Shooting Star, was in service and among other improvements offered the pilot the reassurance of an ejection seat. It was also the first USAF aircraft equipped with an explosive canopy remover. Produced in greater numbers than any other version, many earlier models were at least partly upgraded to "C" standard.

The first jet against jet air combat came on November 8, 1950, when four MiGs were seen to fly into Korean air space and were challenged by F-80Cs of the 51st Fighter-Interceptor Wing. Even though all but one of his guns jammed, Lt Russell J. Brown attacked and destroyed one of the MiGs in mid-air. In spite of this and other air combat successes, the F-80 was replaced by F-84s and F-86s during the conflict, as it had become outclassed, but it continued to serve in the fighter-bomber role.

Although the Shooting Star broke much new ground with the US Air Force, it was not widely exported, the only customers being in South America – Ecuador, Chile, Brazil, Uruguay, Colombia and Peru.

The trainer version, the two-seat T-33, was, however, widely exported and continues to serve in air arms half a century after the single-seat P-80 fighter first flew. The T-33 version was created by extending the fuselage to accommodate the two seats in tandem. Between 1949 and 1959 Lockheed built 5691 T-33s and they served with the air forces of nearly 30 countries.

Lockheed F-80C Shooting Star

First flight: January 8, 1944 (XP-80)

Power: Allison 2449kg/5,400lb-thrust J33-A-35 turbojet engine

Armament: Six 12.7mm/0.5in machine-guns, plus two 454kg/1000lb bombs and eight underwing rockets

Size: Wingspan – 11.81m/38ft 9in
Length – 10.49m/34ft 5in
Height – 3.43m/11ft 3in
Wing area – 22.07m^2/237.6sq ft

Weights: Empty – 3819kg/8420lb
Maximum take-off – 7646kg/16,856lb

Performance: Maximum speed – 956kph/594mph
Ceiling – 14,265m/46,800ft
Range – 1328km/825 miles
Climb – 1524m/5000ft per minute

TOP: **Deployed to Europe during the Berlin Airlift, the Shooting Star first fired its guns in combat during the Korean War, where it was able to hold its own for a time against the MiG-15.** ABOVE: **Tasked with defending the USA, P-80s protected their country until the arrival of the much more able F-86 Sabres.**

LEFT: **Hastily produced to defend the USA against Soviet bombers, the F-94 was derived from the T-33.** BELOW: **A battery of 48 unguided missiles gave the F-94 a powerful punch intended to knock enemy bombers from the sky.**

Lockheed F-94

When the USSR exploded its first atomic bomb in 1949, the USA quickly began to develop a range of interceptors that could tackle the expected Soviet bomber fleets. Some were to be developed for the USAF's Air Defense Command over the long term while others, such as the F-94, were rushed into production as stop-gaps.

The tandem-seat F-94 was one of the earliest radar-equipped jet fighters and eventually made up more than 24 squadrons of the fledgling US Air Defense Command, founded on 21 March 1946 to defend the USA. Based on the T-33, the F-94 was fitted with radar, carried a rear-seat observer and was armed with only four 12.7mm/0.5in machine-guns.

The prototype YF-94 first flew in April 1949 and the first production aircraft were in squadron service by the end of that year, such was the urgency to counter the perceived Soviet threat. The ADC F-94s were kept on three-minute alert for the interception of enemy bombers. With 427kg/940lb of radar kit on board, it needed an afterburner to lift off. Once airborne, the F-94 had a performance on a par with the F-80 but no better.

A total of 853 F-94s were built, and A and B models saw action in Korea,

particularly on night missions, although because of their secret radar, they were initially forbidden to overfly enemy territory. When regulations were relaxed, the F-94 began to score victories over the enemy at night and solely by use of instruments.

Named Starfire in the C variant only, the F-94C had a more powerful engine (and in turn a higher top speed), thinner wing, swept tailplane, longer fuselage and a new airborne interception radar. Armament was beefed up to 24 Mighty Mouse rockets and a further 24 housed in wing launchers. These rockets were unguided and were simply intended to destroy bombers by filling the sky with "lead". As the new generation of interceptors came into service, the F-94 was gradually retired and the type ended its brief but useful career equipping National Guard Units in the mid-1950s.

ABOVE: **This aircraft, 48-356, was the YF-94A prototype, having already served as the T-33 prototype in 1948. It is preserved in the USA at a United States Air Force base.**

Lockheed F-94

First flight: April 16, 1949 (YF-94)
Power: Pratt & Whitney 3969kg/8750lb afterburning thrust J48-P-5 turbojet engine
Armament: 24 69.85mm/2.75in Mighty Mouse air-to-air rocket projectiles, plus a further 24 housed in wing launchers
Size: Wingspan – 12.93m/42ft 5in
Length – 13.56m/44ft 6in
Height – 4.55m/14ft 11in
Wing area – 31.4m²/338sq ft
Weights: Empty – 5761kg/12,700lb
Maximum take-off – 10,977kg/24,200lb
Performance: Maximum speed – 941kph/585mph
Ceiling – 15,665m/51,400ft
Range – 1930km/1200 miles
Climb – 2430m/7980ft per minute

Lockheed F-104 Starfighter

The F-104 was designed by Lockheed based on the experiences of American pilots in the Korean War – high performance was the overriding feature of this aircraft, which was frequently described as a missile with a man in it. The short wing had a maximum thickness of 10.16cm/4in and had a leading edge so sharp that when the F-104 was on the ground, it had to have a safety covering for the protection of ground crews. The Starfighter, once nicknamed "Widowmaker" because of the large number of fatal crashes of the type, found greater use with foreign air forces than with the US Air Force.

Development problems delayed the type's entry into USAF service by two years, and deliveries began in January 1958. The F-104 was the first operational fighter capable of sustained speeds above twice the speed of sound and became the first aircraft ever to hold the world speed and altitude records simultaneously. On May 7, 1958 Major Howard C. Johnson reached an altitude of 27,830m/91,243ft, and on May 16, Captain Walter W. Irwin reached a speed of 2259.3kph/1404.19mph.

On December 14, 1959, an F-104C Starfighter boosted the world's altitude record to 31,534m/103,389ft, becoming the first aircraft to take-off under its own power and exceed the 30,480m/100,000ft barrier.

The F-104G that first flew in October 1960 was an all-new version designed for the Luftwaffe as a fighter-bomber and was the most successful mark.

The US Air Force used only about one-third of the F-104s built, with most going to or being built in Canada, West Germany, Italy, Japan, Belgium, Denmark, Greece, Norway, Spain, Taiwan, Jordan, Pakistan and Turkey. In the USA, the last Air National Guard Starfighters were retired in 1975.

In 1997–8, the Italian Air Force extended the life of their licence-built F-104s to keep them flying half a century after the prototype had its maiden flight.

RIGHT: **The F-104G was a multi-role fighter-bomber version designed to meet a Luftwaffe requirement.** BELOW: **Clearly illustrating its nickname, the sleek lines of the F-104 fuselage were very missile-like. It was the "hot ship" of its time.**

Lockheed F-104G Starfighter

First flight: March 4, 1954 (XF-104)
Power: General Electric 7076kg/15,600lb afterburning thrust J79-GE-11A turbojet engine
Armament: One 20mm/0.78in six barrel cannon, wingtip-mounted Sidewinder air-to-air missiles and up to 1814kg/4000lb of external stores
Size: Wingspan – 6.36m/21ft 9in, excluding wingtip missiles
  Length – 16.66m/54ft 8in
  Height – 4.09m/13ft 5in
  Wing area – 18.22m²/196.1sq ft
Weights: Empty – 6348kg/13,995lb
  Maximum take-off – 13,170kg/29,035lb
Performance: Maximum speed – 1845kph/1146mph
  Ceiling – 15,240m/50,000ft
  Range – 1740km/1081 miles
  Climb – 14,640m/48,000ft per minute

General Dynamics/Lockheed Martin F-16 Fighting Falcon

The F-16 Fighting Falcon, with its origins in the 1972 USAF Lightweight Fighter Program, is one of the best combat aircraft in service today. It is highly manoeuvrable and has proven itself in air-to-air combat and air-to-surface attack. It is a relatively low-cost, high-performance weapons system used by the USAF and a number of other nations.

The single-seat F-16A first flew in December 1976 and became operational with the USAF in January 1979. The F-16B, a two-seat model, has tandem cockpits with a bubble canopy extended to cover the second cockpit. Space for the second cockpit was created by reducing the forward fuselage fuel tank size and reduction of avionics growth space. During training, the forward cockpit is used by a student pilot with an instructor pilot in the rear cockpit.

All F-16s delivered since November 1981 have built-in structural and wiring provisions and systems architecture that permit expansion of the multi-role flexibility to perform precision strike, night attack and beyond-visual-range interception missions. This improvement programme led to the F-16C and F-16D aircraft, which are the single- and two-seat equivalents of the F-16A/B, and incorporate the latest cockpit control and display technology. All active USAF units and many Air National Guard and Air Force Reserve units have converted to the F-16C/D.

The F-16 was also licence-built by Belgium, Denmark, the Netherlands and Norway – who needed to replace their F-104 Starfighters. Final airframe assembly lines were located in Belgium and the Netherlands, and these European F-16s are assembled from components manufactured in the four client countries as well as in the USA. Belgium also provided final assembly of the F100 engine used in the European F-16s. The programme increased the supply and availability of repair parts in Europe and thus improved the Europe-based F-16's combat readiness. Turkey also had an F-16 production line.

In the air combat role, the F-16's manoeuvrability and combat radius exceed that of all potential threat fighter aircraft. It can locate targets in all-weather conditions and detect low-flying aircraft in radar ground clutter. In an air-to-surface role, the F-16 can fly more than 860km/500 miles, deliver its weapons with superior accuracy while defending itself against enemy aircraft, and then return to base. The

TOP: **This early F-16 caused a stir when it visited the UK in the late 1970s. The type was a quantum leap in fighter design.** ABOVE: **The highly manoeuvrable fly-by-wire F-16 is always a favourite at air shows.**

aircraft's all-weather capability allows it to deliver ordnance accurately during non-visual bombing conditions.

In designing the F-16, advanced aerospace science and proven reliable systems from other aircraft such as the F-15 and F-111 were selected. These were combined to simplify the design process and reduce the aircraft's size, purchase price, maintenance costs and weight. The light weight of the fuselage is achieved without reducing its strength – with a full load of internal fuel, the F-16 can withstand up to 9G, which exceeds the capability of other current fighter aircraft. The cockpit and its bubble canopy give the pilot unobstructed

ABOVE: **F-16s will be in service for many years to come.** FAR LEFT: **The USAF Thunderbirds aerobatic team were a great advertisement for the type.** LEFT: **An excellent photograph of an F-16C Fighting Falcon, showing the cockpit area and to its right the exit nozzle of the internal cannon.**

forward and upward vision, and greatly improved vision over the side and to the rear while the seat-back angle was expanded from the normal 13 degrees to 30 degrees, increasing pilot comfort and gravity force tolerance. The pilot has excellent flight control of the F-16 through its fly-by-wire system, where electrical wires relay commands, replacing the usual cables and linkage controls. For easy and accurate control of the aircraft during high G-force combat manoeuvres, a side-stick controller is used instead of the conventional centre-mounted control column. Hand pressure on the side-stick controller sends electrical signals to actuators of flight control surfaces such as ailerons and rudder.

Avionics systems include a highly accurate inertial navigation system in which a computer provides steering information to the pilot. The plane has UHF and VHF radios, plus an instrument (automatic) landing system. It also has a warning system and electronic countermeasure pods to be used against airborne or surface electronic threats.

USAF F-16Cs and Ds were deployed to the Persian Gulf during 1991 in support of Operation Desert Storm, where more sorties were flown than with any other aircraft. These versatile fighters were used to attack airfields, military production facilities, Scud missile sites and a variety of other targets.

In February 1994, Italy-based USAF F-16s, deployed to help NATO keep the peace in Bosnia, engaged and destroyed Serb bombers attacking targets in central Bosnia. Turkish licence-built F-16s also enforced the No Fly Zone over Bosnia. Other F-16 operators include Bahrain, Egypt, Greece, Indonesia, Israel, Pakistan, South Korea, Portugal, Singapore, Taiwan, Thailand and Venezuela. The 4000th F-16 was delivered in May 2000 and production and upgrades will undoubtedly keep the F-16 in the front line for many years to come.

ABOVE: **Belgium was one of the European nations who engaged in a licence-build F-16 programme.**

General Dynamics/ Lockheed Martin F-16A

First flight: January 20, 1974 (YF-16)
Power: Pratt & Whitney 10,824kg/23,830lb afterburning thrust F100-PW-100 turbofan engine
Armament: One 20mm/0.78in cannon, nine hard points to carry up to 5435kg/12,000lb of air-to-air missiles, bombs and rockets
Size: Wingspan – 10m/32ft 10in, including wingtip air-to-air missiles
Length – 15.03m/49ft 4in
Height – 5.01m/16ft 5in
Wing area – 28.9m^2/300sq ft
Weights: Empty – 6607kg/14,567lb
Maximum take-off – 14,968kg/33,000lb
Performance: Maximum speed – 2125kph/1320mph
Ceiling – 15,250m/50,000ft plus
Range – 580km/360 miles
Climb – 15,250m/50,000ft per minute

Lockheed Martin/Boeing F-22 Raptor

The advanced air superiority F-22 Raptor fighter was developed in response to a 1983 United States Air Force request for designs of an Advanced Tactical Fighter – a next generation, air superiority fighter. The designs of current front-line US fighter aircraft are decades old and with so much new technology now available, the US military are keen that replacement aircraft incorporate as many new developments in performance and function as possible.

The Lockheed proposal, the YF-22A, was rolled out on August 29, 1990, and first flew on September 29 having been unofficially named Lightning II, after the famous Lockheed fighter of World War II. More stealthy than the F-15, the YF-22A design was more optimized for manoeuvrability, featuring design elements such as vertical thrust vectoring engine exhausts.

The YF-22 was declared the winner of the competition in April 1991 – the first true F-22 impressive prototype was rolled out on April 9, 1997 and its first flight was on September 7, 1997. Flight tests demonstrate that the F-22 combines good handling characteristics with very high manoeuvrability and the

ABOVE: **The second F-22, pictured here on its first flight on June 29, 1998. The Raptor is considered by many to be the world's most advanced fighter.**

test program is expected to continue through 2003, with operational introduction of the Raptor scheduled for 2005.

The heart of the F-22's electronic capability is the APG-77 radar system which is able to detect an enemy aircraft's radar from distances up to 460km/286 miles. It will then acquire the enemy aircraft as a target it can kill at distances of up to 220km/136 miles – the F-22 radar signal will be very difficult to detect and the stealthy F-22 will be virtually invisible to radar.

If the enemy does manage to detect the signal, they must then get a radar lock on the F-22 to launch an attack – the F-22 radar can also analyze the enemy's radar and send out a jamming burst. Between dealing with active threats, the radar system collects information from the combat area, locates electronic systems, classifies them, and alerts the pilot to possible threats or high-priority targets. The F-22's avionics were designed to enable a lone pilot to undertake missions that normally require a two-man crew.

As a safety measure, the aircraft's eight internal fuel tanks are flooded with nitrogen to reduce the danger of fire from fuel fumes. The gas is produced by an on-board nitrogen generation system from air.

Ground crews can monitor the status of the aircraft systems through a laptop computer that can list faults, undertake diagnosis and even check the oil level.

The F-22 is constructed mainly from composites and titanium alloys. Radar absorbent materials are used to minimize the aircraft's radar signature, and the aircraft's shape is intended to make it less conspicuous to radar. The aircraft's frameless canopy is also designed to reduce radar reflections.

The cockpit control layout is based on high-intensity monitor displays, plus a holographic Head-Up Display (HUD). The cockpit also features HOTAS controls so the pilot can issue commands to the systems without releasing the flight controls.

The Pratt & Whitney F-119-PW-100 engine is very advanced but has been designed for ease of maintenance so that all components can be removed or replaced with one of six standard tools. The engine includes vertical thrust vectoring

ABOVE: **The F-22 is expected to be operational from 2005 and will be capable of achieving air superiority in the most hostile air combat situations.**
BELOW: **Pictured at Edwards Air Force Base, California, in October 1999, the F-22 incorporates all relevant new technologies.**

exhaust nozzles to improve the Raptor's manoeuvrability in low-speed combat and are automatically directed by the F-22's flight control system. The exhaust does not emit visible smoke during normal operations. The engine's supersonic cruise capability allows, without the use of afterburner, rapid location to a combat area, fast exit from the target area as a means of defence and higher launch velocities for munitions.

Despite some official doubts about the need for an advanced fighter that is estimated to cost at least $70 million a unit, the USAF plans to field 339 Raptors. The first squadron will be operational by 2005.

Lockheed Martin/ Boeing F-22 Raptor

First flight: September 29, 1990 (YF-22)
Power: Two Pratt & Whitney 16,095kg/35,438lb afterburning thrust F119-100 turbofans
Armament: One 20mm/0.78in cannon, four AIM-9 Sidewinders carried in side weapons bays. Ventral weapons bay can carry four AIM-120 AAMs or six AIM-120s. Additional ordnance can be carried on four underwing hardpoints
Size: Wingspan – 13.56m/44ft
Length – 18.92m/62ft 1in
Height – 5m/16ft 5in
Wing area – 78m²/840sq ft
Weights: Empty – 14,395kg/31,760lb
Maximum take-off – 27,216kg/60,000lb
Performance: Maximum speed – Mach 2
Ceiling – 15,250m/50,000ft
Range and climb data not published

LEFT: **A US Navy F2H-2 Banshee – note the straight wings.**

McDonnell F2H-3 Banshee

First flight: January 11, 1947
Power: Two Westinghouse 1474kg/3250lb thrust J34-WE-34 turbojets
Armament: Four 20mm/0.78in cannon plus underwing racks for 454kg/1000lb of bombs
Size: Wingspan – 12.73m/41ft 9in
Length – 14.68m/48ft 2in
Height – 4.42m/14ft 6in
Wing area – 27.31m^2/294sq ft
Weights: Empty – 5980kg/13,183lb
Maximum take-off – 11,437kg/25,214lb
Performance: Maximum speed – 933kph/580mph
Ceiling – 14,205m.46,600ft
Range – 1883km/1170 miles
Climb – 2743m/9000ft per minute

McDonnell F2H Banshee

The F2H Banshee, though similar in design and appearance to the company's earlier FH-1 Phantom, was larger and had more powerful twin Westinghouse J34 engines which gave about twice the power of the J30 engines in the FH-1.

Designed to meet the US Navy's exacting requirements for carrier operations, while also satisfying the requirement for high speed and increased rates of climb, the F2H Banshee first flew in January 1947. It became the Navy's standard long-range all-weather fighter and entered US Navy service in 1948 as their second carrier jet fighter, after the FH-1. They served with distinction with the US Navy in Korea in 1950–3 but by the end of the conflict they had been superseded by more advanced designs. That said, Banshees remained in service with US Navy reserve units until the mid-1960s.

The Royal Canadian Navy acquired 39 ex-US Navy Banshees between 1955 and 1958. A total of 805 F2H Banshees were made.

McDonnell F3H Demon

LEFT: **The F3H was planned to be the world's first missile-only fighter.**

McDonnell F3H-2 Demon

First flight: August 7, 1951 (XF3H-1)
Power: Allison 6350kg/14,000lb afterburning thrust J71-A-2E turbojet
Armament: Four 20mm/0.78in cannon and four AIM-7C Sparrow AAMs
Size: Wingspan – 10.77m/35ft 4in
Length – 17.96m/58ft 11in
Height – 4.44m/14ft 7in
Wing area – 48.22m^2/519sq ft
Weights: Empty – 10,039kg/22,133lb
Maximum take-off – 15377kg/33,900lb
Performance: Maximum speed – 1041kph/647mph
Ceiling – 13,000m/42,650ft
Range – 2205km/1370 miles
Climb – 3660m/12,000ft per minute

The F3H Demon was the first swept-wing jet fighter aircraft built by McDonnell Aircraft and also the first aircraft designed to be armed only with missiles rather than guns. The carrier-based, transonic, all-weather Demon fighter was designed with the philosophy that carrier-based fighters need not be inferior to land-based fighters. However, the planned powerplant, the new J40 turbojet, failed to meet its expectations and left early Demons (F3H-1N) under-powered. Production delays were also caused by the Navy's desire for the Demon to be an all-weather nightfighter. And so, although the prototype had flown in August 1951, the radar-equipped Demon did not enter service until March 1956 as the F3H-2N and then with the Allison J71 turbojet as the powerplant.

By the time production ceased in 1959, 519 Demons had been built including the definitive Demon fighter-bomber (F3H-2). At its peak US Navy use, the Demon equipped 11 squadrons.

McDonnell F-101 Voodoo

Developed from the XF-88 prototype interceptor that first flew in 1948, the F-101 Voodoo was conceived as a long-range escort fighter for USAF Strategic Air Command B-36s. The F-101 was never going to have the range to stay with the intercontinental bombers but with the still impressive range of over 2414km/1500 miles, the Voodoo went on to a lengthy career as an interceptor and the first USAF

supersonic reconnaissance aircraft. The prototype F-101A first flew in September 1954, and after entering USAF service in 1957 the F-101 was used in a number of speed and endurance record attempts, which were intended to show the Soviets just how fast and far USAF fighters could go. On November 27, 1957, four RF-101As (reconnaissance

versions) took off from California and after refuelling in flight, two of the aircraft landed at McGuire Air Force Base, New Jersey, while the other two turned around and landed back at March Air Force Base in California on the other side of the continental United States. Meanwhile, Major Adrian Drew, flying an F-101A at Edwards Air Force Base, set a new absolute speed record of 1942.97kph/1207.34mph. All these record-breaking flights earned the Voodoo the nickname "One-Oh-Wonder".

The two-seat all-weather F-101B first flew in 1957. In service it had a Hughes fire-control system and was armed with six Falcon air-to-air missiles, or two Genie nuclear-tipped air-to-air missiles and four Falcons.

Fifty-six surplus Voodoos were transferred to the Royal Canadian Air Force in 1961 as CF-101Bs. A decade later these were replaced by more capable ex-USAF aircraft that continued in RCAF service until 1985. USAF and

RCAF Voodoos guarded the polar approaches to North America against Soviet bombers.

The last US Air Force F-101 was retired in 1971, while the last Air National Guard F-101s were retired in 1983. Reconnaissance versions of the Voodoo were also supplied to the Chinese Nationalist Air Force.

McDonnell F-101B Voodoo

First flight: September 29, 1954 (F-101A)

Power: Two Pratt & Whitney 6749kg/14,880lb afterburning thrust J57-P-55 turbojet engines

Armament: Two MB-1 Genie nuclear-tipped air-to-air missiles and four Falcon air-to-air missiles or six Falcon air-to-air missiles

Size: Wingspan – 12.09m/39ft 8in
Length – 20.54m/67ft 4.75in
Height – 5.49m/18ft
Wing area – 34.19m²/368sq ft

Weights: Empty – 13,141kg/28,970lb
Maximum take-off – 23,768kg/52,400lb

Performance: Maximum speed – 1965kph/1221mph
Ceiling – 16,705m/54,800ft
Range – 2494km/1550 miles
Climb – 11,133m/36,500ft per minute

ABOVE LEFT: **The F-101 Voodoo set a number of speed and endurance records.** BELOW: **The RF-101 was the first USAF supersonic reconnaissance platform.**

McDonnell Douglas F-4 Phantom II

One of the world's greatest ever combat aircraft, the two-seat Phantom was designed to meet a US Navy requirement for a fleet defence fighter to replace the F3H Demon and counter the threat from long-range Soviet bombers. When the F-4 proved faster than their F-104 Starfighter, the United States Air Force ordered the Phantom too.

The F-4 was first used by the United States Navy as an interceptor but was soon employed by the US Marine Corps (USMC) in the ground support role. Its outstanding versatility made it the first US multi-service aircraft flying concurrently with the US Air Force, Navy and Marine Corps. The Phantom excelled in air superiority, close air support, interception, air defence suppression, long-range strike, fleet defence, attack and reconnaissance.

The sophisticated F-4 was, without direction from surface-based radar, able to detect and destroy a target beyond visual range (BVR). In the Vietnam and Gulf Wars alone, the F-4 was credited with 280 air-to-air victories.

Capable of flying at twice the speed of sound with ease, the Phantom was loved by its crews, who considered it a workhorse that could be relied on, that could do the job and get them home safely. F-4s have also set world records for altitude (30,040m/98,556ft on December 6, 1959), speed (2585kph/1606mph on November 22, 1961) and a low-altitude

TOP: **The F-4 Phantom, a truly classic combat aircraft, served US forces until 1996.** ABOVE: **Britain's Royal Navy operated the F-4 from its carriers from 1968.**

speed record of 1452kph/902mph that stood for 16 years. Phantom production ran from 1958 to 1979, resulting in a total of 5195 aircraft. 5057 were made in St Louis, Missouri, in the USA while a further 138 were built under licence by the Mitsubishi Aircraft Co. in Japan. F-4 production peaked in 1967, when the McDonnell plant was producing 72 Phantoms per month.

The US Air Force had 2874 F-4s, while the US Navy and USMC operated 1264. A number of refurbished ex-US forces aircraft were operated by other nations, including the UK, who bought a squadron of mothballed ex-US Navy F-4Js to complement the RAF's F-4Ms.

LEFT: **The Royal Air Force operated F-4s from 1968 until 1992, including some ex-Royal Navy examples.**

Regularly updated with the addition of state-of-the-art weaponry and radar, the Phantom served with 11 nations around the globe – Australia, Egypt, Germany, Greece, Iran, Israel, Japan, South Korea, Spain, Turkey and the UK. Britain's Royal Navy and Royal Air Force both operated Phantoms from 1968 and the last RAF Phantoms were retired in January 1992. The Phantom retired from US military forces in 1996, by which time the type had flown more than 27,350,000km (around 17 million miles) in the nation's service. In May 1998, when the aircraft was celebrating 40 years in the air, the Phantom was still flying in defence of eight nations – Egypt, Germany, Greece, Israel, Japan, South Korea, Spain and Turkey. Israel, Japan, Germany,

Turkey, Greece, South Korea and Egypt have undertaken or plan to upgrade their F-4s and keep them flying until 2015, nearly 60 years after the Phantom's first flight on May 27, 1958.

LEFT: **This German Air Force F-4 is typical of the many examples bought by foreign air arms.** BELOW LEFT: **This fine study of an RAF F-4 shows the impressive weapon load that made the Phantom such a formidable fighter.**

McDonnell Douglas Phantom FGR.2 (F-4M)

First flight: February 17, 1967

Power: Two Rolls-Royce 9305kg/20,515lb afterburns thrust Spey 202 turbofans

Armament: Fighter role – Four Sky Flash or Sparrow medium-range air-to-air guided missiles, four AIM-9 Sidewinder short-range air-to-air missiles and a 20mm/0.79in rotary cannon

Size: Wingspan – 11.68m/38ft 4in
Length – 17.73m/58ft 2in
Height – 4.95m/16ft 3in
Wing area – 49.25m²/530sq ft

Weights: Empty 14,080kg/31,000lb
Maximum take-off – 26,300kg/58,000lb

Performance: Maximum speed – 2230kph/1386mph
Ceiling – 18,300m/60,000ft
Range – 2815km/1750 miles
Climb – 9760m/32,000ft per minute

215

Mikoyan-Gurevich MiG-15

This formidable fighter was designed in the USSR with the benefit of swept-wing research captured from the Germans at the end of World War II. The RD-45 engine, an illegally copied Rolls-Royce Nene turbojet, was far more advanced than contemporary Russian engines and produced a performance that could outclass virtually all NATO's fighters of the time. The MiG-15 was developed for the Project S requirement for an interceptor designed to shoot down heavy bombers and was armed with one 37mm/1.45in cannon and two 23mm/0.9in cannon – German experience in World War II found that cannons larger than 20mm/0.79in were needed to bring down four-engine bombers.

The MiG-15 first flew in December 1947 but it only came to the attention of the West during the Korean War. On November 1, 1950 some USAF P-51 Mustang pilots reported coming under fire from six swept-wing jet fighters that had flown across the Yalu river from Manchuria – the Mikoyan-Gurevich MiG-15 was now in the Korean War and gave the United Nations forces a wake-up call.

After the first combat encounters with Western fighters, the MiG-15bis (improved) version appeared. Its VK-1 engine had 454kg/1000lb more thrust than the RD-45 of the earlier version, was lighter and could carry a greater fuel load. The Russian jets were starting to enjoy relatively easy victories against USAF B-29 bombers, which had previously operated in relative safety. Flying from Chinese bases immune from UN attack, the MiGs were used to defend North Korean installations and represented a major threat to UN air superiority in the north where they created the very dangerous "MiG Alley". UN aircraft could fly freely across the battlefields but faced deadly opposition when they neared areas in range of the MiG bases. The MiGs forced the B-29s to move their operations to night-time.

The USAF was quick to respond to the MiG threat by deploying the F-86A Sabre, the most modern USAF fighter available. Even so, the MiG had a better rate of climb, a tighter turning circle and a much better ceiling than the early three-cannon Sabre. The Sabre's armament of six 12.7mm/0.5in machine-guns was no match for the MiGs, although the Sabre was a steadier gun platform.

The first MiG versus Sabre dogfight took place on December 17, 1950, when four F-86s came upon four MiGs at an altitude of 7620m/25,000ft. Leader of the F-86 section, Lt Colonel Bruce H. Hinton, fired 1500 rounds of ammunition and set fire to one of the MiGs, causing it to crash.

During the Korean War, the NATO Allies were so desperate to examine a MiG at close quarters that they offered a $100,000 reward for any pilot who would defect and bring his MiG-15 with him. When a North Korean pilot, Lt Ro Kun Suk, did defect in September 1953 he was not aware of the prize but was given it anyway.

BELOW: **Developed with captured wartime German data, the MiG-15 is a classic jet fighter aircraft.**

LEFT: **Operating from Chinese bases during the Korean War, the MiG-15s were immune to UN attack on the ground.** BELOW: **The arrival of the MiG-15 in the sky over Korea came as an unpleasant surprise to the West.**

Codenamed "Fagot" by NATO, the MiG-15 became standard equipment with Warsaw Pact air forces until the late 1960s, when it was relegated to training duties. At least 3000 single-seat MiG-15s were built in the former Soviet Union and in Czechoslovakia (as the S-102 and S-103) and Poland (as the LIM1 and 2). In addition, from 1949 over 5000 two-seat MiG-15UTIs (known as the CS-102 and LIM-3 in Czechoslovakia and Poland respectively) were built for operational conversion or training and a number remain in service at the time of writing. More than half a century after it first flew, the MiG-15 is still earning its keep.

RIGHT: **Fifty years after it first took to the air, the MiG-15 remained in service with some air arms in 2000.** BELOW: **Two preserved Korean War adversaries – the MiG-15 in the background and the F-86 Sabre in the foreground.**

MiG-15bis

First flight: December 30, 1947
Power: Klimov 2700kg/5952lb VK-1 turbojet
Armament: One 37mm/1.45in cannon and two 23mm/0.9in cannon
Size: Wingspan – 10.08m/33ft 0.75in
　　　Length – 10.86m/35ft 7.5in
　　　Height – 3.7m/12ft 1.75in
　　　Wing area – 20.6m²/221.74sq ft
Weights: Empty – 3681kg/8115lb
　　　Maximum take-off – 6045kg/13,327lb
Performance: Maximum speed – 1075kph/668mph
　　　Ceiling – 15,500m/50,855ft
　　　Range – 1860km/1156 miles
　　　Climb – 3500m/11,480ft per minute

Mikoyan-Gurevich MiG-17

Design of the MiG-17, initially an improved version of the MiG-15, began in 1949 and the aircraft flew long before the MiG-15's guns were fired in anger over Korea. The development work was particularly focused on the MiG-15's poor handling at high speed and the MiG-17, a completely revised design, introduced longer more swept wings and a taller tail with a greater sweep of the horizontal surfaces.

The prototype MiG-17 first flew in 1950 and production of what NATO codenamed "Fresco-A" began in August 1951. Deliveries began in 1952 but were too late to take part in the Korean War, although in reality the first MiG-17s were not much of an improvement over the MiG-15s.

The F model (NATO codename "Fresco-C") of the MiG-17 had an afterburning engine developed from the illegally copied Rolls-Royce Nene that powered the MiG-15. This represented the first major improvement over the -15, so much so that production began in early 1953 while manufacture of the single-seat MiG-15 was stopped. The MiG-17 could carry no more fuel than the MiG-15 internally but its afterburning engine demanded rather more fuel, consequently MiG-17Fs were rarely seen without two 400 litre/88 gallon drop tanks.

Most -17s produced were F models, the only other versions produced in quantity being night/all-weather fighters developed from the earlier unsuccessful MiG-17P. The first was the MiG-17PF codenamed "Fresco-D" by NATO and equipped with search and ranging radar. In 1956 the MiG-17PFU

TOP: **Designed to replace the MiG-15, early MiG-17s had a minimal performance edge over their earlier cousin.** ABOVE: **MiG-17s remained in service as trainers into the third millennium AD.**

became the first missile-armed fighter in Soviet service, equipped with four ARS-212 (later known as AA-1) "Alkali" air-to-air missiles in place of guns. These missiles were "beam-riding", in that they were guided to a target by a radar beam aimed by the launch target.

The MiG-17 was only produced for five years in the USSR but in that time over 6000 were built, of which some 5000 were MiG-17Fs. The Fresco remained one of the most numerous fighters in Soviet service well into the 1960s and many remained in service as trainers as late as 2000.

At least 9000 MiG-17s were built, the majority of them in the USSR but with production also undertaken in Poland, where around 1000 were built as the LIM-5P. A dedicated ground-attack version known as the LIM-5M was developed in Poland, equipped for bomb-carrying and rocket-assisted take-off. China also licence-produced the MiG-17, as the J-5, well into the 1970s. Two-seat versions of the MiG-17 were only built in China as the Soviet Union believed the two-seat MiG-15 to be a perfectly adequate trainer for the MiG-17 and MiG-19. The Chinese two-seat MiG-17 was made by Chengdu (1060 built between 1966 and 1986) and designated JJ-5. The export JJ-5 was known as the FT-5.

Some Warsaw Pact nations went on to use the type in the ground-attack role, armed with bombs and rockets and the type was supplied to many other nations.

MiG-17s saw action in the Congo and in the Nigerian civil war while the Syrians also made extensive use of the MiG fighter. Perhaps the best-known combat use of the MIG-17 is, however, its actions with North Vietnam from 1965 to 1973. The Soviet fighter was a major thorn in the side of the US Air Force and Navy, whose supersonic fighters were expected to rule the skies over Vietnam. The much lighter and more agile MiG-17 could out-turn any US jet fighter and its guns were more reliable and effective than missiles in close combat. The MiG-17 gave US pilots in Vietnam a kill-to-loss ratio about four times worse than in Korea and directly led to a far-reaching evaluation of US fighter aircraft design and tactics, from which the F-16 was one result.

Often eclipsed by earlier and later MiG designs, the MiG-17 was certainly one of the greatest fighters.

ABOVE: **A number of MiG-17s are kept in flying condition by private collectors in the USA.**

ABOVE: **A preserved example at Titusville, Florida.** BELOW: **This MiG-17 has the tell-tale air intake fairing which housed the aircraft's Izumrud radar equipment.**

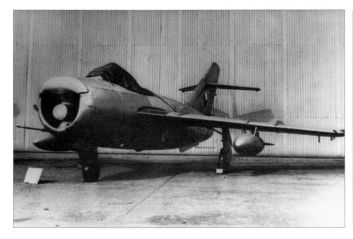

Mikoyan-Gurevich MiG-17F

First flight: January 1950

Power: Klimov 3380kg/7452lb thrust VK-1F afterburning turbojet

Armament: One 37mm/1.46in cannon, two or three 23mm/0.9in cannon plus up to 500kg/1102lb of weapons under wings

Size: Wingspan – 9.63m/31ft 7.25in
Length – 11.26m/36ft 11.25in
Height – 3.8m/12ft 5.5in
Wing area – 22.6m²/243.27sq ft

Weights: Empty – 3930kg/8664lb
Maximum take-off – 6075kg/13,393lb

Performance: Maximum speed – 1145kph/711mph
Ceiling – 16,600m/54,460ft
Range – 1980km/1230 miles with external fuel
Climb – 5000m/16,405ft in 2 minutes, 36 seconds

Mikoyan-Gurevich MiG-19

Like the MiG-17, design of the MiG-19 was underway long before the Korean War (1950–3). Reportedly on a direct order from Stalin, the MiG design bureau sought to create an all-new supersonic fighter and not just a development of an existing type. The resulting aircraft, capable of supersonic speed in level flight, was a truly great fighter.

The MiG-19, Russia's first supersonic fighter, first flew, powered by two Mikulin AM-5 turbojets (the first Soviet-designed

MiG-19S had an all-moving tailplane (which aided stability at all speeds) and was powered by Tumansky RD-9B turbojets, which were essentially renamed but more powerful AM-5s. Air for the engines was drawn in through what appeared to be a single nose intake but was actually split to allow each engine to draw in air through its own intake. This reduced the potential damage caused by bird strike or ingestion of foreign objects on the ground.

The -19S was delivered from mid-1955 and when production ceased in 1959, about 2500 had been built. Among the variants were the all-weather radar-equipped MiG-19PF and the MiG-19PM, armed with missiles

turbojets to be mass-produced), in September 1953 and entered service as the MiG-19P. The type was withdrawn, however, after a series of accidents due to stability problems. The redesigned

in place of guns. NATO codenamed the MiG-19 as "Farmer".

Soviet-built aircraft were supplied to Poland and Czechoslovakia, where they were known as the LIM-7 and S-105

Mikoyan-Gurevich MiG-19SF

First flight: September 18, 1953
Power: Two Tumansky 3300kg/7275lb afterburning thrust turbojets
Armament: Three 30mm/1.18in cannon, plus up to 500kg/1102lb of weapons under the wings
Size: Wingspan – 9.2m/30ft 2.25in
Length – 12.6m/41ft 4in
Height – 3.88m/12ft 8.75in
Wing area – 25m^2/269.11sq ft
Weights: Empty – 5760kg/12,699lb
Maximum take-off – 9100kg/20,062lb
Performance: Maximum speed – 1450kph/901mph
Ceiling – 17,900m/58,725ft
Range – 2200km/1367 miles with drop tanks
Climb – 6900m/22,640ft per minute

respectively. MiG-19s were also licence-built by the Chinese, who recognized the exceptional fighter capability of the MiG-19 and built twice as many as the USSR from 1961. Under the designation Shenyang J-6, China exported to Albania, Bangladesh, Egypt, Kampuchea (Cambodia), Pakistan, Tanzania and Vietnam. Pakistan's J-6s saw extensive combat in its war against India and J-6s were also encountered over Vietnam by US fighters.

LEFT: **This example of a MiG-19, preserved in a Russian museum, was an all-new supersonic fighter from the MiG bureau.** BELOW: **The MiG-19 was the Soviet Union's first fighter capable of supersonic flight.**

Mikoyan-Gurevich MiG-21

The MiG-21, originally designed as a short-range high-performance fighter, has, because of its hard-hitting armament and simple cost-effectiveness, become the most widely used fighter aircraft in the world. Experiences from the air war over Korea influenced the design of the delta-winged MiG-21, which was developed from a series of prototypes that flew in the mid-1950s.

also sold to Arab air forces, who used them against the Israeli Air Force in the Arab-Israeli War (1973). The MiG-21 was popular with pilots because it handled well, was highly manoeuvrable and could fly at twice the speed of sound.

Licensed production was also undertaken in Czechoslovakia and India, while China undertook major unlicensed production, having reverse-engineered (copied) examples they had acquired legitimately. Main shortcomings were limited range and endurance but the -F model came with a centreline 490 litre/108 gallon drop tank, giving the MiG longer legs. 1960 saw the development of the MiG-21PF with a redesigned nose to accommodate the new R1L radar in a moveable conical centrebody in the middle of the nose air intake. This model also introduced the more powerful R-11F2-300 engine for improved performance. Throughout its service life the -21 has been improved

and upgraded, and in 2000 Romania's Aerostar were still offering upgraded MiG-21 Lancers for air defence duties, having upgraded Romanian Air Force MiG-21s. Romania was just one of many countries still operating the MiG-21 almost 50 years after the prototype first flew.

The first MiG-21s (codenamed "Fishbed" by NATO) reached front-line units in the winter of 1957–8, initially armed with only two 30mm/1.18in cannon. The MiG-21F was the first major production version and was exported to the Soviet Union's Warsaw Pact allies as well as to Finland. Large numbers were

ABOVE: **This MiG-21, airbrakes deployed, is a Czech Air Force machine.** LEFT: **A MiG-21MF of the Slovak Air Force.**

Mikoyan-Gurevich MiG-21bis

First flight: Late 1957 (Production MiG-21F)

Power: Tumansky 7500kg/16,535lb afterburning thrust R-25 turbojet engine

Armament: One twin-barrel 23mm/0.9in cannon in underbelly pack and underwing provision for 1500kg/3307lb of weapons, including AA-2 or AA-8 air-to-air missiles and rocket pods

Size: Wingspan – 7.15m/23ft 5.5in
Length – 15.76m/51ft 8.5in
Height – 4.1m/13ft 5.5in
Wing area – 23m²/247sq ft

Weights: Empty – 5200kg/11,465lb
Maximum take-off – 7960kg/17,550lb

Performance: Maximum speed – 2230kph/1385mph
Ceiling – 18,000m/59,050ft
Range – 1160km/720 miles
Climb – 17,680m/58,000ft per minute

221

Mikoyan-Gurevich MiG-23/-27

The disappointing range of the MiG-21 led to a 1965 requirement for a replacement fighter with considerably better endurance. An enlarged MiG-21 and the all-new Ye-23-11/1 were proposed, the latter becoming the prototype MiG-23, which first appeared at the 1967 Aviation Day flypast. Like the MiG-21 before it, the new aircraft was planned in two versions – an interceptor for use with the Soviet Union's PVO air defence forces, and a ground-attack version (the MiG-27) to serve with the USSR's tactical air forces, Frontal Aviation.

The -23 differed from previous production MiG jets by switching the air intake from a centre nose inlet to side inlets, which allowed the search radar to be accommodated in a large nose-cone. The MiG-23MF, known as "Flogger-B" by NATO, was the first production variant, entering Soviet service in 1973 and other Warsaw Pact air arms soon after.

The MiG-23 was not only the USSR's first production aircraft with a variable-geometry "swing-wing", it was also the first swing-wing fighter anywhere. It and the MiG-27 have three sweep positions – minimum (16 degrees) for take-off, low-speed flight and landing; middle (45 degrees) for cruising, and maximum (72 degrees) for high-performance flight.

The MiG-27 ("Flogger-D") fighter-bomber/attack version, can be distinguished from the MiG-23 by its different nose, which slopes away sharply from the cockpit for better pilot view, earning the nickname "ducknose" from its crews. Due to the aircraft's role as a battlefield attack aircraft, the pilot of the -27 is protected from small arms fire by armour on the side of the cockpit. Terrain-avoidance radar relieves the pilot of some of the high workload associated with low-level operations.

Among the operators of the MiG-23/-27 were Poland, Hungary, Bulgaria, East Germany, Romania and Czechoslovakia. Downgraded MiG-23s were exported outside the Warsaw Pact nations to Libya, Syria, Egypt, Ethiopia, India, Cuba, Algeria, Iraq, Afghanistan and North Korea. India's Hindustan Aeronautics produced MiG-27Ms for the Indian Air Force until 1997, finally bringing Flogger production to a close after nearly three decades, with around 4000 aircraft built. MiG-23s and -27s are, however, likely to remain potent aircraft for Russia and many of the nations listed for years to come.

In the late 1980s the US Air Force acquired some ex-Egyptian Air Force MiG-23s for realistic air-combat training of American and NATO pilots.

TOP: **Having "lit the fires", the pilot of this Czech Air Force MiG-23 prepares to accelerate away.**

ABOVE: **More than three decades after it first flew, the MiG-23 is still an effective interceptor.**

Mikoyan-Gurevich MiG-23MF

First flight: 1966
Power: Tumansky 12,500kg/27,550lb afterburning thrust R-29 turbojet engine
Armament: One 23mm/0.9in cannon in belly pod, plus five pylons for air-to-air missiles and rockets
Size: Wingspan – 14.25m/46ft 9in, spread
Length – 16.8m/55ft 1.5in
Height – 4.35m/14ft 4in
Wing area – 28m²/301.4sq ft
Weights: Empty – 11,300kg/24,912lb
Maximum take-off – 18,500kg/40,785lb
Performance: Maximum speed – 2500kph/1550mph
Ceiling – 18,600m/61,025ft
Range – 1300km/808 miles
Climb – 15,240m/50,000ft per minute

Mikoyan-Gurevich MiG-25

The MiG-25 was developed in the early 1960s to counter the threat posed to the Soviet Union by the remarkable US B-70 Valkyrie Mach 3 bomber. Although the B-70 never entered service, the MiG-25 (NATO codename "Foxbat") did and it remains the world's fastest fighter aircraft, capable of Mach 2.8 and up to Mach 3 (3200kph/2000 mph) for short periods. The West was first publicly aware of the Foxbat in April 1965, when it was announced that the prototype had set a new speed record in a 1000km/620 mile closed circuit. The prototype of the reconnaissance version had actually first flown in March 1964. The type subsequently set a number of other records, including an absolute world altitude record of 37,650m/123,524ft.

The high-speed flight environment is a hostile one and aircraft have to be made of special materials to withstand the high temperatures experienced in these operations – the MiG-25 airframe is made of nickel steel and has titanium wing and tail unit leading-edges to withstand the heat generated during very high-speed flight. The MiG-25 is no dogfighter, uses a lot of fuel quickly and needs a very long take-off and landing but it was after all a highly specialized aircraft designed for a very specific purpose – to get very high very quickly.

The interceptor version, MiG-25P, went into production first and entered service in 1970. The later MiG-25PD had look-down/shoot-down radar, more powerful engines and an infra-red search and track capability. Although the B-70 threat never materialized, the MiG-25 did, however, have another high-speed high-altitude target, the USAF SR-71 Blackbird, and it was soon stationed along the eastern and western borders of the USSR to keep the Blackbird at bay. Intercepts were directed by ground control until the powerful on-board radar could lock on to the target. Four of the world's largest, long-range missiles, the AA-6 "Acrid", could then be fired from up to 80km/50 miles away. These missiles, some 6m/19.5ft long, were specially developed to kill the B-70 and were fitted with either infra-red or radar-homing heads.

The reconnaissance MiG-25RB Foxbat entered service about the same time as the interceptor. Four aircraft were stationed in Egypt in 1971 to spy on Israeli positions and were completely immune to the Israeli F-4 Phantoms far below.

Export versions were supplied to Algeria, India, Libya, Syria and Iraq – the only confirmed Iraqi air-to-air victory of the Gulf War of 1991 was scored by a MiG-25 over a US Navy F/A-18 Hornet.

ABOVE: **The MiG-25 was developed into the MiG-31.**
BELOW: **The MiG-25 is made largely of nickel steel and titanium.**

Mikoyan-Gurevich MiG-25P

First flight: March 6, 1964 (Ye-155R-1 prototype)
Power: Two Tumansky 11,000kg/24,250lb afterburning thrust R-31 turbojet engines
Armament: External pylons for four air-to-air missiles, typically four AA-6 "Acrid" air-to-air missiles or two AA-7 "Apex" with two AA-8 "Aphid" air-to-air missiles
Size: Wingspan – 13.95m/45ft 9in
Length – 23.82m/78ft 1.75in
Height – 6.1m/20ft
Wing area – 56.83m^2/611.7sq ft
Weights: Empty – 20,000kg/44,090lb
Maximum take-off – 36,200kg/79,800lb
Performance: Maximum speed – 2975kph/1848mph
Ceiling – 24,385m/80,000ft
Range – 1125km/700 miles
Climb – 15,240m/50,000ft per minute

Mikoyan-Gurevich MiG-29

Over 1200 examples of this very capable, incredibly agile fighter have been built and the type has been exported widely. The MiG-29 was developed in the early 1970s as a high-performance, highly manoeuvrable lightweight fighter to outperform the best the West could offer. The prototype took to the air for the first time in 1977 but it

was a further seven years before the type entered service – ultimately 460 were in Russian service and the rest were exported.

Codenamed "Fulcrum" by NATO, the aircraft has been exported to Bulgaria, Germany, Cuba, Romania, Poland, Slovakia, Peru, Syria, Hungary, Iraq, India, Iran, North Korea, Malaysia and Moldova amongst others. It is not

widely known, but the USA acquired 21 MiG-29s in 1997 from Moldova after Iran had expressed interest in the high-performance fighters. In a unique accord between the USA and Moldova, the aircraft were shipped to the USA to prevent them being acquired by rogue states.

The radar can track ten targets up to 245km/152 miles away and enables look-down-shoot-down capability, while the pilot's helmet-mounted sight allows him or her to direct air-to-air missiles wherever the pilot looks.

The MiG is also designed for rough-field operations – special doors seal off the main air intakes to protect against foreign object ingestion during start up and taxiing. Air is drawn in via louvres in the wingroots instead and as the aircraft takes off the inlet doors open.

The Russians have begun to upgrade some MiG-29s to MiG-29SMT standard by increasing the range and payload,

new computer screens replacing cockpit instruments, as well as improved radar and inflight refuelling capability.

Daimler Chrysler Aerospace modified a number of Polish MiGs for NATO compatibility after that nation joined NATO in 1999, just as they did the East German MiG-29s after German reunification in 1990.

A navalized version, the MiG-29K, was developed but has so far not been produced.

LEFT: **Although it was designed in the early 1970s, the MiG-29 remains a very potent fighter in service around the world.** BELOW: **A fine air-to-air photograph of a Czech Air Force MiG-29.**

Mikoyan-Gurevich MiG-29

First flight: October 7, 1977

Power: Two Klimov 8312kg/18,300lb afterburning thrust RD-33 turbojet engines

Armament: One 30mm/1.18in cannon, six underwing hardpoints carrying 3000kg/6615lb of weapons, including six AAMs or rockets and bombs

Size: Wingspan – 11.36m/37ft 3in
Length – 14.87m/48ft 9in
Height – 4.73m/15ft 6in
Wing area – 38m^2/409sq ft

Weights: Empty – 10,900kg/24,030lb
Maximum take-off 18,500kg/40,785lb

Performance: Maximum speed – 2445kph/1518mph
Ceiling – 18,013m/59,060ft
Range – 3000km/1863 miles
Climb – 19,825m/65,000ft per minute

LEFT: Derived from the formidable MiG-25, the MiG-31 is equipped with a very powerful radar.

Mikoyan-Gurevich MiG-31

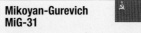

Mikoyan-Gurevich MiG-31

First flight: September 16, 1975 (Ye-155)
Power: Two Aviadvigatel 15,520kg/34,170lb afterburning thrust D-30F6 turbofan engines
Armament: One 23mm/0.9in cannon, four AA-9 "Amos" long-range air-to-air missiles under fuselage, two AA-6 "Acrid" air-to-air missiles and four AA-8 "Aphid" air-to-air missiles on underwing hardpoints
Size: Wingspan – 13.464m/44ft 2in
Length – 22.7m/74ft 5in
Height – 6.15m/20ft 2in
Wing area – 61.6m²/663sq ft
Weights: Empty – 21,825kg/48,115lb
Maximum take-off – 46,200kg/101,850lb
Performance: Maximum speed – 3000kph/1863mph
Ceiling – 20,618m/67,600ft
Range – 720km/447 miles at Mach 2.3 with full armament load
Climb – 10,000m/32,810ft in 7 minutes, 54 seconds

Codenamed "Foxhound" by NATO, the very large MiG-31 was developed from the MiG-25, and replaced the Tu-128 as the main Soviet long-range interceptor. The MiG-31 and its two-man crew was designed to counter low-flying strike aircraft and cruise missiles and is able to engage targets from a considerable distance. Equipped with the long-range AA-9 air-to-air missiles, it is a most effective protector of Russian airspace.

Development began in the 1970s and the prototype MiG-31 (the Ye-155MP) first flew in 1975. The first of around 300 MiG-31s were delivered to the Soviet Air Force from 1979.

Although the Foxhound was inspired by the MiG-25, it is a new all-weather, all-altitude aircraft. Its airframe is composed of nickel steel, light alloy and titanium to cope with the rigours associated with its high performance. The aircraft's sophisticated "Flash Dance" radar, said to be the most powerful fitted to any of the world's fighters, can scan almost 200km/124 miles ahead as well as behind and below. Managed by the back-seater, it can track up to ten targets at once and simultaneously engage four of them having established which present the greatest threat.

Later models had an in-flight refuelling capability which greatly extended the aircraft's endurance and on-board digital datalinks, allowing aircraft to exchange data about targets and tactical situations.

LEFT: The F-2's family connections with the F-16 are clear.

Mitsubishi F-2

First flight: October 1995
Power: General Electric 13,444kg/29,600lb afterburning thrust F110-GE-129 turbofan engine
Armament: One 20mm/0.78in cannon, plus AIM-9L Sidewinders/Mitsubishi AAM-3 air-to-air missiles on wingtips plus underwing hardpoints for weaponry including AIM-7M Sparrow air-to-air missiles
Size: Wingspan – 11.13m/36ft 6in
Length – 15.52m/50ft 10in
Height – 4.96m/16ft 4in
Wing area – 34.8m²/375sq ft
Weights: Empty – 9525kg/21,000lb
Maximum take-off – 22,100kg/48,722lb
Performance: Maximum speed – Mach 2
Ceiling – 15,250m/50,000ft
Range – 830km/515 miles
Climb – not published

Mitsubishi F-2

The Mitsubishi F-2, formerly known as the FS-X, was developed in Japan with the help of the former General Dynamics (now Lockheed Martin) and the similarities between the F-2 and the F-16 are obvious. The type first flew in October 1995 and initial production versions were supplied to the Japan Air Self-Defence Force in 2000. Japan has ordered 130 F-2s to replace the JASDF's Mitsubishi F-1s.

The programme has, however, been dogged by technical problems and by the time the F-2 entered service, each aircraft had cost four times more than a basic F-16.

The Japanese FS-X project was originally intended to produce an indigenous fighter aircraft but in 1987, after considerable US pressure, the F-16 was chosen as the basis of the new aircraft. The F-2 wing is 25 per cent larger than that of the F-16 and an enlarged radome houses a Japanese-designed radar. The fuselage is longer than the F-16 and the fly-by-wire system is all-Japanese due to US reluctance to provide their fly-by-wire software.

The F-2 will initially serve in ground-attack/maritime strike roles but an air defence version is planned to replace Japan's ageing F-4 Phantom fleet.

North American F-86 Sabre

The North American Aviation Company's first jet design was begun in 1944, but following the capture of German research at the end of World War II, the XP-86 was redesigned to incorporate swept-tail surfaces and a swept wing, which would allow supersonic speeds. The prototype of the Sabre flew in 1947 and the aircraft entered service with the US Air Force in 1949. It proved faster than expected: in 1948 an early production F-86 exceeded the speed of sound in a shallow dive, though the aircraft could not achieve this in level flight.

On November 1, 1950, some USAF Mustang pilots on a mission over Korea reported coming under fire by six swept-wing jet fighters that had flown across the Yalu river from Manchuria – the Russian-built Mikoyan-Gurevich MiG-15 was in the Korean War. The USAF were quick to respond to the MiG threat and on 8 November ordered the F-86 Sabre-equipped 4th Fighter Group from the USA to Korea. The F-86A was the most modern USAF fighter available but the Sabre's armament of six 12.7mm/0.5in machine-guns was no real match for the two 23mm/1.09in and one 37mm/1.46in cannon

ABOVE: **North American made full use of wartime German swept-wing research to produce the F-86.** LEFT: **The F-86, the USAF's most modern fighter, was sent to Korea to deal with the MiG-15 threat.**

of the MiG. USAF pilot training and tactics were, however, much better and the Sabre was able to give as much as it got.

The first MiG v. Sabre dogfight took place in December 1950, when four USAF F-86 Sabres came upon four MiGs at an altitude of 7620m/25,000ft. Leader of the F-86 group was Lt Colonel Bruce H. Hinton. He fired on the enemy jets and set fire to one of the MiGs, causing it to crash. On December 22, eight Sabres took on 15 MiGs and in the dogfights that followed from 9145m/30,000ft down to 305m/1000ft, the USAF fighter pilots destroyed no fewer than six of the MiGs. By the end of the Korean War, USAF F-86 Sabres had achieved 757 victories for 103 losses in combat.

The F-86D, virtually a complete redesign on the early Sabres, was an all-weather version fitted with the Hughes fire control system and was essentially a bomber-destroyer. The collision-course radar would take the jet to the target on autopilot and at the right moment the system would extend a box from the belly and unleash 24 70mm/2.75in unguided Mighty Mouse high explosive rockets.

The F-86E was produced from late 1950 and had an "all-flying" tail that was adjustable in flight. Canadian-built versions of the F-86E were supplied to the Royal Canadian Air Force, the RAF and the new Luftwaffe. The RAF received 460 Sabres, all of them flown to the UK in the space of 12 days in December 1952. Britain's Sabres were a much-needed stop-gap while the UK brought its own swept-wing fighters into service and enabled RAF squadrons based in West Germany, the Cold War front line, to provide a totally robust and modern fighter defence against Soviet would-be attackers. In December 1953, No.66 Squadron at Linton-on-Ouse became the first swept-wing unit of RAF Fighter Command when they swapped Meteor F.8s for F-86s. The RAF's Sabres based in West Germany were all replaced by Hunters by the end of May 1956.

Some of the Canadian-built Sabres were later passed on to Italy and Greece under NATO terms to ensure those countries' air forces were well-equipped. Italy's Fiat also licence-built the all-weather F-86K for Italy, France, West Germany, the Netherlands and Norway. For most NATO pilots, the Sabre gave them their first experience of high-speed jet flight. The very capable Sabre, so widely deployed throughout NATO, must have had some deterrence value against the USSR.

Australia's Commonwealth Aircraft Corporation also licence-built the F-86 (as the Sabre Mk 30, 31 and 32) for the Royal Australian Air Force.

The Sabre remained in production until 1957. The US Navy version, known as the FJ-2 Fury, entered service in 1952. Total Sabre and Fury production amounted to over 9500 aircraft. A number of preserved examples continue to fly.

TOP: **The all-weather D model was essentially an all-new Sabre.** ABOVE: **USAF F-86Ds were deployed for all-weather UK air defence between late 1953 and mid-1958.** BELOW: **The Sabre gave many NATO fighter pilots their first high-speed jet experience.**

North American F-86D Sabre

First flight: October 1, 1947 (XP-86)
Power: General Electric 3402kg/7500lb afterburning thrust J47-GE-17B turbojet engine
Armament: 24 70mm/2.75in unguided Mighty Mouse high-explosive rockets
Size: Wingspan – 11.3m/37ft 1in
   Length – 12.29m/40ft 4in
   Height – 4.57m/15ft
   Wing area – 26.76m^2/288sq ft
Weights: Empty – 5656kg/12,470lb
   Maximum take-off – 7756kg/17,100lb
Performance: Maximum speed – 1138kph/707mph
   Ceiling – 16,640m/54,600ft
   Range – 1344km/835 miles
   Climb – 3660m/12,000ft per minute

North American F-82 Twin Mustang

It would be easy to say that this aircraft looks as if it were made of left-over parts at the North American factory but despite its name, this aircraft was not simply two P-51s joined by a new centre wing. The F-82 (originally P-82) was conceived by North American in World War II as a dedicated long-range escort fighter for war in the Pacific. The vast distances between islands in the Pacific

required a fighter type that could fly for hours, yet have its pilot fresh for combat at any time. Development began in 1944 to provide a twin-engine, long-range bomber escort with a pilot and co-pilot/navigator, to reduce fatigue on long-range bomber escort missions.

The Twin Mustang was certainly produced quickly by using the existing P-51 powerplant and some common components including the two modified P-51H fuselages which, combined in a twin-boom configuration, carried the two pilots in separate cockpits. Deliveries of what was the last propeller-driven dayfighter acquired in quantity by the Air Force did not begin until early 1946, but although the Twin Mustang arrived too late for World War II, it had useful post-war Air Force service as an escort fighter and, most importantly, a nightfighter.

Radar-equipped F-82F and Gs were used extensively by Air Defense Command as replacements for the P-61 night-fighter and nine F-82Fs and five F-82Gs were converted as F-82H winterized interceptors for Alaska.

The F-82 had a very successful combat career in the Korean War. Japan-based F-82s were among the first

North American F-82G Twin Mustang

First flight: July 6, 1945
Power: Two Allison 1600hp V-1710-143/145 V-12 piston engines
Armament: Six wing-mounted 12.7mm/0.5in machine-guns, plus up to four 454kg/1000lb bombs under wings
Size: Wingspan – 15.62m/51ft 3in
Length – 12.93m/42ft 5in
Height – 4.22m/13ft 10in
Wing area – 37.9m^2/408sq ft
Weights: Empty – 7256kg/15,997lb
Maximum take-off – 11,608kg/25,951lb
Performance: Maximum speed – 742kph/461mph
Ceiling – 11,855m/38,900ft
Range – 3605km/2240 miles
Climb – 1150m/3770ft per minute

USAF aircraft to operate over Korea and the first three North Korean aircraft destroyed by US forces were shot down by all-weather F-82G interceptors on June 27, 1950. The type flew 1868 sorties in the Korean War before being withdrawn in February 1952.

LEFT: **Developed in World War II, the F-82 saw extensive action in Korea.** BELOW: **The unbelievable but effective configuration of the Twin Mustang – an unusual but potent fighter.**

North American F-100 Super Sabre

The Super Sabre was the world's first supersonic combat aircraft and was developed by North American from 1949 as a successor to the company's highly successful F-86 Sabre. The goal was an aircraft that could exceed Mach 1 in level flight and the F-100 was developed very quickly.

In May 1953 one of the prototypes exceeded the speed of sound on its first flight giving a taste of the performance to come. On October 29, 1953 the first production aircraft set a new world speed record of 1215kph/755mph. Although the first F-100s were delivered to the USAF in 1953, a series of catastrophic inflight failures delayed the F-100A's entry into service for another year. After the wings and fin were reworked to eradicate stability problems, 200 F-100As gave sterling service in the USAF.

The improved and more powerful F-100C and D fighter-bombers reached the Cold War front lines in 1956–7. The C model had in-flight refuelling capability to extend the already impressive range

and a more powerful engine. The F-100D was built in greater numbers than any other version and carried ECM equipment as well as a low-altitude bombing system for "tossing" nuclear weapons. Two-seat and reconnaissance versions were also produced. By the time production stopped in 1959 almost 2300 Super Sabres had been built.

From 1966–71 in the Vietnam War, USAF F-100s saw extensive service in the fighter, reconnaissance and ground-attack roles, flying more missions than the P-51 had in World War II.

Super Sabres retired from USAF service in 1972 but they remained in use with Air National Guard units until 1980. F-100s were supplied to Denmark, France, Taiwan and Turkey, the latter nation finally retiring the type in the mid-1980s.

TOP: **The F-100 was first delivered to the US Air Force in 1953.** ABOVE: **Extensively used in the Vietnam War, the Super Sabre flew many varied types of mission.** LEFT: **USAF F-100s were deployed to Europe in the late 1950s.**

North American F-100D Super Sabre

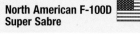

First flight: March 24, 1953
Power: Pratt and Whitney 7711kg/17,000lb afterburning-thrust J 57-P21 turbojet
Armament: Four 20mm/0.78in cannon plus six underwing load points for up to 3402kg/7500lb of weapons
Size: Wingspan – 11.81m/38ft 9in
Length – 15.09m/49ft 6in
Height – 4.95m/16ft 3in
Wing area – 35.77m²/385sq ft
Weights: Empty – 9525kg/21,000lb
Maximum take-off – 15,800kg/34,832lb
Performance: Maximum speed – 1390kph/864mph
Ceiling – 13,716m/45,000ft
Range – 3210km/1995 miles with external drop tanks
Climb – 4877m/16,000ft per minute

Northrop F-5 series

The Northrop F-5 Freedom Fighter is a versatile, low cost, easy to maintain, lightweight supersonic fighter that first flew in 1959. More than 2000 of the 2700 aircraft built were widely exported to over 30 countries friendly to the USA. Deliveries to USAF Tactical Air Command for instructing foreign pilots began in April 1964 and pilots from Iran and South Korea were the first to be trained. A two-place combat-trainer

version, the F-5B, first flew in February 1964, and in 1966–7 a US Air Force squadron of F-5s flew combat missions in South-east Asia for operational evaluation purposes.

Canada and Spain undertook licence production of the F-5 – many Freedom Fighters remain in service with air forces around the world.

The improved F-5E Tiger II appeared in 1972 with more powerful J85 engines which required a wider fuselage. It had much better avionics and an air-to-air fire control radar system as well as a computerized gunsight. Like the F-5 before it, the F-5E attracted interest from foreign air forces, and some 20 foreign air arms had acquired Tiger IIs by the mid-1980s. Although the F-5 may lack all-weather capability, it is relatively cheap, easy to operate, robust and very agile. The first flight of the F-5E was on August 11, 1972 and the first USAF unit to receive the aircraft was the 425th TFS, responsible for training foreign pilots in the F-5 aircraft. Perhaps the best-known use of the Tiger II was as an aggressor aircraft for the USAF. US aggressor pilots were trained in Soviet tactics and used the F5-Es to provide a realistic "enemy" for USAF pilots training in aerial combat skills. Eventually, aggressor squadrons were used to help train pilots of friendly foreign nations. The F-5F was the two-seat combat trainer version of the F-5E. Taiwan, South Korea and Switzerland all produced the Tiger II under licence. Although F-5E production ceased in 1987, the manufacturers have offered

TOP: **This Norwegian Air Force F-5A sports a special scheme for a meet of Tiger squadrons.** ABOVE: **The Swiss Air Force was one of 20 foreign air arms that bought the F-5E.**
BELOW LEFT: **This two-seat USAF F-5F shows how much ordnance could be carried by the type.**

a host of update options which should keep the Tiger II in the front line well beyond 2010.

The ultimate development of the F-5 was the F-20 Tigershark with, among other improvements, 80 per cent greater engine power. The USAF declined the aircraft and this effectively doomed the F-20's export potential.

Northrop F-5E Tiger II

First flight: July 30, 1959 (N-156F F-5 prototype)
Power: Two General Electric 2268kg/5000lb afterburning thrust J85-GE21 turbojets
Armament: Two 20mm/0.78in cannon in nose, two AIM-9 Sidewinder AAMs on wingtip launchers plus up to 3175kg/7000lb of mixed ordnance
Size: Wingspan – 8.13m/26ft 8in
Length – 14.45m/47ft 4.75in
Height – 4.06m/13ft 4in
Wing area – 17.28m²/186sq ft
Weights: Empty – 4410kg/9723lb
Maximum take-off – 11,214kg/24,722lb
Performance: Maximum speed – 1734kph/1083mph
Ceiling – 15,790m/51,800ft
Range – 2483km/1543 miles with drop tanks
Climb – 8754m/28,700ft per minute

Northrop F-89 Scorpion

Northrop F-89D Scorpion

First flight: August 16, 1948

Power: Two Allison 3266kg/7200lb afterburning thrust J-35-A-35 turbojet engines

Armament: 104 Mighty Mouse 70mm/2.75in unguided rockets in wingtip pods or 27 rockets and three Falcon missiles

Size: Wingspan – 18.18m/59ft 8in
Length – 16.41m/53ft 10in
Height – 5.36m/17ft 7in
Wing area – 52.21m²/562sq ft

Weights: Empty – 11,428kg/25,194lb
Maximum take-off – 19,160kg/42,241lb

Performance: Maximum speed – 1024kph/636mph
Ceiling – 14,995m/49,200ft
Range – 4184km/2600 miles
Climb – 1600m/5250ft per minute

The F-89 was an all-weather jet fighter-interceptor designed to replace the P-61 Black Widow and F-82 Twin Mustang. It first flew in August 1948 and had a conventional layout but included what was for the time an unusual design feature called decelerons, a control surface that could operate as a speed brake to allow crews to get into firing position behind a target. While the pilot controlled the aircraft, the back-seat "observer" managed the

radar. The F-89 picked up the unofficial nickname "Stanley Steamer" because of the oversize main landing gear wheels that appeared to be more at home on a locomotive than a fighter.

The definitive F-89 Scorpion, and one version that was built in greater numbers than any other, was the D model, which carried 104 Mighty Mouse 70mm/2.75in unguided rockets in two enormous pods, one on each wingtip. This version also carried the APG-40 radar, which could detect target aircraft up to 80km/50 miles away. The impressive Hughes E-6 fire-control system could then instruct the autopilot on course corrections and even fire the F-89's rockets automatically when in range.

A total of 350 F-89Ds were converted to F-89Js under Project Ding Dong, which saw the aircraft equipped to carry the AIR-2A Genie, an unguided nuclear-tipped air-to-air missile. On July 19, 1957, a Genie was launched from an F-89J, marking the first and only time in history that an air-to-air rocket with a nuclear warhead was launched and detonated. Called Operation Plumb Bob, this test took place at 6100m/20,000ft over Nevada. The rocket was fired at a point approximately 4270m/14,000ft from the F-89 and the Genie covered this distance in 4.5 seconds.

The F-89 was withdrawn from active service in 1959 after protecting the USA, and especially the frozen north, for almost a decade. The last examples of the Air National Guard F-89s were retired from service in July 1969.

LEFT: Note the F-89's twin turbojets almost "bolted on" beneath the fuselage. ABOVE: The F-89 was a large fighter. It protected the USA from Soviet bombers coming from the north. BELOW: As a design the F-89 didn't really break new ground, but it earned its keep as a Cold War all-weather interceptor for over ten years.

Panavia Tornado ADV

The Tornado was produced by a three-nation (UK, West Germany and Italy) consortium, each of which assumed responsibility for the manufacture of specific aircraft sections. The resulting aircraft was a technological, political and administrative triumph, given the problems that had to be overcome. Each nation assembled its own air force's aircraft, and power for all was provided by Rolls-Royce-designed Turbo-Union engines. The strike Tornado was developed and entered service first, while the fighter version was sought as a replacement for the RAF's F-4 Phantoms and Lightnings. The resulting aircraft is an interceptor with a better rate of acceleration than either of these two classic jets. While it cannot manoeuvre as well as the F-16, the Tornado was not designed for manoeuvre. It was made to defend the UK Air Defence Region, a vast area stretching from the south-west approaches up to Iceland, including all of the UK, most of the North Sea, and much of the eastern Atlantic. The Tornado interceptor will be central to the UK's air defence for some years to come.

The Tornado ADV (Air Defence Variant) was designed to an RAF requirement for an interceptor that could perform unrefuelled combat air patrols 563km/350 miles from base, in all weathers and at all altitudes in a hostile electronic warfare environment. In simple terms the main mission envisaged for the Tornado interceptor was to loiter far out over the ocean, beyond the range of land-based radar, waiting to attack Soviet bombers as they approached from over the Arctic.

TOP: **The RAF's Tornado ADV is ideally suited to its primary role of defending the enormous UK Air Defence Region.** ABOVE: **Only the RAF and the Italian and Saudi Arabian air forces operate the ADV.**

Although there is 80 per cent commonality between the airframes, the ADV differs from the strike Tornado in having a 1.36m/4ft 7in longer fuselage. Its sophisticated GEC-Marconi Foxhunter radar can track up to 20 targets while scanning a search area up to 165km/100 miles distant. The chosen armament was the Sky Flash AAM and to achieve the required performance the missiles are carried in tandem semi-recessed pairs under the fuselage centreline.

The Tornado is one of a handful of combat aircraft with variable-geometry or "swing" wings. The wings can move automatically from the swept to the spread position and two interim settings to maximize the aircraft's aerodynamic performance as required at take-off, landing and in high-speed flight.

It has excellent short take-off capability which, together with its on-board Auxiliary Power Unit, makes the ADV well suited for operation from basic forward airfields.

The prototype ADV, the F.2, first flew in 1979 and the first F.2s were delivered to the RAF in November 1984. Due to delays in the development of the Foxhunter radar the aircraft only carried ballast in the nose, and subsequently a version of the radar that did not fully meet RAF standards, until 1989 when the full-specification radar was installed.

Early in production, from the 19th on the production line, all were produced as F. Mk.3s, featuring the RB199 Mk 104 engines, improved afterburners, larger drop-tanks, fully automatic wing-sweep control and provision for four Sidewinders in addition to the four Sky Flash missiles. The F.3 was also 35.5cm/14in longer than the F.2 to accommodate the new engines, carried 891 litres/200 gallons more internal fuel and an inflight refuelling probe was fitted on the port side as standard. However, on September 24, 1987 an F.3 flew direct from Canada to the BAE Systems plant at Warton in the UK without the need to refuel in flight, showing just how long the ADV's legs are.

During the 1980s the RAF Tornado F.3s also assumed the role of an AWACS aircraft as part of the RAF's Mixed Fighter Force plan. Using the Tornado's radar, the navigator was able to direct Hawk trainers towards bogeys, armed with AIM-9 Sidewinder missiles.

Although only Britain wanted the Tornado interceptor version, in 1995 Italy began leasing 24 F.3s from Britain while awaiting delivery of the Eurofighter. These aircraft were modified to carry the Italian Alenia Aspide AAM.

Saudi Arabia is the only export customer and Saudi F.3s, together with RAF ADVs, flew combat patrols throughout the Gulf War (1991) but without seeing action. RAF F.3s subsequently flew as part of the UN Operations Deny Flight/Decisive Edge over Bosnia-Herzegovina, policing the no-fly zone.

In 2000, the RAF F.3s were modified to carry the AMRAAM and ASRAAM missiles and were equipped with the Joint Tactical Information Distribution System (JTIDS), to enable the aircraft to engage multiple targets beyond visual range (BVR).

TOP: **Wings extended to generate maximum lift at take-off, the Tornado is one of the world's few swing-wing aircraft.** ABOVE: **The Tornado fighter variant will defend the UK for years to come.**

BELOW: **Although RAF Tornado fighters were deployed during the Gulf War, they did not see action.**

Panavia Tornado ADV/F.3

First flight: October 27, 1979
Power: Two Turbo-Union 4808kg/10,600lb (7292kg/16,075lb afterburning)-thrust RB199-34R Mk 104 turbofans
Armament: One 27mm/1.05in cannon, four Sky Flash AAMs, plus four AIM-9 Sidewinder AAMs. Italian Air Force F.3 carry Alenia Aspide AAMs instead of Sky Flash
Size: Wingspan – 13.91m/45ft 8in, spread 8.60m/28ft 3in, swept
Length – 18.68m/61ft 4in
Height – 5.95m/19ft6in
Wing area – 26.6m^2/286.3sq ft, at 25 degrees sweepback
Weights: Empty – 14,500kg/31,970lb
Maximum take-off – 27,896kg/61,700lb
Performance: Maximum speed – 2381kph/1480mph
Ceiling – 21,335m/70,000ft
Range – 1853km/1150 miles intercept radius
Climb – 12,200m/40,000ft per minute

Republic F-84 Thunderjet/Thunderstreak

The F-84 aircraft was the USAF's first post-war fighter, and production began in June 1947. It was also the first US Air Force jet fighter capable of carrying a tactical nuclear weapon and the last USAF subsonic straight-wing fighter-bomber to enter service.

F-84s became the standard fighter-escort for USAF Strategic Air Command's bomber force and pioneered the use of aerial refuelling for fighters. During August 1953 F-84Gs, refuelled in mid-air by Strategic Air Command KC-97 tankers, were flown

7216km/4485 miles non-stop from Turner Air Force Base in Georgia, USA, to RAF Lakenheath in the UK, to demonstrate the USAF's long-range fighter-escort capability. Codenamed Operation "Longstride", this was at that point the longest non-stop mass movement of fighter-bombers in history and the greatest distance ever flown non-stop by single-engine jet fighters. F-84s had also been used in two different programmes to provide protection for B-36 Peacemaker bombers.

USAF Thunderjets saw much combat in the Korean War and entered service there in December 1950. Initially assigned to escort B-29 bombers, they were later increasingly used for ground operations. Devastating F-84 raids on dams on May 13 and 16, 1953 caused the loss of all electrical power to North Korea. During that conflict, F-84 pilots flew 86,408 missions, dropped 15,370 tonnes/50,427 tons of bombs, and managed to shoot down or damage 105 North Korean MiG-15 fighters.

The first swept-wing model, the F-84F Thunderstreak, originally designated YF-84A, was first flown on June 3, 1950 and became the only USAF production fighter derived from a straight-wing aircraft.

Under the Mutual Defense Assistance Program, some 2000 F-84s were supplied to many European air forces to bring NATO up to strength during some of the darkest days of the Cold War.

In the USA, the last straight-wing F-84s were retired from the US Air National Guard in 1957 and the last ANG F-84Fs were retired in 1971.

ABOVE: **Designed during World War II, the original straight-wing F-84 entered USAF service in 1947.**
LEFT: **The addition of swept wings in the F model extended the operational life of the F-84 – these are Royal Netherlands Air Force examples.**

Republic F-84F Thunderstreak

First flight: June 3, 1950 (YF-84A)
Power: Wright 15,917kg/7220lb-thrust J65-W-3 turbojet engine
Armament: Six 12.7mm/0.5in machine-guns, plus up to 2722kg/6000lb of external ordnance
Size: Wingspan – 10.24m/33ft 7.25in
  Length – 13.23m/43ft 4.75in
  Height – 4.39m/14ft 4.75in
  Wing area – 30.19m²/325sq ft
Weights: Empty – 6273kg/13,830lb
  Maximum take-off – 12,701kg/28,000lb
Performance: Maximum speed – 1118kph/695mph
  Ceiling – 14,020m/46,000ft
  Range – 1384km/860 miles
  Climb – 2257m/7400ft per minute

Republic F-105 Thunderchief

Republic F-105D Thunderchief

First flight: June 9, 1959
Power: Pratt & Whitney 11113kg/24,500lb afterburning thrust J75-P-19W turbojet
Armament: AIM-9 Sidewinder AAM, one 20mm/0.78in cannon plus up to 6359kg/14,000lb of bombs, mines and air-to-surface missiles
Size: Wingspan – 10.59m/34ft 9in
Length – 19.61m/64ft 4in
Height – 5.97m/19ft 7in
Wing area – 35.77m²/385sq ft
Weights: Empty – 12,474kg/27,500lb
Maximum take-off – 23,967kg/52,838lb
Performance: Maximum speed – 2237kph/1390mph
Ceiling – 12,560m/41,200ft
Range – 1480km/920 miles
Climb – 10,485m/34,400ft per minute

The Republic F-105 Thunderchief is remembered as an outstanding combat aircraft which formed the backbone of United States Air Force tactical air power during the 1950s and 1960s. The F-105 was conceived in 1951 as a Republic private venture high-performance all-weather fighter-bomber to replace the F-84. The USAF,

impressed by the design, ordered two prototypes, the first flying in October 1955. Pure fighters were becoming rarer by this time and so from the outset the F-105 was designed to carry up to 5443kg/12,000lb of mixed, possibly nuclear, ordnance, with 3629kg/8000lb of it carried in an internal weapons bay.

The "Thud", as it commonly became known, was the biggest single-seat, single-engine combat aircraft in history. The F-105, developed from the YF-105A test aircraft, first entered USAF service on May 27, 1958. It was however the F-105B which was first considered operationally ready for USAF service.

The United States Air Force in Europe first received the F-105D on May 12, 1961. The first model of the Thunderchief family to possess genuine all-weather capability, the F-105D was at the time the most sophisticated and complex type to be found in Tactical Air Command's inventory. In appearance the model of the Thunderchief was similar to the earlier F-105B, but possessed a larger nose radome. This contained a radar which permitted the F-105D to perform visual or blind

attacks with a variety of ordnance ranging from air-to-air missiles to conventional "iron" bombs.

F-105 Thunderchief's service in Vietnam was truly impressive, the type seeing action throughout the conflict but half of the 833 F-105s built were destroyed over Vietnam.

LEFT: **Before the F-84 was even in service, Republic were already working on a successor and came up with the excellent F-105.**

BELOW: **The two-seat fighter-bomber version, the F-105F, first flew in 1963.**

LEFT: **The Saab-21 had its origins as a propeller-driven aircraft.**

Saab J21RB

First flight: March 10, 1947
Power: de Havilland 1500kg/3307lb-thrust Goblin 3 turbojet
Armament: One 20mm/0.78in cannon and two 13.2mm/0.53in machine-guns mounted in nose, plus two further machine-guns in wings. Provision for ventral gun pack of eight more 13.2mm machine-guns
Size: Wingspan – 11.6m/38ft 0.75in
Length – 10.45m/34ft 3.5in
Height – 2.95m/9ft 8in
Wing area – 22.2m²/238.97sq ft
Weights: Empty – 3200kg/7055lb
Maximum take-off – 4990kg/11,001lb
Performance: Maximum speed – 800kph/497mph
Ceiling – 12,000m/39,370ft
Range – 720km/447 miles
Climb – 1400m/4600ft per minute

Saab-21

Development of the Saab-21 began in 1941 in response to a need for a Swedish-built fighter/attack aircraft to replace the various obsolete US and Italian fighters then in service with the Swedish Air Force. The resulting Saab-21 has a special place in the history books because it is the only aircraft ever to have seen front-line service propelled by piston and, later, jet power. The Daimler Benz piston-engined version, the J21A, entered service in June 1945, the only pusher-engined fighter to do so in World War II. It was fitted with an early ejection seat to meet the problem of vacating the cockpit unassisted with a snarling propeller blade some 4.58m/15ft behind.

After some problems with adapting the aircraft, the jet-engined J21RA entered service in 1949, with a top speed increase of 160kph/100mph.

Ground-attack versions were produced of both powered types but the Saab-21 is fondly remembered by its pilots for being an excellent fighter, being manoeuvrable, tough and a steady gun platform.

LEFT: **The name of "Tunnan" meaning "the barrel" fitted the J29 perfectly.**

Saab J29F

First flight: September 1, 1948 (prototype)
Power: Flygmotor 2800kg/6173lb RM2B afterburning turbojet
Armament: Four 20mm/0.78in cannon and two RB24 Sidewinder AAMs
Size: Wingspan – 11m/36ft 1in
Length – 10.13m/33ft 2.75in
Height – 3.73m/12ft 3.75in
Wing area – 24m²/258.34sq ft
Weights: Empty – 4300kg/9480lb
Maximum take-off – 8000kg/17,637lb
Performance: Maximum speed – 1060kph/658mph
Ceiling – 15,500m/50,855ft
Range – 2700km/1678 miles
Climb – 3600m/11,810ft per minute

Saab J29 Tunnan

Wartime German swept-wing research directly influenced the design of Saab's second jet fighter, which came to be named "Tunnan" (the barrel) because of its shape. As Saab had no direct swept-wing experience the proposed wing for the J29 was first tested on a Saab Safir aircraft. The test worked well and the first J29 prototype, powered by a Flygmotor licence-built de Havilland Ghost, took to the air on September 1, 1948. Tunnens began to enter service in 1951 and remained in production until 1956. The J29B had larger fuel tanks, while the E model introduced an afterburner and the J29F incorporated all previous improvements. Ground-attack and reconnaissance versions were also developed.

From 1958 the J29 was gradually replaced in Swedish Air Force units by the J32 Lansen, but in 1960 Sweden committed J29s to the UN air component that provided air cover for UN troops in the Belgian Congo. From 1961, Austria took delivery of 30 former Swedish Air Force J29Fs.

TOP: **The Draken was a front-line fighter for over three decades.** ABOVE: **The Draken's double delta-wing planform was very advanced in its day.**

Saab J35 Draken

The remarkable Draken (the dragon) was an aircraft ahead of its time and it could, if it had not been for Sweden's strict export policies, have equipped many air forces around the world. It was designed to satisfy a demanding 1949 Swedish Air Force requirement for an advanced high-performance interceptor, capable of tackling transonic-speed bombers. The specification called for speed 50 per cent greater than new fighters elsewhere, and the ability to operate from roads and other dispersed non-airfield locations. The solution was a futuristic double delta wing that gave strength with low weight and delivered all-round performance, while being able to accommodate fuel, weapons and other equipment. Before the Draken flew, its unique double delta wing was tested on a 70 per cent-scale research aircraft, which proved the viability of the design. The Draken first took to the air in October 1955 and the production version, the J35A, began to reach front-line units of the Swedish Air Force in 1960.

Among its features was a tricycle undercarriage complemented by two retractable tailwheels, deployed to permit a tail-down landing to gain the full aerodynamic braking effect of the wing. This landing technique, coupled with the use of a braking parachute, allowed the Draken to land in 610m/2000ft.

Improved versions appeared throughout the Draken's long operational life, including the J35B, with collision-course radar and increased armament, and the J35D with more powerful engines and improved avionics. The J35F had avionics that were even more advanced, an Aden cannon and the ability to carry Falcon air-to-air missiles instead of Sidewinders. The J35J upgrade of 66 J35Fs produced the ultimate Draken, to keep the type viable until the Gripen was ready to replace it from 1993. Few fighter aircraft remained as capable as the Draken for so long a period.

Reconnaissance versions (with a nose containing five cameras) and training versions were built among the total production run of 606 aircraft. Drakens were also exported to Denmark, Finland and Austria.

Saab J35F Draken

First flight: October 25, 1955

Power: Volvo 7830kg/17,262lb afterburning Volvo Flygmotor RM6C (licence-built R-R Avon 300) turbojet

Armament: One 30mm/1.18in cannon in right wing, two RB 27 and two 28 Falcon missiles, plus up to 1000kg/2205lb of bombs or rockets

Size: Wingspan – 9.4m/30ft 10in
Length – 15.35m/50ft 4.3in
Height – 3.89m/12ft 9in
Wing area – 49.2m²/529.6sq ft

Weights: Empty – 7425kg/16,369lb
Maximum take-off – 12,700kg/27,998lb

Performance: Maximum speed – 2125kph/1320mph
Ceiling – 20,000m/65,615ft
Range – 960km/597 miles with external tanks
Climb – 12,000m/39,370ft per minute

Saab Gripen

This lightweight multi-role fighter is probably the most advanced and capable single-seat fighter in service today. Designed to replace the Swedish Air Force's Viggen and Draken, the Gripen (griffin) first flew in December 1988 and employs the latest advances in aerodynamics, materials and engine technology. From the outset the designers have striven to integrate pilot and machine. The Gripen pilot receives information through an air-to-air Tactical Information Data Link System that permits real-time exchange of data within, and between, tactical air groups. Overall situational awareness is thus maximized, enabling pilots to use their aircraft weapon systems to best effect.

Cockpit ergonomics were exhaustively researched to allow the pilot the maximum amount of time for tactical operation of the aircraft. The cockpit is dominated by three large colour Multi-Function Displays and a wide-angle Head-Up Display – these four displays are the principal flight instruments. The displays are even fitted with light sensors for computer-controlled brightness.

Power is provided by a single Swedish licence-built General Electric F404-GE-400 turbofan engine, which can push the Gripen along at speeds of up to Mach 2, or, crucially, Mach 1 at any altitude. Some 20 per cent by weight of the airframe is made from carbon fibre composites. The Gripen's advanced aerodynamic configuration employs a delta wing and canard foreplanes for short-field operations and to ensure optimum agility at all altitudes, even when fully armed. This manoeuvrability is optimized by the aircraft's fly-by-wire system and the Gripen could probably outmanoeuvre all other current fighters. In these days of stealth, the Gripen has a surprisingly low radar and infra-red signature, improving its air combat survivability chances.

Central to the Gripen's targeting system is the long-range Ericsson PS-05/A multi-mode pulse-Doppler radar, which can track multiple targets simultaneously and provide rapid assessment information to the pilot. This system enables the Gripen to perform equally well in the fighter and the air-to-surface attack role. This truly remarkable aircraft's multi-role

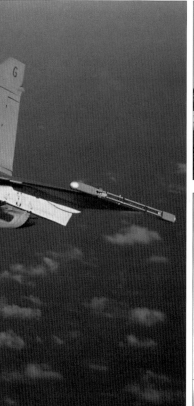

ABOVE: **A fighter for the 21st century, the Gripen is perhaps the most advanced fighter in service today.**

TOP: **The Gripen can operate from 800m/2626ft strips, which is short for such a potent combat aircraft.**
ABOVE: **The Mach 2-capable Gripen is a much sought-after "ride" by today's fighter pilots.**

capability can be realized by the push of a button, effectively changing the Gripen's mission in mid-air.

The aircraft's flexibility is further enhanced by its ability to operate from dispersed sites, including ordinary roads and it can land and take-off from 800m/2625ft strips. An on-board auxiliary power unit allows rapid reaction times even in dispersed locations.

Considerable emphasis has been placed on maximizing component reliability and ease of access for maintenance. Fast turn-round times and in-built test equipment keeps the Gripen's time off-line to a minimum. This results in low life-cycle costs and high availability – this "force multiplier" effect has not been lost on some of the countries expressing interest in export Gripens.

The first of around 200 Gripens began operational service with the Swedish Air Force in June 1997 and the aircraft has also been ordered by the South African Air Force. The Gripen is generally acknowledged as one of the ultimate modern fighters.

Saab JAS 39A Gripen

First flight: December 9, 1988

Power: Volvo Aero Corporation/General Electric 8210kg/18,100lb afterburning thrust RM-12 turbojet

Armament: One internally mounted 27mm/1.06in cannon, one Sidewinder on each wingtip, plus five hardpoints for Sky Flash or Sidewinder AAMs, rockets or bombs

Size: Wingspan – 8.4m/27ft 6in, including wingtip launchers
Length – 14.1m/46ft 3in
Height – 4.5m/14ft 9in
Wing area – 30m²/323 sq ft

Weights: Empty – 6622kg/14,600lb
Maximum take-off – 13,989kg/30,800lb

Performance: Maximum speed – 2126kph/1321mph
Ceiling, range and climb data not published

Saab Viggen

The multi-role Viggen (thunderbolt) was designed to replace the Draken and continued Sweden's desire to remain independent of the East or West for their supply of combat aircraft. The Viggen was, for some time, the most advanced combat aircraft produced in Europe and appeared in fighter, strike and reconnaissance versions. In December 1961 the

Swedish government approved development of Aircraft System 37 which evolved into the Viggen. The basic platform was to be the AJ 37 attack aircraft, to be followed by the S 37 reconnaissance version and finally the all-weather JA 37 fighter.

Design of this ground-breaking aircraft began as far back as 1952 and by 1954 it had grown its distinctive canard wings just to the rear of the cockpit. The canards, working with the wing control surfaces, help generate additional lift during the crucial stages of landing and take-off to reduce the speeds and landing runs required to the minimum. In fact one of the essential requirements of the original specification was that the aircraft could operate from 500m/1640ft runways. Landing

distance is reduced by several means – the Head-Up Display doubles as a precision landing aid, making it possible to aim just 30m/98ft in from the threshold, and the thrust reverser is interconnected with the nose gear, so that it can be selected in the air and will operate as soon as the nose is lowered.

In order to keep the aircraft as small and light as possible, it was decided to install a state-of-the-art navigational computer instead of a human navigator. The aircraft looks a lot heavier than it actually is thanks to the use of honeycomb panels in the aircraft. It is however very strong and is stressed to stand 12G in the tight turns made possible by vast wing area.

The chosen engine for the Viggen, the Pratt & Whitney JT8D-22 designed for the Boeing 727, was licence-built by Volvo in Sweden as the RM8A together with a locally designed afterburner. The fighter version however required that the engine was redesigned, at great cost, to better suit the demands of the fighter mission. The new engine, the RM8B, gave greater thrust at all altitudes and in extreme manoeuvres. The prototype first flew in February 8, 1967 and was described by the test pilot Eric Dahlstrom as being "as simple to fly as a sportsplane". In April 1968 the Swedish Government authorized Viggen production, with the first aircraft being delivered in July 1971.

LEFT: **A JA 37 Viggen, the all-weather Viggen interceptor.** BELOW: **The SF 37 Viggen reconnaissance version carries the night reconnaissance pod on the left under-fuselage pylon.**

LEFT: **The SF 37 reconnaissance version has cameras in the distinctively shaped nose.** BELOW: **The Viggen was a very advanced design, far ahead of other European types of the time.**

The aircraft was designed for simple maintenance from the outset so that conscripts with little training could turn the aircraft around quickly in readiness for its next mission. Refuelling and re-arming by seven ground personnel, of which six were conscripts, had to take less than ten minutes.

The Viggen's one-piece wrap-around windscreen was specially strengthened to survive bird strikes at high speeds and also gives the pilots an excellent forward view. Sweden's numerous dispersed underground hangars dictated that the Viggen's fin be capable of folding down for easier storage.

During the 1960s, the Swedish Air Force were expected to purchase more than 800 Viggens, but the final Viggen production total was 329 built in attack, trainer, two reconnaissance versions and the more powerful JA 37 fighter variant. The last of the Viggens, a fighter, was delivered to the Swedish Air Force in 1990. Since then the Viggen fighter has undergone several upgrades with better radar to track more targets simultaneously, new avionics and cockpit displays and extra weaponry in the form of the AIM-120 AAM.

The Viggen has been gradually replaced in Svenska Flygvapnet (Swedish Air Force) service by the Gripen.

ABOVE: **The last JA 37 interceptor version was delivered to the Swedish Air Force in 1990.** BELOW: **Able to operate from country roads and motorways, the Viggen protected Sweden for almost three decades.**

Saab JA 37 Viggen

First flight: February 8, 1967 (prototype)
Power: Volvo Flygmotor 12,750kg/28,110lb afterburning-thrust RM8B turbofan
Armament: One 30mm/1.18in cannon plus six external hardpoints for 6000kg/13,228lb of ordnance including two Sky Flash and four Sidewinder AAMs
Size: Wingspan – 10.6m/34ft 9.25in
Length – 16.4m/53ft 9.75in
Height – 5.9m/19ft 4.25in
Wing area – 52.2m^2/561.89sq ft, including canards
Weights: Empty – 15,000kg/33,060lb
Maximum take-off – 20,500kg/45,194lb
Performance: Maximum speed – 2195kph/1365mph
Ceiling – 18,290m/60,000ft
Range – 1000km/620 miles
Climb – 10,000m/32,810ft in 1minute, 24 seconds

Sud-Ouest Vautour

The Vautour (vulture) was initially developed as a medium bomber in the early to mid-1950s and from a modern perspective seemed an unusual choice for development as a fighter. The advanced high-performance twin-jet design was first tested in half-scale form in 1949 and the full-scale prototypes began testing in 1951. The trials were so promising that the type, very similar in layout to the Yak-28, was rapidly developed as the S.O. 4050 multi-role combat aircraft.

Three variants of the Vautour were developed: the single-seat cannon and bomb armed Vautour IIA attack aircraft, the two-seat Vautour IIB bomber equipped with a glazed nose for the navigator/bombardier, and the Vautour IIN – the N signifying nuit, or night. The latter was a two-seat all-weather/night attack fighter equipped with an interception radar in the nose, and it took off on its maiden flight on October 16, 1952. A total of 140 examples were ordered by the French but only 70 were produced between 1957 and 1959, armed with rockets, missiles and cannon, and these were mostly based at Tours with an all-weather fighter wing. They were gradually replaced from 1973 by the Mirage F1.

In the late 1950s, Israel wanted to develop a long-range fighter capability to tackle hostile aircraft deep in enemy territory. Following evaluation flights in early 1957 the Israeli Air Force selected the Vautour to replace the de Havilland Mosquito in the long-range attack role and to counter the Arabs' Ilyushin Il-28 light jet bombers. Eighteen Vautour bombers were first exported to Israel, followed by seven of the fighter version. Capable of supersonic speed in a dive, these

TOP: **The similarities between the Vautour and the Yak-28 are clear in this photograph.** ABOVE: **The Vautour IIB bomber version equipped the French equivalent of Strategic Air Command.**

aircraft saw considerable action with the Israeli Air Force (IAF) in the 1967 Six-Day War and were in constant use until 1970.

Two IAF squadrons were equipped with the Vautour – the "Bat" squadron at Tel-Nof operated the IIN variant. The 7 IINs were initially operated as night interceptors (alongside the IAF's Meteor NF.13s until 1960 when these were retired) but after the arrival of the Mirage IIIC in 1963 they were employed as attack aircraft. They did however continue to fly night interceptions as required, for example early in 1964 when they attempted to engage Egyptian MiG-19s.

The first encounter between the IAF Vautours and the MiG-19 had occurred some five years earlier on August 16, 1959 when two Vautours engaged four Egyptian MiGs on the Israeli-Egyptian border. Later in March 1962 a single Vautour chased an Ilyushin Il-28 all the way to Damascus before being ordered to turn back.

TOP: **This French Air Force Vautour IIN was modified to test a new radome installation.** ABOVE: **An unlikely fighter, the Vautour IIN was in front-line service with the Armée de l'Air for around 15 years.**

Sud-Ouest Vautour IIN

First flight: October 16, 1952
Power: Two SNECMA 3503kg/7716lb-thrust Atar 101E-3 turbojet engines
Armament: Four 30mm/1.18in cannon, internal bomb bay with provision for up to 240 unguided rockets, plus underwing pylons for air-to-air missiles or rockets
Size: Wingspan – 15.09m/49ft 6in
Length – 15.57m/51ft 2in
Height – 4.5m/14ft 9in
Wing area – 45m²/484.4sq ft
Weights: Empty – 10,000kg/22,010lb
Maximum take-off – 20,000kg/44,093lb
Performance: Maximum speed – 1105kph/687mph
Ceiling – 15,000m/49,210ft
Range – 3200km/1990 miles
Climb – 3600m/11,800ft per minute

Sukhoi Su-9/11

The dominance of swept-wing fighters in the Korean War stimulated the ultimate development of the configuration – the delta. In the USSR, the TSAGI (National Aerodynamic Research Centre) endorsed the form and encouraged its development. Sukhoi's design bureau produced a prototype delta-winged aircraft, the T-3, and a whole range of nose configurations were tried, but it was the safe option that was chosen for the production aircraft – a circular intake with a small conical centrebody housing the radar.

Production began in 1958 and the first Su-9s joined air defence squadrons in 1959, equipped with four AA-1 "Alkali" air-to-air missiles. Two drop tanks were carried, as the internal fuel capacity of

2145 litres/472 gallons severely limited range. A special version, the T-431, set an altitude record of 28,852m/ 94,659ft in 1959. Su-9s were still in use in the early 1980s and many of the examples retired from service were converted to drones, or pilotless vehicles, and were used as aerial targets to test and train Soviet air defence personnel.

The 1961 Tushino Aviation Day display saw the first appearance of the T-43 prototype, an improved version of the Su-9. By 1965, production of the new version, by then called the Su-11, was underway with a more powerful engine, new radar and improved weaponry. The nose was lengthened and a much larger centrebody was needed to house the new Uragan 5B radar.

ABOVE: **This Su-9 was pictured at the 1967 Soviet Aviation Day display.** BELOW: **A total of 2000 Su-9/11s were built, but the Soviet Union chose to keep them all.**

The new weapons were the long-range Anab air-to-air missiles, carried in pairs, one equipped for infra-red homing (heat seeking) and the other radar-guided.

Combined Sukhoi Su-9/11 production is estimated at 2000 aircraft. None saw service with other Warsaw Pact countries and no examples of this potent fighter were exported.

Sukhoi Su-11

First flight: 1961 (T-43)
Power: Lyulka 10,000kg/22,046lb afterburning thrust AL-7F-1 turbojet
Armament: Two AA-3 Anab long-range air-to-air homing missiles
Size: Wingspan – 8.43m/27ft 8in
Length – 17.4m/57ft 1in
Height – 4.88m/16ft
Wing area – 26.2m^2/282.02sq ft
Weights: Empty – 9100kg/20,062lb
Maximum take-off – 14,000kg/30,865lb
Performance: Maximum speed – 1915kph/1190mph
Ceiling – 17,000m/55,775ft
Range – 1450km/900 miles with drop tanks
Climb – 8230m/27,000ft per minute

Sukhoi Su-15

This very fast single-seat aircraft, codenamed "Flagon" by NATO, served from the 1960s into the 90s. Equipped with long-range air-to-air missiles, the Su-15 was an interceptor, whose sole role was the air defence of the USSR. Around 1500 served with Soviet PVO-Strany home defence units from 1967, deployed in areas where they were only likely to face attacking NATO bombers with little likelihood of ever having to dogfight.

Developed to replace the Su-11, the Su-15 Flagon-A was the first production version and was first seen at the 1967 Aviation Day display – it was clearly a twin-engine development of the Su-11 but with side intakes necessitated by the introduction of the large conical radome. The large rear-warning radar appeared on this model and was common to most of the Flagon family.

Flagon interceptor missions were almost always flown under ground control and this included the most infamous Su-15 mission of all, on September 1, 1983. At 03.26 local time, Su-15 pilot Major Vassily Kasmin launched two AA-3 Anab air-to-air missiles at a Korean Air Lines Boeing 747 airliner, which had strayed 400km/250 miles north of its planned route. The airliner was overflying

ABOVE: **The Sukhoi Su-15 was a very big fighter that protected the Soviet Union and Russia for around 30 years.** BELOW: **This picture of an example preserved in a Russian museum shows the size of the large nose radome.**

Soviet military installations and after reportedly firing warning shots with cannon, the Su-15, under instruction from ground control, attacked from a distance of 800m/2624ft and destroyed the airliner with the loss of all 269 passengers and crew.

The "Flagon-D" was the first version produced in large numbers and differed from the A by having bigger span wings with a kinked leading edge. The E model was also produced in quantity and was powered by more powerful engines (hence the larger air intakes), presumably to reduce the scramble time.

The "Flagon-F" was the ultimate version and entered service in 1975. It introduced bigger engines, gun pods and a more powerful radar, housed in an ogival-shaped radome designed to reduce drag and improve supersonic acceleration.

From the mid-1990s, the Su-15 was replaced by the Su-27 and MiG-31. Two-seat trainer versions and experimental versions with lift jets were also produced.

Sukhoi Su-15 Flagon-F

First flight: 1965

Power: Two Tumansky 7200kg/15,873lb afterburning thrust R-13F2-300 turbojets

Armament: Four AA-3 "Anab" medium-range air-to-air missiles carried on underwing pylons, two AA-8 "Aphid" short-range air-to-air missiles on inboard positions, plus two 23mm/0.9in gun pods

Size: Wingspan – 10.53m/34ft 6in
Length – 21.33m/70ft
Height – 5.1m/16ft 8.5in
Wing area – 36m²/387.5sq ft

Weights: Empty – 11,000kg/24,250lb
Maximum take-off – 18,000kg/39,680lb

Performance: Maximum speed – 2230kph/1386mph
Ceiling – 20,000m/65,615ft
Range – 725km/450 miles
Climb – 10,670m/35,000ft per minute

Sukhoi Su-27 family

The arrival of the long-range Su-27 (codenamed "Flanker" by NATO) gave the USSR a formidable fighter that could escort its bomber force all the way to the UK. This high-performance aircraft, which also had the capability of intercepting aircraft over long distances, came as a shock to NATO planners when it was deployed in the mid-1980s. About 20 per cent larger than the F-15 Eagle, the Su-27 is one of the biggest and most imposing fighters of all time.

Development work began in 1969 under Pavel Sukhoi himself and the prototype first flew in 1977, but early models displayed serious instability problems and it was considerably redesigned. Nevertheless, the Su-27 in service today is considered by many to be the pinnacle of Russian fighter design and the masterpiece of the Sukhoi bureau.

The fast-climbing and superbly manoeuvrable fly-by-wire Flanker can carry up to 10 air-to-air missiles, including the 112km/70-mile-range AA-10C. That amount of missiles gives the Flanker "combat persistence" – it can keep on fighting long after other fighters would have had to turn for home. Huge internal fuel tanks give very long range (up to 4000km/ 2484 miles), with no need for drag-inducing external fuel tanks.

The Su-27's Zhuk radar can track targets while continuing to scan for others and perhaps most importantly gives the aircraft a look-down/shoot-down capability. Very advanced electronics enables the Flanker to detect and destroy an enemy fighter beyond visual range (BVR) at tree-top height, without the need to descend to that level and lose a height advantage. The Su-27 equips air arms in Russia, Belarus, Uzbekistan, Ethiopia, China, Vietnam and the Ukraine

TOP: **The large Su-27 first flew in April 1981 and came as a shock to potential adversaries of the Soviet Union.** ABOVE: **Preparing to land, this Su-27 has deployed its enormous dorsal airbrake which reduces the aircraft's speed most effectively.**

– China also negotiated manufacturing rights to produce its own Su-27s, which began to appear in December 1998.

The Su-27P is a single-seat air defence fighter, the Su-27S is a multi-role version capable of carrying a 4000kg/8820lb bomb load and the Su-27UB is a two-seat operational trainer. Specially modified versions have set more than 40 altitude and climb records.

The Su-30 is a two-seat air defence fighter capable of 10-hour missions and can also serve as an airborne command post for other Su-27s. India and China have ordered these aircraft, which like the derivative Su-37, have canards and thrust-vectoring nozzles for enhanced manoeuvrability.

The Su-27 spawned a whole family of fighter aircraft, including the Su-33, Su-35 and Su-37, but the Su-27 is likely

ABOVE: **This Ukrainian Air Force example shows the huge rear defensive radar boom which effectively gives the type's pilots eyes in the back of their head.**
LEFT: **The excellent Su-27 did much to remove the advantage enjoyed in the early 1980s by US fighter types like the F-15.**

to be the mainstay of the Russian aviation industry for some years to come.

The Russian Navy's carrier arm is equipped with the Su-33 Naval Flanker version (originally the Su-27K), with moveable foreplanes plus folding wings and tailplane. Deployed since 1995 and certainly the most modern fighters in the Russian inventory, Su-33s provide the Russian Admiral Kuznetsov carrier class with air defence. Landing gear is also strengthened and as a naval aircraft it does, of course, have an arrester hook. Because of the lower approach and take-off speeds a number of other changes were made – moveable foreplanes aid manoeuvrability and control in all aspects of flight.

BELOW: **The Su-34 fighter-bomber derivative first flew in 1990, and seats its two-man crew in a side-by-side cockpit.**

Sukhoi Su-27P

First flight: April 20, 1981
(T-10S-1 pre-production prototype)
Power: Two Saturn/Lyulka 12,516kg/27,557lb
afterburning thrust AL-31F turbofans
Armament: One 30mm/1.18in cannon, plus ten
hardpoints for up to ten air-to-air missiles
from AA-8 "Aphids" to AA10Cs
Size: Wingspan – 14.7m/48ft 3in Length – 21.94m/
72ft Height – 5.93m/19ft 6in Wing area – 62m²/667sq ft
Weights: Empty – 16,380kg/36,110lb
Maximum take-off – 33,000kg/72,750lb
Performance: Maximum speed – 2500kph/1553mph
Ceiling – 18,011m/59,055ft
Range – 3680km/2285 miles
Climb – 18,312m/60,040ft per minute

Sukhoi Su-35/37

A version of the Su-27 fitted with canards first flew in May 1985 and was developed into what became the Su-35. The prototype of the first true Su-35, initially designated Su-27M, had its test flight in June 1988. The single-seat Su-35 differed from the Su-27 in a number of ways, apart from the all-moving canard foreplanes. Improved engines provided greater thrust while flight control was managed by a digital fly-by-wire system that boasted quadruple redundancy, that is the systems could find four alternative routes by which to send control commands throughout the aircraft. This kind of system is an insurance against combat damage – on-board systems will simply find another route by which to pass the information.

The extremely efficient Phazotron radar can search over 100km/62 miles, track 24 targets simultaneously and has a terrain-following mode to guide the aircraft automatically over undulating landscapes. Development of this and the fly-by-wire system considerably delayed the overall programme. The Su-35 tailcone also houses a radar, which scans and protects the aircraft's rear. The aircraft is equipped for inflight refuelling and auxiliary fuel tanks are fitted in the two tailfins. The cockpit Electronic Flight Information System (EFIS) consists of three TV screens and a Head-Up Display (HUD).

The Su-37 Super Flanker is a further improvement on the Su-35 and has two-dimensional thrust-vectoring nozzles controlled by the fly-by-wire system. The improved cockpit has a sidestick controller and four LCD multifunction displays. When the Su-37 appeared at the 1996 Farnborough air show piloted by Sukhoi test pilot Eugeny Frolov, it stole the show with the astounding manoeuvres made possible by thrust vectoring. The Su-37 was flipped on its back while flying at 350kph/217mph so that it faced the opposite direction, inverted and almost stationary. After pausing for two seconds (long enough to loose off a missile in combat) the thrust vectoring was used to complete the 360 degree rotation and the aircraft moved off in its original direction of flight at only 60kph/37mph.

Sukhoi's chief designer Mikhail Simonov is so confident about the

TOP: **The Su-37 version has canard foreplanes and agility-enhancing thrust vectoring nozzles.** ABOVE: **The performance and agility of the Su-37 Super Flanker makes it a potent dogfight adversary.**

advantage bestowed by the aircraft's thrust vectoring system, that he challenged any US aircraft to a mock dogfight "… any time, any place!" At the time of writing, the Su-37 was yet to be ordered into production.

Sukhoi Su-35

First flight: June 28, 1988
Power: Two Lyulka 12,500kg/27,557lb AL-31M turbofans
Armament: One 30mm/1.18in cannon and 14 hardpoints to carry a range of missiles and bombs up to 6000kg/13,228lb
Size: Wingspan – 14.7m/48ft 2.75in
Length – 22.2m/72ft 10in
Height – 6.36m/20ft 10in
Wing area – 46.5m²/500sq ft
Weights: Empty – 17,000kg/37,479lb
Maximum take-off – 34,000kg/74,956lb
Performance: Maximum speed – 2500kph/1550mph
Ceiling – 18,000m/59,055ft
Range – 4000km/2484 miles
Climb – not published

LEFT: **The tail-dragging straight-winged Attacker was the Fleet Air Arm's first front-line jet fighter.**

Supermarine Attacker F. Mk I

First flight: July 27, 1946
Power: Rolls-Royce 2271kg/5000lb-thrust Nene 3 turbojet
Armament: Four 20mm/0.78in cannon in wing
Size: Wingspan – 11.25m/36ft 11in
Length – 11.43m/37ft 6in
Height – 3.02m/9ft 11in
Wing area – 21m²/226sq ft
Weights: Empty – 3826kg/8434lb
Maximum take-off – 5539kg/12,211lb
Performance: Maximum speed – 950kph/590mph
Ceiling – 13,715m/45,000ft
Range – 950km/590 miles
Climb – 1936m/6350ft per minute

Supermarine Attacker

The Supermarine Attacker was designed to an RAF specification and combined a Nene jet engine with the laminar wing and landing gear of the piston-engined Spiteful. This approach was taken to bring another British single-seat jet fighter into service as soon as possible. Although the prototype first flew in July 1946, the type did not enter service until August 1951 and then with

the Royal Navy, who maintained interest in the Attacker long after the RAF abandoned it. The Attacker was an unremarkable aircraft and the tailwheel made deck landing difficult, but as the first Fleet Air Arm jet fighter in front-line use, the Attacker provided the Royal Navy with its first foothold in the jet age. The type was phased out of front-line use in 1954.

Attackers were also supplied to the Pakistani Air Force, who operated them as land-based aircraft.

LEFT: **The Scimitar was a large twin-engined fighter and although only produced in limited quantities, it served the Royal Navy well in a variety of roles for a decade.**

Supermarine Scimitar F.1

First flight: January 11, 1957
Power: Two Rolls-Royce 5105kg/11,250lb static thrust Avon 202 turbojets
Armament: Four 30mm/1.18in cannon, wing pylons for up to 96 air-to-air rockets or a range of other stores
Size: Wingspan – 11.33m/37ft 2in
Length – 16.87m/55ft 4in
Height – 5.28m/17ft 4in
Wing area – 45.06m²/485sq ft
Weights: Empty – 10,869kg/23,962lb
Maximum take-off – 15,513kg/34,200lb
Performance: Maximum speed – 1143kph/710mph
Ceiling – 14,020m/46,000ft
Range – 2288km/1422 miles
Climb – 3660m/12,000ft per minute

Supermarine Scimitar

This large and heavy fighter was the Royal Navy's first swept-wing single-seat fighter and was also the first Fleet Air Arm aircraft equipped to carry an atomic bomb. The Scimitar was equally at home carrying out low-level bombing attacks, high-altitude interception with air-to-air missiles and long-range fighter reconnaissance – it represented a quantum leap from the lacklustre Sea

Hawk which it replaced as the Navy's standard single-seat strike fighter.

The first operational squadron equipped with this very capable combat aircraft was No.803, formed at Lossiemouth in June 1958. Although only 76 were produced, the Scimitars gave the Royal Navy real punch and retained their nuclear role until 1969.

LEFT: The Swift was the first swept-wing jet fighter in service with the Royal Air Force, but continued problems led to premature retirement of the type.

Supermarine Swift F. Mk 1

First flight: August 5, 1951
Power: Rolls-Royce 3406kg/7500lb-thrust Avon RA7 turbojet
Armament: Two 30mm/1.18in cannon
Size: Wingspan – 9.85m/32ft 4in
Length – 12.64m/41ft 5.5in
Height – 3.8m/12ft 6in
Wing area – 28.43m^2/306sq ft
Weights: Empty – 5678kg/12,500lb
Maximum take-off – 7721kg/17,000lb
Performance: Maximum speed – 1110kph/690mph
Ceiling – 13,725m/45,500ft
Range – 1175km/730 miles
Climb – 3752m/12,300ft

Supermarine Swift

In 1946 Britain's Air Ministry asked manufacturers to propose a replacement for the Gloster Meteor. Supermarine's entry was a development of its Attacker, but featuring staged improvements including swept wings and tail, tricycle undercarriage and a Rolls-Royce Avon engine, which became the Swift F. Mk 1. This aircraft

was allocated, on a very restricted basis, to No.56 Squadron RAF in February 1954 but only to gain air experience with swept wings. High-speed and high-altitude manoeuvrability and control problems persisted with interim marks, but the FR. Mk 5 did enter RAF front-line service, equipping Nos.2 and 79 Squadrons in RAF

Germany from 1955 until 1961. This version of the Swift, an effective fighter reconnaissance aircraft, was the first reheat-engined swept-wing aircraft in RAF service.

LEFT: The Tu-28P is the largest interceptor ever built, and is some 8.4m/27ft longer than the F-14 Tomcat. This example, complete with dummy AA-5 missiles, is preserved in a Russian museum.

Tupolev Tu-28P

First flight: 1957
Power: Two Lyulka 11,200kg/24,690lb afterburning thrust AL-21F turbojets
Armament: Four AA-5 "Ash" long-range air-to-air missiles
Size: Wingspan – 18.1m/59ft 4.5in
Length – 27.2m/89ft 3in
Height – 7m/23ft
Wing area – 80m^2/861sq ft
Weights: Empty – 25,000kg/55,125lb
Maximum take-off – 40,000kg/88,185lb
Performance: Maximum speed – 1850kph/1150mph
Ceiling – 20,000m/65,615ft
Range – 5000km/3105 miles
Climb – 7500m/25,000ft per minute

Tupolev Tu-28

Codenamed "Fiddler" by NATO, this very large fighter provided the USSR with a long-range fighter capability from the 1960s until its gradual replacement by Su-27s and MiG-31s in the late 1980s. The Tu-28, designed to intercept Western missile-carrying aircraft before they had a chance to launch their deadly weapons, was the world's largest all-weather

interceptor. With a range of more than 3000km/1865 miles, the Tu-28 was deployed to protect the northern Soviet Union and was armed with four AA-5 "Ash" air-to-air missiles.

Production began in the early 1960s and the type entered service in the mid-1960s, although it was unknown to the West until Soviet Aviation Day in 1967. Two crew were carried in tandem.

The aircraft were phased out of service by 1992.

Vought F7U Cutlass

In 1945 the US Navy issued a requirement for a 965kph/600mph carrier-borne fighter. German wartime aerodynamic research data proved very useful to US aircraft designers in the immediate post-war years. Vought (or Chance Vought as it was then known) designers were particularly interested in the work carried out by the Arado company on tailless aircraft and this led directly to the rather unconventional F7U Cutlass, which had a 38-degree swept wing, twin tail fins but no conventional tail surfaces. The Cutlass helped the US Navy break new ground – it was the first supersonic production aircraft in the US Navy inventory.

The F7U-1 was the first version in service but only 14 were built and these

were used for trials and training. The aircraft was very demanding in terms of maintenance and it also had a high accident rate but it was very popular with pilots and could pull 16G manoeuvres when making use of its excellent aerobatics.

The F7U-3 that ultimately equipped 13 US Navy and Marine Corps squadrons ashore and on carriers was not just modified and improved – it was effectively a new design. The F7U-1 version had not been considered robust enough for carrier use so the new model was considerably tougher, being re-stressed throughout. To reduce maintenance time over 100 extra doors and access panels were added. The nose was redesigned, twice, to improve pilot visibility and the tricycle undercarriage nosewheel was both lengthened and strengthened. This new version was introduced into US Navy service from 1954 and the

TOP: **Like the Douglas Skyray, the Cutlass was designed with the benefit of data derived from German wartime aerodynamic research. This Cutlass is preserved at the Museum of Naval Aviation at Pensacola in Florida.** ABOVE: **An F7U-1 Cutlass.** BELOW LEFT: **The Cutlass is surely one of the oddest-looking fighters ever.**

F7U-3M variant was equipped to carry four laser-beam-riding Sparrow air-to-air missiles.

Most were withdrawn from service in 1956–7 as new, more capable aircraft became available. The F7U-3 was just as accident-prone as the F7U-1, with an incredible 25 per cent of all aircraft built being lost in accidents.

Vought F7U-3 Cutlass

First flight: September 29, 1948 (XF7U-1 prototype)
Power: Two Westinghouse 2767kg/6100lb afterburning thrust J46-WE-8A turbojet engines
Armament: Four 20mm/0.78in cannon, plus underwing attachments for rockets
Size: Wingspan – 12.09m/39ft 8in
Length – 13.13m/43ft 1in
Height – 4.46m/14ft 7.5in
Wing area – 46.08m^2/496sq ft
Weights: Empty – 8260kg/18,210lb
Maximum take-off – 14,353kg/31,642lb
Performance: Maximum speed – 1094kph/680mph
Ceiling – 12,190m/40,000ft
Range – 1062km/660 miles
Climb – 3960m/13,000ft per minute

251

Vought F-8 Crusader

The single-seat Crusader naval fighter began life as Vought's response to a 1952 US Navy requirement for a carrier-based supersonic fighter. The prototype first took to the air in March 1955 and exceeded Mach 1 during this initial flight, making it the first fighter designed for shipboard operation to fly faster than sound.

Carrier operations require that aircraft have very robust landing gear, an arrester hook, and folding wings but these features all add to the overall weight and thus can compromise

performance. Vought came up with a brilliant variable-incidence wing, which on take-off and landing could be pivoted up seven degrees. This gave the wing a high angle-of-attack and so reduced approach and take-off speeds. The raised centre section of the wing also acted as a speed brake to reduce landing speed further.

The armament consisted of four 20mm/0.78in cannon, two of the guns on either side of the fuselage. Behind the guns, on each side of the aircraft, was a launch rail for a single Sidewinder air-to-air missile. There were no wing stores pylons on the prototype, but these came on later production models.

The first production version of the F8U-1 Crusader, as it was then named, flew at the end of September 1955 and the US Navy accepted its first operational F8U-1 on December 28, 1956. The US Navy was eager to show off its new fighter and a series of speed and endurance records were bagged by Crusaders in 1956–7. On July 16, 1957 an F8U-1 and an F8U-1P reconnaissance model attempted to set a coast-to-coast speed record. The pilot of the F8U-1P that landed in New York after a flight of 3 hours and 23 minutes was Major John Glenn, later an astronaut and US senator.

The F8U-1E had an improved radar system that gave it limited all-weather capability while the more powerful F8U-2 incorporated a further improved radar and fire-control system, as well as an uprated J57-P-16 engine with 7670kg/16,900lb of afterburning thrust.

Next version was the F8U-2N, with new avionics, including a push-button autopilot, and the uprated J57-P-20 engine, with increased afterburning thrust of 8,170kg/18,000lb. Yet more versions followed. The first F8U-2NE flew at the end of June 1961 and carried an improved search and fire-control radar system for enhanced all-weather operation.

In September 1962, the US Navy introduced an aircraft designation system in line with US Air Force designations, so

ABOVE: **The last of the gunfighters – two US Navy Vought F-8 Crusaders, the top one flying in an inverted position.** BELOW: **The F-8's innovative variable-incidence wing reduced take-off and landing speeds.**

ABOVE: **The French Aéronavale was the main overseas customer for the Crusader, and operated the type until 2000.**

existing Crusader variant designations were changed. The F8U-1 became the F-8A and the later models changed thus: F8U-1E/F-8B, F8U-2/F-8C, F8U-2N/F-8D, F8U-2NE/F-8E, F8U-1P/RF-8A.

One final new-production model was built – the F-8E(FN), built for the French Aéronavale. However, French carriers were smaller than American carriers, and this dictated new engineering, including blown flaps to reduce the aircraft's landing speed.

The Aéronavale operated 42 Crusaders from the carriers *Clémenceau* and *Foch*. The French aircraft also had the capability to carry two Matra R.530 air-to-air missiles and eventually four Matra Magic R.550 heat-seeking missiles, in place of Sidewinders.

The Crusader was used by both US Marine and US Navy detachments during the war in Vietnam, its combat début coming on August 2, 1964. North Vietnamese patrol boats attacked the US Navy destroyer *Maddox* so four Crusaders from the carrier *Ticonderoga* attacked and sank one of the patrol boats. The Marines used the aircraft largely in the attack role, but the US Navy used the Crusader as a dogfighter and in the period 1966–8 shot down at least 18 MiGs.

The Crusader proved so effective that in 1966 a re-engineering programme was established to refurbish and improve the type. Stronger wings and main landing gear plus blown flaps (devised for the French Crusaders) were added to a total of 446 rebuilt.

By 1972, fighter versions of the F-8 were being phased out of US Navy service but in 1978, 25 refurbished US Navy F-8Hs were sold on to the Philippine Air Force as F-8Ps, which finally retired in 1986. The Aéronavale Crusaders were the last of the type in service and were replaced by the Rafale from 2000, bringing more than four decades of Crusader service to an end.

ABOVE: **US Navy F-8s proved to be formidable dogfighters during the Vietnam War.**
LEFT: **The F-8 Crusader was one of the first supersonic fighters, and was a potent combat aircraft for over four decades.**

Vought F-8E Crusader

First flight: March 25, 1955
Power: Pratt & Whitney 8165kg/18,000lb
   afterburning thrust J57-P-20A turbojet engine
Armament: Four 20mm/0.78in cannon,
   four AIM-9 Sidewinder air-to-air missiles,
   or two AGM-12B Bullpup missiles
Size: Wingspan – 10.72m/35ft 2in
   Length – 16.61m/54ft 6in
   Height – 4.8m/15ft 9in
   Wing area – 32.52m²/350sq ft
Weights: Empty – 9038kg/19,925lb
   Maximum take-off – 15,422kg/34,000lb
Performance: Maximum speed – 1800kph/1120mph
   Ceiling – 17,983m/59,000ft
   Range – 966km/600 miles
   Climb – 17,374m/57,000ft in 6 minutes

LEFT: The Yak-17 was the penultimate Yak jet fighter modified from an original piston-powered type.

Yakovlev Yak-17

First flight: Early 1947
Power: Klimov 1000kg/2205lb thrust RD-10A turbojet
Armament: Two nose-mounted 23mm/0.9in cannon
Size: Wingspan – 9.2m/30ft 2.25in
   Length – 8.78m/28ft 9.75in
   Height – 2.1m/6ft 10in
   Wing area – 14.85m²/159.85sq ft
Weights: Empty – 2430kg/5357lb
   Maximum take-off – 3323kg/7326lb
Performance: Maximum speed – 750kph/466mph
   Ceiling – 12,750m/41,830ft
   Range – 717km/446 miles
   Climb – 5000m/16,405ft in 5.8 minutes

The Yak-17 was developed from the earlier Yak-15 which itself had been a conversion of the taildragging Yak-3 piston fighter. The Yak-15 had been the first successful Soviet jet fighter in service having first flown in April 1946. About 200 Yak-15s were built before being succeeded by the much improved Yak-17 of which around 430 were built.

The Yak-17 differed from the Yak-15 by having a retractable tricycle under-carriage (thus eliminating the archaic tailwheel), and a more powerful engine. Structural strengthening also took place, and to improve the aircraft's range, drop-tanks were introduced too. A two-seat conversion trainer variant (YaK-17UTI) was also built.

The Yak-17 was also operated by Poland and Czechoslovakia and was phased out by all air forces by 1955.

LEFT: The Yak-23 took the Yak-15 design as far as it could go.

Yakovlev Yak-23

First flight: June 17, 1947
Power: Klimov 1590kg/3505lb thrust RD-500 turbojet
Armament: Two nose-mounted 23mm/0.9in cannon
   plus one 60kg/132lb bomb
Size: Wingspan – 8.73m/28ft 7.75in
   Length – 8.12m/26ft 7.75in
   Height – 3.31m/10ft 10.3in
   Wing area – 13.5m²/145.32sq ft
Weights: Empty – 2000kg/4409lb
   Maximum take-off – 3036kg/6693lb
Performance: Maximum speed – 975kph/606mph
   Ceiling – 14,800m/48,555ft
   Range – 1200km/745 miles
   Climb – 2041m/6693ft per minute

The Yak-23 was the ultimate development of the Russian Yak-15/-17 family. It differed from the Yak-17 by having the horizontal tail surfaces mounted higher up a much larger fin.

Designed as a lightweight day fighter, the Yak-23 first flew in June 1947 with power provided by an imported Rolls-Royce Derwent. It entered production,

powered by a Soviet copy of the Derwent (the RD-500), in early 1948. 310 were built and many were operated by other Eastern Bloc nations including Bulgaria, Romania, Czechoslovakia and Poland. The last of the barrel-bodied Yaks, this aircraft was always seen as a back up for the advanced swept wing fighters under development at the time

and this wonderfully agile fighter was indeed replaced throughout the Warsaw Pact by the MiG-15 in the mid-1950s.

LEFT: **The Yak-25, equipped with a heavyweight nose radar.**

Yakovlev Yak-25

First flight: June 19, 1952 (Yak-120)
Power: Two Tumansky 2633kg/5798lb-thrust RD-9 turbojet engines
Armament: Two 37mm/1.46in cannon
Size: Wingspan – 11m/36ft 1in
  Length – 15.67m/51ft 5in
  Height – 4.32m/14ft 2in
  Wing area – 28.94m^2/311.51sq ft
Weights: Empty – 7300kg/16,095lb
  Maximum take-off – 10,900kg/24,030lb
Performance: Maximum speed – 1090kph/677mph
  Ceiling – 14,000m/45,900ft
  Range – 2730km/1696 miles
  Climb – 3000m/9800ft per minute

Yakovlev Yak-25

Codenamed "Flashlight" by NATO, the two-seat Yak-25 (not to be confused with the Yak-25 single-engine fighter prototype of 1947) was the Soviet Union's first all-weather radar-equipped jet fighter and took to the air in prototype form (Yak-120) in June 1952. The new aircraft was designed to loiter for up to 2¹⁄₂ hours and carry the new Sokol radar that weighed in at around 500kg/1100lb. Power was provided by two jets slung beneath a swept but untapered wing. Sole armament was a pair of 37mm/1.46in cannon housed under the fuselage.

Although production began in 1953, with the aircraft then designated Yak-25, the radar was not ready for service until late 1955. The type was deployed to protect the far north of the Soviet Union against NATO bombers, and the introduction of the Yak-25 was enough to persuade the USAF that overflights of the USSR were no longer an easy reconnaissance option.

Production ceased in 1958 after 480 had been built. It remained in front-line use until the mid-1960s.

LEFT: **The Yak-28 was a multi-role type, and appeared in a number of versions.**

Yakovlev Yak-28PM

First flight: March 5, 1958 (Yak-129)
Power: Two Tumansky 6128kg/13,492lb after-burning thrust R-11AF-2-300 turbojets
Armament: Two Anab missiles, one infra-red and one radar-homing, plus two short-range air-to-air missiles
Size: Wingspan – 11.64m/38ft 2.25in
  Length – 20.65m/67ft 9in
  Height – 3.95m/12ft 11.5in
  Wing area – 37.6m^2/404.74sq ft
Weights: Maximum take-off – 15,700kg/34,612lb
Performance: Maximum speed – 1890kph/1174mph
  Ceiling – 16,000m/52,495ft
  Range – 2630km/1634 miles
  Climb – not known

Yakovlev Yak-28

At first glance the Yak-28 was similar to the Yak-25 in configuration but it was a wholly new design that first flew in prototype form during 1958 as the Yak-129. First versions developed were bomber/tactical attack aircraft but the Yak-28P was a dedicated all-weather interceptor with tandem cockpits for the two crew. It was designed to operate at low and medium altitude equipped with an Orel radar and armed with two air-to-air missiles, one radar-homing and one beam-riding.

Codenamed "Firebar" by NATO, the Yak-28 was capable of transonic flight and entered service in the winter of 1961–2. The aircraft was upgraded in numerous ways – its engines were uprated to have 6128kg/13,492lb after-burning thrust each and two short-range air-to-air missiles were added to the stores options, gaining the aircraft the designation Yak-28PM. Production ceased in 1967 after 437 fighters had been built and the type was phased out of service in the mid-1980s.

ABOVE: **The Sepecat Jaguar, developed jointly by Britain and France.**

BOMBERS

Introducing bombers

The earliest days of using aircraft as bombers saw pilots tossing small improvised bombs over the side of their aircraft on to a rather surprised enemy below. Hitting the target was more luck than judgement. This is a far cry indeed from the bomber aircraft of today that can fly around the world at several hundred miles an hour and arrive undetected in enemy airspace to drop precision-guided bombs down the chimney of a target and destroy it with no damage to surrounding buildings.

Once it was appreciated that the combination of aircraft and bombs was more than a novelty, military strategists were soon calling for more and bigger bombs to be carried. This required larger aircraft with more than one engine to carry the greater payload. Range then became an issue as the bombers had to be able to reach targets far beyond the front line. Engine technology and performance, as well as a greater understanding of aerodynamics, became considerations as the bombers had to be able to climb to heights away from enemy guns and fighters, or have sufficient speed to outrun the latter. Once the enemy started to try to knock the new bombers out of the sky, they had to defend themselves by carrying machine-guns and cannon. Technological advances saw the monoplane emerge, then largely replace the biplane in bomber fleets by

TOP: **The crew of an RAF Coastal Command B-17 Flying Fortress being briefed in 1943.** ABOVE: **Smoke pours from the remains of a bridge in France destroyed by Allied bombers around D-Day, 1944.**

World War II. Advances in construction techniques brought the use of more metal, specifically lightweight but strong alloys, and less wood and canvas.

The dawn of the jet engine opened up many opportunities for designers, but the long-range piston-engine bombers designed for use in World War II remained the mainstay of post-war bomber forces. Then, as atomic weapons appeared, bomber aircraft no longer had to carry many tons of bombs at a time when one massively destructive bomb would do the same job.

During the Cold War, as the United States and the Soviet Union faced each other across thousands of miles of sea or polar ice caps, the priority was the development of aircraft that could fly as quickly as possible across the world to bomb the enemy. The Cold War has fuelled bomber development since World War II, and most of the bomber aircraft in service around the world today were conceived during the Cold War. Large swept-wing jet bombers such as the Boeing B-47, Tupolev Tu-16, Boeing B-52 and Myasishchev M-4 were the principal bomber aircraft in the opposite inventories. All were good aircraft, but designers sought improvements in performance. The US B-58 Hustler was a Mach 2 nuclear bomber, but it proved to have insufficient range for the job required of it. Both Soviet and US engineers produced the brilliantly innovative variable-geometry designs with "swing wings" – the Tu-22M, F-111 and the B-1B. These aircraft, with wings spread, could cruise to their targets and then, with wings swept, could carry out high-speed, low-level attacks of which their larger fixed-sweep counterparts were simply not capable.

While bomber aircraft have evolved hugely since World War I, so have the weapons they can carry. "Dumb" free-fall conventional bombs are now complemented by "smart" munitions, which can be guided very precisely to a target. Bomber aircraft can also carry air-to-surface missiles, which

TOP: **The ruins of Hiroshima in 1945 bear testimony to the massive destructive power of a single atomic bomb.** ABOVE: **A "smart" bomb being loaded on to an F-117A Nighthawk for Operation Desert Storm of the Gulf War, 1991.**

were used in World War II, allowing them to attack a range of targets from a safe distance, such as troop concentrations, buildings, shipping or radar installations. Nuclear weapons remain an option for a number of nations around the world, but no weapon of this kind has been used in anger since the two raids on Japan in 1945.

The "stealth" aircraft currently in service with the US Air Force (F-117 and B-2) are remarkable examples of aviation technology, and were both produced as a result of the Cold War. Bomber aircraft became so sophisticated that people needed technological aids – radar – to find them. The designers of "stealth" aircraft have used technology to make the planes invisible again, creating the same surprise for the enemy that the manual bombing raids did in the early days of air warfare. These aircraft were well used during the second Gulf War, when coalition air assaults on Iraq were so intense that strike aircraft were "stacked" outside Baghdad 24 hours a day waiting for targets to be assigned.

Bomber aircraft have revolutionized the execution of warfare and its consequences in the sense that they can bring war to people in their homes, whereas once this was something that happened a long way away.

ABOVE: **The futuristic-looking and adventurous delta-winged Avro Vulcan of the Royal Air Force, nicknamed the "tin triangle", first went to war in the Falkland Islands in 1982. It was extremely popular at air shows all over the world.**

The History of Bombers

From the early improvised bombers of World War I to the atomic bombers that ended World War II, and their successors which arguably kept peace during the Cold War, bomber aircraft have been a potent weapon at military leaders' disposal. Bombers evolved from slow short-range machines carrying light bomb loads through to the mighty B-52 Stratofortress which can fly around the world unrefuelled while carrying an enormous amount of weaponry, including "smart" bombs and cruise missiles. The latest generation of bomber aircraft are the "stealth aircraft" which can pass undetected through the most complex air defence systems.

While high speed and high altitude were once the aim of bomber designers, making maximum use of technology is now their goal. Total obliteration of the enemy is no longer the sole aim of bomber aircraft. We live in a very different world to that of almost a century ago when the first bombers lumbered into the air. Television beams live pictures of bombing raids into our homes and every mission can unleash a political storm. "Smart" precision weapons are therefore widely used to minimize avoidable loss of life and collateral damage.

LEFT: **Lockheed P2V Neptune.**

Birth of the bomber

Although the US Army was the first to drop a bomb from an aeroplane in 1910, it was the Italians who first dropped them in anger against the Turks in 1911. Few of the early bombs were purpose-made, and modified artillery shells fitted with fins were common, sometimes tossed over the side of the aircraft or suspended alongside or beneath the aircraft and dropped at the right time (again trial and error played a large part in this) by the removal of a pin or even a piece of string. While nations debated the morals of bombing and the most effective technique, the Italians simply got on with learning the hard way – at war. It is worth considering that aircraft were operating as bombers some years before the evolution of the scouts that became fighters.

> "Another popular fallacy is to suppose that flying machines could be used to drop dynamite on an enemy in time of war."
> William H. Pickering.
> *Aeronautics*, 1908

Before the start of World War I, the Austro-Hungarians, French, Germans and Russians were all developing specialized bomber aircraft to carry ordnance to and then drop it on a target. Britain had experimented with

TOP: **The Russian plane Ilya Mourometz, designed by Igor Sikorsky, was the world's first four-engined aircraft, and could fly over great distances for the time.** ABOVE: **An Italian-operated example of the pioneering Voisin bomber. This version was powered by a 190hp Isotta-Franschini V.4B engine.**

dropping bombs from aircraft pre-war, but did not build dedicated bombing aircraft until after war had broken out. Many different types of aircraft were used for bombing early in the war, some having the ability to carry an observer or bombs in place of the observer. However, the key to making bombing a potential war-winning military tool was to develop an aircraft that could defend itself while carrying a large cargo of bombs to the heart of the enemy's location.

The first true bomber aircraft used in combat was the French-designed Voisin. Of steel frame construction, the Voisin had a crew of two plus up to 60kg/132lb of bombs. Power was provided by a 70hp engine that drove a pusher propeller. The Voisin earned its spurs when attacking Zeppelin hangars at Metz-Frascaty on August 14, 1914. The pioneering aircraft remained in production throughout World War I and was improved constantly, with engine power increasing from 70hp to 155hp. Most impressive was the increase in bomb load up to 300kg/660lb by the end of hostilities.

The French Aviation Militaire began to organize its Voisins into bomber squadrons in September 1914, and eventually had a bomber force of over 600 aircraft which conducted a sustained bombing campaign on the Western Front from May 1915.

On the Eastern Front, the Imperial Russian Air Service soon followed the French lead, and were equipped with the world's first four-engine aircraft, the Ilya Mourometz, designed by Igor Sikorsky. This large aircraft, very advanced for the time, had its first flight in May 1913 and was developed to carry up to 999kg/2200lb of bombs. The most advanced version could remain airborne for five hours at altitudes of around 2743m/9000ft at speeds of 85mph. The type carried out the first of over 400 bombing missions on the Eastern Front in February 1915.

The nations that fought in World War I all had differing views on bombing strategies. Britain's Royal Naval Air Service, Royal Flying Corps and then the Royal Air Force focused on the tactical use of bombing in support of ground troops – the British would also carry out revenge attacks if they felt that the enemy had overstepped the mark.

French planners did not have aircraft in their inventory that would reach Germany, and were in the difficult position of not wanting to bomb areas of France occupied by Germany. In addition, they feared revenge bombing of unoccupied French towns within reach of German aircraft. Meanwhile, Germany was developing aircraft that could cross France and strike at London itself.

TOP: A classic photograph of a World War II RAF bomber over its target during a bombing raid. ABOVE: A detailed photograph of a German Gotha bomber's bomb load. BELOW LEFT: British Avro 504s of the Royal Naval Air Service made an early bombing raid on the Zeppelin factory at Freidrichshafen in November 1914. BELOW: An early propaganda photograph showing a manual bomber delivering a personalized bomb by hand.

Early bombing raids

While the Allies were focusing mainly on military targets for bombing, Germany embraced the concept of the bomber as a psychological weapon to be used against civilians. The experience of the panic caused by early Zeppelin raids over cities spurred the Germans to plan raids against enemy population centres. As early as August 1914 German aircraft were flying over Paris dropping grenades and an invitation to the Paris garrison to surrender. Within six weeks, German Etrich Taube aircraft had dropped 56 bombs, none of them heavier than 4.5kg/10lb, which killed 11 Parisians and injured a further 47.

The Germans' tactical use of bombers in World War I is well illustrated by the 1917 German attack on a British supply train prior to the Battle of Mesines Ridge. As a result of the disruption to their supply of ammunition, British artillery had to cease firing after three hours.

Britain's early bombing successes began with Royal Naval Air Service raids on the Zeppelin sheds at Düsseldorf and Cologne on October 8, 1914. The aircraft used were two Sopwith Tabloids. The plane attacking Cologne failed to find its target due to bad weather and bombed the railway station instead, but the other Tabloid successfully dropped a small number of 9kg/20lb bombs on the airship shed, destroying it and Zeppelin Z.9 in the process. The sheds had been targeted before by B.E.2s on September 22, but bad weather and unexploding bombs meant that the mission failed.

Britain was keen to build a dedicated bomber force, and in December 1914 the Admiralty called for the development of a large hard-hitting bomber described by Commodore Murray F. Sueter as a "bloody paralyser of an aeroplane". The resulting Handley Page O/100 entered service with the Royal Naval Air

LEFT: **A selection of German bombs used during World War I. Size of munitions grew as larger aircraft became available.** BELOW: **The Etrich Taube carried out early raids over Paris in August 1914 during World War I. At the start of the war, Taubes were operated by wealthy individuals as well as by the Imperial German forces.**

Service in November 1916, and was used at first for daylight sea patrols near Flanders. From March the following year, the O/100s focused on night-bombing of German naval bases, railway stations and junctions, and industrial targets.

Attacks against weapon-manufacturing facilities were an effective means of removing a threat at source. In 1915 Allied aircraft set out to attack a factory at Ludwigshafen suspected of manufacturing chlorine gas dropped on Allied troops.

A long-range bomber had always been a German priority so that the British mainland would be within reach. In autumn 1916 the Gotha G.V appeared, and this very capable aircraft gave Germany the ability to strike at Britain itself.

On May 25, 1917, a fleet of 21 Gothas attacked the English coastal town of Folkestone, killing 95 inhabitants. The raid caused widespread panic among a populace who now believed that Germany could rain death from the sky over Britain unopposed. At midday on June 13 another fleet of Gothas dropped bombs on London, and the daily raids continued for a month, largely unopposed by the RNAS and Royal Flying Corps. The effect on civilian morale was considerable and damaging, and workers' productivity levels plummeted. The psychological impact was perhaps as damaging to Britain as the loss of life and physical destruction caused by the falling bombs.

The arrival into service of the Sopwith Camel forced the Gothas to switch to night-bombing, which caused the cost to the Germans to climb. Bombing accuracy fell, accidents happened in night-flying and aircraft were shot down for little gain, so the raids ceased before the end of the war. The raids had been damaging for Britain: 835 civilians were killed, 2000 were wounded and there had been three million pounds worth of damage (an enormous amount of money in 1918). However, the morale and productivity problems among the population were even more damaging, and showed the world that the bomber could be a war-winner.

TOP: **A Gotha G.V bomber. These aircraft spread terror among civilians in southern England following raids on the coast and over London in 1917. Daily daylight raids on the capital began in June 1917, launched from bases in Belgium.**
ABOVE: **Soldiers amidst the remains of a house destroyed by a Zeppelin raid over Kings Lynn in Norfolk, England, in 1915.**
LEFT: **The figures with this upturned Handley Page O/400 give a clear indication of the aircraft's size. Note the bomb-bay cells exposed between the legs of the fixed undercarriage.**

Bomber aircraft technology up to 1945

"When my brother and I built the first man-carrying flying machine we thought that we were introducing into the world an invention which would make further wars practically impossible." So said one of the fathers of powered flight, Orville Wright, in 1917. When the Wright brothers built their pioneering Wright Flyer in 1903 they used wood as the main material for the wings and fuselage, braced by piano wire for added strength. By the end of World War II, just over four decades later, most bombers were all-metal and had ranges and top speeds that the Wrights could only have dreamt of. The Wright Flyer was a biplane, having two pairs of wings, and also a pusher aircraft, that is, the propeller was used to push the aircraft from behind rather than pull it from the front as in later so-called tractor aircraft.

The pusher arrangement was retained for some early bombers such as the German Gothas, but having the back end of a large aero engine facing into the wind did little for the aerodynamics of pushers, so the tractor configuration finally became the standard in fighters, bombers and other aircraft.

As engine technology improved and speeds increased, drag became a serious design consideration on early aircraft, and aircraft frames were increasingly covered and enclosed with taut fabric to achieve streamlining. This technique was used into the mid-1930s, but by the time of World War II most new bomber aircraft were of all-metal "monocoque" construction. Whilst the early canvas-covered bombers got their structural strength from taut metal bracing wires, the metal skin of the monocoque fuselage (and in time the wings and tail), welded or riveted to a light metal interior framework, provided an incredibly strong construction. The downside of this construction was the damage that would be caused by cannon shells hitting

ABOVE: **The Consolidated B-24 Liberator first flew in December 1939, and was produced in greater numbers than any other bomber in history.** LEFT: **The Junkers Ju 52, a famed airliner, equipped the embryonic and clandestine Luftwaffe formed in the 1930s. It made its bomber debut in 1936 during the Spanish Civil War. By the end of that conflict, the type had dropped 6096 tonnes/ 6000 tons of bombs on Republican targets.**

LEFT: **A Bristol Blenheim production line at Filton, 1938. The high-speed Blenheim could outrun most contemporary fighters when it entered RAF service in 1937. The original aircraft from which the Blenheim derived, the Type 142, was the first British stressed-skin monoplane.** BELOW: **This fascinating reference photograph shows the variety of bombs at RAF Bomber Command's disposal by the end of World War II, ranging from small general-purpose bombs to the large "earthquake" bombs used against specialist targets.**

the metal structure – in canvas-covered aircraft the shells could have passed right through the aircraft, causing little damage.

The Wrights chose a biplane configuration for their Flyer, and this form was used in most early bombers because two pairs of wings generated more lift than one. Pre-World War I accidents had led Britain's government to ban the Royal Flying Corps from using the apparently unstable and unsafe monoplane, and it was not until 1936 that the RAF deployed a monoplane bomber – the Avro Anson. The "Annie" incorporated both old and new aircraft construction techniques – it was a monoplane but its fuselage had a metal framework with a fabric covering. It is worth pointing out that the Soviet Tupolev TB-3 four-engined monoplane was in production from 1929.

Engine technology developed at almost breakneck speed in the time between World Wars I and II. The 1916 DH4 had a top speed of 230kph/143mph and was powered by a 250hp Eagle

VIII in-line piston engine. Within a quarter of a century the Wright Double Cyclone (as used in the Grumman Avenger and B-25 Mitchell) was producing 1700hp and the B-29 that carried out the atomic bomb raids had four 2200hp Wright Duplex Cyclone engines.

At the end of World War I, air-cooled radials and in-line piston engines were the dominant engine types, and both had much to commend them. They were developed to the maximum until the jet engine ultimately replaced them both. Germany's Arado Ar 234 pioneered jet bombers in action and carried out raids over Britain in 1944. The Ar 234 was impossible to catch, and more powerful and efficient engines, coupled with improved aerodynamics, enabled bombers to fly higher and faster.

LEFT: **The cockpit of an Avro Lancaster, the most famous of all British bomber aircraft. The "Lanc" was derived from the earlier twin-engine Manchester, and went on to become key to the RAF's night offensive against Germany. Over 7000 Lancasters were built between 1941 and 1945, and two examples survive in flying condition – one in the UK and one in Canada.**

"The bomber will always get through. The only defence is in offence, which means that you have to kill more women and children more quickly than the enemy if you want to save yourselves."
British Prime Minister Stanley Baldwin, November 10, 1932

Bombers of the Spanish Civil War

Between the two world wars in Europe, there was only one major military conflict – the Spanish Civil War fought between the Nationalists under Franco and the Republicans who fought to protect the left-wing government. The Soviet Union was quick to offer aid to the Republicans, the equipment including Polikarpov fighters and the Tupolev SB-2 bomber. Italy, under Mussolini, supported Franco by sending over 700 aircraft, including S.M.79 Sparviero and B.R.20 bombers and S.M.81 bomber-transports. The Nationalists, however, had already asked for assistance from a far more formidable ally – Germany. The Third Reich saw the Spanish Civil War as a great opportunity – it was a means of taking the world's attention away from a re-arming

"Air power may either end war or end civilization."
Winston Churchill, 1933

Germany, but also allowed Germany to test its troops and equipment in combat. A foothold in Spain would also allow Germany a southern launchpad for a later invasion of France.

Around 19,000 German volunteers, most of them Luftwaffe personnel, ultimately fought as part of the fighting force named the Condor Legion. Armed with Germany's latest fighter and bomber types, men and machines were tested under fire. German bombers that saw action included the Heinkel He111, Junkers Ju 52/3m and Ju 87 Stuka, and the Dornier Do17.

While the bomber aircraft of the Condor Legion were used largely in support of ground forces, they were also deployed in the strategic bombing role. While military leaders around the world considered the use of the bomber as a strategic weapon, the Germans were gaining valuable combat experience. Allegedly, Condor Legion bomber crews were initially given tourist maps to locate their targets. Despite amateurish beginnings, on April 26, 1937, the bombers of

BELOW: **The Heinkel He111 flew as part of the Condor Legion, and proved very effective against Republican forces. The He111 achieved infamy as one of the types that carried out the bombing raid against Guernica in April 1937. The aircraft pictured is a Spanish-built CASA 2.111 version.**

LEFT: **The Ju 87 Stuka dive-bomber used Spain as a testing-ground, and proved its worth to military leaders. The Stuka was more than a dive-bomber – sirens were fitted to the undercarriage to generate an ear-splitting screech intended to terrify the enemy beneath it.** BELOW: **A Condor Legion Heinkel He111-B-1, having made a forced landing after a mission.**

ABOVE: **The Italians supplied aircraft in support of Franco, including Savoia Marchetti S.M.81 bomber-transports. This example is pictured on a reconnaissance flight over the Ebro front.** RIGHT: **An impressive line-up of aircraft, including Ju 52s and S.M.81s at a May 1939 review of Nationalist aviation at the end of the campaign at Barajas.**

the Condor Legion attacked the small town of Guernica in northern Spain and changed the world's views of bomber aircraft forever.

For over three hours, Heinkel He111 bombers, accompanied by strafing fighters, dropped 45,000kg/ 100,000lb of high-explosive and incendiary bombs on Guernica, systematically pounding it to rubble. Over 1600 civilians, one third of the population, were killed, and almost 900 more were wounded. Seventy per cent of the town was destroyed and the fires started by the incendiaries burned for three days.

Guernica had no strategic value as a military target, but a German report at the time stated that "...the concentrated attack on Guernica was the greatest success." Guernica had been used to test a new Nazi military tactic – carpet-bombing the civilian population to demoralize the enemy. However, the effect of the attack on Guernica went far beyond the Republican forces. Guernica made some European countries fear they might be next, thus making them more responsive to German demands for capitulation.

The Spanish Civil War ended in March 1939 with the surrender of Republican forces in Madrid. The Condor Legion had been instrumental in securing victory for the Nationalists.

At the post-war Nuremberg trials, the chief of the Luftwaffe Hermann Goering said, "Spain gave me an opportunity to try out my young air force." The Blitzkrieg tactic, later used across Europe, had been refined in Spain. The 19,000 battle-hardened Luftwaffe personnel who rotated through the Condor Legion between 1936 and 1939 were soon in action over Poland, Czechoslovakia, Holland, Belgium and France – Spain had taught them well.

LEFT: **The Heinkel 111 was an effective tactical bomber, but lacked the bomb load to help the Luftwaffe pound Britain into submission.**
BELOW: **A classic wartime photograph of a Luftwaffe He111 over the River Thames and the Rotherhithe and Millwall areas of London.**

The Blitz

When Britain declared war on Germany in September 1939, Luftwaffe raids over London and elsewhere in the nation were widely expected. Large public air-raid shelters were provided, and over a million Anderson do-it-yourself shelters were distributed among those living in large towns and cities. Aware of the fate of those who had already faced the German war machine, around 13 per cent of the population left London in the days following the declaration of war, and many children were evacuated to the country. The panic subsided when the expected attacks did not come, and many of those who had left London returned.

When large-scale bombing raids came in the summer of 1940, they were directed against Royal Air Force Fighter Command as a prelude to invasion, for Hitler knew that he needed air superiority before any invasion could succeed. The success of RAF Fighter Command and the Few in what came to be known as the Battle of Britain is well documented. However, the British victory was due in no small part to a German switch in tactics – Luftwaffe raids against Fighter Command and Britain's air defence capability were largely abandoned in early September and attacks were directed at the nation's capital to erode the morale of the population. The change in tactics may have been brought about by an inept German bomber crew who, on August 24, bombed a residential area of south London apparently in error. This prompted a retaliatory attack by the RAF on the night of August 26. While the RAF raid caused little damage, Hitler was furious, and personally ordered attacks against London on September 4.

The first large-scale air raids on London targeted industrial areas and the docks. Initially these raids took place in daylight and at night, but heavy daytime losses led the Luftwaffe to restrict their attacks to darkness. At night, due to the inadequacies of British night defences at the time, the Luftwaffe were able to operate largely unmolested.

From mid-September, the Luftwaffe bombed the rest of London, including Buckingham Palace. The positive effect on British morale was considerable, uniting Britons of all classes against a common enemy. High morale among Londoners was essential when the Luftwaffe dropped 5385 tonnes/5300 tons of high explosives on London over 24 nights in September 1940.

Air raids continued most nights with up to 400 bombers dropping 406 tonnes/400 tons of high explosives and incendiaries on the capital. Although London's transport infrastructure was constantly disrupted, as were supplies of gas, electricity and water, repairs were effected swiftly to thwart the German aim of bringing chaos to the heart of their enemy. The general resilience of the population, christened the Spirit of the Blitz, meant that for the most part, London not only continued to function effectively, but was determined to fight on, even though by October 1940 around 250,000 people had been made homeless by the Blitz.

Raids on other British cities began in November 1940 and reached as far as Wales, Scotland and Northern Ireland. The Luftwaffe did however continue to make frequent visits to London. On May 10, 1941, 550 Luftwaffe bombers dropped

LEFT: Initially used in raids against Britain, Ju 87s proved to be easy meat for the Spitfires and Hurricanes of RAF Fighter Command, and they were withdrawn from operations against the UK. BELOW: Smoke billows over London, silhouetting Tower Bridge and the Tower of London, following a Luftwaffe raid on the East London Dockland on September 7, 1940.

ABOVE: An iconic image of the Battle of Britain as the Luftwaffe attempt to sweep RAF Fighter Command from the sky over England. The vapour trails were short-lived pointers to the deadly air combat taking place over southern Britain in the summer of 1940. RIGHT: Troops and police examine the wreckage of a German bomber which crashed on London's Victoria railway station during the Blitz.

more than 711 tonnes/700 tons of German bombs and thousands of incendiaries on London in what was probably the worst raid of the Blitz. Nearly 1500 people were killed and around 1800 were seriously injured in the last of the large attacks on London at this stage in the war.

On the night of November 14–15, 1940, around 500 German bombers dropped 508 tonnes/500 tons of high explosives and incendiaries on Coventry, a major industrial city. During the 10-hour onslaught, 550 people were killed, 1000 injured, and many thousands of homes were damaged or destroyed. Coventry Cathedral, left in ruins by the devastating raids, came to symbolize German aggression, and the attack on Coventry gave impetus to the planning of the very large strategic raids by Allied bombers that came later in the war, both in Europe and in Japan.

The German Blitzkrieg technique of waging war failed against Britain because the Luftwaffe was only equipped to fight tactically. The principal German bomber was the twin-engined Heinkel He111 medium-range bomber that carried a maximum bomb load of around 2277kg/5000lb over a relatively short distance. The aircraft was simply not suited for sustained attacks against targets over a long distance. Other German bombers, such as the Junkers Ju 88 and Dornier Do17, were equally unsuited to strategic bombing raids. The British and Americans, however, believed that heavy bombers could win a war. Had the Luftwaffe been equipped with large four-engined heavy bombers like those deployed by RAF Bomber Command or the US Eighth Air Force, then Germany might well have been able to bomb the population of Britain into submission.

271

The Dambusters

No.617 Squadron, the most famous squadron in the Royal Air Force, was formed at Scampton on March 21, 1943, under the command of Wing Commander Guy Gibson. An outstanding pilot and leader, Gibson was allowed to have his pick of crews from other squadrons to fly Lancasters on a special, highly-secret operation. Gibson himself was not told for some weeks that Operation Chastise, codename for the dams raids, involved breaching the Möhne, Eder and Sorpe Dams which held back more than 300 million tons of water vitally important to German industry.

This secret mission required a special bomb which had to be delivered in a highly unusual manner. The bomb had to be spun in the bomb bay of the aircraft at 500rpm so that when it hit the water it would "skip" across the surface rather than sink. The crew had to release the bomb while flying exactly 18.3m/60ft above the water at a speed of exactly 354kph/220mph. The bomb also had to impact the water at exactly 388m/425yd from the dam wall and only a 6 per cent deviation was permissible. The targets under attack were heavily defended, and the raids had to take place at night.

The first Lancaster took off from Scampton shortly before 21:30 hours on May 16, 1943, and Wing Commander Gibson's aircraft, the first to attack the Möhne Dam, released its mine at 28 minutes past midnight. Half an hour later, just after the fifth Lancaster had attacked, Gibson radioed England with the

BELOW: **This Lancaster, preserved in the UK, frequently flies commemorative fly-pasts over the Derbyshire lake that was used to train the Dambusters. The Lancasters used for the mission were specially modified to accommodate the unusual weapon and the equipment required to "spin" it.**

news that the dam had been breached. The remaining aircraft of the Möhne formation then flew on to the Eder Dam. The first two mines failed to breach the dam, but shortly before 2am, when the third Lancaster had attacked, Gibson signalled the codeword "Dinghy", indicating success with the second part of the operation. Other aircraft attacked the Sorpe and Schwelme Dams but did not succeed in breaching them. Just how low the Lancasters flew during the attack is shown by the fact that one had to turn back as it had hit the sea and lost its bomb on the journey to mainland Europe.

Of the 19 Lancasters which took off for the dams raid with their 133 crew, eight planes and 56 men did not return. Five planes crashed or were shot down en route to their targets. Two were destroyed while delivering their attacks and another was shot down on the way home. Two more were so badly damaged that they had to abandon their missions. No.617 Squadron, known from this time onwards as the "Dambusters", had become famous.

The attack had huge propaganda value and made Gibson a national hero. Gibson was awarded the Victoria Cross for bringing round his Lancaster to give covering fire to the Lancasters that were following up his attack on the Möhne Dam. Thirty-one other members of 617 Squadron were also decorated.

Severe flooding occurred where the Möhne Dam was breached. Six small electricity works were damaged and rail lines passing through the Möhne Valley were disrupted. But industrial production was not affected in the long term. When the Eder Dam broke, there were similar results. Kassel, an

ABOVE: **Guy Gibson (left) was a gifted pilot and leader who handpicked his crews for the historic dams mission. He did not survive the war but his version of the dams raids is recorded in his book "Enemy Coast Ahead".**

important arms-producing town, was reached by the flood-water, but little actual damage was done. Had the Sorpe Dam been breached, the damage would have been much greater. The potential for a major disaster was recognized by Albert Speer who commented, "Ruhr production would have suffered the heaviest possible blow."

In the short and long term, the damage done by 617 Squadron was repaired quite quickly. But the most important impact of the raid was that 20,000 men working on the Atlantic Wall had to be moved to the Ruhr to carry out repairs to the damaged and breached dams. This work was completed before the rains of the autumn appeared.

BELOW OPPOSITE AND BELOW, FROM LEFT TO RIGHT: **These stills from a film of a training flight show the spinning bomb falling from the aircraft, striking the water and then bouncing. In the last image of the sequence, pieces of the Lancaster can be seen falling away, having been knocked off by the force of the water thrown up as the bomb hit the water.**

The Mighty Eighth Air Force

O n August 17, 1942, 12 Boeing B-17 Flying Fortress
bombers of the 97th Bomb Group took off from Grafton
Underwood in Northamptonshire, England, to attack targets
in occupied France, on what was to be the first US heavy
bombing mission flown from the UK in World War II.

From 1942 until the end of the war in 1945, the Eighth Air
Force flew B-17 Flying Fortresses and B-24 Liberators in
daylight bombing operations against Germany and Nazi-
occupied Europe. At its peak strength, the Eighth Air Force
could launch more than 2000 four-engine bombers and more
than 1000 fighters on a single mission. For these reasons,
the Eighth Air Force became known as the "Mighty Eighth".

Daytime bombing was especially hazardous, and some
27,000 men of the Eighth Air Force died on operations from
UK bases – the highest casualty rate of any Allied force. The
Eighth's B-17s and B-24s suffered heavy losses over Europe,
especially after the bombing of Germany started in January
1943. The heavy bombers had the range to reach almost any
target in Germany, but in the
early months there were no
Allied fighters with the range
to follow and protect them.
Once the Allied fighter
escorts turned back, the

> "Hitler built a fortress around
> Europe, but he forgot to put
> a roof on it."
> Franklin D. Roosevelt

TOP: **This B-17F named "Hells Angels" became the first Eighth Air Force
bomber to complete 25 combat missions on May 13, 1943. The famed B-17
"Memphis Belle" was the first to complete the 25 missions and return to the
USA.** ABOVE: **Eighth Air Force bombers packed real teeth, as this B-17 waist
gunner shows, with his 12.7mm/0.5in Browning machine-gun. A total of
305 8AF air-gunners achieved "ace" status, being credited with at least five
air kills each.**

Eighth's bombers were vulnerable to attacks by German Luftwaffe fighters. During the spring, summer and autumn of 1943, Eighth Air Force losses of aircraft and aircrew sometimes reached 12 per cent for a day's raid and at one point it became statistically impossible for a bomber crewman to survive a 25-mission tour of duty. The effect that this had on morale was considerable.

When the Eighth Air Force fighters became able to escort the bombers all the way to their targets and back, the losses slowly began to drop back to what were considered to be acceptable levels, although they remained high.

The Eighth also participated in the preparation for the invasion of occupied Europe in June 1944 by bombing German missile sites and defences, and by flying special operations to support French resistance fighters and Allied ground troops. Later in the war, the Eighth also flew humanitarian missions dropping food and supplies to civilians liberated from Nazi rule.

The Mighty Eighth compiled an impressive record during World War II. Seventeen Congressional Medals of Honor went to Eighth Air Force personnel, and by the end of World War II they had been awarded a number of other medals, including 220 Distinguished Service Crosses and 442,000 Air Medals. Many more awards made to Eighth Air Force veterans after the war remain uncounted. There were 261 fighter aces (with five confirmed kills or more) in the Eighth Air Force in World War II. Thirty-one of these aces had 15 or more aircraft kills each. Another 305 enlisted gunners were also acknowledged as aces.

By the end of the war in Europe, the Eighth had fired over 100 million rounds of ammunition and dropped 703,550 tonnes/ 692,470 tons of bombs at a cost of 4162 heavy bombers and 2222 fighter aircraft lost.

The actions of the Mighty Eighth played a major role in disrupting Germany's war economy and transportation system and, ultimately, in the destruction of Nazi Germany.

ABOVE LEFT: **The G-model of the Flying Fortress, equipped with a chin turret, was able to defend itself against head-on attack – a weak spot on earlier models. Flying in box formations, the bombers would provide cover for each other against enemy fighters.** ABOVE: **B-17s raining down bombs on enemy targets.** LEFT: **The B-24 Liberator is often over-shadowed by the B-17, but it was deployed in greater numbers than the Boeing bomber. This photograph taken in the summer of 1944 shows a B-24 sheathed in flames over Austria – it crashed within minutes.**

The Doolittle raid

The April 1942 air attack on Japan, launched from the aircraft carrier USS *Hornet* and led by Lieutenant Colonel James H. Doolittle, was at that point the most daring operation undertaken by the United States in the Pacific War. Though conceived as a diversion that would also boost American and Allied morale, the raid generated strategic benefits that far outweighed its limited goals.

The raid had its roots in a chance remark that it might be possible to launch twin-engined bombers from the deck of an aircraft carrier, making feasible an early air attack on Japan. On hearing of the idea in January 1942, US Fleet commander Admiral Ernest J. King and Air Forces leader General Henry H. "Hap" Arnold responded enthusiastically. Arnold assigned Doolittle to assemble and lead a suitable air group. The well-tested and proven B-25 Mitchell medium

RIGHT: **Doolittle (left) and Captain Mitscher on board the USS *Hornet* just before the historic bombing of Tokyo in April 1942.** BELOW: **The North American B-25 Mitchell was a rugged bomber that made its combat debut by sinking a Japanese submarine on December 24, 1941. The type went on to become one of the most widely used aircraft of World War II, serving with many Allied air forces.**

bomber was selected, and tests showed that it could indeed fly off a carrier while carrying bombs and enough fuel to reach and attack Japan, and then continue to friendly China.

Recruiting volunteer aircrews for the top-secret mission, Doolittle began special training for his men and modifications to their aircraft. The new carrier *Hornet* was sent to the Pacific to carry out the Navy's part of the mission, which was so secret that her Commanding Officer, Captain Mitscher, had no idea of his ship's part in the operation until just before 16 B-25s were loaded on to his flight deck. *Hornet* sailed on April 2, 1942, and headed west to be joined in mid-ocean on April 13 by USS *Enterprise*, which would provide limited air cover.

The plan called for an afternoon launch on April 18, around 643km/400 miles from Japan, but enemy vessels were met before dawn on April 18. The small enemy boats were believed to have radioed Japan with details of the American carriers heading their way, so Doolittle's Raiders had to take off immediately while still more than 965km/600 miles from their target.

Most of the 16 B-25s, each with a crew of five, attacked the Tokyo area, while some bombed Nagoya. Damage to Japanese military targets was slight, and none of the aircraft reached China, although virtually all the crews survived.

Japan's military leaders were nevertheless horrified and embarrassed by the audacious raid. The Americans had attacked the home islands once and could do it again, and so the Japanese were forced to keep more ships and aircraft in the home islands in case of further US attacks.

These significant military resources could have been used against American forces as they attacked island after island while making their way closer to Japan.

Combined Fleet Commander Admiral Isoroku Yamamoto proposed that the Japanese removed the risk of any similar American raids by destroying America's aircraft carriers in the theatre. This move led the Japanese to disaster at the Battle of Midway a month and a half later.

Perhaps the most significant result of the Doolittle mission was the hard-to-quantify but very real effect that it had on American morale. The United States was finally hitting back after Pearl Harbor, and the brave men who were the Doolittle Raiders raised the confidence and morale of all Americans, civilians and military alike.

ABOVE: **The start of the Pacific War – the Japanese attack on Pearl Harbor, on December 7, 1941.** ABOVE RIGHT: **The Doolittle Raiders en route to their mission aboard the *Hornet*.** RIGHT: **An historic photograph of a B-25 leaving the deck of the *Hornet* at the start of the bombing mission over Tokyo. The raid's effects went far beyond the material damage caused by the bombs dropped that day.**

The atomic bomb raids

"Sixteen hours ago, an American airplane dropped one bomb on Hiroshima, Japan, and destroyed its usefulness to the enemy. That bomb had more power than 20,000 tons of TNT. It had more than two thousand times the blast power of the British Grand Slam, which is the largest bomb ever yet used in the history of warfare... It is an atomic bomb. It is a harnessing of the basic power of the universe." US President Harry Truman, August 6, 1945.

In late 1944, the United States began full-scale air raids on Japan, and by late spring 1945, the US 20th Air Force had destroyed or disabled many of Japan's major cities with fire-bombing raids. However, Japanese ground forces in the Pacific continued to fight, and the US military believed the death toll among US personnel would rise dramatically as the Allies moved closer to the Japanese home islands. Meanwhile, two billion US dollars had been spent and 200,000 people were working on the Manhattan Project to produce a super-weapon – the atomic bomb. After a successful test on July 16, 1945, it was decided that one instant devastating blow to a Japanese city might persuade the Japanese to surrender and save perhaps hundreds of thousands of lives on all sides.

In late 1943, Manhattan Project scientists were confident enough to tell the Army Air Forces (AAF) to begin

ABOVE: **The B-29 was the world's most advanced bomber and the only aircraft in the US inventory really capable of carrying out the demanding mission. This B-29, preserved in the USA, is the only flying example of the Superfortress.**
BELOW: **Col. Paul Tibbets (centre, with pipe), commander of the historic mission, pictured with the ground crew of the *Enola Gay* and the aircraft on Tinian. Tibbets was a highly experienced combat pilot who had taken part in early Eighth Air Force raids from Britain. The *Enola Gay* is preserved in the USA.**

preparing for the atomic bomb's use. The B-29, the world's most advanced bomber, was the obvious choice for the delivery vehicle and, under the leadership of Colonel Paul Tibbets, a hand-picked unit trained hard for one job – dropping atomic bombs.

Fifteen specially modified Boeing B-29 Superfortresses were prepared for "special weapons" delivery. The 509th Composite Group was the first USAAF bombardment group to be organized, equipped and trained for atomic warfare, needless to say under complete secrecy. Tibbets emphasized high-altitude flying, long-range navigation and the use of radar in training to prepare the crews for a high-altitude release of the bomb many miles from their base. They also worked on an escape manoeuvre that would avoid the shock wave that could damage or destroy the aircraft.

As part of the training, a 4540kg/10,000lb bomb was dropped, designed to simulate the actual "Fat Man" atomic bomb later dropped at Nagasaki. Loaded with high explosive, these were named "pumpkin" bombs because of their shape and colour. From November 1944 to June 1945, the 509th trained continually for the first atomic bomb drop. In April 1945, the group had moved to a new base on Tinian in the Mariana Islands, only 2333km/1450 miles from Tokyo.

Hiroshima was chosen as the first target, with Kokura and Nagasaki as second and third targets. The attack would occur as soon after August 2 as the weather allowed.

At 08:15 hours on August 6, B-29 *Enola Gay*, piloted by Tibbets, dropped the 4406kg/9700lb atom bomb codenamed "Little Boy" over Hiroshima.

> "My God, what have we done?"
> Robert Lewis, co-pilot of the *Enola Gay*, the B-29 that dropped the first atomic bomb, August 6, 1945

The devastation caused by the bomb brought no response to the demand for unconditional surrender, and conventional bombing raids continued. On August 9, B-29 *Bockscar* dropped the second and only remaining complete atom bomb in the US arsenal, codenamed "Fat Man", over Nagasaki. The primary target had been the city of Kokura, but clouds had obscured it. With fuel running low due to a fuel transfer problem, the pilot Chuck Sweeney proceeded to the secondary target, Nagasaki, a leading industrial centre. When the bomb detonated, it felt as though *Bockscar* was "being beaten with a telephone pole", said a member of the crew.

Japan surrendered unconditionally on August 14, and on August 28, US aircraft began landing the first occupation forces at Tokyo. B-29s were now dropping food, medicine and other supplies to US Allied prisoners. World War II was finally over, but the Atomic Age had dawned.

TOP: *Hiroshima photographed in March 1946, still showing the utter devastation caused by the explosion of the "Little Boy" atomic bomb on August 6, 1945. The bomb exploded 610m/2000ft above the centre of Hiroshima, and 6.5km²/4sq miles of the city were wiped out instantly. Anything beneath was turned to ashes, and only a few concrete buildings survived the blast – but in ruins.*

ABOVE: *Enola Gay returns to its base on Tinian following the first atomic bombing mission. Tibbets said of the raid, "...we had seen the city when we went in and there was nothing to see when we came back."* LEFT: *The mushroom cloud over Nagasaki following the detonation of the "Fat Man" atomic bomb on August 9, 1945. Japan surrendered unconditionally five days later.*

Bomber aircraft development since World War II

The effectiveness of heavy bomber campaigns during World War II and the use of the ultimate weapon, the atomic bomb, meant that from the end of the war until the end of the 1950s, the heavy bomber was central to the military planning of the world's most powerful nations. The protagonists on the world stage were desperate to get a technological edge in case the Cold War ever heated up. Massive retaliation and mutually assured destruction awaited the players in a World War III unless new technology could provide one side with the upper hand and a means of total defeat of the enemy. The period was typified by major investment in experimental programmes, from flying wings to flying saucers. After the war, swept-wing jet bomber aircraft gradually replaced straight-wing piston-powered types, although turboprop bombers remain in front-line Russian service today in the form of the Tupolev Tu-95/142 "Bear" bomber/anti-submarine aircraft.

Greater knowledge of "area rule" (the design approach that produces a fuselage contour with the lowest possible transonic wave drag) came in the 1950s and helped engineers and aircraft designers beat the so-called "sound barrier" and produce aircraft capable of supersonic speeds in level flight. The quest for high speed was typified by the B-58 Hustler.

Jet engine technology progressed rapidly after the war. The Canberra B.2 was powered by the 2952kg/6500lb thrust Avon 101, while the B-47 had 3266kg/7200lb thrust J47-GE-25 turbojets. These bestowed a performance vastly better than the bombers in service just a few years previously. Compare that to the 13,980kg/30,780lb afterburning thrust of the B-1B Lancer's F-101 GE-102 turbofans. Afterburning or reheat capability was developed in the late 1940s to give jet-powered aircraft an emergency boost of energy when required.

The 1957 Soviet launch of the Sputnik satellite sent shockwaves through the Western world as everyone was quick to realize that if a satellite could be launched into space, an atomic device could also be launched using the same missile at London or Washington. There followed in the USA a crash programme in missile development, which culminated in a vast and potent missile arsenal in the USA. One result of this was that funding for the development of the manned bomber, which many thought was becoming a dinosaur, was a fraction

BELOW: **This photograph taken at Boeing's plant in Wichita, Kansas, shows B-47 Stratojets in final assembly. Development of this aircraft began before World War II ended. Stratojets entered USAF service in 1952, and were the USA's best nuclear deterrent in the period before ICBM missiles.**

LEFT: The Panavia Tornado is one of the few variable-geometry or "swing-wing" aircraft to have entered front-line service. The Tornado has been the backbone of the Royal Air Force's bomber capability since the mid-1980s. This Tornado was pictured during the Gulf War, where the type specialized in daring and risky low-level attacks. BELOW: The Rockwell B-1 Lancer was designed to meet a mid-1960s requirement and, having survived cancellation, finally entered service in 1986. This was one of the last long-range strategic bombers to be built, and its impressive low-level high performance allows it to penetrate sophisticated air defences. While no true stealth technology was built into the B-1, it was designed with a small radar profile for such a large and capable aircraft.

ABOVE: The B-2 Spirit is a long-range strategic heavy bomber designed from the outset as a stealthy combat aircraft. It combines reduced infrared, acoustic, electromagnetic, visual and radar signatures, making the aircraft very hard to detect or track. RIGHT: A Lockheed F-117A Nighthawk "stealth fighter" under construction. This aircraft was the world's first to exploit low-observable stealth technology – its surfaces and edge profiles reflect hostile radar into narrow beam signals away from enemy radar detectors.

of that spent on missile forces. Despite the presence of nuclear weapons in the world, which some people saw as a stabilizing factor, large and bloody wars continued to erupt around the world, and strategic bombers were not necessarily the best aircraft to have in the inventory.

The philosophy of massive retaliation seemed inflexible when what was needed was a flexible response, particularly for smaller conventional operations. This was a period of uncertainty in bomber history, and no bomber programmes were initiated and completed in the decade from 1960 to 1970.

Early jet bombers continued to use the materials and construction techniques of piston-powered aircraft. High-speed flight put extreme stresses on airframes,

so engineers looked beyond aluminium and magnesium alloys, and introduced titanium alloys and special steels. Carbon fibre composites are now widely used and are three times as strong while weighing half as much as aluminium alloys.

A truly innovative development of the post-war period was the swing or variable-geometry wing, in which the wings can move automatically from the swept to the spread position to maximize the aircraft's aerodynamic performance as required.

On take-off, the spread position generates more lift and gets the aircraft off the ground sooner. Once in the air, the wings sweep back for high-speed flight. Only a handful of swing-wing bombers, such as the F-111 and the Tornado, have seen service.

Cold War bombers

Cold War rivalry and tensions between the United States/NATO and the Soviet Union/Warsaw Pact fuelled the development on both sides of more efficient and destructive bomber aircraft at almost any cost. Research, design and development were accelerated to a pitch that would have been unlikely had it not been for the Cold War.

In the immediate post-war period the Soviet Union's main bomber programme was the Tu-4, copied from US B-29s acquired during World War II. The Soviets reportedly spent two years carefully dismantling the US aircraft and studying the finest details of both structure and systems. The Tu-4 programme effectively kick-started Soviet post-war bomber development, the helping hand unwittingly given to them by their ideological enemies of the next four decades. The Soviet B-29 copies were produced from 1945 until 1953.

The years of the Cold War saw each side making a technological leap and the other mirroring or trying to improve the aircraft available should World War III have erupted. It was equally important to devise ways of countering new bombers through developing higher-performance fighters, early-warning and anti-aircraft technology,

> "It is an ironic, but accurate fact, that the two strongest powers are the two in the most danger of devastation."
> John F. Kennedy, June 10, 1963

ABOVE: **Royal Air Force Meteor fighters formating on and refuelling from a USAF Boeing KB-29 tanker converted from a standard B-29. Inflight refuelling was a vital means of extending the reach of Cold War combat aircraft – both fighters and bombers. Co-operation of this kind between the USAF and the RAF was common throughout the Cold War, and continues to this day.**

and specifically surface-to-air missiles. The USA usually took the lead, but there were some notable exceptions.

The priority for the USA was to develop a bomber that could strike around the world without the need for forward bases. They wanted the ability to fight the Soviet Union even if Europe fell and they had to launch strikes from the continental USA. The Soviet aim was also to reach its enemy from the other side of the world. One bomber that almost met this requirement, needing only one mid-air refuelling, was the English Electric Canberra-derived Martin B-57. However, the aircraft could not carry the large weapon load required over such vast distances.

Range was not enough: the aircraft also had to be able to avoid the unwelcome attentions of defending fighters by flying either higher or faster, or both. The B-36 had a top speed of 661kph/411mph, which was slower than many fighters of the World War II era. The answer for the USA came in the form of the B-47 Stratojet, Boeing's swept-wing, six-jet-engined design. The Tu-16, which used technology derived directly from the B-29, was the Soviet equivalent of the B-47 Stratojet, both of them first-generation swept-wing jet bombers.

Moscow's 1954 May Day parade fly-past saw the public debut of the Myasishchev M-4 long-range strategic bomber, which gave the Soviets the reach to hit the USA. The mighty Boeing B-52 Stratofortress had had its maiden flight a year earlier and in it the USAF finally got a high-performance bomber with intercontinental range. By the 1960s there were many experts who considered the bomber to be obsolete because new, highly accurate and destructive long-range missiles became available on both sides of the Iron Curtain. Despite this, bomber development continued, not just in the USA and the Soviet Union. Britain's V-bomber force included the highly advanced and complex Vulcan and Victor jet bombers which, although not having intercontinental range, could, with air-refuelling, have reached targets very far away from the UK. Similarly, France's Force de Dissuasion, equipped with high-speed Mirage IV bombers, was created as a potent deterrent against would-be aggressors.

ABOVE: **A picture considered impossible during the Cold War – a USAF B-52 Stratofortress parked near a Tupolev Tu-95 "Bear". These two very different bomber types faced each other across an ideological divide that lasted decades.**

BELOW: **Two classic British bomber types: a Handley Page Victor converted for tanker duties refuels two Blackburn Buccaneers. The Victor was in RAF service as a bomber from 1958 until the late 1970s. The Buccaneer, technically the last-ever all-British bomber, served in the Royal Navy and Royal Air Force from 1960 into the early 1990s.** BOTTOM: **The French were keen to develop their own nuclear deterrent and created the French Strategic Air Command's Force de Dissuasion. Equipped with the potent and high-performance Mirage IV, the force was ready for action around the clock from 1964 to 1996. Here, a Mirage IV refuels from a dedicated KC-135FR tanker.**

In the Tupolev Tu-22M, the Soviet Union created the first swing-wing strategic bomber, a major development. The American equivalent, the Rockwell B-1 project, was cancelled because of fears of rising costs. The Rockwell design was resurrected, and entered service as the highly capable B-1B Lancer. The development in bombers which really did take design into a new age was the unveiling of the Northrop B-2 Spirit, the "stealth bomber", believed to be the most expensive aircraft ever. Inspired by the Northrop Flying Wings of the 1940s, the B-2 was conceived during the Cold War as a long-range heavy bomber that could penetrate the world's most sophisticated air defences undetected and then drop up to 16 nuclear bombs. Aircraft such as the B-2 and the B-52 will be flying for many years to come. In the case of the B-52, the aircraft is expected to remain in service until 2045, a century after the start of the "war" for which it was designed to fight.

BELOW: **The Rockwell B-1 was conceived at the height of the Cold War, but is expected to stay in the front line for many years to come. The type saw extensive action during the 2003 war in Iraq.**

Strategic Air Command

Strategic Air Command (SAC) was established in the USA on March 21, 1946, and in October that year its mission was defined: SAC was to attain an immediate state of combat readiness and to stand by for immediate operations, either alone or jointly with other forces, against enemies of the USA. In addition, SAC was required to develop, test and improve strategic bombardment tactics. Together with Tactical Air Command, SAC formed the offensive element of the USAF that existed for more than four decades.

On October 19, 1948, Lt. General Curtis E. Le May took command of SAC and went on to build it into the most powerful military force ever. Survivability was key to SAC's deterrence capability, so Le May moved the SAC Headquarters to the remote Offutt Air Force Base, Nebraska. SAC personnel were in no doubt as to the importance of their mission when Le May told them, "We are at war now!" Le May's aim was to build SAC into a force that could unleash such firepower and destruction on an enemy that they would no longer have the will or ability to wage war.

After slow development, the advent of the Korean War brought more funds to the USAF, enabling SAC to expand rapidly. Another driving factor in the development of SAC was the growing threat of Soviet military development, principally in the development of the Soviet hydrogen bomb, which was first tested on August 12, 1953.

To reduce the risk to its aircraft from enemy attack, SAC began to disperse them to bases across the USA, and did not have too many concentrated at a single location. In addition, SAC began acquiring bases around the world (in England, Greenland and Spain, among other locations) to improve its aircraft's ability to reach enemies anywhere.

BELOW: **The B-52, one of the greatest combat aircraft ever built, was the aircraft Le May was waiting for. Its entry into service in 1955 gave SAC the ability to fly around the world, strike at targets and fly home again. Although it was designed as a nuclear bomber, the Vietnam War showed the B-52's capabilities as a conventional bomber.**

LEFT: This fine comparison shows the relative size of two of SAC's earliest bombers, the B-29 Superfortress (left) and the B-36 Peacemaker. The B-36 was the largest bomber ever to serve with the USAF, and for a decade in the late 1940s and early '50s, the Peacemaker provided SAC with a long-range strategic bomber deterrent. BELOW: Taken in October 1955, this photograph shows two RB-47s, the reconnaissance variant of SAC's Stratojet bomber.

ABOVE: A SAC KB-50 tanker refuelling an F-101 Voodoo, the fighter conceived as a long-range escort fighter for SAC B-36s. Voodoos would never have the range to go all the way with the bombers, but a range of 2414km/1500 miles still made it a useful defence. RIGHT: The B-58 Hustler joined SAC as a supersonic replacement for the B-47 Stratojet. In 1960, the B-58 became SAC's first operational supersonic bomber.

Initially equipped with tired World War II aircraft types, by the mid-1950s SAC was operating its first all-jet bomber, the B-47 Stratojet. By 1955, SAC was being equipped with the mighty B-52 (still the backbone of the USAF bomber force around half a century later), the B-58 Hustler and, equally importantly, the KC-135 jet tanker, which gave SAC a truly global reach. SAC demonstrated its ability to strike anywhere around the world when three B-52s made a non-stop round-the-world flight. By the late 1950s, SAC was complementing its airborne nuclear forces with ballistic nuclear missiles.

By 1960, a third of SAC's bombers and tankers were on 15-minute ground alert, combat-ready and armed for nuclear war. By July 1961, half of SAC's bombers and tankers were on ground alert while a number of nuclear-armed bombers were constantly airborne. From February 1961, SAC kept an Airborne Command Post in the air at all times, ready to take control of SAC forces in the event of an attack on the SAC HQ at Offut. From 1964 to 1973, SAC bombers flew thousands of bombing missions in South-east Asia, and the Linebacker II campaign in December 1972 is thought to have brought the North Vietnamese back to the peace table.

The collapse of the Soviet Union at the end of the Cold War brought an end to the threat of Soviet aggression. Following the Gulf War in 1991, a restructuring of the United States Air Force brought the stand-down of Strategic Air Command. On June 1, 1992, Strategic Air Command passed into the history books, hailed by many as winners of the Cold War.

Bomber aircraft defences from 1945

Most of the bombers in service in the post-war period had some type of defensive gun armament. B-29s, like their B-17 predecessors, bristled with guns in tail, waist and ventral positions. In the late 1940s and early '50s it was felt that, provided a bomber could fly higher and faster than defending fighters and anti-aircraft fire, it would get to its target unscathed. This was the philosophy behind the wartime de Havilland Mosquito and the jet-powered English Electric Canberra which first flew in 1949 – in bomber configuration, neither type carried defensive armament.

Guns continued to be installed in bombers, although guns in nose positions were omitted as bomber aircraft began to fly higher and faster. The Avro Shackleton may well have been the last front-line bomber in service with this form of

armament. The B-52, however, did retain a group of remotely controlled cannon in the tail, which was only deleted in later versions. Even the high-speed Tupolev Tu-22M had two radar-controlled cannon in its tail. Today the backbone of Britain's bomber force, the Panavia Tornado GR4, has a 27mm/1.05in cannon in the nose.

World War II proved the value of fighter escort for large fleets of bombers, and this no doubt prompted the decision to trial a very unusual defensive installation in the B-36 Peacemaker. The B-36 was so large that its forward bomb

RIGHT: **Few aircraft have had the capability to carry another aircraft for defence, but Strategic Air Command's B-36 Peacemaker could. Trials with an F-85 Goblin were followed by more using an F-86 Thunderstreak.**
BELOW: **The structure of "stealth" aircraft, such as the Lockheed F-117 Nighthawk pictured, and the materials from which they are made, are central to their defence and survivability.**

bay had room to carry a McDonnell F-85 Goblin jet fighter that could protect the bomber from enemy fighters and then return to the aircraft.

However, the unarmed Mosquito approach held good until anti-aircraft missile technology produced missiles that could down a jet aircraft at 18,300m/60,000ft. Most anti-aircraft missiles were fired at targets tracked on radar, which then directed the missile to the vicinity of the target. The missile would switch to its own homing facility and look for a heat source, normally the aircraft's engine jet pipe. The same technique was used by most air-to-air fighter-launched missiles. A hit from a missile was usually enough to bring down any aircraft – warheads varied from high explosive to "shrapnel" types, and some were even nuclear-tipped. Bombers began to employ various means of confusing would-be attackers. Radar-controlled missiles would only function if the radar could find and lock on to its target. Bombers carry electronic jamming devices which will find and jam the appropriate enemy fire control radars of anti-aircraft guns and missiles. On some missions, for example the Libya raids carried out

by the USAF, dedicated jamming aircraft (EF-111s) went in ahead of the main attack force. During the RAF's Black Buck bombing raids on the Falklands, specialized Shrike anti-radar missiles were fired by Vulcan bombers.

Most bombers now carry special rear warning radar to alert crews to unwelcome attention from the rear. On-board equipment detects missile locks from fighter aircraft or missiles. The bomber can then take evasive action and deploy bundles of chaff (strips of metal foil) to create a confusing radar image, and also flares which fire 20 to 30 times around the aircraft, presenting a plethora of brilliantly hot, burning objects that hopefully draw the heat-seeking missile away.

"Stealth" aircraft revolutionized bomber operations because potential enemies at the time relied on defence radars to pick up incoming bombers. Most radars cannot pick up the stealth aircraft and, if they did, heat-seeking missiles would be thwarted thanks to the ingenious cooling and dissipation of hot exhaust gases from the aircraft's engines, which reduced the aircraft's infrared signature. All future bomber aircraft will be made using stealth technology.

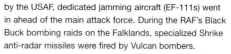

FAR LEFT: In contrast to the hi-tech tail defences of the B-52, the Tu-95 Bear retains two 23mm/0.9in cannon in the tail which can be fired manually. The tail turret is clearly inspired by that of the Tu-4 B-29 copy produced in the Soviet Union in the years following World War II. LEFT: The tail of the B-52 has changed considerably during its time in service. It was initially armed with four remotely controlled 12.7mm/0.5in machine-guns. In the H-model pictured, the tail defence is the 20mm/0.78in "minigun", part of the AN/ASG-21 Defensive Fire Control system. Note also the tail warning and search radomes above the gun.
BELOW LEFT: Even the Mach 2-capable Panavia Tornado carries cannon armament in the nose.
BELOW: Avro Shackleton. The "Shack" was probably the last front-line bomber with nose guns.

287

V-bombers

Britain's V-bombers – the Vulcan, Victor and Valiant – were the last of the Royal Air Force's long-range heavy bombers, and they were Britain's airborne nuclear deterrent from 1955 until 1968.

The concept of the force, not seen as one of mixed aircraft types at first, had its origins in a 1946 Air Ministry Operational Requirement calling for a bomber able to carry a 4542kg/10,000lb atomic bomb to a target 2775km/1725 miles away, from a base anywhere in the world. The aircraft was required to deliver its bomb deep into enemy territory and avoid destruction by enemy aircraft or anti-aircraft defences.

Four very different jet-powered designs from four different companies made it from the drawing board in response to the requirement. Avro and Handley Page both proposed futuristic, aerodynamically adventurous designs judged to be sufficiently risky that Vickers and Shorts were invited to develop their rather simpler and thus less risky designs as something of an insurance policy for the RAF. The Air Staff asked for the Vickers design, ultimately named Valiant, to be produced over the Short Sperrin as the interim aircraft, while the advanced Avro and Handley Page aircraft were developed into the Vulcan and Victor respectively. These aircraft represented a massive technological leap for an air force equipped with Lancasters, Lincolns and latterly old B-29s loaned by the

TOP: **XA901 was a Vulcan B.1 and was one of the earlier Vulcans to be produced. The total number of B.1s built was 45, the last delivered to the RAF in April 1959. The all-white, anti-flash paint scheme was intended to offer some protection against the effects of the flash following a nuclear detonation.**
ABOVE: **Elements of the V-force were rotated overseas to Akrotiri in Cyprus, the location photographed here in 1970. From Cyprus, the bombers would have been able to reach targets beyond the range of UK-based aircraft. Beneath this Vulcan's nose is a tanker version of the Victor bomber.**

Americans. Looking back, it took surprisingly little time – only nine years – for the jet-powered nuclear bombers to reach squadron service.

The V-bombers were effectively designed around Britain's own atomic bomb, which was developed in parallel with the aircraft. Britain's first operational atomic bomb, "Blue Danube", a free-fall plutonium bomb, was available in November 1953, but it was not until 1955 that Britain's first atomic bomber unit, No.138 Squadron, was operational with its Valiants at RAF Wittering. Although the jet-powered Canberra had been in Bomber Command service since 1951, its bomb bay was too small to take the British A-bomb that became available.

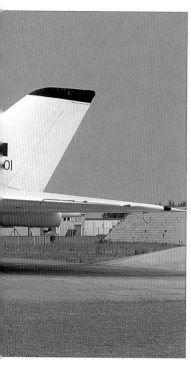

It was January 1957 before the first Vulcans entered service with the RAF's 230 OCU (Operational Conversion Unit) at Waddington, and the type was entering squadron service by the summer. November 1957 saw the Victor deliveries beginning and the Handley Page bomber was in squadron use from April 1958. Ten RAF airfields were updated to become V-bomber bases, while a further 26 were earmarked as V-bomber dispersal bases in times of international tension.

The V-force possessed massive destructive capability, and its credibility as an effective deterrent against would-be aggressors – specifically the Soviet Union – rested on its ability to get airborne and get to the target if required. The V-force perfected the QRA (quick reaction alert), whereby a number of aircraft were fuelled, armed and ready to be airborne in just four minutes, the amount of time it would take for a detected Soviet ballistic missile to impact on UK bases. The credibility of the V-force was in question once Soviet anti-aircraft technology developed to the point that a U-2 spyplane was shot down over the USSR from an altitude of 19,810m/65,000ft in May 1960. The answer was to bring the V-force down to low level, operating below the effective height of most enemy radars, only climbing to an altitude of 3660m/12,000ft to drop the deadly cargo. By now the force was carrying the Yellow Sun hydrogen bomb, which was replaced by the WE177 weapon in the mid-1960s. Later-mark Victors and Vulcans were armed with the Blue Steel stand-off

TOP: The enormous Blue Danube atomic bomb, around which the V-bombers were designed. This all-British weapon was a free-fall plutonium bomb.

ABOVE: The Vickers Valiant was the most conventional of the three V-bomber designs, and was ordered as insurance should the more advanced Victor and Vulcan be problematic. BELOW: The Victor first flew in prototype form just seven years after the end of World War II, yet this aircraft served in the RAF until 1993 when the last tanker versions were retired. The Victor could carry the greatest bomb load of the V-bombers, an impressive 15,890kg/35,000lb.

missile with a range of 161km/100miles. This enabled the V-bombers to improve the launch aircraft's survivability over heavily defended targets.

When the strategic deterrent role passed from the V-force to the Royal Navy's Polaris submarines in 1969, these aircraft remained in front-line service (although the Valiant had been withdrawn by then) and were still very potent weapon platforms with the ability to carry many tons of bombs, including nuclear payloads, if required.

The Falklands Black Buck raids

When Argentina invaded the Falklands in 1982, Britain's campaign to regain the islands was made more difficult because of the sheer distances involved. Once Britain's Task Force was ready to re-take the islands, Argentine air defences on the Falklands had to be disabled. Firstly, the runway at Port Stanley had to be made unusable for Argentine aircraft, as it was assumed that, given time, the Argentine air force would base Mirage and Skyhawk fighters there, which could have made things very difficult for the Task Force. Without a Falklands base, these combat aircraft operating from the Argentine mainland were near the limits of their operating radius. Secondly, Argentine radar sites had to be neutralized so that the British Harriers of the Task Force could not be attacked or detected. The missions had to take place in total secrecy from friendly territory which led the military planners to one choice: Ascension Island, a small British dependency in the Atlantic almost 6436km/4000 miles from the Falklands. There was only one aircraft in the RAF inventory that could carry a heavy bomb load over the considerable distances involved – the Vulcan.

TOP: **The Vulcan finally saw action after almost three decades of service when the type was used to carry out the longest bombing raids ever contemplated.**
ABOVE: **The raid was only possible with a complex series of inflight refuellings from Victor tankers which themselves had to be refuelled to get back to base.**

The missions to the Falklands were codenamed "Operation Black Buck", and five were ultimately flown. Three were directed against the runway at Stanley, while a further two attacked radar sites on the islands. The logistics of these missions are staggering, and with the distance from Ascension to the Falklands a 16-hour round trip of over 12,389km/7700 miles, they were at that point the longest bombing missions in history.

LEFT AND BELOW: **A key aim of the Black Buck missions was to put the Port Stanley runway out of action. This was essential to prevent its use by Argentine Mirage (left) and Skyhawk (below) aircraft which posed a significant threat to the British Task Force. Both were near the end of their range operating from the Argentine mainland, and they could be contained by the British Harriers.**

Each Black Buck Vulcan had to be refuelled numerous times by RAF Victor tankers also operating from Ascension, and some of the tankers themselves had to be refuelled to get home. Although many RAF Vulcans had refuelling probes, they had not been used for some time. There followed a period where serviceable refuelling probes were sought, one apparently coming from a Vulcan in a museum. Because of the great distances involved over the ocean, the Vulcans needed improved navigation aids, which came in the form of equipment allegedly acquired from a British Airways store. In addition, the Vulcan's throttle controls were modified to allow pilots unlimited power from the Olympus engines.

The first Black Buck mission took place from April 30 to May 1, 1982. Loaded with 21 x 454kg/1000lb bombs, two Vulcans took off from Ascension for the eight-hour trip to their target, escorted by no fewer than 11 Victor tankers which had to refuel the bombers or each other to reach the Falklands and return.

One of the Vulcans developed a technical problem and had to return to base, leaving a lone Vulcan – XM607 – to carry out the mission. Dwindling numbers of tankers flew on with the Vulcan while the empty tankers returned to Ascension, many with barely enough fuel to land. The last Victor transferred so

much fuel to the Vulcan that it only had enough left to get within 644km/400 miles of Ascension, and another Victor had to launch to refuel the incoming "dry" tanker.

About 482km/300 miles from Stanley, the Vulcan descended to 92m/300ft above the sea to avoid detection, and about 64km/40 miles out the aircraft climbed to 3050m/10,000ft to begin the bombing run. Then, 16km/10 miles from the target, an anti-aircraft gun radar was detected, but was jammed by equipment on the Vulcan supplied by the Americans. Twenty-one 454kg/1000lb bombs were dropped in a diagonal line across the runway, one hitting the runway dead-centre.

The effect of this and subsequent Black Buck raids was more on Argentine morale than the Argentine military machine. If Vulcans could reach the Falklands, they could reach the Argentine mainland and, as a result, many Argentine fighters were kept back to defend against a possible raid on Argentina. The raids had been a success.

LEFT: **XM607 was one of the Vulcan B.2s that carried out the Black Buck raids. Armed with 21 x 454kg/1000lb bombs, the Vulcan dropped the bombs obliquely across the runway. Argentina then feared that an attack on the mainland might also have been feasible.**

Operation El Dorado Canyon

In 1986, following a number of terrorist attacks on US citizens and interests, US intelligence cited "incontrovertible" evidence that the incidents were sponsored by Libya. On April 14, 1986, the United States launched Operation El Dorado Canyon against Libya. Part of the operation called for UK-based USAF F-111 crews to fly one of the longest combat missions in history.

US President Ronald Reagan wanted to mount a strike against the regime of Libyan leader Colonel Gadaffi, but first sought cooperation from the Western Allies. The USAF's 48th Tactical Fighter Wing in England had been working on plans for a strike, which assumed that the F-111s could fly through French airspace to strike at Libya. Western media speculation about the strike caused the plan to be changed to include support aircraft (EF-111 and US Navy A-7 and EA-6B) to carry out the suppression of enemy defences. The US Navy role in the operation grew, as the raid had to hit Gadaffi hard.

Plans were further complicated when France, Germany, Italy and Spain all refused to cooperate in a strike. Only Britain cooperated by allowing the use of its soil to launch the attack. A radically different plan was drawn up. The F-111s would now navigate over the ocean around France and Spain, pass east over the Strait of Gibraltar and then over the Mediterranean to line up for their bombing run on Libya.

It would be a gruelling round trip of 10,298km/6400 miles, taking 13 hours and needing from eight to twelve inflight refuellings for each of the bombers. The F-111 crews, trained for missions against the Soviet Union, were familiar with 2-hour NATO sorties, so El Dorado Canyon placed a tremendous strain on the crews and the aircraft's complex systems.

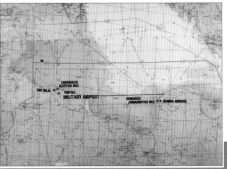

RIGHT: **The map used by Secretary of Defense Weinberger at the White House briefing which told the world of Operation El Dorado Canyon.** BELOW: **An F-111 leaves the runway at RAF Lakenheath in Suffolk, England, to take part in what was then the longest bombing mission in history. The F-111 is a very fast and accurate low-level bomber, but the aircraft was not designed for gruelling 13-hour missions like the Libya raids.**

US planners tabled a joint USAF/USN attack against five major Libyan targets. Two were in Benghazi: a terrorist training camp and a military airfield. The other three targets were in Tripoli: a terrorist naval training base; the former Wheelus AFB; and the Azziziyah Barracks compound, which housed the HQ of Libyan intelligence and also contained one of five residences that Gadaffi was known to have used. Eighteen F-111s were to strike the Tripoli targets, while US Navy aircraft were to hit the two Benghazi sites.

At 17:36 GMT on April 14, 24 F-111s left Lakenheath, six of them spare aircraft set to return after the first refuelling. Five EF-111 electronic warfare aircraft also launched. This was the start of the first US bomber mission from British soil since the end of World War II. The US Navy attack aircraft came from carriers of the Sixth Fleet operating in the Mediterranean. Coral Sea provided eight A-6E medium bombers and six F/A-18C Hornets for strike support. America launched six A-6Es, plus six A-7Es and an EA-6B for strike support. They faced a hazardous flight because Libya's air defence system was virtually on a par with that of the Soviet Union. Timing was critical, and the USAF and USN attacks had to be simultaneous to maximize the element of surprise so that the strike aircraft could get in and out as quickly as possible.

Of the 18 F-111s that headed for Libya, five had aborted en route, so at around midnight GMT, 13 F-111s reached Tripoli. The first three elements hit the Azziziyah Barracks. One element struck the Sidi Balal terrorist training camp while the two remaining elements, armed with parachute-retarded 225kg/500lb bombs, struck Tripoli airport, destroying a number of aircraft in the process. The F-111s carried out their attack at speeds around 740kph/460mph and heights of 60m/200ft.

EF-111As and Navy A-7s, A-6Es, and an EA-6B armed with HARM and Shrike anti-radar missiles flew in defence suppression roles for the F-111s. Across the Gulf of Sidra, Navy A-6E aircraft attacked the Al Jumahiriya Barracks at Benghazi, and to the east the Benina airfield.

News of the attack was being broadcast in the USA while it was underway. One F-111 aircraft was lost over Tripoli, possibly hit by a SAM, and its crew were killed. The F-111s spent only 11 minutes in the area of the targets, then faced a long flight home with yet more inflight refuellings.

The operation was never intended to be a means of toppling Gadaffi, but he is known to have been very shaken when bombs exploded near him. When he next appeared on state television, he was certainly subdued. Most importantly, the raids demonstrated that even in those pre-"stealth" days, the USA had the capability to send its high-speed bombers over great distances to carry out precision attacks. The raid was considered a success, but the situation between the USA and Gadaffi remained unresolved until an uneasy peace was agreed 17 years later.

BELOW: **This photograph, taken on February 12, 1986, shows the deck of the USS *Saratoga* (CV-60) as flight-deck crews prepare EA-6B Prowlers, F-14 Tomcats and A-7 Corsairs for operations in the southern Mediterranean. Tension was high between the USA and Libya, and on March 24, 1986, the US Navy destroyed a SAM site after USN aircraft were targeted unsuccessfully by Libyan missiles.**

BENINA AIRFIELD
15 APR 86

DESTROYED MIG-23/FLOGGER

MIG-23/FLOGGER PIECES

ABOVE: **A still from film taken by a USAF F-111 as the US attack on the military side of Tripoli airport begins. 225kg/500lb bombs were dropped on these Soviet-made Il-76 transports, which the USA believed transported military and subversive materials around the world. The film was shot at night using the F-111's Pave Tack laser-guided delivery system.** LEFT: **Photographs taken by US Navy aircraft on April 15, 1986 show the damage caused at Benina airfield by the previous day's attack carried out by USN aircraft.**

Gulf War bombers

The air campaign against Iraq was launched on January 16, 1991, the day after the United Nations' deadline for Iraqi withdrawal from Kuwait expired. Operation Desert Shield had become Desert Storm. The scale and strength of the Allied air attacks on one night were staggering, and the initial air attack removed much of Iraq's ability to defend itself against further air assaults. The air campaign was conducted by the USA, Saudi, British, French, Italian and Free Kuwaiti, as well as various Arab air forces.

Lockheed F-117 "stealth fighters" flew to the Iraqi capital of Baghdad and destroyed command and control centres. As Baghdad's anti-aircraft defences (seven times greater than that of Hanoi later in the Vietnam War) blazed away at targets it could not see, the F-117s were delivering 907kg/2000lb laser-guided bombs down ventilation shafts and through doorways to destroy underground bunkered facilities. Meanwhile, cruise missiles were also taking out targets with pinpoint accuracy. Seven USAF B-52Gs had taken off from Barksdale Air Force Base, Louisiana, and headed towards the Persian Gulf. They flew a round trip of more than 22,526km/ 14,000 miles, remaining airborne for 35 hours, the longest combat mission in history at that time. The launch of their Boeing AGM-86C conventionally armed cruise missiles (first combat use for the weapon) was one of the opening salvoes

TOP: **Operating from RAF Fairford in Britain, eight USAF B-52s dropped a total of 1176 tonnes/1158 tons of bombs during 60 missions on mainly front-line Republican Guard targets.** ABOVE: **The Republic A-10 Thunderbolt proved to be a modern equivalent of the Hawker Typhoon, carrying out much the same job as the "Tiffie" after D-Day, attacking enemy armour and vehicles. However, the Typhoon was not armed with the A-10's deadly 30mm/1.18in cannon which fires 30 armour-piercing rounds per second.**

of the operation. Iraqi anti-aircraft defences then became targets themselves with scores of US defence suppression types such as the EF-111, F-4G Wild Weasels and EA-6 Prowlers launching anti-radiation missiles or using powerful jammers to cripple enemy electronic sensors.

LEFT: The crew of RAF Victor K2 tanker XH671 head out to their aircraft for another mission in support of Desert Storm combat aircraft. These flying petrol stations were essential for aircraft such as Tornados and Buccaneers. BELOW: An F-111 of the UK-based 48th Tactical Fighter Wing "in theatre" at Taif in Saudi Arabia during the Gulf War. In 2500 Gulf War F-111 missions, these fine aircraft destroyed 2203 targets, including artillery, 13 runways, 245 hardened aircraft shelters and 12 bridges.

For a month, Coalition aircraft pounded away at any targets that might contribute to the Iraqi ground war effort. Precision bombs were used to minimize errors and casualties – a successful strike was one that hit within 3m/10ft of its mark.

In the first day of Desert Storm, 655 Coalition aircraft flew 1322 sorties against communication centres and airfields. Within 24 hours, the Coalition achieved air superiority and was then at liberty to destroy Iraq's command and control centres, and to cut communications between Kuwait and Baghdad.

Once defences were silenced, strike aircraft, including the Jaguar, F-16 and F/A-18, hit airfield complexes with conventional bombs. RAF Tornado bombers specialized in the use of the devastating JP233 runway denial weapon system against Iraqi runways. This weapon had to be used at low level, which led to relatively high losses among the RAF bomber crews. Hardened shelters were not able to protect Iraqi aircraft hidden within because the Coalition bombers were able to direct pinpoint attacks on the structures' doors.

Veteran Royal Air Force Buccaneers, normally deployed in the maritime attack role in the UK, were rushed to the Gulf for overland laser designation (target-marking) missions. Armed with Sidewinder AAMs for self defence, pairs of Buccaneers would operate with four Tornados, all carrying precision-guided bombs and the "Buccs" each carrying a laser pod – two were carried in case one became unserviceable, thus avoiding the entire mission being scrubbed. The Buccaneer flew the first such mission on February 2 against the As Suwaira road bridge. These mixed Tornado/Buccaneer teams destroyed 20 road bridges over the Tigris and Euphrates rivers, very effectively breaking Iraqi supply lines to their invasion forces in Kuwait. Unknown to the Coalition, the Iraqis had run their fibre optic communications cables along the bridges, so every wrecked bridge added to communications chaos among the enemy.

Allied Air Forces then proceeded to pound the Iraqi land forces – specifically the divisions deployed in Kuwait and Southern Iraq. The USAF's veteran B-52 bombers, operating mainly from Diego Garcia in the Indian Ocean, decimated the morale of Iraq's Republican Guard. They delivered some 40 per cent of all the weapons dropped by Coalition forces and flew approximately 1620 combat sorties.

Coalition bombers continued to attack Iraqi targets until the invaders were driven from Kuwait, and on March 3, 1991, Iraq accepted the ceasefire.

> "We have carefully chosen our targets and we've bombed them with precision."
> US Secretary of Defense Dick Cheney, 1991

LEFT: A Royal Air Force Tornado GR1 at its base in Kuwait. The Tornado played a vital strike role during the war, initially tasked with hazardous low-level missions. In all, 1500 bombing raids were carried out by the swing-wing bombers.

A–Z of World War Bombers

1914–45

There were no true bomber aircraft when World War I broke out, but military leaders were quick to realize the value of aircraft that could rain down destruction on their enemies from the air. While early bombing raids saw hand-held munitions tossed over the side of an aircraft, by the end of the Great War aircraft were being produced with the capacity to carry bomb loads of 800kg/ 1760lb over ranges in excess of 1000km/ 621 miles.

The specifications given to designers of new bomber aircraft in World War I were little changed by World War II, except in their magnitude. Some biplanes were still in front-line service. But by the end of World War II, bombers in service included the Boeing B-29, which had a range of 5229km/3250 miles and a top speed of 576kph/358mph. The weapons carried had changed in their destructive capacity. While the Handley Page bombers of World War I would have carried a number of 113kg/250lb bombs on a raid, the B-29 had to carry just one atomic bomb equivalent to 20,320 tonnes/20,000 tons of high explosives to destroy a city. The bomber had become a war-winning weapon.

LEFT: **Bristol Beaufort I.**

LEFT: **Although the D3A did not have a retractable undercarriage, large streamlined fairings over the fixed landing gear were used to make them more aerodynamic.**

Aichi D3A Val ●

First flight: January 1938
Power: One Mitsubishi 1,070hp Kinsei 44 radial piston engine
Armament: Two 7.7mm/0.303in machine-guns in upper forward fuselage plus one in rear cockpit; external bomb load of 370kg/816lb
Size: Wingspan – 14.37m/47ft 2in
Length – 10.20m/33ft 5in
Height – 3.80m/12ft 7in
Wing area – 34.9m²/375.67sq ft
Weights: Empty – 2408kg/5309lb
Maximum take-off – 3650kg/8047lb
Performance: Maximum speed – 385kph/239mph
Service ceiling – 9,300m/30,510ft
Range – 1470km/913 miles
Climb – 3000m/9845ft in 6 minutes

Aichi D3A

This two-seat low-wing monoplane dive-bomber, codenamed "Val" by the Allies, came to prominence on December 7, 1941, when a Japanese Naval Task force launched 183 aircraft, including 51 Aichi D3A-2s, from six aircraft carriers to attack Pearl Harbor's Battleship Row and other US Navy installations on the Hawaiian island of Oahu. One of the D3A-2's victims was the USS *Pennsylvania*.

The D3A first flew in January 1938, and between December 1939 and August 1945 the Aichi company built a total of 1495 aircraft in two main variants. The type D3A-1 entered service with the Imperial Japanese Navy in 1940 and was followed a year later by the D3A-2 which had the more powerful 1300hp Kinsei engine and increased fuel capacity. The D3A-2 was the main production version, with 1016 aircraft

being built by the time it became obsolete at the end of 1942. Over the following years, many were used as training aircraft, but as the war progressed and the Americans moved closer to the Japanese mainland, most of the remaining aircraft were used in kamikaze attacks against US naval ships at Leyte and Okinawa.

LEFT: **The Amiot 143 was probably the ugliest aircraft produced by a nation known for its appreciation of fine forms.**

Amiot 143 ▮▮

First flight: August 1934
Power: Two Gnome-Rhone 870hp Kirs 14-cylinder radial engines
Armament: Four 7.5mm/0.29in MAC 1934 machine-guns, one each in nose and dorsal turrets and fore and aft in ventral gondola; internal and external bomb load of up to 800kg/1761lb
Size: Wingspan – 24.53m/80ft 5in
Length – 18.26m/59ft 11in
Height – 5.68m/18ft 7in
Wing area – 100m²/1076.4sq ft
Weights: Empty – 6100kg/13,426lb
Maximum take-off – 9700kg/21,350lb
Performance: Maximum speed – 310kph/193mph
Service ceiling – 7900m/25,920ft
Range – 1200km/746 miles

Amiot 143

The lumbering Amiot 143 was a more powerful re-engined version of the Amiot 140 of 1931 vintage, and retained the fixed non-retractable undercarriage. This all-metal aircraft, with its distinctive two-deck fuselage, had a wing section so deep that the flight engineer could access the engines in flight. The large aerodynamic fairings that covered the wheels were 2.13m/7ft long.

Five French Groupes de Bombardement were equipped with this type in May 1940 when Germany invaded France and the Low Countries. After carrying out early raids dropping propaganda leaflets on Germany, they were restricted to night-bombing of the advancing German columns. In a rare daylight bombing raid against bridges on May 14, 1940, 12 out of 13 143s were shot down.

At the time of France's surrender, only 50 Amiot 143 aircraft remained, and these subsequently formed part of the French Vichy Air Force. By then obsolete, many were converted for use in the transport role.

LEFT: **The Blitz was the world's first operational jet bomber aircraft.** BELOW: **The development Ar 234s used a launch trolley with a steerable nosewheel and mainwheel brakes for taxiing. As this photograph shows, the trolley was released after take-off. Note the main landing skid beneath the fuselage and the smaller ones below the engine nacelles.** BOTTOM LEFT: **An early Blitz on its launch trolley.**

Arado Ar 234 Blitz

The origins of this type date back to a specification issued by the German Air Ministry in 1940 for a fast turbojet-powered single-seat reconnaissance aircraft. The design proposed by Arado, the Ar 234, went on to become the world's first jet-powered bomber.

The first prototype, the Ar 234V-1, first flew on June 15, 1943. and this was quickly followed by seven other prototypes, all using a launching trolley and landing skid arrangement since the aircraft's fuselage was so narrow that it could not take a conventional undercarriage. Once the aircraft reached 60m/197ft, the launch trolley was released and returned to earth on parachutes for re-use.

The third prototype, Ar 234V-3, was fitted with an ejection seat and had rocket-assisted take-off equipment installed under the wings. During the prototype trials, the launch trolley arrangement had performed very well, but it was soon realized that the aircraft's immobility on landing would be a great disadvantage when it came to operational deployment. Turn-around times would be increased and the aircraft would be vulnerable to enemy air attack. It was therefore decided to abandon the trolley and skid, and all production aircraft had a conventional wheeled undercarriage fitted into the wider fuselage of the production B-series.

Despite being famed as the first jet bombers, early Ar 234s did serve as reconnaissance aircraft that readily avoided enemy interception. Some special examples also equipped an

Arado Ar 234B-2

First flight: June 15, 1943
Power: Two BMW 890kg/1962lb thrust 004B turbojets
Armament: External bomb load of 2000kg/4402lb
Size: Wingspan – 14.11m/46ft 3in
Length – 12.64m/41ft 5in
Height – 4.30m/14ft 1in
Wing area – 26.4m²/284.18sq ft
Weights: Empty – 5200kg/11445lb
Maximum take-off – 9850kg/21,608lb
Performance: Maximum speed – 742kph/461mph
Service ceiling – 10,000m/32,808ft
Range – 1630km/1013 miles
Climb – 6000m/19,685ft in 17.5 minutes

experimental nightfighter unit. However, Germany's fortune and the Blitz's performance soon led to its development as a bomber that entered service with the Luftwaffe in October 1944. Operated by KG76, the aircraft's first operational missions were flown against targets during the Ardennes offensive in December 1944. This jet bomber unit was very active in the early weeks of 1945 by taking part in a ten-day series of attacks against the Ludendorff bridge at Remagen, which had been captured by the Americans. The Blitz was a pioneering aircraft which was closely studied by the Allies post-war.

Armstrong Whitworth Whitley

TOP: **Z9226 was a Whitley Mk V, pictured here during its service with No.10 Squadron, Bomber Command.** ABOVE: **A Bomber Command Whitley crew prepare for another mission. Note the unusual off-centre single machine-gun in the nose turret.**

The Whitley, designed in response to Air Ministry specification B.3/34, was an all-metal twin-engined monoplane bomber with retractable landing gear, and first flew on March 17, 1936. It entered service with the RAF in March 1937, was one of the first heavy night-bombers of the RAF and the first RAF aircraft with a stressed-skin fuselage. The high incidence of the aircraft's wing gave the Whitley a distinctive nose-down flying attitude. During the "phoney war" period, the RAF's Whitley squadrons bore the brunt of leaflet dropping raids over German cities, which resulted in many losses. On March 19, 1940, Whitleys dropped the first bombs on German territory during World War II when they attacked the Hornum seaplane base on the island of Sylt. The Whitley, together with the Wellington and Hampden – lightweights by the standards of later Bomber Command "heavies" – formed the backbone of the early British bomber offensive.

Heavy losses during the winter of 1940–1 and the introduction of four-engine aircraft meant that the Whitley's front-line activities were soon restricted to Coastal Command U-boat patrol duties over the approaches to their bases along the French Atlantic coast. Coastal Command's first success using air-to-surface-vessel (ASV) radar was by a Whitley VII of No.502 Squadron against U-Boat *U-206* in November 1941.

The Whitley I was delivered to the RAF off the drawing board while the Whitley IIs were completed with two-stage superchargers for the engines. The Mark III was part of the second production run. Though similar to the II, this version

Armstrong Whitworth Whitley Mark V

First flight: March 17, 1936
Power: Two Rolls-Royce 1145hp Merlin X piston engines
Armament: One 7.7mm/0.303in machine-gun in nose turret; four in tail turret; up to 3178kg/7000lb bomb load carried in bomb bay and inner wings
Size: Wingspan – 25.6m/84 ft
Length – 21.5m/70ft 6in
Height – 4.57m/15ft
Wing area – 105.63m²/1137sq ft
Weights: Empty – 8785kg/19,350lb
Maximum take-off – 15,209kg/33,500lb
Performance: Maximum speed – 357kph/222mph
Service ceiling – 7930m/26,000ft
Range – 2654km/1650 miles
Climb – 244m/800ft per minute

ABOVE: **The famed Merlin engine did not power Whitleys until the introduction of the Mk IV. The aircraft shown here, undergoing intense but staged servicing, is a Mk III with Armstrong Siddeley Tiger engines.** RIGHT: **RAF Coastal Command operated Whitleys on maritime patrol duties. Initially standard bomber aircraft, such as that pictured, operated in the role. Later the Mk VII, specially equipped with ASV radar, could readily detect enemy vessels below.**

had a retractable ventral "dustbin" turret armed with two 7.7mm/0.303in machine-guns – this version could also carry larger bombs. The final 40 airframes of the second production run were completed as Whitley IVs with the famous Rolls-Royce Merlin engines and an increased fuel capacity.

The Mark V was similar to the Mark IV but replaced the manually operated turret with a Nash and Thompson-powered tail turret with four 7.7mm/0.303in machine-guns. As a result of combat experience, the rear fuselage of this version was also extended by 38cm/15in to improve the rear gunner's field of fire. Other changes included a revised fin shape, the addition of a leading de-icing facility and greater fuel capacity.

The Whitley VII was built specifically to serve with Coastal Command units on maritime reconnaissance duties. The VII was equipped with ASV Mk II radar and can be most readily identified from other versions by the four dorsal radar masts atop the rear fuselage, and numerous aerials carried. This model also differed by having a sixth crew member and extra fuel tankage in the bomb bay and fuselage. Compared to earlier versions with a range of 2011km/1250 miles, this version could reach distances of 3700km/2300 miles.

Earlier Bomber Command versions were phased out of front-line service from 1942, after which they were used as trainers and glider tugs – the aircraft was heavily used for training airborne troops for D-Day. During 1942–3, 15 Whitley Mk Vs were transferred to BOAC and given civil registrations to carry out Gibraltar-to-Malta supply flights. Some Whitleys served in the Fleet Air Arm until 1946 as flying classrooms to instruct on Merlin engine handling and fuel transfer.

ABOVE: **When phased out as bombers, early versions were switched to glider tug and paratroop training, thus playing a part in the success of D-Day.**

LEFT: **The Anson was one of the longest-serving RAF aircraft. This Anson bears the squadron codes of Coastal Command's No.206 Squadron.**
BELOW: **Although the Anson was advanced in some ways, early versions had to be started by hand.**

Avro Anson

The origins of the Anson lay in the Avro 652 light transport airliner that served with Imperial Airways from March 1935. The 652 had been built to meet an Imperial Airways requirement for an aircraft that could transport four passengers over a series of 676km/420 mile journeys at a cruising speed greater than 209kph/130mph. Roy Chadwick, who later worked on Avro's Lancaster and early stages of the Vulcan's design, led the design team to produce what was an innovative aircraft for the time.

The Avro 652 was swiftly adapted to meet a May 1934 Air Ministry requirement for a twin-engine coastal reconnaissance aircraft. The Anson differed from its civil predecessor by having different engines, rectangular, not round, windows and also in having "teeth" in the form of a hand-operated dorsal Armstrong Whitworth turret with a 7.7mm/0.303in Lewis machine-gun. In comparative trials, the Anson was pitted against a military version of the de Havilland Dragon Rapide designed to satisfy the same RAF requirement. The Avro design's greater range and endurance impressed the Air Ministry, and a large order was placed.

The Anson represented a major breakthrough for the Royal Air Force, being the first monoplane in RAF squadron service and also the first to employ the novel retractable undercarriage, even though it was hand-operated.

The prototype first flew in 1935, and Coastal Command's No.48 Squadron at Manston was the first operational Royal Air Force Anson unit. From 1936 until the start of World War II, Ansons served in front-line squadrons of RAF Coastal Command on general reconnaissance and search-and-rescue duties. By the outbreak of war in September 1939, the RAF had 760 Mk Is equipping 10 Coastal and 16 Bomber Command squadrons, where they served as an interim aircraft until other types, such as the Armstrong Whitworth Whitley, Lockheed Hudson and Handley Page Hampden, were available.

The Anson was right in the front line of Britain's defences at the time. On September 5, 1939, an Anson of No.500 Squadron made the first attack of the war on an enemy U-boat. In June 1940, three Ansons, attacked over the Channel by nine Luftwaffe Messerschmitt Bf109s, succeeded in shooting down two and damaging one of the German fighters. Having earned its spurs, the Anson, or "Faithful Annie" as it was nicknamed in RAF service, soon settled down to the more sedate career of a trainer and light transport aircraft, although some remained with Coastal Command in the air-sea rescue role during the war years. The Commonwealth Air Training Plan of 1939 saw almost all British and Commonwealth navigators, air gunners and wireless operators trained on Ansons. Purpose-built Anson trainers had dual controls and trailing edge flaps as well as a hydraulically operated undercarriage.

By the time production ceased in 1952, Avro had made over 8000 Ansons in Britain and a further 2882 in Canada. This was one of the longest production runs of any British aircraft. In addition to the RAF, the type had been operated by 12 other air forces around the world, including those of Australia, Belgium, Estonia, Finland, Egypt and the USA.

After the war, later versions of the Anson were largely used for transport purposes, and in March 1956 the Avro Anson completed 20 years' service with the RAF, rivalling the long service of its company predecessor, the Avro 504 biplane. The official retirement of the Anson from RAF service was on June 28, 1968, when the last six Ansons on the Southern Communications Squadron were withdrawn, setting a record at the time of 32 years in RAF service.

Avro Anson Mk I

First flight: March 24, 1935
Power: Two Armstrong Siddeley 335hp Cheetah IX radials
Armament: One fixed forward-firing 7.7mm/0.303in Lewis machine-gun, plus another in dorsal turret; 163kg/360lb bomb load
Size: Wingspan – 17.22m/56ft 6in
　　　Length – 12.87m/42ft 3in
　　　Height – 3.99m/13ft 1in
　　　Wing area – 43.01m²/463sq ft
Weights: Empty – 2440kg/5375lb
　　　Maximum take-off – 3632kg/8000lb
Performance: Maximum speed – 302kph/188mph
　　　Ceiling – 5790m/19,000ft
　　　Range – 1062km/660 miles
　　　Climb – 293m/960ft per minute

Avro Manchester

The twin-engine prototype Manchester, the Avro 679, was flown from Ringway (now Manchester International Airport) with Avro chief test-pilot Sam Brown at the controls for the first time on July 25, 1939. The aircraft had been designed by Avro chief designer Roy Chadwick to Air Ministry Specification P.13/36, which called for a twin-engine bomber powered by the new Rolls-Royce Vulture engine. Handley Page had also entered the competition for this Air Ministry contract with its H.P.56 project, but owing to the slow development of the Vulture engine, the company decided to change its design to a four-engine aircraft using the Rolls-Royce Merlin V-12 engine. Their project was to become the very successful Halifax.

Even though the Vulture development programme had been constantly delayed by numerous problems, Chadwick still kept faith with the troublesome new engine. In January 1940 the Air Ministry placed an order for 1200 Manchester Mk 1s, and the aircraft entered service

with 5 Group Bomber Command in November 1940 as a replacement for the ageing Handley Page Hampden bomber.

The Manchester had an excellent airframe and should have been a good aircraft for Bomber Command, providing an increased bomb load capacity on existing bomber types, greater range and more defensive armament. Unfortunately, the Rolls-Royce Vulture engine was still very unreliable and also downrated on power from the original specification. As a result, the Manchester suffered a loss rate of 5.8 per cent on operational sorties, and many experienced bomber crews were also killed on training flights. This situation resulted in the Rolls-Royce Vulture engine development project being cancelled, and only 209 aircraft were delivered to the RAF bomber squadrons. Of these, 64 were lost on operations and a further 12 on training flights. The Manchester was withdrawn from service, and the last Bomber Command Manchester mission was a raid on Bremen on the night of June 25–6, 1942.

TOP: **The Manchester, a sound design, was plagued by engine problems, but the type was to metamorphose into one of the greatest bombers ever, the Lancaster.**
ABOVE: **The Manchester entered RAF service only 16 months after its maiden flight, such was the urgency to get bomber aircraft to combat units.**

Avro Manchester Mk 1

First flight: July 25, 1939
Power: Two Rolls-Royce 1760hp Vulture 24-cylinder piston engines
Armament: Eight 7.7mm/0.303in Browning machine-guns in power turrets in nose (2), mid-upper (2) and tail (4); internal bomb bay accommodating a maximum load of 4699kg/ 10,350lb
Size: Wingspan – 27.46m/90ft 1in
Length – 21.34m/70ft
Height – 5.94m/19ft 6in
Wing area – 105.63m²/1137sq ft
Weights: Empty – 13,362kg/29,432lb
Maximum take-off – 25,424kg/56,000lb
Performance: Maximum speed – 426kph/265mph
Ceiling – 5795m/19,000ft
Range – 2623km/1630 miles
Climb – Not available

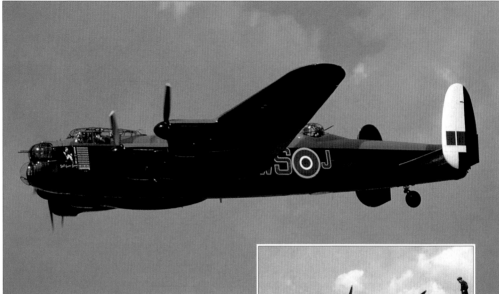

Avro Lancaster

The Avro Lancaster became Great Britain's most famous four-engine bomber during World War II. It was developed from the ill-fated Manchester that suffered from unreliable Rolls-Royce Vulture engines. Even while the Manchester was being produced, the Avro design team, led by Chief Designer Roy Chadwick, investigated a possible four-engine replacement. The proposed four-engine Manchester Mk III, powered by Rolls Royce Merlin XX engines, was discussed with the Air Ministry on February 20, 1940. At first the proposal created little interest because most of the Merlin engine production was needed for Hurricane and Spitfire fighter aircraft. However in July 1940 the Air Ministry requested Avro to go ahead with their project and use as many Manchester components as possible in the new design.

Manchester airframe BT308 was designated project No.683 and fitted with four Rolls-Royce Merlin X engines on extended wings. This prototype model first flew on January 9, 1941 with the Manchester's triple tail fins but without ventral and dorsal turrets.

While the early handling trials were successful, a change in the tail configuration was recommended, and the original type of vertical tail surfaces were replaced by larger endplate surfaces on a wider-span tail-plane with the large central fin deleted. Exhaustive flying tests followed, and the now renamed Lancaster soon revealed its potential with excellent performances. The first production model prototype DG595 flew on May 13, 1941, and was later flown to Boscombe Down for service trials.

TOP: **The Lancaster first flew in combat on March 3, 1942, and was in the front line until the end of World War II. The Lancaster pictured is preserved in the UK by the RAF's Battle of Britain Memorial Flight.**
ABOVE: **This Mk I built by Metropolitan Vickers is being bombed-up prior to a mission.**

On June 6, 1941, Avro received a contract for 454 Lancaster Mk Is powered by four Merlin XX engines, plus two prototype Lancaster Mk IIs fitted with four Bristol Hercules VI engines.

On Christmas Eve, 1941, No.44 (Rhodesia) Squadron based at RAF Waddington in Lincolnshire received the first three production Lancaster Mk Is. The first operation with the Lancaster was carried out on March 3, 1942, when four aircraft of No.44 Squadron were detailed to lay mines in the Heligoland Bight. The Lancasters took off from Waddington at 18:15 hours and all returned safely five hours later.

The early-production Lancasters had a maximum gross take-off weight of 28,602kg/63,000lb and carried a variable bomb load up to a maximum of 6356kg/14,000lb. The bomb load mix depended upon the type of target to be attacked. For example, the bomb load for the demolition of industrial sites by blast and fire was codenamed "Cookie Plumduff" and this consisted of 1 x 1816kg/4000lb, 3 x 454kg/1000lb, plus up to six small bomb carriers loaded with 1.8kg/4lb or 13.62kg/30lb incendiaries. Later, heavier bomb loads would be carried, such as the 3632kg/8000lb Cookie, the 5448kg/12,000lb Tallboy and finally the 9988kg/22,000lb Grand Slam. The defensive armament consisted of a two-gun power turret fitted in the nose and mid-upper position plus a four-gun turret in the tail.

In February 1942 Air Chief Marshal Sir Arthur Harris became head of Bomber Command and prioritized the production of four-engine aircraft for his bomber force. Manufacturing capacity was increased by Avro but Rolls-Royce became concerned that they would not be able to satisfy the ever-increasing demand for the Merlin engines. This situation had been foreseen, and one alternative was to use a different engine – the Lancaster Mk II using the Bristol Hercules was already in the pipeline with an order for 300 placed with Armstrong Whitworth. The second solution was for the Packard Motor Corporation to manufacture the Merlin engine in the USA.

The first Lancaster Mk III powered by the Packard Merlin 28s came off the Avro production lines in August 1942. Although the Packard Merlin-powered Lancaster had almost identical performance to the Mk I, it was given the new designation because of different servicing requirements. The Packard Corporation also shipped Merlins over the Canadian border where the Victory Aircraft Company built 430 Lancaster Mk X aircraft.

With the deployment of the Mk III, a total of 7377 Lancasters were built between October 1941 and October 1945, equipping 57 RAF Bomber Command Squadrons by the end of World War II.

ABOVE: **The Lancaster was the only RAF aircraft able to carry Bomber Command's specialist ordnance such as Tallboy and Grand Slam bombs, as well as the famous "bouncing bomb".** BELOW: **The very large bomb bay of the Lancaster (the bomb bay doors are open in this photograph) enabled it to carry up to 6356kg/14,000lb of bombs. RAF Lancasters were not phased out until December 1953.**

ABOVE: **Post-war, the Lancaster was supplied to the French Navy who used the aircraft for maritime reconnaissance, as did the Royal Canadian Air Force who converted a number of Canadian-built "Lancs" for the same purpose.**

Avro Lancaster Mk I

First flight: January 9, 1941
Power: Four Rolls Royce or Packard 1460hp Merlin XX, 20 or 22s
Armament: Nose and dorsal turrets with two 7.7mm/0.303in Brownings, tail turret with four 7.7mm/0.303in Brownings; normal bomb load 6356kg/14,000lb or 9988kg/22,000lb single bomb with modifications to bomb bay
Size: Wingspan – 31.1m/102ft
Length – 21.1m/69ft 4in
Height – 5.97m/19ft 7in
Wing area – 120.45m²/1297sq ft
Weights: Empty – 16,344kg/36,000lb
Maximum take-off – 30,872kg/68,000lb
Performance: Maximum speed – 443kph/275mph at 4572m/15,000ft
Cruising speed – 322kph/200mph at 4572m/15,000ft
Service ceiling – 6706m/22,000ft
Range – 4072km/2530 miles
Climb – 6096m/20,000ft in 41 minutes, 36 seconds

Boeing B-17 Flying Fortress

In 1934 the United States Army issued a specification for a long-range, high-altitude daylight bomber for its Air Corps. The Boeing Aircraft Company responded with a prototype designated Model 299, powered by four 750hp Pratt & Whitney Hornet engines, which flew for the first time on July 28, 1935. Even though the prototype was destroyed in an accident, the project went ahead, and 13 Y1B-17s and one Y1B-17A were ordered for evaluation. After extensive trials these were designated B-17 and B-17A respectively. By the end of March 1940, the first production batch of 39 B-17Bs was delivered to the Army Air Corps, sporting a modified nose and enlarged rudder. Meanwhile, owing to the expansion of the Air Corps, a further order for 38 B-17Cs was placed. These aircraft were powered by four Wright 1200hp Cyclone engines and also featured other minor internal changes. In 1941, 20 of the B-17Cs were transferred to the RAF in England and designated Fortress Is for evaluation under combat conditions against the new generation of fast German day fighters. While the sleek four-engine all-metal Flying Fortress monoplane was unquestionably the most advanced heavy bomber in 1935, it failed with the RAF under high-altitude daylight bombing conditions by sustaining several losses, not only through enemy action but also because of mechanical and system failure.

Unfortunately for Boeing, by 1941 the B-17 had become outclassed in many respects by the new generation of medium and heavy bombers of Britain and Germany and, more importantly, that of another US aircraft company, Consolidated, whose four-engine B-24 Liberator had greater range, could carry a heavier bomb load and had better defensive armament. To retrieve the design from the verge of obsolescence, Boeing

ABOVE: **A fine air-to-air study of two B-17s preserved in flying condition in the USA. The B-17 first saw action in Europe with the Royal Air Force, who tested early models operationally. The trial was not successful because the once-advanced B-17 design had been overtaken by fighter developments.**

designed a new rear end for the aircraft. The fuselage was lengthened by 1.8m/6ft and deepened towards the rear to incorporate a tail gun position with two machine-guns projecting from the end of the fuselage. These were traversed manually and were aimed with a remote sight from the rear gunner's glazed cabin. A Sperry two-gun power turret sited in the upper fuselage aft of the pilot's cabin gave a field of fire from the horizontal plane to an all-round 75-degree elevation.

Also replacing the original under-gun emplacement just aft of the wing root came a semi-retractable rotating ball turret housing two machine-guns. In addition to the new defensive gun positions, both the hand-held guns firing through the waist openings were retained, plus the one in the radio operator's cabin. The nose armament, a single rifle-calibre machine-gun, remained unchanged, whereas all other weapons were of the larger 12.7mm/0.5in calibre, with greater range and hitting power. With this new ten-gun defensive system, the B-17E truly was a Flying Fortress.

The B-17E, with a crew of ten, was the first Flying Fortress type to see combat in the European Theatre of Operations with the US Army Air Corps. However, one defensive weakness still remained, and that was against head-on attack by high-performance German fighters armed with 20mm/0.78in cannon. A total of 512 B-17Es were built, and after further refinements the F-series entered production in April 1942.

RIGHT: **These preserved Flying Fortresses fly in formation reminiscent of the defensive boxes in which Eighth Air Force B-17s flew for their mutual protection during dangerous daylight missions.**

RIGHT: **These preserved Flying Fortresses fly in formation reminiscent of the defensive boxes in which Eighth Air Force B-17s flew for their mutual protection during dangerous daylight missions.**

Over the next 18 months, 3400 B-17Fs were produced, including 61 long-range reconnaissance aircraft designated F-9s, plus another 19 delivered to RAF Coastal Command as the Fortress II.

The last production run of 86 B-17Fs were fitted with a chin-mounted power-operated Bendix turret, housing a pair of 12.7mm/0.5in machine-guns, which provided the extra fire power to help stave off the Luftwaffe frontal fighter attacks. The Bendix chin turret became a standard production item, and the type was designated B-17G. This variant started to enter service with the US Bombardment Groups in the autumn of 1943 and became the main production type, with 8680 aircraft built by the end of hostilities in Europe. Another 85 B-17Gs served with RAF Coastal Command as Fortress IIIs.

During World War II USAAF B17 Flying Fortresses flew 294,875 sorties to targets all over Europe, dropping 650,240 tonnes/640,000 tons of bombs at a cost of 4483 aircraft missing in action, plus other operational losses of 861.

RIGHT: **The B-17G model introduced the Bendix chin turret mounting two 12.7mm/0.5in machine-guns for defence against head-on attacks.**
BELOW: **Immortalized by the wartime propaganda film "Memphis Belle", many of the world's surviving B-17s – including the aircraft pictured here – came together for the filming of the 1990 blockbuster of the same name.**

Boeing B-17G Flying Fortress

First flight: July 28, 1935
Power: Four Wright 1200hp Cyclone R-1820-97 radial piston engines
Armament: Twin 12.7mm/0.5in machine-guns under nose, aft of cockpit, under centre fuselage and in tail, and single-gun mountings in side of nose, in radio operator's hatch and two waist positions; maximum bomb load 7990kg/ 17,600lb
Size: Wingspan – 31.62m/103ft 9in
  Length – 22.78m/74ft 9in
  Height – 5.82m/19ft 1in
  Wing area – 131.92m²/1420sq ft
Weights: Empty – 13,488kg/29,710lb
  Maximum take-off – 29,737kg/65,500lb
Performance: Maximum speed – 462kph/287mph
  Ceiling – 10,920m/35,800ft
  Range – 3220km/2000 miles
  Climb – 427m/1400ft per minute

Boeing B-29 Superfortress

The B-29 Superfortress, the most advanced bomber produced during World War II, was the result of Boeing's reaction to specification XC-218, which called for a bomber with a range in excess of 8045km/5000 miles that could carry a bigger bomb load at a higher speed than the B-17B. Fortunately for Boeing, design work had been carried out on their next generation of heavy bombers over the preceding two years, and a full-scale mock-up of model 341 had been produced. This was remarkably close to specification XC-218, and so with a small amount of re-work, Boeing were able to submit their design. Three prototypes were ordered, and the first XB-29 flew on September 21, 1942. Meanwhile, a priority order for 1500 aircraft had been placed with Boeing following the Japanese attack on Pearl Harbor. The first YB-29 evaluation aircraft was delivered to the 58th Bombardment Wing in July 1943 and was followed three months later by the first batch of B-29-BW production aircraft. The Superfortress had many advanced features, including remotely controlled gun turrets and a partly pressurized fuselage.

RIGHT: **The B-29 was not used in Europe during World War II, instead being limited to the Pacific theatre.** BELOW: **The B-29 was a major technological leap forward for the USAAF, bringing huge increases in performance with it.**

At the end of 1943 the decision was made to use only the B-29 against the Japanese in the Pacific theatre. In the spring of 1944 the two fully equipped bombardment wings were deployed to bases in India and south-west China. The first bombing mission was flown on June 5 against Japanese targets in Thailand, and was followed a few days later by raids against the Japanese mainland. With the establishment of five air bases on the Mariana Islands in March 1944, the B-29 bombardment wings were able to mount a sustained bombing campaign against mainland Japan. It was from one of these bases in August 1945 that B-29 *Enola Gay* dropped the first atomic bomb on the city of Hiroshima, followed three days later by B-29 *Bockscar* dropping a second on Nagasaki. The Boeing bomber played a vital role in the defeat of Japan, who surrendered on August 14, five days after the Nagasaki raid.

Boeing B-29 Superfortress

First flight: September 21, 1942

Power: Four Wright 2200hp R-3350-57 radial engines

Armament: Four-gun turret over nose, two-gun turrets under nose, over and under rear fuselage, all with machine-guns of 12.7mm/ 0.5in calibre, plus one 20mm/0.78in and two 12.7mm/0.5in guns in tail; up to 9080kg/ 20,000lb bomb load

Size: Wingspan – 43.05m/141ft 3in
Length – 30.18m/99ft
Height – 9.01m/29ft 7in
Wing area – 161.27m²/1736sq ft

Weights: Empty – 31,843kg/70,140lb
Maximum take-off – 56,296kg/124,000lb

Performance: Maximum speed – 576kph/358mph
Ceiling – 9695m/31,800ft
Range – 5229km/3250 miles
Climb – 7625m/25,000ft in 43 minutes

ABOVE: **The B-29's performance and large bomb load made it the only choice for the delivery of the atomic bombs to Japan.** RIGHT: **The B-29 was used extensively during the Korean War, initially in support of ground troops but then more appropriately as a strategic bomber. Back in the USA, the Superfortress was the main aircraft of the fledgling Strategic Air Command.** BELOW: **The Soviet copy of the B-29, the Tu-4, influenced Soviet bomber design for years after they "acquired" it at the end of World War II.**

The B-29 may be famous or infamous for the atomic bomb raids, but the many conventional, largely incendiary, bombing raids carried out by the Superfortresses against Japan ultimately destroyed the centres of a number of large Japanese cities.

After the war, the B-29 became the mainstay of the newly formed USAF Strategic Air Command, and later saw continuous action during the three-year Korean War. Initially used in a tactical bomber role to halt the North Korean ground advance, the USAF B-29s were soon deployed in the role for which they were made – strategic bombing. Operating from bases in Japan, raids were carried out against industrial targets in North Korea.

The basic B-29 design underwent a number of modifications over the years. These variants included the SB-29 for air-sea rescue, the TB-29 trainer and the WB-29

tanker. The Royal Air Force operated the aircraft as the Washington, with 88 ex-USAF examples in service from 1950. Most were returned to the USA in 1954, but some remained in Bomber Command service until 1958.

The Soviet Union managed to produce a copy of the B-29, which was named the Tu-4 in Soviet service. These unlicensed copies were based on US aircraft which fell into Soviet hands at the end of World War II. In a programme unparalleled in ingenuity and audacity, the Soviet Union ultimately produced over 300 of their version. The Soviet Union's post-war atomic bomber fleet was therefore directly related to the three US B-29s which had originally made emergency landings on Soviet territory following bombing missions over Japan. America had given the Soviet Union the aircraft that could have been turned on the USA.

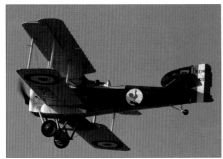

LEFT: **The Bre.14 replaced older types in front-line service from mid-1917. The type often attacked deep behind enemy lines.**

Breguet Bre.14

Breguet Bre.14

First flight: November 21, 1916
Power: One Renault 300hp 12F in-line engine
Armament: One fixed forward-firing 7.7mm/
0.303in machine-gun, twin 7.7mm/0.303in Lewis
machine-guns on mounting in rear cockpit;
underwing racks for up to 40kg/88lb bomb load
Size: Wingspan – 14.36m/47ft 1in
Length – 8.87m/29ft 1in
Height – 3.3m/10ft 10in
Wing area – 47.5m²/511.3sq ft
Weights: Empty – 1030kg/2271lb
Maximum take-off – 1565kg/3450lb
Performance: Maximum speed – 184kph/114mph
Ceiling – 6000m/18,290ft
Range – 700km/435 miles
Climb – 5000m/16,400ft in 39 minutes

The prototype of this highly advanced two-seat light-bomber biplane made its first flight in November 1916, only six months after Breguet's chief engineer Louis Vuillierme began the design. The pilot was Louis Breguet, such was the significance and advanced nature of the aircraft. It was revolutionary for a French combat aircraft, having its engine and propeller at the front and, perhaps most impressively, it was made principally of lightweight Duralumin.

The Bre.14 A.2 production aircraft entered service with the Aeronautique Militaire in the spring of 1917 on the Western Front, and soon established a reputation among French aircrew for being robust and reliable. The principal bomber version used by France's strategic bomber force during World War I was the Bre.14 B.2.

By the end of World War I, orders for nearly 5500 Bre.14s had been placed with the Breguet aircraft manufacturing

company. The aircraft had been so successful after its introduction during the war that by the time the production line closed down in 1926, the total number of aircraft manufactured had reached 8000.

Post-war, it served in a number of roles such as light transport and air ambulance, and the type also pioneered mail routes in French equatorial Africa.

LEFT: **The Bre.19 was well used by Spain in the 1920s and early '30s.**

Breguet Bre.19 A.2

First flight: May 1922
Power: One Lorraine 450hp 12Ed in-line piston
engine
Armament: One fixed forward-firing 7.7mm/
0.303in machine-gun and two more in rear
cockpit; 700kg/1543lb bomb load under wings
Size: Wingspan – 14.83m/48ft 7.75in
Length – 9.61m/31ft 6.25in
Height – 3.69m/12ft 1.25in
Wing area – 50m²/538.31sq ft
Weights: Empty – 1387kg/3058lb
Maximum take-off – 2500kg/5511lb
Performance: Maximum speed – 214kph/133mph
Ceiling – 7200m/23,620ft
Range – 800km/497 miles
Climb – 5000m/16,405ft in 29 minutes,
50 seconds

Breguet Bre.19

This aircraft, which had substantial amounts of aluminium alloy in its structure at an early stage in aircraft design, was built as a reconnaissance/bomber successor to Breguet's Bre.14 of World War I. It flew for the first time in March 1922 and, as a measure of progress, weighed the same as its Breguet predecessor but could carry a payload that was up to 80 per cent greater.

The Breguet company were excellent publicists and had the Bre.19 set countless world records to prove what an effective combat aircraft it was. As a result, in addition to use by the French, the aircraft was widely exported and was operated by nine other air forces. Licence-built versions were produced in Turkey, Belgium, Yugoslavia, Greece, Japan and Spain. Both sides of the

Spanish Civil War used the Bre.19 and the Chinese used the type against the Japanese in Manchuria. Greek Bre.19s were used against invading Italians in October 1940.

Breguet 691/693

The Breguet 690 series of military aircraft stemmed from a 1934 specification for a three-seat heavy fighter, which led to the Bre.690. The prototype twin-engine fighter's performance so impressed that, with war clouds gathering, the Bre.691 light attack variant (with Hispano-Suiza engines), which first flew in 1937, was swiftly put into production. This differed from the fighter version in having a bomb bay in which to carry 400kg/880lb of bombs. One hundred examples of the light bomber were ordered, but before they were all built, a new and improved version, the 693 powered by Gnome-Rhone engines, had appeared. The Bre.695 had American Pratt & Whitney Twin Wasp Junior engines. By the Fall of France, almost three hundred examples of all marks had made it to front-line units. Two French Air Force Groups GBA I/54 and II/54 were first to become fully equipped with the Bre.693. The type made its operational debut on May 12, 1940, attacking advancing German troop columns. Ten of the eleven 693s sent on the mission were destroyed. The crews battled on in spite of the overwhelming and more capable opposition, but

suffered heavy losses against the superior German single-engine fighters. By June 24, 1940, almost half of the Bre.693s in service were lost in the course of over 500 sorties in defence of their country.

The Vichy air force took over the remaining machines, and many of these were in turn seized by the Luftwaffe, who stripped the engines out to power some of their own aircraft. A number were passed on to Italy, who used the aircraft for operational training from 1942–3.

ABOVE, LEFT AND BELOW: **The Bre.690 fighter from which the bomber variants were developed. The ground-attack version had different engines and a bomb bay. Breguet pilots fought bravely against invading German forces, but were swiftly overwhelmed.**

Breguet Bre.693 AB2

First flight: October 25, 1939

Power: Two 700hp Gnome-Rhone 14M Mars 14-cylinder radial engines

Armament: One 20mm/0.78in cannon and two 7.5mm/0.29in fixed forward-firing machine-guns, three 7.5mm/0.29in machine-guns fixed and obliquely rearward firing, plus one trainable; internal bomb load of 400kg/880lb

Size: Wingspan – 15.36m/50ft 5in
Length – 9.67m/31ft 8in
Height – 3.19m/10ft 5in
Wing area – 28.8m²/310sq ft

Weights: Empty – 3010kg/6625lb
Maximum take-off – 5500kg/12,105lb

Performance: Maximum speed – 475kph/295mph
Service ceiling – 8500m/27,885ft
Range – 1350km/839 miles
Climb – 4000m/13,120ft in 7 minutes, 12 seconds

Bristol Blenheim

When the Bristol Blenheim bomber entered RAF service in 1937, it represented a huge leap forward for the service – the Mk I Blenheim was considerably faster than the 290kph/180mph Hind biplane it replaced and could outrun most contemporary fighters, many of which were biplanes. Initially developed as the Type 142, a fast eight-seat passenger plane, the aircraft that became the three-seat Bristol Blenheim bomber flew for the first time in April 1935. Britain First was the name given to the Type 142, which had been ordered by newspaper tycoon Lord Rothermere, who wanted a fast executive transport.

In August 1935 the Air Ministry issued Specification B28/35 covering the conversion of the aircraft to the bomber role, and this was designated Type 142M.

Major modifications followed, including raising the wing from a low to a mid-wing position to allow room for the internal bomb bay. The nose section was also redesigned to accommodate both pilot and observer/bomb-aimer. The third member of the crew was a mid-upper gunner, who was housed in a power-operated dorsal turret with a 7.7mm/0.303in Lewis machine-gun. The pilot could also fire a Browning 7.7mm/0.303in, which was installed in the port wing leading edge.

The Air Ministry placed an initial order for 150 Blenheim Mk Is in September 1935. This was followed with a second order in December 1936 for another 434 aircraft, after a series of successful trials. In March of the following year,

TOP: **Considered to be something of a forgotten bomber, the Blenheim gave the Royal Air Force a bomber aircraft with a performance that was superior to many fighters of the time.** ABOVE: **Over 1000 Blenheims were in service when war broke out, and it was a No.139 Squadron Blenheim that was first to fly over Germany on September 3, 1939.**

Wyton-based No.114 (Hong Kong) Squadron of 2 Group Bomber Command became the first RAF squadron to be equipped with the Blenheim Mk I. A total of 1134 Mk Is were built, with 1007 being on RAF charge by August 1939. This hot-rod bomber brought much interest from overseas customers, and export versions were supplied to Greece, Finland, Turkey, Romania, Lithuania and Yugoslavia.

By the start of World War II, the Mark I had been largely replaced by the Mark IV in UK-based RAF bomber units. The Blenheim Mk IV was basically a Mk I airframe with two Bristol Mercury XV radial engines fitted with de Havilland three-blade variable-pitch propellers. It also had a redesigned and enlarged nose and extra internal fuel tanks.

At the outbreak of war in September 1939, Royal Air Force bomber squadrons had 197 Blenheim Mk IVs on strength. On September 3, a Blenheim IV of Wyton-based No.139 Squadron became the first RAF aircraft of World War II to cross the German border, while flying a reconnaissance mission. On the next day, Blenheims of Nos.107 and 110 Squadrons took part in the RAF's first offensive operation of the war, when they unsuccessfully attacked German naval units in the Elbe Estuary. While at least three bombs struck the pocket Battleship *Admiral Scheer*, they failed to explode. No.107 Squadron lost four of its five aircraft on the raid, and these were Bomber Command's first casualties of World War II.

The defensive shortcomings of the Blenheim soon became apparent when the type suffered heavy losses while taking part in anti-shipping operations in the North Sea. The armament was subsequently increased to five machine-guns. In all, 1930 Mk IVs were built in the UK. Most of No.2 Group Blenheims were replaced in 1941 by the Douglas Boston and the de Havilland Mosquito.

The final British-built version of the Blenheim was the Mk V. Over 940 were built, the majority being the VD tropical variant. These were shipped out to North Africa to support the Eighth Army in the Western Desert but again, the Blenheims suffered appalling combat losses against the Messerschmitt Bf109s and were soon replaced by US-supplied Baltimores and Venturas.

In Canada, the Fairchild Aircraft Company built 676 Blenheims for the Royal Canadian Air Force, and these versions were designated the Bolingbroke Mk I to Mk IV. Finland operated the Blenheim until 1956.

RIGHT: **Blenheim IVs manned by Free French crews saw considerable action in North Africa.** BELOW: **The Blenheim was a versatile aircraft that achieved combat success in the day- and nightfighter as well as the bomber role. The aircraft pictured here is a Mark I nightfighter from RAF Squadron No.141.**

ABOVE: **This No.110 Squadron Blenheim IV sustained damage in air combat, and had to be patched before its next mission.**

Blenheim Mk I

First flight: June 25, 1936
Power: Two Bristol 920hp Mercury XV radial engines
Armament: One 7.7mm/0.303in Browning machine-gun in leading edge of port wing, one 7.7mm/0.303in Vickers machine-gun in dorsal turret; maximum internal bomb load of 454kg/1000lb
Size: Wingspan – 17.7m/58ft 1in
Length – 12.11m/39ft 9in
Height – 3m/9ft 10in
Wing area – 43.57m²/469sq ft
Weights: Empty – 3677kg/8100lb
Maximum take-off – 5675kg/12,500lb
Performance: Maximum speed – 428kph/266mph
Service ceiling – 8320m/27,280ft
Range – 1810km/1125 miles
Climb – 469m/1540ft per minute

Bristol Beaufighter

The Beaufighter came about when the Bristol company simply proposed a versatile, heavily armed aircraft that they thought the Royal Air Force needed. Using major elements of the Beaufort torpedo bomber already in production, the two-seat Beaufighter was produced quickly and joined front-line squadrons at the height of the Battle of Britain in 1940, only 13 months after the prototype first flew. Day fighter versions saw action in the Western Desert and Malta, while RAF Coastal Command also used the "Beau" to great effect, particularly over the Bay of Biscay against Junkers Ju 88s.

The development of combat aircraft relies entirely on the engines available to power the aeroplanes, and it was the improvements to the Bristol Hercules that led to the Beaufighter's development in a host of different roles. More power allowed designers to add more weight to the aircraft in the form of new weaponry, equipment, armour or fuel.

There were two significant Beaufighter developments in 1942 – a trial torpedo installation succeeded, and the type was experimentally and successfully armed with rocket projectiles.

By late 1942, Mk VICs were being completed with torpedo-carrying gear. The Beaufighter was now able to carry and launch a large torpedo (the British 45.7cm/18in or the US 57.2cm/22.5in) against shipping, and the first "Torbeau" unit

TOP: **The Beaufighter T.F. Mk X was a purpose-designed torpedo-carrying version that saw considerable RAF Coastal Command service.**
ABOVE: **T.F. Xs of No.404 Squadron RCAF, which formed part of the Banff Strike Wing in Scotland, carrying out sweeps against enemy shipping in the North Sea.**

was No.254 Squadron based at North Coates. Equipped with Mk VIC torpedo-fighters, the squadron first attacked enemy shipping with the new weapon on April 18, 1943. The Beaufort was soon phased out in favour of the new-found British torpedo-bomber.

The VIC was gradually replaced in Coastal Command service by a new purpose-designed torpedo-bomber version, the Beaufighter T.F. Mk X. This dedicated torpedo-bomber, powered by 1770hp Hercules XVII engines, was probably the best British anti-shipping aircraft in service in the later stages of World War II. The Hercules Mk XVII was developed to optimize the Beaufighter for low-level missions, and achieved peak power at just 152m/500ft. Dive brakes were also soon introduced as an aid in low-level attacks. The Mk X was the main production variant of the Beaufighter, with over 2200 produced. Normally flying with a crew of two, a third crew member could be carried to assist with torpedo-aiming. Using special equipment including a radio altimeter, the Beaufighter could make precision low-level, wave-top height attacks with torpedoes or rockets. Mk Xs ultimately carried the A.I. Mk VIII radar, adapted for use against surface targets, housed in the tell-tale "thimble-nose" radome. The Beaufighter X was an extremely effective anti-shipping aircraft, scouring the waters around Britain for German shipping. In March 1945, aircraft of Nos.236 and 254 Squadrons sank five German U-boats in just two days.

Beaufighters were also heavily used by Australian units on anti-shipping missions. Australia produced their own Beaufighter Xs, some 364 in total, which were known as T.F. Mk 21s. Powered by the Hercules XVIII, the T.F.21s entered service in 1944 and played a key role in the Royal Australian Air Force's support for the Allied advance into the East Indies. These Beaufighters' high-speed, low-level attacks caused the Japanese to nickname them "Whispering Death".

Post-war, a number of Beaufighters remained in RAF service, mainly in the Far East where they retired from front-line duties in 1950. Thirty-five RAF Beaufighters were converted for use as target tugs. Designated T.T.10, these aircraft served in the UK, Middle East and Far East until 1960.

ABOVE RIGHT: **The Beaufighter was originally conceived as a multi-role aircraft, and fighter versions, like the IIF pictured, appeared during the Battle of Britain.**
RIGHT AND BELOW: **When the Beaufighter was equipped for carrying a torpedo later in the war, it became the best British anti-shipping aircraft of the time. Note the four cannon on the underside of the nose.**

Bristol Beaufighter T.F. Mk X

First flight: July 17, 1939
Power: Two Bristol 1770hp Hercules XVII 14-cylinder air-cooled radials
Armament: Four 20mm/0.78in cannon, six 7.7mm/ 0.303in machine-guns, one 7.7mm /0.303in machine-gun in dorsal position; one 726kg/ 1600lb or 965kg/2127lb torpedo, two 227kg/ 500lb bombs, eight 76.2mm/3in rocket projectiles
Size: Wingspan – 17.63m/57ft 10in
 Length – 12.7m/41ft 8in
 Height – 4.82m/15ft 10in
 Wing area – 46.73m²/503sq ft
Weights: Empty – 7082kg/15,600lb
 Maximum take-off – 11,440kg/25,200lb
Performance: Maximum speed – 512kph/318mph
 Service ceiling – 4572m/15,000ft
 Range – 2366km/1470 miles
 Climb – 1524m/5000ft in 3 minutes, 30 seconds

LEFT: **A Beaufort I of No.217 Squadron RAF. With its raised "upper deck", the type is one of the easiest to identify.**

Bristol Beaufort

Bristol Beaufort I

First flight: October 15, 1938
Power: Two Bristol 1113hp Taurus VI 14-cylinder radial engines
Armament: Two 7.7mm/0.303in Vickers K guns in dorsal turret and one in port wing, plus one rearward-firing 7.7mm/0.303in Browning machine-gun under nose; up to 454kg/1000lb of bombs internally and 227kg/500lb externally, or one 728kg/1605lb torpedo semi-recessed
Size: Wingspan – 17.62m/57ft 10in
Length – 13.59m/44ft 7in
Height – 3.79m/12ft 5in
Wing area – 46.73m²/503sq ft
Weights: Empty – 5950kg/13,107lb
Maximum take-off – 9637kg/21,228lb
Performance: Maximum speed – 426kph/265mph
Ceiling – 5032m/16,500ft
Range – 2575km/1600 miles
Climb – 564m/1850ft per minute

Derived from the Bristol Blenheim, the Beaufort was the Royal Air Force's standard torpedo bomber from 1940–3. The Bristol Aeroplane Company started design work in 1935, and the twin Mercury engine prototype made its first flight in October 1938. However, because the Air Staff insisted on a four-man crew which increased the all-up weight, the aircraft's performance proved to be inadequate. After studying a number of engine options, it was decided to use the 1130hp Bristol Taurus engine. Extensive trials followed,

and the Beaufort Mk I went into service with RAF Coastal Command in 1939. Nos.22 and 42 Squadrons became fully operational with the Mk I Beaufort in August 1940, carrying out mine-laying and attacks against shipping off the French and Dutch coast. On April 6, 1941, both these squadrons attacked and seriously damaged the German battlecruiser *Gneisenau* in Brest Harbour. For his actions during the raid, Flying Officer Kenneth Campbell of No.22 Squadron was posthumously awarded the VC.

In 1939, plans were made to manufacture the Beaufort in Australia to serve with the RAAF in the south-west Pacific. However, because of the difficulty of supplying the Taurus engine from Britain, locally made Pratt & Whitney Twin Wasp engines were fitted.

A total of 2080 Beauforts were built, including the 700 made in Australia.

LEFT: **This Mark B.1 Brigand was converted to T.4 standard for training.**

Bristol Brigand B.1

First flight: December 4, 1944
Power: Two Bristol 2810hp Centaurus 57 radial engines
Armament: Four 20mm/0.78in cannon; up to 907kg/2000lb of bombs, rockets or a torpedo
Size: Wingspan – 21.9m/71ft 10in
Length – 14.15m/46ft 5in
Height – 5.33m/17ft 6in
Wing area – 66.7m²/718sq ft
Weights: Empty – 11,622kg/25,600lb
Maximum take-off – 17,706kg/39,000lb
Performance: Maximum speed – 576kph/358mph
Service ceiling – 7930m/26,000ft
Range – 4506km/2800 miles
Climb – 456m/1500ft per minute

Bristol Brigand

The robust Brigand, unpopular with some crews, was the last twin-piston-engine bomber to serve in the Royal Air Force. Originally designed as a long-range torpedo bomber to replace the Beaufighter, the Brigand had the wings and tail of Bristol's unsuccessful Buckingham bomber just as the Beaufighter had those of the Beaufort. In addition, it retained the Buckingham's twin Centaurus engines.

The aircraft first flew in December 1944, and although some were made as torpedo bombers, the type was mainly built as a light bomber for use in tropical climates to better suit the needs of the post-war RAF.

The Brigand light bomber first entered RAF service in early 1949 in Iraq, but the type is best known for its four years of bombing and rocket firing action against terrorists in Malaya from 1950–4.

However, Brigands were also used against the Mau Mau in Kenya. The RAF took delivery of 143 Brigands, a small number of which served in weather reconnaissance and radar training.

LEFT: **A Ca.133T transport version of the very useful type.**

Caproni Ca.133

The three-engine Caproni Ca.133 was developed from the Ca.101 bomber/ transport series of aircraft. Three engines, relatively low weight and a large wing meant the aircraft could operate from short and primitive airstrips. Over 500 aircraft were built, and the type was first used in action by the Italians in Ethiopia in 1936. During the Spanish Civil War the Nationalists operated ten of the bombers, while the Italians used the type as a paratroop aircraft for their 1939 invasion of Albania.

The Ca.133 was numerically an important aircraft for the Italians when that nation joined World War II in 1940. Fourteen bomber squadrons were equipped by the type, principally protecting Italy's African interests, but if caught by enemy fighters, these aircraft were easy prey. When the aircraft were obsolete as bombers, many served as ambulances as well as transports. The Ca.148 18-passenger transport was developed from the Ca.133, and served the Italian Air Force after the war.

Caproni Ca.133

First flight: 1935
Power: Three Piaggio 460hp Stella P VII C16 radial piston engines
Armament: Four 7.7mm/0.303in machine-guns in dorsal and ventral turrets and waist positions; up to 500kg/1100lb bomb load
Size: Wingspan – 21.24m/68ft 8in
Length – 15.36m/50ft 4.75in
Height – 4m/13ft 1in
Wing area – 65m²/699.65sq ft
Weights: Empty – 4194kg/9240lb
Maximum take-off – 6691kg/14,740lb
Performance: Maximum speed – 265kph/165mph
Service ceiling – 5500m/18,044ft
Range – 1350km/838 miles
Climb – 286m/940ft per minute

This short take-off and landing aircraft was a workhorse. Even though the British RAF fighter squadrons in the Libyan western desert considered the Caproni Ca.133 to be easy prey, the aircraft continued to provide a valuable service to the Italian armed forces as a bomber, troop carrier and ambulance right up to the Italian surrender in 1943.

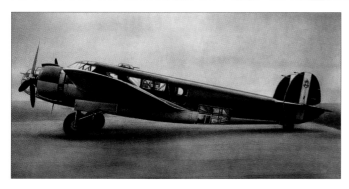

LEFT: **Photographed in November 1930, a Ca.135bis, the version that was exported to Hungary.**

Caproni Ca.135

First flight: April 1, 1935
Power: Two Piaggio 1,000hp P.XI RC40 14-cylinder radial piston engines
Armament: One 12.7mm/0.5in machine-gun in nose and dorsal turret and one in ventral position; bomb load of 1600kg/3527lb carried internally or beneath wings
Size: Wingspan – 18.80m/61ft 8in
Length – 14.40m/47ft 2in
Height – 3.40m/11ft 1in
Wing area – 60m²/645.84sq ft
Weights: Empty – 6106kg/13,450lb
Maximum take-off – 9556kg/21,050lb
Performance: Maximum speed – 440kph/273mph
Service ceiling – 7000m/22,965ft
Range – 2000km/1240 miles
Climb – 4000m/13,120ft in 13 minutes, 20 seconds

Caproni Ca.135

The Caproni Ca.135 was designed to meet a Regia Aeronautica fast medium-bomber specification, and flew in prototype form in 1935. This aircraft was a case of the old meeting the new as it was a monoplane but with wooden wings and a fuselage covered with metal at the front and fabric to the rear.

Ultimately, the type was never bought for the Italian Air Force and was only produced for export. Peru was an early customer and had 32 examples while Hungary purchased 180 Ca.135s for its Air Force in 1937, and used them against the Soviet Union. However, once the aircraft had entered service, it soon

became obvious that the Ca.135 was not a great aircraft, and the type was soon relegated to training and transport duties.

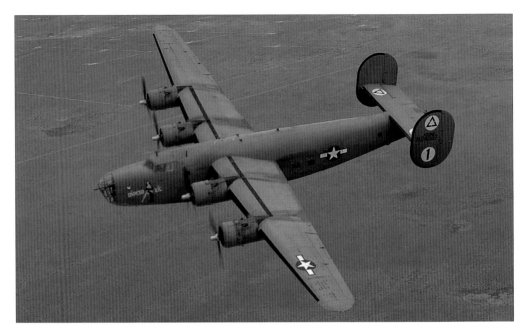

Consolidated B-24 Liberator

With the growing possibility of war erupting in Europe, in 1939 the US Army Air Corps expressed an interest in the Consolidated Aircraft Corporation's ideas for a new four-engine, long-range, high-flying heavy bomber. As a result, a contract for one prototype was placed with the Company in March 1939, and the aircraft was designated the XB-24. The flying surfaces that were the bases of the XB-24 design had been proven in the 1930s with Consolidated's PBY flying boat. The prototype construction advanced quickly over the next few months, and the aircraft took off on its maiden flight from Lindbergh Field, California, on December 29, 1939. It was powered by four 1200hp Pratt & Whitney R-1830-33 radial engines and could carry 3632kg/8000lb of bombs in its capacious fuselage. For defensive armament it had six hand-operated 7.7mm/0.303in Browning machine-guns. The B-24 was the first American heavy bomber with a tricycle undercarriage.

Seven pre-production YB-24 aircraft, ordered for US Army Air Corps evaluation, were soon coming off the San Diego assembly line in early 1941. These aircraft were re-designated XB-24Bs because they were fitted with Pratt & Whitney 1200hp R-1830-41 engines and General Electric B-2 turbo superchargers for high-altitude flight. Other modifications included an increase to the tail span of 0.6m/2ft. The first nine production B-24A Liberators were delivered to the USAAC in May 1941. These were quickly followed by a further development batch of nine aircraft designated B-24Cs, which differed from earlier versions by having three power turrets.

TOP: **Often overshadowed by the B-17, the B-24 was in fact produced in greater numbers than any other bomber ever.** ABOVE: **Liberator IIIs (B-24Ds) stationed at Aldergrove in Northern Ireland, April 1943. Note the aerials fixed to the port wing and nose.**

Further modifications followed before the first main production model, the B-24D, started to be delivered to the various Army Air Corps Bombardment Groups. This variant had a take-off weight increased to 25,424kg/56,000lb and was powered by Pratt & Whitney R-1830-43 engines, giving a top speed of 487kph/303mph at 7625m/25,000ft. Armament was now ten 12.7mm/0.50in machine-guns and a bomb load of 3995kg/8800lb. Range was also increased by 1046km/650 miles, giving a total range of 4586km/2850 miles.

Consolidated B-24D Liberator

First flight: December 29, 1939

Power: Four Pratt & Whitney 1200hp R-1830-65 radial engines

Armament: Two gun turrets in nose, tail, upper fuselage aft of cockpit and under centre fuselage, and single manual guns in waist (beam) positions, totalling 10 12.7mm/0.5in machine-guns; normal bomb load of 3995kg/ 8800lb

Size: Wingspan – 33.35m/110ft
Length – 20.47m/67ft 2in
Height – 5.49m/18ft
Wing area – 97.36m²/1048sq ft

Weights: Empty – 15,436kg/34,000lb
Maximum take-off – 29,510kg/65,000lb

Performance: Maximum speed – 467kph/290mph
Service ceiling – 8540m/28,000ft
Range – 3220km/2000 miles
Climb – 6100m/20,000ft in 22 minutes

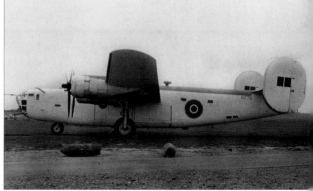

In September 1942, the 93rd Bombardment Group became the first B-24D bombardment group to join the Eighth Air Force in England. A month later, the 44th BG arrived in the UK, also equipped with B-24s. By the end of the war in Europe, 3800 Liberators had been accepted by the Eighth Air Force. Of these, almost a third were lost in action over enemy territory.

In all, five production plants produced 19,256 Liberators between May 1941 and the end of hostilities in 1945. The Ford Motor Company, using mass-production techniques perfected for the automobile industry, built 6792 at its Willow Run plant alone.

Although the B-24 was more technologically advanced than the B-17, it is often eclipsed in history by the Boeing bomber. The facts are however quite clear – the B-24 was produced in greater numbers than any bomber in aviation history.

In August 1943, B-24s carried out one of the most famous USAAF bombing raids of World War II. Fifty-six out of

TOP: **Post-war, the B-24 was used by other nations. This is a Royal Canadian Air Force B-24.** ABOVE LEFT: **This B-24, Diamond Lil is preserved in the USA by the Commemorative (formerly Confederate) Air Force as a tribute to the aircrew who made the ultimate sacrifice in defence of freedom.** ABOVE: **In RAF service, the B-24G was designated Liberator G.R.V.**

179 bombers were lost during the mission, a daring low-level attack on the Romanian oil fields, which supplied one-third of the Third Reich's high-octane fuel. Only the Liberator could reach these targets from the nearest friendly airfields in North Africa.

France had ordered 120 Liberators, but fell to the Germans in 1940 before the aircraft were delivered. Royal Air Force Coastal Command was quick to appreciate the long range of the B-24, and took over the French order. The first RAF Liberator took to the air in January 1941. The Liberator played a key role in the RAF's war against German U-boats in the Battle of the Atlantic.

Consolidated PBY-5A Catalina

The Consolidated Aircraft Corporation received a contract for a prototype flying boat from the US Navy in February 1928. The aircraft was designated XPY-1, and was designed for alternative installations of either two or three engines. However, it was the initial configuration that ultimately evolved into the most outstanding monoplane flying boat of the 1930s, the PBY Catalina.

The contract for the construction of the PBY prototype was issued to Consolidated in October 1933, and the aircraft flew for the first time in March 1935. Aircraft were delivered to the US Navy's Patrol Squadrons from October 1936. As part of a training exercise and also to demonstrate the aircraft's long-range endurance capabilities, Patrol Squadron VP-3 flew a non-stop round-trip mission from San Diego, California, to the Panama Canal Zone in 27 hours, 58 minutes, covering a distance of 5297km/3292 miles.

The PB1s were powered by 850hp Pratt & Whitney R-1830-64 engines, but in 1937 the engines were upgraded to 1000hp, and 50 aircraft were ordered, designated PB-2s. The third variant, the PB-3, was delivered to the Soviet Union in 1938 along with a manufacturing licence. The Soviet PB-3 was powered by two Russian-built 950hp M87 engines, and designated GST. The PB-4 variant also appeared in 1938 with large mid-fuselage blister observation and gun positions.

In April 1939, the US Navy ordered a prototype amphibious version that could land on water or land (with a retractable undercarriage), designated XPBY-5A. After service evaluation

TOP AND ABOVE: **The Royal Air Force made extensive use of the Catalina during World War II, having first evaluated the type in July 1939. The aircraft shown at the top of the page is in fact a Canso, the amphibious version which could operate from land or sea thanks to a retractable undercarriage.**

tests, orders were placed by the US Navy. The Royal Air Force had already shown interest in the type, aware of the gathering war clouds in Europe and the need to patrol British waters far from land. One aircraft was flown over from the USA for RAF evaluation, and as soon as war was declared 30 examples of the amphibious version were ordered. These were delivered to the RAF in early 1941 and were in service almost immediately, named the Catalina by the British. The US Navy also adopted the name Catalina in 1942. During a patrol on May 26, 1941,

LEFT: The PBY was the most numerous and the most successful flying boat of World War II. It entered US Navy service in 1936 and equipped 21 patrol squadrons by the start of the war. BELOW: The Catalina's ingenious retractable floats became the aircraft's wingtips when retracted.

ABOVE: US Navy Catalina amphibians (PBY-5As) tied down at their Aleutian bases, World War II. RIGHT: RAF Catalinas operated in the Atlantic, Mediterranean and the Indian Ocean, and took part in the protection of Arctic convoys while based in Russia.

a Catalina of No.209 Squadron operating from Castle Archdale in Northern Ireland spotted the German battleship *Bismarck* once Royal Navy ships had lost the enemy ship.

The RAF had 650 Catalinas, and many served in the Atlantic. Two Royal Air Force Catalina pilots who operated in the Atlantic were awarded the Victoria Cross for gallant attacks on German submarines in the open sea. British "Cats" also operated in Ceylon and Madagascar patrolling the Indian Ocean, while aircraft operating from Gibraltar were on station for the 1942 Allied landings in North Africa. The last U-boat sunk by RAF Coastal Command was destroyed by a No.210 Squadron Catalina on May 7, 1945.

The PBY-5A variant was used widely during World War II by a number of countries. Canadian-built versions of the flying boat were also produced, and were known as "Cansos" by the Royal Canadian Air Force. Further development of the Catalina led to the fitting of more powerful 1200hp engines, revised armament and search radar equipment. By the end of production in 1945, over 4000 Catalinas had been made, making it the most-produced flying boat in history.

Catalinas were operated by many air arms around the world, including Australia, Brazil, France, the Netherlands, New Zealand, South Africa and the Soviet Union. A number remain in civilian use today, and are popular attractions at air shows.

Consolidated PBY-5 Catalina

First flight: March 1935
Power: Two Pratt & Whitney 1200hp R-1830-92 Twin Wasp 14-cylinder radial engines
Armament: Two 12.7mm/0.5in machine-guns in bow turret and one in each beam blister, one 7.62mm/0.3in machine-gun in ventral tunnel; war load of up to 1816kg/4000lb of bombs, mines or depth charges, or two torpedoes
Size: Wingspan – 31.7m/104ft
Length – 19.45m/63ft 10in
Height – 6.15m/20ft 2in
Wing area – 130m²/1400sq ft
Weights: Empty – 9493kg/20,910lb
Maximum take-off – 16,080kg/35,420lb
Performance: Maximum speed – 288kph/2135mph
Ceiling – 4480m/14,700ft
Range – 4095km/2545 miles
Climb – 189m/620ft per minute

Consolidated Vultee PB4Y-2/P4Y-2 Privateer

Consolidated PB4Y-2 Privateer

First flight: September 1943
Power: Four 1350hp Pratt & Whitney R-1830-94 Twin Wasp 14-cylinder radials
Armament: Twelve 12.5mm/0.50in machine-guns; up to 2725kg/6000lb of bombs
Size: Wingspan – 33.53m/110ft
  Length – 22.73m/74ft 7in
  Height – 9.17m/30ft 1in
  Wing area – 97.4m²/1048sq ft
Weights: Empty – 17,018kg/37,485lb
  Maximum take-off – 29,510kg/65,000lb
Performance: Maximum speed – 381kph/237mph
  Service ceiling – 6309m/20,700ft
  Range – 4505m/2800 miles
  Climb – 332m/1090ft per minute

After seeing the threat that German U-boats posed to Britain, the importance of effective and hard-hitting long-range maritime reconnaissance/anti-submarine aircraft was appreciated early in World War II. The US Navy wanted a purpose-designed aircraft for the job rather than a converted bomber, having already operated a maritime version of the hugely successful B-24 Liberator designated the PB4Y-1.

Three B-24Ds were taken from the San Diego B-24 production line and rebuilt with a fuselage dramatically extended by 2.1m/7ft. The whole interior of the aircraft was changed substantially, and armament was changed to better suit the intended role. Engine cowlings were changed and turbochargers were deleted from the engines because the Privateers were to operate at relatively low altitude. The other obvious modification was the very large single tail fin in place of the B-24's distinctive twin-fin arrangement.

The prototype XPB4Y-2 Privateer flew in September 1943, and an order was placed for 1370 aircraft. Deliveries began in July 1944, and the aircraft were used exclusively in the Pacific theatre, where they patrolled in support of amphibious operations. At war's end, 736 had been delivered, when the rest of the order was cancelled.

Post-war, six US Navy squadrons continued to fly Privateers, and the aircraft flew numerous missions during the Korean War, at which time it was redesignated the P4Y-2. It was used increasingly as a Cold War electronic intelligence-gathering platform.

Eleven served with the US Coast Guard (designated P4Y-2G) to deal with the USCG's developing search-and-rescue mission, then retired from the military in the early 1960s. A number fly on in the USA as fire-bombers because their capacious fuselage can carry huge amounts of water and fire-inhibitors.

TOP, ABOVE AND BELOW: **The Privateer was essentially a single-finned, lengthened B-24 Liberator developed specifically during World War II for the US Navy. The type was only used in the Pacific, and one unit was equipped with pioneering anti-shipping glide-bombs – a primitive "smart" weapon.**

LEFT: **The Alcione (kingfisher) was used on both sides – pro-Allies and Axis – in Italy. The model pictured is the Z.1007bis, which was the major production version.**

CRDA/CANT Z.1007 Alcione

CRDA/CANT Z.1007bis Alcione

First flight: May 1937
Power: Three Piaggio 1000hp P.XIbis RC 40 14-cylinder two-row radial engines
Armament: One 12.7mm/0.5in Breda-SAFAT machine-gun in both dorsal and ventral position, one 7.7mm/0.303in machine-gun in each beam hatch position; 2000kg/4410lb bomb load or two 454kg/1000lb torpedoes
Size: Wingspan – 24.8m/81ft 4in
Length – 18.4m/60ft 4in
Height – 5.22m/17ft 1.5in
Wing area – 70m²/753.47sq ft
Weights: Empty – 8626kg/19,000lb
Maximum take-off – 13,633kg/30,029lb
Performance: Maximum speed – 450kph/280mph
Service ceiling – 8082m/26,500ft
Range – 1795km/1115 miles
Climb – 472m/1550ft per minute

Cantieri Riuniti dell'Adriatico (CRDA), also known as CANT, specialized in flying boats, one of which was the three-engine Z.506B Airone twin-float seaplane. A landplane version was an obvious development to investigate, and this flew for the first time in May 1937. Following successful testing, the aircraft was put into widespread production, and was built totally of wood. The Z.1007 became one of the most important bombers in the Italian Air Force inventory. The Z.1007bis and Z.1007ter were the main production versions, with 526 built – while the ter version had the more powerful 1175hp Piaggio P.XII engines, it carried a lighter 1000kg/2205lb bomb load. There were also subvariants of the bis, with Serie I–III having a single fin and Serie IV–IX being twin-fin aircraft. Like so many medium bombers designed in the mid-1930s, the Alcione fared very badly against modern fighters. In spite of this, the aircraft were well-used in the Italians' Greek and Balkan campaigns, throughout the Mediterranean and even over the Russian front.

LEFT: **A Condor of the 11th Bombardment Squadron from March Field, California, pictured in July 1932.**

Curtiss B-2 Condor

First flight: July 1927
Power: Two Curtiss 600hp GV-1570 in-line piston engines
Armament: Six 7.62mm/0.3in machine-guns; up to 1138kg/2508lb bomb load
Size: Wingspan – 27.43m/90ft
Length – 14.43m/47ft 4.5in
Height – 4.95m/16ft 3in
Wing area – 138.97m²/1496sq ft
Weights: Empty – 4222kg/9300lb
Maximum take-off – 7078kg/15,591lb
Performance: Maximum speed – 212kph/132mph
Ceiling – 5215m/17,100ft
Range – 1296km/805 miles
Climb – 259.3m/850ft per minute

Curtiss B-2 Condor

The Curtiss XB-2 was a direct development of the Martin MB-2 (NBS-1) built by Curtiss, and used steel tubing instead of wood for the construction of the fuselage. The XB-2 prototype was ordered by the US Army in 1926 and the first flight took place in July 1927. The aircraft's engines had distinctive tall radiators which jutted up above the engine nacelles. The aircraft also featured unusual defences in that each nacelle had a gunner's position at the rear, which it was hoped would offer a better field of fire than fuselage positions.

The B-2 had twin rudders and twin horizontal stabilizers, which even by 1927 standards were somewhat outmoded. Twelve aircraft were finally ordered at a unit cost of 76,373 US dollars – this was a great deal of money, and had initially caused the Army to favour other designs, as had the size of the B-2, which made it too big for hangars of the time. Nevertheless, from 1929 these B-2s equipped the 11th Bombardment Squadron and constituted the US's only heavy bomber capability for a time. Canvas-covered biplanes like the B-2 soon became obsolete.

Curtiss SB2C Helldiver

The Curtiss SB2C was the second Curtiss US naval aircraft to be called Helldiver, but shared little but a name with the earlier aircraft. The Helldiver is another aircraft whose contribution to the final Allied victory is often underestimated. Said to be a handful at low speeds, the two-man Helldiver first flew in December 1940 but did not see action until November 1943 when it took part in a carrier strike against Rabaul. The Helldiver became the most successful Allied dive-bomber of World War II, and certainly made a major contribution to the successful outcome of the war in the Pacific. The aircraft had good range, making it a very useful weapon for action in the great expanse of the Pacific. The aircraft packed a significant punch and could carry 454kg/1000lb of bombs under its wings, while a torpedo or further 454kg/1000lb could be carried in the internal bomb bay.

Later improvements to this already more than capable combat aircraft included an uprated Wright Cyclone engine and hardpoints for carrying rocket-projectiles.

The Helldiver saw considerable action in the battles of the Philippine Sea and Leyte Gulf, and played a significant part in the destruction of the Japanese battleships *Yamato* and *Musashi*. As the Allies moved towards the Japanese home islands, Helldivers were active in the Inland Sea and helped deal the deathblow to the Japanese Navy.

Post-war, Helldivers were the only bombers in the US Navy, and continued to equip USN units until 1948, when the Douglas Skyraider was introduced.

Other post-war operators of the Helldiver included the Italian, Greek and Portuguese navies. Helldivers fought on with the French Navy and were used by them in Indo-China. Thailand took delivery of six Helldivers in 1951, and retired the aircraft in 1955.

TOP AND ABOVE: **After an unimpressive service debut, the Helldiver became the standard US Navy "scout-bomber" for the remainder of World War II.**

Curtiss SB2C-4 Helldiver

First flight: December 18, 1940

Power: One Wright 1900hp Wright R-2600-20 Cyclone radial engine

Armament: Two 20mm/0.78in cannon in wings, two 7.62mm/0.3in machine-guns in rear cockpit; 454kg/1000lb of bombs or a torpedo carried internally, plus an additional 454kg/1000lb of bombs and rocket projectiles carried under wings

Size: Wingspan – 15.16m/44ft 9in
Length – 11.17m/36ft 8in
Height – 4.01m/13ft 2in
Wing area – 39.2m²/422sq ft

Weights: Empty – 4788kg/10,547lb
Maximum take-off – 7543kg/16,616lb

Performance: Maximum speed – 434kph/270mph
Service ceiling – 8875m/29,100ft
Range – 1987km/1235 miles
Climb – 549m/1800ft per minute

de Havilland/Airco DH4

LEFT: **DH4s stationed in France during World War I.**

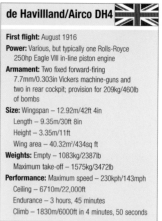

de Havillland/Airco DH4

First flight: August 1916
Power: Various, but typically one Rolls-Royce 250hp Eagle VIII in-line piston engine
Armament: Two fixed forward-firing 7.7mm/0.303in Vickers machine-guns and two in rear cockpit; provision for 209kg/460lb of bombs
Size: Wingspan – 12.92m/42ft 4in
Length – 9.35m/30ft 8in
Height – 3.35m/11ft
Wing area – 40.32sq²/434sq ft
Weights: Empty – 1083kg/2387lb
Maximum take-off – 1575kg/3472lb
Performance: Maximum speed – 230kph/143mph
Ceiling – 6710m/22,000ft
Endurance – 3 hours, 45 minutes
Climb – 1830m/6000ft in 4 minutes, 50 seconds

The DH4 was arguably the most successful light bomber to see action during World War I. The biplane was designed by Geoffrey de Havilland in response to a 1914 War Office requirement for a two-seat day bomber for service with the Royal Flying Corp (RFC) and Royal Navy Air Service (RNAS). Some have compared the aircraft's versatility in World War I to that of its de Havilland successor, the twin-engine Mosquito, whose many applications in World War II are well documented.

The DH4 was originally designed around the 200hp Beardmore-Halford-Pullinger engine. However, there were many development problems with the new engine, so no fewer than seven different engine types were fitted to production aircraft. Various sub-contractors to de Havilland built 1449 aircraft in the UK and in the USA a further 4846 were produced by three US companies. These US models were powered mainly by the 400hp Packard Liberty engine. The DH4 entered front-line service in 1917.

de Havilland/Airco DH9A

LEFT: **This DH9A, E8673, was built by the Aircraft Manufacturing Co. Ltd.**

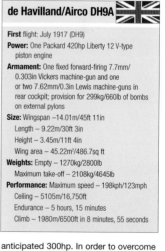

de Havilland/Airco DH9A

First flight: July 1917 (DH9)
Power: One Packard 420hp Liberty 12 V-type piston engine
Armament: One fixed forward-firing 7.7mm/ 0.303in Vickers machine-gun and one or two 7.62mm/0.3in Lewis machine-guns in rear cockpit; provision for 299kg/660lb of bombs on external pylons
Size: Wingspan –14.01m/45ft 11in
Length – 9.22m/30ft 3in
Height – 3.45m/11ft 4in
Wing area – 45.22m²/486.7sq ft
Weights: Empty – 1270kg/2800lb
Maximum take-off – 2108kg/4645lb
Performance: Maximum speed – 198kph/123mph
Ceiling – 5105m/16,750ft
Endurance – 5 hours, 15 minutes
Climb – 1980m/6500ft in 8 minutes, 55 seconds

The DH9 was derived from the successful DH4, and first entered Royal Flying Corps service with No.103 Squadron in December 1917. The following March, it went into action on the Western Front with No.6 Squadron, but the engine was found to be underpowered. With a full bomb load of 299kg/660lb mounted on external pylons, it could only climb to around 4575m/15,000ft, which was 2135m/ 7000ft lower than the DH4 it replaced. There was also a very high rate of engine failure during bombing operations.

The disappointing performance was found to be entirely due to the problematic BHP engine, which only developed 230hp instead of the anticipated 300hp. In order to overcome the problem, the BHP engine was replaced by the 420hp Packard Liberty engine. These models, designated DH9A, went on to be some of the finest bomber aircraft of World War I.

de Havilland/Airco DH10 Amiens

The DH3 produced in 1916 was a large twin-engined pusher configuration biplane heavy bomber. The design was not put into production, and both prototypes were scrapped within a year. The Royal Flying Corps still needed heavy bombers with the range to hit strategic German targets well beyond the front line, and the situation was made more pressing when Germany began its Gotha bomber raids in daylight over London in 1917. Geoffrey de Havilland, realizing that there was not time to start to design a new aircraft from scratch, revisited the DH3 design and used it as the basis for the new bomber aircraft.

The DH10 was similar in layout to the DH3, but was bigger overall and much more robust. The design was swiftly translated into a real aircraft, powered by two BHP 230hp in-line engines in pusher arrangement. The prototype Amiens I (serial C8658) had its maiden flight on March 4, 1918. The trailing edges of the wing had the tell-tale cut-out to allow clearance for the pusher propeller blades. Two other prototypes had the engines installed in the tractor configuration, with the propellers facing forwards. The tractor prototypes were powered by the 360hp Rolls-Royce Eagle VIII (Amiens II, serial C8659, first flight April 20) and the 400hp Liberty 12 (Mk III). In both tractor and pusher configuration, the power plants were positioned between the wings mounted on struts. The fourth prototype had the Liberty engines mounted right on the lower wing, and the performance improved – this version was designated Amiens IIIA or DH10A. Test-flights proved the worth of the design, and the aircraft could fly faster while carrying twice the bomb load of the DH9.

TOP: **The second Amiens prototype. Developed from the earlier DH3, the DH10 arrived just too late to see action during World War I.** ABOVE: **The Amiens IIIA, also known as the DH10A.**

This very capable aircraft was delivered too late for service in World War I, and only eight had been delivered to No.104 Squadron of the then Royal Air Force by the time of the Armistice. Had the war progressed, the aircraft would have been sure to prove its worth in combat.

The original wartime order had been for 1291 aircraft to be built by seven different companies and most were cancelled at the war's end. Some 220 were built, half being the IIIA version engined with either Liberty or Eagle power plants.

Post-war, the Amiens equipped No.216 Squadron in Egypt until it was succeeded by the Vimy in 1923. In Europe the type was well known for its airmail activity, which began in 1919

with No.120 Squadron flying between Hawkinge and Cologne, significantly improving communications with the British Army of the Rhine. In May 1919 an Amiens became the first aircraft to haul mail at night. In June 1921, DH10s pioneered the mail service between Cairo and Baghdad, reportedly using tracks in the desert to assist with navigation.

No.60 Squadron (originally No.97), based at Risalpur on the North West Frontier of India, was the only Royal Air Force unit to use the Amiens bomber in anger. In November 1920 and January 1922 the type was used to carry out bombing raids against rebels in India. The type was replaced there by the DH9A in 1923.

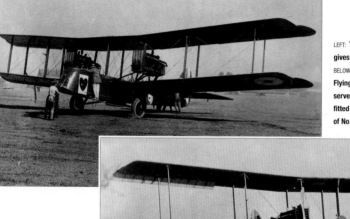

LEFT: **The gentleman peering into the cockpit gives a good idea of the DH10's size.**
BELOW: **Around 220 DH10s were built for Royal Flying Corps/Royal Air Force use, and they served until the early 1920s.** BOTTOM: **A DH10 fitted with tropical radiators, believed to be of No.216 Squadron, based in Egypt.**

de Havilland/Airco DH10 Amiens Mk III

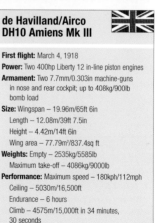

First flight: March 4, 1918
Power: Two 400hp Liberty 12 in-line piston engines
Armament: Two 7.7mm/0.303in machine-guns in nose and rear cockpit; up to 408kg/900lb bomb load
Size: Wingspan – 19.96m/65ft 6in
Length – 12.08m/39ft 7.5in
Height – 4.42m/14ft 6in
Wing area – 77.79m²/837.4sq ft
Weights: Empty – 2535kg/5585lb
Maximum take-off – 4086kg/9000lb
Performance: Maximum speed – 180kph/112mph
Ceiling – 5030m/16,500ft
Endurance – 6 hours
Climb – 4575m/15,000ft in 34 minutes, 30 seconds

de Havilland Mosquito

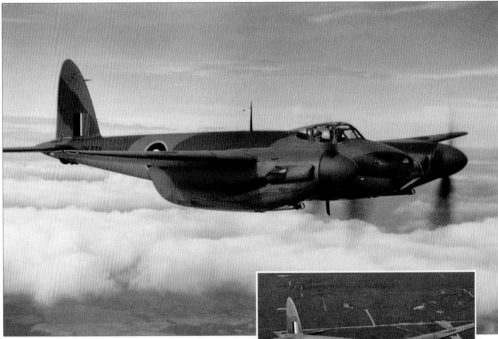

Dubbed the "Wooden Wonder", the Mosquito became the most versatile aircraft to see action during World War II. The Mosquito was a true multi-role combat aircraft which started life in late 1938 as a private venture outline design for a bomber/reconnaissance aircraft that could fly so fast and so high that no defensive armament would be needed.

The wooden construction was chosen because it was very strong when laminated and also kept down the weight, thus providing an excellent high-performance airframe. Another advantage of using wood was that furniture manufacturers could be subcontracted to make the fuselage, wings and tail-plane without disrupting Britain's already overstretched aircraft industry. Wood construction also avoided the use of strategic materials.

Even so, it was only after the start of World War II that Britain's Air Ministry seriously considered the proposal – and then with some caution – but in November 1940 the Mosquito first flew and convinced the sceptics that it was indeed a remarkable aircraft. Priority production was ordered for the bomber version, and meanwhile the photo-reconnaissance and fighter prototypes were prepared.

The first Mosquito prototype was in the Bomber configuration and with its clean airframe and powerful Merlin engines, the aircraft soon proved that it had exceptional

TOP AND ABOVE: **The Mosquito, the "Wooden Wonder", was one of the first true multi-role aircraft, equally at home in bomber, fighter, nightfighter and photo-reconnaissance roles. The aircraft pictured at the top of the page is a B.Mk V, serial DK338.**

performance and handling characteristics. The Mosquito remained the fastest combat aircraft in the world until 1944. Successful service trials quickly followed and the original March 1940 order for 50 aircraft was subdivided into ten Photo-Reconnaissance Mark Is, ten Bomber Mark VIs and 30 Nightfighters Mark II.

The first Mosquitoes to enter service with the RAF were the Photo-Reconnaissance models in September 1941, and these were used for deep penetration missions over Germany and occupied Europe. During these operations the Mosquito crews found that they were able to outpace all the latest German fighter aircraft.

On November 15, 1941, No.105 Squadron, which was based at RAF Swanton Morley in Norfolk, received its first Mosquito B.IV bomber. However, production of the new aircraft was slow, and it was not until May 1942 that the Squadron flew its first operational sorties to Cologne.

In mid-1943, the B.IX was introduced with increased bomb capacity and the "Oboe" navigational aid for Pathfinder duties. These specialist bombers would lead RAF Bomber Command's Pathfinder Force over enemy territory and lay down target markers. This greatly improved the accuracy of Bomber Command raids and made a significant contribution to the RAF's strategic night-time bomber offensive against the Third Reich.

Fighter-bomber versions were also developed, and the FB.Mk VI became the most widely used of all Mosquito fighters. This version was a day or night intruder, able ultimately to carry up to two 227kg/500lb bombs as well as the usual fighter armament. RAF Coastal Command was quick to see the potential of the type and soon began to use the VI, armed with underwing rockets, as a maritime strike aircraft.

Mosquito crews soon acquired a reputation for the ability to deliver their bomb loads with pinpoint accuracy over both short and long distances. This was ably demonstrated on

February 18, 1944, when 19 Mosquitoes blasted open a German jail at Amiens, which held French resistance fighters. Later, in October 1944, the Gestapo HQ at Aarhus University, Jutland, was bombed with such precision that Danish Resistance leaders were able to escape.

In all, 7781 Mosquitoes were built in some 50 variants before production ceased in 1950. The B35 was the ultimate bomber variant of the "Mossie", and it remained in service with RAF Pathfinder units until being replaced by the jet-powered Canberra in 1953. Versions of the Mosquito remained in front-line service with the RAF until December 15, 1955. The Mosquito was a truly magnificent British aircraft.

ABOVE: **The Mosquito had a bomb-carrying capability that staggered crews of heavy bombers. Here, an aircraft of No.692 Squadron based at Gravely in the UK is being loaded with a 1817kg/4000lb bomb for a wartime mission.** LEFT: **A Mosquito B.Mk IX.** BELOW: **The DZ313 was a B.Mk IV Mosquito powered by Merlin 21 engines.**

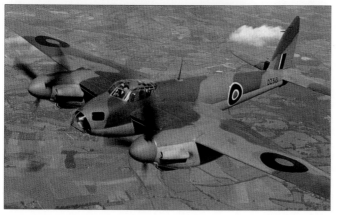

de Havilland Mosquito B.IV

First flight: November 25, 1940
Power: Two Rolls Royce 1230hp Merlin 21 12-cylinder liquid-cooled in-line piston engines
Armament: 908kg/2000lb bombs
Size: Wingspan – 16.51m/54ft 2in
    Length – 12.47m/40ft 10in
    Height – 4.66m/15ft 3in
    Wing area – 42.18m²/454sq ft
Weights: Empty – 5947kg/13,100lb
    Maximum take-off – 10,160kg/22,380lb
Performance: Maximum speed – 612kpg/380mph
    Service ceiling – 9455m/31,000ft
    Range – 1963km/1220 miles
    Climb – 878m/2880ft per minute

Dornier Do17

In 1932 the German Ordnance Department issued development guidelines to a number of leading German aircraft companies for the design and construction of a twin-engine medium bomber with a retractable undercarriage. Dornier designated the project Do17, and covered up the military aspects of the development by describing the aircraft as a fast mail-plane for Deutsche Lufthansa and also a freight carrier for the German State Railways.

On May 17, 1933, the go-ahead was given for the construction of two prototypes, one a high-speed commercial aircraft and the other for "freight" with special equipment – in other words, a bomber. The Do17 bomber prototype first flew in November 1934, and its superior performance caused much concern outside Germany.

At the International Air Show at Dübendorf, Switzerland in 1937, the Do17 MV1 proved to be the leader in its class. It even outpaced a number of European countries' front-line day fighters, including those of France and Czechoslovakia.

The first military examples, the Do17E high-speed bomber and the Do17F long-range reconnaissance aircraft, entered

service with the Luftwaffe and saw action during the Spanish Civil War. Both variants were powered by two BMW VI 12-cylinder V-type engines, the Do17F having extra fuel tanks and two bomb bay cameras.

Further development of the Do17 E- and F-types led to the Do17M medium bomber and the Do17P reconnaissance model powered by Bramo 323 radial engines. The definitive variant was the Do17Z, with an extensively glazed cockpit, "beetle" eye, glazed nose and uprated Bramo 323 A-1 engines.

Nicknamed the "Flying Pencil", over 500 Do17Z models were built. Although this aircraft could outpace most contemporary fighters when it entered service with the Luftwaffe in 1938, it soon became obsolete after suffering heavy losses during the Battle of Britain. Nevertheless early in the war, as the Nazis swept through Poland, Norway, the Low Countries and France, the Do17 medium bomber was a key weapon in the German arsenal.

TOP: **The Do17 "Flying Pencil", combat-tested during the Civil War in Spain, was one of the Luftwaffe's most important bomber types.**

ABOVE: **The Do17Z was the main production version, and entered Luftwaffe service in 1938.**

Dornier Do17Z-2

First flight: November 23, 1934 (prototype)
Power: Two BMW Bramo 1000hp 322P Fafnir 9-cylinder radial engines
Armament: One or two 7.92mm/0.31in machine-guns in the windscreen, nose, dorsal and ventral positions; internal bomb load of 1000kg/2205lb
Size: Wingspan – 18m/59ft
  Length – 15.8m/51ft 10in
  Height – 4.60m/15ft 1in
  Wing area – 55m²/592sq ft
Weights: Empty – 5210kg/11,467lb
  Maximum take-off – 8590kg/18,906lb
Performance: Maximum speed – 410kph/255mph
  Ceiling – 8200m/26,905ft
  Range – 1500km/932 miles
  Climb – 3000m/9843ft in 8 minutes, 40 seconds

Dornier Do217

At the beginning of 1938 manufacturing specification No.1323 was issued to Dornier for a fast, flexible aircraft that could be used as a medium bomber, long-range reconnaissance or smoke-laying aircraft.

The Do217 was derived from the highly successful Do17/215 series of bombers but was very different to the earlier aircraft. In order to get a quick flying prototype, Dornier modified a Do17-M by adding the Do17Z all-round vision cockpit and increasing the size of the fuselage to enlarge the bomb bay capacity.

The Do217 V-1 prototype first flew in October 1938 but crashed seven days later during single-engine flying tests. The second prototype, Do217 V-2, carried on with the flying-test schedule over the following three months. On February 25, 1939, the third prototype took to the air powered by two Jumo 211-A engines in place of the in-line DB 601s. The Jumo engines were now regarded as essential if the desired performance was to be achieved, and they were fitted to the next two prototypes. However, many other power plants were tried before a final decision was made to use two BMW 801 radials on production models.

TOP AND ABOVE: **The Do217, although mainly inspired by the earlier Do215, was a larger aircraft and differed considerably in many ways. The Do217 could carry the greatest bomb load of all the Luftwaffe bombers of the period.**

The 217 was initially developed as a bomber that carried a greater load than any German bomber of the time. The first production run started at the end of 1940 with the Do217 E-1 medium bomber variant. It was followed by the E-2 and E-3 versions, which differed from the E-1s in their defensive armament and were intended for dive-bombing operations. The Do217 E-4 was identical to the E-2 version apart from a heavy machine-gun in the nose. Other sub-variants included the E-2/R-4 torpedo bomber, the E-2/10 maritime patrol and the E-5, which was capable of carrying radio-controlled air-to-surface missiles.

Dornier Do217 E-2

First flight: October 4, 1938
Power: Two BMW 1580hp 801ML 14-cylinder radial piston engines
Armament: One 20mm/0.78in cannon in lower port side of nose, one 13mm/0.5in machine-gun in dorsal turret and one in ventral step position, one 7.92mm/0.31in machine-gun in nose and one in each side of cockpit; 4000kg/8804lb bomb load
Size: Wingspan – 19m/62ft 4in
Length – 18.20m/59ft 8in
Height – 5.03m/16ft 6in
Wing area – 57m²/613.5sq ft
Weights: Empty – 8855kg/19,490lb
Maximum take-off – 16,465kg/36,239lb
Performance: Maximum speed – 515kph/320mph
Ceiling – 9000m/29,530ft
Range – 2800km/1740 miles
Climb – 210m/690ft per minute

Other variants followed, including the three-seat 217J fighter-bomber and nightfighter versions. Both differed from the 217 bomber by having a solid nose in place of the bomber version's "greenhouse" nose for a bomb-aimer.

The J-1 was a fighter-bomber, operational from February 1942, armed with four nose-mounted 7.92mm/0.31in machine-guns and four 20mm/0.78in cannon in addition to dorsal and ventral gun positions, each mounting a pair of 13mm/0.51in guns.

Douglas B-18 Bolo

The twin-engine B-18 Bolo was the first Douglas medium bomber, and was derived from the successful twin-engined DC-2 commercial transport. The B-18 was intended to replace the Martin B-10 in USAAC service. During Air Corps bomber trials at Wright Field in 1935, the B-18 prototype competed with the Martin 146 (an improved B-10) and the four-engine Boeing 299, forerunner of the B-17 Flying Fortress. Surprisingly, only 13 YB-17s were ordered at first as the Army General Staff chose the less costly Bolo and, in January 1936, ordered 133 of the Douglas bombers. Later, 217 more were built as B-18As with a "shark" nose in which the bomb aimer's position was extended forward over the nose gunner's position.

In addition to 133 B-18s, 217 improved B-18As were built, 20 of which were transferred to the Royal Canadian Air Force and designated Digby 1s. During the winter of 1939–40, over 100 B-18As were upgraded to the B-18B standard by installing specialist radio equipment for maritime patrol operations in American and Caribbean waters. These aircraft were used to seek and report the position of German U-boats operating off the US east coast.

The B-18 Bolos were the most numerous US bombers deployed outside the country as the United States entered World War II.

Many B-18s were destroyed by the Japanese at Pearl Harbor on December 7, 1941, and by early 1942 improved aircraft replaced the Bolo as a front-line bomber. Many B-18s were then used as transports or for paratroop training, or modified as B-18Bs for going on anti-submarine duty.

TOP : **The distinctive Douglas tail points to the Bolo's DC-2 origins.** ABOVE: **This often overlooked bomber was the main type in US use pre-war.** BELOW LEFT: **The bomb aimer's position was over the nose gunner's position, giving the Bolo the so-called "sharknose" look.**

Douglas B-18A Bolo

First flight: April 1935
Power: Two Wright 1000hp R-1820-53 Cyclone 9-cylinder radial engines
Armament: One 7.62mm/0.30in machine-gun in nose, dorsal and ventral positions; up to 2951kg/6500lb of bombs
Size: Wingspan – 27.28m/89ft 6in
Length – 17.63m/57ft 10in
Height – 4.62m/15ft 2in
Wing area – 89.65m²/965sq ft
Weights: Empty – 7409kg/16,321lb
Maximum take-off – 12,563kg/27,673lb
Performance: Maximum speed – 346kph/215mph
Service ceiling – 7,285m/23,900ft
Range – 1931km/1200 miles
Climb – 3048m/10,000ft in 9 minutes, 54 seconds

Douglas SBD-5 Dauntless

Douglas SBD-5 Dauntless

First flight: July 1935
Power: One Wright 1200hp R-1820-60 Cyclone 9-cylinder radial engine
Armament: Two 12.7mm/0.5in fixed forward-firing machine-guns in upper part of the forward fuselage, two trainable 7.62mm/0.3in machine-guns in rear cockpit; external bomb or depth charge load of 1021kg/2250lb
Size: Wingspan – 12.66m/41ft 6in
Length – 10.09m/33ft 1in
Height – 4.14m/13ft 7in
Wing area – 30.19m²/325sq ft
Weights: Empty – 2963kg/6521lb
Maximum take-off – 4858kg/10,700lb
Performance: Maximum speed – 410kph/255mph
Ceiling – 7786m/25,530ft
Range – 2519km/1565 miles
Climb – 457m/1500ft per minute

The most successful American dive-bomber of World War II had its origins in a 1934 Northrop proposal for a new US Navy dive-bomber based on the Northrop A-17 light attack bomber.

A prototype was ordered and first flew in July 1935, designated XBT-1. After a series of service trials, an order was placed for 54 BT-1 models. The first production batch was fitted with the 825hp Wright R-1535-94 engine. However, the last one off the production line was fitted with a 1000hp R-11820-32 engine and designated XBT-2. Further modifications followed, and after the Northrop Corporation became a division of Douglas in August 1937, the aircraft was redesignated XSBD-1.

It was June 1940 before the US Marine Corps started to receive a batch of 57 Dauntless SBD-1s with their distinctive, large perforated flaps. A few weeks later, the US Navy ordered 82 SBD-2 aircraft with increased fuel capacity, protective cockpit armour and autopilot. After further modifications, the Navy received over 400 SBD-3s during the summer of 1941. By the end of the year, the Dauntless formed the attack element of the US Navy's carrier-based air group in the Pacific. After the Japanese strike on

Pearl Harbor, the SBDs operated from the US aircraft carriers *Lexington* and *Yorktown* during the early months of 1942. They carried out numerous offensive operations against enemy shipping and island shore installations in the build-up to the battle of the Coral Sea. During this battle, the SBDs were joined by the Douglas TBD Devastator torpedo aircraft, and together they attacked and sank the Japanese light carrier *Shoho* and damaged the fleet carrier *Shokaku*. This was followed in June 1942 by the Battle of Midway, where SBDs from the carriers *Enterprise*, *Hornet* and *Yorktown* had a major success by sinking the Japanese carriers *Akagi*, *Kaga* and *Soryu*, and damaging the *Hiryu* so badly that it had to be scuttled. By the end of the battle, Japan had lost most of its capital ships in the Pacific.

In October 1942 the SBD-4 made its appearance fitted with radar and radio navigation equipment. This was followed in large quantities by the SBD-5, which had a more powerful 1200hp engine. One SBD-5 was fitted with a 1350hp R-1820-66 engine and used as a prototype for the SBD-6. This was the last Dauntless variant to be produced, and it appeared in early 1944.

ABOVE: **The Dauntless inflicted massive damage on enemy ships in the Pacific war, serving the US Navy and Marine Corps throughout World War II.**
BELOW: **This photograph shows the SBD's trademark perforated flaps.**

Douglas A-20 Boston/Havoc

The story of the Douglas DB-7 family of combat aircraft is complicated by the variety of names by which the numerous bomber, nightfighter and intruder versions were known. The complex DB-7/A-20/Havoc/Boston story began with Douglas submitting their DB-7 to meet a 1938 US Army

TOP: **The solid-nosed A-20G was the most numerous and main operational variant of the series serving in Europe, the Mediterranean and the Pacific, mainly in the low-level attack role.** ABOVE: **An RAF Boston III – note the forward gun blister fairing housing just above the nosewheel, containing the 7.7mm/0.303in machine-guns.**

specification for an attack aircraft. The result was an advanced and complex design which incorporated the novel nosewheel undercarriage arrangement for better pilot visibility on the ground. The aircraft also featured a highly unusual emergency second control column for the rear gunner's use in the event of the pilot being incapacitated.

France placed an order for 100 DB-7 models in February 1940, and some of these aircraft did see service with the French Armée de l'Air. Some of these aircraft flew to Britain to fight on against the Nazis, while some remained to be used by the Vichy Air Force. However, the principal early user of the Douglas design in Europe was the Royal Air Force, with whom the Havoc nightfighter/intruder version entered service in April 1941. A three-seat intruder version carried a 908kg/2000lb bomb load for use against targets in France, and was certainly a nuisance to the enemy under cover of darkness.

The first of the DB-7 series to serve as an RAF bomber was the Boston III variant (USAAF A-20C). This daylight bombing role was the one for which the aircraft was first designed. The first IIIs arrived in the UK from the USA in the summer of 1941 and soon replaced the Blenheims of No.2 Group, carrying out anti-shipping missions as well as bombing raids. A total of 781 Boston IIIs were delivered to the RAF, and the first to enter service did so with No.88 Squadron at Swanton Morley in October 1941. They saw action for the first time on February 12, 1942, and went on to fly many missions against targets in France, Belgium and the Netherlands, frequently flying perilously low to avoid enemy defences. They also took part in attacks on the German warships *Scharnhorst*, *Prinz Eugen* and *Gneisenau*, when they took part in the famous channel dash. The IIIs also served with the RAF in Italy, Tunisia and Algeria. On July 4, 1942, RAF Bostons attacked airfields in Holland – this raid was unusual because six of the aircraft involved were flown by crews of the US Eighth Air Force, giving the Mighty Eighth its first taste of battle in Europe. As more heavy bombers entered RAF service, the Bostons were restricted to tactical operations.

As part of the D-Day operations, British-based Bostons of the Second Tactical Air Force generated smoke screens over the invasion beaches.

1944 also saw the introduction of the Boston IV (the A-20G in USAAF service) and the Boston V (USAAF A-20H) distinguished from earlier versions by its power-operated gun turret. This version served with the RAF in the Second Tactical Air Force until the end of war in Europe in close co-operation with advancing ground troops. In USAAF service, the A-20G served with the Ninth Air Force in Europe, the Twelfth in the Mediterranean and in the Pacific with the Fifth Air Force. Around half of all the A-20G models produced were supplied to the Soviet Union. Total production of all versions was 7478 aircraft.

ABOVE: **USAAF Havocs first saw action when they came under attack during the Japanese strike at Pearl Harbor in December 1941.**

RIGHT: **An early A-20A Havoc.** BELOW: **BD121 was built as a Boston I, then converted to Havoc intruder standard. Note the flame damper exhausts and matt black paint for maximum concealment at night.**

Douglas Boston IV/A-20G

First flight: October 26, 1938 (Douglas 7B prototype)

Power: Two Wright 1700hp R-2600-23 14-cylinder radial engines

Armament: Six 12.7/0.50in machine-guns in the nose, two in dorsal position and one in ventral position; bomb load of 1816kg/4000lb

Size: Wingspan – 18.69m/61ft 4in
Length – 14.63m/47ft 11in
Height – 5.36m/17ft 7in
Wing area – 43.11m²/464sq ft

Weights: Empty – 7256kg/15,984lb
Maximum take-off – 12,348kg/27,200lb

Performance: Maximum speed – 546kph/339mph
Service ceiling – 7869m/25,800ft
Range – 3380km/2100 miles
Climb – 3048m/10,000ft in 7 minutes, 6 seconds

Douglas A-26/B-26 Invader

There are some combat aircraft that have served in two major wars, but few have served in three conflicts spread over more than two decades. The Invader did just that in World War II, Korea and Vietnam.

In 1940, before it could get detailed information on combat experiences in Europe, the USAAF issued a requirement for an attack aircraft to be built in three different prototype forms – attack, nightfighter and bomber. After the prototypes had flown (the XA-26 bomber version was first to fly, on July 10, 1942) it was the attack version that was selected first for production under the designation A-26B. Armed with six machine-guns in the solid nose and up to 14 more in remotely controlled turrets or underwing gunpacks, the heavily-armed Invader could also carry up to 1816kg/4000lb of bombs. This was a formidable and fast ground-attack aircraft – it was in fact the fastest American bomber of World War II.

The A-26B made its debut in the European theatre with the US Ninth Air Force in November 1944. The destructive power of the aircraft was used to maximum effect by bombing, ground strafing and launching rocket attacks in advance of the Allied ground forces as they fought their way through Europe. The aircraft was also used for dropping allied agents into enemy territory. Invaders had entered service in the Pacific at the same time.

1945 saw the entry of the A-26C into front-line service, and this version differed by having only two guns in a glazed nose and room for a bomb-aimer's position. This version saw little

TOP: **The A-26 was the fastest bomber the USA had in its World War II inventory.**
ABOVE: **The Invader served in three major conflicts of the 20th century, and had three designations in its service life.**

use before the end of the war, by which time 1091 examples had been built compared to 1355 B-models.

In the immediate post-war period, some Invaders were converted for use as target tugs for the US Navy, designated JD-1 (later the UB-26J). In 1948, USAF A-26 aircraft were redesignated B-26, not to be confused with the unrelated Martin B-26 Marauder withdrawn from USAF service in 1948.

LEFT: *My Baby*, B-26B, pictured in Korea in 1950. Note the nose, bristling with guns. BELOW: Equally potent armament can be seen in the nose of this French Air Force Invader pictured in Indo-China, March 1951.

In 1950, USAF Invaders took part in the first (and three years later the last) combat mission of the Korean War, where over 450 Invaders – both B-26B and B-26C models saw extensive USAF service, principally as night-intruders. Meanwhile, France also used them in Indo-China against the Viet Minh.

As tensions grew in Vietnam, Invaders were deployed to South Vietnam in 1962 and although they were painted in South Vietnamese markings, the aircraft flew into combat with US crews on board. After an aircraft disintegrated in mid-air due to wing stress problems, the B-26 was withdrawn from Vietnam. However, the USAF was keen to not lose the capability of the B-26 and invited On Mark Engineering, a company who had already carried out civilian conversions of the B-26, to produce a very heavily armed, dedicated counter-insurgency (COIN) version for use in South-east Asia. Low-hour airframes were extensively converted, essentially producing 40 brand new aircraft, the B-26K. These rebuilt aircraft saw extensive use in Vietnam in the ground-attack and interdiction roles until 1970, often flown by men younger than the aircraft itself.

The Invader's identity crisis was further complicated in 1966, when the B-26K was redesignated the A-26A for political reasons. The USAF wanted to base B-26K Invaders in Thailand, but the Thai government did not want bombers operating from their country. The B-26K was simply redesignated the A-26A, an attack aircraft, which was acceptable to the Thai government.

Some air forces still had Invaders as front-line aircraft into the late 1970s. When the fast Invader was declared surplus, many were well-used for civilian purposes, from executive transports to firebombers and crop-sprayers.

ABOVE: The A/B-26 Invader family of aircraft served extensively around the world, with some still on active duty into the 1970s.

Douglas B-26B Invader

First flight: July 10, 1942
Power: Two Pratt & Whitney 2000hp R-2800-27 18-cylinder radial piston engines
Armament: Ten 12.7mm/0.50in machine-guns mounted in nose, dorsal and ventral turrets; bomb load of 1816kg/4,000lb
Size: Wingspan – 21.34m/70ft
Length – 15.42m/50ft
Height – 5.64m/18ft 6in
Wing area – 50.17m²/540sq ft
Weights: Empty – 10,373kg/22,850lb
Maximum take-off – 15,890kg/35,000lb
Performance: Maximum speed – 571kph/355mph
Service ceiling – 6740m/22,100ft
Range – 2253km/1400 miles
Climb – 610m/2000ft per minute

LEFT: **Operating from land and sea, the Fairey III served the RAF and Royal Navy into the 1930s.**

Fairey III family

Originally a World War I twin-float seaplane, this general-purpose biplane aircraft was converted by Fairey into a landplane, the Fairey IIIA. This entered Royal Navy service as a two-seat carrier-borne bomber. The IIIB was a floatplane version, while the IIIC had a much more powerful engine. The Fairey IIID was the second most numerous variant produced, and appeared in RAF landplane but mainly Royal Navy floatplane versions. In the spring of 1926, four RAF Fairey IIIDs carried out a 22,366km/13,900-mile long-distance

formation flight from Northolt (near London) to Cape Town and back through Greece, Italy and France. IIIDs were exported to Australia, Portugal, Sweden and the Netherlands.

The Fairey IIIF, a much-improved development of the IIID, was the most numerous variant, with 597 aircraft produced. This aircraft, again in landplane and floatplane versions, gave sterling service in the RAF and Fleet Air Arm in Britain and overseas from 1927 until the mid-1930s. The obvious successor to the excellent IIIF was another IIIF which

is what the RAF's Fairey Gordon and Royal Navy Seals were. The two-man Gordon was a IIIF fitted with a different engine and other minor changes, while the Seal was a three-seat naval version with a float conversion option and an arrestor hook. Members of this family of aircraft served from World War I through to the early days of World War II – quite an achievement.

Fairey IIIF Mk IV

First flight: March 19, 1926
Power: One Napier 570hp Lion XIA 12-cylinder V-type engine
Armament: One 7.7mm/0.303in Vickers machine-gun in front fuselage and one 7.7mm/0.303in Lewis gun in rear cockpit; provision for 227kg/500lb bomb load under lower wing
Size: Wingspan – 13.94m/45ft 9in
Length – 11.19m/36ft 8.6in
Height – 4.26m/14ft
Wing area – 40.74m²/438.5sq ft
Weights: Empty – 1762kg/3880lb
Maximum take-off – 2743kg/6041lb
Performance: Maximum speed – 193kph/120mph
Service ceiling – 6710m/22,000ft
Range – 644km/400 miles
Climb – 305m/1000ft per minute

LEFT: **A visit to the USA by Richard Fairey brought the D-12 engine to Britain.**

Fairey Fox I

First flight: January 3, 1925
Power: One Fairey 480hp Felix (licence-built Curtiss D-12) piston engine
Armament: One fixed forward-firing 7.7mm/0.303in Vickers machine-gun and one on flexible mount in rear cockpit; up to 227kg/500lb bomb load
Size: Wingspan – 11.58m/38ft
Length – 9.50m/31ft 2in
Height – 3.25m/10ft 8in
Wing area – 30.1m²/324.5sq ft
Weights: Empty – 1184kg/2609lb
Maximum take-off – 1869kg/4117lb
Performance: Maximum speed – 251kph/156mph
Service ceiling – 5185m/17,000ft
Range – 1046km/650 miles
Climb – 5795m/19,000ft in 39 minutes, 45 seconds

Fairey Fox

The Fairey Fox was designed around a licence-built copy of the compact but powerful American Curtiss D-12 engine. The powerplant's comparatively small cross-section permitted almost unprecedented streamlining of the aircraft's nose, which reduced drag and in turn allowed higher speed. The prototype Fairey Fox light bomber biplane first flew on January 3, 1925, and was soon shown to be 81kph/50mph faster than existing

Royal Air Force bombers. Perhaps more alarmingly, the wood and fabric Fox could outpace contemporary fighters too.

In August 1926, No.12 Bomber Squadron, based at RAF Northolt, became the only RAF squadron, due to peacetime military economies, to be fully equipped with the Fox. It was replaced with Hawker Harts in RAF service in 1931. However, Avions Fairey in Belgium undertook production and built a further

178 aircraft. Nine Belgian Air Force squadrons were equipped with Foxes at the time of the German invasion in May 1940, and the crews of these aircraft fought bravely against a bigger enemy.

Fairey Hendon

The Fairey Hendon is often overlooked by historians due to the small numbers of the type that ultimately entered Royal Air Force service. Built to meet a 1927 Air Ministry specification for a heavy night-bomber, the Hendon (known as the Fairey Night Bomber until three years later) first flew in November 1931. Unusually for the time, it was a monoplane and carried its bombs internally. The twin-fin arrangement allowed room for a defensive tail position from which a gunner could provide effective rear defence. Production aircraft also featured enclosed cockpits, which were far from standard, while the engines appeared in streamlined nacelles which, along with a fixed but streamlined undercarriage, minimized drag.

The prototype, powered by Bristol Jupiter engines, crashed during tests which led to some delays in its development. The aircraft was repaired and re-engined with more powerful Rolls-Royce Kestrel engines, but the biggest delay was official dithering over what was an advanced design for the period. The decision to produce the

ABOVE: **K5085 was built by Fairey at their Stockport plant as a Hendon II with enclosed cockpit and nose turret.** RIGHT: **An early Hendon with Fairey Gordons in the background.**

aircraft was delayed, incredibly, for four years, by which time the design was verging on obsolescence.

Production Hendons (Mark II) were finally built between September 1936 and March 1937, but only 14 aircraft were built as a further order for 60 was cancelled. Power was provided by Kestrel VI engines, and the Mark II also had a turret for the nose gunner.

When the type eventually made it into service, the 14 aircraft were allocated to No.38 Squadron (based at Mildenhall and later Marham) and later to No.115 Squadron, which formed from the nucleus of a No.38 flight. The Hendon, with its all-metal fabric-covered structure, was the first monoplane in RAF squadron service.

The Fairey Hendon night-bomber quickly became obsolete and was replaced by the Vickers Wellington just before the start of World War II.

Fairey Hendon II

First flight: November 1931
Power: Two Rolls-Royce 600hp Kestrel VI in-line piston engines
Armament: Three 7.7mm/0.303in Lewis guns in nose, dorsal and tail positions; up to 753kg/1660lb of bombs carried internally, or alternatively 15–20 troops
Size: Wingspan – 31.03m/101ft 9in
Length – 18.53m/60ft 9in
Height – 5.72m/18ft9in
Wing area – 134.43m²/1447sq ft
Weights: Empty – 5799kg/12,773lb
Maximum take-off – 9080kg/20,000lb
Performance: Maximum speed – 251kph/156mph
Service ceiling – 6557m/21,500ft
Range – 2188km/1360miles
Climb – 286m/940ft per minute

Fairey Swordfish

The Swordfish holds a special place in aviation history because it is one of the few combat aircraft to be operational at both the start and end of World War II. This remarkable aircraft was also the last British military biplane in front-line service, and had the distinction of serving longer than the aircraft intended to replace it in Fleet Air Arm service. The "Stringbag" was developed from an earlier failed Fairey design and first flew in April 1934, designated TSR (torpedo spotter reconnaissance).

After successful service trials, a contract to supply 86 Swordfish Mk Is to the Royal Navy's Fleet Air Arm was signed. The Swordfish entered service with No.825 Squadron in July 1936, and over the next three years a further 600 aircraft were delivered, equipping 13 Fleet Air Arm squadrons. During World War II another 12 squadrons were formed.

The wartime exploits of this deceptively frail-looking aircraft are legendary. Its first major action was against the Italian naval base at Taranto on November 11, 1940. HMS *Illustrious* launched 21 Swordfish of Nos.815 and 819 Squadrons to make a night attack on the Italian fleet. During the raid the Swordfish destroyed three battleships, two destroyers, a cruiser and other smaller ships for the loss of only two of the attacking aircraft. The attack crippled the Italian fleet and eliminated the opportunity for Italian warships to bolster German naval strength in the Mediterranean.

Other notable actions include the crippling of the German battleship *Bismarck* in May 1941. Swordfish from the Royal Navy carriers HMS *Victorious* and HMS *Ark Royal* were involved in the search for the German battleship. The first Swordfish attack, led by Lieutenant Commander Esmonde,

LEFT: **Each of these D-Day period Swordfish bears stripes on both sets of wings and the fuselage, giving the aircraft a zebra-like appearance. There were few Allied biplanes in the front line at the time of D-Day.** BELOW: **The "Stringbag" was involved in many notable World War II actions, the most famous of which is probably the Swordfish attack on the Italian fleet at Taranto.**

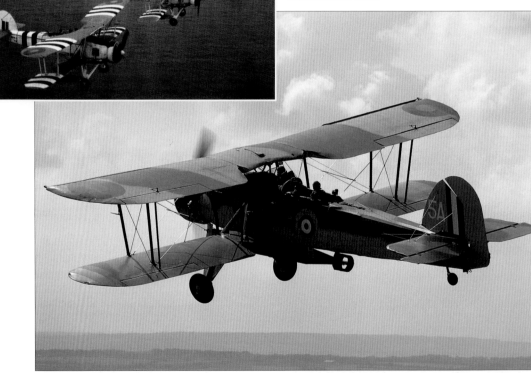

was launched from *Victorious* but none of the torpedoes from the nine aircraft caused serious damage. During the second attack, delivered by 20 Swordfish from the *Ark Royal*, a torpedo severely damaged *Bismarck's* rudder, greatly limiting the ship's manoeuverability. The pursuing British task force was then able to catch and finally sink *Bismarck* with naval gunfire.

Then in February 1942, crews of No.825 Squadron carried out a gallant attack against the *Scharnhorst*, *Gneisenau* and *Prinz Eugen*, during which all six aircraft were shot down. Only five of the 18 crew members survived. For his bravery and leadership under fire, Lieutenant Commander Esmonde, veteran of the *Bismarck* mission and leader of the attack, was posthumously awarded the Victoria Cross.

While the Mk I was an all-metal, fabric-covered aircraft, the Mk II Swordfish which entered service in 1943 had metal-clad lower wings to enable the aircraft to fire rocket projectiles.

Later the same year, ASV (air-to-surface-vessel) radar was installed between the aircraft's fixed undercarriage legs on Mk IIIs, while the Mk IV had an enclosed cockpit.

During the desperate Battle of the Atlantic, there were simply not enough aircraft carriers to escort Allied convoys across the ocean. As a stopgap measure to provide some protection for the convoys, Britain converted grain ships and oil tankers to become MAC ships (Merchant Aircraft Carriers). Grain ships, fitted with a 122m/400ft flight deck, a below-deck hangar and lift, operated four Swordfish. The tankers had a 140m/460ft flight deck but no hangar in which to accommodate their three Swordfish – the MAC Swordfish suffered considerable wear and tear.

From 1940 all development and production of the Swordfish passed from Fairey to the Blackburn Aircraft Company, which built 1699 of the 2391 aircraft produced. The last RN Swordfish squadron disbanded in May 1945.

ABOVE: **The Swordfish outlasted the aircraft intended to replace it in Fleet Air Arm service, the Albacore.** LEFT: **An excellent air-to-air study of Swordfish, complete with 45cm/18in torpedo. Note the bomb shackles beneath the wing.** BELOW: **Thirteen Fleet Air Arm squadrons were equipped with the "Stringbag" when war broke out.**

Fairey Swordfish Mk I

First flight: April 17, 1934
Power: One Bristol 690hp Pegasus IIIM3 9-cylinder air-cooled radial engine
Armament: One fixed 7.7mm/0.303in Browning machine-gun in the nose and one flexible 7.7mm/0.303in Vickers or Lewis machine gun in the rear cockpit; one 45cm/18in 731kg/1610lb torpedo or one 681kg/1500lb mine or bombs
Size: Wingspan – 13.87m/45ft 6in
      Length – 10.87m/35ft 8in
      Height – 3.76m/12ft 4in
      Wing area – 56.39m²/607sq ft
Weights: Empty – 2134kg/4700lb
      Maximum take-off – 3409kg/7510lb
Performance: Maximum speed – 222kph/138mph
      Service ceiling – 5029m/16,500ft
      Range – 1658km/1030 miles unloaded
      Climb – 3050m/10,000ft in 15 minutes, 2 seconds

Fairey Battle

The Fairey Battle which first flew on March 10, 1936 was initially known as the Fairey Day Bomber. It had its origins in a 1932 Air Ministry specification, and was a single-engine light bomber with a crew of three, designed to replace the Hind and Hart biplanes in Royal Air Force service. This low-wing stressed-skin monoplane was the epitome of modern aircraft design in the mid-1930s, replacing fabric-covered biplanes and boasting a retractable undercarriage, variable-pitch propellers and a cockpit canopy. Impressively, it could carry twice the bomb load over the twice the distance of the aircraft it was to replace. Nevertheless when it went to war, it was an aircraft out of time and proved to be under-powered and inadequately armed for modern air combat.

The famous Merlin engine is forever linked to the Battle of Britain duo, the Spitfire and Hurricane, but the Fairey Battle was the first aircraft to be fitted with the new high-performance Rolls-Royce engine. The five main marks of the Battle (I–V) were designated thus depending which version of the Merlin engine, I to V, was used for power.

Battles entered RAF service in May 1937 and ultimately equipped 15 RAF bomber squadrons. By the time Britain entered World War II in September 1939, over 1000 aircraft were in service with the RAF.

TOP: **Three Stockport-built Fairey Battle Is of No.218 Squadron, Royal Air Force. The Battle could carry a much greater bomb load than those aircraft that it replaced, but it was underpowered.** ABOVE: **K4303, the Battle prototype, pictured over a Fairey airfield. Note that this aircraft has a propeller spinner fitted, but service aircraft did not have this refinement.**

When Britain sent the Advanced Air Striking Force to France in September 1939, ten squadrons of Battles were the main offensive component. On September 20, 1939, a Battle of No.88 Squadron claimed the first German aircraft downed on the "western front". However, the Battle was no match for nimble monoplane fighters, and was simply no longer suited to unescorted daylight missions. On September 30, 1939, when four out of five Battles of No.150 Squadron were shot down by Bf109s, unescorted missions ceased.

Fairey Battle Mk I

First flight: March 10, 1936
Power: One Rolls-Royce 1030hp Merlin
    12-cylinder piston engine
Armament: One 7.7mm/0.303in machine-gun in
    leading edge of starboard wing and one in rear
    cockpit; bomb load of 454kg/1000lb
Size: Wingspan – 16.45m/54ft
    Length – 12.90m/42ft 4in
    Height – 4.57m/15ft
    Wing area – 39.2m²/422sq ft
Weights: Empty – 3018kg/6647lb
    Maximum take-off – 4899kg/10,792lb
Performance: Maximum speed – 414kph/257mph
    Service ceiling – 7930m/26,000ft
    Range – 1609km/1000 miles
    Climb – 280m/920ft per minute

TOP: **Over 1000 Battles were in RAF service when war broke out, and the type was sent into action early in the conflict. All was well until the Battle faced the best Luftwaffe fighters on the day and suffered heavy losses. By 1941 most were being used for training.** ABOVE: **On one operation in May 1940, 40 out of 71 aircraft were lost on a daylight raid against enemy targets.** RIGHT: **The Fairey P4/34, inspired by the Battle and resembling a scaled-down version of it, began as a light bomber prototype. The aircraft was developed into a two-seat fighter for the Royal Navy, the Fulmar.**

When the Blitzkrieg reached France in May 1940, these Battles were thrown into the thick of the fighting in desperation, doing battle with the most modern German fighters, and they suffered terrible losses. On May 10, operating at heights of around 76m/250ft, the Battles attacked German ground forces with delayed-fuse bombs and suffered high losses from ground fire – 13 of 32 aircraft were lost. On May 14, a force of 71 Battles was sent to bomb German bridges at Sedan and only 31 aircraft returned to their bases.

By the end of June 1940, all Battles were recalled to Britain but the type continued to be used for attacks against enemy-held Channel ports as well as the crucial raids against the German invasion barges in the Channel ports in September 1940.

Once removed from front-line duties, Battles were used as training aircraft, target-tugs and for teaching air gunnery. A dedicated two-cockpit Battle Trainer, a truly strange-looking aircraft, helped many British and Commonwealth pilots earn their wings.

Eight hundred were shipped to Canada and 400 to Australia for these purposes under the Empire Air Training Scheme (EATS). Battles remained in Royal Australian Air Force use until 1949.

Battles were also exported to Turkey (29), South Africa (190 plus) who used them in action in East Africa, and Belgium where 18 were built under licence by Avions Fairey. These Belgian Battles suffered the same fate at their RAF counterparts as they bravely fought against much more modern aircraft.

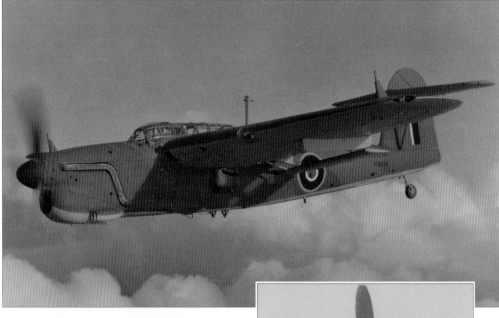

Fairey Barracuda

The Fairey Aviation Company's response to Specification S.24/37 for a Fairey Albacore replacement was the three-seat Barracuda, which had its maiden flight on December 7, 1940. Testing highlighted some shortcomings that were resolved in the second prototype, but this did not fly until June 1941. Britain's aviation industry was focusing on the production of fighters and bombers at the time, and the new torpedo bomber just had to wait. Service trials were therefore not complete until February 1942, after which the more powerful Merlin 32 was fitted. The new engine was required to cope with the increasing weight of the Barracuda due to a beefing-up of the structure and additional equipment to be carried. The re-engined Barracuda became the Mark II, the main production variant of the type. The Mark IIs began to enter service in early 1943, the first 12 Mark IIs going to No.827 Squadron, then re-forming at Stretton. By May 1943, many squadrons of the Fleet Air Arm became fully equipped with Barracuda Mk IIs and then joined carriers of the home and Far Eastern fleets. The Barracuda has a number of claims to fame – it was the first British carrier-based monoplane of all-metal construction to enter service with the Fleet Air Arm, as well as being the first monoplane torpedo bomber. A total of 1688 Barracuda Mk IIs were built by Fairey, as well as Westland, Blackburn and Boulton Paul.

The Barracuda Mark III (912 examples built by Fairey and Boulton Paul) was developed to carry air-to-surface-vessel radar in a radome blister under the rear fuselage, and first flew

TOP: **A fine air-to-air study of a Fairey (Heaton Chapel-built) Barracuda Mk I.** ABOVE: **A great visual explanation of the below-deck space saving that can be achieved by having naval aircraft with folding wings.**

in 1943. The radar enabled the Barracuda to track its prey much more effectively. In European waters, Mark IIIs equipped with ASV radar flew anti-submarine patrols from small escort carriers, using rocket-assisted take-off to get clear of the short decks.

In April 1944, the carriers *Victorious* and *Furious* sent 42 Barracudas to carry out a dive-bombing attack on the German pocket battleship *Tirpitz*, then at anchor in Kaa Fjord, Norway.

The Barracudas were part of Operation Tungsten, the aim of which was the destruction of the enemy ship. The Barracudas had practised long and hard for the operation, and attacked in a steep dive despite heavy defensive flak. They scored 15 direct hits with armour-piercing bombs for the loss of only two aircraft. *Tirpitz* was so damaged in the raid that it was out of action for three months, and the Navy was able to channel its resources elsewhere, at least for a time.

Nos.810 and 847 Squadrons, Fleet Air Arm, which were embarked on HMS *Illustrious*, introduced the Barracuda to the Pacific theatre of operations in April 1944, when they supported the US Navy in a dive-bombing attack on the Japanese installations on Sumatra.

In all, 17 operational Fleet Air Arm squadrons were equipped with Barracudas during World War II. Wartime production of the Fairey Barracuda totalled 2541 aircraft. In 1945, production started on the more powerful Mk V, later designated the TF.5, but only 30 models of this variant were built and were used as trainers during the post-war period.

No fewer than 2572 Barracudas of all marks were delivered to the FAA. Barracudas were also operated by the French and Dutch Fleet Air Arms.

ABOVE RIGHT: **The Barracuda was instrumental in severely damaging the *Tirpitz* during April 1944.** RIGHT: **The ultimate Barracuda, the Mk V appeared too late for war use, and was destined for post-war training instead.** BELOW: **With the carrier deck crew watching intently, a Fleet Air Arm Barracuda prepares to catch the arrestor wire with its hook.**

Fairey Barracuda Mk II

First flight: December 7, 1940
Power: One Rolls-Royce 1640hp Merlin 32 V-12 piston engine
Armament: Two 7.7mm/0.303in Browning machine-guns in rear cockpit; one 735kg/1620lb torpedo or one 454kg/1000lb bomb beneath fuselage, or four 204kg/450lb or six 113kg/250lb bombs, depth charges or mines under wings
Size: Wingspan – 14.99m/49ft 2in
Length – 12.12m/39ft 9in
Height – 4.60m/15ft 1in
Wing area – 34.09m²/367sq ft
Weights: Empty – 4245kg/9350lb
Maximum take-off – 6401kg/14,100lb
Performance: Maximum speed – 367kph/228mph
Ceiling – 5060m/16,600ft
Range – 1851km/1150 miles
Climb – 1524m/5000ft in 6 minutes

LEFT: **The Farman can only be described as an amazing looking contraption, but it did carry out a daring night raid on Berlin.**

Farman F.220 series

The unmistakable Farman F.220 series of heavy bombers might have been one of the older designs in Armée de l'Air service, but it was still the only four-engined bomber in the Allied inventory of 1940.

The series had its origins in the F.210 of 1930, which began the distinctive box cross-section fuselage retained by descendent bombers for the next decade. The aircraft had a very high

wing, and four radial engines arranged in back-to-back pairs so that each engine nacelle had both a pusher and puller propeller. Despite its ungainly appearance, its performance was good for the time. When war broke out, the F.221 and the F.222 versions carried out leaflet raids over Germany, and during the fight for France the aircraft carried out 63 bombing missions over Germany and occupied France. The series

reached its technological peak with the F.223 (renamed NC.223 when the Farman company merged), one of which carried out an epic and courageous night-bombing attack on Berlin on the night of June 7–8, 1940.

Farman F.222.2

First flight: October 1937
Power: Four Gnome-Rhone 920hp 14N 14-cylinder radial piston engines
Armament: One 7.5mm/0.29in machine-gun in nose, dorsal and ventral turrets; up to 3900kg/8584lb bomb load
Size: Wingspan – 36m/118ft 1.25in
Length – 21.45m/70ft 4.5in
Height – 5.2m/17ft 0.3in
Wing area – 186m²/2002sq ft
Weights: Empty – 10,800kg/23,770lb
Maximum take-off – 18,700kg/41,159lb
Performance: Maximum speed – 360kph/224mph
Ceiling – 8000m/26245ft
Range – 2200km/1367 miles
Climb – 3000m/9840ft in 9 minutes, 40 seconds

LEFT: **The M.F.11 was the first military trainer in Australia, and this example is preserved in that country.**

Farman M.F.11 Shorthorn

First flight: 1914
Power: One Renault 70hp 8-cylinder piston engine
Armament: One machine-gun for the observer; up to eighteen 7.3kg/16lb bombs on underwing racks
Size: Wingspan – 16.15m/53ft
Length – 9.5m/31ft 2in
Height – 3.9m/12ft 9.5in
Wing area – 57m²/613.56sq ft
Weights: Empty – 550kg/1210lb
Maximum take-off – 840kg/1849lb
Performance: Maximum speed – 100kph/62mph
Ceiling – 3800m/12,470ft
Endurance – 3 hours, 45 minutes
Climb – 90m/295ft per minute

Farman M.F.11 Shorthorn

The Maurice Farman M.F.11 (S.11 in British service) was developed from the earlier M.F.7 known as the Longhorn due to the long structural "horns" that supported the forward elevator. The M.F.11 was therefore inevitably known as the Shorthorn as it lacked the forward elevator. This was replaced by a hinged elevator attached to the tail.

The aircraft first flew in 1914 and was of pusher configuration, so lent itself to reconnaissance and bombing. Adopted by most of the Allied air arms, the Shorthorn was often equipped with dual controls and was used as a trainer throughout the war. The M.F.11 was available with floats for operation from calm water.

Britain's Royal Naval Air Service took delivery of around 90 examples. One aircraft piloted by the daring Commander Samson made a lone night attack against enemy targets at Ostend. He dropped 18 7.3kg/16lb bombs, having used the flare from a Very pistol to illuminate his targets below.

Fiat B.R.20 Cicogna

This aircraft was one of a long line of Italian combat aircraft designed by Rosatelli from 1919, all designated with the prefix B.R. for Bombardamento Rosatelli. The B.R.20 was designed and entered production remarkably quickly, and the prototype had its maiden flight in February 1936. Incredibly, the Cicogna (stork) equipped combat units by the end of that year. The B.R.20 was an advanced all-metal aircraft for the time, and Italy's Aviazione Legionaria took the type into action in support of the Nationalists during the Spanish Civil War. It flew alongside German Heinkel 111s, proved to be very effective, and could hold its own when faced with the fighters of the day. Spain purchased 25 of their own and also negotiated a manufacturing licence which was never taken up.

The aircraft was successfully exported to Venezuela and also to Japan, which operated 85 examples in China under the designation Type 1 Model 100. By the time Italy entered World War II in 1940, the B.R.20 was effectively obsolete.

The improved and streamlined B.R.20M (M for modificato) accounted for around half of the 602 B.R.20s built, and featured heavier defensive armament and protective armour.

Well known for its use in the Balkan and Western Desert campaigns, this Italian bomber was actually deployed against the British mainland for a brief spell, a fact that is often overlooked. Keen to promote joint military operations with the Germans and possibly believing German propaganda that the RAF would

ABOVE: **The B.R.20 was the subject of an unusual trade agreement with Japan – 85 of the bombers were supplied in exchange for large deliveries of soya beans.** BELOW LEFT: **This once-advanced bomber was obsolete by 1940.**

be a pushover, Mussolini sent a fleet of B.R.20 bombers escorted by Italian fighters to the Channel coast for operations against England.

On November 1, 1940, a formation of around ten B.R.20s, escorted by 40 CR42 fighters, set course to attack the docks at Harwich. Eight of the bombers were claimed as destroyed by the RAF and the Italians withdrew within weeks.

Fiat B.R.20 Cicogna

First flight: February 10, 1936
Power: Two 1000hp Fiat A.80 engines
Armament: One 12.7mm/0.5in machine-gun in nose, dorsal and ventral turret; internal bomb load of 1600kg/3522lb
Size: Wingspan – 21.56m/70ft 8in
Length – 16.68m/54ft 8in
Height – 4.75m/15ft 7in
Wing area – 74m²/796.5sq ft
Weights: Empty – 6500kg/14,306lb
Maximum take-off – 10,340kg/22,758lb
Performance: Maximum speed – 440kph/273mph
Ceiling – 8000m/26,250ft
Range – 2750km/1709 miles
Climb – 6000m/19,685ft in 25 minutes

Focke-Wulf Fw200

The Fw200 Condor maritime reconnaissance bomber aircraft had its origins in a Deutsche Lufthansa airliner. The Fw200 was a low-wing, all-metal, four-engine monoplane with fully retractable undercarriage which could carry 26 passengers. The aircraft was a headline-grabber in 1937, and set numerous records pre-war for non-stop flights from Germany to New York and Tokyo. Finland, Denmark and Brazil ordered the airliner but the military capabilities of the large aircraft were not lost on the Japanese who were the first to ask for a military long-range maritime-reconnaissance version. This development prototype, known as the Fw200V-10, had a large below-floor cabin grafted on to the underside of the fuselage, which carried the aircraft's bomb load as well as defensive machine-guns. The aircraft's obvious applications came to the attention of the Luftwaffe, who then requested a prototype of their own, the Fw200C, for evaluation. As World War II broke out and the Luftwaffe needed a long-range maritime-patrol and attack aircraft, their prototype version was pressed into production.

TOP AND ABOVE: **The military potential of the Fw200 was apparently first considered by the Japanese. Had Germany developed the Condor into a heavy bomber early in the war and produced large numbers, this could have been a major threat to Britain. However, the Luftwaffe were more concerned with tactical aircraft than "heavies".**

The first Luftwaffe unit to receive the Condor (and its main operator for the war) was Kampfgeschwader (KG) 40 in April 1940. With a crew of five (pilot, co-pilot and three gunners), the Condor flew its first mission against British shipping on April 8, 1940, while operating from Denmark. Two months later, the unit was transferred to France, from where it operated until

Focke-Wulf Fw200C-3 Condor

First flight: July 27, 1937 (civil model)

Power: Four BMW-Bramo 1200hp 323R-2 Fafnir 9-cylinder radial engines

Armament: One 7.92mm/0.31in gun in forward dorsal turret, one 13mm/0.5in gun in rear dorsal position, two 13mm/0.5in guns in beak positions, one 20mm/0.78in gun in forward position of ventral gondola and one 7.92mm/0.31in gun in aft ventral position; maximum bomb load of 2100kg/4622lb

Size: Wingspan – 32.85m/107ft 9in
Length – 23.45m/76ft 11in
Height – 6.30m/20ft 8in
Wing area – 119.85m²/1290sq ft

Weights: Empty – 17,005kg/37,428lb
Maximum take-off – 24,520kg/53,968lb

Performance: Maximum speed – 360kph/224mph
Service ceiling – 6000m/19,685ft
Range – 3560km/2212 miles
Climb – 200m/656ft per minute

ABOVE: **Operating from France, and not in huge numbers, the Fw200s caused great losses to British shipping.** BELOW RIGHT: **The Condor could also act as an airborne command post, directing U-boats towards allied shipping.**

late 1944. By the end of September 1940, the Condors had sunk 91,440 tonnes/90,000 tons of Allied shipping, and Churchill soon referred to these aircraft as "the scourge of the Atlantic".

By December 1940, 36 aircraft were operational, and during 1941, 58 Mk C-2s were built, fitted with bomb racks in the outboard engine nacelle and beneath the wing. Structural problems with the Condor's rear fuselage manifested themselves early in the aircraft's career, with a number simply breaking their backs on landing. An improved, strengthened version with much more powerful engines, the Fw200C-3, was being built by mid-1941.

As the Condor became more numerous and crews learned the art of maritime surveillance and attack, the aircraft became a major threat to Allied shipping – 328,185 tonnes/323,016 tons (116 ships) were sunk during April 1941 alone. The radius of operation could be extended even further as long-range fuel tanks would increase endurance from the normal 9 hours, 45 minutes to 18 hours.

The final version of the Condor to see service was the Fw200C-6 armed with a Henschel Hs293B air-to-surface missile beneath each wing. The total wartime Fw200 production was 252 aircraft.

Despite the relatively small numbers, the Condor fleet proved to be a major concern for the Allies – not only could the Condor attack a ship on its own, it could also direct U-boats towards convoys. The Condor's reign ended in late 1944 as the Allies overran Luftwaffe bases in France. Surviving Fw200s earned their keep as transports. The chief of the Gestapo, Heinrich Himmler, had a Condor as his personal transport. Well armoured, the VIP transport boasted a large leather chair, as well as a personal escape hatch for the occupant.

ABOVE: **The "scourge of the Atlantic", as Churchill once described the Condor fleet, was only stopped when the Allies seized their French bases after D-Day.**

Gotha bombers

TOP AND ABOVE: **The Gotha was one of the first bombers able to take the war far beyond the front line and right to the heart of the enemy's homeland. Gotha raids on London in 1917–18 caused panic and damage to morale.**

As a result of unexpected and seemingly unstoppable bombing raids by German bombers over London in 1917–18, for some civilians the word "Gotha" became synonymous with terror. Development of the series of bombers began in 1915 with the Gotha G.II, which entered service on the Eastern Front in the autumn of 1916. Repeated engine failures led to its withdrawal and the appearance of the G.III with two machine-guns and the more reliable Mercedes D IVa engine. By December 1916, 14 were in front-line service, each able to carry a 400kg/880lb bomb load.

The Germans had been keen to carry out sustained bombing raids over London, and were able to do this with their Zeppelin airships until British defences got the measure of their hydrogen-filled adversaries. A heavier-than-air alternative was needed, and so the Gotha G.IV was conceived. Some sources claim the aircraft's development was greatly helped by the capture of a brand new Handley Page O/400 in early 1917.

The G.IV was made of wood and steel, and covered with plywood and fabric. An unusual feature was the "firing tunnel" tested on some G.IIIs, which enabled the gunner to fire down "through" the floor to defend the aircraft's rear most effectively by eliminating the blind-spot favoured by stalking fighter aircraft. Power was provided by two Mercedes D.IVa in-line piston engines mounted between the wings and driving pusher propellers. To give clearance to the spinning wooden prop blades behind the wings, the trailing edge of the upper wing had a large section removed. When testing proved the soundness of the aircraft's design, production began by Gotha, LVG and Siemens-Schuckert.

When formations of Gothas headed to hostile territory they were able to cover each other with defensive fire from their two 7.92mm/0.31in Parabellum machine-guns, something lone Zeppelin raiders lacked on their 51 bombing raids over Britain in World War I. The G.IV was able to carry up to 500kg/1100lb of bombs in cradles beneath the wing, and two primitive rectangular bomb bays between the pilot and the rear crewman contained up to six bombs, each stacked one on the other so that as the lowest bomb was released, all of the rest followed.

The first large Gotha raid on Britain took place on May 25, 1917, when 21 Gothas bombed Folkestone in Kent, killing almost 100 civilians. Within three weeks, the first daylight raid on London was carried out by a formation of 14 Gothas. The raids continued each day, with the Gothas flying at heights of 3050–4880m/10,000–16,000ft up the Thames Estuary, too high for the defenders to reach them. However, to achieve these altitudes the Gothas had to reduce their bomb load, which was at its maximum on night raids when lower altitudes were safer. The raids against southern England were launched mainly from the German bases St Denis Westrem and Gontrode in Belgium. These airfields were frequently attacked by British bombers trying to remove the threat to the homeland at source. The Gotha raids were costly in lives but were also damaging financially and psychologically for the civilians who experienced the raids. By early 1918, the raiders were suffering heavy losses to the guns of the fast-climbing British S.E.5a and Sopwith Camel defending fighters, even at night.

August 1917 had seen the introduction of the G.V, an improved version of the IV which featured more aerodynamic engine nacelles to reduce drag. The final versions in service were the G.Va, with a biplane tail assembly and a shorter nose, and the G.Vb which had a nose wheel for improved landing safety on night operations.

The 22 Gotha raids on Britain had seen these early bombers drop a remarkable total of 84.3 tonnes/83 tons of bombs on the country.

TOP RIGHT: **A Gotha V, featuring more streamlined engine nacelles.**
RIGHT: **The Gotha G.VII was produced as a long-range reconnaissance aircraft, with the nosegun position deleted and the engines repositioned closer to the fuselage and in a puller configuration.** BELOW: **Formations of Gothas were early users of the box formation best associated with the Eighth Air Force bombers of World War II. The Gothas positioned themselves to provide mutual cover against enemy aircraft.**

Gotha G.V

First flight: Early 1917
Power: Two Mercedes 260hp D IVa in-line piston engines
Armament: Two 7.92mm/0.31in machine-guns on mounts in nose and dorsal positions; up to 500kg/1100lb bomb load
Size: Wingspan – 23.7m/77ft 9in
Length – 11.86m/38ft 11in
Height – 4.3m/14ft 1.25in
Wing area – 89.5m²/963.4sq ft
Weights: Empty – 2740kg/6030lb
Maximum take-off – 3975kg/8748lb
Performance: Maximum speed – 140kph/87mph
Ceiling – 6500m/21,325ft
Range – 500km/311 miles
Climb – 3000m/9840ft in 28 minutes

Grumman Avenger

Grumman's large single-engine torpedo bomber certainly lived up to the name "Avenger" given to it on the day that Japan attacked Pearl Harbor. Procured in great quantities, the type saw action with Allied air arms in virtually all theatres of operation in World War II. Of the 9836 aircraft produced, 2290 were built by Grumman (and designated TBF) while the remaining TBM models were manufactured by the General Motors Eastern Division.

The Avenger was designed in just five weeks, and was first flown on August 1, 1941. With a three-man crew, the aircraft featured an internal weapons bay, gun turret and a rear defensive gun position. A door on the right-side rear of the wing allowed access into the rear fuselage, which was packed with equipment, flares, parachutes and ammunition. At the lower level, the bombardier was provided with a folding seat from which he could either man the lower rear machine-gun, or face forward and aim the aircraft for medium-altitude level bombing. The pilot sat in a roomy and comfortable cockpit above the leading edge, and enjoyed an excellent view.

Only one aircraft returned from the six that made the Avenger's combat debut at the Battle of Midway in June 1942. Despite this poor start, the Avenger went on to become one of the great naval combat aircraft of World War II, being involved in the destruction of more than 60 Japanese warships. It was the first US single-engined aircraft able to

TOP AND ABOVE: **The Grumman Avenger and Tarpon, one and the same. The Royal Navy quickly dropped the Tarpon name and standardized on the original US one. The excellent Avenger was designed in just five weeks.**

carry the hard-hitting 560mm/22in torpedo (as well as depth charges, rockets and bombs) and was also the first to boast a power-operated gun turret. Torpedoes launched by US Navy Avengers were largely responsible for the sinking of the large Japanese battleships *Yamato* and *Musashi*.

The Royal Navy received 402 Avengers (TBF-1Bs) under the Anglo-American Lend-Lease arrangement with the first squadron, No.832 Squadron (on board HMS *Victorious*), being equipped in early 1943. Although originally designated Tarpon Mk I for British service, they were later redesignated Avenger Mk I. Around 330 TBM-1s were also supplied to the Royal Navy, and designated Avenger Mk II.

Delivery of the TBM-3 began in April 1944, with the Royal Navy receiving the 222 TBM-3 aircraft designated Avenger Mk III by the British. Torpedo bomber versions remained in

ABOVE AND RIGHT: **Although the Avenger had a shaky combat debut during the Battle of Midway, it was soon shown to be among the best naval fighting aircraft ever produced. Avengers lived up to their name and were solely or partly responsible for the destruction of over 60 Japanese naval targets.**

RN service until 1947 and then, in 1953, the Royal Navy began acquiring anti-submarine versions designated the Avenger AS Mk IV or AS Mk V. The Avenger finally retired from the Royal Navy in 1962.

In 1951, the Royal Canadian Navy anti-submarine units were re-equipped with wartime Avengers which had been overhauled and updated. In 1955, a further eight Avengers entered Canadian service in the Airborne Early Warning role, carrying large and powerful equipment. New Zealand acquired two squadrons of Grumman Avengers, which were used as dive-bombers by Nos.30 and 31 Squadrons. Secondary roles undertaken by the Kiwi Avengers included the spraying of Japanese gardens with diesel oil and target drogue towing.

Post-war, the type was also adapted to a wide variety of civilian uses, including crop-spraying and water-bombing. During 1947 an Avenger was used for trials of aerial seed-sowing and fertilizing in New Zealand. With an additional auxiliary fuel tank converted into a hopper installed in the bomb bay, it could carry 1017kg/2240lb of fertilizer.

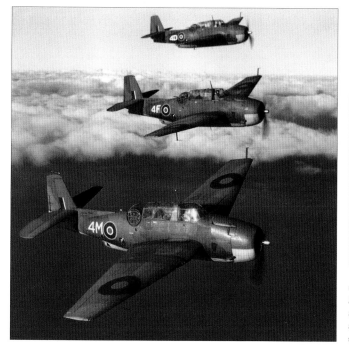

Grumman TBM-3 Avenger

First flight: August 1, 1941
Power: One Wright 1900hp R-2600-20 radial engine
Armament: Two 12.7mm/0.5in fixed forward-firing machine-guns in the upper part of the forward fuselage, two trainable 7.62mm/0.3in machine-guns in rear cockpit; external bomb or depth charge load of 1021kg/2250lb
Size: Wingspan – 16.51m/54ft 2in
Length – 12.48m/40ft 11in
Height – 5m/16ft 5in
Wing area – 45.52m²/490sq ft
Weights: Empty – 4787kg/10,545lb
Maximum take-off – 8124kg/17,895lb
Performance: Maximum speed – 444kph/276 mph
Ceiling – 7625km/25,000ft
Range – 1609km/1000 miles
Climb – 328m/1075ft per minute

LEFT: **Three Avengers of No.846 Squadron, Fleet Air Arm, pictured in December 1943. Torpedo-armed British Avengers served until 1947, but anti-submarine versions flew on in Fleet Air Arm service until 1962.**

353

Handley Page Halifax

RAF Fighter Command's Hurricane was always overshadowed by the Spitfire, and in Bomber Command the Halifax was regularly eclipsed by the Lancaster, despite the Handley Page bomber's significant contribution to the Allied victory in World War II. The Halifax preceded the Lancaster into Bomber Command service and was the first four-engine RAF "heavy" to drop bombs on Germany in World War II.

Originally designed as a twin-engine monoplane to Specification P.13/36 using the ill-fated Rolls Royce Vulture engine, the Halifax underwent a radical redesign in 1937. The aircraft was uprated with four 1280hp Merlin X engines and defensive armament for the seven-man crew, which was comprised of two 7.7mm/0.303in Browning machine-guns in the nose turret, two in beam positions and four in the rear turret. The prototype first flew in October 1939, the first production aircraft entering service with RAF Bomber Command a year later with No.35 Squadron of No.4 Group. The Halifax's first bombing operation saw six aircraft of No.35 attack enemy targets in Le Havre, France, on the night of March 11–12, 1941.

The Halifax Mk I was built in three groups, Series I, II and III, the difference being the permitted take-off weight of each. The Series III also had an increased fuel capacity. The Mk II was again made in three series. The Series I was powered by four 1390hp Merlin XX engines and had increased fuel capacity. The two hand-held machine-guns in the aircraft's waist positions were deleted and replaced by a Boulton Paul twin-gun turret in the dorsal position. Flame-damping exhaust muffs were removed to improve performance, and the little-used nose turret was also eliminated. The Halifax II Series IA was powered by 1460hp Merlin 22 engines housed in low-drag cowlings. For forward defence, a single machine-gun was mounted through a redesigned Perspex nose cone and a four-gun low-drag dorsal turret was also fitted. Later production Series IA aircraft also introduced the rectangular vertical tail

surfaces that became synonymous with the Halifax. These modifications raised the aircraft's speed by 32kph/20mph compared with the Mk I.

The next major development was the Mk III model, which was powered by four 1615hp Bristol Hercules XVI radial engines. The first example flew in July 1943. Other modifications included a retractable tail wheel and an H2S radar scanner in a blister beneath the lower rear fuselage or a ventral gun as standard. On later production examples, extended wingtips were introduced, thereby raising the span to 31.76m/104ft 2in. This new wing was used on all subsequent Halifax variants. The Halifax Mk IV was a project only and by the time the ultimate Mk VI and VII bomber versions were produced in 1944, the Halifax was showing its age and very few were produced. In 1944 some Mk IIIs, Vs and VIIs were converted for paratroop-dropping and glider-towing in preparation for the D-Day offensive.

A total of 6176 aircraft were built and, although overshadowed by the Avro Lancaster, the Handley Page Halifax proved to be a far more versatile aircraft in that it could be adapted to many different roles. The Halifax squadrons of the RAF flew 82,773 operational sorties for the loss of 1884 aircraft (2.2 per cent) during World War II. The last Halifaxes were phased out of Royal Air Force and French Armée de l'Air service in 1952.

RIGHT: **A Halifax Mk I of No.76 Squadron.** BELOW: **An aircraft of No.10 Squadron. Although in the shadow of the "Lanc", the Halifax was produced in great numbers and played a key role in the ultimate Allied victory.**

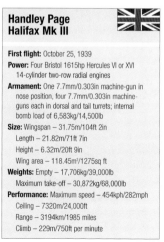

Handley Page Halifax Mk III

First flight: October 25, 1939

Power: Four Bristol 1615hp Hercules VI or XVI 14-cylinder two-row radial engines

Armament: One 7.7mm/0.303in machine-gun in nose position, four 7.7mm/0.303in machine-guns each in dorsal and tail turrets; internal bomb load of 6,583kg/14,500lb

Size: Wingspan – 31.75m/104ft 2in
Length – 21.82m/71ft 7in
Height – 6.32m/20ft 9in
Wing area – 118.45m²/1275sq ft

Weights: Empty – 17,706kg/39,000lb
Maximum take-off – 30,872kg/68,000lb

Performance: Maximum speed – 454kph/282mph
Ceiling – 7320m/24,000ft
Range – 3194km/1985 miles
Climb – 229m/750ft per minute

LEFT: **The squadron code "KM" identifies these Hampden Mk Is as aircraft of No.44 Squadron.**
BELOW: **Men of a No.83 Squadron Hampden leaving their aircraft after a flight early in World War II.**

Handley Page Hampden

The Handley Page Hampden prototype H.P.52 first flew in June 1936, and after Royal Air Force trials and various modifications, the type entered service with No.5 Group, RAF, during the summer of 1938. This five-seat medium bomber was so fast and manoeuvrable that Handley Page initially presented it to the RAF as a fighter-bomber. The pilot had a fixed forward-firing gun in addition to the aircraft's three manually operated Lewis guns for all-round defence. This defensive system gave the Hampden the edge over its British rivals because it didn't suffer from the drag and weight penalties of heavy gun turrets. In fact, the Hampden bomb load was almost equal to that carried by the bigger Whitley and Wellington, and it was almost as fast as the Blenheim medium bomber.

By the start of World War II, eight RAF squadrons were fully operational and took part in the early raids against German naval shore installations and shipping in the North Sea. However, daylight raid formations over enemy territory soon encountered opposition from fast German single-engine fighters, and the Hampden squadrons suffered heavy losses. In fact, casualties were so high that the Hampdens were taken off operations until they could be equipped with much better armament and armour. By then the decision had been taken that RAF Bomber Command would become mainly a night-raiding force, which no doubt saved many Hampden crews' lives.

Nicknamed the "Flying Suitcase" because of the cramped crew positions in a very narrow fuselage, the Hampden had a successful career with No.5 Group during the summer of 1940, bombing Germany itself, mine-laying and bombing invasion barges in continental ports along the English Channel. It had a separate and successful career as a long-range torpedo bomber with RAF Coastal Command until late 1943.

A total of 1430 Hampden medium bombers were built before the type was replaced in RAF squadron service by the Avro Manchester from 1941.

Handley Page Hampden Mk II

First flight: June 21, 1936
Power: Two Bristol 1000hp Pegasus XVIII 9-cylinder radial engines
Armament: One 7.7mm/0.303in machine-gun in port side of forward fuselage, one in nose position, two in dorsal and two in ventral positions; bomb load of 1816kg/4000lb
Size: Wingspan – 21.08m/69ft 2in
Length – 16.33m/53ft 7in
Height – 4.55m/14ft 11in
Wing area – 62.06m²/668sq ft
Weights: Empty – 5348kg/11,780lb
Maximum take-off – 8515kg/18,756lb
Performance: Maximum speed – 409kph/254mph
Ceiling – 5795m/19,000ft
Range – 3034km/1885 miles
Climb – 300m/980ft per minute

LEFT: **Daylight raids early in the war showed that the Hampden had defensive deficiencies.**

Handley Page Heyford

The Heyford was the last biplane bomber in RAF service and even looked dated when new, its fixed spatted landing gear doing nothing to improve its appearance. The Heyford's wings were of metal frame with fabric covering, while the fuselage was half metal (forward) and half fabric-covered. Despite this, the Heyford was the most important British bomber of the mid-1930s.

Three prototypes were ordered for evaluation in 1927, the first having its maiden flight in June 1930. Successful testing led to the type being ordered, and when production ended in July 1936, 15 Heyford Mk I, 21 Heyford Mk IA, 16 Heyford Mk II and 70 Heyford Mk III aircraft had been delivered. The marks differed little except in the type of engines installed, all Rolls-Royce Kestrels.

Perhaps the most striking visual feature of the bomber was that its fuselage was mounted on the upper wing. This gave the pilot and defensive gunners an excellent field of vision. To protect the aircraft's blind spot below and to the rear, a retractable ventral "dustbin" turret could be lowered from beneath the rear fuselage.

The centre section of the lower wing was thick enough to contain cells for the carriage of bombs. It is a matter of opinion if the proximity of the bomb cells to the ground made for speedy re-arming since armourers had to lie on the ground beneath the aircraft to secure the bombs in place.

The first unit to be equipped with the type in November 1933 was No.99 Squadron based at Upper Heyford. Nos.7, 9, 10, 38, 78, 97, 102, 148, 149 and 166 Squadrons followed.

As Whitleys and Wellesleys appeared from 1937, the Heyford was gradually phased out, the last being replaced by Wellingtons in 1939. The type continued to be used for training purposes until being finally retired in July 1941.

TOP: **K3500, Heyford I of 99 Squadron. The aircraft was lost after an engine failure at night in May 1937. Note the bomb shackles under the wing.**

ABOVE: **A Heyford crew of No.10 Squadron poses for the camera. The gunner's exposed position cannot have been a popular one.**

Handley Page Heyford Mk IA

First flight: June 1930 (prototype)
Power: Two Rolls-Royce 575hp Kestrel IIIS 12-cylinder piston engines
Armament: Three 7.7mm/0.303in machine-guns in nose, dorsal and ventral "dustbin" positions; up to 1589kg/3500lb bomb load
Size: Wingspan – 22.86m/75ft
Length – 17.68m/58ft
Height – 5.33m/17ft 6in
Wing area – 136.56m²/1470sq ft
Weights: Empty – 4177kg/9200lb
Maximum take-off – 7672kg/16,900lb
Performance: Maximum speed – 229kmh/142mph
Ceiling – 6405m/21,000ft
Range – 1481km/920 miles with reduced bomb load
Climb – 213m/700ft per minute

Handley Page O/400

Given that powered flight was so new, Handley Page's World War I series of large night-bombers was a remarkable achievement. The Handley Page O/400 was a refinement of the earlier O/100, which was designed to an Admiralty specification for a dedicated bomber aircraft – at the time (1914) this was a revolutionary idea. O/100s were operational in France in 1916, and revision of the design (increased fuel capacity and better engines) led to the hugely successful O/400 bomber. Five hundred and fifty were built in Britain and a further 100 were produced in the USA. The 0/400 was a very large aircraft, and in daylight would have been easy prey for capable German fighters. It was therefore used as a night-bomber and could carry ordnance up to the size of the 749kg/1650lb bomb, the heaviest used by the British during World War I.

Charged with attacking enemy industrial targets, the 0/400s would fly in fleets of up to 40 a night. These raids were the first true strategic bombing raids in history, and the large Handley Page bombers were seen by some military leaders as the future of waging war. More than 400 O/400s operated with the Royal Air Force before the Armistice of November 1918, equipping Nos. 58, 97, 115, 207, 214, 215 and 216 Squadrons of the RAF. In August 1918 an O/400 was attached to No.1 Squadron of the Australian Flying Corps serving in the Middle East. No.1 worked with T.E. Lawrence, whose Arab associates, impressed by the sheer size of the aircraft, reportedly called it "The Father of all aeroplanes".

The type served in the RAF until late 1919, when it was replaced by the Vickers Vimy. Post-war, ten O/400s were converted from military to civil configuration and used in the UK by Handley Page Transport Ltd.

Handley Page O/400

First flight: December 17, 1915
Power: Two Rolls-Royce 360hp Eagle VIII Jupiter VIII piston engines
Armament: Various bomb loads, sixteen 50.8kg/112lb bombs or one 749kg/1650lb bomb, two 7.7mm/0.303 Lewis Guns in nose, two Lewis guns in mid-upper position, and single Lewis firing through lower rear trapdoor
Size: Wingspan – 30.48m/100ft
 Length – 19.17m/62ft 10.75in
 Height – 6.72m/22ft 0.75in
 Wing area – 153.1m²/1648sq ft
Weights: Empty – 3859kg/8502lb
 Maximum take-off – 6065kg/13,360lb
Performance: Maximum speed – 157kph/98mph
 Service ceiling – 2590m/8500ft
 Range – 1046km/650 miles
 Climb – 3048m/10,000ft in 40 minutes

Hawker Typhoon

The Typhoon was designed around the new Rolls-Royce and Napier 24-cylinder 2000hp engine then under development, and flew for the first time in February 1940. Development and production problems delayed the Typhoon's delivery to the RAF until August 1941, when it became the RAF's first 643kph/400mph fighter. However, the extent of engine and structural problems in its early days was such that the large Hawker fighter was almost withdrawn from service. Instead, the problems were resolved and a use was found for the Typhoon's high low-level speed. Luftwaffe Focke-Wulf 190s had been carrying out hit-and-run raids along Britain's south coast, and the Typhoon, with its top speed of 663kph/412mph, was the only British fighter that could catch them. Typhoons destroyed four raiders within days of being deployed.

Following the success of night raids over occupied France in November 1942, the fighter was employed increasingly for offensive duties, strafing enemy airfields, shipping, roads, railways and bridges. From 1943, "Tiffies" went on the offensive, attacking targets in

France and the Low Countries, and when carrying rocket projectiles, they proved to be truly devastating aircraft.

Just prior to D-Day (June 6, 1944), Typhoons attacked German radar installations. These high-risk daylight attacks against heavily defended targets robbed the enemy of their radar "eyes" when they needed them most.

Relentless day and night attacks by RAF Typhoons on German communications targets greatly aided the D-Day operations. The aircraft that was once almost scrapped from RAF service eventually equipped no fewer than 26 squadrons of the 2nd Tactical Air Force. The Typhoon's original bomb load of 227kg/500lb gradually increased to 908kg/2000lb, the heaviest payload of any fighter-bomber. With eight 27.2kg/60lb rocket projectiles beneath the wing in which were buried four 20mm/0.78in cannon each firing 600 rounds per minute, at low level the "Tiffie" was a monster that harried German ground forces throughout Normandy. Later Typhoons had the bubble cockpit canopy in place of the earlier "glasshouse" framed cockpit, which improved visibility.

TOP AND ABOVE: **Although designed as a pure fighter, it will be as a ground-attack type that the Typhoon will perhaps be best remembered. The "Tiffie" inflicted massive damage on German forces before, during and after the D-Day landings. Note the rockets beneath the wing of the aircraft pictured immediately above.**

Hawker Typhoon IB

First flight: May 27, 1941 (Production IA)
Power: Napier 2180hp Sabre IIA 24-cylinder sleeve-valve liquid cooled piston engine
Armament: Four 20mm/0.78in cannon in outer wings and racks for eight rockets or two 227kg/500lb bombs
Size: Wingspan – 12.67m/41ft 7in
Length – 9.73m/31ft 11in
Height – 4.67m/15ft 4in
Wing area – 25.92m²/279sq ft
Weights: Empty – 3995kg/8800lb
Maximum take-off – 6015kg/13,250lb
Performance: Maximum speed – 663kph/412mph
Ceiling – 10,736m/35,200ft
Range – 821km/510 miles (with bombs)
Climb – 914m/3000ft per minute

Heinkel He111

The prototype of the Heinkel He111 first flew in February 1935 and owed many of its design features to the earlier single-engine He70 which set eight world speed records in 1933. Designed in 1934 as a twin-engine high-speed transport and revealed to the world as a civil airliner in 1935, the He111 was in fact secretly developed as the world's most advanced medium bomber. Six He111 C-series airliners went into service with Lufthansa in 1936 but even the airliner versions served a military purpose, as two He111s in Lufthansa markings flew secret photographic reconnaissance missions over the Soviet Union, France and Britain.

It took the installation of 1000hp Daimler-Benz DB 600A engines and the improved all-round performance they bestowed to make the He111 a viable military aircraft. The first mass-produced bomber versions, the He111 E and He111 F, were desperately effective in the testing-ground that was the Spanish Civil War, where, as part of the Condor Legion, they flew in support of the Fascists. The effectiveness of Blitzkrieg tactics was due in no small part to the Heinkel bomber – the bombing of Guernica sent a clear message around the world about the military might of the Luftwaffe. The speed of the He111 enabled it to outpace many of the fighter aircraft pitted against it in Spain, but this led the Germans to assume incorrectly that their bombers would reign supreme in the European war that was to come.

ABOVE AND BELOW: **A German bomber, built in Spain post-war, powered by British engines. These aircraft were Spanish licence-built CASA 2.111s, and served the Spanish Air Force into the 1960s. These were the "Heinkels" that appeared in the film "Battle of Britain".**

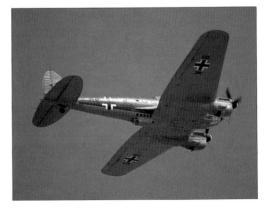

However, the Heinkel's shortcomings were exposed when it came up against the more modern fighters of the Royal Air Force – the Spitfire and the Hurricane. Although by sheer weight of numbers, the He111s did inflict much destruction on Britain during the early stages of World War II, losses mounted and the Heinkel was soon restricted to night operations and other specialized missions.

Under cover of darkness during the Blitz of 1940–1, the He111 continued to perform as an effective bomber, inflicting serious blows against its British enemies, including the devastating raids on Coventry.

Due to a German decision to focus on mass production of existing weapons rather than invest in development of newer ones, the He111 laboured on long after it should have been retired. He111s were developed for use as torpedo bombers, glider tugs and troop transports, and in the last year of the war they served as air launch platforms for V1 flying bombs targeted against British cities. Perhaps the strangest development of the He111 was the joining of two aircraft at the wing, with an additional section of wing containing a fifth engine. Twelve examples of this truly strange-looking aircraft were produced as tow aircraft for the large Messerschmitt Me321 transport gliders. By the end of World War II, however, the He111 was used mainly as a transport aircraft.

By the end of 1944, over 7300 He111s had been built for the Luftwaffe, while a further 236 were licence-built by the Spanish manufacturer CASA. The Spanish machines (designated CASA 2.111) were identical to the He111 H-6 produced in Germany and half were powered by Junkers engines supplied from Germany. The rest of the Spanish aircraft, built post-war, had Rolls-Royce Merlin engines. Spain continued to operate the Heinkel bombers until 1965.

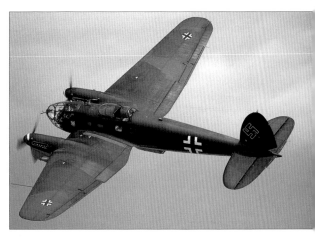

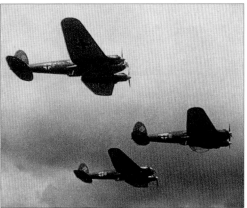

ABOVE RIGHT: **The Spanish machines were the same as the He111 H-6.** RIGHT: **The real thing – a formation of Luftwaffe He111s.** BELOW: **Groundcrew attending to a Luftwaffe He111 early in World War II.**

Heinkel He111 H-16

First flight: February 24, 1935 (prototype)
Power: Two Junkers 1350hp Jumo 211F piston engines
Armament: One 20mm/0.78in MG FF cannon in nose, one 13mm/0.51in MG131 gun in dorsal position, two 7.92mm/0.31in MG15 guns in rear of ventral gondola and two 7.92mm/0.31in MG81 guns in each of two beam positions; up to 2500kg/5503lb of bombs carried internally and externally
Size: Wingspan – 22.60m/74ft 1in
  Length – 16.40m/53ft 9in
  Height – 4m/13ft 1in
  Wing area – 86.50m²/931.07sq ft
Weights: Empty – 8680kg/19,105lb
  Maximum take-off – 14,000kg/30,814lb
Performance: Maximum speed – 436kph/271mph
  Service ceiling – 8390m/27,500ft
  Range – 1950km/1212 miles
  Climb – 4500m/14,765ft in 30 minutes

Heinkel He177

Had the Nazis produced an atomic bomb, as the Luftwaffe's only heavy bomber it was the He177 Greif (griffon) that would have carried it. At the end of World War II a sole aircraft undergoing modification for the role was discovered in Czechoslovakia. Given the number of these aircraft that had to turn back from missions due to engine problems, the bomb might have posed more of a threat to Germany than anywhere else. Of all the aircraft in the Luftwaffe's World War II inventory, the He177 had the greatest military potential and caused the greatest amount of trouble to its air and ground crews.

In many ways, it is surprising that the aircraft made it to production at all because it was proposed to meet a baffling 1938 requirement for a large, long-range heavy bomber and anti-shipping aircraft that could deliver a sizeable 2000kg/4402lb bomb load in medium-angle dive-bombing attacks. It has to be borne in mind that while the Allies embraced the concept of strategic air power as a means of waging war, the Luftwaffe was always a tactical air power adjunct to German land forces. That different philosophy explained the lack of large, heavy bombers in the wartime Luftwaffe.

RIGHT AND BELOW: **Having emerged from an ill-considered specification, the He177 proved to be the only German four-engined "heavy" of World War II. In mid-1944, there were raids on the Eastern Front of up to 90 of these troublesome aircraft.**

At a glance, the six-seat He177 has two engines, but on closer inspection each Daimler-Benz DB-610 engine is in fact a pair of coupled DB605 engines driving a single propeller shaft. The designers decided that was a good way to reduce drag, but any benefits were far outweighed by the innumerable problems caused by these troublesome engines which regularly caught fire in the air, even at cruising speeds. Six out of the eight prototypes crashed and out of the first 35 pre-production A-0 models, built mainly by Arado, many were written off through take-off accidents or fires in flight. A further 130 A-1 versions were built by Arado, while Heinkel were responsible for the production of the A-3 and A-5 versions, of which 170 and 826 respectively were constructed.

The aircraft itself was essentially a good design, and the slim tubular fuselage and long wings gave a range of 5500km/3417 miles – far beyond anything else in the Luftwaffe inventory. The engine was the design's Achilles

heel, and plagued its service record. The type in A-1 form was first used in action by KG (*Kampfgeschwader*) 40 for maritime strike and reconnaissance missions from bases in France. The aircraft could carry an impressive range of anti-shipping ordnance, including the Henschel Hs 293 missile, which was guided after launch to its target by the bombardier's joystick in the gondola beneath the nose. The missile "pilot" followed the missile's course thanks to flares at the rear of the missile. Torpedoes and sea mines could also be deployed.

During January to March 1944 the Luftwaffe's KG40 and KG100 carried out what were known as the Steinbock raids. These revenge raids were in response to the Allies' escalating attacks against German cities and were aimed at London. The planners knew the single most effective way that the aircraft could attack and hope to evade interception by the Royal Air Force's increasingly efficient nightfighter force. The aircraft climbed to around 9000m/29,527ft over the coast of Europe and then, at full power, began a shallow dive towards Britain. By the time the aircraft were over England they were at speeds of around 700kph/435mph, which made the aircraft hard to catch but did little for bombing accuracy. The raids were ineffective and although of the 35 aircraft that took part in the numerous raids only four were destroyed by British defences, many had to turn back repeatedly with engine fires and other malfunctions.

Following the D-Day landings, He177 anti-shipping missions from France ceased, but the type was still in use as a missile launch platform against the Allies in early 1945.

On the Eastern Front, KG4 and KG50 were first to use the He117 in the pure bomber role, and some aircraft were also fitted with huge 50mm/2in or even 75mm/2.93in anti-tank guns.

ABOVE: **An He117 A-5/R2 carrying a Henschel Hs 293A anti-shipping missile. The weapon could be carried on a special pylon fitted beneath the forward bomb bay or beneath the wing.** RIGHT AND BELOW: **The RAF evaluated certain captured enemy aircraft. Note that in both these photographs the Luftwaffe markings have been overpainted with RAF roundels, and broad D-Day invasion-type stripes have been applied to the wings and rear fuselage to deter friendly would-be attackers. The aircraft pictured on the right has had "Prise de Guerre" painted on its side.**

Heinkel He177 A-5

First flight: November 19, 1939
Power: Two Daimler-Benz 2950hp DB 610A piston engines
Armament: Three 7.92mm/0.31in machine-guns, three 13mm/0.51in machine-guns and two 20mm/0.78in cannon in nose, tail, dorsal and ventral gondola positions; up to 1000kg/2201lb of bombs and two anti-shipping missiles
Size: Wingspan – 31.44m/103ft 1.75in
Length – 20.4m/66ft 11.25in
Height – 6.39m/20ft 11.75in
Wing area – 102m²/1097.95sq ft
Weights: Empty – 16,800kg/36,976lb
Maximum take-off – 31,000kg/68,231lb
Performance: Maximum speed – 490kph/304mph
Ceiling – 8000m/26,245ft
Range – 5500km/3417 miles
Climb – 260m/853ft per minute

Ilyushin Il-2 Shturmovik

During the 1930s, the Soviet government was very interested in developing a dedicated purpose-designed anti-tank aircraft. Various projects came to nothing, then in 1938, as war seemed inevitable, a team under Sergei V. Ilyushin at the Soviet Central Design Bureau (TsKB) produced a new design, a two-seat aircraft designated the TsKB-55 which first flew in December 1939. The Ilyushin design was then redesignated BSh-2, for Bronirovanni Shturmovik or Armoured Assault Aircraft. Although some of the aircraft, now designated Il-2, did reach front-line units by the time of the June 1941 German invasion, the new and unfamiliar aircraft had little impact. By now the Soviets were concerned that many of

ABOVE AND BELOW LEFT: **More Il-2s were built than any other aircraft in history. When told of production problems with the type, Stalin said the tough, hard-hitting aircraft were "needed by the Red Army like it needs air or bread". The large hollow above the engine directed air to the engine's radiator intake.**

their aircraft factories might be overrun by the Germans, so development and production of the Il-2 ceased while the factories were relocated beyond the Urals. This was a massive undertaking, and all the more remarkable because Il-2s were coming off the new refined production lines only two months after the relocation of the production facilities.

This heavily-armoured ground-attack monoplane was the backbone of the Soviet ground-attack units during World War II and was one of the most formidable aircraft used in the conflict. Perhaps the key to the aircraft's success was its survivability due to the extraordinary amounts of protective armour which was not installed but was part of the aircraft's structure itself, guarding the pilot, engine, fuel tank, cooling system and bomb bays.

The aircraft first flew in single-seat form on October 12, 1940, and went on to be the most produced aircraft in history, with more than 36,000 built. The heavily armoured Il-2 reached front-line units in May 1941. Though devastating against ground targets, the aircraft was no match for modern fighter aircraft when Soviet fighter cover was not available, and it

suffered heavy losses from the Luftwaffe. The solution was proposed in February 1942 – the two-seat Il-2m3, which was in fact the original configuration proposed by Ilyushin. The second crewman manned a 12.7mm/0.5in machine-gun for rear protection but he was not as protected by armour as the pilot and was seven times more likely to be killed in action. The forward-firing armament of two 20mm/0.78in cannon was also replaced by two high-velocity 23mm/0.9in cannon.

On November 19, 1942, the Red Army launched a counterattack against the German offensive in Stalingrad, and their white Shturmoviks were the masters of the air. Over the following four days the Il-2s carried out around 1000 sorties attacking German armour, artillery and troops. The Ilyushin aircraft was a key part of the Soviet counterattack which led to the German surrender at Stalingrad on February 2, 1943.

The Il-2m3 had four small bomb bays that could carry up to 192 2.5kg/5.5lb PTAB anti-tank bomblets which the aircraft would scatter over enemy columns. It was also equipped with the DAG-10 grenade launcher which would eject small aerial mines on parachutes in the path of pursuing aircraft.

By mid-1943, Shturmovik pilots had perfected their tactics. Flying in groups of eight to twelve aircraft in open country, they would attack soft targets such as personnel or soft-skinned vehicles by simply skimming in as low as 5m/16ft. Against armoured columns, they would attack straight down the column or weave across it repeatedly, scattering the PTAB anti-tank bombs from as low as 100m/320ft. Bunkers or emplacements were attacked using dive-bombing techniques. To tackle armour formations on a battlefield, the Il-2s would form their "circle of death" above and around the enemy below. Aircraft would peel off it, turn and attack the tanks below almost at their leisure, knowing that a large part of the sky above was protected by the encircling Il-2s. Ground fire less than 20mm/0.78in calibre held no fear for the well-armoured Shturmoviks. The attacks would continue until the aircraft expended fuel and ammunition.

The Il-2's contribution to the pivotal Soviet victory at Kursk was considerable. The aircraft destroyed 70 tanks of the 9th Panzer Division in just 20 minutes, killed 2000 men and destroyed 270 tanks of the 3rd Panzer Division in just two hours, and virtually wiped out the 17th Panzer Division.

TOP AND ABOVE: **The rear gunner of Il-2m3 frequently had the aft cockpit canopy removed to improve his or her field of fire. The aircraft in the foreground immediately above bears the legend "Avenger".** BELOW LEFT: **The Il-10 replaced the Il-2 in production in 1944. With fighter-like handling, the Il-10 was a major redevelopment of the Il-2, which remained in service in the Eastern Bloc into the late 1950s.**

Ilyushin Il-2m3 Shturmovik

First flight: March 1941 (production Il-2)
Power: One Mikulin 1720hp Am-38F piston engine
Armament: Two 23mm/0.9in wing-mounted machine-guns and one 12.7mm/0.5in machine-gun for gunner; up to six 100kg/220lb bombs or two 250kg/551lb bombs plus eight rocket projectiles under outer wing
Size: Wingspan – 14.6m/47ft 10.75in
Length – 11.65m/38ft 2.5in
Height – 4.17m/13ft 8in
Wing area – 38.5m²/414.42sq ft
Weights: Empty – 4525kg/9959lb
Maximum take-off – 6360kg/13,998lb
Performance: Maximum speed – 410kph/255mph
Service ceiling – 6000m/19,690ft
Range – 765km/475 miles
Climb – 5000m/16,405ft in 12 minutes

Ilyushin Il-4

Always overshadowed by its Western counterparts, the Il-4 was produced in great quantities, and was one of the best bomber aircraft of World War II. It was derived from the Ilyushin DB-3, a record-breaking long-range bomber that first flew in prototype form in 1935. The second prototype, the TsKB-30, amazed the world when it flew from Moscow to Canada, a distance of 8000km/4971 miles. The DB-3 served in great numbers with the Long Range Aviation and Naval Aviation elements of the Soviet Air Force, and carried out early bombing raids on Germany in World War II. The 7.62mm/0.3in rifle-calibre armament of the DB-3 proved inadequate against Finnish fighters in the 1939–40 Winter War, but was never significantly improved.

An improved version, the DB-3F, was developed in 1938, one of the requirements being that assembly was to be very straightforward for mass production. The new version bore little resemblance to its predecessor, having a streamlined and extensively glazed nose. It was also more heavily armoured than its predecessor, more so when it saw action because the gunners proved to be a popular target for enemy fighter pilots.

Test-flights were concluded by June 1939 and the type, redesignated Il-4 in 1940, was ordered into production. After the German invasion, production had been disrupted by moving the lines to the safety of Siberia. During the production run in 1942, wood was introduced in place of some metal components made of scarce light alloys. Metal was reintroduced as soon as it became available. Manufacture of the Il-4 continued until 1944, by which time 5256 had been built.

TOP AND ABOVE: **The Ilyushin DB-3 bomber was a record-breaker, and its defensive armament (7.62mm/0.3in) was one of the aircraft's few shortcomings.**

A fourth crew member, the "hatch" gunner, was added to improve defence, and two external fuel tanks were also added, which resulted in an 18 per cent increase in the fuel and an additional 600km/373 mile range. The outer wing was redesigned with leading-edge sweepback, thus improving stability and control. New, more efficient propellers and bigger split-flaps were installed to improve short-field operations.

The Il-4 was used for long-range bombing missions, but was equally efficient hauling its maximum bomb load of 2500kg/5502lb over short distances to attack tactical targets. The first Soviet bombing raid on Berlin was carried out by naval Il-4s on the night of August 8–9, 1941.

LEFT: **The upper gun turret of the DB-3F was fitted with a 12.7mm/0.5in machine-gun.** BELOW: **These aircraft were the backbone of Soviet long-range bomber capability.**

ABOVE: **The Il-4 proved itself to be among the best bomber aircraft produced by the Soviet Union in World War II. Note the very thick flying suits worn by the crew in this photograph, and also the machine-gun in the centre of the aircraft's nose.**

Il-4 crewman Lieutenant I.M. Chisov was thrown clear of his exploding aircraft following a German fighter attack in January 1942. Without a parachute, he fell 6710m/22,000ft into a snow-filled ravine and, though badly injured, lived to tell the tale.

The Il-4 was also developed as a mining and torpedo bomber equipped with a 940kg/2069lb torpedo for attacks against German shipping in the Baltic. Some pilots were happy to carry two of these heavy weapons at the same time. These naval Il-4s were also equipped with six RS-82 rocket projectiles beneath the wing for suppression of flak ships and other defences.

The type remained in Soviet military use after the end of World War II into the 1950s, and was given the NATO codename "Bob". An improved version, the Il-6, was designed for high-altitude operations powered by two 1500hp diesel engines, but was never flown.

Ilyushin Il-4

First flight: 1939
Power: Two 1100hp M-88B radial piston engines
Armament: One 12.7mm/0.5in and two 7.62mm/ 0.3in machine-guns on mounts in nose and dorsal positions; up to 2500kg/5502lb bomb load
Size: Wingspan – 21.44m/70ft 4.25in
Length – 14.8m/48ft 6.75in
Height – 4.1m/13ft 5.5in
Wing area – 66.7m²/717.98sq ft
Weights: Empty – 5800kg/12,766lb
Maximum take-off – 11,300kg/24,871lb
Performance: Maximum speed – 430kph/267mph
Ceiling – 9700m/31825ft
Range – 3800km/2361 miles
Climb – 270m/886ft per minute

Junkers Ju 52/3m

The Junkers Ju 52/3m is one of the greatest aircraft ever built. Though simple and unwieldy by modern standards, with a fixed undercarriage and corrugated construction, the robust Junkers was built in great numbers and served in a variety of roles from bomber to ski-equipped airliner. It equipped no fewer than 30 airlines pre-war and remained in service with a Swiss airline half a century after the type first flew.

The 3m (for three engines or *Motoren*) was developed from a single-engine version of the same aircraft, the Ju 52. The 3m version first flew in April 1932 and quickly became the standard aircraft of Lufthansa, accounting for three-quarters of its fleet. The military applications of this rugged and capable aircraft were clear to the German militarists, who encouraged the development of a military bomber-transport version. The Ju 52/3mg3e, powered by three BMW 525hp 132A-3 engines, could carry six 100kg/220lb bombs. It had a faired gun position on top of the fuselage rear of the wing and a primitive "dustbin" turret, each mounting a 7.92mm/0.31in machine-gun. As a transport, it could carry 18 troops or 12 stretchers.

This version became the first type to equip the first bomber group of the fledgling and secretly developing Luftwaffe, and it debuted as a bomber in 1936 during the Spanish Civil War with Germany's Condor Legion. Initially the Junkers ferried more than 10,000 Moroccan troops to Spain in support of the

TOP: **The "Tante Ju" (Auntie) Junkers, developed throughout its service, was the aerial workhorse of Nazi Germany.** ABOVE: **The Ju 52/3m was the standard airliner of Lufthansa, making up most of its fleet in the mid-1930s. The aircraft pictured here is still operated by the German airline and appears at air shows around Europe.**

Fascists, but then began bombing Republican targets and supporting ground troops battling for control of Madrid.

In March 1937 the Ju 52s, which were then considered to be slow, were tasked with night-time bombing of Republican-held territory. For the rest of the war the Ju 52 was used for moving large numbers of troops and supplies. That said, by the end of the war the Junkers bombers had dropped 6096 tonnes/6000 tons of bombs – the Ju 52 had played an important part in Franco's victory.

By the outbreak of World War II, the Ju 52 was obsolete as a bomber but was used on a vast scale as a transport aircraft. Over 1000 Ju 52s were in service with the Luftwaffe

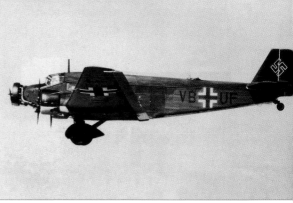

LEFT: **The Ju 52 had a fixed undercarriage – one of its recognition features, together with the type's corrugated metal skin.**

at the start of World War II, but at peak, around 5000 examples of the rugged workhorse were used by the Third Reich. Hitler himself used a Ju 52 as his private transport for a time. Ju 52s transported the attacking army and their supplies during the German invasions of Norway, Denmark, France and the Low Countries in 1940.

In May 1941, around 500 Ju 52s took part in the huge airborne assault by the Germans on the island of Crete. Numerous versions appeared during the war with improved radio equipment, auto pilot and different self-defence armament. Minesweeper and glider tug versions also saw service. The Ju 52 was used on all fronts on which the Third Reich fought, and was a vital part of the Nazi war machine.

However, production of the aircraft was not limited to Germany. In post-war France, 400 examples of a version designated the AAC 1 Toucan were built, a number of them serving in the French Air Force and Navy. These French machines saw active service in the Algerian and Indo-China conflicts. Meanwhile in Spain CASA, who also produced a version of the Heinkel He111, built 170 aircraft designated C-352-L. An often forgotten Ju 52 fact is that ten reconditioned examples captured from the Luftwaffe flew with British European Airways in the immediate post-war years.

ABOVE LEFT: **Each aircraft in this formation of Ju 52s has its ventral "dustbin" gun turret deployed – another unpopular gunner position.** ABOVE: **The type was improved constantly (the aircraft shown here has streamlined housings over the wheels), and appeared in a multitude of versions.**

Junkers Ju 52/3mg3e

First flight: October 13, 1930 (Ju 52 single-engine version)

Power: Three BMW 725hp 132A-3 radial piston engines

Armament: One 7.92mm/0.31in machine-gun each in dorsal position and retractable ventral "dustbin" turret; 500kg/1100lb bomb load

Size: Wingspan – 29.24m/95ft 11.5in
Length – 18.9m/62ft
Height – 5.55m/18ft 2.5in
Wing area – 110.5m²/1189sq ft

Weights: Empty – 5720kg/12,589lb
Maximum take-off – 10,500kg/23,110lb

Performance: Maximum speed – 265kph/165mph
Service ceiling – 5900m/19,360ft
Range – 1000km/620 miles
Climb – 3000m/9840ft in 17 minutes, 30 seconds

Junkers Ju 87 Stuka

The Stuka (short for *Sturzkampfflugzeug* or dive-bomber) is one of the best-known wartime Luftwaffe-combat types and certainly the easiest to recognize with its inverted gull wings and fixed undercarriage. Like many Luftwaffe aircraft, the Ju 87 was designed to provide tactical support to the army in land actions.

Although dive-bombing was used as an attack technique in World War I, no aircraft in that conflict was specifically designed for the role. Junkers developed the first dedicated dive-bomber, the K47, in the 1920s and test-flew the aircraft in 1928. Most of these aircraft were exported to China amidst great secrecy because Germany was still bound by the post-World War I agreement that it should not be producing weapons of war.

German strategists saw the potential of the dive-bomber as an effective weapon when used in close support of ground forces, reducing the enemy's resistance before ground forces advanced. Still amidst great secrecy, Germany decided to manufacture dedicated dive-bomber aircraft, and in 1933 Henschel developed the Hs123 while Junkers continued to work on their K47. The Henschel design was a biplane, but the Ju 87 (derived from the K47) was a single-engine monoplane which broke with the Junkers tradition of corrugated skin construction. The prototype was powered, ironically as later events proved, by a Rolls-Royce Kestrel engine, and had its

TOP: **Shortly before World War II began, the new Ju 87B had re-equipped all Luftwaffe Stukageschwaden.** ABOVE: **Evaluated under combat conditions in Spain, the Stuka became a key aircraft in the Blitz strategy.**

maiden flight in May 1935. The Luftwaffe were very impressed by the potent new dive-bomber and, with testing complete, the Stuka began to enter service in 1937. These early Stukas were sent to Spain and the Civil War for operational evaluation with the German Condor Legion.

In the first production version, the Ju 87A-1, a single fin replaced the two of the prototype, dive brakes were fitted to the outer wings, and the British engine was replaced by a Junkers Jumo 210Ca 640hp engine. The A-2 model can be identified by the larger undercarriage fairings and was powered by the supercharged 680hp Jumo 210Da.

By early 1939, all the A-series aircraft were relegated to training duties, and all dive-bomber units began equipping with the more powerful Ju 87B series, powered by the 1200hp

Jumo 211Da direct-injection engine. More streamlined spats over the landing gear appeared, and the latest Stukas were now equipped with an automatic dive control. The B-2 was improved further and could carry up to 1000kg/2200lb of bombs. The D-series fitted with the 1410hp Jumo 211J-1 engine introduced more armour to protect the crew. Various sub-types saw action, including night ground-attack versions armed with cannon. From 1942, the Ju 87G-1 dedicated anti-tank version was in action on the Eastern Front.

The Stuka's automatic dive control enabled the pilot to pre-set a pull-out height should he black out in the course of a steep dive-bombing attack. On commencing the dive attack, the pilot adjusted the dive angle manually by referring to red indicator lines painted on the canopy showing 60, 75 and 80 degrees from horizontal. The pilot would visually aim the aircraft at his target until a signal light on the altimeter illuminated, telling the pilot to press the bomb-release button on the top of the control column. The automatic pull-out would commence as the bombs left their cradles. The bombs would follow the same course to the target as the aircraft had during its dive, while the pilot would experience around 6g as the aircraft automatically levelled out to begin its climb skywards.

The rear gunner operated a machine-gun which might keep defending fighters at a safe distance, but a Stuka was easy prey for fast modern fighters. With air superiority achieved and against obsolete fighters in Poland and the Low Countries the Stuka was able to hold its own, but when it came up against the Hurricanes and Spitfires of the RAF large numbers were destroyed on cross-Channel missions. The Ju 87 had a slow top speed and could not climb away quickly. Accordingly, it was withdrawn from operations against the UK, but the type continued to serve in Greece, Crete, North Africa, Malta and on the Eastern Front.

The Stuka was more than a dive-bomber – it was also a psychological weapon. The wheel covers were fitted with sirens that would wind up as the aircraft went into their dive – this created terror among the enemy below. Whistles were also known to be fitted on to the fins of the bombs to ensure a similar effect as the ordnance fell. The total number of Stukas produced was around 5700 aircraft.

ABOVE: **A D-series Stuka, complete with extra armour for crew protection.**
RIGHT: **A Ju 87B, the version which introduced automatic dive control.**
BELOW: **Unmistakable with its inverted gull wings – the Stuka.**

Junkers Ju 87D-1

First flight: 1940
Power: One Junkers 1410hp Jumo 12-cylinder piston engine
Armament: Two 7.92mm/0.3in machine-guns in wings and two in rear cockpit; up to 1800kg/3962lb bomb load
Size: Wingspan – 13.8m/45ft 3.5in
Length – 11.5mm/37ft 8.75in
Height – 3.9m/12ft 9.5in
Wing area – 31.9m²/343.38sq ft
Weights: Empty – 3900kg/8584lb
Maximum take-off – 6600kg/14,526lb
Performance: Maximum speed – 410kph/255mph
Ceiling – 7290m/23,915ft
Range – 1535km/954 miles
Climb – 5000m/16,405ft in 19 minutes, 48 seconds

Junkers Ju 88

Said by many to be the most important German bomber of World War II, the Ju 88 was in front-line service from the start to the end of the war. The Ju 88 is widely described as the "German Mosquito", because like the de Havilland aircraft, the Ju 88 was an extremely versatile design and was developed from a bomber for use in the dive-bomber, torpedo-bomber, close support, reconnaissance, heavy fighter and nightfighter roles.

In January 1936, the ReichsLuftMinisterium (RLM, the German Air Ministry) released specifications for a new fast bomber that could carry a bomb load of over 500kg/1100lb. The Junkers Flugzeug und Motorenwerke company responded with the Junkers Ju 88, designed largely by two American nationals employed for their expertise in stressed-skin construction. Construction of the prototype began in May 1936 with the first flight of the Ju 88-V1 taking place on December 21, 1936. A total of five prototypes were built, and one, the Ju 88-V5, made several record-breaking speed flights. In 1937, the specification was modified to include dive-bombing capabilities as well as an increased payload and range. The Ju 88-V6 was the first prototype built to meet the new specification, and it flew on June 18, 1938. In the autumn of 1938, the RLM chose the Ju 88 to become the latest bomber to join the Luftwaffe, and the Ju 88A production version began to reach front-line units in 1939. When war did eventually break out in September 1939, it was the Ju88A-1

TOP: **The Ju 88 was without doubt the most versatile aircraft operated by the Luftwaffe in World War II, and was in production throughout the conflict.**

ABOVE: **The fastest of the principal German bombers, the Ju 88 was found to have poor defensive armament.**

that entered service, although the first recorded mission was not flown until later in that month. The arrival of the Ju 88 was a significant boost to Germany's bomber forces, and although it was heavier than both the Dornier Do17 and the Heinkel He111, even when it carried a substantial bomb load, it was still the fastest of the three. Unlike other Luftwaffe bomber types such as the Heinkel He111, the Ju 88 was not battle-tested in the Spanish Civil War.

The strong and manoeuvrable Ju 88 was a key Luftwaffe aircraft in the 1940 Battle of Britain but in spite of its speed, it suffered at the guns of the faster British fighters. Although the Ju 88 had an extensive battery of machine-guns for defence, all forward machine-guns except that operated by the pilot had to be operated by the flight engineer who had to leap from one gun to another as British fighters assaulted the aircraft. As a result of combat experiences, the bomber was modified to carry extra defensive guns as well as more armour to protect the crew.

The A-series was the standard bomber version of the Ju 88. About 20 Ju 88As were sold to Finland in 1939, and mass production of the Ju 88 started in 1940 with the A4. Large numbers of the Ju 88A-4 were built with longer wings to carry heavier bomb loads of up to 2500 or 3000kg/5502 or 6603lb. Despite this, the 88 continued to operate successfully from rough fields. By the end of the war, 17 different subtypes of the Ju 88A had been designed. One of the most bizarre came from a 1944 RLM request to Junkers to develop a composite aircraft consisting of a fighter aircraft mounted on top of an unmanned heavy bomber aircraft. This Mistel combination aircraft was then flown to the target, where the fighter's pilot released the bomber, which was filled with explosives and plummeted to earth while the fighter returned to base. These Mistel weapons used old Ju 88s coupled to Messerschmitt Bf109s or Focke-Wulf Fw190s. About 85 Mistel combinations were built by the end of the war but only a few missions were flown.

ABOVE: **The aircraft pictured here is a Ju 88A-5. Bombing, dive-bombing, nightfighting and reconnaissance were all roles carried out by the great varieties of Ju 88s produced during the war.**

RIGHT: **A Ju 88A-4 pictured over the Eastern Front in 1943.**
BELOW: **The large "glasshouse" nose of the Ju 88 gave the crew excellent forward vision.**

Junkers Ju 88A-4

First flight: December 21, 1936 (Ju 88 prototype)
Power: Two Junkers Jumo 1340hp 211J-1 piston engines
Armament: One 7.9mm/0.308in machine-gun in front cockpit, one 13mm/0.51in or two 7.9mm/0.308in machine-guns in front nose, two rearward-firing 7.9mm/0.308in machine-guns in rear cockpit and one 13mm/0.51in or two 7.9mm/0.308in machine-guns at rear of gondola beneath nose; up to 3600kg/7923lb carried internally and externally
Size: Wingspan – 20m/65ft 7in
Length – 14.4m/47ft 2.6in
Height – 4.85m/15ft 11in
Wing area – 54.5m²/586.6sq ft
Weights: Empty – 9860kg/21,041lb
Maximum take-off – 14,000kg/30,814lb
Performance: Maximum speed – 433kph/269mph
Ceiling – 8200m/26,900ft
Range – 2730km/1696 miles
Climb – 400m/1312ft per minute

373

Kawanishi H8K

When Japan first went to war with the Allies, its standard
maritime patrol flying boat was the Kawanishi H6K.
The type performed well in the early stages of the war in the
reconnaissance and bombing roles until it came up against
Allied fighters, when it suffered severe maulings. It had entered
service in 1938 and, thinking ahead, the Japanese Navy
immediately issued a specification for a replacement with a
30 per cent higher speed and 50 per cent greater range.

The requirement called for a long-range aircraft with better
performance than Britain's Short Sunderland or the American
Sikorsky XPBS-1. The designers produced one of the finest
military flying boats ever built, and certainly the best of
World War II.

To give the aircraft the required range, it carried eight
small unprotected fuel tanks in the wings and a further six
large tanks in the fuselage or, more correctly, hull. The hull
tanks were partially self-sealing and also boasted a carbon
dioxide fire extinguisher system. Ingeniously, the tanks were
placed so that if any leaked, the fuel would collect in a fuel

TOP: **The H8K entered Imperial Japanese Navy service in late 1941
and first flew into action in March the following year.** ABOVE: **Fitted
with beaching gear, this H8K, codenamed "Emily" by the Allies, is
undergoing engine runs.**

"bilge" and then be pumped to an undamaged tank. The
aircraft was a flying fuel tank, with 15,816 litres/3479 gallons
being a typical fuel load and accounting for some 29 per cent
of the take-off weight. The aircraft positively bristled with
defensive armament – 20mm/0.78in cannons were carried
in powered nose, dorsal and tail turrets, with two more in
opposite beam blisters. A further three 7.7mm/0.303in
machine-guns were in port and starboard beam hatches and
in the ventral position. The crew positions were well armoured.

ABOVE: **The H8K was the fastest flying boat of World War II.** ABOVE RIGHT: **The Japanese boat was larger overall than the famed Sunderland used by the RAF.** RIGHT: **Well armed and with excellent overall performance, the H8K was a formidable opponent for Allied fighter aircraft.**

The Navy was appropriately impressed with the aircraft, but flight-testing of the H8K in late 1940 was far from uneventful, and numerous features of the aircraft had to be revised. The heavy aircraft's narrow hull, for example, caused uncontrollable porpoising in the water – when the nose lifted from the water's surface, the whole aircraft became unstable. The design team revised the hull, and production of the H8K1 (Navy Type 2 Flying Boat Model 11) began in mid-1941. Total production was a mere 175 aircraft produced in the H8K1, H8K2 (improved engines, heavier armament and radar) and 3H8K2-L (transport) versions.

The H8K was powered by four 1530hp Kasei 11s or 12s. The latter bestowed better high-altitude performance and powered late-production H8K1s. The aircraft's offensive load, carried under the inner wing, was either two 801kg/1763lb torpedoes, eight 250kg/550lb bombs, or 16 60kg/132lb bombs or depth charges.

The H8K made its combat debut on the night of March 4–5, 1942. The night-bombing raid on the island of Oahu, Hawaii, was over so great a distance that even the long-range H8K had to put down to refuel from a submarine en route. Although bad weather meant that the target was not bombed, the raid showed that the H8K was a formidable weapon of war. It was the fastest and most heavily defended flying boat of World War II, and one which Allied fighter pilots found hard to down in aerial combat.

The H8K's deep hull lent itself to the development of a transport version, the H8K2-L, with two passenger decks. The lower deck reached from the nose to some two-thirds of the fuselage, while the upper deck extended from the wing to the back of the hull. Seats or benches could accommodate from 29 passengers or 64 troops in differing levels of comfort. Armament was reduced, as was fuel-carrying capability with the removal of the hull tanks.

Kawanishi H8K2

First flight: Late 1940

Power: Four Mitsubishi 1850hp Kasei radial engines

Armament: 20mm/0.78in cannon in bow, dorsal and tail turrets and in beam blisters, plus four 7.7mm/0.303in machine-guns in cockpit, ventral and side hatches

Size: Wingspan – 38m/124ft 8in
Length – 28.13m/92ft 4in
Height – 9.15m/30ft
Wing area – 160m²/1722sq ft

Weights: Empty – 18,380kg/40,454lb
Maximum take-off – 32,500kg/71,532lb

Performance: Maximum speed – 467kph/290mph
Ceiling – 8760m/28,740ft
Range – 7180km/4460 miles
Climb – 480m/1575ft per minute

Lockheed Hudson

TOP: **The Hudson was specifically designed to meet an urgent British requirement for a coastal reconnaissance bomber, but also went on to serve the USAAF.** ABOVE: **The Hudson also served with the RAAF, RNZAF and RCAF.**

The Lockheed Hudson, the first American-built aircraft to be used operationally by the RAF during World War II, was designed to meet an urgent 1938 British requirement for a long-range maritime patrol bomber and navigation trainer. Lockheed's response, after five days and nights of frenzied work, was a militarized version of the proven Lockheed 14 Super Electra. The original Lockheed Model 10 Electra was a ten-seat civil airliner which first flew in February 1934. The larger and more powerfully engined Super Electra carried 12 passengers and first flew in July 1937. Howard Hughes made a high-profile round-the-world trip in a Super Electra, and it was this type of aircraft that took Prime Minister Chamberlain to meet Hitler in September 1938. In June 1938 the British Purchasing Commission placed an order for the Lockheed aircraft, stipulating that 200 aircraft had to be delivered by the end of December 1939. A further 50 aircraft would be bought if they could be delivered by the same date.

The Hudson was an all-metal mid-wing monoplane with an eliptical cross-section fuselage and a transparent nose for bomb-aiming. Fowler flaps were fitted to improve short-field performance. The crew normally consisted of a pilot, navigator, bomb-aimer, radio operator and gunner. Armament consisted of a bomb load of up to 454kg/1000lb (in later models) and up to seven machine-guns in nose, dorsal turret, beam and ventral hatch positions.

The first flight of a Hudson I (as a modified existing aircraft there was no need or time for a prototype) was on December 10, 1938, and the first of the RAF's aircraft arrived at Liverpool docks within two months. It may be hard to believe now, but the Hudson was considered something of a hot-rod compared to the Anson it replaced in RAF service. It climbed at 366m/1200ft per minute compared to the 220m/720ft per minute of the Anson, and had a top speed around 30 per cent greater than that of the "Annie". The Hudson Mk I began squadron service with RAF Coastal Command's No.224 Squadron in the summer of 1939, and by September No.233 Squadron was also equipped, soon followed by No.220. Shortly after war broke out, Hudsons also equipped

LEFT: **The first American-built aircraft used in action by the RAF during World War II.**
BELOW LEFT: **A Hudson of No.85 Squadron RAF.**
BELOW: **Hudsons and A-29s saw action in the Mediterranean, Pacific, Indian Ocean, Carribbean and Atlantic.**

Nos.206 and 269 Squadrons. All these aircraft flew vital maritime patrol and anti-shipping missions in defence of the UK. At peak strength, the RAF's Hudson force amounted to 17 squadrons.

The Hudson earned its spurs on October 8, 1939, when a No.224 Squadron Hudson Mk I shot down a Dornier Do18D flying boat off Jutland, the first German aircraft to be claimed by the RAF during the war. In early 1940, Hudsons began to be equipped with air-to-surface-vessel radar. Based at Aldergrove in Northern Ireland, Hudsons carried out dedicated anti-submarine patrols from August 1940. The Hudson's first victory against a U-boat occurred on August 27, 1941, when an aircraft operating out of Iceland bombed and damaged *U-570* which, following strafing attacks, surrendered. A total of 25 U-boats were put out of the war by RAF Hudsons.

Hudsons also took part in more conventional operations, with 35 participating in the RAF's second "thousand bomber" raid. The Hudsons of No.161 Squadron took part in top-secret operations delivering (and retrieving) agents, arms and other supplies into enemy territory under cover of darkness.

Total production amounted to 2584, and Hudsons were also operated by the RCAF, RAAF and RNZAF fighting in the Mediterranean, South Pacific, Indian Ocean, North Atlantic and Caribbean. China, Portugal and Brazil also purchased the

Lockheed bomber. The USAAF had 490 (as the A-29), the US Navy 20 (as the PBO-1), and a further 300 were military trainers (AT-18) in the USA. It was US Navy PBO-1s that sank the first two U-boats destroyed by US forces, and a Hudson that destroyed the first for the USAAF.

Lockheed Hudson Mk I

First flight: December 10, 1938
Power: Two Wright 1100hp GR-1820-G-102A radial piston engines
Armament: Two forward-firing 7.7mm/0.303in machine-guns, plus two others in dorsal turret; up to 635kg/1400lb bomb load
Size: Wingspan – 19.96m/65ft 6in
Length – 13.51m/44ft 4in
Height – 3.61m/11ft 10in
Wing area – 51.19m²/551sq ft
Weights: Empty – 5280kg/11630lb
Maximum take-off – 7945kg/17,500lb
Performance: Maximum speed – 396kph/246mph
Ceiling – 7625m/25,000ft
Range – 3154km/1960 miles
Climb – 3048m/10,000ft in 6 minutes, 18 seconds

Martin bomber series

The Martin Model 123 was designed and built as a private venture by the Glenn L. Martin Company of Baltimore, Maryland. The aircraft, which first flew in January 1932, was hugely influential because it broke with many design traditions and set new standards for US military combat types – it was the USAAC's first all-metal monoplane bomber.

The Model 123 was a mid-wing, all-metal monoplane, and the monocoque fuselage had corrugated top and bottom surfaces. The fuselage was sufficiently deep to allow the carriage of bombs in an internal bomb bay, as opposed to the external racks of many bombers in service at the time. The main landing gear retracted backwards to be semi-recessed into the rear of the engine nacelles. In this version, three of the crew of four sat in separate open cockpits atop the fuselage.

The US Army were interested in Martin's new "hot ship", and under the designation XB-907 the aircraft was extensively tested at Wright Field. Its speed of 317kph/197mph was ahead of all the fighters in USAAC service at the time.

The aircraft was returned to Martin for modifications, including the addition of a front gun turret in place of the far-from-popular open gun position in the nose.

However, the pilot's cockpit and the dorsal gunner positions remained open to the elements. The designation was changed to XB-907A when it was returned to the Army for more tests, then in January 1933 the Army ordered 48 production versions with enclosed cockpits, designated YB-10.

The type entered squadron service in June 1934. The major production version was the B-10B powered by 775hp Wright R-1820-33s, and production B-10B deliveries began in December 1935.

The B-12 was the same as the B-10 but was powered by Pratt & Whitney engines and had the ability to carry an auxiliary fuel tank in the bomb bay.

The B-10s and derivatives remained in service with US Army bombardment squadrons until aircraft like the B-17 were available in the late 1930s, by which time it was obsolete. No US Army B-10s participated in any combat during World War II, but export aircraft (Model 139) supplied to the Netherlands saw action against the Japanese in 1942. Other export customers were Argentina, China, the Soviet Union, Siam and Turkey. The sole remaining Martin B-10 is preserved by the United States Air Force Museum.

TOP AND ABOVE: **An advanced US bomber for the time, the B-10 served until being replaced by the next generation of bombers like the B-17. Dutch and Chinese examples were used for missions against the Japanese. Although the type was outmoded by then, it still enjoyed some successful missions. The aircraft pictured above is preserved by the United States Air Force Museum.**

Martin B-10B

First flight: January 1932 (Model 123)
Power: Two Wright 775hp R-1820-33 Cyclone radial piston engines
Armament: Three 7.62mm/0.3in machine-guns in nose and rear turrets and in ventral position; up to 1026kg/2260lb bomb load
Size: Wingspan – 21.49m/70ft 6in
Length – 13.64m/44ft 9in
Height – 4.7m/15ft 5in
Wing area – 62.99m²/678sq ft
Weights: Empty – 4395kg/9681lb
Maximum take-off – 7445kg/16,400lb
Performance: Maximum speed – 343kph/213mph
Ceiling – 7381m/24,200ft
Range – 1996km/1240 miles
Climb – 567m/1860ft per minute

LEFT: **Few Marylands remained in Britain, and the type became the first US-supplied bomber used by the RAF in North Africa.**

Martin Maryland

The Martin 167 Maryland was built to a USAAC specification, but the type was only operated by France and Britain. It was designed for both reconnaissance and bombing, and four squadrons of the French Air Force were equipped with the type at the time of the German invasion in May 1940.

Britain ordered its own Marylands and took delivery of diverted French orders

after France fell. This required all the considerable labelling in the aircraft to be changed from French to English. These early aircraft were designated Maryland Is in RAF service and were followed by the more powerfully engined Maryland IIs. A total of 225 aircraft served with the Royal Air Force and virtually all served in the Middle East.

Malta-based Marylands provided valuable reconnaissance cover in the region, and those of the Desert Air Force's Nos.39 and 223 Squadrons were effective light bombers. The type also equipped four South African Air Force squadrons active in the Western Desert.

Martin Maryland Mk II

First flight: March 14, 1939
Power: Two Pratt & Whitney 1200hp R-1830-S3C4G Twin Wasp radial piston engines
Armament: Four 7.7mm/0.303in wing-mounted machine-guns, plus two more in dorsal and ventral positions; up to 908kg/2000lb bomb load
Size: Wingspan – 18.69m/61ft 4in
Length – 14.22m/46ft 8in
Height – 4.57m/14ft 11.75in
Wing area – 50.03m²/538.5sq ft
Weights: Empty – 5090kg/11,213lb
Maximum take-off – 7631kg/16,809lb
Performance: Maximum speed – 447kph/278mph
Ceiling – 7930m/26,000ft
Range – 1947km/1210 miles
Climb – 546m/1790ft per minute

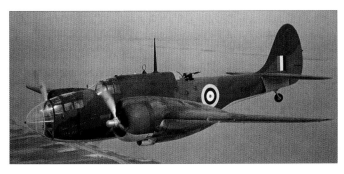

LEFT: **A Baltimore I in flight. Of the RAF's first batch of 400 aircraft, 41 were lost at sea in transit.**

Martin Baltimore Mk IV

First flight: June 14, 1941
Power: Two Wright 1660hp R-2600-19 Cyclone 14 radial piston engines
Armament: Four 7.7mm/0.303in wing-mounted machine-guns, two or four more in dorsal turret, two 7.63mm/0.3in in ventral position; up to 908kg/2000lb bomb load
Size: Wingspan – 18.69m/61ft 4in
Length – 14.8m/48ft 5.75in
Height – 5.41m/17ft 9in
Wing area – 50.03m²/538.5sq ft
Weights: Empty – 7018kg/15,460lb
Maximum take off 10,260kg/22,600lb
Performance: Maximum speed – 491kph/305mph
Ceiling – 7106m/23,300ft
Range – 1530km/950 miles
Climb – 4572m/15,000ft in 12 minutes

Martin Baltimore

Unlike the Maryland, the Baltimore was designed specifically to meet Royal Air Force requirements. Although it was developed from the Maryland and had the same wing, the Baltimore had more powerful engines and, most apparently, a deeper fuselage to allow better communication between the crew. Despite this, the narrow fuselage made movement around the aircraft in an emergency almost impossible. The RAF ordered 400 in May 1940 but 1575 were

ultimately produced for them. They were used solely in the Mediterranean, the first joining No.223 Squadron.

The crew of four consisted of a pilot, navigator/bomb-aimer, top gunner and a radio operator who also manned the ventral gun position. Baltimore Marks I to IV had 1600hp Wright GR-2600-A5B radial engines, while the V and VI had the upgraded 1700hp Wright engines.

Desert Air Force Baltimores flew day and night bombing missions in support

of ground troops in the North African campaign. Later, the type was used for intensive bombing ahead of invading Allied troops in Italy.

Martin Mariner

Martin had a history of producing flying boats, and in 1937 the company began work on a design to replace the Consolidated Catalina in US Navy service. Martin's Model 162, naval designation XPBM-1 (Experimental Patrol Bomber Martin 1), had a deep hull and shoulder-mounted gull wings, a flat twin-fin tail and inward-retracting wing floats. The gull wing design was used to produce the greatest possible distance between the engines and sea water. A less than half-scale single-seat version was produced to test the aerodynamics of the design, and its success led to the first flight of the full-scale prototype XPBM-1 in 1939.

The XPBM-1 prototype first flew in February 1939 and test-flights called for a redesign of the tail, which resulted in the dihedral configuration that matched the angle of the main wings. The aircraft had been ordered before the test-flight, so the first production model, the PBM-1, appeared quite quickly in October 1940 with service deliveries being complete by April 1941. By now the type was named Mariner. The PBM-1 had a crew of seven and was armed with five 12.7mm/0.5in Browning machine-guns. One gun was mounted in a flexible position in the tail, one was fitted in a flexible mount on each side of the rear fuselage, another was fitted in a rear dorsal turret and one was fitted in a nose turret. In addition, the PBM-1 could carry up to 908kg/2000lb of bombs or depth charges in bomb bays that were, unusually, fitted in the engine nacelles. The doors of the bomb bays looked like those of landing gear, but the Mariner was not amphibian at this stage.

In late 1940 the US Navy ordered 379 improved Model 162Bs or PBM-3s, although around twice that number were actually produced. This order alone required the

TOP: **A PBM-1 Mariner in flight, with power provided by two Wright R-2600-6 Double Cyclones.** ABOVE: **A Mariner being serviced in the Iwo Jima area, World War II. The PBMs were the eyes of the US fleet since landplanes based in the Marianas did not have the range for the required ocean patrol coverage.**

US government-aided construction of a new Martin plant in Maryland. The -3 differed from the -1 mainly by the use of uprated Pratt & Whitney 1700hp R-2600-12 engines, larger fixed wing floats and larger bomb bays housed in enlarged nacelles. Nose and dorsal turrets were powered on this version. Early PBM-3s had three-bladed propellers, but production soon included four-bladed propellers.

The PBM-3C, rolled out in late 1942, was the next major version, with 274 built. It had better armour protection for the crew, twin gun front and dorsal turrets, an improved tail turret still with a single gun, and air-to-surface-vessel radar. In addition, many PBM-3Cs were fitted with an underwing searchlight in the field.

US Navy Mariners saw extensive use in the Pacific, guarding the Atlantic western approaches and defending the Panama Canal. It was concluded that most Mariners were not likely to encounter fighter opposition, so much of the defensive armament was deleted – once the guns, turrets

LEFT: **A Mariner being prepared for hoisting by a US Navy seaplane tender, believed to be at the time of the Korean War.** BELOW: **US Navy Mariners flying over the Brazilian capital of Rio de Janeiro as they escorted an Allied convoy into port.** BOTTOM LEFT: **The pilot of a US Navy PBM-3S starts his port engine as crewmen stand by in case of fire at a Caribbean naval air station, 1944. The large protuberance above the cockpit area is a powerful anti-submarine search radar.**

and ammunition were removed, the weight saving resulted in a 25 per cent increase in the range of the lighter PBM-3S anti-submarine version. However, the nose guns were retained for offensive fire against U-boats and other surface targets. Despite this development, a more heavily armed and armoured version, the PBM-3D, was produced by re-engining some 3Cs. Larger non-retractable floats and self-sealing fuel tanks were also a feature of this version.

Deliveries of the more powerfully engined PBM-5 began in August 1944, and 589 were delivered before production ceased at the end of the war. With the PBM-5A amphibian version (of which 40 were built), the Mariner finally acquired the tricycle landing gear. The Mariner continued to serve with the US Navy and US Coast Guard into the early 1950s, and over 500 were in service at the time of the Korean War. The USCG retired its last Mariner in 1958.

Martin PBM-3D Mariner

First flight: February 18, 1939 (XPBM-1)
Power: Two Wright 1900hp R-2600-22 Cyclone radial piston engines
Armament: Eight 12.7mm/0.5in machine-guns in nose, dorsal, waist and tail positions; up to 3632kg/8000lb of bombs or depth charges
Size: Wingspan – 35.97m/118ft
Length – 24.33m/79ft 10in
Height – 8.38m/27ft 6in
Wing area – 130.8m²/1408sq ft
Weights: Empty – 15,061kg/33,175lb
Maximum take-off – 26,332kg/58,000lb
Performance: Maximum speed – 340kph/211mph
Ceiling – 6035m/19,800ft
Range – 3605km/2240 miles
Climb – 244m/800ft per minute

Martin B-26 Marauder

In 1939 the US Army Air Corps issued a demanding specification for a high-speed medium bomber, and Martin's Model 179 proposal was so impressive that the aircraft was ordered into production off the drawing board. The aircraft was a shoulder-wing monoplane with a spacious circular cross-section fuselage for a crew of five and a retractable tricycle landing gear for improved visibility on the ground.

The first aircraft flew on November 25, 1940, and the first B-26s went to the 22nd Bomb Group at Langley Field, Virginia. This was quite a transition because the B-26 weighed two and a half times as much as the B-18 it was replacing, and had a landing speed that was 50 per cent greater. Although the original specification was exceeded, the aircraft did exhibit difficult low-speed handling, which led to an early high accident rate. Modifications improved low-speed performance and revisions to training overcame the problem, and on December 8, 1941, the day after the Japanese attack on Pearl Harbor, the USA deployed B-26s to Australia.

The first B-26 mission flown was by the 22nd Bomb Group on April 5, 1942. Taking off from Garbutt Field, Australia, the aircraft first staged through an airfield near Port Moresby, New Guinea, before attacking the Japanese base at Rabaul in New Britain.

The A-model carried more fuel, heavier armament and could carry a torpedo for maritime attack. On June 4, 1942, during the Battle of Midway, four Marauders set off to carry out the type's first torpedo attack in action against Japanese

ABOVE: **In May 1943, the B-26 became the principal medium bomber of the US Ninth Air Force in Europe. The aircraft pictured here was restored to flying condition, and appears at US air shows.**

carriers. The torpedo runs began at 244m/800ft, the aircraft then dropping down to around 3m/10ft above the sea while under heavy attack from Japanese fighters. Two B-26s were lost in the attack, the other two were seriously damaged and none of the torpedoes found their mark. The conclusion drawn from this rare tragic chapter in B-26 history was that the type was simply unsuited to this form of attack.

By November 1942 the B-26Bs (with bigger engines, more armour and, in later aircraft, bigger wings) and B-26Cs (B-models produced in Nebraska) began to see action in North Africa with 12 units of the US 12th Air Force. These aircraft, operating in a tactical bomber role, supported Allied ground forces as they fought through Corsica, Italy, Sardinia, Sicily and then southern France.

B-26s of the US Ninth Air Force, initially based in Britain in support of the D-Day landings, ranged over northern Europe attacking airfields, roads, bridges, railroads and V-1 flying bomb facilities. Despite early safety issues, the Marauder went on to have the lowest attrition rate per sortie of any American aircraft operated by the US Air Forces in Europe.

Under Lend-Lease, the Royal Air Force ordered a total of 522 Marauders and deployed them all, like the Martin Maryland and Baltimore before them, only in the Mediterranean theatre

RIGHT: Because the B-26 was ordered straight from the drawing-board, there were no prototypes, but most of the first batch of 201 were retained for testing and training. The aircraft shown here is a JM-1, a US Navy/Marine Corps target tug/trainer version of the B-26B.

and with the South African Air Force. No.14 Squadron was the first RAF unit to be equipped in August 1942, and was operational within two months. RAF B-26s also supported Allied forces in Sicily, Sardinia and Italy, and by the end of March 1944 had dropped a total of 18,288 tonnes/18,000 tons of bombs. In March 1943 six squadrons of Free French Air Force Marauders became operational. Flying alongside other Allied B-26s, the French Marauders supported the Allied invasion of southern France in August 1944.

By the end of the war, the B-26 had flown 129,943 operational sorties in the European and Mediterranean theatres alone, dropping 172,092 tonnes/169,382 tons of bombs in the process and destroying 402 enemy aircraft.

ABOVE: Unit cost for the B-26 was 261,000 US dollars when it first entered service. This was reduced to 192,000 US dollars by 1944 owing to the numbers in production and refinement of the production lines. LEFT: Deliveries to the air force began in 1941, and the type was deployed to Australia the day after Pearl Harbor to combat any further Japanese aggression.

ABOVE: The Marauder I in RAF service was equivalent to the B-26A, and had a shorter wing than later models.

Martin B-26B Marauder

First flight: November 25, 1940
Power: Two Pratt & Whitney 1920hp R-2800-43 radial piston engines
Armament: 12.7mm/0.5in machine-guns in nose, tail, top turret and fixed forward-firing on side of fuselage
Size: Wingspan – 21.64m/71ft
Length – 17.75m/58ft 3in
Height – 6.55m/21ft 6in
Wing area – 61.13m²/658sq ft
Weights: Empty – 10,896kg/24,000lb
Maximum take-off –16,798kg/37,000lb
Performance: Maximum speed – 454kph/282mph
Ceiling – 6405m/21,000ft
Range – 1851km/1150 miles
Climb – 4572m/15,000ft in 13 minutes

Mitsubishi G4M

The G4M, codenamed "Betty" by the Allies, was the Japanese Navy's principal heavy bomber of World War I. It was designed to an extremely exacting 1937 Imperial Japanese Navy specification for a land-based bomber capable of carrying a full bomb load over 3704km/2000 nautical miles. The performance was hard to achieve and came largely at the cost of protection of the crew (in terms of armour and defensive armament) and the aircraft's fuel tanks, which were contained in the aircraft wing but without armour or the ability to self-seal when damaged.

Nicknames such as "One-Shot Lighter" and the "Flying Cigar" were coined on both sides, reflecting the aircraft's tendency to explode in flames when hit in combat – the aircraft was not popular with its crews.

The prototype first flew in October 1939 and, being a basically sound design, the type progressed through flight-testing with production beginning in late 1940. The type, now designated Navy Type 1 Attack Bomber Model 11, began to reach front-line units in the summer of 1941. The next

production version, the G4M1 Model 12, was powered by the Kasei 15 engine, which provided better performance at altitude. Late 1942 saw the appearance of the improved GM42 Model 22 with a new laminar-flow wing, larger tailplane and power provided by 1800hp Mitsubishi Kasei 21 engines.

Perhaps the type's most famous action took place on December 10, 1941, three days after the attack on Pearl Harbor. G4Ms and G3Ms of the 22nd Air Flotilla sank two British capital ships, the *Prince of Wales* and the *Repulse*, off the coast of Malaya. The two ships were the first capital ships ever to be sunk by air attack at sea while free to evade. In March 1942, G4Ms made the first bombing attacks on the port of Darwin in northern Australia.

A number of earlier models were designated G4M2e Model 24J when modified to carry the MXY-7 Okha piloted kamikaze missile. Due to the great weight increase, the G4M2e was very

RIGHT: **In service from mid-1943, the G4M2 was a refined version of the Japanese bomber but lacked the range of the earlier versions.**
BELOW: **G4M1s – the original version of Japan's numerically most important bomber, in service throughout the Pacific war.**

Mitsubishi G4M3 Model 34

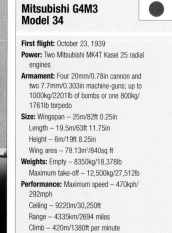

First flight: October 23, 1939
Power: Two Mitsubishi MK4T Kasei 25 radial
  engines
Armament: Four 20mm/0.78in cannon and
  two 7.7mm/0.303in machine-guns; up to
  1000kg/2201lb of bombs or one 800kg/
  1761lb torpedo
Size: Wingspan – 25m/82ft 0.25in
  Length – 19.5m/63ft 11.75in
  Height – 6m/19ft 8.25in
  Wing area – 78.13m²/840sq ft
Weights: Empty – 8350kg/18,378lb
  Maximum take-off – 12,500kg/27,512lb
Performance: Maximum speed – 470kph/
  292mph
  Ceiling – 9220m/30,250ft
  Range – 4335km/2694 miles
  Climb – 420m/1380ft per minute

ABOVE: **In the G4M3, the designers remedied the earlier versions' tendency to ignite so readily when hit in combat.** RIGHT: **The great range of the earlier G4Ms was only achieved at the expense of protective armour for the crew.** BELOW: **This "Betty", pictured near Singapore, was captured by the RAF in Malaya. In addition to RAF roundels, the aircraft bears the letters ATAIU SEA for Allied Technical Air Intelligence Unit, South-east Asia. The aircraft is being evaluated but flown by Japanese naval pilots under the close armed supervision of RAF officers.**

slow when carrying the weapon, and the combination had a disastrous combat debut on March 21, 1945, when most were shot down by carrier-based Allied fighter aircraft before they could launch their missiles.

Long range was not a prime concern once the Allies began to force their way towards Japan itself, and in the G4M3 Model 34, which first flew in early 1944, self-sealing fuel tanks and protective armour for the crew were introduced. Only 60 had been built by the end of the war.

In August 1942, Rabaul-based G4Ms flew the first counter-attacks against US forces invading Guadalcanal. Of 26 aircraft in the attack, at least 17 were shot down in a single raid. One aircraft damaged by ground fire made a suicide attack on the

transport ship *George F. Elliott*. G4Ms operated throughout the six-month battle for Guadalcanal and suffered heavy losses.

By early 1943, the Japanese Navy had developed new techniques using "Betties" for night torpedo attack. On the night of January 29–30, 1943, during the Battle of Rennell Island, G4Ms successfully torpedoed and sank the heavy cruiser *Chicago*, and in February 1944 a Betty torpedoed the US carrier *Intrepid*. On August 19, 1945 it was two G4M1s that carried the Imperial Japanese delegation to discuss the final requirements for Japan's surrender with the Allies.

Mitsubishi built a total of 2416 G4Ms, including prototypes, in addition to 30 G6M1 escort fighter versions manned by crews of ten who had no fewer than 19 guns at their disposal.

North American B-25 Mitchell

TOP: **The B-25 made its combat debut in early 1942, and the type remained in the front line throughout World War II.** ABOVE: **FV914, an RAF Mitchell II (B-25D) looses its bomb load. The Mk II was the main version of around 800 examples operated by the RAF.**

In the late 1930s, the US Army was looking for an "Aircraft-Bombardment Type-Medium" to fill the gap in its inventory between its light and heavy bombers. North American's response was the NA-40, which developed into the B-25 Mitchell, one of the most widely used aircraft of World War II. The B-25 entered USAAF service in 1941 and was in action until the end of the war, but the type will forever be known as the aircraft that carried out the April 1942 Doolittle raid against Tokyo from the carrier USS *Hornet*. However, the first action of a B-25 was probably the sinking of a Japanese submarine on Christmas Eve 1941. The Mitchell was named after Colonel "Billy" Mitchell who was court-martialled in the 1920s for his far-sighted views on US air power and strategic bombing.

Early production versions were eclipsed by the much-redesigned B-25C/D, which was the same aircraft built at different locations – C-models were built by North American at Inglewood while Ds were produced at NA's Dallas plant. In total some 3909 examples of the C/D were built, and 533 were supplied to the Royal Air Force as Mitchell IIs. Under the Lend-Lease deal between Britain and the USA, the RAF acquired a total of over 800 examples of this robust and reliable bomber. The B-25 first entered RAF service with Nos.98 and 180 Squadrons in September 1942, and from August 1943 they operated as part of the Second Tactical Air Force, carrying out pre-D-Day attacks on targets in Northern France as well as on V-1 "doodlebug" sites in the Pas de Calais. A total of 870 C/Ds were also supplied to the Soviet Union.

The next production variant was the B-25G, which was developed from a C-model modified to carry a US Army 75mm/2.93in field gun in the nose. This seemingly far-fetched proposal resulted in the production of 405 examples which

North American B-25H Mitchell

First flight: August 19, 1940 (production B-25)
Power: Two Wright 1700hp R-2600-13 radial
  piston engines
Armament: One 75mm/2.93in cannon, fourteen
  12.7mm/0.5in machine-guns; up to 1362kg/
  3000lb bomb load or one 908kg/2000lb torpedo,
  plus up to eight rocket projectiles
Size: Wingspan – 20.6m/67ft 7in
  Length – 15.54m/51ft
  Height – 4.8m/15ft 9in
  Wing area – 56.67 m²/610sq ft
Weights: Empty – 9068kg/19,975lb
  Maximum take-off – 16,365kg/36,047lb
Performance: Maximum speed – 442kph/275mph
  Service ceiling – 7259m/23,800ft
  Range – 4344km/2700 miles
  Climb – 4572m/15,000ft in 19 minutes

ABOVE: **The Doolittle raid is the best-known B-25 mission, but the bomber carried out countless vital missions while serving with the USAAF, USN, USMC and RAF.** RIGHT: **The heavily armed B-25J was produced in greater numbers than any other version.**

carried 21 6.81kg/15lb shells for use against ground targets and shipping. The improved B-25H carried a lighter 75mm/2.93in gun but also had four 12.7mm/0.5in guns in the nose, a further four in blisters on the sides of the nose, two more in a dorsal turret and in the tail, two in the waist positions, as well as a bomb load of 1362kg/3000lb and up to eight rocket projectiles fired from beneath the wings. One thousand examples of this hard-hitting B-25 version were built, and they saw extensive service in the Pacific.

The most numerous version of all was the B-25J, with more than 4300 examples delivered before the end of the war. This example lost the 75mm/2.93in gun but retained the other armament of the H-model. This version saw action in the Pacific, the Mediterranean and in South-east Asia. In RAF service this version was known as the Mitchell III.

The B-25 was one of the most widely used aircraft of World War II, serving with the United States Army Air Forces, Navy and Marine Corps, and was supplied to the USSR, Britain, China, Australia, Canada, France and the Netherlands.

In January 1943, B-25s were ordered by the US Navy for the US Marine Corps. Their 706 B-25s (C,D, H and J-models) were designated PBJs, and supported marine landings during the island-hopping campaigns of the drive to the Japanese home islands.

Post-war, in addition to equipping smaller air forces, many B-25s were used as training and light transport aircraft. The last B-25 in US military service was a VIP transport retired on May 21, 1960. The aircraft's stability and ease of adaptation led a number to be used as camera ships for the film industry, and some fly on in this role today.

ABOVE: **The B-25 was widely operated post-war, and a number of B-25s are preserved by collectors and museums.**

Short Stirling

The Short S.29 Stirling was one of 11 designs proposed by numerous aircraft manufacturers to satisfy the Air Ministry Specification B12/36. This called for a four-engined heavy bomber that could carry a bomb load of 6356kg/ 14,000lb over a distance of 4827km/3000 miles. The wingspan of the new bomber was not to exceed 30.5m/100ft so that the aircraft could comfortably pass through the doors of most Royal Air Force hangars of the time. It was this limitation that really defined much of the Stirling's operating parameters. The wings did not have the lifting ability to carry a fully laden Stirling to the ideal higher altitudes, but at low altitude, the aircraft was the fastest of the RAF's heavies.

The Stirling was Short's first aircraft with a retractable undercarriage, as the company was more used to producing flying boats with hulls and floats. To test the soundness of their design Shorts first produced a half-scale prototype, which flew in September 1938. In testing, it was decided to increase the length of the undercarriage legs to increase the wing's angle of attack, which would in turn reduce take-off and landing runs. The solution was not without problems – the large and complex undercarriage led to a number of accidents in service. In addition, production Stirlings stood over 7m/nearly 23ft high as a result. It is worth noting that unlike the Lancaster (derived from the twin-engine Manchester) and the Halifax (originally to be powered by two Vulture engines), the Stirling was designed from the outset as a four-engined machine.

TOP: **The Stirling III was the standard RAF bomber version from 1943.**

ABOVE: **The long undercarriage legs of the Stirling are clear in this photograph – the ground crew are dwarfed by the machine.**

The Stirling was the first of the RAF's new four-engined bombers to fly, the full-size prototype first taking to the air in May 1939. At the end of the maiden flight, a brake locked on landing and the resulting crash wrote off the aircraft. The second prototype's first flight was almost as eventful when an engine failed on take-off. Despite these shaky beginnings, the Stirling reached front-line units in August 1940 when No.7 Squadron at RAF Leeming took delivery of the new heavy bomber. The type made its combat debut, again with No.7 then based at Oakington, on the night of February 10–11, 1941, when three aircraft dropped 56 227kg/500lb bombs on oil storage tanks near Rotterdam. RAF Stirlings attacked Berlin for the first time in April 1941 and the type participated in all the 1942 thousand-bomber raids.

Some shortcomings of the original design were addressed in the Mark III, powered by Hercules XVI engines, which became the standard Bomber Command version in 1943–4. However, by mid-1943 the Stirling was sustaining higher losses than other heavies, and one source states that within five months of being introduced, 67 out of 84 aircraft delivered were lost to enemy action or written off after crashes. During the year, the Stirlings were gradually phased out of the RAF's main bomber force and moved to attacks on less well-defended targets and less dangerous duties such as mine-laying. The Stirling's final Bomber Command operation was flown by No.149 Squadron against Le Havre on September 8, 1944.

However by mid-1944 the Stirlings had found a new lease of life as troop-carriers and glider-tugs, and they performed great service on D-Day. RAF Stirling units in action on D-Day were Fairford-based Nos.90 and 622, and from Keevil Nos.196 and 299 Squadrons.

As the Allies fought their way through Europe after D-Day, Stirlings were also used in support of the RAF's Second Tactical Air Force transporting 120 22.7 litre/5 gallon jerry cans full of petrol at a time. In addition to glider-tug duties, the Stirling was used to drop food supplies and ammunition to the French resistance, and also to drop airborne troops.

Post-war, a number of Stirling Vs (a dedicated transport version built for RAF Transport Command) were used as passenger aircraft between England and the continent for a brief time.

RIGHT: **Stirlings of No.7 Squadron, probably at Oakington in Cambridgeshire.**
BELOW: **Two Stirlings of No.7 Squadron fly across the flat open spaces of East Anglia.**

ABOVE: **The Stirling was a large aircraft but due to its construction, the largest bomb it could carry was 1816kg/4000lb. Here, an armourer prepares a "cookie" bomb prior to loading it aboard the waiting aircraft.**

Short Stirling Mk III

First flight: May 14, 1939 (full-size prototype)
Power: Bristol 1650hp Hercules XVI radial engines
Armament: Eight 7.7mm/0.303in machine-guns in nose, dorsal and tail turrets; up to 6356kg/14,000lb bomb load
Size: Wingspan – 30.2m/99ft 1in
Length – 26.59m/87ft 3in
Height – 6.93m/22ft 9in
Wing area – 135.63m²/1460sq ft
Weights: Empty – 19,613kg/43,200lb
Maximum take-off – 31,780kg/70,000lb
Performance: Maximum speed – 435kph/270mph
Ceiling – 5185m/17,000ft
Range – 950km/590 miles with full bomb load
Climb – 244m/800ft per minute

Short Sunderland

The Sunderland is a rare type of military aeroplane – one that was derived from a civil aircraft. Based upon the Short C Class "Empire" flying boats operated by Imperial Airways in the 1930s, the Short "Sunderland" became one of the Royal Air Force's longest serving operational aircraft over the next two decades. One of the finest flying boats ever built, during World War II the Sunderland played a decisive role in the defeat of German U-boats in the Battle of the Atlantic.

Although the first flight of the prototype Sunderland took place in October 1937, the Air Ministry was already familiar with the aircraft's successful civilian counterpart, and had placed an order in March the preceding year.

In early June 1938 the first batch of production Sunderland Mk Is were delivered to No.230 Squadron based in Singapore. The Sunderland replaced the RAF's mixed fleet of biplane flying boats and represented a huge leap in capability.

By the outbreak of World War II in September 1939, three Coastal Command squadrons had become operational and were ready to seek out and destroy German U-boats. The Sunderland also became a very welcome sight to the many seamen from sunken vessels and airmen who had had to ditch their aircraft. When the British merchant ship *Kensington Court* was torpedoed 113km/70 miles off the Scillies on September 18, 1939, two patrolling Sunderlands had the entire crew of 34 back on dry land just an hour after the ship sank.

TOP: **This Sunderland was converted to "Sandringham" civilianized standard post-war, although some would say that life aboard a Sunderland was quite civilized. Few RAF combat aircraft have ever had a kitchen or, more correctly, a galley.** ABOVE: **A Mark II built by Shorts at Rochester, operated by No.10 Squadron. This Australian squadron became part of Coastal Command at the start of World War II, and operated in the Atlantic.**

The Sunderland, with its crew of ten, was heavily armed and became known to the Luftwaffe as the Flying Porcupine. Many times during the war a lone Sunderland fought off or defeated a number of attacking aircraft.

Although Sunderlands did engage in many a "shoot-out" with German vessels, sometimes the sight of the large aircraft was enough to have an enemy crew scuttle their boat – such was the case on January 31, 1940, when the arrival of an aircraft from No.228 Squadron prompted the crew of U-Boat *U-55* to do just that.

At the end of 1940 the Mk II was introduced, with four Pegasus XVIII engines with two-stage superchargers, a twin-gun dorsal turret, an improved rear turret and ASV (air-to-surface-vessel) Mk II radar. The most numerous version was the Mk III that first flew in December 1941. This variant had a modified hull for improved planing when taking off. This was

LEFT: **This Sunderland III, W3999, was the first production machine of the version, and had its maiden flight on December 15, 1941. The III had a dorsal gun turret as standard, as well as a refined hull.** BELOW LEFT: **A Sunderland V of No.230 Squadron. The Mk V entered RAF service in early 1945 and remained the standard RAF flying boat until 1959.** BELOW: **At home on water or in the air, the Sunderland's ability to find and destroy U-boats made it a key aircraft in the fight against Nazi Germany.**

followed by a larger and heavier version designated the Mk IV/Seaford. After evaluation by the RAF, the project of the flying boat was abandoned.

The Sunderland Mk V was the final version, and made its appearance at the end of 1943. It was powered by four 1200hp Pratt & Whitney R-1830-90 Twin Wasp engines and carried ASV Mk VI radar. By the end of the final production run in 1945 a total of 739 Sunderlands had been built, and after World War II, many continued to serve with the British, French, Australian, South African and New Zealand air forces.

Post-war, RAF Sunderlands delivered nearly 5080 tonnes/5000 tons of supplies during the Berlin Airlift, and during the Korean War they were the only British aircraft to operate throughout the conflict. During the Malayan Emergency RAF Sunderlands carried out bombing raids on land against terrorists.

The Sunderland finally retired from the Royal Air Force on May 15, 1959, when No.205 Squadron flew the last sortie for the type from RAF Changi, Singapore, where the illustrious operational career of the Sunderland flying boat had begun 21 years earlier. However, the last air arm to retire the type from military service was the Royal New Zealand Air Force in March 1967. A total of 749 Sunderlands were built between 1937 and 1946.

Short Sunderland Mk V

First Flight: October 16, 1937 (prototype)
Power: Four Pratt & Whitney 1200hp R-1830 Twin Wasp 14-cylinder air-cooled radials
Armament: Eight 7.7mm/0.303in Browning machine-guns in turrets, four fixed 7.7mm/0.303in Browning machine-guns in nose, two manually operated 12.7mm/0.5in machine-guns in beam positions; 2252kg/4,960lb of depth charges or bombs
Size: Wingspan – 34.36m/112ft 9in
Length – 26m/85ft 3in
Height – 10.01m/32ft 11in
Wing area – 138.14m²/1487sq ft
Weights: Empty – 16,798kg/37,000lb
Maximum take-off – 27,240kg/60,000lb
Performance: Maximum speed – 343 kph/213mph
Ceiling – 5456m/17,900ft
Range – 4795 km/2980miles
Climb – 256m/840ft per minute

Tupolev SB

ABOVE: **The SB was built in great numbers, and was the first stressed-skin aircraft built in the Soviet Union. The radial engines were later replaced with in-line powerplants, which bestowed better performance.** BELOW LEFT: **The SB was widely used, seeing action in the Spanish Civil War, and with the Chinese Air Force against Japan. Czech machines were seized by the Luftwaffe and used as target tugs.**

This aircraft is often incorrectly referred to as the SB-2, which is more a Western corruption of the designation SB-2-M100A meaning SB with 2xM100A engines. It was designed to a 1933 Soviet Air Force specification for a fast light bomber with a maximum level speed of 330kph/205mph, a ceiling of 8000m/26,250ft, range of 700km/434 miles and the ability to carry a 500kg/1100lb bomb load. The Tupolev ANT-40 SB (*skorostnoy bombardirovschik* or high-speed bomber) incorporated elements of earlier Tupolev designs and was of metal stressed-skin construction.

This fast, well-armed bomber first flew on April 25, 1934, with power provided by two US Wright Cyclone radials. After a landing accident it was rebuilt and re-engined with Soviet M-87 engines.

Production began in 1935, with early aircraft powered by 750hp M-100 engines and then 860hp 100As. The SB-2bis was the last production version, and first flew in October 1936 with power provided by two 960hp M-103s. Around 6650 SBs were built in total before production ended in late 1940.

SBs were supplied to the Republican forces during the Spanish Civil War. While some nations used Spain as a testing ground, providing aircraft and manpower free of charge, the Soviet Union required hard currency before allowing their aircraft to take part. SBs also saw action during the Nomonhan Incident, a border skirmish that became a small war against the Japanese in Mongolia during 1939. The type was also used against Finnish forces during the Winter War, but was beginning to show its age when faced with fast and agile fighters.

At the start of Operation Barbarossa, the German invasion of the Soviet Union in June 1941, 71 out of 82 Bomber Air Regiments operated the type. Many were lost when attacked by Luftwaffe fighters when having no fighter protection of their own. The SB was one of the Soviet Air Force's primary bombers until its withdrawal began in 1943, by which time it was operating largely at night.

Czechoslovakia imported a number of SBs and then produced its own licensed version known as the B-71. Among a number of variants, Tupolev produced a civil transport, the PS-40, for Aeroflot.

Tupolev SB-2bis

First flight: April 25, 1934
Power: Two 960hp M-103 piston engines
Armament: Six 7.62mm/0.3in machine-guns; up to 600kg/1320lb bomb load
Size: Wingspan – 20.33m/66ft 8.5in
   Length –12.57m/41ft 2.75in
   Height – 3.25m/10ft 8in
   Wing area – 56.7m²/610.33sq ft
Weights: Empty – 4768kg/10,494lb
   Maximum take-off – 7880kg/17,344lb
Performance: Maximum speed – 450kph/280mph
   Ceiling – 7800m/25,590ft
   Range – 2300km/1429 miles
   Climb – 400m/1310ft per minute

Tupolev TB-3 M-17

First flight: December 22, 1930
Power: Four 715hp M-17F piston engines
Armament: Eight 7.7mm/0.303in machine-guns in nose and dorsal positions, and in two retractable underwing "dustbins"; up to 2000kg/4402lb bomb load
Size: Wingspan – 39.5m/129ft 7in
Length – 24.4m/80ft 0.75in
Height – 8.2m/26ft 9in
Wing area – 230m²/2475.8sq ft
Weights: Empty – 10,967kg/24,138lb
Maximum take-off – 17,200kg/37,857lb
Performance: Maximum speed – 197kph/122mph
Ceiling – 3800m/12,470ft
Range – 1350km/839 miles
Climb – Not known

Tupolev TB-3

This large four-engined low-wing bomber was the most advanced bomber in the world for a time. It made its maiden flight on December 22, 1930, and production was underway within a year. The first service aircraft were delivered to the Soviet Air Force in early 1932.

Everything about this aircraft was big and it had a heavier maximum take-off weight than any other aircraft at the time. The TB-3s had a corrugated metal covering similar to that used by Junkers. The wings were so thick they contained "crawl-ways" giving access to the engines during flight. The pilot and co-pilot sat side by side in an open cockpit with separate windscreens.

Continually modified, over 500 of these bombers remained in service at the time of the German invasion in 1941, and some carried out night-bombing attacks against the invaders. Paratroop conversions could carry up to 35 troops in the fuselage and wings.

Tupolev Tu-2S

First flight: January 29, 1941 (prototype ANT-58)
Power: Two 1850hp Ash-82FNV radial piston engines
Armament: Two 20mm/0.78in cannon, three 12.7mm/0.5in machine-guns; up to 4000kg/8804lb bomb load
Size: Wingspan – 18.86m/61ft 10.5in
Length – 13.8m/45ft 3.5in
Height – 4.55m/14ft 11in
Wing area – 48.8m²/525.3sq ft
Weights: Empty – 7474kg/16,450lb
Maximum take-off – 11,360kg/25,003lb
Performance: Maximum speed – 550kph/342mph
Ceiling – 9500m/31,170ft
Range – 1400km/870 miles
Climb – 700m/2300ft per minute

Tupolev Tu-2

This potent medium bomber, initially known as the ANT-61, first entered Soviet Air Force service in 1942, and from the outset it proved to be a key weapon in the Soviet inventory. It was fast, very well armed, handled well and needed few upgrades or improvements during its service life. The Tu-2S, the second main production version, differed from earlier examples by having uprated engines, greater bomb load and heavier gun armament.

Unlike many of its contemporaries, the Tu-2 continued to serve after World War II and saw considerable use with North Korea during the Korean War. Wartime production was around 1100 but a further 1400 were built post-war.

Some Communist nations operated the type until 1961, which speaks volumes for the quality of the design of this bomber which had the NATO reporting name of "Bat".

Vickers Vimy

In 1917, the British were developing bombers capable of bombing the German heartland. Had World War I not come to an end in November 1918, these bombers, among them the Vickers Vimy, would have formed strategic bomber fleets attempting to pound Germany into submission. Although the war came to an end before the Vimy saw action, the type continued to serve in the RAF as a front-line bomber until the late 1920s.

The biplane Vimy was a large aircraft for its day with a wingspan of over 20m/68ft, and the prototype B9952 first flew on November 17, powered by two 207hp Hispano-Suiza engines. Of wooden construction and fabric-covered, the Vimy had a crew of three and could carry a bomb load in excess of a ton – this was a far cry from the hand-held bombs thrown overboard from the early World War I bombers.

Although many aircraft contracts were cancelled at the war's end, the Vimy continued to be supplied to the Royal Air Force. The main production version of the Vimy was the Mark IV powered by Rolls-Royce Eagle VIII engines, and some 240 were built – the first were delivered to the RAF in France in 1918 and the last batch were delivered to the RAF in 1925. The Vimy did not enter service fully until July 1919 when it joined No. 58 Squadron stationed in Egypt. In Britain, the first of the home squadrons to be equipped with the Vickers bomber was No.100 based at Spittlegate. No.7 Squadron was formed in June 1923 to operate Vimys, and was the Royal Air Force's UK-based heavy bomber until being augmented by the Vimys of Nos.9 and 58 Squadrons in 1924. By 1925 the Vimy

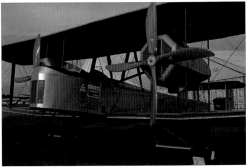

TOP: **A replica of Alcock and Brown's famous Atlantic-crossing Vimy. The Vimy's performance on that epic flight demonstrated the greatness of the design.**

ABOVE: **The Vimy was built for deep bombing missions into Germany, but some of these aircraft continued to fly in RAF service long after the end of the Great War.**

was being replaced by Vickers Virginias, but the aircraft of No.502 stationed in Northern Ireland remained in front-line service until 1929. The type was used increasingly for mail services, as a trainer and for parachute training. The Vimy design was also developed into the Vimy Commercial with an all-new large-diameter fuselage – a dedicated version was produced as the Vimy Ambulance for moving wounded personnel. The Vickers Vernon bomber-transport derivative became the first aircraft designed specifically for troop-carrying, and served mainly in Iraq in the mid- to late 1920s.

On June 14, 1919, the Vimy flew into the history books when a Vimy IV owned by the Vickers company and the thirteenth off the production line took off from Newfoundland

ABOVE AND LEFT: **Alcock and Brown's flight was an epic for its day. On their return to Britain, they became national heroes, having finally beaten the Atlantic.**

ABOVE: **Vimys did not reach RAF units until the end of October 1918, and then only three machines were delivered.** ABOVE LEFT: **This Vimy was built by Vickers at Bexley, and was powered by Salmson engines.**

and headed eastward across the Atlantic. The two-man crew were Royal Air Force officers Captain John Alcock, who served as pilot, and Lieutenant Arthur Whitten-Brown, navigator. Also aboard the aircraft were around 3927 litres/865 gallons of highly flammable aviation fuel. For the transatlantic flight the Vimy was specially adapted – all military equipment was removed and the cockpit was widened so that the two fliers could sit side by side on a narrow wooden bench with a thin cushion for comfort. Once alterations had been made to Alcock and Brown's Vimy, the aircraft was dismantled, crated and transported to Newfoundland.

The epic, trailblazing flight, averaging 190km/118 miles per hour, was far from uneventful – the pair faced snow, ice and fog, as well as extreme tiredness. Then at 08:40 hours the next morning, after a 16-hour flight, Alcock and Brown sighted Ireland, and within minutes prepared to land. The aircraft landed in a bog and nosed over, sustaining damage, but the pioneering airmen were unhurt. As well being knighted and feted throughout their country, Alcock and Brown won the Daily Mail newspaper's prize of 10,000 pounds offered in 1913 for the first successful crossing of the Atlantic.

Vickers Vimy IV

First flight: November 30, 1917
Power: Two Rolls-Royce 360hp Eagle VIII in-line piston engines
Armament: Two Lewis guns, one each in nose and mid-upper positions; 1124kg/2476lb of bombs
Size: Wingspan – 20.7m/68ft
Length – 13.3m/44ft
Height – 4.7m/15ft
Wing area – 124m²/1330sq ft
Weights: Empty – 3225kg/7104lb
Maximum take-off – 5675kg/12,500lb
Performance: Maximum speed – 166kph/103mph
Service ceiling – 3660m/12,000ft
Range – 1448km/900 miles
Climb – 110m/360ft per minute

Vickers Virginia

The Virginia was the standard heavy night-bomber of the Royal Air Force from 1924 until 1937, a long service in those inter-war days. Structurally it differed little from the Vimy developed by Vickers in World War I, but its performance was slightly better than its predecessor and it could carry a greater bomb load. The type was designed to meet Air Ministry specification 1/21, and first flew at Brooklands in November 1922. RAF service deliveries began in late 1924, the first recipient units being Nos.7 and 58 followed by No.9. The

three squadrons took part in the famous Hendon Display in 1925, and the Virginias were popular participants at the annual show through to 1937.

The Virginia was modified considerably during its service career so that the final version in service, the X, was quite different to the early Marks. The prototype Virginia (J6856) had its Lion engines housed in rectangular nacelles, but production aircraft all featured smaller, oval-section nacelles. A total of 124 were built for the RAF in ten versions, and Marks I to V can be identified by the dihedral on the bottom wing only. The Mark VII introduced a lengthened and redesigned nose. The Mark X was the first version not to be of wooden construction, instead being all-metal with a fabric covering – this model accounted for 50 of the 124 aircraft built.

It was the Virginia that introduced the auto-pilot into RAF service, and when the type was replaced by newer bombers, it continued to serve as a parachute trainer, with jump-off platforms added to the rear of the engines. Some were still flying as engine test-beds in 1941.

TOP: **The Virginia was still a front-line bomber in 1937. Within seven years, the RAF was operating jet fighters.** ABOVE: **A Virginia taking part in early inflight refuelling experiments with a Westland Wapati.**

ABOVE: **The roar of the Virginia's noisy Lion engines could be heard from miles away.**

Vickers Virginia Mk X

First flight: November 24, 1922
Power: Two Napier 580hp Lion VBW-12 piston engines
Armament: One 7.7mm/0.303in machine-gun in nose and two more in the tail; up to 1362kg/3000lb bomb load
Size: Wingspan – 26.72m/87ft 8in
Length – 18.97m/62ft 3in
Height – 5.54m/18ft 2in
Wing area – 202.34m²/2178sq ft
Weights: Empty – 4381kg/9650lb
Maximum take-off – 7990kg/17,600lb
Performance: Maximum speed – 174kph/108mph
Ceiling – 4725m/15,500ft
Range – 1585km/985 miles
Climb – 152m/500ft per minute

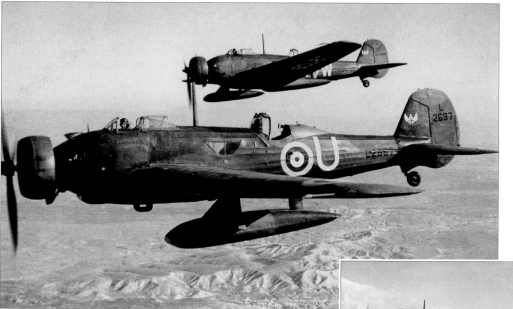

Vickers Wellesley

The Vickers Wellesley was the first of the Vickers designs, and the first RAF aircraft to employ the unique geodetic construction developed by Barnes Wallis. Vickers had designed a biplane bomber to meet a 1931 general-purpose requirement G.4/31, and then as a private venture developed a monoplane derivative which became the Wellesley. The prototype flew on June 19, 1935, and sufficiently impressed the Air Ministry that in September an order was placed for 96 aircraft to specification 22/35, which was written around the Wellesley. As well as the unusual geodetic construction, the bomber carried innovative streamlined bomb panniers under the wings, thereby simplifying construction. In a 14-month production run which began in March 1937, a total of 176 examples were built.

The Wellesley entered RAF service in April 1937 with No.76 Squadron at Finningley, and ultimately equipped six UK-based Bomber Command squadrons. By the start of the war,

however, only four examples remained in service with Bomber Command in Britain, a hundred Wellesleys having been transferred to the Middle East. In an often overlooked episode of World War II, East Africa-based aircraft saw action against the Italians in 1940. The type also carried out maritime reconnaissance in the region until 1941.

The Wellesley is perhaps best known for its record-breaking flight undertaken in 1938 from Egypt to Australia. Three aircraft of the Long Range Development Flight set off on November 5, 1938, from Ismalia, Egypt. One had to abort en route but two Wellesleys, L2638 and L2680, flew non-stop to Darwin, Australia, covering 11,524km/7162 miles in a little over 48 hours and set a new world long-distance record. These aircraft only differed from service aircraft by having extra fuel tanks, accommodation for a third crew member and a Pegasus XXII in place of the usual XX. In service aircraft, the Mark II designation covered aircraft with a large continuous canopy over both cockpits.

TOP AND ABOVE: **The Wellesley was used in anger against Italian forces in 1940. Note the innovative bomb panniers carried beneath the aircraft's wings. The aircraft pictured here are Mk Is.**

Vickers Wellesley

First flight: June 19, 1935
Power: One Bristol 925hp Pegasus XX
Armament: One forward-firing 7.7mm/0.303in machine-gun in right wing, plus one in rear cockpit; up to 908kg/2000lb bomb load carried in underwing panniers
Size: Wingspan – 22.73m/74ft 7in
Length – 11.96m/39ft 3in
Height – 3.75m/12ft 4in
Wing area – 58.5m²/630sq ft
Weights: Empty – 2891kg/6369lb
Maximum take-off – 5039kg/11,100lb
Performance: Maximum speed – 286kph/178mph
Ceiling – 10,065m/33,000ft
Range – 4168km/2590 miles
Climb – 366m/1200ft per minute

Vickers Wellington

The Wellington was built using a unique and ingenious geodetic construction developed by the brilliant Barnes Wallis, who later developed the bouncing bomb. The aircraft's geodetic fuselage was built of a large criss-cross metal mesh which gave the aircraft incredible strength. This meant that fabric-covered Wellingtons came home with very large holes in them caused by flak or cannon fire when other aircraft would have broken up in mid-air. The "Wimpy", as the type was nicknamed (after J. Wellington Wimpy of the Popeye cartoons), first reached front-line service in October 1938 with No.99 Squadron at Mildenhall. The Wellington was the principal bomber of Bomber Command at the start of World War II with six squadrons on strength, and remained so until the four-engined heavies joined the force later in the war. On September 4, 1939, along with Blenheims, 14 Wellingtons of Nos.9 and 149 Squadrons flew the first offensive RAF bombing raid of the war against Germany.

The Wellington was Vickers' response to the British Air Ministry's 1932 specification B.9/32 for a twin-engined medium bomber. After its first flight in June 1936, the Wellington caused a stir when it made a public appearance at the annual Hendon air display later that year. The large streamlined monoplane bomber was a great advance on the biplanes that had been the norm.

The first production version to enter service was the I, which differed greatly from the prototype K4049. The fuselage shape was refined, and a retractable tailwheel was fitted together with gun turrets. The IA saw some armament changes

TOP: **This Wellington II served with No.104 Squadron RAF. The Mark II was a Mark IC, but powered by 1145hp Merlin X engines, and 400 examples were built.**
ABOVE: **The groundcrew of this Wellington had a novel means of recording the number of missions on the aircraft nose, taking inspiration from a popular beer advertisement of the period.**

but the Mark IC, of which 2685 were built, introduced beam guns instead of a ventral gun, and larger mainwheels were fitted. By mid-1941, more powerfully engined Wellington Mk IIs and Mk IIIs had entered service. As the Wellingtons flew on their daylight missions over enemy territory, the official belief was that when flying in formation the bombers would be able to defend themselves without fighter escort against marauding fighters. The reality was very different and Wellingtons, with their unsealed fuel tanks, proved to be very vulnerable. On December 18, 1939, Wellingtons of Nos.9, 37 and 149 Squadrons were sent to carry out a mission against the

LEFT: **Wellington ICs of No.311 Squadron. This photograph pre-dates the unit's transfer to Coastal Command in April 1942.** BELOW: **Wellingtons entered Coastal Command service in the spring of 1942. These Mk XIIIs had A.S.V. masts on the "spine" to search for submarines.**

ABOVE: **The end of the line – the Wellington X was the final bomber version, with over 3800 built. Post-war, many were converted to T.10 standard with a faired nose and the turret deleted.**

Schillig Roads and Wilhelmshaven. They were attacked by Luftwaffe fighters, and ten of the bombers were destroyed and three badly damaged. After this mission highlighted the aircraft's vulnerability, the Wellington was switched to night operations.

The Wellington proved to be a very successful night-bomber, and carried out bombing raids deep into Germany and Italy. The night of August 25–6, 1940 saw Wellingtons of Nos.99 and 149 Squadrons join Hampdens and Whitleys on Bomber Command's first attack on the heart of the Third Reich, Berlin. The Cologne raid of May 30, 1942 saw no fewer than 599 Wellingtons take part in the mission.

In September 1940, Wellingtons joined No.202 Group as the RAF's first long-range bombers in the Middle East. The type also saw use in the North African and Greek campaigns, and in 1942 India-based Wellingtons became the RAF's first long-range bombers operating in the Far East.

The Wellington fought on in Europe until it carried out its last offensive mission on the night of October 8–9, 1943 against Hanover. However, the "Wimpy" did continue to serve as a bomber elsewhere, and on March 13, 1945, aircraft of No.40 Squadron dropped 1816kg/4000lb "cookie" bombs on Trevisio in the Italian theatre.

Mention must also be made of the Coastal Command Wellingtons, fitted with 14.63m/48ft metal hoops that were used for exploding enemy mines in the sea below by generating a strong magnetic field. Coastal Command Wellingtons also carried out anti-submarine duties, the first enemy vessel being sunk on July 6, 1942.

Post-war, many converted Wellingtons continued to serve as training aircraft into the mid-1950s. In all 11,461 Wellingtons were built, the last of which was rolled out on October 13, 1945.

Vickers Wellington IC

First flight: June 15, 1936

Power: Two Bristol 1000hp Pegasus XVIII radial engines

Armament: Two 7.7mm/0.303in machine-guns in nose and tail turrets, two in beam positions; up to 2043kg/4500lb bomb load

Size: Wingspan – 26.26m/86ft 2in
Length – 19.68m/64ft 7in
Height – 5.31m/17ft 5in
Wing area – 78.04m²/840sq ft

Weights: Empty – 8424kg/18,556lb
Maximum take-off – 12,939kg/28,500lb

Performance: Maximum speed – 378kph/235mph
Cceiling – 5490m/18,000ft
Range – 4104km/2550 miles
Climb – 320m/1050ft per minute

Vultee Vengeance

The Vengeance was designed for the Royal Air Force, who considered that, following the combat successes of the Luftwaffe's Stuka during the Spanish Civil War and the Blitzkrieg, a dedicated purpose-designed dive-bomber should be in the RAF inventory. However, by the time the Vengeance was ready to enter service, the RAF had seen the vulnerability of the German dive-bomber through the gunsights of British fighters during the Battle of Britain. Accordingly, the RAF decided that the Vengeance was not suited to the European theatre but was appropriate for operations in the Far East and against challenging targets in Burma.

History has not been kind to the aircraft but in fact it was a very capable, stable and accurate bombing platform. In Burma, often operating out of range

of friendly fighter cover, Royal Air Force and Indian Air Force Vengeances played a key role in the battles against the Japanese for Imphal and Kohima, and carried out precision bombing raids against key bridges used for moving supplies to the Japanese.

The Royal Navy's Fleet Air Arm received a total of 113 Vengeances, 88 of which had been delivered by the end of August 1945, and the rest by early 1946. No FAA aircraft saw action; they were used mainly as target tugs.

The Royal Australian Air Force took delivery of great numbers of the Vengeance from 1942, some 342 in total. The RAAF operated the type in combat in New Guinea, and after withdrawal from front-line service, the Australian aircraft flew as target tugs and communications aircraft until they

ABOVE: **Vengeance Mk III of No.84 Squadron, Burma 1944.** BELOW LEFT: **RAAF Vengeance dive-bombers of No.24 Squadron returning from a raid on Alexishafen airstrip, February 27, 1944.**

were retired in 1946. Some of the Australian machines were modified for pesticide spraying in late 1945.

The Free French Air Force operated the Vengeance in North Africa, and the aircraft was also supplied to Brazil. The USAAF commandeered some of the aircraft intended for British use but these aircraft did not see combat. By the end of production in 1944, 1528 aircraft had been built in total.

Vultee A-35B Vengeance

First flight: July 1941 (first RAF aircraft)
Power: One Wright 1700hp Double Row Cyclone R-2600 radial piston engine
Armament: Six 7.7mm/0.303in machine-guns in wings and rear cockpit; bomb load of 908kg/2000lb
Size: Wingspan – 14.63m/48ft
  Length – 12.12 m/39ft 9in
  Height – 4.67 m/15ft 4in
  Wing area – 30.84sq m/332sq ft
Weights: Empty – 4676kg/10,300lb
  Maximum take-off – 7445kg/16,400lb
Performance: Maximum speed – 449kph/279mph
  Service ceiling – 6800m/22,300ft
  Range – 1931km/1200 miles
  Climb – 366m/1200ft per minute

Yokosuka D4Y2

First flight: November 1940
Power: One Aichi 1400hp Atsuta 32 piston engine
Armament: Two 7.7mm/0.303in forward-firing and one 7.92mm/0.31in rear-firing machine-gun; up to 800kg/1761lb bomb load
Size: Wingspan – 11.5m/37ft 8.75in
Length – 10.22m/33ft 6.25in
Height – 3.74m/12ft 3.25in
Wing area – 23.6m²/254sq ft
Weights: Empty – 2440kg/5370lb
Maximum take-off – 4250kg/9354lb
Performance: Maximum speed – 550kph/342mph
Ceiling – 10,700m/35,105ft
Range – 1465km/910 miles
Climb – 820m/2700ft per minute

Yokosuka D4Y Suisei

Yokosuka was the location for the Imperial Japanese Navy's First Naval Air Technical Arsenal, which began to design a carrier-based single-engine dive-bomber in 1938. The resulting Suisei (comet), based on the Heinkel He118, was unusual as it was one of few Japanese combat types to be powered by a liquid-cooled engine, in this case a licence-built copy of the German DB 601.

In service from autumn 1942, the type served initially in the reconnaissance role (D4Y1-C), with the dedicated dive-bomber version (D4Y1) entering service in 1943. The type did not fare well against high-performance Allied fighters, and many fell to their guns due to poor protection for the crew and the lack of self-sealing fuel tanks. A total of 2038 were built, the D4Y2 having a more

powerful engine while the D4Y4 was a kamikaze suicide-bomber version which carried one 800kg/1761lb bomb. The Allied codename allocated to all versions was "Judy".

Yokosuka P1Y1 Ginga

First flight: Spring 1943
Power: Two Nakajima 1820hp Homare 11 radial piston engines
Armament: Two 20mm/0.78in cannon, one forward-firing, one rear-firing; up to 800kg/1760lb bomb load
Size: Wingspan – 20m/65ft 7.5in
Length –15m/49ft 2.5in
Height – 4.3m/14ft 1.25in
Wing area – 55m²/592sq ft
Weights: Empty – 7265kg/15,990lb
Maximum take-off – 13,500kg/29,713lb
Performance: Maximum speed – 547kph/340mph
Ceiling – 9400m/30,840ft
Range – 5370km/3337 miles
Climb – 650m/2133ft per minute

Yokosuka P1Y1

This aircraft was built to a 1940 Imperial Japanese Navy requirement for a fast, low-flying medium bomber with the ability to launch torpedo attacks. The prototype P1Y flew in August 1943 and showed great potential, but problems with development delayed its entry into service until early 1945 as the Navy Bomber Ginga (Milky Way) Model II.

Over 1000 were built but this potent combat aircraft was dogged by maintenance problems that stopped the bomber, which could outrun fighters at low level, being a thorn in the Allies' side. It was a complex machine and experienced, well-trained maintenance personnel were in short supply. The aircraft's range at over 5000km/

3105 miles was very impressive, but among other roles the Ginga was used as a suicide-bomber before the end of the war in the Pacific. The Allied codename for the bomber was "Frances".

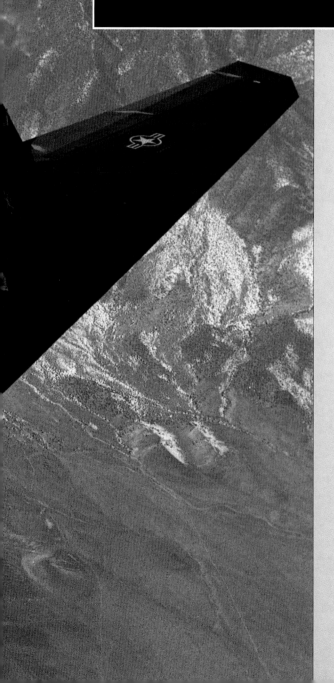

A–Z of Modern Bombers

1945 to the Present Day

The devastating atom bomb raids on Japan that brought World War II to a close guaranteed, at least for a time, the future development of bombers in nations developing such weapons for themselves. Atomic weapons would only be effective if an efficient means of delivery was available. As the Cold War began, the immediate need on all sides was for bomber aircraft that could travel considerable distances, outperform enemy defences and then bomb effectively. Jet technology and greater understanding of aerodynamics led to bomber aircraft flying higher and faster, up to twice the speed of sound. The Cold War forced the development of new technology in many directions, perhaps most spectacularly in "stealth".

By the late 1950s and early '60s, anti-aircraft defence developments, notably SAM missiles and the development of intercontinental ballistic missiles, called the very need for bombers into question. However, ongoing conventional warfare the world over has proved the need for aircraft that can be operated flexibly. Very high speed is no longer a prerequisite for bombers, whereas survivability in today's highly sophisticated air warfare environment is vital.

LEFT: **Lockheed F-117 Nighthawk.**

Aermacchi MB-339

Aermacchi MB-339C

First flight: August 12, 1976
Power: One licence-built Rolls-Royce 1998kg/
    4400lb thrust Viper 680-43 turbojet
Armament: Up to 1816kg/4000lb of external
    weapons including bombs, rockets, cannon
    pods, anti-shipping missiles and air-to-air
    missiles
Size: Wingspan – 11.22m/36ft 10in
    Length – 11.24m/36ft 11in
    Height – 3.99m/13ft 1in
    Wing area – 19.3m²/207.7sq ft
Weights: Empty – 3313kg/7297lb
    Maximum take-off – 6356kg/14,000lb
Performance: Maximum speed – 902kph/560mph
    Ceiling – 14243m/46,700ft
    Range – 2035km/1263 miles
    Climb – 9150m/30,000ft in 6 minutes, 40 seconds

The origins of the MB-339 advanced trainer/light attack aircraft date back to the mid-1950s when the hugely successful MB-326 trainer (and later light attack aircraft) was first designed. By the 1970s Aermacchi were considering a successor, and the MB-339 was born. The airframe shares a lot of its structure with the MB-326K light attack aircraft, with the forward fuselage redesigned to allow the tandem seating to be staggered vertically enabling the instructor to see over the pupil.

The resulting aircraft is stronger and has an uprated powerplant compared to the MB-326. Six hardpoints carrying up to 1816kg/4000lb give this nimble aircraft a powerful punch. The first prototype, I-NOVE, flew on August 12, 1976, and the first production MB-339A trainer was delivered to the Italian Air Force on August 9, 1979. Other customers included New Zealand, Argentina, Dubai, Ghana, Malaysia, Nigeria and Peru. Perhaps the most high-profile user of the MB-339 are the Italian Frecce Tricolori aerobatics display team.

The MB-339AM was a proposed maritime strike version, while the Viper 680-powered MB-339B is enhanced for the ground-attack role. The MB339-K (also known as the Veltro 2), was a single-seat attack version yet to be produced. The next ground-attack version was the MB-339C. Also powered by the Viper 680-43, this version first flew on December 17, 1985, and can carry air-to-air and air-to-ground missiles as well as bombs. The first production customer for the C-model was the Royal New Zealand Air Force, who received their first three aircraft in April 1991.

The MB-339 FD is the latest and most advanced version of the MB-339 in service, and is equipped with self-defence systems for more realistic operational training and for increasing the aircraft survivability in combat.

TOP: **A Royal New Zealand Air Force MB-339. The advanced trainer was seen by many nations as a means of acquiring cost-effective ground-attack capability.** ABOVE: **MB-339Cs.** BELOW: **An Italian Air Force MB-339A.**

LEFT: **A Brazilian Air Force AMX performing a ground-attack demonstration. The aircraft is a fine example of technological and manufacturing co-operation between two nations thousands of miles apart.** BELOW: **The International AMX-T two-seat version.**

AMX International AMX

The AMX fighter-bomber originated from a requirement from the Italian Air Force for a ground-attack aircraft to replace its G91 and F-104s, and the Brazilians' need to replace their MB-326s.

A special consortium was set up to produce this very capable aircraft in both Italy and Brazil. Italian companies Alenia and Aermacchi produce around 70 per cent of the aircraft and Brazilian company Embraer is responsible for 30 per cent. Alenia manufactures the central section of the fuselage, radome, ailerons, spoilers and tail surfaces. Aermacchi is responsible for the forward fuselage, integration of the guns (one 20mm/0.78in cannon in Italian aircraft and two 30mm/1.18in cannon in Brazilian) and avionics, the canopy and the tail structure. Embraer is responsible for the air intakes, wings, leading edge slats, flaps, wing pylons and external fuel tanks. Elements are made in both countries and then shipped to the other as each has final assembly facilities. Power is provided by a non-afterburning

Rolls-Royce Spey 807 turbofan built under licence.

The prototype first flew in 1984 and the first AMX aircraft was delivered to the Italian Air Force in January 1989 and to the Brazilian Air Force in 1990. In total, 192 aircraft, 155 single-seaters and 37 AMX-T two-seaters have been delivered to Italy and Brazil. In December 2002, the Venezuelan Air Force signed a contract for 12 AMX-T aircraft.

Although the primary role of the AMX is ground attack, the aircraft is also highly effective in the air defence mission – in fact, so much so that in 1999, Italian Air Force AMXs were deployed as part of the NATO forces in Operation Allied Force against Serbia.

The AMX Advanced Trainer Attack (AMX-ATA) is a new AMX two-seater, multi-mission attack fighter for combat roles and advanced training. AMX-ATA incorporates new sensors, a forward-looking infrared, helmet-mounted display, a new multi-mode radar for anti-air and anti-ship capability, and new

weapon systems, including anti-ship missiles and medium-range missiles. The Venezuelan Air Force ordered eight AMX-ATAs in 1999 for the advanced trainer and attack aircraft role.

AMX International AMX

First flight: May 15, 1984
Power: One licence-built Rolls-Royce 5008kg/ 11,030lb thrust Spey 807 turbofan
Armament: One 20mm/0.78in cannon (two 30mm/ 1.18in in Brazilian aircraft); weapons load of up to 3800kg/8364lb comprising bombs, rockets and air-to-air missiles
Size: Wingspan – 8.87m/29ft 2in
Length – 13.23m/43ft 5in
Height – 4.55m/14ft 11in
Wing area – 21m²/226.1sq ft
Weights: Empty – 6700kg/14,747lb
Maximum take-off – 13,000kg/28,613lb
Performance: Maximum speed – 915kph/568mph
Ceiling – 13,008m/42,650ft
Range – 1852km/1150 miles
Climb – 3126m/10,250ft per minute

Avro Lincoln

The Lincoln, originally known as the Lancaster IV, was produced to meet a British Air Ministry requirement for a Lancaster replacement. In 1943, Air Ministry planners were turning their thoughts to developing a long-range bomber force (Tiger Force) for action in the Pacific. These new aircraft had to be able to cover the vast distances between likely take-off points and targets.

Elements of the Lancaster were indeed featured in the new design, and the family resemblance is clear, but the aircraft was a sufficiently different design to be named Lincoln instead. A larger fuselage was carried by a new wing and the aircraft was protected by heavier armament. The increased weight required a stronger undercarriage assembly. The prototype, with Captain Brown at the controls, took to the air for the first time at Ringway, Manchester, on June 9, 1944.

Lancaster production had to remain high, so Lincolns did not reach RAF squadrons until August 1945. World War II ended before the Lincoln made it to the Pacific theatre, but the aircraft equipped post-war Bomber Command in the difficult and tense period before the jet-powered V-Bombers were available.

Lincolns went on to equip around 20 squadrons of RAF Bomber Command but it was soon realized that the Lincoln was somewhat lacking in a world increasingly dominated by jets. This led to partial replacement in RAF service by hastily

TOP: **The Lancaster connection is clear, but there was much that was new about the Lincoln.** ABOVE: **The Lincoln I began to reach RAF units in August 1945.**

acquired ex-USAF B-29s. However, Lincolns did see action against communist terrorists in Malaya in 1950 and Mau-Mau dissidents in Kenya from 1953. Lincolns were finally replaced in the RAF by the V-Bombers from 1955. The last Lincolns in RAF service were used in radar development trials until May 1963.

Australia undertook construction of what was designated the Lincoln Mk 30 at the Government Aircraft Factory (GAF), and the first GAF Lincoln, A73-1, flew in March 1946. The first four were assembled mainly from British parts but the rest were manufactured locally. The GAF Lincolns were powered by both British and Australian engines. A number of special "heavy-lift" aircraft were known as Mk 30As. Twelve aircraft were completed as long-nosed Mk 31s, the nose housing three crew. The Lincoln GR.31 was a unique Australian version developed for anti-submarine work. Royal Australian Air Force Lincolns also took part in the Malayan Emergency.

In the latter stages of World War II, Canada had also ordered home production of the Lincoln to equip Canadian bomber units destined for the Pacific. When war ended, production was stopped after only six aircraft had been started. Post-war, the RCAF evaluated the Lincoln but chose not to produce or buy any more. The only export customer for British-built Lincolns was the Argentine Air Force, which acquired 30 Lincoln Mk IIs in 1947.

TOP: **The Lincoln II, or B.2 as it was known in service, differed from the Mk I in its engines, which were Merlin 66, 68A or 300s.** RIGHT: **For the tense years after World War II while the new jet bombers were developed, the Lincoln was Bomber Command's main weapon.** BELOW: **RAF Lincolns were used in combat in Malaya and Kenya.**

Avro Lincoln

First flight: June 9, 1944
Power: Four Rolls-Royce 1750hp Merlin 85 in-line piston engines
Armament: Two 12.7mm/0.5in machine-guns each in turrets in tail, nose and dorsal position; up to 6356kg/14,000lb of bombs
Size: Wingspan – 36.58m/120ft
 Length – 23.86m/78ft 3.5in
 Height – 5.27m/17ft 3.5in
 Wing area – 132m²/1421sq ft
Weights: Empty – 19,522kg/43,000lb
 Maximum take-off – 34,050kg/75,000lb
Performance: Maximum speed – 475kph/295mph
 Service ceiling – 9302m/30,500ft
 Range – 2366km/1470 miles
 Climb – 245m/800ft per minute

Avro Shackleton

TOP: **The Shackleton protected Britain's interests on land, sea and in the air for over three decades.** ABOVE: **The Shackleton prototype, VW126, which had its maiden flight on March 9, 1949.**

During World War II, Britain learned that enemy submarines could wreak havoc with seaborne supply routes in the Atlantic. While surface vessels can be effective against submarines, they can only patrol a relatively small area, and they themselves are at risk from submarines. In contrast, RAF Coastal Command's Lend-Lease Fortresses, Liberators and Catalinas were able to range over vast areas of ocean on a single patrol, and destroyed around 200 German submarines.

Realizing the strategic necessity for effective maritime reconnaissance aircraft in the RAF inventory, and mindful of the fact that Lend-Lease types would be returning to the USA, the Air Ministry issued a 1946 requirement for a British replacement. Avro's design, which became the Shackleton, was selected, possibly because the new aircraft was to employ some elements of the already familiar Avro Lincoln bomber. The Lincoln's wings and undercarriage were mated to a new design fuselage and the aircraft was powered by the higher-performance Griffon engines which turned six-blade contra-rotating propellers. Because of the very long duration of maritime patrol missions, crew comfort was taken seriously, as was soundproofing to protect the ten-man crew against the horrific noise levels generated by four snarling Griffons. Despite the best efforts of the designers, the main wing spar, which passed straight through the fuselage, continued to be a major obstacle when moving from the front to the rear of the aircraft, as had been the case on both the Lincoln and the Lancaster before it.

The first of three Shackleton M.R.1 prototypes, VW126, took to the air on March 9, 1949. The M.R.I and M.R.IA (denoting differing powerplant detail) began to enter RAF service in February 1951. This first Shackleton version is easy to identify thanks to the large "chin" radome, which proved to be problematic as it failed to provide the ideal 360-degree cover and was susceptible to bird-strike. In the Mk 2 Shackleton, which entered RAF service in late 1952, the radar was moved back to the ventral position and was housed in a retractable radome. The nose of this version was also lengthened, and acquired a bomb-aimer's and a nose-gunner's position armed with two 20mm/0.78in Hispano cannons.

When the Shackleton M.R.3 entered service in late 1957, it introduced the tricycle undercarriage, much to the pilots' delight. Crews had voiced concerns over landing the tail-dragger versions because the Shackleton was a heavy aircraft to land with a tailwheel – several tons heavier than

Avro Shackleton M.R.2

First flight: June 17, 1952
Power: Four Rolls-Royce 2455hp Griffon 57A V-12
   piston engines
Armament: Two pairs of 20mm/0.78in cannon;
   maximum weapons-bay load of 8172kg/
   18,000lb of bombs or depth charges
Size: Wingspan – 36.58m/120ft
   Length – 26.59m/87ft 3in
   Height – 5.1m/16ft 9in
   Wing area – 132m²/1421sq ft
Weights: Empty –25,379kg/55,900lb
   Maximum take-off – 39,044kg/86,000lb
Performance: Maximum speed – 500kph/311mph
   Ceiling – 6405m/21,000ft
   Range – 5440km/3380 miles
   Climb – 260m/850ft per minute

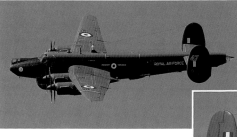

ABOVE: **Normally based at Lossiemouth in Scotland, this Shackleton AEW2 is pictured at Gibraltar.** LEFT: **The AEW2 Shackletons flew on long after their anticipated retirement, while a replacement was finalized.** BELOW: **The MR3 carried extra fuel for its long overwater flights in tip-tanks at the end of the wing.** BOTTOM: **The M.R.3 introduced the tricycle undercarriage, while the mid-upper turret of earlier versions was deleted.**

a Lancaster, for example. The tricycle gear also made taxiing rather less stressful for those on the flightdeck and probably for those on the ground too. More efficient braking, a greater fuel load, full sound insulation (needed on an 18-hour mission), a galley and rest area were all introduced in the Mark 3. It was this version that was exported to South Africa, whose No.35 Squadron operated them until 1984.

As more equipment was carried, the all-up weight rose sharply, so to assist with take-off from shorter runways, two Viper jet engines (similar to those used to power the BAC Strikemaster) were fitted to the outboard engine nacelles from 1966. The stresses caused by the use of this modification ultimately shortened the flying life of the Mk 3 aircraft.

The 1956 Suez crisis marked the Shackleton's "combat" debut, providing anti-submarine cover for the British and French ships below. "Shacks" were frequently involved in colonial policing and saw action in Oman, Kuwait and Borneo, but over the years the type also carried out humanitarian and relief missions in areas affected by natural disasters as far afield as Jamaica, Belize and Morocco. The Shackleton, with its long endurance and ability to carry a great deal of rescue equipment, made it an excellent search-and-rescue (SAR) platform.

However, the Shackleton's principal role was the tracking of potentially hostile vessels on and below the surface of the sea. For hunting submarines the aircraft carried a radar which could detect a submarine's snorkel as it broke the sea surface up to 56km/35 miles away.

From the late 1960s, Shackletons were gradually replaced by Nimrods in the maritime reconnaissance role, but the old Avro aircraft continued to fly into the 1980s, modified to serve in the airborne early warning (AEW) role, guarding mainly the northern approaches to Britain.

Avro Vulcan

The Vulcan, surely one of the most remarkable-looking aircraft ever built, seemed to owe more to the inhabitants of other planets than the German wartime research which influenced its design. The aircraft was Avro's futuristic and adventurous response to a 1946 Air Ministry Operational Requirement calling for a bomber able to carry a 4540kg/ 10,000lb atomic bomb to a target 2775km/1725 miles away.

The Avro Type 698 was conceived as a high-altitude atomic bomber, and was the first four-engine delta-wing aircraft. The unconventional wing shape was chosen because it combines good load-carrying capabilities and high subsonic speed at altitude. To help gain data for the radical new design, several "mini-Vulcans" research aircraft were built – the Avro Type 707s. Gradually the design was changed before the well-known Vulcan layout was finalized. What had been a flying wing with wingtip fins acquired a single central fin, the nose was extended and a distinct fuselage section evolved.

The prototype VX770 flew in August 1952, piloted by Wing Commander Roly Falk, and in 1953 the type 698 was officially named the Vulcan. Spectacular Farnborough appearances followed, the most amazing being a full roll at the 1955 show.

After a redesign of the wing and the addition of more powerful engines, the Vulcan B.1 entered RAF service in February 1957, and became operational with No.83 Squadron at Waddington in July of the same year. Britain's nuclear

TOP: **VX770, the Vulcan prototype, was powered by 2952kg/6500lb thrust Avon turbojets, a long way from the 9080kg/20,000lb thrust Olympus engines that powered the later B.2.** ABOVE: **Vulcan B.1, pictured with its fellow V-bomber, the Victor.**

deterrent force had to be effective and hard-hitting, and it became clear that the B.1 was increasingly vulnerable to the improved Soviet defences it would have to overcome if it were to strike deep into the Soviet Union. To increase the chances of the RAF crews reaching their objectives, the Vulcan B.2 was proposed, with more powerful engines, an electronic warfare (ECM) suite in an enlarged tailcone, and an inflight refuelling capability, along with an improved, larger wing. Some B.1s had a few B.2 improvements incorporated and were designated B.1As. With a longer range, the ability to carry a heavier bomb load (two nuclear weapons instead of one) and greatly improved self-defence capability, the B.2 ensured that the British nuclear strike force was a very real threat to the Soviet Union.

Even with the new and improved B.2, the delivery of free-fall nuclear weapons into the heart of the Soviet Union was probably still a one-way ticket for Vulcan crews. To improve their survivability, a stand-off nuclear missile – the Blue Steel – was developed, which could be launched 161km/100 miles away from the target. Blue Steels were carried partially recessed in the Vulcan's modified bomb bay.

Due to the improvements in Soviet air defence technology, the Vulcans became increasingly vulnerable at high level over enemy territory. The solution was to bring the Vulcan force down to low level, and the aircraft in service were upgraded to B.2A standard. More powerful Olympus engines were fitted, together with terrain-following radar in the nose and a warning radar atop the fin. The Vulcan's role changed when Royal Navy Polaris-equipped submarines took on responsibility for Britain's strategic nuclear deterrent, and they were switched to a tactical low-level penetration role.

However, it was with conventional weapons that the Vulcan first went to war in 1982, when it was used against Argentine positions on the Falkland Islands in what were then the longest bombing raids in history. Vulcans also served in strategic reconnaissance and air-refuelling tanker roles before being withdrawn from service in 1984 to be replaced by Tornadoes. Avro built 144 Vulcans in total, a small number considering the impact that the design had on the aerospace world, and the affection felt for the "tin triangle" by air-show fans the world over.

ABOVE RIGHT: **The Vulcan B.2 was able to carry two nuclear bombs and had increased survivability compared to earlier Vulcans.** RIGHT: **The Vulcan bomb bay carried extra fuel tanks in later versions, but was originally designed to carry the enormous Blue Danube bomb.** BELOW: **Compare the kinked leading edge wing of this B.2 to the pure delta of the prototype.**

Avro Vulcan B.2A

First flight: August 30, 1952 (Avro 698 prototype)
Power: Four Rolls-Royce 9080kg/20,000lb thrust Olympus 301 turbojets
Armament: Twenty-one 454kg/1000lb bombs, nuclear bombs or one Blue Steel stand-off missile
Size: Wingspan – 33.85m/111ft
Length – 30.5m/99ft 11in
Height – 8.26m/7ft 1in
Wing area – 368m²/3964sq ft
Weights: Empty – Approximately 37,682kg/83,000lb (Mk 1)
Maximum take-off – 113,500kg/250,000lb
Performance: Maximum speed – 1038kph/645mph
Ceiling – 16775m/55,000ft
Range – 5550km/3450 miles
Climb – Not published

411

BAC/BAE Strikemaster

The origins of the BAC 167 Strikemaster can be traced back to the piston-powered Hunting/Percival Provost basic trainer which first flew in 1950. Hunting swiftly proposed a jet-powered successor to the Provost – the Jet Provost – as a basic jet trainer for the Royal Air Force. Retaining the wings and tail of the original piston aircraft, the Jet Provost also introduced a tricycle undercarriage. From the mid-1950s, the "JP" was the RAF's standard basic jet trainer until it was finally retired in 1993, having being replaced by the Tucano.

The final production version of the Jet Provost was the Mk. 5 which introduced, among other refinements, a pressurized cabin. Following some exports of the Mk 5, it was this version that the manufacturers BAC (Hunting became part of the British Aircraft Corporation in 1961) developed as a private venture into a dedicated combat aircraft, the Strikemaster, which, as a two-seater, still retained a trainer capability.

The Strikemaster first flew in October 1967, and boasted side-by-side ejection seats and the ability to carry 1362kg/3000lb of ordnance on eight underwing hardpoints. Armament

included free-fall or retarded bombs, gun packs or napalm. Alternatively, a reconnaissance pod, extra fuel tanks or a gun camera could be carried.

The aircraft's simplicity coupled with exceptionally good manoeuvrability and handling were features of the bomber, which attracted numerous overseas customers. Powered by a Rolls-Royce Viper turbojet, the aircraft was designed for operation from rough and short airstrips.

Customers for this very capable combat aircraft, which appeared in a variety of export versions, included Oman (Mk 82 and 82A), Singapore (Mk 84), Botswana, Ecuador (Mk 89), Kenya (Mk 87), Kuwait (Mk 83), New Zealand (Mk 88), Saudi Arabia (Mk 80 and 80A), Sudan (Mk 55) and South Yemen.

RIGHT: **This Strikemaster is painted in the colours of the Singapore Air Defence Command.** BELOW: **The Royal Saudi Air Force was a major customer for the Strikemaster.**

Apart from training, the Strikemaster was most commonly used for ground-attack and counter-insurgency operations. The aircraft of Ecuador, Oman and South Yemen are known to have seen combat – all 20 of the Sultan of Oman's Strikemasters have sustained battle damage.

Between 1968 and 1977, the Royal Saudi Air Force took delivery of a total of 47 Strikemasters in three separate batches. All the aircraft were used for training purposes at the King Faisal Air Academy in Riyadh until 1997, making the Strikemaster one of the longest serving aircraft in RSAF history.

Of the 16 Strikemasters acquired by the Royal New Zealand Air Force (where the aircraft was nicknamed "Blunty") in 1972, use of the aircraft was restricted after 1981 when cracks were discovered in the wing and tail structures of most RNZAF aircraft. The rigours of flying through low-level turbulence and high usage were given as the likely causes. Replacing the wings of all their aircraft was considered too costly by the RNZAF, who retired them in 1992. Similar problems with the Strikemasters of Ecuador caused the grounding of their fleet for months at a time, while causes were identified and where possible remedied.

The final batch of new Strikemasters was delivered to Sudan in 1984. In all, 146 Strikemasters were sold around the world and many have now been refurbished for civilian use, surviving as "warbirds" in Britain, the USA and Australia.

BELOW LEFT: **In this view of an RNZAF Strikemaster, the side-by-side seats can be clearly seen.** BELOW: **The Strikemaster was one of the first small but capable and affordable trainer/ground-attack aircraft available to smaller nations. There was clearly a demand for this type, and the Strikemaster satisfied that for many nations.**

ABOVE: **An Omani Strikemaster armed with bombs and rockets – the aircraft supplied to Oman saw considerable action.**

BAC Strikemaster

First flight: October 26, 1967
Power: One Rolls-Royce 1548kg/3410lb thrust Viper Mk 535 turbojet
Armament: Two 7.62mm/0.3in machine-guns; maximum bomb load of 1362kg/3000lb
Size: Wingspan – 11.23m/36ft 10in
Length – 10.27m/33ft 8.5in
Height – 3.34m/10ft 11.5in
Wing area – 19.85m²/213.7sq ft
Weights: Empty – 2812kg/6195lb
Maximum take-off – 5221kg/11,500lb
Performance: Maximum speed – 760kph/472mph
Ceiling – 12,200m/40,000ft
Range – 2224km/1382 miles
Climb – 1601m/5250ft per minute

British Aircraft Corporation TSR.2

Few British aircraft have stirred as much controversy or strength of feeling as the TSR.2. The project's cancellation in 1965 was seen by many commentators as a political step that became the deathblow for Britain's troubled aviation industry.

The TSR.2 (Tactical Strike and Reconnaissance) was initially designed to meet a demanding 1957 Royal Air Force requirement for a Canberra tactical bomber replacement with terrain-following radar, advanced inertial navigation, supersonic speed at low level and Mach 2 at high altitude. In addition, the new aircraft would ideally have the capability to be operated from short, rough landing strips.

Despite the facts that the requirement become more demanding as development progressed, and that most of the TSR.2's systems were totally new to the British aviation industry, the aircraft began to take shape.

TSR.2's form was of course dictated by the missions it was designed to carry out, but by way of comparison it was longer than an Avro Lancaster but had a smaller wingspan than a Spitfire fighter. The short wingspan was essential for supersonic performance at very low altitude but would fail to generate sufficient lift for it to operate from short strips. The solution was to fit the aircraft with the most powerful blown flaps ever made, which used high-speed air blown over the flaps to make the wing produce massive amounts of lift at take-off and landing.

The TSR.2 carried equipment that is now commonplace but was extremely advanced for the time. A projected moving map, head-up display (HUD), one of the first terrain-following radars and a canopy coated with gold alloy to reflect nuclear

TOP: **XR219, the prototype TSR.2, during its test programme.** ABOVE: **The TSR.2 was equipped with pioneering terrain-following radar, which would have guided the aircraft at heights of 91m/200ft at the speed of sound.**

flash were all cutting-edge features of this remarkable aircraft. The avionics – purpose-designed for the aircraft – would have used forward- and side-looking radar and other systems to feed updated position and steering information to the pilot's HUD, the navigator, the weapon arming and release systems and the autopilot simultaneously. If the whole system had failed, the aircraft would have been automatically put in a climb. Among the materials used in the aircraft's construction were aluminium-copper alloys, aluminium-lithium alloys and ultra-high tensile steel.

The first flight of prototype XR219 took off from Boscombe Down on September 27, 1964, with Roland "Bee" Beamont at the controls and Don Bowen as navigator. The Olympus

BAC TSR.2

First flight: September 27, 1964
Power: Two Bristol Siddeley 14982kg/33,000lb thrust Olympus 22R turbojets
Armament: Up to 1816kg/4000lb of weapons on underwing pylons; proposed bomb load of up to 2724kg/6000lb
Size: Wingspan – 11.28m/37ft
Length – 27.13m/89ft
Height – 7.32m/24ft
Wing area – 65.03m²/700sq ft
Weights Empty – 90,000kg/198,090lb
Maximum take-off – 188,000kg/413,788lb
Performance: Maximum speed – 2390kph/1485mph
Ceiling – 17,080m/56,000ft
Range – 4827km/3000 miles
Climb – 15,250m/50,000ft per minute
(these figures may not have been achieved in testing but are in the aircraft's specification)

ABOVE LEFT: **XR222, the fourth TSR.2, is preserved at the Imperial War Museum Duxford in the UK.** LEFT: **XR222 prior to its "completion", at least for display purposes, at the Imperial War Museum Duxford.** BELOW LEFT: **During the 24 flights made by XR219, the aircraft's capabilities were clear to the crew.** BELOW: **A rare view of the "hotseat", the pilot's cockpit of TSR.2.**

engines being developed for TSR.2 had some problems (including exploding examples) that had not been resolved before this first flight. The team were keen to get the aircraft into the air as soon as possible in the hope that its remarkable performance would silence the critics. Consequently it was decided that one test-flight could be made with the imperfect engines that were considered likely to explode at more than 97 per cent power. The 14-minute test-flight was uneventful and the aircraft was shown to be responsive and stable.

During further test-flights, the extremely complex aircraft showed that it had the potential to become one of the most formidable strike aircraft in the world. The aircraft made 24 flights and accumulated 13 hours and 9 minutes of flight time, including some at supersonic speeds, before the TSR.2 project was cancelled by the new Labour government on April 6, 1965. The government cited spiralling costs and the minimum 3-year delay in the TSR.2 reaching squadron service as reasons for the decision. The RAF never did receive an alternative to the TSR-2 as a supersonic strike successor to the Canberra.

BAE Systems Harrier

British innovation in aircraft design is perhaps best demonstrated by the Harrier. This truly remarkable aircraft, constantly improved and updated since its first uncertain hovering flight in October 1960, is still the only single-engined vertical or short take-off and landing (V/STOL) in service.

During the Cold War it was obvious that the West's military airfields would have been attacked very early in any offensive. Dispersal of aircraft and equipment was one option of response – the other was the Harrier, with its ability to operate from any small piece of flat ground. The fact that an aircraft can fly straight up with no need for forward movement still leaves spectators stunned over four decades after the prototype first flew.

The Harrier can take off and land vertically by the pilot selecting an 80-degree nozzle angle and applying full power. At 15–30m/50–100ft altitude, the nozzles are gradually directed rearwards until conventional wingborne flight is achieved. The key to the Harrier's vertical take-off lies with the vectored thrust from the Harrier's Pegasus engine, directed by four jet nozzles controlled by a selector lever next to the throttle in the cockpit. The nozzles swivel as one, directing thrust from directly to the rear to just forward of vertical. While hovering or flying at very low speeds, the aircraft is controlled in all lanes of movement by reaction control jets located in the nose, wing and tail. These jets are operated by the Harrier's conventional rudder pedals and control column.

The Harrier GR1 first entered squadron service with the RAF in October 1969, and many were subsequently upgraded to GR3 standard, with more powerful engines and a tail warning radar to alert the pilot to hostile missiles locking on

TOP: **An RAF GR7. The Harrier is one of the all-time great combat aircraft. The basic soundness of the concept has lent itself to many upgrades and improvements.** ABOVE: **Radar-equipped AV-8Bs of the Spanish Navy operating from the carrier** *Principe de Asturias*. **These aircraft were similar to those operated by the Italian Navy and USMC aircraft.**

to his aircraft. GR3s of No.1 Squadron RAF were in action during the 1982 Falklands War. They carried out ground-attack operations using cluster and "smart" bombs, with weapon loads of up to 1362kg/3000lb. The Squadron flew more than 150 missions, with two aircraft lost to heavy anti-aircraft fire at Goose Green.

Early in the Harrier's operational life, the US Marine Corps expressed an interest in the aircraft, leading to more than a hundred being built as the AV-8A by McDonnell Douglas in the USA. The USMC continues to operate Harriers today, the AV-8B variant being roughly equivalent to the RAF's GR7. US Marine Corps AV-8Bs took part in Operation Desert Storm in 1991. The other customer for the early Harrier was the Spanish Navy, which ordered the US-built AV-8A, and subsequently sold some of the aircraft on to the Thai Navy in 1996.

ABOVE: **The GR7 is the RAF equivalent of the American-designed AV-8B.**
LEFT: **The Harrier gives its operators unparalled strike flexibility.**

The second-generation GR5 and GR7 versions replaced the original Harrier GR3s in the late 1980s/early 1990s in the offensive support role. The GR7 is, in essence, a licence-built American-designed AV-8B Harrier II fitted with RAF-specific navigation and defensive systems as well as other changes, including additional underwing pylons for Sidewinder missiles. The improved design of the GR7 allows the aircraft to carry twice the load of a GR3 over the same distance or the same load over twice the distance. The first flight of the Harrier GR7 was in 1989, and deliveries to RAF squadrons began in 1990. A total of 96 aircraft were ordered, including 62 interim GR5s which were later modified to GR7 standard.

The Harrier GR7 is capable of operating throughout the full spectrum of ground-attack operations by day and night. The aircraft carries forward-looking infrared (FLIR) equipment which, when used in conjunction with the pilot's night-vision goggles (NVGs), provides a night, low-level capability. The Harrier T10, a two-seat trainer version of the GR7, came into service in 1995 and can be used operationally.

Recent operational deployments for the Harriers have been to Italy in support of NATO and UN operations in Bosnia and Serbia, and to the Gulf embarked on Royal Navy aircraft carriers, where they complemented the Royal Navy's own Sea Harriers.

Plans in 2002 announced the withdrawal of the Sea Harrier by 2006, with the Harrier GR7/GR9s being operated by both RAF and Royal Navy squadrons.

The Harrier continues to be upgraded. New Pegasus 107 engines, giving more thrust at higher temperatures, make the aircraft Harrier GR7As even more efficient. Also, a major upgrade to the aircraft's avionics and weapons systems will enable the Harrier to carry a variety of current and future weapons. These include Maverick air-to-surface missiles, Brimstone anti-armour missiles and Sidewinder air-to-air missiles for self-defence. A new, stronger composite rear fuselage will also be fitted. These aircraft will become Harrier GR9s, while those with the uprated engines and weapons systems will be Harrier GR9As. The programme also includes an upgrade of the two-seater T10 aircraft to the equivalent GR9 standard known as the Harrier T12.

RAF Harriers saw service in Kosovo and in the 2003 invasion of Iraq. On March 22, 2003, alongside aircraft of the USAF and USN, the RAF were heavily involved in attacks against key Iraqi targets, including Baghdad. One of the RAF raids featured the first operational use of the RAF's Maverick missile. A Harrier GR7 pilot launched one of the missiles against a mobile SCUD missile launch site some 322km/200 miles into Iraq. It successfully engaged and destroyed the target.

ABOVE: **The Harrier GR7 can carry up to 4903kg/10,800lb of ordnance under its wings and fuselage.**

BAE Systems Harrier II GR7

First flight: October 21, 1960 (P1127)
Power: One Rolls-Royce 9765kg/21,500lb thrust Pegasus Mk5 turbofan
Armament: Two 25mm/0.90in cannon; up to 4903kg/10,800lb bombs, missiles or rockets
Size: Wingspan – 9.25m/30ft 4in
Length – 14.36m/47ft 1in
Height – 3.55m/11ft 7.75in
Wing area – 21.37m²/230sq ft
Weights: Empty – 6973kg/15,360lb
Maximum take-off – 14,074kg/31,000lb
Performance: Maximum speed – 1058kph/661mph
Ceiling – 15,250m/50,000ft plus
Range – 11,861km/7370 miles
Climb – Not available

Blackburn Buccaneer

The Buccaneer was at one point the most advanced high-speed low-level strike aircraft in the world. It had its origins in the July 1953 Naval Staff Requirement NA.39 which called for a long-range carrier-borne strike aircraft capable of carrying a nuclear weapon beneath enemy radar cover and attacking enemy shipping or ports.

Blackburn's N.A.39 design, the B-103, was the successful contender and the development contract was awarded in 1955 – the first of 20 pre-production aircraft took to the air on April 30, 1958, and also appeared at that year's Farnborough air show. The B-103 prototype was powered by 3178kg/ 7000lb thrust Gyron turbojets, not the much more powerful Spey of later models. The carrier aircraft elements of the design, such as folding wings, folding nose catapult fittings and arrestor hook, were introduced from the fourth aircraft onwards. The aerodynamically advanced aircraft incorporated many innovations, including a rotary bomb-bay door (intended to avoid the drag of conventional bomb-bay doors and weapons carried beneath the aircraft) and a split tail cone which opened to act as airbrakes. The aircraft also had a cutting-edge boundary layer control system in which air from the engines was forced through slits on the wings' leading edges, producing much more lift than that wing would normally give. Increasing the wings' efficiency meant the aircraft could land at lower speed and carry more ordnance.

The miniature detonating cord (MDC), which shatters the cockpit canopy prior to ejection, is now standard on most British fast jets, and was pioneered on the Blackburn design. It was actually developed to aid escape in the event of underwater ejection.

TOP: **Buccaneer S.1 XK534 from the Fleet Air Arm Trials Unit at Lossiemouth. Painted overall in anti-flash white, this was the 18th pre-production aircraft.** ABOVE: **The Buccaneer's wings are able to fold up through 120 degrees from a hinge.**

Royal Navy carrier trials began in January 1960 and the first B-103 deck landing took place on HMS *Victorious* on the 19th of the month. Having given the aircraft the name Buccaneer in 1960, the Navy took delivery of the first production version, the S.1, in July 1962. HMS *Ark Royal* sailed with the first operational Buccaneer squadron, No.801, and its anti-flash white Buccaneers only six months later in January 1963. The Cold War was at one of its chilliest phases and Britain wanted nuclear-capable aircraft in service as soon as possible.

The S.1 was soon shown to be under-powered, and in some conditions the Gyrons could barely lift a loaded Buccaneer off the deck within safety margins. Consequently, Fleet Air Arm Scimitars fitted with inflight refuelling equipment were detailed to refuel the partly fuelled and therefore lighter Buccaneers shortly after they left the deck. Forty S.1s were built before production switched to the next Mark. The improved S.2 was the principal production version (84 were built) and had a greater range than the earlier version thanks to the more powerful but less thirsty Spey engines. Service S.2s are most easily recognized by the fixed refuelling probe forward of the cockpit.

The S.2s served in the Royal Navy's front line from January 1967 until the last S.2s left the deck of the *Ark Royal* in November 1978. However, the Buccaneer's career was far from over as the first of almost 90 aircraft had begun service with the Royal Air Force in October 1969, filling the gap in the RAF inventory left by the scrapping of TSR.2 and the cancellation of the intended F-111 purchase for the RAF.

Twenty-six of the aircraft were new-build while a further 62 Royal Navy examples were gradually transferred into RAF service. In addition to retaining a nuclear strike capability, Buccaneers were also tasked with anti-shipping missions from land bases. RAF Germany, right in the nuclear front-line, first welcomed No.15 Squadrons Buccaneers early in 1971. Tornados began to replace the Germany Buccaneers in 1983 but two squadrons tasked with maritime strike remained in service in Scotland. In 1991 some of these aircraft were "called up" for service in the

first Gulf War, where they acted as laser designators for laser-guided bombs dropped by Tornados. To give it an even longer range for these special missions, the "Bucc" was fitted with a 2000 litre/440 gallon fuel tank carried in the bomb bay.

TOP RIGHT: **Buccaneers served on Royal Navy carriers from 1962 until 1978.**
MIDDLE RIGHT: **Some Royal Navy aircraft were transferred to the RAF, while others were brand new aircraft. Some of these retained a nuclear strike capability based in Germany.** RIGHT: **The last Buccaneers in RAF service were those retained for the maritime strike role.** BELOW: **The last British bomber was tasked with demanding Gulf War missions shortly before its retirement.**

Blackburn Buccaneer S.2

First flight: April 30, 1958 (B-103 prototype)
Power: Two Rolls-Royce 5039kg/11,100lb thrust Rolls-Royce Spey 101 turbofans
Armament: One nuclear bomb or four 454kg/ 1000lb conventional bombs carried internally
Size: Wingspan – 13.41m/44ft
Length – 19.33m/63ft 5in
Height – 4.95m/16ft 3in
Wing area – 47.82m²/514.7sq ft
Weights: Empty –13,620kg/30,000lb
Maximum takeoff – 28,148kg/62,000lb
Performance: Maximum speed – 1038kph/ 645mph
Ceiling – 12,200m/40,000ft plus
Range – 3218km/2000 miles
Climb – 9150m/30,000ft in 2 minutes

Boeing B-47 Stratojet

As World War II was drawing to a close, the US Army Air Forces were considering replacements for the aircraft types then in service. Development of a new subsonic, high-altitude, medium-range bomber began in 1945 with four US contractors in the running. The Boeing design, the six-jet XB-47 (first flight December 1947), with the performance of contemporary jet fighters, won the competition and became the first jet-powered swept-wing bomber in service. Its six turbojet engines (so many were needed because of the poor power output of early jets) were housed in pods slung beneath the 35-degree swept-back wings, the inboard pods housing two engines each while a single engine was positioned towards the tip of each wing. Early versions at maximum take-off weight needed additional thrust from 18 solid-fuel booster rockets in the aft fuselage.

B-47s began entering the USAF inventory in 1952 and, in the days before intercontinental ballistic missiles, the fast nuclear-armed bomber was the best deterrent the USA had. Apart from the swept wings and profusion of engines, the aircraft incorporated many novel features, including a remote-controlled tail gun turret and a bicycle-type retractable main landing gear with single, two-wheel legs on the forward and aft fuselage. Outrigger wheels that retracted into the two-engine pod cowling provided added stability. The B-model was the first production version in service but was supplanted by the B-47E, the ultimate bomber version.

The three-man B-47 was a heavy aircraft in its day, and although it was a medium-range bomber, it was heavier than any strategic bomber aircraft of World War II. A tail chute was used to slow down the aircraft during landings, one of the first aircraft to use the technique. The B-47 could carry a 9080kg/20,000lb bomb load that limited the aircraft to a maximum of two nuclear weapons of the early 1950s. However, so many B-47s were manufactured, they did represent a more than credible deterrent or threat to the Soviet Union. Conventional weaponry options included 6129kg/13,500lb or eight 454kg/1000lb bombs.

The B-47 had a 5792km/3600 mile range which required Strategic Air Command to make use of forward bases in friendly nations such as Britain, Spain and Morocco, as well as

ABOVE: **The B-47 was a great technological leap for US military aviation. The main bomber at the time of the B-47's first flight was the B-29.** LEFT: **At its peak use, the B-47 equipped 28 SAC Bomb Wings, each with 45 aircraft.**

LEFT: The large swept wings, 1-2-2-1 engine layout and the fighter style canopy make the B-47 one of the easiest aircraft to identify. BELOW: An early B-47 assisted by 18 rockets at take-off. BOTTOM: Over 2000 B-47s were built, and they provided the USA with a credible nuclear deterrent.

Alaska, to be within striking distance of the USSR. In addition, the B-47 was later equipped with an air-refuelling capability and 36-hour missions were flown to show the world the reach of the SAC bomber. However, when some foreign hosts chose to withdraw their offer of forward bases, the usefulness of the B-47 was reduced because there was insufficient tanker support to allow great numbers of B-47s to operate from the continental USA.

Also, as with Britain's V-force, the B-47 role was changed in the mid-1950s due to the development of effective Soviet surface-to-air missiles (SAMs), and the aircraft's structure was strengthened so that it could be used as a low-level bomber avoiding Soviet radars.

Some B-47s were modified for reconnaissance use (RB-47) and, as space was at a premium in the airframe, these versions were not capable of carrying bombs as well as reconnaissance equipment. However, the RB-47B could be converted back to bomber configuration.

By 1956, B-47 deployment peaked, with over 1300 equipping 28 SAC wings, while around 250 RB-47s were in SAC service in the same period. The B-47 was gradually phased out in the early 1960s. About 400 were in service in 1964 and by 1966 the last B-47 had been phased out. The retirement of the B-47 was balanced by the large numbers of strategic nuclear missiles then joining the US arsenal. A total of 2039 B-47s were built.

Boeing B-47E Stratojet

First flight: December 17, 1947
Power: Six General Electric 3269kg/7200lb thrust J47-GE-25 turbojets
Armament: Two 20mm/0.78in cannon in remote-controlled tail turret; up to 9080kg/20,000lb of bombs
Size: Wingspan – 35.36m/116ft
  Length – 33.48m/109ft 10in
  Height – 8.51m/27ft 11in
  Wing area –132.66m²/1428sq ft
Weights: Empty – 36,663kg/80,756lb
  Maximum take-off – 89,973kg/198,180lb
Peformance: Maximum speed – 975kph/606mph
  Ceiling –12,352m/40,500ft plus
  Range – 5794km/3600 miles
  Climb – 1326m/4350ft per minute at maximum power

Boeing B-52 Stratofortress

The B-52 is surely one of the greatest combat aircraft of all time, remaining in front-line service almost six decades after the USAF specification for what became the B-52 was released in 1946. The USAF wanted a bomber with a 16,090km/10,000-mile range and a speed of over 804kph/500mph. Boeing initially proposed a conventional design with piston engines to achieve the range. As the US Air Force wanted the aircraft to fly as high and fast as possible to drop atomic weapons, Boeing revised the design with eight jet powerplants and swept wings.

The prototype first flew in 1952 and ever since entering service in 1955, the B-52 has been in the front line. The first operational version was the B-52B, and in 1956 a B-model dropped the first air-dropped hydrogen bomb over Bikini Atoll. In an attempt to demonstrate the reach of the USAF Strategic Air Command, three B-52Bs made a non-stop flight around the world in January 1957, with the help of five inflight refuellings.

A total of 744 B-52s were built with the last, a B-52H, delivered in October 1962. Only the H-model is still in the Air Force inventory and is assigned to Air Combat Command and the Air Force Reserves. The first of 102 B-52s was delivered to Strategic Air Command in May 1961.

The B-52 could bomb the Soviet Union from bases in the continental USA and was a key element in SAC's deterrence of the Soviet Union. To ensure the survivability of the SAC deterrent against a pre-emptive Soviet strike, the SAC B-52 force was dispersed and rotated. In addition, a given number

TOP: **A B-52D. The B-52 is a truly great military aircraft. Despite being in service for half a century, there is still no other aircraft in the US inventory that can do the job of the B-52, and on the same scale.** ABOVE: **The bomb-carrying capacity of the "Buff" is considerable – 27,240kg/60,000lb of weaponry can be trucked and dropped on a target.**

of B-52s was kept on standby ready for take-off and, for a time, in the air ready to begin attacks on Soviet targets. From 1958 until 1968, ten to twelve USAF B-52s were airborne at all times. At the time of the 1962 Cuban missile crisis, 70 aircraft were kept aloft at all times for one month. Following two crashes in which radioactivity was released from the nuclear bombs aboard, the airborne alert ceased.

The B-52, with its cavernous bomb bay and great lifting capability, has been armed with free-fall hydrogen bombs and parachute retarded bombs as well as stand-off nuclear

LEFT: **The B-52G was a complete structural redesign with a distinctive short fin.** BELOW: **The H-model is the version still in USAF use today, and will be for some years to come.** BOTTOM: **Inflight refuelling during the Gulf War. The conflict gave the old but potent bomber the opportunity to get into the record books with the longest bombing mission in history.**

missiles, including the AGM-86B. Of course, the aircraft has never used nuclear weapons in anger. During the Vietnam War, however, USAF B-52s dropped almost 3 million tons of bombs. The bomb bay of the D-model was modified so that it could carry up to 108 conventional bombs, which meant that each aircraft could carry around 27.4 tonnes/27 tons per aircraft.

Two decades after its missions over Vietnam, the B-52 took part in the Gulf War. Seven B-52s armed with AGM-86 cruise missiles flew 22,500km/14,000 miles (and into the history books) from the USA to carry out the first air strike of the war – this was the longest combat mission ever flown. During the conflict, 80 B-52s flew 1624 sorties, dropping 26,111 tonnes/ 25,700 tons of bombs, accounting for 40 per cent of the total dropped during the war. In 2003, USAF B-52s operating from a base in Britain carried out numerous bombing raids on targets in Iraq, demonstrating that the '52 was still a potent front-line combat aircraft 51 years after the type first flew.

Today, the B-52s of USAF Air Combat Command remain a key means of delivering US air power with worldwide precision navigation capability. The aircraft is also highly effective when used for ocean surveillance, and can assist the US Navy in anti-ship and mine-laying operations. In two hours, two B-52s can monitor 362,600km²/140,000sq miles of ocean surface.

The B-52 is capable of dropping or launching the widest array of weapons in the US inventory. This includes gravity bombs, cluster bombs, precision-guided missiles and joint direct attack munitions. Updated with modern technology, the B-52 will be capable of delivering the full complement of joint developed weapons – current engineering analysis shows the B-52's life span to extend beyond the year 2045. The B-52 will be kept flying because there is nothing else in the US inventory that can carry out the B-52 mission on the same scale.

Boeing B-52D

First Flight: April 15, 1952
Power: Eight Pratt & Whitney 5493kg/12,100lb thrust J57-P-19W turbojets
Armament: Four 12.7mm/0.5in machine-guns in tail; maximum of 108 conventional bombs up to 27,240kg/60,000lb
Size: Wingspan – 56.4m/185ft
Length – 47.7m/156ft 6in
Height – 12.75m/48ft 3.7in
Wing area – 371.6m²/4000sq ft
Weights: Empty – 85,806kg/189,000lb
Maximum take-off – 204,300kg/450,000lb
Performance: Maximum speed – 893kph/555mph
Ceiling – 13,725m/45,000ft
Range – 11,861km/7370 miles
Climb – Not available

423

Boeing/McDonnell Douglas/Northrop F/A-18 Hornet

With its excellent fighter and self-defence capabilities, the F/A-18 was intended to increase strike mission survivability and supplement the F-14 Tomcat in US Navy fleet air defence. The F/A-18 played a key role in the 1986 US strikes against Libya. Flying from the USS *Coral Sea*, F/A-18s launched high-speed anti-radiation missiles (HARMs) against Libyan air-defence radars and missile sites, thus silencing them during the attacks on military targets in Benghazi.

The F/A-18's advanced radar and avionics systems allow Hornet pilots to shift from fighter to strike mode on the same mission with the flip of a switch, a facility used routinely by Hornets in Operation Desert Storm – they fought their way to a target by defeating opposing aircraft, attacked ground targets and returned home safely. This "force multiplier" capability gives the operational commander more flexibility in employing tactical aircraft in a rapidly changing battle scenario.

The F/A-18 Hornet was built in single and two-seat versions. Although the two-seater is a conversion trainer, it is combat-capable and has a similar performance to the single seat version, although with reduced range. The F/A-18A and C are single-seat aircraft, while the F/A-18B and D are dual-seaters. The B-model is used primarily for training, while the D-model is the current Navy aircraft for attack, tactical air control, forward air control and reconnaissance squadrons.

In November 1989, the first F/A-18s equipped with night-strike capability were delivered, and since 1991, F/A-18s have been delivered with F404-GE-402 enhanced performance engines that produce up to 20 per cent more thrust than the previous F404 engines. From May 1994, the Hornet has been equipped with upgraded radar – the APG-73 – which substantially increases the speed and memory capacity of the radar's processors. These upgrades and improvements help the Hornet maintain its advantage over potential enemies and keep it among the most advanced and capable combat aircraft in the world.

Apart from the US Navy and Marine Corps, the F/A-18 is also in service with the air forces of Canada, Australia, Spain, Kuwait, Finland, Switzerland and Malaysia.

Canada was the first international customer for the F/A-18, and its fleet of 138 CF-18 Hornets is the largest outside the USA. The CF-18s have an unusual element to their paint scheme in that a "fake" cockpit is painted on the underside of the fuselage directly beneath the real cockpit. This is intended to confuse an enemy fighter, if only for a split second, about the orientation of the CF-18 in close air combat. That moment's hesitation can mean the difference between kill or be killed in a dogfight situation.

TOP: **The Hornet/Super Hornet family of aircraft have given their operators an exceptional combination of capabilities – few aircraft can fight, not just evade, enemy aircraft and then carry out devastating pinpoint attacks.** ABOVE: **Aircraft operated by Spain were designated EF/A-18. This is a single-seat A-model.**

The F/A-18E/F Super Hornet was devised to build on the great success of the Hornet, and having been test-flown in November 1995, entered service for evaluation with US Navy squadron VFA-122 in November 1999.

The Super Hornet is 25 per cent larger than its predecessor but has 42 per cent fewer parts. Both the single-seat E and two-seat F-models offer increased range, greater endurance, more payload-carrying ability and more powerful engines in the form of the F414-GE-400, an advanced derivative of the Hornet's current F404 engine family that produces 35 per cent more thrust.

Structural changes to the airframe increase internal fuel capacity by 1634kg/3600lb, which extends the Hornet's mission radius by up to 40 per cent. The fuselage is 86.3cm/34in longer and the wing is 25 per cent larger with an extra 9.3m²/100sq ft of surface area. There are two additional weapons stations, bringing the total to 11.

In the words of its manufacturers, "The Super Hornet is an adverse-weather, day and night, multi-mission strike fighter whose survivability improvements over its predecessors make it harder to find, and if found, harder to hit, and if hit, harder to disable."

The first operational cruise of the F/A-18 E Super Hornet was with VFA-115 on board the USS *Abraham Lincoln* on July 24, 2002, and the type was first used in combat on November 6, 2002, when they participated in a strike against hostile targets in the "no-fly" zone in Iraq.

ABOVE: **A US Marine Corps F/A-18D drops a bomb over a bombing range in Nevada.** BELOW LEFT: **A fine air-to-air study of USMC Hornets.** BELOW: **USMC Hornets. The type is operated by a number of other nations outside the USA, on four different continents.** BOTTOM: **The Super Hornet is bigger and better than the original design.**

Northrop F/A-18E Super Hornet

First flight: November 18, 1995
Power: Two General Electric 9988kg/22,000lb thrust afterburning F414-GE-400 turbofans
Armament: One 20mm/0.78in cannon, eleven hardpoints carrying up to 8058kg/17,750lb of weapons, including AIM-7, AIM-120 AMRAAM, AIM-9 air-to-air missiles or other guided weapons, bombs and rockets
Size: Wingspan – 13.62m/44ft 9in
Length – 18.31m/60ft 1in
Height – 4.88m/16ft
Wing area – 46.5m²/500sq ft
Weights: Empty – 13,426kg/29,574lb
Maximum take-off – 29,937kg/66,000lb
Performance: Maximum speed – 1915kph/1189mph
Ceiling – 15,250m/50,000ft plus
Combat radius – 2225km/1382 miles
Climb – Not published

Breguet Alizé

Breguet Alizé

First Flight: March 26, 1955 (prototype)
Power: One Rolls-Royce 1975hp DartRDa21
turboprop
Armament: Two anti-shipping missiles carried
beneath the folding wings, or a combination
of depth charges, bombs or rockets; acoustic
torpedo, three 160kg/352lb depth charges
housed in internal bomb bay
Size: Wingspan – 15.6m/51ft 2in
Length – 13.86m/45ft 6in
Height – 5.00m/16ft 4.75in
Wing area – 36.00m²/387.51sq ft
Weights: Empty – 5700kg/12,546lb
Maximum take-off – 8200kg/18,048lb
Performance: Maximum speed – 518kph/322mph
Ceiling – 8000m/26,245ft plus
Range – 2500km/1553 miles
Climb – 420m/1380ft per minute

ABOVE: **Alizé prepares to take off from a French carrier.**
LEFT: **This French Navy Alizé's retractable radome is seen in the stowed position beneath the roundel.** BELOW: **Sporting a French Navy 1990s low-visibility paint scheme.**

The carrier-borne anti-submarine Alizé (tradewind) was derived from the Vultur carrier-based attack aircraft designed for the French Aeronavale but never produced for service. The Alizé was an extensive redesign of the earlier type and had its first flight on October 5, 1956.

The crew of three consisted of pilot, radar operator and sensor operator. The pilot was seated in front to the right, the radar operator in front to the left, and the sensor operator sat sideways behind them. Landing gear retracted backwards into nacelles in the wings. The Alizé, powered by the Rolls-Royce Dart RDa.21 turboprop driving a four-bladed propeller, could patrol for over 5 hours.

The aircraft was armed with a potent array of torpedoes, depth charges, bombs, rockets and missiles. A total of 89 examples of the Alizé were built between 1957 and 1962, including

prototypes. The Aeronavale operated 75 from March 1959 on board the carriers *Clemenceau* and *Foch*.

The Aeronavale upgraded the Alizé in the 1980s and '90s with the latest avionics. The aircraft was simply not able to hunt modern nuclear-powered submarines effectively, so was limited to maritime surface patrol duties.

The Aeronavale operated 24 examples until 1997, and in the spring of 1999, aircraft flying off the carrier

Foch were used operationally during the NATO air campaign against Serbia over Kosovo. The Alizé was finally withdrawn from Aeronavale service in 2000 with the retirement of the *Foch*.

The Indian Navy operated the Alizé (at least 12 examples) from shore bases and from the light carrier *Vikrant*. The type was used for reconnaissance and patrol during India's 1961 occupation of Portuguese Goa, and was also used for anti-submarine patrol during the Indo-Pakistan War of 1971. During this conflict, one Alizé was shot down by a Pakistani F-104 Starfighter in what must have been a most unusual air-combat episode. The Alizé was gradually relegated to shore-based patrol duties in the 1980s, and was finally phased out in 1991, replaced by ASW helicopters.

LEFT: **The German Navy have operated Atlantics since the mid-1960s.**
BELOW: **The improved Atlantique 2.**

Breguet/Dassault Atlantic

In 1956, NATO began to consider a maritime patrol aircraft capable of hunting Soviet nuclear submarines, to replace the ageing Lockheed Neptune. Fourteen countries took part in studies to produce an aircraft that could fly for 18 hours at 300 knots and carry all the equipment and ordnance needed to search for and destroy Soviet submarines. Out of the 25 put forward, Breguet (now Dassault Aviation) proposed the Atlantic, which was ultimately ordered by France (40 aircraft), Germany (20), and later by the Netherlands (9) and Italy (18). Construction was carried out by a consortium of manufacturers across the four nations.

The first Atlantics were delivered to the French Navy in October 1965 and equipped four squadrons who operated them in the maritime reconnaissance role. However, the French aircraft were also used for land reconnaissance over Mauritania and Chad, and during the first Gulf War.

As well as advanced optical equipment, the Atlantic was fitted with highly advanced avionics systems – largely British and American – including a Thomson underfuselage radar able to locate submarines on the surface. Other equipment included a magnetic anomaly detector (MAD) to sense the magnetic fields generated by the metal mass of submerged submarines.

The aircraft could also drop acoustic buoys in a search area which, with the equipment on board, would form a submarine acoustic detection network in which a vessel could be easily located. Having identified a target, the Atlantic could then use a variety of equipment to attack, including bombs, depth charges, homing or acoustic torpedoes, plus a variety of missiles armed with conventional or nuclear warheads.

The French Navy were so impressed by the capability of the Atlantic that they ordered the much-improved Atlantique Mark 2, 28 examples of which were finally delivered between 1989 and 1997.

One of the radars carried on the Mark 2 is so sensitive it can detect a submarine periscope above the surface. The Mark 2's acoustic detection system uses buoys that can not only locate submarines, but will also compare the findings with its database to identify the class, nationality and threat level of the "bogey".

In the event of an enemy attack, the aircraft also has electronic counter-measures to deceive infrared and radar homing missiles. The Atlantique 2 can carry eight torpedoes or two Exocet missiles, or eight pods containing a raft and survival equipment for any survivors of a sinking.

A fully up-to-date glass cockpit Atlantique Mark 3 will be entering French Navy service in 2007, while Germany and Italy hope to replace their original Mark Is with 3s by 2010.

ABOVE: **A view inside the Atlantique 2, which is equipped with the very latest electronic surveillance and processing equipment.**

Breguet/Dassault Atlantic

First flight: October 21, 1961
Power: Two Rolls-Royce 6106eshp Tyne 21 turboprops
Armament: Up to 6000kg/13,206lb of bombs, depth charges, torpedoes, mines and missiles carried in weapons bay or on underwing pylons
Size: Wingspan – 37.42m/122ft 9in
Length – 33.63m/110ft 4in
Height – 11.35m/37ft 3in
Wing area – 120.34m²/1295sq ft
Weights: Empty – 25,300kg/55,685lb
Maximum take-off – 46,200kg/101,686lb
Performance: Maximum speed – 6481kph/403mph
Ceiling – 9150m/30,020ft
Range – 9075km/5635 miles
Climb – 746m/2450m per minute

Convair B-36 Peacemaker

The Convair B-36 Peacemaker was physically the largest bomber to ever have gone into service with the United States Air Force, and during the late 1940s and early '50s, it was the USAF's long-range strategic bombing deterrent. Although it never saw combat, reconnaissance versions flew near or possibly over the Soviet during the height of the Cold War in the mid-1950s.

The B-36 was conceived in the early years of World War II, when the US feared that its ally Britain may have been invaded by Germany. The USA knew that if it was drawn into the war in Europe it would need a means of carrying out attacks from the continental USA. In search of an aircraft capable of carrying out bombing raids over unprecedented distances, on April 11, 1941 the US Army Air Corps invited designs for a bomber with a 724kph/450mph top speed, a cruising speed of 442kph/275mph, a ceiling of 13,725m/45,000ft and a maximum range of 19,308km/12,000 miles. Consolidated's design, the Model 35, had twin fins and rudders, and four or six engines were suggested. To speed up the intercontinental bomber project, the requirements were scaled down to a 16,090km/10,000-mile range, cruising speed of between 386–483kph/240–300mph, and a service ceiling of 12,200m/40,000ft.

In late 1941, Consolidated (later Convair) was asked to proceed to prototype stage (two aircraft) using six engines, and the aircraft was designated XB-36. The aircraft proposed

by Consolidated was staggering in its proportions. The slightly swept-back wing spanned 70.1m/230ft with a wing area of 443.32m²/4772sq ft. At that stage the aircraft was powered by six 28-cylinder Pratt & Whitney R-4360 Wasp Major air-cooled radials, each driving a 5.8m/19ft three-bladed Curtiss propeller, unusually, in pusher configuration. These engines were accessible in flight through the truly enormous 2.29m/7.5ft thick wing root. The four bomb bays could carry 20,884kg/46,000lb of bombs, compared to the 9080kg/20,000lb of bombs of the B-29. The fuselage of the aircraft was 49.4m/162ft long, and the crew moved from front to rear through a 0.64m/25in diameter, 24.4m/80ft pressurized tunnel using a wheeled trolley.

In early 1943, the USA faced losing its bases in China to the invading Japanese, so the mighty Convair bomber, with its planned global reach, became an even more important project. Therefore, a June 1943 order was placed for 100 examples of the huge bomber, with the prototype to be ready by September 1944 and service deliveries within a year. Development delays with the engines, among other aspects of the project, almost doomed the aircraft, then Allied progress in the Pacific war reduced the project's priority status. Even when Germany surrendered, the B-36 project stayed alive because the USA needed a means of delivering their atom bomb against potential enemies around the world.

The prototype finally flew, almost two years late, on August 8, 1946. At the time, there were only three runways in the USA strong enough to take the weight of the behemoth bomber, which was the heaviest and largest land-based aircraft to have flown.

BELOW: **Instead of the normal bare-metal finish, this B-36B carries so-called "Arctic red" test markings. The aircraft was operated by the 7th Bomb Group.**

Strategic Air Command ultimately had ten wings equipped with B-36 Peacemakers. A-models were unarmed and used as training aircraft, whereas the B-36B was a nuclear bomber.

As more equipment and fuel increased the weight of the aircraft, the piston engines – developed to produce all the power they could – were augmented by four 2452kg/5400lb thrust turbojets, leading to the "six turning, four burning" description of the B-36's later powerplant arrangements. This model, produced as the B-36D, was complemented by 64 B-models converted to D standard. This ten-engined

version was the template for later, more powerful and better-equipped bomber versions.

When production ended in August 1954, 383 aircraft had been built for the USAF. From 1958, the B-36 was replaced in Strategic Air Command by the Boeing B-52. In the ten or so years that the B-36 was in front-line service, it gave the USA a global reach, leaving potential enemies in no doubt that they could be attacked by America. If one accepts that deterrence kept the peace at this time in the Cold War, then the B-36 could indeed have no better name than "Peacemaker".

ABOVE: **The B-36D, "six turning and four burning".**
LEFT: **The RB-36D was a reconnaissance version of Convair's "Big Stick" – the endurance and carrying power of the aircraft allowed it to undertake strategic reconnaissance missions.** BELOW LEFT: **The scale of the B-36 can be best appreciated by considering the 2.13m/7ft-high tunnel that passed within the wings to allow inflight maintenance of the outer engines.**

Convair B-36J Peacemaker

First flight: August 8, 1946 (YB-36)
Power: Six Pratt & Whitney 3600hp R-4360-53 radial piston engines and four General Electric 2452kg/5400lb thrust J47-19 turbojets
Armament: Sixteen 20mm/0.78in cannon in fuselage tail and nose turrets; maximum bomb load of 20,884kg/46,000lb
Size: Wingspan – 70.1m/230ft
Length – 49.4m/162ft 1in
Height – 14.22m/46ft 8in
Wing area – 443.32m²/4772sq ft
Weights: Empty – 77,650kg/171,035lb
Maximum take-off – 186,140kg/410,000lb
Performance: Maximum speed – 661kph/411mph
Service ceiling – 12,169m/39,900ft
Range – 10,945km/6800 miles
Climb – 677m/2220ft per minute

Convair B-58 Hustler

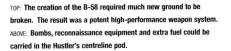

TOP: **The creation of the B-58 required much new ground to be broken. The result was a potent high-performance weapon system.**
ABOVE: **Bombs, reconnaissance equipment and extra fuel could be carried in the Hustler's centreline pod.**

The delta-winged B-58 was designed as a supersonic replacement for the USAF's B-47, and the prototype's first flight took place on November 11, 1956. The aircraft went supersonic for the first time on December 30 that year. A total of 116 aircraft were built, including 30 test and pre-production aircraft, and the aircraft reached squadron service in 1960, becoming the Strategic Air Command's and the world's first operational supersonic bomber.

The B-58 was first designed to meet an exacting requirement, and the design team had to make great advances to meet it. The aircraft had to fly at Mach 2 (the first bomber to do so) at high-altitude, carry and accurately drop nuclear weapons, and be as small as possible to have the smallest possible radar signature. The aircraft, all of its equipment and weaponry were for the first time seen as an entire weapons system in USAF procurement, and Convair was responsible for making it all work together. This new approach required the breaking of much new ground, and did lead to delays.

There were many "firsts" associated with the B-58 Hustler. It was the first aircraft to have heat-resistant, stainless-steel honeycomb sandwich skin panels in the wings and fuselage, and was the first bomber with a weapons pod to be jettisoned

after bombing. The B-58 was the first supersonic aircraft with engine pods mounted outboard on the thin delta wing, which had a 60-degree sweep.

Crew consisted of a pilot, navigator and defensive systems operator seated in tandem. Each crew member also had a unique escape ejection capsule – these were retrofitted when it was realized that simple ejection seats would not protect crews ejecting at supersonic speeds. To improve the crew's chances of surviving ejection, a high-speed, high-altitude capsule ejection system was installed that would allow safe ejection at supersonic speeds up to altitudes of 21,350m/70,000ft.

When required, the individual crew member's capsule closed airtight clam-shell doors, activating independent pressurization and oxygen supply systems. The crew member could then eject the capsule or remain encapsulated in the event of cabin pressure or oxygen loss until the aircraft reached a lower altitude. The pilot's capsule contained a control stick and other equipment so that he could continue to fly the aircraft from inside the capsule. After ejection, the capsule was lowered by parachute, and shock absorbers were included to soften the landing. On water, the airtight capsule would float, and additional flotation bags could turn the capsule into a life raft.

The thin fuselage had no room for a bomb bay, so the aircraft was fitted with a unique large streamlined centreline weapons pod, which included a fuel tank as well as a nuclear bomb or reconnaissance equipment. It was the pod and access to it on the ground that necessitated the B-58's very tall undercarriage legs. Four bombs could be carried beneath the wing if the pod was removed, but with the associated loss of a fuel tank, this could only have been over shorter ranges.

Although the Hustler had a greater range than the B-47 it was intended to replace, it still needed forward bases to be able to hit the Soviet Union. The alternative was to refuel the B-58 inflight to give it a greater reach, and all bomber versions were built with this facility. The B-58 set many high-speed records, flying for up 20 hours on routes around the world thanks to inflight refuelling. These missions were not just for the record books but also had some sabre-rattling potential, showing the Soviet Union just how far the aircraft could and would fly if needed. However, the B-58's range problem was made worse by the tactical need to bring the bombers down to low level. Soviet anti-aircraft missile defences were improving, so even the high- and fast-flying B-58 could not avoid them. As a result, the B-58 crews switched tactics and trained, very effectively, to penetrate Soviet defences at low level beneath enemy radar, resulting in an increase in fuel consumption and associated range penalties.

TOP: **This aircraft is a YB-58A production prototype. The non-standard red and white paint scheme identifies the aircraft as a test aircraft.** ABOVE: **The Hustler had to have long undercarriage legs to give clearance to the weapons pod.**

Eighty-six Hustlers were operational in Strategic Air Command from 1960, but the aircraft was phased out after only ten years due to high operating costs, operational limitations and the limited opportunities for development of the design. An interesting B-58 offshoot was a plan (which stayed on the drawing board) to produce a supersonic passenger-carrying version with a wider fuselage and room for 52 seats.

ABOVE: **The TB-58A was an operational trainer with the middle cockpit adapted for use by an instructor. Seven aircraft were converted to this standard. Notice how high the aircraft sits with the pod removed.**

Convair B-58 Hustler

First flight: November 11, 1956
Power: Four General Electric 7082kg/15,600lb afterburning thrust J79-5B turbojets
Armament: One 20mm/0.78in cannon in tail; payloads (including pod) of up to 8830kg/ 19,450lb of nuclear or conventional weapons
Size: Wingspan – 17.32m/56ft 10in
  Length – 29.49m/96ft 9in
  Height – 9.58m/31ft 5in
  Wing area – 143.35m²/1543sq ft
Weights: Empty – 25224kg/55,560lb
  Maximum take-off – 74,002kg/163,000lb
Performance: Maximum speed – 2128kph/ 1322mph
  Ceiling – 19,520m/64,000ft
  Range – 8248km/5125 miles
  Climb – 5310m/17,400ft per minute

Dassault Mystère/Super Mystère

Developed from the Dassault Ouragan, France's first jet fighter, the Mystère was essentially an Ouragan with swept wing and tail surfaces, and first flew in 1951. The production version, the Mystère II, was among the first swept-wing aircraft in production in western Europe, and entered Armée de l'Air service between 1954 and 1956 powered by the SNECMA Atar, the first French turbojet to be used in military aircraft. A Mystère IIA was the first French aircraft to break Mach 1

in controlled flight (in a dive), on October 28, 1952. The Armée de l'Air ordered 150 Mystère IICs, and the last was delivered in 1957, by which time the type was already being relegated to advanced training duties. Even as the Mystère was becoming operational, the better Mystère IV was already flying. Mystère IIs remained in use as advanced trainers until 1963.

The Mystère IV was a new aircraft, having few common parts with the Mark II – it had a new oval-section fuselage, thinner wings with greater sweep, and new tail surfaces. The first prototype was flown in September 1952, powered by a Hispano-built Rolls-Royce Tay 250 turbojet, as were the first 50 production examples – later examples were powered by the Hispano-Suiza Verdon. The production contract for 225 Mystère IVAs for the Armée de l'Air was paid for by the USA as part of the NATO Military Assistance Program. The first production Mystère IVA flew in late May 1954, and the type entered service with the Armée de l'Air the following year. The Mystère IVA remained a first-line fighter with the Armée de l'Air until the early 1960s, but continued to serve as an operational trainer until 1980.

ABOVE: **Marcel Dassault started to design jet fighters two years after being freed from a Nazi concentration camp. The Mystère was developed from his first design, the Ouragan, and ultimately led to the Mystère IVA pictured.**

LEFT: **The IVA was a very basic combat jet by today's standards, but it served the French Air Force well into the 1980s.**

ABOVE: **A Mystère IVA of the Armée de l'Air EC 8 (8th Fighter Wing). Note the open airbrakes.**
LEFT: **The ultimate Mystère – the Super Mystère first flew in 1955, and was exported to Honduras and Israel.** BELOW: **This Super Mystère was photographed at an annual NATO "Tiger Meet".**

Sixty Verdon-powered Mystère IVAs ordered by the French were sold on to Israel, and the first batch of 24 arrived in April 1956, just in time for the war with Egypt in October. In the hands of skilled Israeli pilots, they proved more than a match for Egyptian MiG-15s. The Indian Air Force also bought 110 all-new production Verdon-powered Mystère IVAs. First delivered in 1957, they equipped five squadrons and were used in the close-support role during the 1965 Indo-Pakistan war. Indian Mystère IVAs served until 1973.

The ultimate Mystère was the Super Mystère which, like the Mystère IV, was largely a new aircraft. It was bigger and heavier than previous Mystères and was the first European production aircraft capable of transonic flight. The first prototype flew in March 1955 and had wings with a 45-degree sweepback and an F-100-like oval air intake. The prototype exceeded Mach 1 in level flight the day after it first took to the air. A total of 180 Super Mystère B2s were built for the Armée de l'Air, the last delivered in 1959. They were switched to the attack role once the Mirage III was available, and remained in French service until late 1977.

In 1958, 36 Super Mystères bought by the French were sold on to the Israelis who used them to counter the Soviet-designed and built MiG-19s favoured by Arab nations. In the early 1970s, the Israelis upgraded surviving Super Mystères by retrofitting a non-afterburning Pratt & Whitney J52-P8A turbojet, and 12 of these uprated Super Mystères were sold to Honduras, who operated them until 1989. Their retirement brought the operational career of the Mystère series to an end.

Dassault Mystère IVA

First flight: February 23, 1951 (Mystère prototype)
Engine: Hispano-Suiza 3500kg/7703lb thrust Verdon 350 turbojet.
Armament: Two 30mm/1.18in cannon; two 454kg/1000lb bombs or twelve rockets
Size: Wingspan 11.12m/36ft 6in
　Length – 12.85m/42ft 2in
　Height 4.60m/15ft 1in
　Wing area – 32m²/344.46sq ft
Weights: Empty – 5886kg/12,955lb
　Maximum take-off – 9500kg/20,909kg
Performance: Maximum speed – 1120kph/696mph
　Ceiling – 15,000m/49,200ft
　Climb – 2700m/8860ft per minute
　Range – 912km/570 miles

Dassault Etendard and Super Etendard

Dassault's private venture Etendard (standard) was designed to meet the needs of both French national and NATO programmes for new light fighters reflecting air-combat experiences of the Korean War. Various versions did not get beyond the prototype stage, but then the Etendard IV drew the attention of the French Navy as a multi-role carrier-based fighter, leading to the development of the Etendard IV M specifically for the Navy – the first naval aircraft developed by Dassault.

The Etendard IV M made its maiden flight in May 1958, and between 1961 and 1965 the French Navy took delivery of 69 Etendard IV Ms that served on the French carriers *Foch* and *Clemenceau*, as well as 21 reconnaissance/tanker Etendard IV Ps. The Etendard IV M continued to serve in the French Navy until July 1991, by which time they had logged 180,000 flying hours and made 25,300 carrier landings.

The search for an Etendard replacement led Dassault to propose the Super Etendard, an updated, improved aircraft based on the Etendard IV M, but a 90 per cent new design.

Designed both for strike and interception duties, it featured the more powerful Atar 8K-50 engine and a strengthened structure to withstand higher-speed operations. The weapons system was improved through the installation of a modern navigation and combat management system centered on a Thomson multi-mode radar. The wing had a new leading edge and revised flaps which, together with the newer engine, eased take-off with greater weight compared to the Etendard.

The aircraft prototype made its maiden flight October 28, 1974, and the first of 71 production aircraft were delivered from mid-1978, again for service on the aircraft carriers *Foch*

TOP: **The Super Etendard was derived from the earlier Etendard, but was a 90 per cent new aircraft.** ABOVE: **The Etendard IVP had a fixed refuelling probe and could carry a "buddy pack" to become an inflight tanker.**

and *Clemenceau*. One hundred Super Etendards were planned for the Navy, but spiralling costs called for a reduction of the order. Armed with two 30mm/1.18in cannon, the Super Etendard could carry a variety of weaponry on its five hard points, including two Matra Magic AAMs, four pods of 18 68mm/2.68in rockets, a variety of bombs or two Exocet anti-ship missiles. A number were also modified to carry the Aerospatiale ASMP nuclear stand-off bomb.

The Argentine Navy's use of the Super Etendard/Exocet combination during the Falklands War of 1982 proved devastating against British ships – Argentina had ordered 14 Super Etendards from Dassault in 1979, but only five aircraft and reportedly five missiles had been delivered by the time France embargoed arms shipments to Argentina. These five strike fighters, despite having pilots unwilling to engage the agile British Harriers in air combat, nevertheless proved to be a very potent element of the Argentine inventory.

On May 4, 1982, two Super Etendards took off from a base in Argentina, preparing to attack the British task force. After three hours and an inflight refuelling, the aircraft located and launched an attack on the British ships. One of the Exocets found and severely damaged the frigate HMS *Sheffield*, which

sank on May 10. On May 25, two Exocet-equipped Super Etendards again attacked the task force, this time sinking the *Atlantic Conveyor* with its cargo of nine helicopters.

A handful of Super Etendards were supplied to Iraq in October 1983 when the Iraqis were desperate to cripple Iran by attacking tankers in the Persian Gulf with Exocets. Around 50 ships were attacked in the Gulf in 1984, the majority of the actions apparently carried out by Iraqi Super Etendards.

Production of the Super Etendard ended in 1983, but from 1992 a programme of structural and avionics upgrading was undertaken to extend the service life of the "fleet" until 2008.

ABOVE RIGHT: **The Etendard flew on with the French Navy until 1991.**
RIGHT: **An excellent on-deck view showing French Etendards and Super Etendards at sea.** BELOW: **French Navy Super Etendards are expected to remain in service at least until 2008.**

Dassault Super Etendard

First flight: October 28, 1974
Power: SNECMA 5000kg/11,005lb afterburning thrust Atar 8K-50 turbojet
Armament: Two 30mm/1.18in cannon; 2100kg/4622lb of weapons, including Matra Magic AAMs, AM39 Exocet ASMs, bombs and rockets
Size: Wingspan - 9.6m/31ft 6in
Length – 14.31m/46ft 11.5in
Height – 3.86m/12ft 8in
Wing area – 28.4m²/305.71sq ft
Weights: Empty – 6500kg/14,306lb
Maximum take-off – 12,000kg/26,412lb
Performance: Maximum speed – 1205kph/749mph
Ceiling – 13,700m/44,950ft
Range – 650km/404 miles
Climb – 6000m/19,685ft per minute

Dassault Mirage III family

The delta-wing Mirage III was certainly one of the greatest combat aircraft ever, and was produced in greater numbers than any other European fighter. The success of this aircraft brought France to the forefront of the military aircraft industry. It started as a Dassault private venture, and first flew in November 1956, having benefited from the testing of the small Mirage I experimental delta aircraft. After some refinements to the wing design, it reached twice the speed of sound in level flight in October 1958. The aircraft's capability soon caught the attention of the French Air Force, who quickly ordered the high-performance aircraft. Foreign air forces were also very interested in the Mirage, and orders from Israel and South Africa followed in late 1960. By now the first production aircraft, the Mirage IIIC single-seat air defence fighter, was coming off the production line for the Armée de l'Air, and the first were delivered in July 1961.

The Mirage IIIE was a long-range fighter-bomber version powered by the SNECMA Atar 9C turbojet. While the IIIC was a dedicated interceptor, the IIIE was designed and equipped for both air defence and all-weather ground attack, and French versions were equipped to carry a nuclear bomb. It was widely exported and was also built under licence in Australia and Switzerland. Although France has retired its IIIs, many air forces still operate the type, having upgraded it in many ways – Swiss and Brazilian IIIs, for example, have acquired canard wings.

The IIIE spawned the Mirage 5 ground-attack fighter, essentially a simplified version designed as a daytime clear-weather ground-attack fighter in response to an Israeli Air Force request. The need for sophisticated radar was considered not to be so great in the Middle East, so when the Mirage 5 first flew in May 1967, it was minus the Cyrano radar. The delivery to Israel was stopped for political reasons by Charles de Gaulle, and the aircraft instead served as the Mirage 5F in the Armée de l'Air. Israel decided to go it alone and developed its Mirage III into the Kfir.

RIGHT: **A Swiss Mirage III demonstrates its dramatic rocket-assisted take-off technique.** BELOW: **An Armée de l'Air Mirage IIIE armed with an AS.37 anti-radar missile.**

Dassault Mirage 50

First flight: May 1969
Power: One SNECMA 7210kg/15,869lb
  afterburning thrust Atar 9K-50 turbojet
Armament: Two 30mm/1.18in cannon; up to
  4000kg/8804lb of rockets, bombs and guided
  weapons
Size: Wingspan – 8.22m/27ft
  Length – 15.56m/51ft 1in
  Height – 4.5m/14ft 9in
  Wing area – 35m²/375sq ft
Weights: Empty – 7150kg/15,737lb
  Maximum take-off – 14,700kg/32,354lb
Performance: Maximum speed – 2338kph/
  1452mph
  Ceiling – 18,011m/59,094ft
  Range – 2410km/1496 miles
  Climb – 11,168m/36,642ft per minute

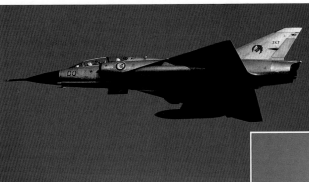

ABOVE LEFT: **The excellent Mirage III can carry up
to 4000kg/8804lb of ordnance.** LEFT: **Although
French Mirage IIIs were retired some time ago,
the type remains in use in Switzerland and Brazil.**
BELOW: **Swiss Mirage IIIs received a canard wing
as part of an upgrade programme.** BOTTOM: **An
early French Mirage III. This type was produced
in greater numbers than any other fighter of
the period.**

However, some 450 Mirage 5s were exported to other
nations, and more advanced avionics were offered later.
Belgium built their own Mirage 5 bombers and upgraded
them in the 1990s to keep them flying until 2005.

The Mirage 50 multi-mission fighter was created by
installing the more powerful Atar 9K-50 engine in a Mirage 5
airframe. It first flew in April 1979, and boasted head-up
displays and a more advanced radar than the Mirage III. Chile
and Venezuela both ordered Mirage 50s. Dassault offers the
Mirage 50M upgrade for existing Mirage IIIs and 5s, but several
operator nations have undertaken local upgrade programmes
with improved avionics and the addition of canard foreplanes.

In the 1967 and 1973 Arab-Israeli wars, the Israeli Mirage
IIIs outclassed Arab-flown MiGs and generated lots of export
sales, but Mirage pilots admit that the type did not have
a great sustained turn capability due to the aerodynamic
idiosyncrasies of the delta wing. Indeed, three Mirages were
shot down by comparatively pedestrian Iraqi Hunters during
the Six Day War of 1967. Nevertheless, the Mirage III series
gave many air forces their first combat aircraft capable of
flying at twice the speed of sound, and many upgraded
examples will be flying for some years.

437

Dassault Mirage IV

The Mirage IV strategic nuclear bomber was developed in the late 1950s, following a 1954 decision that France wanted an independent nuclear deterrent force. The aircraft was a two-seat, twin-jet engine supersonic bomber with an effective range of up to 4500km/2795 miles but only with inflight refuelling. The delta wing of the Mirage IV clearly carried on that of the Mirage III, though on a much larger scale. The Mirage IV was developed as a weapon system, with Dassault being the prime contractor for the complete system – aircraft, navigation, attack management system, as well as the casing and release system for the nuclear bomb.

The Mirage IV 01 made its maiden flight powered by two 6000kg/13,206lb SNECMA Atar 09 turbojets on June 17, 1959, with Roland Glavany at the controls. In July the aircraft achieved speeds of Mach 1.9. Three pre-production aircraft were then built, the first taking to the air in October 1961, this time powered by 6400kg/14,086lb thrust Atar 9C engines. Each of the three aircraft was used for trials and development of the aircraft's navigation, inflight refuelling and bombing systems.

However, it was more than two and a half years before the first Mirage IV-A was delivered to the French Air Force in February 1964. At the time of its delivery, the Mirage IV was the only aircraft in the world that could fly at twice the speed

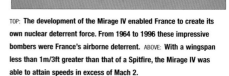

TOP: **The development of the Mirage IV enabled France to create its own nuclear deterrent force. From 1964 to 1996 these impressive bombers were France's airborne deterrent.** ABOVE: **With a wingspan less than 1m/3ft greater than that of a Spitfire, the Mirage IV was able to attain speeds in excess of Mach 2.**

of sound for sustained periods. Fifty Mirage IV-As were ordered in 1959 and a further 12 in 1964, and they were all delivered by 1966.

Assigned to French Strategic Air Command, CFAS (Commandement des Forces Aeriennes Stratégiques), nine and later six dispersed air bases housed these aircraft, which were France's airborne nuclear deterrent from 1964 until the Mirage IV was retired as a strategic bomber in 1996. The aircraft had dedicated KC-135FR tanker aircraft assigned to the Mirage IV units, although Mirage IVs could also be fitted with "buddy" inflight refuelling packs themselves. The aircraft were kept at readiness in hardened shelters from which they could start their take-off run. For short-field take-off, the aircraft were also fitted with 12 booster rockets, six beneath each wing, and special fast-drying chemicals were developed for hardening soft surfaces from which the heavy aircraft could then operate.

Dassault Mirage IV-A

First Flight: June 17, 1959

Power: Two SNECMA 7000kg/15,407lb thrust Atar
9K turbojets

Armament: One 60-kiloton AN 22 nuclear bomb or
one 30- or 150-kiloton 900kg/1980lb ASMP
stand-off nuclear air-to-surface missile or up to
7200kg/15,847lb of conventional bombs or
anti-radar missiles

Size: Wingspan – 11.85m/38ft 11in
Length – 23.5m/77ft 1in
Height – 5.65m/18ft 6in
Wing area – 78m²/839.6sq ft

Weights: Empty – 14,500kg/31,914lb
Maximum take-off – 31,600kg/69,551lb

Performance: Maximum speed – 2338kph/1451mph
Ceiling – 20,000m/65,620ft
Range – 2500km/1552 miles
Climb – 11,000m/36,090ft in 4 minutes, 15 seconds

ABOVE: **Some of the fleet were upgraded to IV-P standard, and could carry a
stand-off weapon.** RIGHT: **Rocket-assisted take-off was required to get the
aircraft airborne from shorter runways, and was important for dispersed
operations.** BELOW: **A Mirage IV-A in full flight. The IV-As were kept in hardened
shelters from which they could begin their take-off run.**

In common with other major air forces around the world,
the French Air Force had to respond to the increased
sophistication of air defences. As a result, they switched to
flying their bombers at low level to avoid enemy radar and
surface-to-air missiles. The Mirage IV's structure was modified
to cope better with the stresses caused by high-speed,
low-level flying and the 60 kiloton AN 22 nuclear weapon
carried semi-recessed under the fuselage, and was modified
for low-level use and to increase the chances of aircraft and
crew survivability.

The aircraft were frequently upgraded during their time in
service, and 12 were modified for the reconnaissance role by
fitting cameras and SLAR (side-looking airborne radar).

Nineteen aircraft were modified to IVP standard in the late
1980s by the inclusion of inertial navigation and rear-warning
radar. This version could also carry the Aerospatiale ASMP
stand-off nuclear missile, which could be launched up to
250km/155 miles from the target. In June 1996, the Mirage
IVPs were retired from the nuclear role and five aircraft were
retained for strategic reconnaissance duties.

439

de Havilland Venom

The Venom was proposed by de Havilland as a Vampire successor, and was initially designated Vampire FB.8. The aircraft had to be substantially altered to accommodate the new more powerful Ghost engine and so the aircraft was given its own identity – the Venom. The first production version, the FB.1, was delivered to the RAF in December 1951, followed by the improved ejection-seat-equipped FB.4 version. The Venom ultimately equipped 19 squadrons of the Royal Air Force, serving in Germany, India and the Far East. The Germany-based Venoms were a vital element of the West's Cold War defences at the time.

Licence-built versions were produced as FB.50s in Switzerland, where some remained in service until the early 1980s. British-built versions were also exported to Iraq and Venezuela.

Two-seat radar-equipped all-weather/nightfighter versions were also produced, and the Venom NF.2 entered RAF service in 1953. Emergency escape from this version was virtually impossible as there were no ejection seats for the two crew and the heavy hinged canopy had to be lifted manually. The NF.3 had an American radar and, perhaps more importantly for Venom nightfighter crews, a quick-release canopy.

The de Havilland Sea Venom FAW Mk 20 gave the Royal Navy an interim radar-equipped, all-weather fighter force between the piston-engined Sea Hornet and the appearance of the advanced Sea Vixen. Later improvements led to the FAW Mk 21 and 22. The Sea Venom was also operated by the Australian Navy, and in France SNCASE built a redesigned Sea Venom, including a single-seat version for the French Navy, who called it the Aquilon.

Royal Navy Sea Venoms, in concert with RAF Venom fighter-bombers, saw action during the Suez crisis in 1956.

TOP: **A Venom FB.4 wearing "Suez stripes".**
ABOVE RIGHT: **During the Suez operations, three squadrons of RAF Venom FB4s flew close air support missions.** ABOVE: **A Sea Venom FAW Mk 21.**

de Havilland Venom FB.4

First flight: September 2, 1949 (Venom prototype)
Power: de Havilland 2406kg/5300lb thrust Ghost 105 turbojet
Armament: Four 20mm/0.78in cannon; provision for two Firestreak air-to-air missiles or 908kg/2000lb of bombs or eight 27kg/60lb rocket projectiles
Size: Wingspan – 12.7m/41ft 8in
    Length – 10.06m/33ft
    Height – 2.03m/6ft 8in
    Wing area – 25.99m²/279.75sq ft
Weights: Empty – 3995kg/8800lb
    Maximum take-off – 6950kg/15,310lb
Performance: Maximum speed – 961kph/597mph
    Ceiling – 14,640m/48,000ft
    Range – 1730km/1075 miles
    Climb – 36.7m/7230ft per minute

Douglas A-3 Skywarrior

In the late 1940s, a whole new class of aircraft carrier was under development by the US Navy, the super-carrier Forrestal-class. These large carriers would be able to operate large aircraft and give the US Navy the opportunity to take its air power to a new level. The Navy called for a large new strategic bomber to operate from the supercarriers, and Douglas came up with the A3D, at 31,780kg/70,000lb the world's largest and heaviest carrier-borne aircraft when it was designed. It flew in October 1952, and became the Navy's first twin-jet nuclear bomber.

The nuclear bomb aspect was challenging because details of the weapon were top secret, and designers had to guess the appearance and weight of the nuclear bombs to be carried aboard. In its vast internal bomb bay it could carry up to 5448kg/12,000lb of weaponry. Also, the internal bomb bay had to be accessible from the cockpit so that the crew could arm the nuclear device during flight.

Due to its size, it was soon named "Whale" by its crews, and in 1962 the aircraft was redesignated A-3.

The first production version, the A-3A (A3D-1), with a radar-controlled tail turret and a crew of three, entered service with the Navy Heavy Attack Squadron One in 1956. After flying a few conventional bombing missions over North and South Vietnam, Skywarriors were used as carrier-based aerial-refuelling tankers and as reconnaissance aircraft covering the Ho Chi Minh trail. As advancing technology rendered its old role obsolete, the resilient aircraft continued to evolve. It was used for electronic countermeasures, photographic reconnaissance, crew training and as a VIP transport. A few US Navy Skywarriors even served in the 1991 Gulf War.

A revised USAF version was named Destroyer, and designated B-66. Built in bomber, photo-reconnaissance, electronic countermeasures and weather reconnaissance versions, the B-66 was active in the Vietnam War.

TOP: **The largest and heaviest carrier aircraft of its day, the A-3 Skywarrior.** ABOVE: **The "Whale" was a significant element of the US nuclear deterrent for a time.**

Douglas A-3B Skywarrior

First Flight: October 28, 1952 (XA3D-1)

Power: Two Pratt & Whitney 4767kg/10,500lb thrust J57-P-10 turbojets

Armament: Two 20mm/0.78in cannon in remotely controlled rear turret; up to 5448kg/12,000lb of bombs

Size: Wingspan – 22.1m/72ft 6in
Length – 23.27m/76ft 4in
Height – 6.95m/22ft9.5in
Wing area – 75.43m²/812sq ft

Weights: Empty – 17,891kg/39,409lb
Maximum take-off – 37,228kg/82,000lb

Performance: Maximum speed – 982kph/610mph
Ceiling – 12,505m/41,000ft
Range – 1690km/1050 miles
Climb – 1100m/3600ft per minute

441

Douglas Skyraider

The Skyraider can be rightly considered to be one of the greatest combat aircraft ever. Designed during World War II as a replacement for Douglas's own Dauntless dive-bomber, this rugged aeroplane fought in both Korea and Vietnam. The prototype XBT2D-1 first flew on March 19, 1945, and in February 1946 became the AD-1 Skyraider, the biggest single-seat aircraft in production. Designed around Wright's R-3350 engine, the Skyraider was created with the benefit of considerable combat experience. The designers' aim was to produce a very versatile aircraft which could absorb considerable damage and carry the widest range of available weaponry. Built like a big fighter, the Skyraider carried all of its weaponry beneath its folding wings.

Following carrier trials in early 1946, the Skyraider formally entered US Navy front-line service with VA-19A in December 1946. Production of consistently improved versions continued, and four years into manufacturing, 22 variants had appeared. Production continued for 12 years, and when it ceased in 1957, 3180 Skyraiders had been delivered to the US Navy.

Korea is often thought of as a jet war, but the Skyraider's 10-hour loiter capability and great weapon-carrying capacity considerably outclassed any jet then in service. The US Navy was hugely impressed by its performance.

Among the versions soon appearing were the AD-2 with increased fuel and a more powerful engine, and the AD-3 with a revised canopy, improved propeller and landing gear. The AD-4 had the more powerful 2700hp R-3350 engine and greatly increased load-carrying capacity, the AD-4W was a three-seat airborne early warning variant (used by the Royal

TOP: **A Royal Navy Skyraider AEW1. The type equipped two Fleet Air Arm units until 1960, and was used during the November 1956 Suez campaign.**
ABOVE: **Skyraiders were at home carrying out high-risk low-level missions. Here, an AD-1 drops napalm in Vietnam.**

Navy Fleet Air Arm), while the AD-5 was a four-seat, multi-role version. The Skyraider was strengthened to carry more and more equipment and ordnance, and the AD-5 could operate at all-up weights of 11,350kg/25,000lb. The AD-5 could also be adapted for casualty evacuation or for transporting 12 troops. The AD-6 was a much-improved single-seat attack version, while the AD-7 had a 3050hp engine and even more reinforcement to the wings and undercarriage.

Douglas A-1H (AD-6) Skyraider

First Flight: March 19, 1945 (XBT2D-1)
Power: One Wright 2700hp R-3350-26WA radial piston engine
Armament: Four wing-mounted 20mm/0.78in cannon; up to 3632kg/8000lb of ordnance carried under wings and on one fuselage hardpoint
Size: Wingspan – 15.25m/50ft 0.25in
Length – 11.84m/38ft
Height – 4.78m/15ft 8.25in
Wing area – 37.19m²/400sq ft
Weights: Empty – 5433kg/11,968lb
Maximum take-off – 11,350kg/25,000lb
Performance: Maximum speed – 518kph/322mph
Ceiling – 8692m/28,500ft plus
Range – 2116km/1315 miles
Climb – 870m/2850ft per minute

ABOVE: **Fifty-four airframes were converted to EA-1F standard for electronic countermeasures duties.** LEFT: **The AD-4 version was built to carry a much greater war load, and the AD-4B was cleared to carry nuclear weapons.**
BELOW: **Thought obsolete by doubters even before it entered service, the Skyraider confounded everyone with a production run in a myriad of variants and an outstanding combat record in two major conflicts.**

AD-4Ns saw considerable action with the French Armée de l'Air in Algeria, and these machines were retired in 1965. By now the USA was embroiled in Vietnam, and following trials the Skyraider was found to be the ideal close support aircraft needed for tackling difficult ground targets. Again, the hard-hitting aircraft's loiter capability made it an obvious choice for this type of warfare. The US Air Force, Navy and Marine Corps all operated Skyraiders in Vietnam, as did the US-trained South Vietnam Air Force. The aircraft also served as forward air control (FAC) platforms, helicopter escort and rescue support missions. Never considered a dogfighter, the Skyraider had four 20mm/0.78in cannon in the wings, and US Navy Skyraider pilots are known to have shot down at least two MiG-17 jets over Vietnam.

In 1962, new tri-service aircraft designations were introduced so all the designations of Skyraiders then in service were changed. The AD-5 was the A-1E, the AD-5N the A-1G while the AD-6 and AD-7 became the A-1H and A-1J respectively.

As well as Britain and France, Skyraiders were also supplied to Chad, who used them in combat up to the late 1970s. The aircraft that had entered service when piston-engined warplanes were considered by some to be obsolete was therefore still fighting more than a quarter of a century after it first entered service.

ABOVE: **The A-1E/AD-5 was a redesigned multi-role aircraft with a side-by-side cockpit.**

English Electric/BAC/Martin B-57 Canberra

When it comes to long-service records in the Royal Air Force, there is one aircraft that leads the field – the English Electric Canberra. More than half a century after the type first entered RAF service in 1950, photo-reconnaissance versions continue to be a vital element of the RAF's intelligence-gathering capability.

The Canberra was Britain's first jet bomber and was designed in the Mosquito tradition, so that its high and fast flying capability was intended to keep the aircraft safe from defending fighter aircraft – no defensive armament was to

be carried. The Canberra was every bit as versatile as the Mosquito it succeeded, and served with distinction as a light bomber, advanced trainer, intruder and photo-reconnaissance platform.

The first Canberra prototype, VN799, took off from Warton on May 13, 1949, with famous test-pilot Roland Beamont at the controls. It exhibited excellent manoeuvrability at all altitudes and handled well at low speed. Refinements to the original design led to the B.2 version, which first flew in April 1950 and became the RAF's first jet bomber when it entered service at RAF Binbrook in May 1951 with No.101 Squadron. The RAF needed lots of Canberras, and production was beyond the capability of English Electric. Consequently, rival manufacturers Avro, Handley Page and Shorts all built Canberras to meet the demand. A more powerful version, the B.6, entered RAF service in 1954–5, and Canberras saw combat over Malaya and during the 1956 Suez Crisis.

An indication of the aircraft's greatness is the fact that early in its career, the Canberra was selected for licensed production in the USA for the US Air Force. The first of

TOP: **WK163 was a Canberra B.2 that was fitted with Scorpion rocket engines to attain a record-breaking altitude.** LEFT: **The USAF sought an aircraft with good manoeuvrability and flexibility, and found it in the Canberra. Licence-built as the Martin B-57 Canberra, around 400 were built in the USA.**

around 400 aircraft (bomber and reconnaissance versions) was rolled out of the Martin plant on July 20, 1953. These American Canberras saw extensive service in Vietnam.

Canberras were also built under licence in Australia for the RAAF. These versions, known as MK20s, were based on the British B.2 version but had increased internal fuel capacity and a crew of two. In September 1958 Canberras from No.2 Squadron RAAF became the first Australian jet bombers in combat when they carried out an attack against terrorists in Northern Malaya. Then in 1967, No.2 was sent to Vietnam as part of Australia's military commitment to the war. Operating as part of the USAF's 35th Tactical Fighter Wing, Squadron 2's Canberras flew 6 per cent of the Wing's sorties but inflicted 16 per cent of the damage. Overall, 11,963 sorties were flown in Vietnam, and 76,389 bombs dropped for two aircraft lost.

The Canberra's distinguished RAAF career ended on June 30, 1982, when No.2 Squadron flew its Canberras for the last time.

English Electric and its subcontractors built over 750 Canberras, and many were exported. In the early 2000s, Canberra remained in service with Argentina, India, Peru and even NASA (B-57s).

Photo-reconnaissance versions were developed early on, and it was the PR.9 version that remained in service with the RAF in 2004. In 2003, Canberras of No.39 Squadron conducted 56 reconnaissance sorties over Iraq in support of British and Coalition forces.

The PR.9's equipment had evolved over its time in service. A variety of daytime "wet" cameras can be carried for medium and higher-level vertical and oblique photography. An electro-optical long-range oblique photographic sensor (EO-LOROP) can also be carried, which records imagery in digital format on magnetic tape for interpretation on the ground. The PR.9 also carries navigation equipment that 1960s navigators could only have dreamt of, as well as defensive systems such as jammers and chaff and flare dispensers.

ABOVE: **USAF B-57s saw extensive use in the Vietnam War, mainly flying night intruder missions. The aircraft pictured here is a multi-role bomber/ reconnaissance/trainer/tug B-57E.** RIGHT: **When the RAF Canberra's bombing days were over, some were converted for ECM training. The aircraft in this photograph is a T.17.** BELOW: **The Canberra is an all-time classic combat aircraft. This model is an E.15 used for high-altitude calibration of ground radar.**

English Electric/BAC Canberra B.6

First Flight: May 13, 1949 (prototype)
Power: Two Rolls-Royce 3405kg/7500lb afterburning thrust Avon 109 turbojets
Armament: 2724kg/6000lb of bombs carried internally, plus two 454kg/1000lb bombs or gun pods under wings
Size: Wingspan 19.51m/64ft
Length – 19.96m/65ft 6in
Height – 4.75m/15ft 7in
Wing area – 89.19m²/960sq ft
Weights: Empty – 10,108kg/22,265lb
Maximum take-off – 24,062kg/53,000lb
Performance: Maximum speed – 973kph/605mph
Ceiling – 14,634m/48,000ft plus
Combat radius – 1779km/1105 miles
Climb – 1220m/4000ft per minute

Fairchild Republic A-10 Thunderbolt II

In the early 1970s, when the USAF was considering an aircraft capable of halting a Soviet armoured thrust in Central Europe, they looked back at their experiences in Korea and Vietnam where aircraft modified for use in the close air support role had exhibited many shortcomings. Instead, they needed a purpose-designed aircraft that could carry a heavy weapons load, have good endurance and be able to withstand damage from ground fire.

The answer was the remarkable A-10, designed from the outset to tackle Warsaw Pact armour in Europe. Combining accurate firepower and survivability, the A-10 was designed to fly low and relatively slowly across the battlefield to take out enemy armour and artillery in the very hostile, low-level battlefield environment. The aircraft has high-lift wings fitted with large control surfaces, making the aircraft very manoeuvrable, while its short take-off and landing capability permitted operations in and out of rough field locations near front lines.

All the aircraft's controls are duplicated and designed to work even if hydraulic pressure is lost due to enemy fire. The aircraft's fuel tanks are filled with fire-retardant foam, and the A-10's pilot sits in a "bathtub" of titanium armour for protection against shrapnel and small arms fire.

The aircraft can survive direct hits from armour-piercing and high explosive projectiles up to 23mm/0.9in calibre. Self-sealing fuel cells are protected by internal and external foam. Remarkably, many of the aircraft's parts are interchangeable left and right, including the engines, main landing gear and fins.

TOP: **The arrival of the A-10 over a battlefield is bad news for an enemy. The aircraft was created to destroy armour and artillery, and does so most effectively.** ABOVE: **This view shows how the aircraft's engines can be masked by the wing from below, thus preventing a lock from an infrared weapon.**

The primary weapon of the A-10 is the nose-mounted GAU-8/A 30mm/1.18in seven-barrel cannon which, together with its ammunition, takes up much of the aircraft's internal space. This is the most powerful gun ever fitted to an aircraft, firing 35 rounds of controversial depleted uranium armour-piercing ammunition per second. One hit from this extremely potent weapon can destroy a tank a mile away from the aircraft. The aircraft can also carry a range of bombs, rockets and missiles, including the Maverick anti-armour missile.

LEFT: Designed to halt Soviet armour, the A-10 entered front-line service in 1976. Note the 30mm/1.18in cannon protruding from the nose.
BELOW: Feeding the beast – belts of 30mm/1.18in ammunition are loaded for the A-10's devastating 30mm/1.18in cannon. 1350 rounds are carried.

ABOVE: This A-10 is carrying Sidewinder air-to-air missiles for self defence. Eleven hardpoints can carry an array of ground-attack weaponry.
RIGHT: The A-10 is likely to remain in service until at least 2010.

Turbofan engines were chosen to power the aircraft because they give off less heat than conventional jet engines, thus making them less vulnerable to heat-seeking weapons. The engines were also positioned high on the upper rear fuselage, protecting them from ground fire. Using night-vision goggles, A-10 pilots can conduct their missions as efficiently during darkness as in daylight.

The A-10 entered US Air Force service in 1976 and remained in the Cold War front line until the late 1980s. Although trained for war in Europe, USAF A-10 pilots first saw action in the Gulf War of 1991 when 144 A-10s were deployed to Saudi Arabia. During the A-10's 8100 Gulf War missions, around 24,000 missiles, rockets and bombs were fired or dropped and one million rounds were fired by A-10 cannon. A-10s launched 90 per cent of the total number of the AGM-65 Maverick missiles used.

USAF A-10s were credited with the destruction of over 1000 Iraqi tanks, 1200 artillery pieces and 2000 vehicles, as well as two helicopters in air-to-air combat with air-to-air missiles. Only six aircraft were lost in the war, all to ground-launched enemy missiles.

A-10s were also in the vanguard of the 2003 invasion of Iraq, and are expected to remain in the USAF inventory until 2010.

Fairchild Republic A-10 Thunderbolt II

First Flight: May 10, 1972
Power: Two General Electric 4115kg/9065lb thrust TF34-GE-100 turbofans
Armament: One GAU-8/A 30mm/1.18in cannon; up to 7264kg/16,000lb of weapons, including free-fall or guided bombs, Maverick missiles or Sidewinder anti-aircraft missiles on underwing and underfuselage points
Size: Wingspan – 17.53m/57ft 6in
Length – 16.26m/53ft 4in
Height – 4.42m/14ft 8in
Wing area – 24.18m²/260.28sq ft
Weights: Empty – 9780kg/21,541lb
Maximum take-off – 22,700kg/50,000lb
Performance: Maximum speed – 706kph/439mph
Ceiling – 9302m/30,500ft plus
Range – 926km/576 miles
Climb – Not available

Fairey Gannet

During the course of World War II, the Royal Navy had learned the value of carrier-based anti-submarine aircraft. For the post-war years the Navy needed a modern aircraft to tackle the submarine threat posed by any potential enemy. In 1945 the Fleet Air Arm issued a requirement, GR.17/45, for a carrier-based ASW (anti-submarine warfare) aircraft which could both hunt and kill submarines.

Of two cosmetically similar designs built to prototype standard, it was the Fairey design that ultimately won the contract, having flown for the first time on September 19, 1949. The aircraft had a deep barrel-like fuselage to accommodate both sensors and weapons for hunting and killing enemy craft. Power came from an Armstrong-Siddeley Double Mamba engine which was actually two turboprop engines driving a shared gearbox. This in turn drove a contra-rotating propeller system. The Double Mamba was chosen because one of the engines could be shut down for more economical cruising flight. Conventional twin-engined aircraft exhibit problematic handling if one engine fails, resulting in what is known as asymmetric flight. In this situation, the working engine forces its side of the aeroplane ahead of the other side, resulting in crabbing flightpath, as well as major concerns on landing. If one Double Mamba failed, this would not be an issue for the pilot of a Gannet.

The Fairey 17 began carrier-deck trials in early 1950, and on June 19 that year the aircraft made the first landing of a turboprop aircraft on a carrier, HMS *Illustrious*. The Admiralty then requested that search radar be included, as well as a

TOP: **The Gannet prototype, September 1949.** ABOVE: **The Gannet was a large aircraft and the wings had to fold twice to fit it into underdeck hangars.**

third seat for the operator, resulting in a third modified prototype which flew in May 1951. When Fairey's aircraft won the competition to go into production, the name "Gannet" was given to the aircraft. The Gannet, brimming with equipment and weapons, was a technically complicated aircraft, an example being the wings that folded not once but twice for under-deck stowage. Because of development delays, the Gannet AS.1 did not enter FAA service until 1955, some ten years after the requirement was first issued.

The fuselage had a big weapons bay to accommodate two torpedoes or other munitions, up to a total of 908kg/2,000lb. A retractable radome under the rear fuselage housed the search radar. When the extendable "dustbin" radome was added, it led to lateral instability in flight, which was remedied by the addition of two auxiliary finlets to the horizontal tailplane. Simply raising the height of the vertical tailplane would have had the same effect, but would have exceeded below-deck hangar height limits. The Gannet's crew of three sat in tandem, with pilot, observer/navigator and radio/radar operator each in their own cockpits, the radio/radar operator's seat facing the tail of the aircraft.

A number of Gannets were operated by foreign air arms. Deliveries to the Royal Australian Navy for carrier operations began in 1955 (phased out in 1967), while the former West German naval air arm operated Gannets from shore bases, phasing them out in 1965. Indonesia obtained refurbished Royal Navy examples.

A total of 181 Gannet AS.1s were built, together with 38 Gannet T.2 conversion trainers for training pilots on the idiosyncrasies of the aircraft and its unique powerplant. In 1956, the improved 3035hp Double Mamba 101 was introduced into Gannets on the production line. Aircraft thus powered were designated AS.4 and T.5 for the trainer version. The Gannet AS.6 was the AS.4 with a new 1961 radar and electronics fit.

Fairey were also contracted to produce an airborne early warning (AEW) Gannet to replace the Douglas Skyraider in Fleet Air Arm service. Designated AEW.3, these were new-build dedicated early-warning aircraft with a huge radar installation mounted on the underside of the fuselage beneath the cockpit. This version, which served until 1977, carried a pilot and two radar plotters who were housed in a rear cabin.

ABOVE: **Points to note on this Gannet AS.4 are the large port exhaust from the Double Mamba, the arrestor hook and the two red finlets.** BELOW: **Note the large radome beneath the Gannet AEW.3.** BOTTOM: **The AEW Gannets were retired from RN service in 1977.**

Fairey Gannet AS.1

First flight: September 19, 1949 (prototype)
Power: One Armstrong Siddeley 2950eshp Double Mamba 100 turboprop
Armament: Up to 908kg/2000lb of torpedoes and depth charges
Size: Wingspan – 16.56m/54ft 4in
Length – 13.11m/43ft
Height – 4.18m/13ft 8.5in
Wing area – 44.85m²/482.8sq ft
Weights: Empty – 6841kg/15,069lb
Maximum take-off – 9806kg/21,600lb
Performance: Maximum speed – 499kph/310mph
Ceiling – 7625m/25,000ft
Range – 1518km/943 miles
Climb – 670m/2200ft per minute

General Dynamics F-111

The F-111 was originally intended to be a fighter to equip both the US Air Force and Navy. Following a difficult development period during which the Navy dropped out of the programme, the remarkable variable-geometry aircraft, with its confusing fighter designation, became a highly effective all-weather interdictor.

The F-111 was the first production aircraft in the world with "swing wings", which gave the aircraft the flexibility to land and take off with straight wings and for low-speed flight, but to fly at high supersonic speeds with the wings swept.

TOP: **An Upper Heyford-based F-111E launches an attack on a British bombing range.** ABOVE: **The F-111 terrain-following radar enables the aircraft to fly very fast and very low to deliver its weapons.**

The F-111A entered USAF service in October 1967. Once early in-service problems were ironed out, the F-111 became a formidable long-range bomber which could deliver conventional or nuclear weapons from low altitude. The F-111 weapons system also featured a groundbreaking automatic terrain-following radar that guided the aircraft at a pre-set height following the ground contours. The aircraft could fly itself over all types of terrain by day or night, whatever the weather.

The wings and much of the fuselage rear of the crew compartment contained fuel tanks. Using internal fuel only, the aircraft had a range of more than 4000km/2500 miles. External fuel tanks could be carried on the wing pylons for additional range, and could be jettisoned if necessary.

The F-111 could deliver conventional or nuclear weapons and could carry up to two bombs or additional fuel in the internal weapons bay. External ordnance included combinations of bombs, missiles and fuel tanks. The loads nearest the fuselage on each side pivoted as the wings swept back, keeping ordnance parallel to the fuselage. Outer pylons did not move, but could be jettisoned for high-speed flight.

The F-111E model had modified air intakes to improve the engine's performance at speeds above Mach 2.2. Most USAF F-111Es served with the 20th Fighter Wing based at RAF Upper Heyford, England, in support of NATO. On January 17, 1991, F-111Es deployed to Incirlik Air Base, Turkey, carried out some of the first bombing raids of Operation Desert Storm. More than 100 F-111 aircraft of different versions joined the first strikes against Iraqi targets, both as bombers and radar jammers. As the war progressed, the F-111s were employed in precision attacks with laser-guided weapons on hardened aircraft shelters and bunkers. Later in the war, the F-111s were used against enemy tanks at night.

The F-111F had improved turbofan engines, giving 35 per cent more thrust than those of the F-111A and E. The last F-model was delivered to the Air Force in November 1976. The F-model equipped RAF Lakenheath's 48th Fighter Wing, and had been proven in combat over Libya in 1986.

Development of the EF-111A Raven began in January 1975 when the Air Force made a contract with Grumman Aerospace to modify two F-111As to serve as electronic warfare platforms.

One of the F-111's design innovations was its unique crew escape module, a requirement stipulated by the US Navy but retained in the ultimate Air Force model. The pilot and weapons system officer sit side by side in the

air-conditioned, pressurized module and therefore have no requirement for ejection seats or pressure suits. If the crew pulled the "eject" handles on the centre console, a rocket motor blasts the "pod" clear of the aircraft and it descends by parachute. The module could be fired even at ground level or under water. Flotation bags were fitted to the watertight and airtight module for a water landing.

F-111Cs were an export version supplied to the Royal Australian Air Force, the F-111's only export client. When production ceased in 1976, a total of 562 F-111s had been built.

TOP RIGHT: **The F-111 was the first production aircraft with a variable sweep wing.** ABOVE: **The RAAF was the only non-US operator of the F-111.**
RIGHT: **An F-111 with wings unswept for relatively low-speed flight.**
BELOW: **The crew escape module was one of the F-111's many innovations.**

General Dynamics F-111F

First flight: December 21, 1964 (F-111A)
Power: Two Pratt & Whitney 11,395kg/25,100lb afterburning thrust TF30-P-100 turbofans
Armament: One 20mm/0.78in cannon; one 340kg/750lb nuclear or conventional bomb or two 340kg/750lb bombs in internal bomb bay, plus up to 11,350kg/25,000lb of bombs, rockets, missiles or fuel tanks on four under-wing pylons
Size: Wingspan – 19.2m/63ft, spread 9.74m/32ft, swept
Length – 22.4m/73ft 6in
Height – 5.22m/17ft 1in
Wing area – 48.77m²/525sq ft
Weights: Empty – 21,417kg/47,175lb
Maximum take-off – 45,400kg/100,000lb
Performance: Maximum speed – 2655kph/1650mph
Service ceiling – 17,995m/59,000ft plus
Range – 4707km/2925 miles
Climb – 6710m/22,000ft per minute

Grumman A-6 Intruder/EA-6 Prowler

The Grumman A-6 Intruder, a two-seat, all-weather, subsonic, carrier-based attack aircraft, was designed for a 1957 US Navy competition for a new long-range, low-level tactical strike aircraft. While the performance of the subsonic A-6 was not spectacular, it was superbly suited to the particular attack role for which it was carefully tailored. The A-6 prototype made its first test-flight in April 1960, and was followed by 482 production A-6As delivered to the US Navy from early 1963. From night flights over the jungles of Vietnam to Desert Storm missions above heavily-fortified targets in Iraq, the Grumman A-6 Intruder developed a work-horse reputation, and was the subject of many tales of daring aviation during its 34-year career as the US Navy's principal medium-attack aircraft. The aircraft's ruggedness and all-weather mission capability made it a formidable asset to US Navy and Marine Corps air wings throughout its service. The strengths of the Intruder included its capability to fly in any weather and its heavy weapons payload – two traits highlighted on the big screen in the action film "Flight of the Intruder". A little-known fact is that the Intruder delivered more ordnance during the Vietnam War than the B-52.

A tough and versatile aircraft, the A-6 was called upon to fly the most difficult missions, with flying low and alone in any weather its speciality. The all-weather attack jet saw action in every conflict the USA has been involved in since Vietnam. With the ability to carry more ordnance, launch a wider variety of state-of-the-art smart weapons, conduct day or night strikes over greater distances on internal fuel than any carrier-borne aircraft before or since, and provide mid-air refuelling

TOP AND ABOVE: **The Intruder served the US Navy and Marine Corps through Vietnam, the Libya raids and the Gulf War – it is one of the greatest combat aircraft.**

support to other carrier jets, the Intruder is considered by some to be the most versatile military aircraft of modern times.

In 1986 the A-6E, an advanced upgraded development of the A-6A, proved that it was the best all-weather precision bomber in the world in the joint strike on Libyan terrorist-related targets. With US Air Force F-111s, A-6E Intruders penetrated sophisticated Libyan air defence systems, which had been alerted by the high level of diplomatic tension and by rumours of impending attacks. Evading over 100 guided missiles, the strike force flew at low level in complete darkness, and accurately delivered laser-guided and other ordnance on target.

No guns of any kind were carried aboard the A-6, and the aircraft had no internal bomb bay. However, a wide variety of stores could be mounted externally, including both conventional and nuclear bombs, fuel tanks and an assortment of rockets and missiles. As with all versatile attack aircraft, many combinations of payload and mission radius were available to the A-6E. For example, a weapons load of 945kg/2080lb, consisting of a Mark 43 nuclear bomb, could be delivered at a mission radius of 1432km/890 miles. For that mission, four 1362 litre/300 gallon external tanks would have been carried. Alternatively, a bomb load of 4648kg/10,296lb could be delivered at a mission radius of 724km/450 miles with two 1362 litre/300 gallon external tanks.

The EA-6B Prowlers were developed from the EA-6A, which was an Intruder airframe intended primarily to be an electronic countermeasures and intelligence-gathering platform. These aircraft were initially designed to fly in support of the Intruders on Vietnam missions. However, the EA-6B is a significant aircraft in its own right and provides an umbrella of protection for strike aircraft (by suppressing enemy air defences), ground troops and ships by jamming enemy radar, electronic data links and communications. At the same time, the Prowler is gathering tactical electronic intelligence within the combat area.

Intruders left US Navy service in the late 1990s but Prowlers will fly on for the foreseeable future.

ABOVE RIGHT: **The A-6 was responsible for dropping more bombs during the Vietnam War than the mighty B-52.**
RIGHT: **Note the fixed refuelling probe on the nose of this A-6.**
BELOW: **The Grumman Prowler was based on the Intruder, and has evolved into an aircraft which, in its own way, can disable enemy electronic defences.**

Grumman A-6E Intruder

First Flight: April 19, 1960 (YA-6A)
Power: Two Pratt & Whitney 4222kg/9300lb thrust J52-P-8B turbojets
Armament: Up to 8172kg/18,000lb of nuclear or conventional ordnance or missiles
Size: Wingspan – 16.15m/53ft
Length – 16.69m/54ft 9in
Height – 4.93m/16ft 2in
Wing area – 49.13m²/528.9sq ft
Weights: Empty – 12104kg/26,660lb
Maximum catapult take-off – 26,604kg/58,600lb
Performance: Maximum speed – 1035kph/644mph
Ceiling – 12,932m/42,400ft
Range – 1627km/1011 miles
Climb – 2621m/8600ft per minute

Handley Page Victor

It is hard to believe that while some at Handley Page were working on the Halifax during World War II, others were thinking about a tailless flying-wing jet-powered bomber. Shortly after the end of the war, the futuristic concept aroused the interest of the Air Ministry and the design evolved into an aircraft with a fuselage and a tail but with an innovative crescent-shaped wing. It took five years to get the design from the drawing board into the air – the prototype HP80 Victor WB771 took flight at Boscombe Down on Christmas Eve 1952.

As testing continued, more orders came from the RAF for the high-performance bomber, and in early 1956 the first Victor B.1 rolled off the production line. Capable of speeds in excess of the speed of sound in a shallow dive, the first Victors were delivered to the RAF in November 1957, and Bomber Command declared them operational in April 1958 with No.10 Squadron. The second production batch had a larger tailcone to accommodate tail warning radar, and refined engines, and these aircraft were designated B.1A. The Victor was now a nuclear bomber and part of Britain's V-force with the Vulcans and Valiants. However, with a bomb load of up to 15,890kg/ 35,000lb, the Victor could carry a much greater bomb load than the other V-bombers.

The improved Mk 2 variant with Rolls-Royce Conway engines (and thus redesigned wing roots and intakes), larger wing, modified tailcone and new electrical system among

TOP: **Painted in overall anti-flash white, the Victor, with the other V-bombers, was the UK's nuclear deterrent in the late 1950s.**

ABOVE: **The Victor's unusual crescent wing was groundbreaking. The Victor pictured here is a B(SR).2.**

other modifications, was finally put into production, and the first Victor B.2 flew in February 1959. As Soviet anti-aircraft defences improved, so the V-force had to modify its tactics to remain a credible deterrent. The B.2s became low-level, high-speed bombers, and also began to carry the Blue Steel stand-off nuclear missile.

The last B.2 was completed in April 1963, the year that RAF Victors were deployed to Singapore in a show of force to Indonesia, who threatened the British protectorate of Malaysia. As the B.2s replaced the earlier Marks in service, the B.1s and B.1As were converted into air-refuelling tankers (BK.1 and BK.1A).

LEFT: **Tanker trio – three Victors pictured a month before the type was retired in 1993.** BELOW LEFT: **Refuelling an RAF Jaguar en route to the Gulf, 1991.** BELOW: **This Victor K.2 is without its underwing refuelling pods. Note the large fuel tank hanging under the wing, and the inflight refuelling probe.**

The first converted Victor tanker flew on April 28, 1965. Special reconnaissance versions of the aircraft were also produced – nine B.2s were completed as B(SR).2s, and were excellent reconnaissance aircraft with bomb bays filled with cameras and massive flash units. The standard Victor remained in service as a nuclear bomber until 1975.

Further conversions of "surplus" Victor bombers resulted in the K.2 tanker, which entered service in May 1974. A total of 24 conversions were carried out, and the K.2s were expected to fly until around 1988.

It was as a tanker that the Handley Page bomber finally went to war. The very long-range 1982 Black Buck Vulcan bombing missions against Argentine forces on the Falklands were only possible due to 11 Victor tankers refuelling the bomber and themselves on the outward leg from Ascension. In a less well-known aspect of the Falklands campaign, Victor XH675 carried out a 11,263km/7000-mile, 14-hour and 45-minute reconnaissance mission, radar-mapping the South Atlantic.

Handley Page Victor B. Mk 2

First flight: December 24, 1952
Power: Four Rolls-Royce 9352kg/20,600lb thrust Conway 201 turbofans
Armament: One Blue Steel stand-off missile or up to 15,890kg/35,000lb of conventional bombs
Size: Wingspan – 36.57m/120ft
Length – 35.03m/114ft 11in
Height – 8.57m/28ft 1.5in
Wing area – 241.3m²/2597sq ft
Weights: Empty – 51,864kg/114,240lb
Maximum take-off – 101,242kg/223,000lb
Performance: Maximum speed – 1038kph/645mph
Ceiling – 18,300m/60,000ft
Range – 7400km/4600 miles

The dwindling Victor tanker fleet was forced into the spotlight in early 1991 when coalition forces set about ousting Iraqi invaders from Kuwait. Eight tankers refuelled RAF and US combat aircraft on 299 sorties. The Victor was finally retired from RAF service on October 15, 1993. Eighty-six Victors had been produced in all.

Hawker Siddeley/British Aerospace Nimrod

TOP: **The Nimrod is the only jet-powered, long-range maritime patrol and ASW aircraft.** ABOVE: **Somewhere in that shape lies the trailblazing de Havilland Comet jet airliner.**

D esign work on the Nimrod began in June 1964 with the aim of replacing the RAF's ageing Shackleton maritime reconnaissance aircraft.

Based on the airframe of the world's first jet airliner, the de Havilland Comet, the production Nimrod was a new-build aircraft with a shorter, modified, pressurized fuselage. The addition of a weapons and operational equipment bay 15.8m/ 52ft in length under the main fuselage gave the aircraft its unique double-decker cross-section and enabled it to claim the biggest bomb bay of any NATO aircraft.

In 1965, the British Government gave the Nimrod project the go-ahead and two prototypes, conversions from civil Comets, first flew in 1967. The first production Nimrod MRI, XV226, had its maiden flight in June 1968 and the Nimrod entered Royal Air Force service in 1969.

The Nimrod was a revolutionary concept for a maritime patrol aircraft, a class typically powered by turboprops. The Nimrod combined the advantages of high altitude and comparatively high-speed capability from its jet powerplants coupled with low wing-loading and good low-level manoeuvrability.

The Nimrod has an enviable reputation for its anti-submarine warfare capabilities, surface surveillance and anti-shipping roles. In the anti-submarine warfare (ASW) role, prop-engined aircraft produce vibrations that are easily detectable by submarines, whereas the Nimrod's jet noise is virtually undetectable.

This very versatile aircraft can carry a variety of stores, including the Stingray torpedo, Harpoon anti-ship missile and Sidewinder infrared missile for self-defence or targets of opportunity. The aircraft can also carry its own chaff/flares suite for decoying incoming missiles.

Hawker Siddeley/British Aerospace Nimrod MR2

First Flight: May 23, 1967
Power: Four Rolls-Royce 5511kg/12,140lb thrust Spey 250 turbofans
Armament: 6129kg/13,500lb of mixed maritime weaponry carried in bomb bay, including Harpoon anti-ship missiles, rocket/gun pods or pairs of Sidewinder AAMs carried under wing
Size: Wingspan – 35m/114ft 10in
Length – 38.63m/126ft 9in
Height – 9.05m/29ft 8.5in
Wing area – 197m²/2121sq ft
Weights: Empty – 39,362kg/86,700lb
Maximum take-off – 80,585kg/177,500lb
Performance: Maximum speed – 926kph/575mph
Ceiling – 12,810m/42,000ft
Range – 8045km/5000 miles plus
Climb – Not available

ABOVE: **The Nimrod's jet flight is difficult to detect from under water.**
RIGHT: **Note the inflight refuelling probe atop the nose and the magnetic anomaly detector boom projecting from the tail. The latter is just one means of detecting submerged submarines.**

In the early 1980s, the type was upgraded to MR2 standard, principally by updating and improving the aircraft's surveillance equipment. For the aircraft's role in Operation Corporate during the 1982 Falklands War, an inflight refuelling probe became standard. Royal Air Force Nimrods have seen service all over the world and played a pivotal role in the Falklands and Gulf conflicts.

The Nimrod currently carries out three main roles: anti-surface unit warfare (ASUW), anti-submarine warfare (ASW) and search-and-rescue (SAR). It has an unrefuelled endurance of around 10 hours.

After a quarter of a century in service, the Nimrod MR2's airframe and systems are to undergo a dramatic upgrade to MR4 standard, which will extend the type's operational life by a further 25 years. An 80 per cent new aircraft, the MR4 will be 30 per cent heavier than the MR2, carry 30 per cent more fuel and have twice the patrol endurance. The 18-strong fleet of MR4s is expected to be in service by 2009.

One less well-known aspect of the Nimrod story is the Nimrod R1. Three Nimrods were adapted to R1 standard in the early 1970s following the retirement of Comet 2Rs, and have been constantly upgraded ever since. The maritime reconnaissance equipment was removed and replaced with highly sophisticated and sensitive systems for reconnaissance and the gathering of electronic intelligence (ELINT). The ability of the Nimrod to loiter for long periods, following a high-speed dash to the required area of operation, makes the aircraft ideally suited to this task. RAF R1s have been quietly and secretly gathering information in trouble spots and on potential enemies of the UK since 1974.

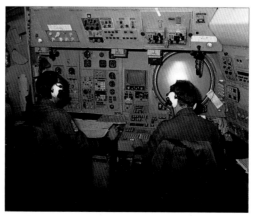

ABOVE: **The Nimrod MR2 has a crew of 13 – three on the flight deck and the rest manning the banks of equipment carried on board.**

457

Ilyushin Il-28

The Il-28 was the Soviet Air Force's first jet bomber to enter service. The aircraft, codenamed "Beagle" by NATO, has been described as Soviet's Canberra owing to its longevity and adaptability.

The Il-28 first flew on August 8, 1948, and the aircraft was in front-line service within two years. Twenty-five pre-production models took part in the 1950 Moscow May Day fly-past, an

TOP: **Now a museum piece, the Il-28 was a groundbreaking addition to the Soviet inventory – the USSR's first jet bomber.** ABOVE: **Despite its unchallenging appearance, the Il-28 proved to be a major weapon for the Soviet Union.**

annual spectacle which was awaited with some trepidation on the part of western analysts during the Cold War. Production of this fine aircraft went on until around 1960, and some 10,000 were finally built by the Soviet Union and under licence in China until 1969. Design work on this medium bomber began around the end of World War II, and the aircraft's shape seemed to owe more to the past than the future. Straight-winged, the Il-28 did, however, have a highly swept-back tail fin and tailplanes for better control in high-speed dives.

Power for the prototype was provided by two RD-10 turbojets developed from wartime German Junkers Jumo engines, but production versions were powered by Klimov VK-1s, a Soviet version of the reliable British Nene engine supplied pre-Cold War.

The engines were mounted in pods beneath the wings in the same way that the Jumos had been mounted on the wartime Arado Blitz bomber. While the pilot had a rounded fighter-looking bubble canopy, the navigator/bombardier's bombsight was housed in a World War II-style greenhouse nose. At the base of the tail fin was a defensive powered gun turret which looked very similar to that of a B-17 or B-29, and housed two 23mm/0.9in cannon. The rear gunner also served as radio operator for the aircraft. Two 23mm/0.9in cannon were fixed in the nose for front defence.

LEFT: **A rare picture of a Chinese-built Il-28, the H-5, in service with the Romanian Air Force.** BELOW: **Wartime German jet aircraft development certainly influenced some aspects of the Il-28 design, such as the engines slung beneath the wing. The prototype was, in fact, powered by engines derived from German Jumos.** BOTTOM: **A flight of "Soviet Canberras".**

Using the bomb bay and external hardpoints, the aircraft could carry up to 3000kg/6603lb of ordnance. Wing-tip fuel tanks gave the aircraft extended range. The Il-28R variant was a tactical reconnaissance version with cameras mounted in the bomb bay, but could also carry out electronic intelligence gathering. The Il-28T was the torpedo bomber in service with the Soviet Navy.

The Beagle was retired from the Soviet Air Force and Navy front line in the 1980s but continued to serve as target tugs and ECM (electronic countermeasures) platforms – Finland and East Germany operated the dedicated unarmed target-towing version.

The Il-28 was also operated by a number of export customers, having been sold to over 20 countries including Afghanistan, Egypt, Hungary, Iraq, North Korea, Poland and Yemen. Nigeria's controversial use of their six Il-28s against Biafran civilians in 1968 shocked the world.

Many Arab air forces operated the type, and when 50 examples of this very capable bomber arrived in Egypt in the mid-1950s, tensions between Egypt and Israel rose. During the 1956 Suez crisis and subsequent conflicts in 1967 and 1973, Egyptian Il-28s were targeted on the ground before they could be used against Israel.

Earlier, during the 1962 Cuban Missile Crisis, Soviet Il-28s being assembled on Cuba posed enough of a threat to the USA that the aircraft, as well as the notorious missiles, had to be removed.

Over 500 were sold to China, who also licence-built the aircraft – their domestic version, the H-5, remained in front-line service into the late 1990s. Bomber versions continued to be used by former Soviet satellite and client states well into the 1990s.

Ilyushin Il-28

First flight: August 8, 1948
Power: Two Klimov 2700kg/5942lb thrust VK-1 turbojets
Armament: Two 23mm/0.9in cannon in nose and two in tail turret; maximum bomb load of 3000kg/6603lb carried internally and externally
Size: Wingspan – 21.45m/70ft 4.5in
Length – 17.65m/57ft 10.75in
Height – 6.7m/21ft 11.8in
Wing area – 60.8m²/654.47sq ft
Weights: Empty – 12,890kg/28,569lb
Maximum take-off – 21,000kg/46,221lb
Performance: Maximum speed – 900kph/559mph
Ceiling – 12,300m/40,355ft
Range – 2180km/1355 miles
Climb – 900m/2953ft per minute

Lockheed P2V Neptune

Even before the USA entered World War II, it was clear that the US Navy would need a land-based patrol bomber with better performance and armament than the types then available, such as the Hudson and Ventura. The Navy needed an aircraft designed specifically for day or night anti-submarine warfare and anti-shipping operations. Lockheed began work on designing such an aircraft before the Navy managed to issue an official requirement. In the confusion following America's joining the war, the US Navy was only interested in proven and available aircraft types, so Lockheed continued to develop their design with no official support. However, by early 1943 the Navy began to look for the next generation of maritime patrol aircraft and asked Lockheed to proceed to prototype stage. The XP2V-1 first flew on May 17, 1945, and was followed by 14 production versions of the P2V-1, which began to enter US Navy service in March 1947. The designers introduced many production refinements with the aircraft, for example trying to keep much of the fuselage shape curving in only one direction, thus allowing the use of shaped skins which would fit in any number of areas on the fuselage instead of just one. The aircraft was designed to be

manufactured into easily accessible subassemblies, keeping assembly time to a minimum. The Neptune thus became an easy aircraft to service – for example, a complete engine change could be done in 30 minutes and an outer wing panel in 79 minutes.

However, the Neptune had made a name for itself before it entered service. From September to October 1946, a modified Neptune named Truculent Turtle flew 18,100km/11,250 miles non-stop from Western Australia to Columbus, Ohio, in 55 hours and 15 minutes, and captured the world long-distance record.

Over 30 variants of the P2V appeared before production ceased in 1962. After the P2V-1, the improved and more powerfully engined P2V-2, with the ability to carry sonobuoys, was the next significant version. However, the major production version was the P2V-5, first flown on December 29, 1950.

RIGHT: **Test-flown during World War II, the Neptune was finally retired from active duty four decades later. The aircraft pictured here is a Dutch Navy machine.** BELOW: **An excellent air-to-air study of a US Navy P2V. Note the remotely controlled searchlight on the tip of the starboard wingtip fuel tank.**

Powered by 3250hp R-3350 engines, this version carried additional fuel in ingenious large wingtip tanks. Apart from 1589 litres/350 gallons of fuel, the forward portion of the starboard wingtip tank housed a powerful moveable searchlight that was linked to the movement of the nose turret guns. The port wingtip tank had APS-8 search radar mounted in its forward portion, and both tanks could be jettisoned in an emergency. The P2V-5 could carry a 3632kg/8000lb bomb load of mines, torpedoes, bombs or depth charges, as well as 16 rockets beneath the wings. An APS-20 radar was mounted in the underbelly position just aft of the nose-wheel doors. The increase in ASW and ECM (electronic countermeasures equipment) required an increase in the aircrew to nine men, and the P2V-5's range was 7642km/4750 miles.

In addition to the US Navy, the P2V-5 was supplied to Argentina, Australia, Brazil, the Netherlands and Portugal. Fifty-two P2V-5s were delivered to the Royal Air Force in 1952. Designated Neptune MR.1s, the aircraft were delivered with nose, dorsal and tail turrets. Twenty-seven were later modified, and the nose and tail turrets replaced with the clear plexiglass nose and MAD boom in the tail. The Neptune entered service with No.217 Squadron and also equipped Nos.36, 203 and 210 Squadrons. The aircraft were returned to the USA in 1957 when the RAF's Shackleton force was up to strength.

The P2V-7 was the final Neptune version off the production line. First flown on April 26, 1954, it was powered by two piston engines augmented by two turbojets. With a dash speed of 586kph/364mph, this version was the fastest of the Lockheed-produced Neptunes. The APS-20 search radar, with its larger radome, was mounted further forward than on the P2V-5s.

By the 1970s, P2Vs had been phased out from all US Navy Fleet Patrol Squadrons but remained in service with Reserve Patrol Squadrons. In April 1978, the last reserve unit re-equipped with the P-3 Orion, thus ending over three decades of P2V Neptune operations with the US Navy.

Kawasaki had assembled some 48 P2V-7s in Japan and went on to produce a developed turboprop-powered version, designated P-2J, with a longer fuselage to carry more equipment. The turboprops were again augmented by two turbojets. A total of 83 P-2Js were built by Kawasaki, with the first delivered in October 1969. These aircraft, the last operational Neptunes in the world, were finally retired in 1985.

TOP: **A P2V-7 of French Aéronavale unit Escadrille 12S.** TOP RIGHT: **A Dutch Navy Neptune.** ABOVE: **An RAF crew gaining experience of one of 50 P2V-5 Neptunes allocated to Britain and Australia before flying the aircraft to the UK.**

Lockheed P2V-7 Neptune

First Flight: May 17, 1945 (XP2V-1 prototype)
Power: Two Wright 3500hp R-3350-32W radial piston engines and two Westinghouse 1543kg/3400lb thrust J34-WE-36 turbojets
Armament: Two 12.7mm/0.5in machine-guns in dorsal turret; up to 3632kg/8000lb of bombs, depth charges or torpedoes
Size: Wingspan – 31.65m/103ft 10in
Length – 27.94m/91ft 8in
Height – 8.94m/29ft 4in
Wing area – 92.9m²/1000sq ft
Weights: Empty – 22,670kg/49,935lb
Maximum take-off – 36,272kg/79,895lb
Performance: Maximum speed – 649kph/403mph
Ceiling – 6710m/22,000ft
Range – 5930km/3685 miles
Climb – 366m/1200ft per minute

Lockheed P-3 Orion

The P-3C Orion is one of the all-time great military aircraft. Developed quickly in a time of national need from the existing Lockheed Electra airliner, the Orion has been protecting the maritime interests of the USA and other P-3 customers for over four decades, and remains a potent submarine killer.

In 1957, the US Navy issued an urgent requirement for a long-range maritime reconnaissance and anti-submarine warfare (ASW) aircraft to replace the ageing P2V Neptune. Lockheed's answer was a modified Electra airliner airframe, which first flew in November 1959. Structurally, the aircraft differed in that the Orion was 2.24m/7ft 4in shorter and had a weapons bay for carrying mines, torpedoes, depth charges or even nuclear weapons.

The aircraft entered the US Navy inventory in July 1962, and more than 30 years later it remains the Navy's sole land-based ASW aircraft. It has gone through one designation change (P3V to P-3) and three major models – P-3A, P-3B and P-3C, the latter being the only one now in active service. The last Navy P-3 came off the Lockheed production line in April 1990.

The P-3 Orion built its reputation as the ultimate submarine-finder during the Cold War. From the Cuban Missile Crisis to the end of the Soviet Union, the Orion carried out round-the-clock, low-profile patrols to keep the USA and NATO ahead of the Soviets.

The P-3 can be equipped with a variety of sophisticated detection equipment. Infrared and long-range electro-optical cameras plus special imaging radar allow the Orion, with no

TOP: **The P-3 is still among the best ASW aircraft in the world, almost half a century after its first flight.** ABOVE: **A Royal Netherlands Navy P-3.**

defensive armament, to monitor activity from a safe distance. It can stay airborne for very long periods, and its four powerful Allison T56-A-14 engines can fly at almost any altitude.

In addition to submarine-hunting, the P-3 is called upon for peacekeeping and relief missions around the world. When civil war flared in Liberia, P-3s were the eyes and ears of forces protecting the US Embassy. In Somalia, P-3s monitored street operations in Mogadishu from well off-shore. In Rwanda, P-3s tracked large groups of refugees to help pinpoint relief efforts. Then, in Operation Desert Storm, P-3s logged more than 12,000 hours in 1200 combat surveillance sorties.

The current US Navy force of 12 active and seven reserve squadrons supports requirements for 40 P-3Cs to be continuously forward-deployed around the world, ready

RIGHT: **The US Navy will continue to operate P-3s for some years to come. This aircraft has opened the doors of its weapons bay, which can contain torpedoes, nuclear depth charges and mines.** BELOW: **This photograph of a US Navy P-3 shows the area beneath the fuselage aft of the wing, consisting of over 50 chutes from which a variety of stores can be dispensed.** BELOW RIGHT: **The P-3 has now become a battlefield surveillance platform over land and sea.**

to support global US Navy operations. In addition to US Navy use, P-3s were exported to Australia, Chile, Greece, Iran, the Netherlands, New Zealand, Norway, Portugal, South Korea, Spain and Thailand. Some were also built in Japan by Kawasaki, and the Canadian Armed Forces operate a version known as the CP-140 Aurora.

US Navy P-3s were active in Afghanistan in late 2001, where the aircraft used data links to provide real-time video and other sensor data to land forces.

The role of the Orion has evolved from being simply a maritime anti-submarine aircraft to being a battlefield surveillance platform at sea or over land. The aircraft's long range and loiter time proved to be invaluable assets for the Allies during Operation Iraqi Freedom because it can view the battle area and instantaneously provide that information to ground troops.

The P-3C has advanced submarine-detection sensors such as directional frequency and ranging (DIFAR) sonobuoys and magnetic anomaly detection (MAD) equipment. The avionics system is integrated by a computer that supports all of the tactical displays and monitors for the 11 crew members, and can automatically launch weapons, as well as providing flight information to the pilots. The aircraft can carry a variety of weapons internally and on wing pylons, such as the Harpoon anti-surface missile, the Mk 50 torpedo and the Mk 60 mine. From the Cold War to today's tensions, the P-3 was there, and it is likely to remain in service around the world for the foreseeable future.

Lockheed Martin P-3C Orion

First Flight November 25, 1959 (YP-3A)

Power Four Allison 4910eshp T-56-A-14 turboprop engines

Armament 9080kg/20,000lb of ordnance, including cruise missile, Maverick (AGM 65) air-to-ground missiles, Mk 46/50 torpedoes, rockets, mines, depth bombs and special weapons

Size Wingspan – 30.36m/99ft 6in
Length – 35.6m/116ft 10in
Height – 10.27m/33ft 7in
Wing area – 120.77m²/1300sq ft

Weights Empty – 27,917kg/61,491lb
Maximum take-off – 64,468kg/142,000lb

Performance Maximum speed – 750kph/466mph
Ceiling – 8631m/28,300ft
Range – 4405km/2738 miles
Climb – 594m/1950ft per minute

Lockheed S-3 Viking

The S-3 Viking in service today is an all-weather, carrier-based patrol/attack aircraft, which provides protection for the US fleet against hostile surface vessels while also functioning as the Carrier Battle Groups' primary tanker. The S-3, one of the most successful of all carrier aircraft, is extremely versatile and is equipped for many missions, including day/night surveillance, electronic countermeasures, command/control/communications warfare, as well as search-and-rescue (SAR). Its versatility has made it known as the "Swiss Army Knife of Naval Aviation".

In the late 1960s, the deployment of Soviet deep-diving nuclear powered submarines caused the US Navy to call for a new breed of carrier-borne US Navy ASW aircraft to succeed the Grumman S-2. Lockheed, in association with Vought Aeronautics, proposed the S-3A, which came to be called Viking.

To keep the aircraft aerodynamically clean and avoid reducing its top speed, as many protuberances as possible were designed to retract. Thus, the inflight refuelling probe, the magnetic anomaly detection boom at the rear of the aircraft and some sensors retract for transit flight. The small four-man aircraft has folding wings, making it very popular on carriers due to the small amount of space it takes up relative to the importance of its mission. With its short, stubby wings, the Viking was something of a wolf in sheep's clothing and could have given a very good account of itself had the Cold War heated up. Carrying state-of-the-art radar

TOP: **Developed to counter a specific Soviet threat, the Viking is considered to be the ultimate sub-killer.** ABOVE: **An S-3B of VS-31 "Topcats" aboard the USS** *John F. Kennedy***, Arabian Sea, April 2004.**

systems and extensive sonobuoy deployment and control capability, the S-3A entered US Navy service with VS-41 in February 1974. In total 187 were built and equipped 14 US Navy squadrons.

In the mid-1980s, the aircraft was completely refurbished and modified to carry the Harpoon missile, the improved version being designated the S-3B. While the S-3A was primarily configured for anti-submarine warfare, the S-3B has evolved into a premier surveillance and precision-targeting platform for the US Navy, and has the most modern precision-guided missile capabilities. It does so many things so well – surface and undersea warfare, mine warfare, electronic reconnaissance and analysis, over-the-horizon targeting, missile attack, and aerial tanking – that its current mission is summed up by the US Navy as being simply "Sea Control".

ABOVE: **The Viking has an internal weapons bay which can carry bombs, depth charges, mines and torpedoes, while missiles, rocket pods, bombs, flare dispensers or mines can be carried on two underwing hardpoints.**

The S-3B's high-speed computer system processes and displays information generated by its targeting-sensor systems. To engage and destroy targets, the S-3B Viking employs an impressive array of airborne weaponry, including the AGM 84 Harpoon Anti-Ship Missile, AGM 65 Maverick Infrared Missile and a wide selection of conventional bombs and torpedoes. Future Viking aircraft will also have a control capability for the AGM 84 stand-off land-attack missile extended range (SLAM-ER). The S-3B provides the fleet with a very effective fixed-wing "over the horizon" aircraft to combat the significant and varied threats presented by modern maritime combatants.

On March 25, 2003, an S-3B from the "Red Griffins" of Sea Control Squadron Thirty-eight (VS 38) became the first such aircraft to attack inland and to fire a laser-guided Maverick missile in combat. The attack was made on a "significant naval target" in the Tigris River near Basra, Iraq. VS-38 was embarked in the USS *Constellation*.

The Viking, easy to update with the latest avionics and surveillance equipment, will be flying with the US Navy for many years to come.

TOP: **The aircraft carries a long magnetic anomaly detection boom which can be extended from the rear of the aircraft to aid submarine-detection.**
ABOVE: **An S-3A of VS-22 "The Checkmates" from USS *Saratoga*.**
BELOW: **The S-3B's mission, neatly summed up by the US Navy, is "Sea Control".**

Lockheed S-3B Viking

First Flight January 21, 1972
Power Two General Electric 4211kg/9275lb thrust TF-34-GE-400B turbofan engines
Armament Up to 1793kg/3950lb of ordnance, including AGM-84 Harpoon, AGM-65 Maverick and AGM-84 SLAM missiles, torpedoes, rockets and bombs
Size: Wingspan – 20.93m/68ft 8in
    Length – 16.26m/53ft 4in
    Height – 6.93m/22ft 9in
    Wing area – 55.55m²/598sq ft
Weights Empty – 12,099kg/26,650lb
    Maximum take-off – 23,852kg/52,539lb
Performance Maximum speed – 834kph/518mph
    Ceiling – 12,200m/40,000ft
    Range – 3706km/2303 miles
    Climb – 1280m/4200ft per minute

Lockheed Martin F-117A Nighthawk

Usually and erroneously referred to as the "stealth fighter", the F-117A Nighthawk bomber was the world's first operational aircraft designed to exploit low-observability stealth technology. This precision-strike aircraft can penetrate high-threat airspace undetected and then use laser-guided weaponry against critical targets.

The F-117A was developed by Lockheed Martin after lengthy work on stealth technology was carried out in secret from 1975. Development of the F-117A began in 1978, and it

TOP: **Developed in incredible secrecy, the "stealth fighter" was the world's first operational aircraft built with stealth technology.** ABOVE: **Braking parachutes trailing, a pair of F-117As during a visit to the UK.**

was test-flown in 1981, but it was not until 1988 that its existence was publicly announced. The first F-117A was delivered in 1982, and USAF Air Combat Command's first F-117A unit, the 4450th Tactical Group, achieved operational capability in October 1983. Lockheed Martin delivered the last of 59 aircraft to the Air Force in July 1990, and five additional test aircraft were retained by the company.

The aircraft's surfaces and edge profiles are optimized to reflect hostile radar into narrow beam signals, directed away from enemy radar detectors. All the doors and opening panels on the aircraft have saw-toothed forward and trailing edges to reflect radar. The aircraft is constructed principally of aluminum, with titanium used for areas of the engine and exhaust systems. The outer surface of the aircraft is coated with a radar-absorbent material (RAM) and for stealth reasons, the F-117A does not rely on radar for navigation or targeting. Instead, for navigation and weapon aiming, the aircraft is equipped with a forward-looking infrared (FLIR) and a downward-looking infrared (DLIR) with laser designator, supplied by Raytheon.

The F-117 is powered by two low-bypass General Electric F404-GE-F1D2 turbofan engines. The rectangular air intakes on both sides of the fuselage are covered by gratings that are coated with radar-absorbent material. The wide and flat structure of the engine exhaust area reduces the infrared and radar detectability of the aft section of the engine. The two large tail fins slant slightly outwards to provide an obstruction for ground-based radars to the infrared and radar returns from the engine exhaust area.

Before a flight, mission data is downloaded on to the IBM AP-102 mission-control computer, which integrates it with the navigation and flight controls to provide a fully automated flight management system. After take-off, the pilot can hand over flight control to the mission programme until within visual range of the mission's first target. The pilot then resumes control of the aircraft for weapon delivery. The aircraft is equipped with an infrared acquisition and designation system (IRADS), which is integrated with the weapon delivery system. The pilot is presented with a view of the target on the head-up display. After the strike, the weapon delivery and impact is recorded on the aircraft's internally-mounted video system, which provides real-time damage assessment.

The F-117A can employ a variety of weapons, including the BLU-109B low-level laser-guided bomb, GBU-10 and GBU-27 laser-guided bomb units, AGM-65 Maverick and AGM-88 HARM air-to-surface missiles.

The F-117A first saw action in December 1989 during Operation Just Cause in Panama, but it was the type's actions in the first Gulf War that grabbed the headlines. On their first trip into theatre, the F-117s flew non-stop from the USA to Kuwait, an air-refuelled flight of approximately 18.5 hours – a record for single-seat combat aircraft that stands today.

In January and February 1991, the F-117A attacked the most heavily fortified targets during Desert Storm, and it was the only coalition jet allowed to strike targets inside Baghdad's

city limits. The F-117A, which normally packs a payload of two 908kg/2000lb GBU-27 laser-guided bombs, destroyed and crippled Iraqi electrical power stations, military headquarters, communications sites, air-defence operation centres, airfields, ammunition bunkers and chemical, biological and nuclear weapons plants.

Although only 36 F-117As were deployed in Desert Storm, and accounted for 2.5 per cent of the total force of 1900 fighters and bombers, they flew more than a third of the bombing runs on the first day of the war. In all, during Desert Storm this remarkable aircraft conducted more than 1250 sorties, dropped more than 2032 tonnes/2000 tons of bombs, and flew for more than 6900 hours. Although more than 3000 anti-aircraft guns and 60 surface-to-air missile batteries protected Baghdad, the Nighthawks owned the skies over the city and, for that matter, the country.

In March 24, 1999, F-117As led the NATO Operation Allied Force air strikes against Yugoslavia. During the campaign, one F-117 was lost, having being tracked by virtually antique Russian long wavelength radars. Normally the only time the aircraft's stealthiness can be compromised is when it gets very wet or opens its bomb bays.

Nighthawks are officially expected to remain in USAF service until 2020, but with updating, the aircraft is likely to be around for much longer.

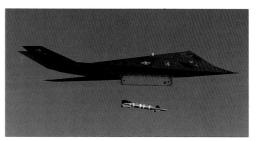

RIGHT: **The principal weapon carried by the F-117 is the precision laser-guided GBU-27 bomb.** BELOW: **The F-117, with its unprecedented form, was so radical that it has challenged how we think combat aircraft should look.**

Lockheed Martin F-117A Nighthawk

First Flight: June 18, 1981
Power: Two General Electric 4903kg/10,800lb
thrust F404-GE-F1D2 non-afterburning turbofans
Armament: Up to 2270kg/5000lb of smart or
free-fall weapons can be carried internally
Size: Wingspan – 13.3m/43ft 4in
Length – 20.1m/65ft 11in
Height – 3.78m/12ft 5in
Wing area – 105.9m²/1140sq ft
Weights: Empty – Approximately 13,620kg/30,000lb
Maximum take-off – 23,835kg/52,500lb
Performance: Maximum speed – High subsonic
Ceiling – Unpublished
Range – Intercontinental with air-refuelling
Climb – Unpublished

McDonnell Douglas A-4 Skyhawk

From 1954, Douglas (and later McDonnell Douglas) built 2960 Skyhawks in a production run that lasted a quarter of a century. Designed as a small and therefore cost-effective lightweight carrier-borne high-speed bomber, the Skyhawk was affectionately nicknamed "the scooter" or "Heinemann's Hot Rod" after Douglas designer Ed Heinemann. He had been working on a compact jet-powered attack aircraft design which the US Navy ordered for evaluation – this was the XA4D-1, and the first of nine prototypes and development aircraft flew in June 1954. Development was swift and the Navy were eager to acquire this new and very capable combat aircraft. Chosen as a replacement for the venerable Skyraider,

ABOVE: **The A-4's designer Ed Heinemann championed the concept of a small, light and relatively cheap jet bomber, and his "scooter" is still in service with some air arms half a century after the type's maiden flight. This photograph shows the TA-4J tandem trainer.** BELOW LEFT: **A Royal Australian Navy A-4G.**

the Skyhawk provided the US Navy, US Marines Corps and friendly nations with a manoeuvrable but powerful attack bomber that had great altitude and range performance, plus a remarkable and flexible weapons-carrying capability.

Production deliveries of A-4As began in September 1956. The A-4 was first delivered to the US Navy's VA-72 attack squadron on October 26, 1956. Its small size allowed it to fit on an aircraft carrier lift without needing to have folding wings, thus saving weight and extra maintenance. The Skyhawk was roughly half the empty weight of its contemporaries and could fly at 1089km/677mph at sea level. US examples of the aircraft were nuclear-capable.

The Skyhawk was progressively developed with more powerful engines – early A–C models had been powered by the Wright J65, a licence-built copy of the British Armstrong Siddeley Sapphire engine. The A-4C was followed by the A-4E, a heavier aircraft powered by Pratt & Whitney's J52 engine. The A-4F was the last version to enter US Navy service and was easily identified by its dorsal avionics "hump". The ultimate development of the Skyhawk was the A-4M, known as the Skyhawk II, specifically designed for the US Marines. This model that first flew in 1970 had a larger canopy for better pilot view, and had a maximum take-off

LEFT: **The A-4D2 version had a more efficient engine, beefed-up rear fuselage and powered rudder, and introduced the fixed inflight refuelling probe.** BELOW: **The "camel's hump", which appeared on later A-4s, housed all-weather navigation and weapons-delivery avionics.** BOTTOM: **Two-seat trainer versions of the A-4 were produced to train both pilots and radar intercept officers.**

weight twice that of the early A-4 versions. Power for this "super" Skyhawk came from a J52-P-408, and the Skyhawk II was in production until 1979. The US Navy's Blue Angels flight demonstration aerobatics team flew the A-4 Skyhawk II from 1974 until 1986.

The Skyhawk's combat career began on August 4, 1964, with the first American carrier-launched raids on North Vietnam. The A-4s were soon performing most of the Navy's and Marine Corps' light air attack missions over Vietnam.

Skyhawks were also operated by the armed forces of Argentina, Australia, Israel (who used them extensively in the 1973 Yom Kippur war), Kuwait, Singapore, Indonesia, Malaysia and New Zealand, and they remained active with several air services into the 2000s.

Argentina was the first export customer for the Skyhawk, operating A-4Ps and A-4Qs which were modified B and C-models respectively. These aircraft, acquired in the mid-1960s, were later complemented by A-4Rs which were ex-USMC A-4Ms. Argentine Skyhawks were the most

destructive strike aircraft to engage British Forces during the 1982 Falklands War. Operating from mainland bases, the Skyhawks carried out many attacks against British shipping. On May 12, a Skyhawk raid put HMS *Glasgow* out of action, and on May 21, the Skyhawks attacked the British invasion force landing at San Carlos. On May 25, Argentine Skyhawks attacked and sank HMS *Coventry*. The cost of these actions was high, with Argentina losing ten A-4s to anti-aircraft defences and fighters in a matter of days.

McDonnell Douglas A-4M Skyhawk II

First flight: June 22, 1954 (XA4D-1 prototype)
Power: One Pratt & Whitney 5079kg/11,187lb thrust J52-P408 turbojet
Armament: Two 20mm/0.78in cannon in wing roots; up to 4156kg/9155lb of bombs or air-to-surface and air-to-air missiles
Size Wingspan – 8.38m/27ft 6in
Length – 12.27m/40ft 4in
Height – 4.5m/15ft
Wing area – 24.2m²/260sq ft
Weights: Empty – 4751kg/10,465lb
Maximum take-off – 11,123kg/24,500lb
Performance: Maximum speed – 1100kph/683mph
Ceiling – 11803m/38,700ft
Range – 1480km/920 miles
Climb – 3142m/10,300ft per minute

McDonnell Douglas F-4 Phantom II

The F-4, one of the world's greatest-ever combat aircraft, was designed to meet a US Navy requirement for a fleet defence fighter to replace the F3H Demon and to counter the threat from long-range Soviet bombers. The US Air Force also ordered the Phantom when the F-4 was shown to be faster than their high-performance F-104. The F-4 was first used by the US Navy as an interceptor, but was soon employed by the US Marine Corps in the ground support role. Its outstanding versatility made it the first US multi-service aircraft to fly with the US Air Force, Navy and Marine Corps concurrently. The remarkable Phantom excelled in air superiority, close air support, interception, air defence suppression, long-range strike, fleet defence, attack and reconnaissance.

The sophisticated F-4 was, without direction from surface-based radar, able to detect and destroy a target beyond visual range (BVR). In the Vietnam and Gulf Wars alone, the F-4 was credited with 280 air-to-air victories. As a bomber, the F-4 could carry up to 5.08 tonnes/5 tons of ordnance and deliver it accurately while flying at supersonic speeds at very low level.

Capable of flying at twice the speed of sound with ease, the Phantom was loved by its crews, who considered it a workhorse that could be relied on, that could do the job and get them home safely. F-4s have also set world records for altitude (30,059m/98,556ft on December 6, 1959), speed (2585kph/1606mph on November 22, 1961) and a low-altitude speed record of 1452kph/902mph that stood for 16 years.

Phantom production ran from 1958 to 1979, resulting in a total of 5195 aircraft. Of these, 5057 were made in St Louis,

TOP: **The F-4, a jack of all trades and master of them all, is considered by many to be the greatest ever combat aircraft. This photograph shows an F-4G optimized to neutralize hostile radars.** ABOVE: **Germany's F-4F fleet will remain in service until 2015.**

Missouri, in the USA, while a further 138 were built under licence by the Mitsubishi Aircraft Co. in Japan. F-4 production peaked in 1967 when the McDonnell plant was producing 72 Phantoms per month. The USAF acquired 2874 while the US Navy and Marine Corps operated 1264.

The F-4 was used extensively by the USA in Vietnam from 1965 and served in many roles including fighter, reconnaissance and ground attack. A number of refurbished ex-US forces

ABOVE: **An F-4E releases its bombs.** RIGHT: **The F-4 has set world records for speed and altitude.** BELOW: **The Phantom has served both the Royal Air Force and the Royal Navy. Britain retired its last Phantom in 1992.**

aircraft were operated by other nations, including the UK, who bought a squadron of mothballed ex-US Navy F-4Js to complement the RAF's F-4Ms.

Regularly updated with the addition of state-of-the-art weaponry and radar, the Phantom served with 11 nations around the globe – Australia, Egypt, Germany, Greece, Iran, Israel, Japan, South Korea, Spain and Turkey. Britain's Royal Navy and Royal Air Force both operated Phantoms from 1968, and the last RAF Phantoms were retired in January 1992. For a time, RAF F.G.R.2 Phantoms with the ability to carry 11 454kg/1000lb bombs were based in Germany in the tactical nuclear bomber role.

1996 saw the Phantom's retirement from US military forces, by which time the type had flown more than 27,350,000km/ around 17 million miles in the nation's service. Israel, Japan, Germany, Turkey, Greece, Korea and Egypt have undertaken or plan to upgrade their F-4s and keep them flying until 2015, nearly 60 years after the Phantom's first flight.

McDonnell Douglas Phantom F.G.R.2 (F-4M)

First flight: February 17, 1967
Power: Two Rolls-Royce 9313kg/20,515lb afterburning thrust Spey 202 turbofans
Armament: One 20mm/0.78in cannon; eleven 454kg/1000lb free-fall or retarded conventional or nuclear bombs, 126 68mm/ 2.65in armour-piercing rockets, all carried externally
Size: Wingspan – 11.68m/38ft 4in
Length – 17.73m/58ft 2in
Height – 4.95m/16ft 3in
Wing area – 49.25m²/530sq ft
Weights Empty – 14,074kg/31,000lb
Maximum take-off – 26,332kg/58,000lb
Performance: Maximum speed – 2230kph/ 1386mph
Ceiling – 18,300m/60,000ft
Range – 2815km/1750 miles
Climb – 9760m/32,000ft per minute

McDonnell Douglas/Boeing F-15

The F-15 Eagle, designed to succeed the legendary F-4 Phantom, is a highly manoeuvrable, all-weather combat aircraft originally designed to gain and maintain US Air Force air superiority in aerial combat. It is probably the most capable multi-role fighter in service today.

The first F-15A flight was made in July 1972, and the test-flight of the two-seat F-15B trainer was made in July 1973. The first USAF Eagle (an F-15B) was delivered to the US Air Force in November 1974, while the first Eagle destined for a front-line combat squadron was delivered in January 1976, and some squadrons were combat-ready by the end of the year.

In the fighter role the Eagle's air superiority is achieved through a mixture of incredible manoeuvrability and acceleration, range, weapons and avionics, and in the strike role it can penetrate enemy defences and outperform and outfight any current potential enemy aircraft. The F-15's manoeuvrability and acceleration are due to its high engine thrust-to-weight ratio and low wing-loading. Low wing-loading (the ratio of aircraft weight to its wing area) is a vital factor in manoeuvrability and, combined with the high thrust-to-weight ratio, enables the aircraft to turn tightly without losing airspeed in the process.

The F-15E Strike Eagle, which first flew in July 1980, is a two-seat, dual-role fighter for all-weather, air-to-air and deep interdiction missions – the rear cockpit is reserved for the weapon systems operator (WSO) and incorporates an entirely new suite of air-to-ground avionics. On four television-like screens, the WSO can display information from the radar, electronic warfare or infrared sensors, monitor aircraft or weapon status and possible threats, select targets, and use an electronic "moving map" to navigate. Two hand controls are used to select new displays and to refine targeting information. Displays can be moved from one screen to another, chosen from a "menu" of display options.

While earlier models of the Eagle were purely air-to-air combat aircraft, the E-model is a dual-role fighter. It can fight its way to a target over long ranges, destroy enemy ground positions, and fight its way back out. The F-15E performs day

TOP: **Preparing to land, with massive dorsal airbrake extended, this Israeli F-15 shows some of the weapon-carrying ability of the type.** ABOVE: **An F-15E Strike Eagle of the 48th TFW based at Lakenheath, UK.**

and night all-weather air-to-air and air-to-ground missions including strategic strike. Its engines incorporate advanced digital technology for improved performance, and acceleration from a standstill to maximum afterburner takes less than four seconds. Although primarily a bomber, the F-15E is equally at home performing fighter and escort missions.

The F-15E became the newest fighter in USAF Tactical Air Command when the 405th Tactical Training Wing accepted delivery of the first production model in April 1988. Strike Eagles were among the first US aircraft in action during the first Gulf War, and they spearheaded an attack on Iraqi forces on January 16, 1991.

The F-15E can carry an external payload of up to 11,123kg/ 24,500lb, including fuel tanks, missiles and bombs. Considered to be the most advanced tactical fighter aircraft in the world, the F-15E is the fifth version of the F-15 to appear since 1972.

More than 1500 F-15s have been produced for the USA and international customers Israel, Japan and Saudi Arabia. The F-15I Thunder, a strike version designed for Israel, was built in the USA, the first of 25 Thunders arriving in Israel in January 1998.

TOP: The dual-role Strike Eagle can battle its way to a target like a fighter, and then carry out a devastating bombing attack. ABOVE: The Strike Eagle was designed to succeed the long range F-111. LEFT: The F-15 can operate in all weather, day or night. BELOW: Fighter escort or strike missions – both are specialities of the F-15E.

McDonnell Douglas F-15E

First flight: July 27, 1972

Power: Two Pratt & Whitney 13,211kg/ 29,100lb afterburning thrust F100-PW-229 turbofans

Armament: One 20mm/0.78in cannon; 11,123kg/ 24,500lb of external store, including free-fall, retarded, guided, nuclear or conventional bombs, as well as missiles

Size: Wingspan – 13.04m/42ft 9.5in
Length – 19.44m/63ft 9.5in
Height – 5.64m/18ft 6in
Wing area – 56.48m²/608sq ft

Weights: Empty – 14,528kg/32,000lb
Maximum take-off – 36,774kg/81,000lb

Performance: Maximum speed – 2655kph/ 1650mph
Ceiling – 19,215m/63,000ft
Range – 4445km/2760 miles
Climb – 15,250m/50,000ft per minute

Mikoyan-Gurevich MiG-27

The MiG-21's range never lived up to expectations, and led to a 1965 requirement for a replacement with considerably better endurance. An enlarged MiG-21 and the all-new Ye-23-11/1 were proposed, the latter becoming the prototype MiG-23 which first appeared in 1967. Like the MiG-21, the new aircraft was proposed in two versions – an interceptor for use with Russia's PVO air defence forces and a ground-attack version, the MiG-27, to serve with Russia's tactical air forces, Frontal Aviation.

The MiG-23 was not only Russia's first production aircraft with a variable-geometry "swing wing"; it was also the first swing-wing fighter anywhere. It and the MiG-27 have three sweep positions: minimum (16 degrees) for take-off, low-speed flight and landing; middle (45 degrees) for cruising; and maximum (72 degrees) for high-performance flight. The aircraft's swing wings are high-mounted, and the single engine is fed by rectangular box-like air intakes forward of the wing roots.

The MiG-27 is an improved but simplified version of the close air-support and ground-attack MiG-23, designed to fly at a slower speed and lower altitude, carrying a larger weapon load with better radar and precision missile-aiming equipment. The MiG-27 (known to NATO as Flogger-D) can be distinguished from the MiG-23 by a different nose (housing a laser rangefinder and other sensors) which slopes away sharply from the cockpit for better pilot view, earning the nickname "Ducknose" from its crews. The MiG-27 pilot is seated higher for better visibility, and the nose has a flattened glass underside, which contains the TV tracker unit and laser rangefinder/designator.

The MiG's multi-barrel GSh-6-N-30 30mm/1.18in autocannon has been likened to the A-10's Vulcan cannon, and is a very potent ground-attack weapon which can spew out 900 rounds of 30mm/1.18in shells over an effective range of 2000m/6562ft.

Due to its role as a battlefield attack aircraft, the pilot of the MiG-27 is protected from small-arms fire by armour on the side of the cockpit. Terrain-avoidance radar relieves the pilot of some of the high workload associated with low-level operations. The MiG-27 lacks the MiG-23's air-to-air radar, relying instead on fighter cover over the battlefield to perform its mission. It also has a different engine, different landing gear, and a navigation/attack system tailored to the ground-attack mission in all weathers. The carriage of various reconnaissance pods means that the aircraft can carry out tactical reconnaissance missions. The MiG-27 has reportedly also been operated from Soviet aircraft carriers.

ABOVE: **The last of the line, an Indian-manufactured MiG-27M Flogger in Indian Air Force service.** LEFT: **Note the rocket pods on this Czechoslovakian Air Force machine.**

LEFT: **Although some MiG-27s have become museum exhibits, the type remains in front-line use with many nations.** BELOW: **The MiG-23/27 was the Soviet Union's first variable-geometry aircraft.** BOTTOM: **Indian-built Floggers are known as Bahadur (Valiant).**

Among the operators of the MiG-23/-27 were Poland, Hungary, Bulgaria, East Germany, Romania and Czechoslovakia. Downgraded MiG-23s were exported outside the Warsaw Pact nations to Libya, Syria, Egypt, Ethiopia, India, Cuba, Algeria, Iraq, Afghanistan and North Korea. Russian MiG-27 production was completed in the mid-1980s, but India's Hindustan Aeronautics produced MiG-27Ms (locally named Bahadur or Valiant) for the Indian Air Force until 1997, finally bringing Flogger production to a close after nearly three decades, with around 4000 examples built.

MiG-27s were used in combat in Afghanistan by the Soviets from 1979 until 1989. Iraqi machines were used in the Iran-Iraq War between 1980 and 1988, and again briefly during the Gulf War of 1991.

Mikoyan-Gurevich MiG-27

First flight: 1972

Power: One Tumansky 11,500kg/25,311lb afterburning thrust R-29B-300 turbojet

Armament: One 30mm/1.18in cannon in belly; seven pylons for carrying up to 4000kg/8804lb of ordnance, including air-to-air missiles, Kh-29 air-to-surface missiles, AS-7 "Kerry" air-to-surface missiles, rockets and napalm tanks, conventional or tactical nuclear bombs

Size: Wingspan – 13.97m/45ft 10in, spread
Length – 17.08m/56ft
Height – 5m/16ft 5in
Wing area – 37.4m²/402.1sq ft

Weights: Empty – 11,910kg/26,214lb
Maximum take-off – 20,300kg/44,680lb

Performance: Maximum speed – 1885kph/1170mph
Ceiling – 14,008m/45,960ft
Range – 1080km/670 miles
Climb – 12,007m/39,395ft per minute

Myasishchev M-4

Development of a Soviet intercontinental bomber capable of striking US-territory began in the early 1950s. In March 1951, a new design bureau led by Vladimir Myasishchev was established to organize the development and manufacture of a bomber with a range of up to 12,000km/7452 miles, a maximum speed of 900kph/559mph, and the ability to carry a payload of 5000kg/11,005lb. Myasishchev's response was a swept-wing bomber powered by four jet engines buried in the wing roots. While Tupolev believed that only turboprops could provide the great range required to do the job with their Tu-95, Myasishchev instead opted for turbojets.

The high-power engines needed for the production aircraft were still in development, so the prototype, completed in December 1952, was fitted with four AM-3A turbojet engines developed by Mikulin. The prototype had its first flight on January 20, 1953. It achieved a top speed of 947kph/588mph and an altitude of 12,500m/41,012ft, but failed to achieve the required range. Despite this, production of the M-4 began in Moscow in 1955, and it became the Soviet Union's first operational four-jet strategic bomber. The M-4 made its first public appearance in a fly-past over Moscow on May 1, 1954, and was given the NATO codename "Bison". Features of the aircraft included two main undercarriage units arranged in tandem on the fuselage centreline plus twin-wheel outriggers, which retracted into the wingtips. The nose and tail units of the aircraft were pressurized for crew comfort.

The M-4/2M "Bison A" was the original free-fall nuclear bomber version produced, and can be easily identified by the typical Soviet "greenhouse" glazed nose. Many were later

TOP: **With air-refuelling, the M-4 could have attacked the continental USA from Soviet bases with ease.** ABOVE: **The "Bison" was an enormous aircraft – this aircraft is seen at the July 1967 Aviation Festival at Moscow's Domodedovo Airport.**

converted into tankers by the addition of a hose-reel unit in the bomb bay and were used to extend the range of other M-4s, as well as Tu-95s.

Range was always the issue with the M-4, so more powerful VD-7 engines were installed, together with an increase in fuel capacity, resulting in an increased range of up to 11,850km/7359 miles. Air-refuelling increased range even further up to 15,400km/9563 miles, which made these aircraft the first strategic bombers capable of delivering their payload deep into enemy territory and returning to base. The first flight of this version, designated M-4/3M, took place in March 1956, and service deployment started in 1958.

The M-4/3M/M-6 ("Bison-B" to NATO) had a slightly larger wing than the A, a longer nose fitted with a refuelling probe, greater fuel load, more thrust and an improved bombing/

navigation system. Although this version was primarily a free-fall strategic bomber, it could also serve as a tanker when fitted with removable bomb-bay refuelling kit.

The reliability of the VD-7 engines caused concerns and consequently, between 1958 and 1960, the M-4 was fitted with new RD-3M-500A engines – this version is known as the M-4/3MS.

In 1960, the M-4/3MD bomber version was developed, with a slightly larger wing, a redesigned, sharper nose, shorter and relocated nose refuelling probe, and a larger tail radome. Known to NATO as the "Bison-C", this aircraft was principally a free-fall strategic bomber, but could also serve as a tanker.

In the late 1970s a single 3M bomber was converted for transporting the huge components for the Energiya-Buran space launch system to the Baikonur launch site. Propellant tanks and even the Buran orbiter itself were placed on external mounting points on top of a strengthened fuselage. A new two-fin tail was added to the aircraft for extra stability.

The aircraft carried out a total of 150 flights in the early 1980s. A total of 93 aircraft were built, and the 3M bombers remained in Soviet service until the end of the 1980s, when they were scrapped in accordance with strategic force reductions treaty agreements.

ABOVE RIGHT: **The "Bison C" had a short refuelling probe on the nose, and with its great range, it was suited to the reconnaissance role.**
RIGHT AND BELOW: **These two photographs were taken from US Navy aircraft 16 years apart, and little seems to have changed. The Soviet bomber gets close to US interests and an F-4 goes to escort the Bison away. The picture on the right is a "Bison C", while the aircraft below is a "Bison B", with a longer refuelling probe. The M-4 was one of the earliest Soviet aircraft equipped for IFR.**

Myasishchev M-4/3M

First flight: January 20, 1953
Power: Four Soloviev 13,000kg/28,613lb thrust D-15 turbojets
Armament: Six defensive 23mm/0.9in cannon; up to 9000kg/19,809lb of various munitions carried in internal bomb bay
Size: Wingspan – 50.48m/165ft 7.5in
Length – 47.2m/154ft 10in
Height – 14.1m/46ft
Wing area – 309m²/3326sq ft
Weights Empty – 80,000kg/176,080lb
Maximum take-off – 170,000kg/374,170lb
Performance: Maximum speed – 900kph/560mph
Ceiling – 15,000m/49,200ft
Range – 11,000km/6835 miles
Climb – Not available

North American A3J/A–5 Vigilante

In November 1953, North American Aviation began work on a design project for an all-weather long-range carrier-based strike aircraft capable of delivering a nuclear weapon at speeds of up to Mach 2. To meet the needs of the design, the team proposed an aircraft so advanced in many ways that it is fair to say that when the Vigilante appeared, no other aircraft had incorporated so many technological innovations.

The first prototype, the YA3J-1, was rolled out on May 16, 1958, and was officially named Vigilante. The first flight took place on August 31, 1958, and the aircraft went supersonic for the first time on September 5. A second prototype entered the test-flight programme in November that year. The first production A3J-1s soon followed, and the sixth Vigilante constructed made 14 launches and landings on the USS *Saratoga* in July 1960.

The demands made on an aircraft flying at twice the speed of sound are considerable, and special measures have to be taken to ensure that systems continue to function in this very harsh environment. In the case of the Vigilante, pure nitrogen was used instead of hydraulic fluid in some of the airframe's hottest areas. The Vigilante was structurally unusual in that major elements were made of titanium to protect against aerodynamic heating, and the wing skins were machined as one piece from aluminium-lithium alloy – gold plate was used as a heat-reflector in the engine bays.

Advanced aerodynamic features included a small high-loaded swept wing with powerful flaps and a one-piece powered vertical tail. Revolutionary fully variable engine inlets were fitted to slow down supersonic air to subsonic speed

TOP: **The highly advanced Vigilante gave the US Navy a Mach 2 strike capability.** ABOVE: **An RA-5C is readied for launch from the flight deck of the USS *Forrestal* in the Atlantic Ocean.**

before it reached the engine, thus producing maximum performance from the engines at any speed. A fully retractable refuelling probe was built into the forward port fuselage ahead of the pilot's cockpit.

The A3J-1 Vigilante also featured some extremely advanced electronics for the time, including the first production fly-by-wire control system which, although a mechanical system, was retained as back-up. Bombing and navigation computations were carried out by an airborne digital computer and the aircraft had the first operational head-up display (HUD). The aircraft's radar had early terrain-avoidance features, lessening the pilot's workload at low level.

ABOVE: **The RA-5Cs were either all new or converted from the nuclear strike A-5A.** RIGHT: **During the Vietnam War, US Navy RA-5Cs were the "sharp" end of the world's most advanced military reconnaissance system.**

In December 1960, the Vigilante set a new world altitude record for its class when it carried a 1000kg/2403lb payload to a height of 27,893m/91,451ft, exceeding the then record by 6.4km/4 miles.

The Vigilante's nuclear weapon was stored in a unique internal weapons bay without bomb-bay doors in the aircraft belly. Instead of the nuclear bomb being dropped, the weapon (mounted in a long duct that extended back between the two engines) was ejected to the rear during release. This was a complex system, and was prone to technical problems.

The first squadron deployment occurred in August 1962 aboard the USS *Enterprise* on its first cruise, and in September that year the A3J-1 was redesignated A-5A under the new Tri-Service designation system. Shortly thereafter, the US Navy's strategic deterrent mission was assumed by nuclear-powered submarine Polaris missiles, and further procurement of the A-5A was halted after only 59 had been

built. Most were returned to North American for conversion to RA-5C standard – 53 were eventually rebuilt as RA-5Cs and were joined in service by 55 new production aircraft. The RA-5C retained the bomber version's very high-speed performance and was capable of electromagnetic, optical and electronic reconnaissance. The type was used to great effect by the US Seventh fleet during carrier air wing operations in the Vietnam War. The US Navy's last RA-5C fleet squadron was disbanded in September 1979.

RIGHT AND BELOW: **The RA-5C could carry out photographic, electronic and electromagnetic reconnaissance.**

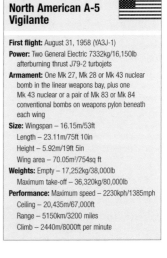

North American A-5 Vigilante

First flight: August 31, 1958 (YA3J-1)
Power: Two General Electric 7332kg/16,150lb afterburning thrust J79-2 turbojets
Armament: One Mk 27, Mk 28 or Mk 43 nuclear bomb in the linear weapons bay, plus one Mk 43 nuclear or a pair of Mk 83 or Mk 84 conventional bombs on weapons pylon beneath each wing
Size: Wingspan – 16.15m/53ft
Length – 23.11m/75ft 10in
Height – 5.92m/19ft 5in
Wing area – 70.05m²/754sq ft
Weights: Empty – 17,252kg/38,000lb
Maximum take-off – 36,320kg/80,000lb
Performance: Maximum speed – 2230kph/1385mph
Ceiling – 20,435m/67,000ft
Range – 5150km/3200 miles
Climb – 2440m/8000ft per minute

North American F-100 Super Sabre

The Super Sabre was the world's first supersonic combat aircraft, and was developed by North American from 1949 as a successor to the company's highly successful F-86 Sabre. North American had considered ways to significantly improve the performance of the F-86 Sabre to achieve supersonic speeds in level flight. Design progressed to the Sabre 45, the "45" coming from the angle of the wings' sweepback – the new aircraft was soon designated F-100 Super Sabre.

The aircraft, which made great use of heat-resisting titanium for the first time, was developed very quickly. At Edwards Air Force Base on May 25, 1953, the prototype exceeded the speed of sound on its first flight, giving a taste of the

ABOVE AND BELOW LEFT: **The F-100 Super Sabre, the world's first supersonic combat aircraft. Early problems were rectified, and from early 1955 the type became a key USAF type.**

performance to come. On October 29, 1953, with Lieutenant Colonel Pete Everest at the controls, the first production aircraft set a new world speed record of 1215kph/755mph over a 15km/9.3 mile course at an altitude of around 30m/98ft above the ground.

In 1954, the US Air Force's 479th Fighter Wing became the world's first supersonic air combat unit. However, a series of catastrophic inflight failures led to the type being grounded until early 1955. After the wings and fin were reworked to eradicate stability problems, 200 F-100As went on to give sterling service in the USAF. On February 26, 1955, test-pilot George F. Smith ejected from an F-100 at supersonic speed, believed to be the first person to do so.

Eisenhower's administration was keen to build its nuclear forces, and the USAF's Tactical Air Command was tasked with delivering nuclear weapons – hitherto the sole responsibility of Strategic Air Command. The F-100 was the only likely candidate in the inventory, so from early 1954 design work began on the fighter-bomber F-100C.

The improved and more powerful F-100C and later D fighter-bombers reached the Cold War front lines in 1956–7. The C-model had inflight refuelling capability to extend the already impressive range, and a more powerful engine. On August 20, 1955 an F-100C, piloted by Colonel Horace Hanes, set the world's first supersonic speed record of 1323kph/822mph.

The D-model is thought to be the first dedicated fighter-bomber version since the C was a fighter simply modified for the job. The F-100D (first flight on January 24, 1956) was built in greater numbers than any other version and carried ECM equipment as well as a low-altitude bombing system for "tossing" nuclear weapons. It also featured the first autopilot designed for a supersonic jet. A total of 1274 D-models were built in 19 production blocks.

From 1964 to 1971 in the Vietnam War, USAF F-100s saw extensive service in the fighter, reconnaissance and ground-attack roles, flying more missions than the manufacturer's P-51 Mustang had in World War II. The first F-100 Vietnam mission took place on June 9, 1964. Operating from Da Nang in South Vietnam, they were ordered to bomb a target in the Plaines des Jarres in Laos. Super Sabre operations were mainly conducted from four modern bases built for USAF aircraft – Bien Hoa, Phan Rang, Phu Cat and Tuy Hoa. Although the F-100 was not well suited to the extreme structural loads produced during low-level high-speed bombing, the F-100D alone flew 360,283 sorties between 1964 and 1971. During this time, only 186 aircraft were lost to anti-aircraft fire, and none in air combat. Due to the comparatively short range of the aircraft, it was primarily operated over South Vietnam.

Super Sabres retired from USAF service in 1972, but remained in use with Air National Guard units until 1980. F-100s were supplied to Denmark, France, Taiwan and Turkey, Turkey finally retiring the type in the mid-1980s.

Two-seat and reconnaissance versions were also produced, and by the time production stopped in 1959, almost 2300 Super Sabres had been built.

TOP: **The F-100C fighter-bomber enabled the USA to increase its nuclear forces very rapidly.** ABOVE: **This F-100 wears a typical gaudy pre-Vietnam USAF livery.** BELOW: **Denmark operated single-seat F-100Ds and F-100F two-seat trainers.**

North American F-100D Super Sabre

First flight: May 25, 1953 (prototype)
Power: Pratt & Whitney 7718kg/17,000lb afterburning thrust J57-P21 turbojet
Armament: Four 20mm/0.78in cannon; six underwing load points for up to 3405kg/7500lb of weapons
Size: Wingspan – 11.81m/38ft 9in
Length – 15.09m/49ft 6in
Height – 4.95m/16ft 3in
Wing area – 35.77m²/385sq ft
Weights: Empty – 9534kg/21,000lb
Maximum take-off – 15,813kg/34,832lb
Performance: Maximum speed – 1390kph/864mph
Ceiling – 13,725m/45,000ft
Range – 3210km/1995 miles with external drop tanks
Climb – 4877m/16,000ft per minute

Northrop Grumman B-2 Spirit

When the Northrop B-2 Spirit was rolled out of its hangar and first shown to the world on November 22, 1988, expressions such as "futuristic" and "otherworldly" were used to describe it. These were coincidentally the same terms used to describe Northrop's revolutionary YB-49 flying-wing bomber of 1947.

The B-2 Spirit "stealth" aircraft is a strategic long-range heavy bomber whose all-altitude, low-observable stealth technology gives it the capability to penetrate the world's most sophisticated air defences. Conceived during the Cold War, the B-2 was designed to slip through enemy radar defences without being detected and then drop up to 16 nuclear bombs on key targets. Its first flight was July 17, 1989.

The B-2's low observability is derived from a combination of reduced infrared, acoustic, electromagnetic, visual and radar signatures. These signatures make it difficult for even the most sophisticated defensive systems to detect, track and engage the B-2. While many aspects of the aircraft's low observability remain classified, the B-2's composite graphite-epoxy materials, special coatings (such as radar-absorbent paint on its leading edge) and flying-wing design are all known to contribute to its "stealthiness".

The B-2's low-observability means that it does not need a fleet of support aircraft (jammers, anti-radar aircraft or fighter escort aircraft) to accomplish a mission, and its large payload allows it to do the work of many smaller attack aircraft. The revolutionary blending of low-observability technologies with

TOP: **The number of claimed UFO sightings generated by the B-2, especially during its top-secret development years, are probably high. Even knowing what this flying object is, it still appears other-worldly.** ABOVE: **A rare view of the B-2 with its bomb-bay doors open.**

high aerodynamic efficiency and large payload gives the B-2 important advantages over existing bombers. Its low observability gives it greater freedom of action at high altitudes, thus increasing its range and providing a better field of view for the aircraft's top-secret sensors. The US Air Force has published a representative mission scenario showing that two B-2s armed with precision weapons can do the job that 75 conventional aircraft would normally be required to carry out.

Northrop Grumman B-2 Spirit

First flight: July 17, 1989
Power: Four General Electric 7854kg/17,300lb thrust F-118-GE-100 engines
Armament: 18,160kg/40,000lb of weapons, including free-fall or retarded conventional or nuclear (strategic or tactical) weapons carried in two rotary launcher assemblies
Size: Wingspan – 52.12m/172ft
Length – 20.9m/69ft
Height – 5.1m/17ft
Wing area – Approximately 464.5m²/5000sq ft
Weights: Empty – 69,780kg/153,700lb
Maximum take-off – 170,704kg/376,000lb
Performance: Maximum speed – 915ph/568mph
Ceiling – 15,250m/50,000ft
Range – 9654km/6000 miles
Climb – Not available

ABOVE: **Radar-absorbent paint on the aircraft's leading edge adds to the B-2's "invisibility" to radar.** RIGHT: **During the development of the B-2, some of the testing team of the 1947 YB-49 were consulted about the handling characteristics of the 1940s flying wing.**

The B-2 has a crew of two, a pilot in the left seat and mission commander in the right, so only four crew members are put at risk in this mission, compared to 132 in the conventional.

Capable of delivering both conventional and nuclear munitions, the B-2 brings massive firepower to bear in a short time anywhere on the globe through previously impenetrable defences, and threatens its most valued and heavily defended targets. The unrefuelled range of the B-2 is approximately 9654km/6000 miles.

The B-2 made its combat debut on March 24, 1999, as part of Operation Allied Force when two aircraft dropped 32,908kg/2000lb joint direct-attack munitions (JDAMs) on Serbian targets during a marathon 31-hour, non-stop mission from Whiteman Air Force Base in Missouri, USA. The combination of its all-weather precision capability and the aircraft's ability to penetrate lethal defences put the enemy's high-value fixed targets at risk. Over the course of Operation Allied Force, 45 B-2 sorties by a total of six aircraft delivered 656 JDAMs on critical targets in the then Federal Republic of Yugoslavia. The B-2 was responsible for destroying 33 per cent of all Serbian targets in the first eight weeks.

During Operation Enduring Freedom in Afghanistan, the B-2 flew a total of six missions on the first three days of the war. Each sortie took 70 hours, including the flight to Afghanistan, a turn-around at Diego Garcia for a new crew and the flight back to Whiteman AFB, home of the B-2.

This remarkable aircraft, each costing around 1.2 billion US dollars, gives the USA the edge over potential enemies whose targets, if detectable, can without doubt be attacked by the 21 B-2s of the US Air Force.

Panavia Tornado IDS

Originally known as the Multi-Role Combat Aircraft (MRCA), the Tornado came about as a joint venture between the UK, Italy and Germany, with each nation assuming responsibility for the manufacture of specific aircraft sections. A new tri-national company, Panavia, was set up in Germany to build the Tornado, and the resulting aircraft was a technological, political and administrative triumph, given the problems that had to be overcome. Each nation assembled its own air force's aircraft, and power for all was provided by Rolls-Royce-designed Turbo-Union engines.

The first aircraft took to the air on August 14, 1974 at Manching, Germany. The initial RAF requirement was for 220 Tornado GR1 strike aircraft, and the first of these entered service with the Tri-national Tornado Training Establishment (TTTE) at RAF Cottesmore in 1980. The first front-line squadron to re-equip with the Tornado was IX Squadron at Honington from June 1982. Nuclear-capable Tornado GR1s eventually equipped a total of ten front-line squadrons deployed in Britain and Germany ready for war with the Warsaw Pact.

The Tornado is one of the world's few variable-geometry aircraft whose "swing wings" enable optimum performance at any speed. Swept forward to 25 degrees, wing slats and flaps can be extended providing high lift for take-off and landing. Once the aircraft becomes airborne, the wings are swept back to 45 degrees for normal flying or 67 degrees for high-speed operations.

TOP: **Tornado GR1 – the pod at the tip of the port wing is a Sky Shadow ECM pod, while beneath the tip of the starboard wing sits a chaff and flare dispenser.** ABOVE: **The RAF's first swing-wing combat aircraft, the Panavia Tornado.**

GR1s were upgraded to GR4 standard by adding forward-looking infrared (FLIR), a wide-angle head-up display (HUD), improved cockpit displays, night-vision goggle (NVG) compatibility, new avionics and weapons systems, updated computer software and global positioning system (GPS). The upgrade also allowed for carriage of the Storm Shadow stand-off missile, Brimstone advanced anti-armour weapon, advanced reconnaissance pods and the thermal imaging airborne laser designator (TIALD) targeting pod. A separate programme covered an integrated Defensive Aids Suite, consisting of the radar warning receiver, Sky Shadow radar jamming pod and BOZ-107 chaff and flare dispenser. These upgrades enable the Tornado to operate in the harshest air defence environments.

ABOVE: **RAF Tornados were in the thick of the Gulf War air campaign in 1991, with six lost to SAM missiles.** ABOVE RIGHT: **The radar-transparent nose cone houses the Tornado's ground-mapping and terrain-following radar.** RIGHT: **With wings in the fully-swept position, the Tornado bomber can reach speeds of up to 2336kph/1452mph.**

The heart of the Tornado GR4's navigation and attack system is the main computer, which takes its primary reference from an inertial navigation system (INS) supplemented by global positioning system (GPS). Targeting information can come from the FLIR, TIALD, laser ranger and marked target seeker (LRMTS) or visually. Among the Tornado's available weaponry are Paveway laser- or GPS-guided bombs, ballistic or retarded "dumb" 454kg/1000lb bombs, Cluster Bomb Units (CBU), Storm Shadow, Brimstone, Air-Launched Anti-Radiation (ALARM) and Sidewinder missiles, and a single 27mm/1.05in cannon. A dedicated reconnaissance version, the GR4A, is also in RAF service.

The Tornado GR4 is optimized for low-level penetration of enemy airspace for precision attacks against high-value targets. The GR4 has fly-by-wire flight controls with mechanical back-up, and can operate in all weather conditions, using terrain-following radar (TFR) and ground-mapping radar (GMR) to guide the aircraft and identify the target.

In 1991, RAF Tornados played a vital strike role in the Gulf War, carrying out more than 1500 bombing raids over Iraq. Six Tornados were lost, half in low-level strikes, and all were downed by surface-to-air missiles.

A year later, Tornados of 617 Squadron, the famous Dambusters, participated in Operation Fural, patrolling no-fly zones in southern Iraq.

In January 2003, Royal Air Force Tornados were assigned to Operation Telic, the Coalition liberation of Iraq. This operation marked a number of firsts for the GR4: No.617 Squadron debuted the Storm Shadow stand-off missile, and Enhanced Paveway II and III GPS-guided bombs were used, as were improved ALARM II anti-radar missiles. The Tornado is expected to remain the backbone of Britain's air-strike capability for many years to come.

Panavia Tornado GR4

First flight: October 27, 1979
Power: Two Turbo-Union 7298kg/16,075lb afterburning thrust RB199-103 turbofans
Armament: One Mauser 27mm/1.05in cannon, plus Sidewinder missiles carried for self-defence; up to 8172kg/18,000lb of ordnance, including Paveway 2 or 3 laser-guided bombs, ballistic or retarded "dumb" 454kg/1000lb bombs, Cluster Bombs, Storm Shadow, Brimstone, Air-Launched Anti-Radiation Missile (ALARM)
Size: Wingspan – 13.91m/45ft 8in, spread 8.60m/28ft 3in, swept
Length – 16.70m/54ft 10in
Height – 5.95m/19ft 6in
Wing area – 26.6m²/286.3sq ft at 25 degrees sweepback
Weights: Empty – 13,901kg/30,620lb
Maximum takeoff – 27,975kg/61,620lb
Performance: Maximum speed – 2336kph/1452mph
Ceiling – 15,250m/50,000ft
Range – 2778km/1726 miles
Climb – 9150m/30,000ft in 2 minutes

Republic F-105 Thunderchief

The Republic F-105 Thunderchief – the "Thud" – was the first purpose-designed supersonic tactical fighter-bomber to be developed, and it is widely considered to be one of the greatest-ever single-engine jet-powered combat aircraft. It was also the biggest single-seat, single-engine combat aircraft in history, boasting a large internal bomb bay and unique forward-swept engine inlets in the wing roots. This potent and versatile aircraft could also fly at speeds in excess of Mach 2. The F-105 was the only jet fighter to refuel from a side-fuselage boom, and was the first jet fighter to be armed with a Vulcan 20mm/0.78in cannon.

The F-105 developed from a project begun in 1951 by Republic Aviation to find a supersonic tactical fighter-bomber to replace the F-84. The primary mission for the large F-105 was to be capable of a nuclear strike. The prototype first flew in October 1955, but the first production version, the F-105B of which 75 were built, did not enter US Air Force service until May 1958. On December 11, 1959, an F-105B flown by

Brigadier General Joseph Moore set a new world speed record of 1957.32kph/1216.48mph over a 100km/62-mile closed circuit. Perhaps the greatest tribute to the Thud is that in May 1963, the F-105B was chosen to replace the F-100C Super Sabres as the standard aircraft of the crack USAF Thunderbirds Flight Demonstration Team.

The first flight of the F-105D all-weather strike fighter, the first Thunderchief version to possess true all-weather capability, was made on June 9, 1959, and deliveries to the USAF followed within a year. The F-105D looked similar to the earlier B-model, but had a larger nose radome containing a radar that enabled the aircraft to carry out visual or blind attacks with missiles or bombs. The US Air Force in Europe first received the F-105D in May 1961, and the type equipped two tactical fighter wings based in Germany.

No C or E-models were produced; the F-105F was a two-seat, dual-purpose trainer-fighter, while the G-series were modified F-models equipped with a comprehensive electronic

RIGHT: **The "Thud" was the largest single-seat combat aircraft in history.** BELOW: **The F-105F was a two-seat trainer, but with combat facility.**

countermeasures suite. F-105Gs were nicknamed "Wild Weasels" and were tasked with clearing the way for heavy bombers by jamming enemy radar and eliminating surface-to-air missile sites.

The F-105 was the backbone of USAF tactical air power in the Vietnam War and the D-model carried out more air strikes against North Vietnam than any other aircraft in the US aircraft inventory. From 1965 to 1968, three-quarters of all US air strikes against Vietnam were carried out by F-105s. By the end of the war, the versatile F-105 was credited with 25 MiG kills, but was also found to have suffered more losses than any other US type. Over half of all the D-models built (610) were destroyed in the war, and F-105 pilots were thought to have only a 75 per cent chance of surviving 100 missions over North Vietnam.

Production of the F-105 ended in 1964 after a total of 833 aircraft had been built, but unlike many US fighters, the type was never exported to foreign countries. The F-105 continued in USAF service until as late as 1980, but some continued to serve in the Air Force Reserve and the Air National Guard until 1984.

Republic F-105D Thunderchief

First Flight: October 22, 1955 (YF-105A)
Power: One Pratt & Whitney 10,896kg/24,000lb afterburning thrust J75-P-19W turbojet
Armament: One 20mm/0.78in cannon; 6356kg/14,000lb of mixed ordnance carried internally and externally
Size: Wingspan – 10.59m/34ft 9in
　　　Length – 19.61m/64ft 4in
　　　Height – 5.97m/19ft 7in
　　　Wing area – 35.77m²/385sq ft
Weights: Empty – 12,485kg/27,500lb
　　　Maximum take-off – 23,988kg/52,838lb
Performance: Maximum speed – 2237kph/1390mph
　　　Ceiling – 12,566m/41,200ft
　　　Range – 3846km/2390 miles
　　　Climb – 10,492m/34,400ft per minute

ABOVE LEFT: **The F-105D carried out more bombing missions than any other US type.**
ABOVE: **The F-105G "Wild Weasel" was a dedicated anti-radar aircraft which could jam and destroy enemy radar.**
LEFT: **Over half of all F-105Ds built fell to North Vietnam defences during the war.**

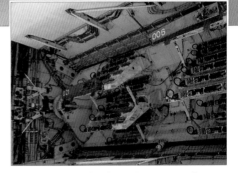

Rockwell B-1 Lancer

The B-1 was designed as a nuclear weapons delivery system in response to a 1965 USAF requirement for a high-speed, low-level replacement for the B-52. Construction of the first prototype B-1A began in late 1972, and the prototype flew on December 23, 1974. By the end of June 1977, three prototypes had made 118 flights with 646 hours of flying time. Spiralling costs led to the project's cancellation in 1977 but interestingly, flight tests of the four B-1As continued until 1981.

High-level military and political lobbying led to the B-1's resurrection by the Reagan administration in 1982. The improved production version which first flew on October 18, 1984 was the B-1B. This differed from the B-1A by having updated avionics, strengthened undercarriage, ejection seats instead of the original crew-escape pod, and the ability to carry weapons externally. The first B-1B was delivered to Dyess Air Force Base, Texas, in June 1985, and operational capability was achieved on October 1, 1986. The last of 100 B-1Bs was delivered on May 2, 1988, each with a unit cost of 200 million US dollars.

The Rockwell B-1B was one of the last long-range strategic bombers to be built, and is capable of penetrating very sophisticated defences. The aircraft is the backbone of America's long-range bomber force, providing massive and rapid delivery of precision and non-precision weapons against any potential adversary anywhere around the globe on short notice. The B-1 uses shorter runways and flies lower and faster than the B-52, can carry more than twice the bomb load, and has a smaller radar profile than the Boeing bomber, making radar detection harder for the enemy.

TOP: **The B1-B, among the last of the true long-range strategic bombers.** ABOVE: **Inside the capacious bomb bay of the Lancer, which can carry up to 34,050kg/75,000lb.**

The ongoing Conventional Mission Upgrade Program is significantly enhancing the B-1B's capability. This increases the aircraft's accuracy and survivability by integrating "smart" and stand-off weapons and onboard countermeasures. The B-1B AN/ALQ 161A defensive avionics system detects and counters enemy radar threats, including missiles attacking from the rear. It defends the aircraft by applying the appropriate countermeasures, such as electronic jamming or dispensing chaff and flares.

The B-1B's radar and inertial navigation equipment enable its crew to navigate globally, update mission profiles and target co-ordinates inflight, and precision-bomb without the need for ground-based navigation aids. Numerous upgrades and modifications have been carried out or are under consideration to keep the Lancer at the technological forefront.

B-1s were used extensively in the 2003 war in Iraq. Operating from Guam, B-1s would head for Iraq, and when nearing Iraqi airspace, drop down to low level while maintaining a high speed. After striking a target or targets, the aircraft would then rendezvous with a tanker for mid-air refuelling. On April 7, 2003 a B-1 was doing just that when an airborne control aircraft made contact, telling the crew, "this is the big one", and directed them to a new high-priority target which had to be struck within ten minutes. Intelligence sources had learned that a high-level Iraqi leadership meeting was underway in a suburb of Baghdad. Prompt action was required to possibly remove the leadership of the enemy regime, and the B-1 was the weapon for the task. The aircraft found the location and dropped four precision-guided 908kg/2000lb bombs on the target – within ten minutes.

Within that time, the crew had planned an escape route, assessed enemy air defences, maintained contact with airborne and ground controllers, selected appropriate weapons and dialled-in the target's co-ordinates. Due to the suburban location, prevention of civilian casualties and collateral damage was a primary concern. To reduce the danger to innocent people and nearby property, mission planners chose the precise Version 3 of the GBU-31 joint direct attack munition (JDAM). The bomb is a hard-target penetrating bomb that buries itself before exploding, thus minimizing fragmentation into surrounding locations. The B-1's global-positioning system guided JDAMs to strike within 12m/40ft of the target. During the 2003 campaign over Iraq, B-1s used around 2100 JDAMs against airfields, bunkers and leadership targets, with a claimed successful targeting of 99 per cent.

TOP: **With wings in the fully swept position, the B-1 can maintain speeds in excess of Mach 1.** ABOVE: **Dropping parachute-retarded bombs.** BELOW: **A B-1B of the 28th Bomb Wing, Ellsworth AFB.**

Rockwell B-1B Lancer

First Flight: October 18, 1984
Power: Four General Electric 13,974kg/30,780lb afterburning thrust F-101-GE-102 turbofans
Armament: Maximum internal bomb load of 34,050kg/75,000lb of conventional or nuclear weapons, cruise missiles or smart weaponry
Size: Wingspan – 41.8m/137ft, unswept 24.1m/79ft, swept
Length – 44.5m/146ft
Height – 10.4m/34ft
Wing area – 181m²/1950sq ft
Weights: Empty – 87,168kg/192,000lb
Maximum take-off – 216,558kg/477,000lb
Performance: Maximum speed – 1448kph/900mph plus
Ceiling – 9150m/30,000ft plus
Combat radius – 9654km/6000 miles
Climb – Not available

Sepecat Jaguar

This potent fighter-bomber was originally designed to meet a joint 1965 Anglo-French requirement for a dual-role advanced/operational trainer and tactical support aircraft. The aircraft was to be built and operated by both countries. The Royal Air Force initially intended to use the aircraft purely as an advanced trainer to replace its Hawker Hunter and Folland Gnat trainers, but this was later changed to the offensive support role on cost grounds.

The finished aircraft was capable of flight in excess of the speed of sound, and could be armed with a tactical nuclear weapon. Often dismissed as obsolete, the Jaguar is still able to deliver a heavy payload over great distances and with considerable accuracy in most weathers.

The Jaguar, coincidentally developed in parallel with Concorde, another Anglo-French project, was the first example of an aircraft developed by Britain with a partner nation for use by the RAF and another air force. Britain built Jaguar wings, tails and the rear fuselage, while France produced the centre and forward fuselage sections.

The French prototype flew on September 8, 1968, while the first Jaguar to be built in Britain, XW560, had its maiden flight at Warton in October 1969. With Wing Commander Jimmy Dell at the controls, the aircraft went supersonic on its first flight.

The British and French air forces each placed orders for 200 aircraft, the RAF opting for 165 single-seat and 35 two-seat aircraft. Deliveries to the RAF began in 1973 and more

TOP AND ABOVE: **When the RAF first considered what became the Jaguar, they were only looking for an advanced trainer. Four decades later, the "Jag" is serving the RAF as a counter-air, close-support and tactical-reconnaissance aircraft.**

than three decades on, the Jaguar continues to equip RAF as well as Armée de l'Air units.

The Jaguar has a robust landing gear designed for use from rough forward airstrips for war in Europe – Royal Air Force Jaguars with full bomb loads were test-operated from lengths of European motorway, which might have been used instead of airfields had the Cold War heated up. The Jaguar force of RAF Germany held the line in West Germany until the Tornado GR1 entered service.

In the early 2000s, the RAF's Jaguar fleet underwent a major upgrade programme and was designated the Jaguar GR3 (T4 for the two-seat variant). The upgrade included improved avionics, including global positioning system (GPS), night-vision goggles (NVG) helmet-mounted sight and new head-up display (HUD) and head-down displays (HDD).

RIGHT: **RAF Jaguars are all based at RAF Coltishall.**
MIDDLE RIGHT: **During the Cold War, the RAF's Jaguars frequently trained in Arctic conditions, but the type's engines are now being upgraded for high and hot operations.**
BELOW RIGHT: **The wingspan of the Jaguar is considerably less than that of the famous Spitfire.** BELOW: **The RAF Jaguar fleet, recently upgraded to GR3 standard, can carry retard and freefall bombs, as well as the Paveway II and III laser-guided bombs.**

The Jaguar is capable of carrying 454kg/1000lb retard and freefall bombs, cluster munitions, laser-guided bombs, rocket and two 30mm/1.18in Aden cannon. For self-defence, two AIM-9L Sidewinder air-to-air missiles can be mounted on the over-wing hardpoints, and may be launched via the helmet-mounted sight system. These are complemented by a rear warning radar, an electronic countermeasures (ECM) pod to jam enemy radar, as well as chaff and flare dispensers to confuse radar and heat-seeking missiles respectively.

The aircraft can carry an external fuel tank on the centreline pylon, or two tanks beneath the wings. In the reconnaissance role, the externally mounted Jaguar Reconnaissance Pod can provide horizon-to-horizon coverage from medium and low level.

RAF and French Jaguars participated extensively in the 1991 Gulf War, and British aircraft have been subsequently involved in many operations in the Middle East and the Balkans. The type regularly deploys for exercises to North America, Europe and the Middle East, operating in diverse conditions from the desert to the Arctic Circle. On February 6, 2003, RAF Jaguars were deployed to the Gulf for action against Iraq again, and carried out many missions as part of the liberation of Iraq.

In August 1976, an export version named Jaguar International first flew. The type was ultimately exported to Ecuador, Oman, Nigeria and India.

Sepecat Jaguar

First Flight: September 8, 1968
Power: Two Rolls-Royce Turboméca 3650kg/ 8040lb afterburning thrust Adour 104 turbofans
Armament: Two 30mm/1.18in cannon; 4540kg/ 10,000lb of mixed ordnance carried externally, plus overwing pylons for air-to-air missiles
Size: Wingspan – 8.69m/28ft 6in
Length – 16.83m/55ft 2.5in
Height – 4.89m/16ft 0.5in
Wing area – 24.18m²/260.28sq ft
Weights: Empty – 7000kg/15,407lb
Maximum take-off – 15,700kg/34,555lb
Performance: Maximum speed – 1699kph/ 1056mph
Ceiling – 13,725m/45,000ft plus
Combat radius – 1408km/875 miles
Climb – Not available

Sukhoi Su-25

The single-seat Su-25 first flew in 1975, and became a hard-hitting ground-attack aircraft first tested in battle during the Soviet invasion of Afghanistan. The aircraft was designed for combat against NATO forces, and is the only dedicated close-support aircraft in the Russian inventory. Its job was to help control the main battle area by launching devastating precision attacks on mobile or stationary enemy ground forces while loitering over the high-risk battle area. The Su-25 can also engage low-speed air targets.

The aircraft was designed for the same purpose as the US A-10 and, like its American counterpart, is a very rugged aircraft. However, the Su-25 is smaller than the A-10, and can fly around 273kph/170mph faster than the American aircraft. Although many aircraft are claimed to be suitable for forward-location rough-field operations, the Su-25 really is. All servicing equipment, including a fuel pump, can be stored in a container carried beneath the aircraft's wing. The aircraft's engines have the remarkable capability to run, at least for short flights, on most fuels to be found in a combat environment, including aviation fuel, petrol and diesel.

Like the A-10, the Su-25 is armed with a devastating 30mm/1.18in cannon for attacking armour. The twin-barrel gun is installed in the port underside of the fuselage and can fire its 250 rounds at a rate of 3000 rounds per minute. SPPU-22 gun pods can be carried on the underwing pylons, each housing GSh-23 23mm/0.9in twin-barrel guns with 260 rounds of ammunition.

The aircraft's ten pylons can carry up to 4400kg/9684lb of ordnance, from self-defence air-to-air missiles to anti-shipping missiles, anti-tank munitions and cluster bombs. Air-to-ground

TOP AND ABOVE: **The Su-25, born in the Cold War, is still in use, largely with air forces in the former Eastern bloc. Even so, some have been relegated to museum pieces (above).**

missiles carried include Kh-23 (NATO codename AS-7 Kerry), Kh-25 (AS-10 Karen) and Kh-29 (AS-14 Kedge). The air-to-air missiles carried on the smaller outboard pylons are the R-3S (AA-2D Atoll) and the R-60 (AA-8 Aphid). The aircraft can be fitted with S-24 240mm/9.3in or S-25 330mm/13in guided rockets, UB-32A pods for 57mm/2.22in S-5 rockets and B-8M1 pods for 80mm/3.12in S-8 rockets.

Aircraft and pilot survivability were central to the design. The pilot, like that of the A-10, sits within a thick titanium "bathtub" for protection against ground fire and shrapnel. While many combat aircraft have cable-activated control surfaces, the Su-25 use heavy-duty pushrods that are much less likely to be severed by a stray bullet. The Su-25 carries a total of 256 decoy flares, which it fires 32 at a time when carrying out an attack run to confuse heat-seeking missiles launched from the ground or the air.

Early examples of the Su-25 were rushed to Afghanistan in 1980 for combat evaluation, and a number of modifications to production aircraft were introduced as a result. The engines were originally close together, and attacks by missiles or anti-aircraft fire led to both catching fire even if only one was damaged. Subsequently, engines were well separated and housed in protective stainless steel bays to safeguard against nearby explosions. Following Afghan Stinger missile attacks that ruptured fuel tanks, the tanks on later aircraft were foam-filled to prevent explosions, as well as being armoured on the underside.

Although the Su-25 was known to the West by its NATO codename "Frogfoot", Soviet pilots called the aircraft "Gratch" (rook) due to that bird's ability to get at hard-to-find targets.

Variants of the Su-25 are operated by the Russian Air Force, Russian Naval Aviation forces, Afghanistan, Angola, Belarus, Bulgaria, the Czech Republic, Georgia, Kazakhstan, North Korea, Peru, the Slovak Republic and the Ukraine. The export variant of the aircraft is known as the Su-25K, and an upgraded Su-25K, known as the "Scorpion", has been developed jointly by Tbilisi Aerospace Manufacturing (TAM) of Georgia with Elbit of Israel. The Su-25UTG is the two-seater aircraft-carrier variant fitted with an arrester hook deployed on the 50,800 tonne/50,000-ton Russian Navy aircraft carrier *Admiral Kuznetsov*.

LEFT: **An Su-25 with underwing stores. This aircraft is based at Pardubice in Czechoslovakia with the 30th Attack Regiment, 1992.** BELOW: **One of the most amazing features of the Su-25 is its ability to run on petrol, diesel or aviation fuel.** BOTTOM LEFT: **The Su-25's ten pylons can carry a devastating array of weaponry.**

Sukhoi Su-25

First flight: February 22, 1975
Power: Two Tumanski 4500kg/9904lb thrust R-195 turbojets
Armament: One 30mm/1.18in cannon; up to 4400kg/9684lb of air-to-air, air-to-surface, anti-tank, anti-radiation missiles, plus guided and cluster bombs, rockets, rocket pods, gun packs, ECM pods and drop tanks
Size: Wingspan – 14.36m/47ft 1.5in
Length – 15.53m/50ft 11.5in
Height – 4.8m/15ft 9in
Wing area – 33.7m²/362.75sq ft
Weights: Empty – 9500kg/20,909lb
Maximum take-off – 17,600kg/38,738lb
Performance: Maximum speed – 975kph/606mph
Ceiling – 7000m/22,965ft
Range – 1249km/776 miles
Climb – 3482m/11,415ft per minute

Tupolev Tu-22/Tu-22M

The Tu-22 had its beginnings in a 1955 study to produce a supersonic bomber capable of penetrating the most modern air defences at high altitude and high speed to deliver nuclear weapons. The aircraft flew for the first time in September 1959 and went on to become Russia's first successful supersonic bomber. Typically of the time, the aircraft was unknown to the West until its first public appearance in 1961 when ten examples, one of them carrying a cruise missile, took part in a fly-past. This no doubt sent NATO analysts into a frenzy, and they soon codenamed the aircraft "Blinder".

The three-man Tu-22 (pilot, navigator and radio operator/gunner) is most easily recognized by the unusual position of its engines at the base of its fin. The tail also housed a radar-controlled 23mm/0.9in cannon for defence.

ABOVE: Since first taking to the air in 1964, the Tu-22M has become a key bomber in the Russian inventory. BELOW LEFT: The original Tu-22, from which the Tu-22M was derived, has its engines located at the base of its fin. The Tu-22 was not a swing-wing aircraft like the Tu-22M.

About 300 Tu-22s were built between 1960 and 1969, the first version being the Tu-22 "Blinder-A" bomber/reconnaissance version carrying free-fall nuclear bombs. The Tu-22K "Blinder-B" was a missile-carrying version armed with AS-4 missiles and a large guidance radar mounted under its nose. The Tu-22R "Blinder-C" was a daylight reconnaissance version with six "windows" in the bomb bay for three pairs of long-range cameras. The Tu-22U "Blinder-D" was a trainer version with the instructor pilot seated in a separate raised cockpit, and the Tu-22P "Blinder-E" was an ECM (electronic countermeasures) version based on Tu-22R. Once the Tu-22s were past their best as bombers, most surviving examples were converted into jamming platforms.

Apart from Russia, who used the Tu-22 into the late 1980s, the type was also operated by Ukraine, Libya and Iraq. The Tu-22 saw action in a number of conflicts, including the Soviet invasion of Afghanistan and the Iran-Iraq War. Iraq used their aircraft against Kurdish rebels in the 1980s, while Libya used their Tu-22s against Chad and Sudan.

Once in service, the Tu-22 offered no great advantage over the Tu-16 that it was intended to replace. The Tu-22 was not built in great numbers, reportedly because of problems with reliability, and Tupolev sought to revise the aircraft's design to produce a much better performance. It was this study

LEFT: **Derived from the Tu-22, the Tu-22M is an all-new aircraft.** BELOW: **The "swing-wing" Tu-22M can achieve speeds in excess of 1930kph/1200mph.** BOTTOM: **The Tu-22M-3 is the most versatile model, and can carry out a range of very different missions.**

which resulted in the Tu-22M ("Backfire" in NATO-speak), originally a swing-wing version of the Tu-22 which became an all-new aircraft.

The engines on the Tu-22M were changed to the much more powerful Kuznetsov units and were repositioned to the more conventional location in the rear fuselage. The Tu-22M prototype, much altered from the original Tu-22 design, first flew on August 30, 1964. It was another five years before NATO became aware of the new aircraft and was able to codename it "Backfire-A". The first production version (of a total run of around 500 aircraft) was the Tu-22M-2 "Backfire-B", but then in 1980 production switched to the Tu-22M-3 "Backfire-C", fitted with more powerful engines and having revised air intakes. Most importantly, this version can carry a number of Kh-15 (NATO "Kickback") missiles which can be

configured for anti-radar, anti-shipping, conventional or nuclear missions. Around 300 examples of the M-2 have been built, and they are still very much in front-line service with both Russia and the only other operator, Ukraine. A small number of the ECM version, the Tu-22MR, were also built.

Tupolev Tu-22M-3

First flight: August 30, 1964
Power: Two KKBM Kuznetsov 25,051kg/55,137lb thrust NK-2512MV turbofans
Armament: One 23mm/0.9in cannon in tail; 24,000kg/52,824lb of conventional munitions in bomb bay or three Kh-22 missiles or ten Kh-15 missiles
Size: Wingspan – 34.28m/112ft 6in, spread 23.3m/76ft 6in, swept
Length – 42.46m/139ft 4in
Height – 11.05m/36ft
Wing area – 175.8m²/1892.4sq ft
Weights Empty – 54,000kg/118,854lb
Maximum take-off – 124,000kg/272,924lb
Performance: Maximum speed – 2000kph/1242mph
Ceiling – 13,226m/43,394ft
Combat radius – 4000km/2485 miles
Climb – Not available

Tupolev Tu-95

The Tu-95 (NATO codename "Bear") was probably the most successful post-war Soviet bomber design. In an age of jet-powered bombers, the turboprop-powered Tu-95 had a remarkable range capability and flew at speeds not far behind those of its "enemy" counterparts.

The Tu-95 had an interesting ancestry because its fuselage profile was that of the earlier Tu-4 bomber, which was an unofficial copy of the American B-29 Superfortress. For many, the Bear is an icon of Cold War tension since it was frequently photographed probing UK airspace, escorted by an RAF fighter.

Development of the Tu-95 began in the early 1950s as the Soviet Union looked to increase the reach and destructive capability of their bomber fleet. KB Tupolev proposed an aircraft with four turbo-prop engines that would provide a range of more than 13,000km/8073 miles and speeds of more than 800kph/497mph at altitudes of 10,000m/32,810ft.

The aircraft's 35-degree swept wings (unique in a propeller-driven aircraft) were made with the experience of developing the swept wing for the Tu-16 jet bomber.

As with many aircraft, the success of the design hinged totally on an effective powerplant. The design of the Tu-95 called for turboprops with a power output of around 10,000hp, while the most powerful Russian turboprop available at the time only generated 4800hp. Engine designers Kuznetsov had the job of getting the prototype Bear in the air, and their stop-gap solution while the awesome NK-12 was developed was to use eight engines arranged in pairs, producing 12,000hp in a

TOP: **As the Spitfire represents the Battle of Britain, so the "Bear" is a Cold War icon.** ABOVE: **The Bear stands tall, 12.12m/39ft 9in high. Note the refuelling probe on this Tu-95H, the ultimate bomber variant.**

tractor and pusher configuration. The eight TV-2 engines, effectively pulling and pushing the aircraft simultaneously, were powerful enough to get 95/1, the Tu-95 prototype, into the air for the first time on November 12, 1952.

The second prototype, 95/2, equipped with four of the hugely powerful TV-12 engines (the most powerful production turboprops ever), was completed in June 1954 and first flew on February 16, 1955. The engines drove contra-rotating propellers, which were used for maximum fuel economy and range.

Production of the aircraft, now formally designated Tu-95, started in January 1956, with the Tu-95M (known to NATO as the "Bear A"), a high-altitude, free-fall nuclear bomber capable

LEFT: **The belly of the Bear, courtesy of a NATO fighter.**
BELOW: **Note the contra-rotating props on this Tu-95H escorted to a UK air show by an RAF Tornado F.3.**
BOTTOM: **The H-model can carry six cruise missile internally, and even ten more under its wings.**

of carrying 9000kg/19,809lb of bombs in its 14.2m/46ft 7in bomb bay over the aircraft's maximum design range. The Tu-95M carried six radar-controlled, turret-mounted AM-23 guns for self-defence. Powered by more fuel-efficient NK-12M engines, deliveries to service units began in October 1957. This was very bad news for NATO because it meant that the Soviet Union now had intercontinental capability.

Most "Bear As" were later converted to AS-3 missile-carrying "Bear B" standard, while around a dozen A-models were converted to Tu-95U configuration for training purposes.

Further versions of the aircraft included the Tu-95K2 "Bear G" which carried two Kh-22 "Kitchen" missiles, one beneath each wing. With a range of up to 460km/286 miles, these 350-kiloton missiles, along with the AS-3, gave the Tu-95 a stand-off capability and improved the aircraft and crew's survivability. The final bomber version of this long-serving but formidable aircraft was the Tu-95MS (the "Bear H"), which carries six Kh-15 "Kent" cruise missiles in its bomb bay and, remarkably, a further ten on underwing pylons.

Maritime reconnaissance variants also appeared while the Tu-142, a dedicated anti-submarine version, was developed with a longer fuselage and a ventral search radar radome. The Tu-142 carries sonobuoys to detect submarines, as well as torpedoes and mines for attack. Ten Tu-142s entered service with India in April 1988 for the long-range surface-surveillance and anti-submarine warfare missions.

An interesting spin-off from the Tu-95 was the Tu-114 airliner. The Tu-95's wing and engines were joined to an enormous fuselage that could carry up to 220 passengers. The airliner debuted at the Paris Air Show in 1959 and entered Aeroflot service in 1961. Thirty examples of the airliner were built, and these served until October 1976.

Tupolev Tu-95MS

First flight: November 12, 1952 (prototype)
Power: Four KKBM Kuznetsov 15,000eshp NK-12MV turboprops
Armament: Two 23mm/0.9in cannon in tail; sixteen Kh-55 "Kent" cruise missiles carried in bomb bay and under wings
Size: Wingspan – 51.1m/167ft 8in
Length – 49.5m/162ft 5in
Height – 12.12m/39ft 9in
Wing area – 297m²/3197sq ft
Weights: Empty – 90,000kg/198,090lb
Maximum take-off – 188,000kg/413,788lb
Performance: Maximum speed – 828kph/514mph
Ceiling – 12,500m/41,010ft
Range – 12,800km/7949 miles
Climb – Not available

Tupolev Tu-160

The impressive Tu-160 (NATO codename "Blackjack") is the most modern strategic bomber in the Russian inventory, and is the heaviest and most powerful bomber ever. It was designed to operate from subsonic speeds at low altitudes to speeds in excess of Mach 1 at high altitudes. Two weapons bays can accommodate a range of munitions, from strategic cruise missiles, short-range guided missiles and nuclear or

ABOVE: **The heaviest bomber ever built – the Tu-160.** BELOW LEFT: **The "Blackjack" can carry a range of weapons, including bombs, mines and nuclear and conventional missiles. Only 36 were ever produced.**

conventional bombs to mines. Similar in layout to the B-1B, with "swing" or variable-geometry wings, work on the Russian aircraft began in 1973 in direct response to the proposed Rockwell bomber. However, the Tu-160 is much bigger and heavier than the B-1, and can fly faster and much further. The Tu-160 was known to the West even before its first flight on December 19, 1981, thanks to a US spy satellite which spotted the aircraft on the ground at its base. Tupolev built two prototypes and one mock-up, which was used for static tests.

Production began in 1984 and, although initial plans called for the construction of 100 aircraft, when production was stopped in 1992, only 36 bombers had been built due to Strategic Arms Limitation restrictions.

The aircraft is powered by four NK-321 25,000kg/55,025lb thrust turbofans mounted in pairs beneath the fuselage centre section, can climb up to 70m/230ft per second and reach heights of over 18,000m/59,000ft. Terrain-following radar guides the aircraft at high speeds at low level, and all four crew members have ejection seats. The bomber, which is controlled by a fighter-style control column and a fly-by-wire

system, can be refuelled in flight using a probe-and-drogue system. The variable-geometry wings can shift from 20 degrees up to 65 degrees and allow flight at both supersonic and subsonic speeds.

The Tu-160 can carry up to 12 Kh-55 long-range missiles and Kh-15 short-range missiles as well as free-fall nuclear and conventional weapons. The bomber is not equipped with any defensive armament, but carries an extensive electronic countermeasures facility.

Deployment of the bombers began in May 1987. Until the end of 1991, 19 Tu-160 bombers served in Ukraine and, on the collapse of the old USSR, the aircraft became Ukrainian property. The aircraft and associated air-launched missiles were subsequently the subject of intense negotiation because Russia wanted the aircraft back. A deal was finally struck in exchange for the cancellation of an enormous gas bill between the two countries.

In July 1999, the Russian Ministry of Defence reportedly ordered one Tu-160 strategic bomber, and the cost was said to be 45 million roubles.

Studies have also been conducted on the aircraft's use as a launch platform for the Burlak space-launch vehicle, which is designed to carry payloads of up to 500kg/1100lb in polar orbits. The launch vehicle would be carried beneath the fuselage of the aircraft, which would give it a head start to a high altitude, thus eliminating the need for excessive heavy fuel loads for launch from the earth's surface.

TOP: **Looking in better shape than the airworthy example opposite, this Tu-160 was photographed in 1999.** ABOVE: **With wings swept and looking like a B-1B, the large Tu-160 can exceed Mach 1.** BELOW: **This large bomber is only in service in limited numbers with Russia and the Ukraine.**

Tupolev Tu-160

First flight: December 19, 1981

Power: Four Kuznetsov 25,000kg/55,025lb thrust NK-321 turbofans

Armament: Up to 16,500kg/36,316lb of ordnance can be carried in two internal weapons bays or under wings, including six Kh-55 long-range missiles or twelve Kh-15 short-range missiles or free-fall nuclear or conventional weapons

Size: Wingspan – 55.7m/182ft 9in, unswept 35.6m/116ft 9in, swept
Length – 54.1m/177ft 6in
Height – 13.1m/43ft
Wing area – 360m²/3875sq ft

Weights: Empty – 110,000kg/242,110lb
Maximum take-off – 275,000kg/605,275lb

Performance: Maximum speed – 2220kph/1378mph
Ceiling – 15,006m/49,235ft
Range – 12,300km/7638 miles
Climb – 4203m/13,780ft per minute

Vickers Valiant

Designed to satisfy the same specification that resulted in the Vulcan and Victor, the Valiant was clearly a less risky design than its fellow V-bombers. It was this fact that appealed to the Ministry of Supply, who saw the Valiant as a safer, fall-back aircraft should the futuristic Avro and Handley Page designs have failed.

The Vickers Type 660 prototype, WB210, first flew on May 18, 1951, with Vickers' chief test-pilot "Mutt" Summers at the controls. The Valiant (the name was given in June 1951) was a clean, conventional high-wing aircraft with its four engines cleverly buried in the wing roots; their intakes were blended into the leading edge of the wing.

The Valiant B.1 first entered service in June 1954 with 232 Operational Conversion Unit at RAF Gaydon, the first V-bomber base. While the fledgling Valiant crews were trained

ABOVE: **The Valiant prototype, WB210, pictured in May 1951. At this stage the aircraft was the Vickers B9/48. It was named a month later.**
BELOW LEFT: **Painted in overall anti-flash white, Valiant B. Mk 1, XD827.**

(many were converting from the piston-powered Avro Lincoln), the first Valiant squadron, No.138, was formed and became fully operational at Wittering in July 1955.

The Valiant's potential as a long-range strategic reconnaissance platform was spotted early, and 11 B(PR) Mk 1 variants were produced. These could carry up to eight cameras instead of munitions in the bomb bay, although the type did retain its bombing capability. First deliveries of these aircraft to No.543 Squadron at RAF Wyton started in June 1955. A true multi-role version was then produced (14 examples), the B(PR)K.1. Similar to the B(PR).1, this version could also mount a removable refuelling system in the bomb bay, making it a bomber/tanker/reconnaissance aircraft. Total production of all marks was 104.

On October 11, 1956, at an altitude of 10,675m/35,000ft over Maralinga, Australia, Valiant B.1 WZ366 carried out the first air-drop of a British nuclear weapon. The Blue Danube bomb detonated at 229m/750ft and produced a yield of 3 kilotons, equivalent to 3048 tonnes/3000 tons of TNT.

In October 1956, Valiants became the first of the V-bombers to drop bombs (mercifully conventional) when they went into action against the Egyptians. The RAF were keen to test their new strategic bombers in operational conditions, and the Egyptian nationalization of the Suez Canal had presented the opportunity. Valiants of Nos.138, 148, 207 and 214 Squadrons were deployed to RAF Luqa on Malta, and the first Valiant raids against Egyptian airfields were carried out on October 31.

In March 1957, four Valiants of No.49 Squadron were detached to take part in the controversial Christmas Island hydrogen bomb tests. On May 15, Valiant B.1 XD818 dropped a prototype hydrogen bomb at 11,895m/39,000ft over Malden Island. The tests finally proved that Britain had a working high-yield bomb and was indeed still a major player on the world stage. Valiants were also used to air-test and launch scale versions of the Blue Steel stand-off missile that was to equip the Vulcan and Victor.

By 1962, Soviet Air Defences were considered to be too effective for the operation of high-level nuclear bombers, and along with the other V-bombers, the Valiant was switched to low-level tactical operations in 1962–3. While the advanced Victor and Vulcan adapted well to the change in role, the Valiant fleet was silently and literally cracking up. Following an emergency landing of Valiant WP217 on August 6, 1964, examination of this and other Valiants showed that the majority of Valiants had suffered significant stress fractures as a result of operating in harsh low-level conditions. The entire Valiant fleet was grounded while the cost of repairing or replacing the aircraft's spars was considered. With the Vulcan and Victor still in service, the cost of keeping the Valiants flying was deemed to be too high. All Valiants were withdrawn from service in January 1965.

TOP: **WZ395 on approach to Filton, June 1960. The airfield near Bristol was one of Bomber Command's V-bomber dispersal airfields.** ABOVE LEFT: **Valiants were fully operational from July 1955.** ABOVE: **WZ392 was a multi-role Valiant B(PR)K.1.**

Vickers Valiant B. Mk 1

First Flight: May 18, 1951
Power: Four Rolls-Royce 4563kg/10,050lb thrust Avon turbojets
Armament: Conventional or nuclear bomb load of up to 9534kg/21,000lb
Size: Wingspan – 34.85m/114ft 4in
    Length – 32.99m/108ft 3in
    Height – 9.8m/32ft 2in
    Wing area – 219.43m²/2362sq ft
Weights: Empty – 34,450kg/75,881lb
    Maximum take-off – 63,560kg/140,000lb
Performance: Maximum speed – 912kph/567mph
    Ceiling – 16,470m/54,000ft
    Range – 7242km/4500 miles plus
    Climb – 1220m/4000ft per minute

Glossary

AA Anti-aircraft

AAF Army Air Forces (USAAF)

AAM air-to-air missile

Aerodynamics study of how gases, including air, flow and how forces act upon objects moving through air

AEW airborne early warning

AFB Air Force Base

Afterburner facility for providing augmented thrust by burning additional fuel in the jet pipe

AI Airborne Interception (radar)

Ailerons control surfaces at trailing edge of each wing used to make the aircraft roll

AMRAAM advanced medium-range air-to-air missile

Angle of attack angle of a wing to the oncoming airflow

ASR Air Sea Rescue

ASRAAM advanced short-range air-to-air missile

ASUW anti-surface unit warfare

ASV air-to-surface-vessel – pertaining to this type of radar developed during World War II

ASW anti-submarine warfare

AWACS Airborne Warning and Control System

Biplane an aircraft with two sets of wings

Blister a streamlined, often clear, large fairing on aircraft body housing guns or electronics

BVR beyond visual range

Canard small winglets attached to forward fuselage

Canard wings two small horizontal surfaces on either side of the front of an aircraft

CAP combat air patrol

Ceiling the maximum height at which an aircraft can operate

CFAS Commandement des Forces Aeriennes Stratégiques – French Strategic Air Command

CRT cathode ray tube

Delta wing a swept-back triangular-shaped wing

Dihedral the upward angle of the wing formed where the wings connect to the fuselage

DLIR downward-looking infrared, of targeting and navigation

Dorsal pertaining to the upper side of an aircraft

Drag the force that resists the motion of the aircraft through the air

ECM electronic countermeasures

Elevators control surfaces on the horizontal part of the tail, used to alter the aircraft's pitch

ELINT electronic intelligence

EO-LOROP electro-optical long-range oblique photographic sensor

ESHP equivalent shaft horsepower

FAA Fleet Air Arm

Faired housed inside a streamlined covering

FBW fly-by-wire

FG Fighter Group (USAAF)

Fin the vertical portion of the tail

Flaps movable parts of the trailing edge of a wing used to increase lift at slower air speeds

FLIR forward-looking infrared, of targeting and navigation

G the force of gravity

GAF Government Aircraft Factory (Australia)

Geodetic metal "basketwork" construction

GPS global positioning system

HARMs high-speed anti-radiation missiles

HOTAS hands on throttle and stick

HP horsepower

HUD Head-Up Display

IFF identification friend or foe

IFR inflight refuelling

JDAMs joint direct-attack munitions

Jet engine an engine that works by creating a high velocity jet of air to propel it forward

Leading edge the front edge of a wing or tailplane

MAC Merchant Aircraft Carrier

Mach speed of sound – Mach 1 = 1223kph/760mph at sea level

MDC miniature detonating cord

Monoplane an aircraft with one set of wings

Nacelle streamlined housing, typically containing weights

NATO North Atlantic Treaty Organization

NVG night-vision goggles

OCU Operational Conversion Unit (RAF)

Pitch rotational motion in which an aircraft turns around its lateral axis

Port left side when looking forward

QRA quick reaction alert

Radome protective covering for radar made from material through which radar beams can pass

RAAF Royal Australian Air Force

RAF Royal Air Force

RATO rocket-assisted take-off

RCAF Royal Canadian Air Force

Reheat *see* Afterburner

RFC Royal Flying Corps

RLM ReichsLuftMinisterium – the German Air Ministry

RNAS Royal Naval Air Service

RNZAF Royal New Zealand Air Force

Roll rotational motion in which the aircraft turns around its longitudinal axis

Rudder the parts of the tail surfaces that control an aircraft's yaw (its left and right turning)

SAC Strategic Air Command (USAF)

SAM surface-to-air missile

SAR search-and-rescue

SLAM-ER stand-off land-attack missile extended range

SLR side-looking airborne radar

Starboard right side when looking forward

STOL short take-off and landing

Supersonic indicating motion faster than the speed of sound

Swing wing a wing capable of variable sweep, e.g. on Panavia Tornado

Tailplane horizontal part of the tail, known as horizontal stabilizer in North America

TFW Tactical Fighter Wing (USAF)

Thrust force produced by engine which pushes an aircraft forward

Triplane an aircraft with three sets of wings

TsKB Soviet Central Design Bureau

UHF ultra high frequency

UN United Nations

USAAC United States Army Air Corps

USAAF United States Army Air Forces

USAF United States Air Force

USAFE USAF Europe

USN United States Navy

V/STOL vertical/short take-off and landing

Variable geometry *see* Swing wing

Ventral pertaining to the underside of an aircraft

VHF very high frequency

Acknowledgements

The author would like to give special thanks to Mike Bowyer, Peter March, Kazuko Matsuo and Hideo Kurihara for their help with picture research.

The publisher would like to thank the following individuals and picture libraries for the use of their pictures in the book (l=left, r=right, t=top, b=bottom, m=middle, um=upper middle, lm=lower middle). Every effort has been made to acknowledge the pictures properly, however we apologize if there are any unintentional omissions, which will be corrected in future editions.

Aerospace Publishing: 212t.

Alan Beaumont: 259b; 289m; 290b; 314t; 321br; 329tl; 332t; 332m; 352b; 399bl; 409um; 411t; 413tr; 414b; 418t; 420b; 422t; 424b; 431m; 435t; 441b; 443t; 449b; 455br; 469t; 471b; 479t; 481t; 503.

BAE Systems: 34b; 40t; 41t; 48t; 49bl; 49br; 162t; 163lm; 163b; 188t; 199um; 233m.

B.J.M. & V. Aviation: 217t.

Michael J.F. Bowyer: 31l; 53b; 59t; 64t; 66b; 69b; 71; 72t; 82b; 93bl; 95m; 101bl; 107m; 113mr; 161m; 164t; 164b; 165t; 166b; 167t; 167m; 168t; 169m; 169b; 171b; 174b; 175m; 175b; 176t; 177lm; 177b; 180b; 181m; 183um; 183b; 187m; 187b; 193b; 195m; 197lm; 198m; 206b; 207t; 208t; 208b; 212b; 215t; 227t; 227m; 228t; 229b; 231tl; 231tr; 233b; 234t; 234b; 239t; 241b; 252t; 434b; 437b.

P.J. Bryden, Wessex Aviation: 418b; 449t; 449m; 453b; 481b; 501br.

Francis Crosby Collection: 66t; 80b; 87b; 92t; 120b; 153b; 185b; 204b; 256–7; 289t; 300t; 300b; 301t; 301m; 301b; 303b; 304b; 308t; 314b; 317t; 319br; 328b; 340t; 345m; 359t; 368b; 371b; 377bl; 379t; 379b; 383b; 391br; 399t; 408b; 410t; 412b; 414t; 415bl; 415br; 417tl; 417b; 440b; 448t; 448b; 454t; 490t; 490b; 491t; 491mr; 491b; 500t.

Ken Duffey: 244b.

Chris Farmer: 170t; 172b; 178t; 179b; 197um; 201m; 201b; 220b, 306; 307t; 324t; 353tr; 386t; 387m; 394t; 424t; 469m; 471m; 488t; 502b.

Imperial War Museum Photograph Archive: 12t (CT 906); 12b (COL 195); 13t (TR 38450); 13m (CT 442); 16t (Q 67436); 16b (Q 67062); 17t (Q 67832); 18t (Q 69593); 18r (Q 42283); 19m (Q 114172); 19b (Q 64214); 20tr (Q 28180); 21tr (Q 68415); 21b (TR 516); 23tl (CH 3513); 23tr (EA 34177A); 24r (Q 63125); 25t (FRA 102960); 25m (TR 22); 25b (FRA 102079); 26t (HU 2742); 25l (GER 530); 28 (TR

137); 29tl (HU 1215); 29tr (HU 50153); 29b (CH 1299); 30b (CL 2332); 31tr (CH 16117); 31br (CH 16607); 33tl (TR 285); 33tr (NYF 18669); 33m (NYF 74296); 33b (A 9423); 36b (A 32268); 37br (A 31917); 38 (CT 62); 41m (CT 68); 42 (CT 72); 45t (CT 391); 47t (CT 57); 52tr (Q 61061); 56t (CH 886); 56b (CH 1101); 57t (COL 187); 57bl (CH 5105); 57br (TR 868); 58b (MH 165); 61t (Q79081); 61m (Q 68344); 61b (Q 11993); 62t (Q 66585); 64b (MH 5698); 65b (TR 978); 67tl (Q 11897); 68b (ATP 12184F); 69t (HU 1642); 70 (HU 2703); 73t (HU 2840); 75t (MA 6711); 75lm (HU 2395); 75b (MH 4190); 76b (Q 33847); 78b (Q 63153); 85tl (TR 284); 85tr (A 11644); 85b (A 24528); 87t (NYF 28563); 89m; 91tr (CH 5093); 91m (C 1291); 91b (CH 17331); 94t (HU 4985); 95t (MH 4880); 96m (MH 4881); 102t (EA 15161); 103t (OEM 5182);

105b (Q 63808); 107tr (CH 15662); 107b (HU 2742); 108b (HU 5181); 109m (HU 2741); 109b (MH 4908); 110 (CT 842); 117tl (HU 63024); 117tr (HU 63022); 117bl (CF 899); 117br (HU 63021); 120t (C 1378); 121tr (Q 55974); 129m (CH 7059); 129b (NYP 21768A); 137m (HU 31375); 137br (EA 25060); 139um (Q 60550); 139b (Q 60608); 140t (Q 07104); 140m (Q 67249); 140b (Q 69650); 143tl (Q 67556); 143tr (Q 27508); 143bl (Q 57660); 143br (HU 68205); 145t (HU 39323); 146m (Q 67061); 148t (COL 188); 149tl (CH 24); 149m (TR 23); 149b (PMA 20625); 151t (EMOS 1214); 151br (CH 5005); 153um (A 25442); 153lm (A20026); 155m (RR 2219); 158b (CT 800); 159b (A 32830); 163um (CT 440); 165b (GLF 1082); 167b (GLF 1003); 184tr (ATP 15053C); 185t (Imperial War Museum

Duxford); 185mr (A 34406); 186bl (COL 50); 186br (CAM 1473); 191 (CT 816); 198b (CT 915); 199t (CT 913); 199m (CT 916); 199lm (ATP 21301B); 200t (ATP 13595C); 215b (CT 70); 253m (A 33984), 258t (TR 1082); 258b (CL 1005); 263t (CL 047); 267m (CA 15856); 269tl (GER 18); 270r (C 5422); 271tl (MH 5591); 272bl (FLM 2340); 272br (FLM 2360); 273t (TR 1127); 273bl; 273br (FLM 2363); 274t (NY 1313); 275tr (HU 4052); 312b (CH 364); 313t (CH 372); 320b (CM 6241); 329b (EMOS 884); 334b (CH 6531); 335b (CH 2786); 341tl (A 3532); 342t (C 2116); 343bl (CH 762); 345t (EMOS 1318); 345b (A 21286); 354b (C 5101); 355t (CH 10598); 355m (CH 3389); 355b (CH 4435); 356tl (CH 3478); 356tr (CH 256); 356b (MH 4859);

386b (CIA 12842); 388b (CH 12677); 389t (CH 17887); 389m (CH 5177); 389b; 390b (CH 7502); 391t (MH 5150); 398b (CH 10247); 399br (CMA 4680); 400t (CF 204).

Key Publishing Ltd: 54b; 55b; 104t.

Cliff Knox: 17um; 20b; 22; 30t; 35m; 39bl; 43b; 45b; 58t; 60b; 72b; 77b; 86bl; 90t; 90b; 91tl; 102b; 103m; 106t; 121b; 126t; 142t; 146b; 152t; 153t; 154b; 174t; 180t; 181b; 190t; 192t; 201t; 209ml; 214t; 217lm; 222b; 224t; 227b; 233t; 237t; 241t; 246t; 247b; 252b.

Kokujoho Magazine: 206tr; 124um; 124lm; 171t; 195b; 225b; 248b.

Hideo Kurihara: 116b; 122t,

330b; 365t; 372t; 374t; 374b;
375tl; 375tr; 375b; 383t;
384t; 384b; 385t; 401t; 401b;
429m; 430t.

Andrew March: 221b, 437um.

Daniel J. March: 32t; 43lm;
67tr; 182b; 198t; 248t, 404b.

Peter R. March: 10–11; 14–15;
17lm; 17b; 18l; 19t; 20tl; 24l;
26b; 27tr; 27br; 31bl; 32b; 34t;
35t; 36t; 37tr; 37bl; 40b; 43t;
43um; 44t; 44b; 45m; 46t; 47b;
49t; 50–1; 52tl; 54t; 55t; 59b;
60t; 62b; 63b; 65t; 68t; 73m;
75um; 76t; 77t; 78t; 79b; 80t;
81t; 81m; 81b; 82t; 83t; 84t;
84b; 86t; 87m; 88t; 88bl; 89t;
89b; 92b; 93br; 94b; 95b; 96b;
97t; 98t; 98b; 99t; 99m; 100m;
103b; 104b; 105t; 106b; 107tl;
108t; 109t; 111t; 112t; 112b;
113ml; 113b; 114b; 115; 116t;
119t; 119b; 120tl; 122b; 123b;

124t; 125b; 126m; 126b; 127t;
127b; 128t; 128b; 131t; 132t;
135t; 135m; 136t; 136b; 137t;
137bl; 138t; 138b; 139t; 141t;
141b; 142b; 144b; 145b; 146t;
147t; 147m; 147b; 148b; 149tr;
150b; 152b; 154t; 154m;
156–7; 158t; 160t; 160m; 160b;
161b; 162b; 163t; 168t; 169t;
170b; 172t; 173t; 173b; 175t;
176b; 177t; 177um; 178b;
179tr; 179m; 181t; 182t; 183t;
183lm; 184b; 186t; 187t; 188b;
189t; 189m; 189b; 190m; 192bl;
192br; 194t; 194b; 195t; 197b;
199b; 200b; 202b; 203t; 204t;
205t; 206tl; 207b; 209t; 209mr;
209b; 210; 211t; 211b; 213t;
213b; 214b; 215m; 216;
217um; 217b; 218t; 218b;
219t; 219m; 220t; 221t; 222t;
223t; 223b; 224b; 225t; 226t;
226b; 228t; 229t; 229m; 230t;
230m; 230b; 231b; 232t; 232b;
235t; 235b; 236b; 237b; 240t;
241um; 241lm; 242t; 243b;

245t; 245b; 246b; 247t; 247m;
249t; 249b; 250t; 250b; 251t;
253t; 253b; 254t; 254b; 255t;
255b; 266t; 272t; 281tl; 283tl;
287bl; 288b; 289b; 291b; 295b;
296–7; 298t; 300l; 303t; 304t;
305m; 307m; 308b; 309t;
309bl; 310t; 312t; 313b; 315m;
316t; 316b; 319bl; 320t; 321tr;
322t; 324t; 325t; 331t; 333b;
334t; 335t; 336t; 336b; 337t;
337b; 340b; 341tr; 341b; 343t;
346b; 352t; 353tl; 359b; 360t;
360b; 361t; 365m; 365b; 366t;
366b; 368t; 369t; 369br; 370t;
376b; 377t; 377br; 378t; 378b;
382; 383um; 383lm; 387t;
387b; 388t; 391bl; 395tr; 396m;
404t; 405b; 407b; 408t; 409lm;
409b; 410b; 411m; 411b; 412t;
413tl; 413b; 415t; 415m; 416t;
417tr; 419lm; 412t; 412b; 424b;
423t; 423m; 425ml; 425mr;
425b; 426m; 426b; 427t; 428;
431t; 431b; 432b; 433t; 433m;
433b; 434t; 436t; 437lm; 438b;

439t; 439m; 439b; 440t; 440m;
443ml; 443b; 444t; 445t; 445b;
446t; 446b; 447bl; 447br;
450t; 451ml; 451mr; 451b;
453t; 454b; 455t; 455bl; 456t;
458t; 459tl; 459tr; 459b; 460t;
461t; 461tr; 462t; 463t; 463bl;
463br; 465l; 465tr; 467t; 467b;
468t; 468b; 470t; 471t; 472b;
473t; 473mr; 473b; 475t; 479tl;
479b; 480t; 480b; 481m; 482t;
482b; 483b; 484t; 485tr; 485b;
486t; 486b; 489t; 489m; 489b;
491ml; 492t; 492b; 493t; 493m;
493b; 494t; 494b; 495b; 496b;
497m; 497b; 498t; 498b; 499t;
499m; 499b; 500b; 501t; 501bl;
502t; 504; 505t; 508; 509; 510.

Brian Marsh: 285bl; 483t.

**Martin-Baker Aircraft
Company:** 48b.

Maru Magazine: 100t; 100b;
122t; 125tr.

Ministry of Defence: 159t.

Northrop Grumman: 21tl; 83b; 86br; 88br; 193t; 194t.

Bruce Robertson: 52b; 63t; 67b; 73b; 99b; 101t; 111b; 114t; 118t; 118b; 124t; 125tl; 132b; 132t; 134b; 135b; 144t; 155t; 155b; 156t; 161t; 184tl; 183m; 190b; 202t; 203b; 205b; 219b; 236t; 242b; 244t; 251m; 251b.

Rolls-Royce: 39br.

Saab: 13b; 35b; 41b; 238; 239b; 505t.

Geoff Sheward: 129t; 133t; 133b; 166t; 179tl; 196; 197t; 243t; 322m; 419um; 419b; 445m; 453m; 464t; 469b; 473ml; 484b; 485tl.

Brian Strickland Collection: 53t; 74; 79t; 93t; 96t; 97b;

101br; 113t; 130; 131b; 139lm; 151bl; 185ml; 271tr; 271bl; 277l; 278b; 279l; 299tl; 299tr; 325t; 328t; 329tr; 338t; 349b; 351t; 351b; 354t; 357t; 363t; 364t; 371tl; 373m; 380b; 393b; 395br; 397t; 398t.

TRH Pictures: 259t; 259m; 260–1; 262t; 262b; 263m; 263bl; 263br; 264t; 264b; 265t; 265m; 265b (Mars); 266b (Ted Nevill); 267t; 267b (Ted Nevill); 268 (Alan Landau); 269tr (Art-Tech); 269bl (Art-Tech); 269br (Art-Tech); 270l (Alan Landau); 271br; 274b; 275tl; 275b; 276t; 276b (Ted Nevill); 277tr; 277br; 279tr; 279br; 280; 281tr; 281bl; 281br; 282; 283tr (Ted Nevill); 283bl; 283br; 284a; 284b; 285tl; 285tr; 285br; 286t (Fairchild); 286b (Alan Landau); 287tl (Ted Nevill); 287tr; 287br; 288t; 290t (Colin Smedley); 291t; 291m; 292t; 292b; 293t; 293bl; 293br; 294t; 294b; 295tl

(Jon Davison); 295tr (Colin Smedley); 298b; 299b; 302r; 305t (Richard Winslade); 305b; 309br; 310b; 311tl; 311tr; 311b; 313m; 315b; 317t (Art-Tech); 317b (Art-Tech); 318b; 319t; 321tl; 321bl; 322b; 323t; 323b; 326t; 326b; 327t; 327m; 327b; 330t; 331b; 332b; 333t; 335m; 337m; 338b; 339t; 339b; 342b; 343br; 344t; 344b; 346t; 347t; 347b; 348t; 348b; 349t; 349m; 350t (Art-Tech); 350b (Art-Tech); 351m (Art-Tech); 353b; 357b; 358t; 358b; 361m; 361b; 362t; 362b; 363m; 363b; 364b; 367t; 367bl; 367br; 369bl; 370b; 371tr; 372b; 373t; 373b; 376t; 380t; 381t; 381m; 381b; 385bl; 385br; 390t (Colin Smedley); 392t (Art-Tech); 392b (Art-Tech); 393t; 394b (Ted Nevill); 395tl (Ewan Partridge); 395bl; 396t; 396b; 397b (Public Domain); 400b; 402–3; 404m; 405t; 406t; 406b; 407t; 407m; 409t; 416b;

419t; 420t; 421m; 423b; 425t; 426t; 427m; 427b; 429t; 429b; 430b; 432t; 435m; 436b; 438t; 441t; 442t; 442b; 444b (Ted Nevill); 447tr; 450b (Jon Davison); 452t; 452b; 457b (Ted Nevill); 458b; 460b; 461b; 464b (Jim Winchester); 465m; 465b; 466t; 474t; 474b (Art-Tech); 475m (Art-Tech); 475b (Art-Tech); 476t (Art-Tech); 476b (Art-Tech); 477t (Art-Tech); 477m (Art-Tech); 477b; 478t; 478b; 479tr; 487tl; 487tr; 487b; 488b (Ted Nevill); 495m (Guy Taylor); 496t; 497t; 505b.

USAF: 46b; 162m.

Nick Waller: 278t; 307b; 318t; 435b; 437t; 443mr; 447tl; 451t; 456t; 457t; 457m; 462b; 466b; 470b; 472t; 495t.

Index

Key to flags

For the specification boxes, the national flag that was current at the time of the aircraft's use is shown.

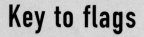

Australia

Brazil

Canada

Czechoslovakia

France

Germany: World War I

Germany: World War II

Germany

India

Israel

Italy

Japan

Netherlands

Poland

Romania

South Africa

Spain

Sweden

Taiwan

United Kingdom

United States of America

USSR